TENNYSON'S RAPTURE

Tennyson's Rapture

TRANSFORMATION IN THE
VICTORIAN DRAMATIC MONOLOGUE

CORNELIA PEARSALL

OXFORD
UNIVERSITY PRESS
2008

OXFORD
UNIVERSITY PRESS

Oxford University Press, Inc., publishes works that further
Oxford University's objective of excellence
in research, scholarship, and education.

Oxford   New York
Auckland   Cape Town   Dar es Salaam   Hong Kong   Karachi
Kuala Lumpur   Madrid   Melbourne   Mexico City   Nairobi
New Delhi   Shanghai   Taipei   Toronto

With offices in
Argentina   Austria   Brazil   Chile   Czech Republic   France   Greece
Guatemala   Hungary   Italy   Japan   Poland   Portugal   Singapore
South Korea   Switzerland   Thailand   Turkey   Ukraine   Vietnam

Copyright © 2008 by Oxford University Press, Inc.

Published by Oxford University Press, Inc.
198 Madison Avenue, New York, New York 10016

www.oup.com

Oxford is a registered trademark of Oxford University Press

Library of Congress Cataloging-in-Publication Data
Pearsall, Cornelia
Tennyson's rapture : transformation in the Victorian
dramatic monologue / by Cornelia Pearsall.
p. cm.
Includes bibliographical references and index.
ISBN 978-0-19-515054-4
1. Tennyson, Alfred Tennyson, Baron, 1809–1892—
Criticism and interpretation. 2. Dramatic monologues—
History and criticism. 3. Politics and literature—Great
Britain—History—19th century. I. Title.
PR5592.D68 P43 2007
821'.8—dc22   2007000225

2 4 6 8 9 7 5 3 1

Printed in the United States of America
on acid-free paper.

For John

ACKNOWLEDGMENTS

Perhaps it is fitting that a book concerned with transformations has undergone so many of its own. John Hollander has championed this project through many of its stages, informing it with his intellectual vitality and generosity. I first wrote about Victorian poetry with Harold Bloom and next with John Guillory, and though not a word here will be familiar to them, this book owes much to their extraordinary tuition. This project has been enlightened by conversations about poetry or about the Victorian period, sometimes over the course of many years or, indeed, many years ago, with Charles Berger, Leslie Brisman, Robert Caserio, Geoffrey Hartman, Linda K. Hughes, Gerhard Joseph, Linda Peterson, Hilary Schor, Warwick Slinn, Kathryn Bond Stockton, Herbert Tucker, Frank Turner, Elizabeth von Klemperer, Barry Weller, and especially Joseph Bristow and Yopie Prins. With her gift for posing questions that require complex answers, Lauren Berlant asked me about the relation of contemporary beliefs in the rapture to this book; answering her led to the research and writing of the entire second chapter.

At Oxford University Press, Elissa Morris was an exceptionally supportive acquiring editor. This book has benefited significantly from the rigor and responsiveness of two anonymous readers. Humanities editor Shannon McLachlan, assistant editor Christina Gibson, production editor Linda Donnelly, and copyeditor Judith Hoover have been assiduous in their efforts, and I am thankful to them for their thoughtful work in seeing this project to fruition. I am particularly grateful for the gracious resourcefulness of librarians at Smith College, Yale University, and the Tennyson Research Centre in Lincolnshire.

Yale University's Beinecke Library granted permission to reprint a revised version of my essay "Tennyson and the Rapture of 'Tithonus,'" pp. 104–21 from *Never Again Would Birds' Song Be the Same: Essays on Early Modern and Modern Poetry in Honor of John Hollander*, ed. Jennifer Lewin (New Haven: Beinecke Library, Yale University, 2002). Several short extracts from my article "The Dramatic Monologue," pp. 67–88 in *The Cambridge Companion to Victorian Poetry*, ed. Joseph Bristow (Cambridge: Cambridge Univ. Press, 2000), are reprinted by permission of Cambridge University Press.

At Smith College, friends and colleagues in several departments and programs have supported this work in many ways. Michael Gorra, Betsey Harries, and Marilyn Schuster gave me valuable suggestions at an earlier stage. Justina Gregory read all of the chapters on classical monologues as I wrote them, saving me when she could from error and sustaining me more than she could know at an especially critical period of composition. My student research assistant Molly Hamer was instrumental in helping with several final aspects of the production of this book, in particular the drafting of abstracts for Oxford Scholarship Online. The insightful curiosity of my students has taught me again and again how much there is still to discover in Victorian poetry.

This project and much else has been illuminated by the friendship and beautiful example of Annie Boutelle, Nancy Mason Bradbury, Rosetta Marantz Cohen, Dana Leibsohn, Karen Traub, and long ago of Wilma Harvey and above all Janet Trubenbach. My mother, Marilyn Meyer Pearsall, a philosophy professor, taught me to think in critical ways, and my father, Robert Brainard Pearsall, an English professor, taught me poetry's centrality to life; I am still learning their lessons. The inspiration of my brother, Anthony Pearsall, and sister, Sarah Pearsall, scholars themselves, has been unfailing. John Rogers supported this project through each of its many incarnations, always seeing what might be best in it, from its earliest to its final version. This book's dedication to him is small recompense for his dedication to it. I wrote the majority of *Tennyson's Rapture* as my daughter Lily was beginning to speak; I have finished it as my daughter Adeline is beginning to write. I thank them both for teaching me daily the value and the beauty of every word.

CONTENTS

TENNYSON'S RAPTURE

INTRODUCTION

Rapt Oration

In *Tennyson's Rapture* I explore Alfred Tennyson's intimate relation to his age through a detailed focus on poetic form, in particular the poet's manifold uses of the dramatic monologue, a genre whose Victorian incarnation he essentially invented. A notoriously elusive genre to define, the dramatic monologue ultimately may be characterized less by its technical elements than by the range of transformations it represents. "Rapture" is a word that signifies aggressive, often transgressive, acts of seizure or rapine, as well as submission to ravishing transport or exaltation; I argue that this poet's major dramatic monologues can be seen to explore these and other mechanisms of radical transformation. At the same time, I track certain processes in these poems of rigorous ratiocination, also in the cause of articulating and effecting processes of change, reading against a critical tradition that views Tennyson as overwhelmed by his own lyric abundance, unknowing in his affect and his effects, stupefied. In searching through the worlds, Victorian and ancient, of Tennyson's dramatic monologues, I focus on a number of his contemporaries, including a wide range of theologians, classicists, explorers, philosophers, and politicians. I investigate some of the poet's major works within such seemingly disparate and yet surprisingly intertwined contexts as nineteenth-century reform politics, classical scholarship, sexological theory, and evangelical writings on the rapture (I follow Victorian theologians in not capitalizing the term). While Tennyson's poetry is at the center of my study, I examine closely the poet's consequential and revealing converse with a range of contemporaries, including Thomas Carlyle, William Gladstone, John Stuart Mill, and Heinrich Schliemann. My readings of Tennyson's verse draw as well from the illuminating resources of Victorian anecdote, attending to myriad conversations, debates, and pronouncements taking place in college rooms in Cambridge, on country walks in Sussex, at dinner parties in London. Reading his poetry within the intersecting spheres of Victorian social and intellectual life helps to restore Tennyson to his densely interwoven contexts but also to reanimate the contexts themselves, to renovate some of the central issues, whether poetic or political, of Victorian culture.

Focusing on a quartet of major dramatic monologues, I seek to establish less a single definition or set of formal requirements for the genre than a set of recurrences, a sequence of rhetorical and thematic patterns. These four poems span nearly the length of Tennyson's career, representing the uses to which this poet put this genre over the course of more than half a century. "St. Simeon Stylites," "Ulysses," "Tithonus," and "Tiresias," the works that most concern this study, were all begun in 1833. Although some parts of these poems may predate the death of his friend Arthur Henry Hallam in Vienna on September 15, 1833, all were substantially developed in the aftermath of that staggering loss. After telling revisions, the first two were published in 1842, and the other two reached their final forms, respectively, in 1860 and 1883. Within two months of Hallam's death, Tennyson performed a vigorous reading of "St. Simeon Stylites" for friends. This monologue of an early Christian martyr can appear the odd man out among the classical company of the three other foundational dramatic monologues, but I hope to show that the ambition for rapture, variously conceived, motivates the speech and actions of each of these speakers. Tennyson called "Tithonus" and "Tiresias" "pendent" to "Ulysses," partly because he transferred lines from one to another in the course of devising the monologue that from the beginning achieved a priority in Tennyson's oeuvre. The author dictates with the term "pendent" that these works in some sense form a community whose context gives them fuller and clearer significance. In so doing, he creates a genre that he does not name.

My first chapter forwards a model for reading the dramatic monologue, whether those of Tennyson or this genre's many other Victorian practitioners, drawing on resources ranging from classical oratorical treatises to contemporary performativity theory. The five subsequent chapters center on this poet's four originary dramatic monologues. These poems are often read in isolation, whether as fully autonomous set pieces or in the context only of other examples of the genre. Hearing them in conversation with other Tennyson poems not of their kind can help us to understand more fully their internal concerns and their external operations within the poet's oeuvre and his culture. These first four dramatic monologues were conceived in the poet's period of greatest shock after Hallam's death, as of course was *In Memoriam*, a text that is especially useful in establishing a preliminary sense of Tennyson's conception of rapture. In section 87, Tennyson describes a return to Cambridge University, where he wanders through town before pausing outside the Trinity College rooms of Arthur Henry Hallam, the subject of his elegy. "Another name was on the door: / I lingered" (87.17–18),

Tennyson tells us, before returning through memory, if not the denominated door, to the interior

> Where once we held debate, a band
>> Of youthful friends, on mind and art,
>> And labour, and the changing mart,
> And all the framework of the land. (87.21–24)[1]

In these debates about philosophy, aesthetics, economics, and political organization among the undergraduate association known as the Cambridge Apostles, Tennyson's friends aimed their discursive arrows with variable success, until Arthur Hallam himself rose to speak: "And last the master-bowman, he, / Would cleave the mark" (87.29–30). No one could vie with his oratorical skills, least of all the admiring poet, who refused to enter these verbal contests. Lingering outside the door, Tennyson recollects the speaker, but also the audience:

> A willing ear
> We lent him. Who, but hung to hear
> The rapt oration flowing free
>
> From point to point, with power and grace
> And music in the bounds of law. (87.30–34)

The "rapt oration" Tennyson recalls seems wholly to absorb the orator, who is in a state of exaltation as he speaks, because of his speech, caught up in the "power and grace" of his own discursive performance. But the "rapt oration" also transports its auditors, who are themselves "rapt," entranced and borne away by Hallam's oratorical prowess.

As Hallam moves to the conclusion of his free-flowing speech, his auditors witness a transformation not only of his discursive but of his physical self, watching "The God within him light his face, / And seem to lift the form, and glow / In azure orbits heavenly-wise" (87.36–38). Hallam appears to enter a state of religious transcendence, illuminated and elevated by God, his eyes ("azure orbits") planets themselves. But there is a suggestion here that this transport might be less benign, and less Christian, than it initially seems. The appearance of a god who "lifts" a young person's physical form and carries it into heavenly "orbits" connotes, as Tennyson well knew, the vision of a rapture of a mortal by an immortal, like that of Ganymede by Zeus or Tithonus by Aurora. These desirable young men are rendered sexual prey or plunder, reminding us that the definition of the Latin root *raptus* is "to seize" and that the experience of rapture can be eroticized and violent. Early in *In Memoriam*, Tennyson describes Hallam's sudden death in 1833, at the age of twenty-two, as an abduction: the lurking "Shadow feared of men" interrupted the "fair companionship" of these friends by enwrapping Hallam in the folds of his "mantle dark and cold." Tennyson imagines a protesting but silenced Hallam, whom he addresses directly as he describes how the Shadow "dulled the murmur on thy lip, / And bore thee where I could not see / Nor follow" (22.12, 13, 14, 16–18). Priscilla Johnston likens this theft of Hallam, who is borne away suddenly and seemingly irretrievably, to Aidoneus's rapture of Persephone, and indeed the abduction of Persephone is an exemplary event represented in Tennyson's first extant poem, a translation of Claudian's "Rape of Proserpine" (c. 1824), and his late dramatic monologue "Demeter and Persephone" (1889).[2] At this moment of being borne away, even Hallam's eloquence fails; it is Tennyson who is left to struggle with the physical, psychic, and discursive challenges posed by rapture.

In Hallam's rooms at Cambridge, Tennyson participated in his friend's state of discursive transport, one so associated with Hallam, I would argue, that the poet's two major scenes of reunion with the dead man in *In Memoriam* are predicated on rapture. Section 95, widely considered the climax of the elegy, recounts the poet's dramatic posthumous intercourse with Hallam. In the course, again, of "lingering" ("By night we lingered on the lawn" [95.1]), Tennyson experiences being suddenly overtaken:

> And all at once it seemed at last
> The living soul was flashed on mine,
>
> And mine in this was wound, and whirled
>   About empyreal heights of thought,
>   And came on that which is, and caught
> The deep pulsations of the world. (95.35–40)

For the first twenty years after this elegy's publication in 1850, the lines describing the entity that "flashed" read, "*His* living soul was flashed on mine, / And mine in *his* was wound" (emphasis added). Troubled that he might have been "giving a wrong impression," Tennyson replaced the "living soul" of Hallam with that of a being he defined indefinitely in conversation as "the Deity, maybe" (*Poems*, 2:413n). Whether it is a man or a deity that catches the poet up and whirls him into the highest heavens is a critical distinction, of course, given the potential homoerotic implications of the pronoun "his," but Tennyson never wavered in his account of the sensation itself. The poet laments the inadequacy of his report with the exclamation "Vague words!" (95.45), but his description is extraordinarily precise, apparently because it was a recurrent experience of his. "I have often had that feeling of being whirled up and rapt into the Great Soul" (*Poems*, 2:413n), Tennyson commented to his son. Though it is impossible not to identify the "Deity" and "Great Soul" to which Tennyson refers as the Judeo-Christian God, his avoidance of the obvious term can leave us with a suggestion of Zeus's rapture of Ganymede. And yet the experience of being suddenly and without warning caught or whirled up into the air is one that echoes as well Paul's New

Testament prophecy that the Lord shall descend and take up the dead: "Then we which are alive and remain shall be caught up together with them in the clouds, to meet the Lord in the air" (1 Thessalonians 4:17, King James Version). This verse is the scriptural foundation for all twentieth- and twenty-first-century rapture predictions, popularized by numerous Internet Web sites and by Tim LaHaye's series of *Left Behind* books, which have sold more than 42 million copies.[3] The modern history of the Christian doctrine of the rapture, however (which I review in chapter 2), is rooted in Britain in the late 1820s and early 1830s, in theological movements of which Hallam and Tennyson were closely aware.

In Memoriam 103 describes a second scene of mystical reunion with Hallam. Tennyson dreams he is traveling on "a little shallop" with the Muses, when they come upon a massive figure of Hallam on the deck of "A great ship" (103.19, 40). He greets them, and Tennyson "fell in silence on his neck," leading the Muses to accuse the poet of abandonment: "So rapt I was, they could not win / An answer from my lips" (103.44, 49–50). This silence is broken by the easy sociality of Hallam, who invites the "maidens" to join them, with biblically inflected language ("Enter likewise ye") (103.6, 51). Hallam intercedes with the Muses on behalf of a poet rendered speechless, returning Tennyson to them, that is, to his own voice. Whether into silence or into speech, it is to a discursive state that the poet is rapt. The rapture of *In Memoriam* 95 is occasioned by Tennyson's reading that night on the lawn the "noble letters of the dead" (95.24), many of which this book discusses, suggesting the physical transport consistently caused by Hallam's words. In the course of being "whirled / About," Tennyson catches "The deep pulsations of the world, / Æonian music measuring out / The steps of Time" (95.40–42), entering into a cosmological rhythmic state that at once defies and keeps time, surely an ideal situation for a poet. Although rapture in Tennyson involves being caught up into another sphere, it differs from the experience of self-instigated transcendence to which Tennyson was also attracted, a condition best represented by the well-known account of his ability to enter into a trance by way of the incantatory repetition of his own name. In these particular elegiac narratives, rapture is instigated by Hallam's language, which in turn inspires Tennyson's.

The catalyst of rapture tends in Tennyson to be some external agent, whether welcomed or resisted. Richard Chenevix Trench, one of Hallam and Tennyson's fellow Cambridge Apostles, whose intense attraction to the nascent movement of rapture theology in the early 1830s I trace in my second chapter, articulated this notion in his influential collection of lectures, *On the Study of Words*, originally published in 1851 and reprinted twenty-seven times by the turn of the century. He distinguishes rapture and its synonyms in his introductory lecture:

> We declare that the good which will really fill our souls and satisfy them to the uttermost, is not in us, but without us and above us, in the words which we use to set forth any transcending delight. Take three or four of these words— "transport," "rapture," "ravishment," "ecstacy,"—"transport," that which *carries*

us, as "rapture," or "ravishment," that which *snatches* us out of and above ourselves; and "ecstacy" is very nearly the same, only drawn from the Greek.[4]

"Synonyms are words of like significance in the main, but with a certain unlikeness as well; with very much in common, but also with something private and
particular, which they do not share with one another," Trench observes in a later
lecture.[5] The capacity to distinguish between discursive likeness and unlikeness
has theological implications, with direct relevance for a reading of the heresy of
Christian similitude in "St. Simeon Stylites," and for reading the genre of the dramatic monologue more generally.

The "private and particular" aspect of rapture is its sense of being not only
carried but "snatched" away, caught up unexpectedly "out of and above ourselves."
Rapture would appear to be a state in which agency and power are ceded in a
forced and silencing passivity, constituting a submission to being overwhelmed
physically, psychically, and discursively. This seems to be the experience the Prince
undergoes in the course of his "weird seizures" (1.14, 81) throughout *The Princess*,
often considered a reference to the epilepsy to which some of Tennyson's immediate family members were subject. These seizures carry the Prince into an involun-
tary suspension, during which "all things were and were not" (3.173, 4.545), but
the condition of rapture is more frequently associated in Tennyson's poetry with
states of intellectual perception and discursive power. Tennyson especially admired
in Hallam what he terms in *In Memoriam* his "All-subtilising intellect" (85.47),
and two of his avatars for his friend in the elegy are husbands whose absorption
in abstract thought estranges them from their wives, a situation that proves fatal
for the eponymous speaker of Tennyson's 1868 dramatic monologue "Lucretius,"
whose wife Lucilia cannot abide his dedication to Epicurean philosophy. Another
figure for Hallam in *In Memoriam* is a husband who is invariably "rapt in matters
dark and deep" (97.19), his intense intellectual preoccupation supported by a loving wife, herself a figure for Tennyson. Still another obsessively engrossed spouse
and figure for Hallam is King Arthur, who in *Idylls of the King* infuriates a less
indulgent mate, and is bitterly described by Guinevere as "Rapt in this fancy of
his Table Round" ("Lancelot and Elaine," 129).

These examples show the rapt thinker as emotionally detached, but more
often in Tennyson, the state of being "rapt" is a social one, and indeed an auditory
one, as it is a state into which an audience is transported, propelled by discursive
and even lyrical skills. Princess Ida describes to the Prince a golden brooch the
school awards in metaphysics, which features an image of "Diotima, teaching him
that died / Of hemlock," as Socrates himself lends a willing ear, "She rapt upon
her subject, he on her" (*The Princess*, 3.285–86, 287). A scene of collective reverie
occurs at the end of *The Princess*, as the group of storytelling college friends
is reduced to silence by a communal vision of the future of humankind: "we
sat / But spoke not, rapt in nameless reverie, / Perchance upon the future man"

(Conclusion, 107–9). In another poem representing Tennyson's undergraduate friendships, also written in the aftermath of Arthur Hallam's death, it is the poet who enraptures his auditors. In "The Epic," the frame for "Morte d'Arthur" (1842), a young poet reads an excerpt from an abandoned Arthurian epic while his friends "Sat rapt" (277).

Whether Diotima by Socrates, the poet by his friends, or Hallam by Tennyson, the scene is the same: an inspired or enraptured speaker is witnessed by auditors who are simultaneously participants, enraptured themselves. The auditor (or reader, as when Tennyson reads Hallam's letters) is at once immobilized ("*Sat rapt*") and yet so caught up rhetorically as to experience the sensation of being caught up physically. These poems narrate this process, but Tennyson's major dramatic monologues go further, seeking not only to describe these effects of discursive rapture, but to provoke them, certainly for the auditors in the poems, possibly for those beyond it. This process governs the logic of the dramatic monologue, though rapture is just a part of the complex range of ambitions articulated by these speakers. In the course of the discursive events whose memories haunt the mourning Tennyson, Hallam is transformed, but he also seeks consciously and ambitiously to bring about transformations in others: this is the hallmark of a performance of rapt oration. The speaker is changed by the performance, as are his auditors, but so too may be some larger situation or circumstance, since the subject for a momentous oration might include or encompass, as Tennyson recalled outside Hallam's college door, "labour, and the changing mart, / And all the framework of the land." While *In Memoriam* and other poems narrate pivotal scenes of being carried away, the experience of discursive rapture underwrites as forcefully the poems that are the subject of this book, the set of intricately intertwined dramatic monologues developed in the immediate wake of Hallam's death.

The dramatic monologue, I argue throughout the two chapters of part 1, responds to charges early in the Victorian period of poetry's removal from social or political consequence. Although Tennyson is often considered conservative in both his person and his poetry, I show that he meets utilitarianism's liberal ideologies with consistent articulations of radical if staggered transformation, themselves indebted to his overlooked affiliation with Whig political positions. In producing a poetics of efficacious lyric, Tennyson engages a range of Victorian theories of oratory (including Hallam's), probing the ambitions inherent in the art of persuasive public speaking. Drawing from the logic of the consequential language that J. L. Austin termed the performative, in the first chapter I investigate the alliances in Tennyson's practice between oratory, long associated with political discourse, and the seemingly apolitical form of the dramatic monologue. Both involve discursive performances that seek to be efficacious or desire to provoke transformation. The monologic speaker seeks rhetorical exhibition or display, but also the accomplishment of some urgent ambition, however subtle or covert. Dramatic monologues, bound as they are to the theatrical dynamism inherent in the pairing of a speaker with an audience, are distinguished by their transformative effects, those they dramatize within the internal world of the poem and those they represent in the world beyond their dramatic bounds. This effect is particular to the genre itself, which everywhere engages the matter of similitude, including whether and when the ideologies suggested by the poem are like those of the poet. On a formal level, these poems make particular use of similes, which can function theatrically, performing their functions by calling attention (through the use of terms such as "like" and "as") to the performance of their functions. In this, they are like (so to speak) the dramatic monologue: the trope resembles the genre. In their resemblance to efficacious speech, Tennyson's dramatic monologues force our interrogation of the broader capacities of poetry, insistently, if anxiously, raising the possibility of larger transformations in Victorian culture that such poems might instigate, instantiate, or interrogate.

Laying the foundation for the detailed readings that occupy this book, I argue that a significant generic consistency of any dramatic monologue is its speaker's recurring ambition for rhetorical efficacy, for the accomplishment of some effect in the course of the monologue, through the medium of the monologue itself. In making this case, I deviate significantly from other critics of the genre who, following Robert Langbaum's widely influential book, *The Poetry of Experience* (1957), hear in these monologues gratuitous speech that is unintentionally self-revealing. I maintain instead that these poems constitute efficacious, highly intentional articulations: something happens during the course of a dramatic monologue because of the deliberate operations of the dramatic monologue itself. Tennyson's speakers attempt through complex discursive machinations to alter circumstances by altering—even enrapturing—persons, to effect social and political transformations by inciting personal ones.

The speaker of a dramatic monologue seeks to accomplish something in the monologue, by way of the monologue itself; this ambition to have an effect characterizes the Victorian instantiation of this genre. It is significant for my readings of Tennyson's dramatic monologues, therefore, that they were conceived in the wake of Hallam's death, but also that they were conceived in the wake of the passage of the 1832 Reform Act. In the first chapter I establish the relevance of Tennyson's political stances for his poetic practices, and in subsequent chapters I probe each dramatic monologist's political associations and ambitions. "The Victorians were not entirely free from humbug," one historian observes, "but they never humbugged themselves into thinking that they were democrats. Politically they were never democrats, if by a political democracy is meant a form of government controlled by a numerical majority of the population. We know how reluctantly the franchise was extended by the three Reform Acts of 1832, 1867 and 1884." After 1832, one in twenty-four men had the vote; after 1867, one in twelve; and after 1884, one in seven.[6] Variously conceived in 1833 and completed in 1842, 1860, and 1883, the monologues on which I focus position themselves in the arena of the era's ongoing reform agitation. Tennyson also never humbugged himself into thinking he was a democrat; his political representations, in their ad-mixture of conservative and liberal elements, were complex and considered, and demand our closer scrutiny.

This project draws from a sufficiently wide array of fields—pursuing the relevance for these poems of aspects of Victorian theological, political, scholarly, and sexological debate, just to name some larger categories—that it seems im-portant to note that my focus on a particular kind of poem that a particular poet wrote is nevertheless unwavering. In reading a set of dramatic monologues that are far-ranging in their references to ancient and contemporary texts and questions, I have tried to follow these speakers where they list—a critical illusion, no doubt, but one fostered by a genre that seeks to represent the speech of specific persons in specific situations. Minute details in Tennyson's dramatic monologues are often born of compendious referentiality, far more than has been sufficiently explored, and this study attempts to follow the diverse but consistently interlocking paths toward which dramatic speakers appear to point. The speaker of Tennyson's first dramatic monologue, "St. Simeon Stylites," the subject of chapter 2, points toward the development of rapture theology in the late 1820s and early 1830s, a context for the poem and the poet that has been entirely overlooked. This theological in-novation was closely followed by a number of Tennyson's closest friends among the Cambridge Apostles, including Hallam. My reading investigates the speaker's rhetorical aims and effects, scrutinizing the performance of this highly struc-tured monologue. I thus use Simeon as an exemplar of more general arguments I make about the genre in chapter 1, though, as we shall see, the monologue itself rigorously interrogates the responsibilities of exemplarity. Just as its speaker rises confidently on his high pillar, the monologue rises to the challenge of its own ex-ample: this first Victorian dramatic monologue may be the most ambitious, since it attempts to provoke nothing less than the rapture itself.

Victorian dramatic monologists voice efficacious language, consistently test-ing the rhetorical power of their own speech. There is no greater monument to the efficacy of poetic language, and its foundational relation to civic life, than Homer's Troy, the fabled city whose teasing presence informs a crucial strain of Tennysonian poetics. Tradition holds Troy to have been built to the music of Apollo's lyre but doomed to rapine, an end that is itself the product of a violent rapture. In "Leda and the Swan" (1923), William Butler Yeats recalls the swift and sudden seizure of a mortal by a god. The rape of Leda, "caught up" by Zeus, engenders two daughters, one of whom is Helen, held responsible by many for the downfall of Troy: "A shudder in the loins engenders there / The broken wall, the burning roof and tower" (11, 9–10).[7] In the two chapters that comprise part 2 I undertake a critical archaeology of Victorian Troy in order to unearth the subterranean ambitions and implications of an interrelated set of Tennyson's classical dramatic monologues. In excavating this poem's complex representations of democratic social change, I draw from sources as diverse as a youthful epistolary debate between Hallam and Gladstone regarding the oratorical prowess and political import of Homer's Ulysses and a dinner party conversation during which Tennyson and Gladstone bickered over Homeric translation. These and other contextual sources inform an extended new reading in chapter 4 of one of the seminal poems of this poet and the Victorian age.

Criticism is only beginning to account for the complex ways Tennyson's classicism inflected his poetics. We have some excellent studies of his sources and influences and have established that in writing about the classical world he was, as so often writers do, simply writing about what he knew, but we have not sufficiently questioned the profound lyric and generic consequences of his allegiances to classical material.[8] In *Culture and Anarchy* (1869), Matthew Arnold declares a "Hellenising" tendency to be "the master-impulse even now of the life of our nation and of humanity," and its force is everywhere evident in Tennyson's early trinity of classical dramatic monologues.[9] Far from being a specialized subject, Homeric textual criticism in particular was widely deployed, in these years of intense public debate over democratic reform, to support competing notions of ideal civic organization.

I explore Tennyson's relationships to a number of his contemporaries to illuminate some of his most consequential poems. Perhaps his most revealing personal and professional relationship was with Gladstone, the period's reigning political figure, whose life and interests intersect with the poet's at a remarkable number of contact points. An especially sharp intersection involved Arthur Hallam, who was Gladstone's closest friend at Eton and Tennyson's closest friend at Cambridge; throughout this study I trace the varying degrees of this triangle. One of his century's foremost public speakers, Gladstone can be understood to enjoy some authority on the subject of oratory; I look to him also for his insights and opinions on the writings of Homer, a subject about which he was also extraordinarily knowledgeable. Gladstone was not the period's subtlest or most respected Homeric scholar, but he was its most prolific. His voluminous writings on the subject are useful for this study partly because they present some fairly standard or widely held views, and partly because they could be controversial and indeed eccentric. The prime minister's Homeric writings present a prime example of the ways Victorian readers addressed classical study to highly contentious, and often highly personal, purposes.[10]

In considering the relation of the dramatic monologue to transformative and efficacious speech, I draw from Gladstone's theories and practice of oratory, which have acute relevance for our understanding of some aspects of Tennyson's own career and literary enterprises. Queen Victoria, whose relations with Gladstone were generally strained, noted in her diary after his death, "He had a wonderful power of speaking and carrying the masses with him."[11] Walter Bagehot, in an 1860 essay on Gladstone, articulated a danger inherent in this "power": "The higher faculties of the mind require a certain calm, and the excitement of oratory is unfavorable to that calm." Rationality can be overtaken by rapture, as auditors may get "carried away," and so may the orator, because the "force which carries away his hearers must first carry away himself," a transport Bagehot likens to a "kind of seizure."[12]

Tithonus's Troy and Tiresias's Thebes are the classical world's song-built cities, raised to the music, respectively, of Apollo and Amphion. I argue in the two chapters of part 3 that in Tennyson's dramatic monologues devoted to these two figures—poems that have always stood as notable examples of Tennyson's technical virtuosity—these speakers attempt to mimic the potency of songs that can compel civic organization. Both speakers recall in their monologues the ways in which their words have apparently failed in accomplishing their intentions (Tithonus demanded immortality instead of eternal beauty; Tiresias mouths unheeded prophecies), and both must now fashion words that will attain release from such spectacularly failed selves.

Tithonus had been a prince of Troy before his rapture by a celestial lover, and he is descended from a Trojan line of extraordinary male beauty. This genealogy is central, I argue in chapter 5, to the aesthetics of Tennysonian lyric, so often charged with being "feminine," a quality associated with being beautiful but ineffectual. Male beauty appears to unfit its possessors for civic action or responsibility, to supplant social efficacy with sensuous languor. I explore the wide implications of the self-conscious beauty of Tennysonian language not only for the genre of the dramatic monologue but also for Victorian conceptions of lyric itself. Employing Hallam's theory of "sympathy" and late Victorian sexological theories of aesthetic identification, I analyze the operations of the rapture that provokes but may also be a product of Tithonus's monologue.

In the final chapter I examine the implications for these two dramatic monologues of a range of Victorian articulations of the contradictory aspects of aristocratic indifference and aristocratic responsibility. I also pursue the consequences of Tiresias's architectonic figurations for his own discursive ambitions. Like Tithonus, he laments his impotence while concurrently seeking oratorical and indeed political power. Even as Tiresias desires to be borne away to Elysium, he aggressively tethers the speaking self to the threatened walls of a song-built city. The genre of the dramatic monologue is everywhere concerned with the mechanics of personal and political transformation; each speaker links the exceptional alterations he seeks or endures to broader social upheavals. The speaker in Tennyson's dramatic monologue "Lucretius," for example, associates his own riven identity with the fracturing Roman polity, lamenting "The Commonwealth, which breaks / As I am breaking now!" (241–42). Every major Tennysonian dramatic monologist similarly recognizes, as did the poet, the profound homology between his own transformations, willing or unwilling, and those of the society to which he is so intimately bound or from which he is rapturously borne away.

PART I

The Performance of the
Dramatic Monologue

Dramatic monologues represent suasive speech: speakers attempt to provoke transformation by way of their monologues, in the course of their monologues. In this study I look to Victorian theories of oratory, of public eloquence that aims to persuade, but it is important to distinguish the suasive ambitions of the dramatic monologue from the larger phenomenon of this period's oratorical practice. Oratory has its own ancient lineage, like poetry, and indeed like the dramatic monologue, which can be seen as rooted in Ovid's *Heroides* and the English literary tradition from Chaucer to Felicia Hemans.[1] In his 1831 "Essay on the Philosophical Writings of Cicero," Tennyson's friend Arthur Henry Hallam made the argument, however, that oratorical eloquence was to some degree like poetry in the rhetorical and linguistic pleasure it can offer. Oratory, he writes, "is an art, circumscribed by definite laws which have their origin in the creative power of genius."[2] I draw throughout this book from Hallam's theories of suasive speech, since he was notable not only in his practice but in his theorizations of the rhetor's art. My purpose here is not to review the history of oratory or its range of Victorian uses, but to study Tennyson's monologic representation of the practice of public eloquence, a central concern in his poetry throughout his career. Dramatic monologues may not seek to be directly influential as an instance of political oratory might; rather, they work to dramatize the complex operations of efficacious speech.

In the year when Tennyson began writing the dramatic monologues that most occupy this book, all poems that offer performances of efficacious speech, John Stuart Mill proposed a highly influential theory regarding the absolute distinction between poetry and suasive speech, or eloquence. Mill's well-known 1833 essay, "What Is Poetry?" forwards this claim:

> Poetry and eloquence are both alike the expression or utterance of feeling. But
> if we may be excused the antithesis, we should say that eloquence is *heard*, poetry
> is *overheard*. Eloquence supposes an audience; the peculiarity of poetry appears
> to us to lie in the poet's utter unconsciousness of a listener. Poetry is feeling
> confessing itself to itself, in moments of solitude. . . . Eloquence is feeling pouring
> itself out to other minds, courting their sympathy, or endeavouring to influence
> their belief or move them to passion or action.[3]

Mill uses the word "eloquence" rather than oratory, but we can certainly hear in
his term the idea of efficacious public discourse. The poet's language, Mill claims,
is never intended for or even aware of an audience; the poet has no designs on an
auditor or eavesdropper. Eloquence or suasive speech, on the other hand, seeks not
only to appeal to "other minds," but also to change those minds, to influence or
move them "to passion or action." Mill's own eloquence goes far in carrying his
point, but just as he was propounding this distinction, Tennyson was producing
the dramatic monologues that represent its collapse.

"*All* poetry is in the nature of soliloquy," Mill generalizes (emphasis added),
conceding nevertheless that poets do make their work public: "It may be said that
poetry which is printed on hot-pressed paper, and sold at a bookseller's shop, is a
soliloquy in full dress and on the stage." This staged soliloquy may appear in public, but it is overheard in the way that a staged soliloquy is: the poetry itself must at
least act as if it were unaware of an audience, forwarding, in a sense, not private or
solitary musings, but the illusion of them. The illusion can never take a different
turn, that is, imagine that there is some auditor (not necessarily a reader) whom
the monologist addresses: "No trace of consciousness that any eyes are upon us
must be visible in the work itself. The actor knows that there is an audience
present; but if he act as though he knew it, he acts ill." Speakers who do address
themselves to an auditor transform their discourse into some other mode:

> But when he turns round, and addresses himself to another person; when the act
> of utterance is not itself the end, but a means to an end,—viz., by the feelings
> he himself expresses, to work upon the feelings, or upon the belief or the will of
> another; when the expression of his emotions, or of his thoughts tinged by his
> emotions, is tinged also by that purpose, by that desire of making an impression
> upon another mind,—then it ceases to be poetry, and becomes eloquence.[4]

Many have recognized Mill's theory of a divorce of poetry from direct concourse
with the world as a severing of poetry from rationality or, indeed, consequence.[5]
He specifically contrasts poetry with speech seeking to be efficacious, to change,
influence, or impress "another mind." Poetry must cede rhetorical ambition; if it
articulates or indicates some purpose or aim on the part of its speaker, then it is
not merely altered, it is nullified: it "ceases to be poetry, and becomes eloquence."
And this generic transformation can work in the opposite direction, Mill argues
in "The Two Kinds of Poetry," also published in 1833. An orator may pass "into

the poet" not by becoming impassioned but by ceasing to seek to persuade, by forgoing, in the course of the speech, "the desire of attaining the premeditated end which the discourse has in view."[6] Although dramatic monologues, in the central distinction that the genre insists on, do not present the affirmations of the poet himself, we shall see that they represent a speaker who advocates on behalf of a range of interests, who dramatizes the "desire of making an impression upon another mind."

Poetry is "the natural fruit of solitude and meditation; eloquence, of intercourse with the world," Mill insists.[7] In attending to such Tennysonian monologists as St. Simeon Stylites, Ulysses, Tithonus, and Tiresias, I look at the ways in which these speakers appear to be exceptionally solitary, cut off from humanity in some of the most extreme ways imaginable. Simeon on his pillar, Ulysses in his legendary stature, Tithonus in his cursed immortality, Tiresias with his void prophetic voice: none of these speakers can find an equivalent for himself or the state in which he finds himself at the start of his monologue. But at the moment each begins to speak, he enters "intercourse with the world," imagines an audience that may be affected by his speech, who indeed must be affected by it if he is to attain the range of transformations he seeks. Dramatic monologists express a suasive imperative: each conceives, because each must, of the uses and indeed the necessity for his eloquence, the verbal felicity that can constitute suasive force. At the least, each speaker desires to set in motion a series of transformations by means of argument, reasoning, entreaty, threats, promises, and the like, as well as by various nonverbal means (movement or gesture, for example) to which his monologue adverts. The transformations a speaker incites by way of the monologue are articulated within the monologue, in the course and by way of its enunciation. These monologues are urgent; it is essential that this speech take place in its particular moment, and in each case the end is conclusive. A monologist's eloquence not only, in Mill's terms, "supposes an audience," but also creates one as he or she speaks. Although a speaker may address himself to a desperate situation, the suasive mode in which each speaks precludes merely issuing orders. Rather, speakers employ a range of oratorical tools; their monologues move across a spectrum of tones, as suasive speech often does, laboring to command an audience in several senses of the term.

In chapter 1 I examine the performance of the Victorian dramatic monologue. I forward a new claim about the functioning of the genre, both in its content—the kinds of speakers and speeches it tends to feature—and in terms of its form, in particular the revealing structural element of simile. I review a series of subjects that have long dominated criticism of this genre, including the issues of *intention* (of the poet and of the speaker), *reception* (by auditors and by readers), and *context* (both internal and external to the poem). Having established that the dramatic monologue constitutes a poetics that represents suasive speech, I turn to investigate a political stance that manifests itself in Tennyson's poetic practice.

I explore Tennyson's widely overlooked or discounted political affiliations, arguing that the poet's ideological commitments have direct bearing on the subjects of his poems as well their sound. If ever a speaker sought to court the sympathy of "other minds," it is St. Simeon Stylites, the subject of chapter 2 and the first test case for the theory of the genre I propose. This anchorite endeavors desperately to work upon "the will of another," indeed, of many others, including God, the saints, and his human auditors. And yet Simeon, balanced high atop his pillar, is less *overheard*, in Mill's sense, than *heard overhead*, and it is in the ingenuity of this discursive contrivance that he stands as fit model for the genre he invents by his very speaking.

1

THE POETICS AND POLITICS OF
THE DRAMATIC MONOLOGUE

Every Victorian dramatic monologue represents an oratorical performance, that is, dramatizes the effort to persuade, functioning not as an oration but drawing for its effects from the resources of suasive speech. Contrary to the long-standing critical assumption that sees dramatic monologists as inadvertent in their revelations and ignorant of the consequences of their speech, my argument holds that each speaker is keenly aware of the potential effects of his or her discourse (not all of which can be controlled) and through it seeks to accomplish highly complex aims. The element of performance is of course inscribed in the very term for the genre (a relatively late coinage): dramatic monologues represent theatrical events. In these poems, a speaker engages in a performance, generally addressing an audience (though this itself may be an ambiguous entity), accompanying his or her speech with appropriate gestures, varying intonations, and a range of theatrical strategies. Dorothy Mermin has observed the genre's emphasis on communication, noting, "A dramatic monologue with or without an auditor is a performance: it requires an audience." But she does not read the theatrical element as also causative, seeking transformations; in her view, "The monologue lacks the resources to develop the temporal dimension, the notion of life as a continuing process of growth and change."[1]

I hope to show, to the contrary, that dramatic monologues are highly elastic in their ability to represent transformation, and that each speaker seeks, moreover, to perform or effect some goal in the course of the monologue's temporal development. Tracking the discursive methods by which Tennyson's speakers work to accomplish various goals—some apparent, others subtle and less readily perceptible, all exceedingly ambitious—is in large measure the aim of this book. And we might see dramatic monologues also as "performative," in J. L. Austin's sense of the term. Austin's philosophy of speech acts can help to clarify the processes that

19

we shall observe in the monologues I work with most intensively. In *How to Do Things with Words*, Austin identifies the category of performative utterances, which accomplish an act by their enunciation. The marriage vow "I do," a statement that is a description but also an act, is the best-known example of this linguistic kind. With a performative utterance, according to Austin, "the issuing of the utterance is the performing of an action."[2] My readings of Tennyson's major dramatic monologues argue that these speeches are indeed acts: they articulate a speaker's goals, but the monologues themselves also come to perform these goals in the course of the monologue, by way of the monologue. In attending to the performance of this speech we shall look not only at the transformations it accomplishes within the fictive situation of the monologue, but also at its effects in the world external to the monologues, the world of this poet and his Victorian readers.

POETICS: PERSUASIVE SIMILITUDE

The ambition for forceful rhetorical efficacy is one Tennyson and his dramatic speakers know intimately. Given what I am claiming is this genre's unflagging exploration of the causes and effects of eloquent performances, it should not be surprising that what A. Dwight Culler identifies as "the first book on the dramatic monologue" was by an elocution instructor, Samuel Silas Curry.[3] President of Boston's School of Expression, Curry, in his 1908 *Browning and the Dramatic Monologue*, stresses the form's overtly theatrical and even oratorical elements, the modes in which they might be literally performed. He also suggests in passing that the poems themselves seek some effect: "There is some purpose at stake; the speaker must...cause decisions on some point of issue."[4] This early recognition of the genre's dramatization of suasive speech has become obscured, with significant implications for our understanding of this poetic kind.

Culler suggests that the genre's origins lie in the classical rhetorical form of *prosopopoeia*, or impersonation, a term he feels Tennyson "would have used, in all likelihood," for these productions. Culler notes examples of prosopopoeia in Tennyson's juvenilia, defining this exercise as "an ancient rhetorical form in which the poet or orator imagined what a particular historical or literary character might have said in a certain situation and then presented that character as actually speaking." In his study of the dramatic monologue, Alan Sinfield points to Quintilian's definition of impersonation in his *Institutio Oratoria*, a standard text in schooling for both Romans and Victorians, especially in training for public speaking.[5]

This classical precedent is a crucial one if we are to understand Tennyson's attraction to producing what his friend John Sterling called in 1842 "a kind of monological personation."[6] Culler reminds us that these impersonations constituted for the Victorians "an important exercise in the literary education of youth, for it was of value to the schoolboy in helping him realize the situation in his Greek and Latin classics."[7] While the final four chapters of this book center on Tennyson's monologues based on classical literature, it is important to note that Quintilian's *Institutio Oratoria*, titled in some English translations *The Education of the Orator*, had as its aim instruction in acts of public eloquence and efficacious speech and was enormously influential. Gladstone's biographer John Morley observed that his subject "had seriously studied from early days the devices of a speaker's training. I find copied into a little note-book many of the precepts and maxims of Quintilian on the making of an orator."[8] Quintilian regards prosopopoeia or impersonation as "the most difficult of tasks," in part because of the variety of speakers and occasions it must command: "For the same speaker has on one occasion to impersonate Caesar, on another Cicero or Cato." Referring to Cicero, Quintilian notes that he was able to "represent the character of all to whom he gave a voice so that though they spoke better than they could by nature, they still might seem to speak in their own persons." The exercise of prosopopoeia is indispensable for a range of discursive enterprises. "For orators," Quintilian notes, "of course it is absolutely essential," and he also contends that it is "of the greatest use to future poets and historians." It is crucial, then, to hear in these "fictitious speeches of historical persons" not only a dramatic performance but powerful persuasive representations.[9]

Intention

In arguing throughout this book that Tennyson's dramatic monologists rise in the power of extraordinary acts of rapt oration to effect some massive transformation of their situations, I diverge markedly from established arguments regarding both Tennyson's speakers and the genre more generally. Critics tend to characterize Tennyson's speakers as overwhelmed and incapacitated by a combination of character and circumstance. This claim has a distinguished history, aspects of which I discuss in subsequent chapters. Recent proponents include Matthew Campbell, who hears in Tennyson's dramatic monologists an "unwilled powerlessness," suggesting "the ways in which mastery and power can be cruelly inhibited."[10] "Tennyson depicts a self alienated and excluded from the world of choice and action," Isobel Armstrong argues.[11] Herbert F. Tucker maintains that this incapacitation is the hallmark of Tennyson's poetics: "His speakers remain the victims of circumstance in a double sense: they regard themselves as heirs of a past they cannot control, and at the same time they invest the present scene of aftermath with an enveloping power that dissolves the will." He states that Tennyson's career "makes sense as a series of just such submissions to an inevitable doom," an argument with which I differ considerably, especially with regard to this poet's use of this genre.[12]

In *The Poetry of Experience* Robert Langbaum puts this highly familiar claim of the impotence of dramatic monologists in these terms: "Most characteristic of Tennyson is a certain life-weariness, a longing for rest through oblivion. This emotional bias is all the more powerful because it appears to be subconscious."[13] Following so abiding a critical assumption of the poet's lack of agency or insight as to either the causes or effects of his poetry, it is but a step to the equally persistent assumption that his speakers are similarly incapacitated and unconscious. Campbell writes, "Tennyson's monologists reveal more than they wish to say," exhibiting "a sudden sense of being carried away."[14] The claim that these speakers have been in some sense or another unwillingly and even unknowingly carried away, in terms of their past experiences and present discourse, is one that I explore and seek to redefine. I argue that Tennyson's speakers do describe and enter into complex experiences of transport, even rapture, but that the speakers themselves knowingly, even willfully, set these transformations into motion by the force of an insistently ambitious discourse.

This critical consensus regarding the fundamental discursive powerlessness of Tennyson's speakers runs parallel to a similarly unwavering critical claim regarding dramatic monologists more generally, namely, that they possess neither command nor even full cognition of the effects of their speech. Langbaum, the most influential theorist of the genre, claims that these monologues are in themselves superfluous and unnecessary; he hears in these works "a superabundance of expression, more words, ingenuity and argument than seem necessary for the purpose." He adds that the "impression of gratuitousness is heightened by the fact that the speakers never accomplish anything by their utterance, and seem to know from the start that they will not."[15] Critics have long joined him in his claim; Adena Rosmarin also remarks the tendency of each speaker to have "more traits than he needs," writing of each dramatic monologist, "He is a convincing person when he is *not* perfectly adapted to his function, to the suasive exigencies of his immediate situation. The bulk of any monologue is in this sense gratuitous, at times even at odds with the speaker's attempt to persuade the narratee."[16]

The primary corollary of the argument that the dramatic monologue is unnecessary for its speaker is that it is counterproductive for him, since dramatic monologists, it is claimed, invariably reveal far more than they can intend. Alan Sinfield's overview of the genre makes this element prescriptive: a dramatic monologue "should include a first-person speaker who is not the poet and whose character is unwittingly revealed," as well as "an ironic discrepancy between the speaker's view of himself and a larger judgment which the poet implies and the reader must develop."[17] Rosmarin's study of the genre also sees ironic distance as the central effect of a dramatic monologist's speech: "His lessons are always inadvertent and never masterly, although, of course, it is his inadvertence that composes the very substance of the poet's masterly design. It is his failure to know himself that makes our edification and pleasure possible."[18] The claim that these are invariably poems representing what Sinfield terms "unwitting character revelation,"[19] in which characters have little purpose in speaking and little sense of the import or revelations of their speech—being, in a sense, overmastered by circumstances as well as by their own discourse—is a primary critical formulation regarding this genre.

Countering this perspective on the dramatic monologue as presenting speech that is unwitting, inadvertent, or unintentional, I argue that a major feature of this poetic genre is its assumption of rhetorical efficacy. Speakers are highly intentional: they desire to achieve some purpose, looking toward goals that they not only describe in the course of their monologues, but also labor consistently to achieve through the medium of their monologues. In reading these poems, I propose, the crucial starting point is to ask what each speaker seeks to perform, what processes he or she seeks to set in motion or ends he or she seeks to attain. My tendency, it might be well to state here, is to assume that they do attain their goals in some measure. Dramatic speakers achieve in particular various kinds of transformation and transportation, as witnessed by the internal evidence of the monologues themselves. Although certain specified ambitions often provide the precondition of a monologue, the reason for the speech itself, we must also track other, less tangible or visible goals that a speaker might attain by way of the monologue. This speech is the result and the articulation of a powerful sense of imperative: it is for urgent reasons that the monologist begins, and the monologue expresses a powerful command of a speaker's discourse and ultimately, I believe, of his or her situation. Ulysses seeks a crew to ferry him to a "newer world," for example, a destination that we shall see is surprisingly specific; but what are the less easily described goals, not only for the voyage but also for the dramatic monologue? While I focus on Tennyson, the dramatic monologues of Robert Browning, the Victorian poet most closely associated with the genre, are as clearly and consistently products of discursive ambitions, as are those of Amy Levy, Dante Gabriel Rossetti, Augusta Webster, and other Victorian poets. In each, the speaker has clear goals he or she intends as a result of the monologue, as well as tacit or less proximate aims.[20]

Austin distinguishes among the locutionary act, which is the act of producing an utterance; the illocutionary act, which can consist of asking, assuring, warning, promising, announcing, pronouncing, appealing, identifying, describing, and the like; and perlocutionary acts, which are illocutionary acts that have specific consequences (so that a threat will warn its auditor, or an argument may convince). Both the illocutionary and the perlocutionary, as utterances that perform acts either in the course of the utterance itself or as a later consequence of the utterance, stress the idea of efficacious language. Acts represented in dramatic monologues, as we shall see, tend to be performed both in the monologue and by way of the monologue. While Austin's studies of a range of linguistic enterprises can sound like the sorts of discursive efforts in which dramatic monologists are engaged—promising, pretending, and making excuses, for example—his insights may be particularly helpful on the subject of intentionality, long a vexed issue for this genre.[21]

I have noted the dominant critical claim that dramatic monologues by any Victorian poet exhibit speakers who reveal themselves in unwitting ways in the course of the monologue, so that the revelations that occur are considered unconscious or accidental, thus wholly subverting any discernible discursive intentions. This claim of language having unusually inadvertent consequences has been made of Tennyson's relation to his poetry as well. Summing up a critical view whose tradition I consider more closely in chapter 4, Harold Bloom remarks the "gap" between Tennyson's "intention and the actual achievement," which he does not consider altogether unfortunate.[22] Austin suggests, however, that one's "idea" of what one is "doing," or one's intention, is "as it were a miner's lamp on our forehead which illuminates always just so far ahead as we go along." Such a light can illuminate what is otherwise darkness, but only to a limited degree: "It will never extend indefinitely far ahead." He continues, "All that is to follow, or to be done thereafter, is not what I am intending to do, but perhaps consequences or results or effects thereof."[23] By this logic, we might understand that dramatic monologists have intentions, and these themselves have consequences and effects, not all of which are anticipated but all of which follow not from unwitting or inadvertent articulations, but from intentional ones. An example that I consider in greater detail in part 3, Tithonus's demand to the gods, "Give me immortality," is not the unintentional misstatement of someone who really sought eternal youth, but a deliberate, intentional request, albeit one with a range of not entirely anticipated results. A dramatic monologue can neither dictate nor describe all of its effects—what speech ever could?—but a range of premeditated and prescribed consequences arises from the speech act that is the monologue, resonating within the monologue and often well beyond it.

In their landmark essay "The Intentional Fallacy" (1946), W. K. Wimsatt and Monroe C. Beardsley insist, "The design or intention of the author is neither available nor desirable as a standard for judging the success of a work of literary art." Although they do not compare literary and oratorical speech, we have seen that John Stuart Mill, who also radically dissociates poetic from intentional discourse, does. The design or intention of an orator is of course largely manifest. An orator intends to convince auditors of some way of thinking or acting, and the oration must be judged at least in part by whether it attains any of its suasive ends. But in this it is perhaps like poetry after all. Wimsatt and Beardsley assert, "Judging a poem is like judging a pudding or a machine. One demands that it work."[24] The poem, like the pudding or machine, must perform some intended function, and it is precisely this ambition for efficacy that dramatic monologues represent. Tennyson's dramatic speakers, drawing on the associations of oratory, also seek to convince auditors of some way of thinking or acting.

Each poem constitutes a performance in several senses: as a dramatic utterance in a dramatic situation, but also as an utterance that intends to accomplish some function. These poems do not endeavor to voice a narrowly defined intention of Tennyson's, it is important to stress. Rather, they articulate *fictions of intention*, specifically the intention to persuade. Tennyson's Ulysses, for example, is attempting to convince his auditors to embark with him on a journey; this is the speaker's intention, we know, not the poet's. Ulysses seeks, indeed, to persuade his auditors of far more than the necessity of quitting Ithaca's shore, and with every word this speaker utters, Tennyson dramatizes the range and results (not all of which can be anticipated) of efficacious speech. The poet intends that his dramatic monologists speak intentionally.

Reception

The critical response to the genre of the dramatic monologue has often centered, in what has been not only a self-reflective but a radically self-reflexive process, on the critical response to the genre of the dramatic monologue. The genre itself renders the question of its own reception a dominant one, as the discourse of a dramatic monologist forces attention on what responses it is likely to prompt from named or implied auditors internal to the poem, as well as readers external to the poems. Sinfield observes, "The silent auditor is the most artificial and peculiar feature of dramatic monologue,"[25] though the presence of this figure of reception may itself be one of the clearest marks of the oratorical bent of the genre, presenting as it does some person or group whom the speaker is seeking to persuade. The auditor is entirely necessary to the monologue, then, serving in some sense as its instigator, as the catalyst (or the excuse) for the discourse itself.

The significant body of criticism occasioned by the dramatic monologue has often attempted to establish a taxonomy of this poetic form's defining characteristics, the signs by which the genre announces itself. Some critics have debated classifications and intricately argued distinctions among such terms as "expressive lyric," "dramatic lyric," "lyrical dramas," "mask lyric," and "monodrama."[26] And yet, as Tucker wisely remarks, "'Dramatic monologue' is a generic term whose practical usefulness does not seem to have been impaired by the failure of literary historians and taxonomists to achieve consensus in its definition."[27] In *Kinds of Literature*, Alastair Fowler argues, "The identification of genre is curiously retroactive," and certainly the term "dramatic monologue" did not attain currency until late in the nineteenth century; Browning, a foremost practitioner of the genre, appears never to have employed the phrase.[28] Intermediary terms used by poets, often as titles for collections, such as "Dramatic Lyrics," "Dramatic Romances," "Dramatic Idylls," "Dramatic Studies," "Dramatis Personae," as well as "Monodrama," indicate their own attempts to place and even to formalize literary production that was for some time unnamable.

Armstrong rightly urges readers of the dramatic monologue to move past the genre's "technical features" in order to "see what this dramatic form enabled the poet to explore."[29] In determining a definition of the dramatic monologue that admirably seeks to avoid grounding a definition of the genre merely in what he terms "mechanical resemblance," Langbaum distinguishes what he considers to be "an effect peculiarly the genius of the dramatic monologue," arguing, in the most influential theoretical claim regarding this genre of the past half century, for the necessary presence in the poems of "the tension between sympathy and moral judgment."[30] Encountering Browning's paradigmatic "My Last Duchess," for example, a reader is divided, Langbaum argues, between understanding and even identifying with the speaker's position and rendering moral judgment about what the speaker appears to reveal. Langbaum's focus, therefore, is chiefly on reception, and he is surely right to recognize the centrality of the effects of these words on auditors or readers. Indeed, the very fact that this genre demands that we define not what it is but what it does, or accomplishes rhetorically, points to its persuasive energies. As I have suggested, however, these effects of reception are broader and still more complex than the dichotomy Langbaum posits.

We still have much to learn about the fluid relationship between auditors and speakers, since as the monologues themselves show, neither role is a definitive one for a person or character to hold. Certainly, each speaker is profoundly and unflaggingly attentive, reading every movement or implied word of his or her auditor, scrutinizing the slightest gestures in what are invariably exchanges, however subtle and possibly nonverbal. Auditors, for their part, are actors throughout, since their responses, whether direct or inferred, can dictate or direct what monologists say at any given point. Gladstone in 1875 provided an admirer with a list of rules for the art of speaking. His final instruction reads, "Remember that if you are to sway an audience you must besides thinking out your matter, watch them all along."[31] The strategy of the century's most popular orator obtains for the speakers to whom we shall be attending: in the exchange occasioned by their suasive speech, monologists and auditors are jointly active in the production of the monologue and subject to its transformative effects. Dramatic monologues invent a fiction of a speaker's dictating his or her reception, and consequently speakers are always occupied with the acceptable limits of their rhetorical stances. The poet, too, was always acutely mindful of his reception, and the impact of the genre's reception on the production of these poems is discernible, we shall see, in the poems themselves.

Context

Austin reminds us that with any performative utterance, "the occasion of the utterance matters seriously" because "the words used are to some extent to be 'explained' by the 'context' in which they are designed to be or have actually been spoken in a linguistic interchange.[32] In *How to Do Things with Words*, he distinguishes what he calls constatives, which provide descriptive statements or establish facts (and which may be true or false), from performatives, which accomplish an act by their enunciation, such as the marriage vow "I do." A performative utterance must take place in a particular context, outside of which the words will not carry the same force or significance. Mary Louise Pratt comments that speech act theory makes it possible to examine utterances for "their surface grammatical properties" but also for "the context in which they are made, the intentions, attitudes, and expectations of the participants, the relationships existing between participants, and generally, the unspoken rules and conventions that are understood to be in play when an utterance is made and received."[33] Judith Butler develops the implications of this argument for the philosophical and linguistic question of hate speech, observing, "That the speech act is a bodily act means that the act is redoubled in the moment of speech: there is what is said, and then there is a kind of saying that the bodily 'instrument' of the utterance performs."[34] In reading dramatic monologues through the prismatic lens of context, we shall seek to understand the nature of their locutions by understanding the complexity of their situations and stations, the associations and bodily instruments each speaker wields even before he or she begins to speak.

Oratorical theorists have long incorporated physical setting and corporal presence in defining oratorical practice. In *Institutio Oratoria*, Quintilian reviews a tradition of theories regarding the aims and practices of oratory, which invariably center on the arts of persuasion; he stresses in particular the frequency with which Cicero "defined the duty of an orator as 'speaking in a persuasive manner.'"[35] Quintilian objects, however, "But many other things have the power of persuasion, such as money, influence, the authority and rank of the speaker, or even some sight unsupported by language, when for instance the place of words is supplied by the memory of some individual's great deeds, by his lamentable appearance or the beauty of his person."[36] A dramatic monologist seeks to carry away his or her auditor by rational argument, but draws on appeals to *pathos* and *ethos* as much as to *logos*. The suasive performance is enhanced by the depth of knowledge and breadth of referent that we may already possess regarding a speaker. An example Quintilian provides of a useful set piece for students practicing the art of prosopopoeia is Priam's speech to Achilles in the last book of the *Iliad*, and I return to the centrality of Trojan modes of suasive speech in my discussion of "Tithonus." Priam's success in ransoming the body of his dead son Hector is dependent not only on his words, nor even on the Trojan riches he proffers, but on his appearance (which Achilles takes special note of), his personal history as the father of many sons who have been killed by Achilles, his stature as ruler of Troy, the respect due to his old age, and the image he calls to Achilles' mind of his own father. In parts 2 and 3 of this book I discuss the poems of Tennyson's that are wholly bound to narratives of Troy in order to understand more fully the range of suasive elements these speakers employ and embody. These persuasive monologues draw their potency from factors in some cases "unsupported by language," such as the attention accorded to Ulysses' rank as well as "the memory" he invokes of his "great deeds," or the spectacle of Tithonus's "lamentable appearance," itself accentuated by his auditor's and his own memory of the former "beauty of his person." A speaker such as Ulysses derives much of his rhetorical force from the fact that his auditors, and Tennyson's readers, know at least the broad outlines of his story, and perhaps far more than that. All dramatic monologists have biographies, even those characters invented by a poet rather than selected from literary or historical sources, and part of our work as readers must be to reclaim each speaker's history, in both its original and its Victorian contexts, prior to its representation in his or her monologue.

Simile

Quintilian's example of Priam's suasive resources merits dwelling upon. Homeric eloquence is a subject that fascinated Tennyson, so this example is particularly resonant for my study, but here I would like to consider less the details of the example than the form of *exemplum* itself. Oratorical instruction from its earliest history has drawn examples from literary texts, offering selected moments for study as a central tool of practical training, and surely the form of the dramatic monologue, speech that is set apart from but always in colloquy with larger narratives (known or implied), resembles the exemplary abstracted prosopopoeic texts of rhetorical schooling. But we must also attend to the resonance of the tool of exemplum: the rhetorical set piece—a speech of Priam or Ulysses, for example—is established precisely *as* an example, an object of imitation. The exercise of dramatic similitude is thus at the heart of prosopopoeia. Orators and poets in training—the Victorian ones, certainly—were to attain the capacity for speaking like a character, preferably one drawn from a Greek or Latin text. Both orators and poets therefore can depend for their effects on a gift for speaking likenesses. And indeed *likeness*, the trope of simile, appears to be necessary to the exercise itself, as students labor to speak like Priam or Ulysses. While my readings of Tennyson's poems pay attention to actual similes, I want here to make the broader claim that this figure of speech serves as a structuring device for the genre of the dramatic monologue more generally.

The attempt even to categorize the genre of the dramatic monologue, classifying the works that belong to it and that do not, has often hamstrung criticism of the poems. Robert Langbaum observes, "No one has quite known what to do with the dramatic monologue except to classify it, to distinguish kinds of dramatic monologues and to distinguish the dramatic monologue from both the lyrical and dramatic or narrative genres." "Such classifications," he grimly concludes, "have a way of killing off further interest in the subject."[37] Generic identification is always dependent on resemblance, as works are assembled into identifiable kinds in conjunction with other works they are like and in contrast to those with which they are unlike. The concept of genre itself functions by the logic of similitude; we mark a range of individual texts as sufficiently "like" one another to merit grouping together. That this literary-historical organizational principle was for so long the most distinctive and inescapable feature of critical discussions of this particular genre, however, answering what appears to have been an implicit invitation made to critics by these poems to classify them, itself bespeaks the genre's organizing principle of similitude.

Recognizing that "the dramatic monologue is unprecedented in its effect," Langbaum determines, "Its effect distinguishes it, in spite of mechanical resemblance, from the monologues of traditional poetry." While I join him in wishing to move past enumerating what he terms "objective criteria" for generic inclusion, I want nevertheless to press further on the issue of resemblance.[38] We can understand the unprecedented effect of this genre by understanding the operations of resemblance itself, that is, very specifically, the trope of simile. The *New Princeton Encyclopedia of Poetry and Poetics* offers this standard definition of simile: "A figure of speech most conservatively defined as an explicit comparison using 'like' or 'as.'" "The function of the comparison," the definition continues, "is to reveal an unexpected likeness between two seemingly disparate things."[39] I should note that although "like" and "as" are the most common links between the entities compared, the trope is not dependent exclusively on these particular connectives. As one theorist of the simile has stated, "To understand the potential range of similes, the entire connective paradigm must be explored," and thus similes could be understood to follow also from such connective phrases as "as one might," "as though," "as if," "the way," "seemingly," "seem to," "the way that," as well as transitive and intransitive verbs such as "recall," "echo," "recreate," "copy," "speak," "suggest," "depict," "imitate," and "resemble."[40] The entry on simile in the *Princeton Encyclopedia* concludes, "At the very least, the current exploration into the range of simile suggests that it may be a far more pervasive aspect of both language and perception than has previously been thought."

Simile is "probably the 'oldest readily identifiable poetic artifice in European literature,'" according to the *New Princeton Encyclopedia*. We might again draw an example of this trope from the *Institutio Oratoria* of Quintilian, which itself, according to Marsh H. McCall in his book on the subject, "offers the most complete and perceptive discussion of comparison in antiquity." Quintilian distinguishes simile from metaphor in these terms: "On the whole metaphor is a shorter form of simile, while there is this further difference, that in the latter we compare some object to the thing which we wish to describe, whereas in the former this object is actually substituted for the thing. It is a comparison when I say that a man did something *like a lion*, it is a metaphor when I say of him, *He is a lion*." McCall posits that Quintilian's choice of example follows from Aristotle, who employs a similar Homeric description, contrasting a simile concerning Achilles in motion, as a hero who "leapt on the foe as a lion," with a metaphor, "the lion leapt."[41] Although Quintilian acknowledges the importance of the conjunctive terms "like" and "as," the distinction is founded on more than whether an introductory word of comparison is used. Fundamental identity is determined by the comparative trope employed. The metaphor works by substitution, by the homology between what is described and what it is compared to; simile works not only to connect but also to separate, acknowledging two separate identities.

We can witness the metaphoric effect of identificatory substitution in the work of Tennyson's Romantic precursors, in which the speaking *I* of the poem is often taken to be indivisible from the poet. While examples abound from the Romantic poets with whose work Tennyson was intimate, let us take an example from Tennyson's own *In Memoriam*.[42] In one of the elegy's best-known stanzas, Tennyson declares a metaphoric relation between himself and a crying infant: "But what am I? / An infant crying in the night: / An infant crying for the light: / And with no language but a cry" (54.17–20). The mourning poet is not *like* a wordless wailing newborn, he *is* one; the infantile identification is wholesale, rendering the elegy itself an inchoate primal wail. That Tennyson's use of similes was precise is clear throughout his poetry, as we shall see, and witnessed also by his conversation. William Allingham records in his diary an 1863 walk with Tennyson at Farringford, where, he writes, "we went down and walked about the grounds, looking at a cedar, a huge fern, an Irish yew." Allingham continues, "Then we went down the garden, past a large tangled fig-tree growing in the open—'It's like a breaking wave,' says I. 'Not in the least,' says he." Tennyson is decisive, and dismissive, making clear his exacting standards for any claim of resemblance. That the poet's knowledge of the range of acceptable similes is definitive is not challenged by Allingham, who comments on Tennyson's terse disagreement, "Such contradictions, *from him*, in noway disagreeable."[43]

The logic of the simile is the logic of the retention of a separation of identity for comparable but unlike entities, and this logic is a defining aspect of the genre of the dramatic monologue. Any Victorian dramatic monologue establishes the identity of a speaker who is distinct from the poet; this every critic of the genre has agreed on. The most renowned declaration of this separation comes from Robert Browning, who in a note at the beginning of *Dramatic Lyrics* (1842), a collection of what we now term dramatic monologues, called the poems, "though often Lyric in expression, always Dramatic in principle, and so many utterances of so many imaginary persons, not mine."[44] In thus introducing a volume of poetry of which he identifies himself as the author, Browning actively disavows words he concurrently acknowledges to be his own. The author is the poet, of course, on the most literal level, because the duke of Ferrara speaks Browning's words, just as Ulysses speaks Tennyson's words. The first implication

of Browning's discursive division, then, is that these monologues resemble separable utterances, and the monologists resemble speaking individuals, with striking
verisimilitude. These speakers are thus from the start understood to be figures of
resemblance. (We might note that the speakers in Browning who are concerned
with artworks are themselves generally obsessed with the challenges of achieving
representational verisimilitude, strongly valuing apt resemblances in painting and
sculpture.)

In considering this question of discursive resemblance, it is useful to return to
Austin's description of intention as, "as it were," a minor's lamp, which he uses to
make his argument about the range and limits of intention. In thus employing
the simile, he exemplifies Quintilian's point that similes are a crucial component
of suasive language. And yet it merits noting that this and other metaphors and
similes that animate his discussion are surprising, because Austin largely excludes
poetic language from his theories of performative utterances, attempting in a sense
to quarantine the disease of dramatic language: "As utterances our performatives
are also heir to certain other kinds of ill which infect all utterances. And these
likewise, though again they might be brought into more general account, we
are deliberately at present excluding." He claims, "A performative utterance will,
for example, be *in a peculiar way* hollow or void if said by an actor on the stage,
or if introduced in a poem, or spoken in soliloquy." His example of the hollow
or void seems especially relevant to dramatic monologues, which draw for their
effects precisely from their association with the categories he provides, that is, the
resources of theatrical performance, poetry, and soliloquy. He shifts from calling such usage "peculiar" to calling it "special," explaining, "Language in such
circumstances is in special ways...used not seriously, but in ways *parasitic* upon
its normal use—ways which fall under the doctrine of the *etiolations* of language.
All this we are *excluding* from consideration."[45] "Austin's parasite has gone on
to enjoy a distinguished career in literary theory and criticism," Andrew Parker
and Eve Sedgwick comment; Jacques Derrida and others have argued that what
Austin excludes "as anomalous, exceptional, 'nonserious'" is iterability itself.[46] But
Austin's distinction echoes Mill's distinction between the *heard* and the *overheard*,
the suasive and the poetical, which in turn echoes a distinguished line of philosophical approaches to the question of what things poetry appears to be doing, or
not doing, with its words.

"The self of a dramatic monologue, after all, is the most elaborate illusion
of the text, the product of a speech act and not its producer," Tucker argues,[47]
but I see the mechanisms of the dramatic monologue operating differently. The
question Austin set into motion was how we might distinguish language in its
"ordinary" efficacious uses and in its "nonserious" or "parasitic" uses, a divide the
dramatic monologue bridges. Pratt suggests that in order to distinguish "between
the fictional speaker of a work of literature and its real-world speaker, the author,"
we follow Richard Ohmann in calling certain literary works "imitation speech

acts." This position risks confirming Austin's suggestion that literary instances are secondary, false, or parasitic, but is nevertheless helpful in recognizing that performativity can itself be theatrically performed by way of dramatic similitude.[48] Dramatic monologists seek to cause effects in the course of their speaking; what they perform are the mechanics and imperatives of persuasive speech, thus attaining an illusion also of some of its performative consequences.

Each dramatic monologist speaks, then, in the *likeness* of a speaker. This similitude can help account for the fact that readers of these poems have so often attempted to determine what views most closely represent the poet's. A significant critical occupation, from the earliest appearance of any of these poems, has been uncovering which beliefs articulated by the speakers are those of the poet, thereby arguing for Browning's endorsement of the aesthetic theories of Fra Lippo Lippi, say, or Tennyson's endorsement of the political views of the speakers of *Locksley Hall* or *Maud*. But in seeking to identify an exact equivalence of views—for instance, that the pro-war views of the speaker in *Maud* are Tennyson's—readers have engaged in what we could call a metaphoric fallacy. Rather than being identical with a poet's views, we might instead insist that the views of a dramatic speaker can only be *like* the views of the poet. And the question of discursive or ideological likeness attends these assemblies of dramatic monologists, as readers have quite reasonably tended to cluster these poems by resemblance, affiliating Browning's Renaissance art poems "My Last Duchess," " Pictor Ignotus," "Andrea del Sarto," and "Fra Lippo Lippi," for example, or Tennyson's classical monologists, as the poet himself did, in calling "Tithonus" and "Tiresias" "pendent" to "Ulysses," and thus making patent their likeness. Although Tennyson had not yet conceived his dramatic monologues during Hallam's lifetime, the poet's friend, reading Tennyson's "Mariana" (1830), nevertheless recognized that the female character's voice arose from an accretion of likenesses. Hallam wrote to Tennyson's sister Emily in an appreciation that must have sounded to the poet after his friend's death like an assignment, "Alfred's Mariana grew up by assimilative force, out of the plaintive hint left two centuries ago by Shakespeare."[49]

And yet, in spite of the centrality of likeness, or "assimilative force," to monologic identity, the genre demands still more insistently that we always recognize the *unlikeness* of the speaker and the poet. Alan Sinfield offers a capacious definition with which most readers would agree, determining "to consider all first-person poems where the speaker is indicated not to be the poet as dramatic monologue." The defining feature of the genre, therefore, is its insistence on an absolute separation between poet and speaker: the speaker of the poem is not the poet. Sinfield considers this an example of a "feint," arguing that the dramatic monologue "feigns because it pretends to be something other than what it is: an invented speaker masquerades in the first person which customarily signifies the poet's voice." Sinfield's distinction between speaker and poet is instructive, but it risks inviting moral judgment against the speaker, not on the basis of the content of the monologue (as Langbaum does) but on the form, so that any monologist is, by dint of the genre itself, false, even potentially mendacious, working chiefly to dupe the reader. "My Last Duchess," for example, "is experienced throughout by the sophisticated reader as a set-up."[50] The impression speakers give of attempting to manipulate auditors (and readers) is due to the oratorical underpinning of the genre; this in itself indicates how strongly every monologist labors to attain rhetorical command of situations.

The issue of the judgment of dramatic speakers by readers and internal auditors has been a bugbear of criticism of this genre: we have too often heard these speakers only to judge them. This critical emphasis on judgment has limited our ability to understand the full range of what these speakers are saying; in desiring to apprehend speakers, as we might criminals, we have failed fully to comprehend them. Indeed, with dramatic monologues, we often arrive as auditors at a moment that is past the point when judgment over past deeds would be a particularly apposite or at least unanticipated response: speakers tend to voice the expected judgment directly in their monologues. Browning's artists, for example (including Pictor Ignotus, Andrea del Sarto, and Fra Lippo Lippi), all announce clearly the judgments that stand already on their lives and works. And yet these judgments are not offered because the actions of this speaker are at an end or completed, but because, indeed, he is moving toward some future goal—Browning's duke attaining his next duchess, Tennyson's Ulysses embarking on his journey, to take the best-known examples—that will require a successful rhetorical performance to accomplish. Thus the monologue itself is the most forceful action in which the speaker engages: it represents the *summa*—the highest point and also the summation—of all his ambitions. Internal auditors and readers are to be affected by this speech in ways the speaker closely intends; if anything, the auditors—ourselves included—are being assessed, even judged, continuously by the speaker, as all the asides and verbal elbowing throughout the majority of dramatic monologues attest. We in turn must attempt to assess this discourse in the way that we weigh the effects of any speech or oratory; our judgment is thus a rhetorical or aesthetic matter as much as a moral one.

I maintain in each of my readings that these speakers are entirely authentic in their discourse, that in every case each speaker means what he says, in ways that are calculating but not necessarily therefore duplicitous. I argue, indeed, that the genre does invoke the notion of duplicity in the most literal manner, namely, that of a dualism of speakers (the monologist and the poet) who are coexistent and concurrent, due less to feigning than to structuring along the lines of simile. Metaphor produces or reflects radical and, many theorists have claimed, wholesale identity: two distinct entities (the poet and the speaker of a poem in the first person, for example) are one. Simile announces a sharp differentiation between the two conjoined entities. The connective language stresses, and even magnifies or exaggerates, an essential separation: to say that Achilles is "like" a lion is to announce that he is not one. The conjunction "like" highlights the difference between the entities, dividing the two elements being compared.

The standard definition of simile as a yoking together of unlike things can illuminate Browning's now classic definition of the dramatic monologue: these utterances are "not mine," but they are *like* "mine." In a study of Wallace Stevens's use of simile, J. V. Brogan reminds us, "In simile...one thing is said only to resemble another, never to *be* another; the two are always two and yet are joined *as* one by that resemblance."[51] Two unlike discourses, those of the poet and of the dramatic monologist, are conjoined, actively maintaining both resemblance and unlikeness. And this antithesis extends to the experience of the reader, since we can now see how Langbaum's influential distinction between sympathy and judgment itself operates under the logic of simile. A reader responds, he argues, with sympathy regarding those views of a monologist he considers *like* his own, and with judgment regarding those views he considers *unlike* his own (Langbaum consistently assumes a male reader—like himself, as it were).[52] The monologue is dependent for a variety of its effects, then, on its creation of dramatized situations of simile.

I am placing a considerable emphasis on the foundational significance of the trope of simile to the genre of the dramatic monologue, but it is important to acknowledge that simile is traditionally considered subordinate to metaphor. As the *Princeton Encyclopedia* reminds us, "One of the most interesting and salient facts about simile is that in Western culture, at least, there has been a traditional prejudice against simile in favor of metaphor." Though simile and metaphor tend to be viewed along a hierarchical scale, each trope performs vital and distinct functions, so that we might view simile as being like metaphor (knowing that the comparison affirms their unlikeness) rather than less than metaphor. Aristotle is credited with establishing this ranking, having argued that simile is inferior for two reasons, namely, that its locutions are longer, so "less pleasing," and that, because simile "does not affirm that this *is* that, the mind does not inquire into the matter."[53]

For Quintilian, simile seems never to have been negligible in its uses or effects; he consistently argues that for the functional purposes of oratory, simile is a highly purposive trope. Similes have long been charged with serving chiefly as poetic ornament, an issue my discussion of "Tithonus" will take up, but Quintilian stresses the particular use of simile for establishing proof, due to its capacity for presenting apt comparisons. Alexander Bain's *English Composition and Rhetoric* (1869) can help us to understand further how the ambition for efficacious speech, whether in poetry or oratory, is connected to the trope of simile. Like Quintilian, Bain has great admiration for the possibilities inherent in simile, declaring, "The intellectual power named Similarity, or Feeling of Agreement, is the chief inventive power of mind." He notes that this skill is particular to "great poets" and uses as an example lines from the *Iliad*: "The eloquence of Ulysses is described by the help of a similitude—

Soft *as the fleeces of descending snows*
The copious accents fall with easy art;
Melting they fall, and sink into the heart![54]

I shall return in chapter 3 to this simile because the oratorical brilliance of Homer's Ulysses has direct bearing on that of Tennyson's Ulysses, but it merits noting here that Bain considers the capacity for recognizing and making comparisons—and the chief example he gives is a simile—to be a distinguishing feature of *poesis*, or making, itself. More than a century later, Steven G. Darian has also claimed that the conscious use of simile can inspire highly original conceptual work. He argues, "The simile process provides not just literary embellishment but a tool for serious thinking, scientific and otherwise. As such, it transcribes a paradigm of the creative act itself, whether in poetry or physics. The history of science might approximate a continuous revelation of hidden analogies between two unlike things or matrices." Darian offers as an example "Newton's discovery 'that the moon behaved like an apple.'"[55]

The relation between simile (the yoking together of unlike things) and rhetoric can be seen, then, as especially close. Oratory, the art of persuasive speech, may be necessary in the first place because of a disjunction or dissimilarity between a speaker and an audience. As Bain points out, "It is supposed that the persons addressed do not, at the outset, see a subject as the speaker sees it, otherwise they would not need persuading." For this reason, a requirement for successful oratory, as Bain puts it in capital letters, is "KNOWLEDGE OF THE PERSONS ADDRESSED." Without this knowledge of an audience's separation from a speaker who desires to form some conjunction between differing views, rhetoric becomes impotent, because, he declares, "inattention to the character of the persons addressed will render nugatory the oratorical efforts of the highest genius." The fundamental challenge faced by an orator is best expressed through the trope of simile; Bain explains, "The Means of Persuasion may be stated, in general terms, as *the assimilating of the object desired with the principles of action of those addressed.*"[56] The rhetorical efforts work through making a successful comparison, recognizing the essential difference in identities between the speaker and the audience that makes the oratorical occasion necessary, even as the audience is being prompted to assimilate the speaker's views.

Similes and metaphors are both tropological agents, altering the identity of the object or person to which they refer. Whether the man is a lion or is like a lion, he is now, due to the trope, conceived of differently (indeed, conceived of by way of prior difference), turned from one identity to another. What simile can do is underscore this transformation while simultaneously undercutting it. Simile "equates one thing with another...while dividing one thing from another," as

Brogan puts it. In at once positing and negating identification, simile can perform something not easily accomplished, and contradictory: in Brogan's words, it can "fragment and unite": "The simultaneous sustaining of both poles is made by positing, semantically, an identity even as this identity is denied."[57]

The logic of the Victorian dramatic monologue is therefore similar to—like—the logic of simile. As I have suggested, this is due to the maintenance of a necessary distinction between the poet and the speaker, but it is also due to the similar performance of both the genre and the trope. Certainly, a dramatic monologue can constitute in a formal sense, whatever the circumstance or setting, a performance. Defining simile, Bain writes, "Simile or Comparison consists in likening one thing to another formally or expressly."[58] The comparison, because made expressly and explicitly, one might say self-consciously, calls attention to its own performance. The simile, in straining credulity, renders any comparison theatrical. *Metaphora* (Latin *translatio*), meaning "to carry across," might seem the more appropriate figure of speech to be favored by Tennyson's generic practice, since this "carrying over" could be understood to correspond with the "carrying away" of rapture. But rapture is consistently understood by him to take place between unlike beings (a god and a man, for example) whose dissimilarity, as we shall see, is vital to the complex experience of seizure.

Both the trope of simile and the genre of the dramatic monologue seek to perform transformation. Due to the articulated comparison of a simile, an identity announces its alteration by the simile itself, and identities and situations are dramatically altered in the course of a dramatic monologue by way of the monologue itself. Oratory, according to Alexander Bain, "avails itself of the poetic charms,"[59] and we might add as a corollary that poetry avails itself, when it chooses, of oratorical devices. Dramatic monologists enact instances of oratorical similitude, making use of the tools of oratory (including the simile) to perform for an audience—whether an audience is one or many, real or imagined, present or absent. Speakers intend through this speech to perform or attain some result, including and especially, in the case of a range of Tennysonian monologists, the effect of discursive rapture. Oratorical performances and dramatic monologues have in common a driving ambition for rhetorical efficacy. Both discursive forms seek transformation, broadly and diversely conceived, with the most representative examples of the genre being distinguished by their transformative effects. The genre must ultimately be defined less by its technical elements than by the processes it initiates and unfolds. In a Victorian dramatic monologue a speaker seeks a host of transformations—of his or her circumstances, of his or her auditors, of his or her self, and possibly all these together—in the course of the monologue, and ultimately attains these by way of the monologue. Dramatic monologues exhibit the mechanics and imperatives of persuasive speech, drawing particularly on the logic of similitude. Gladstone, attending to the speakers of Homeric epic, vigorously praises the "great and diversified oratorical resources of the Poet."[60] The poet to whom he refers is Homer, the significance of whose oratorical representations for both Tennyson and Gladstone I consider. But we must attend to the great and diversified oratorical resources of the Victorian poet as well.

POLITICS: WHIG POETICS

Due to the oratorical performance of the dramatic monologue—the ambition of each of its speakers to attain some suasive goal in the monologue, by way of the monologue—the genre is especially suited to political articulation. Before developing the centrality of transformational oratory to this genre in greater detail in the chapters to follow, it is necessary to clarify the political stances of the poet and their direct effect on his poetics. Representing a line of critical consensus, Robert Langbaum insists, "To understand the essential Tennyson, the only Tennyson who can interest us, we must discard the Victorian image [of the laureate] for the image, proposed by Harold Nicolson a generation ago, of the brooding recluse of the Lincolnshire wolds and the talented misfit of Cambridge."[61] Too summarily discarded, this Victorian image must now be retrieved, not to supplant in turn the figure of the recluse of the wolds (itself also a Victorian image), but to understand how continuous are this poet's representations of the wolds and the world. On the matter of the civic relevance of Tennyson's poetry, in particular, nineteenth-century readers were generally capable of reading this poet more broadly and fully than twentieth-century readers have been. The Victorian image of this Victorian poet can therefore teach us about the complex social workings of this poetry and the culture that valued it so highly.

The issue of Tennyson's political affiliations is unusually vexed. Because these have been generally ill-defined, we tend to call them indeterminate and indefinable and to attribute to Tennyson a vague ideological confusion, rejecting the possibility that he may have held coherent and consistent political opinions. Tennyson biographer Robert Bernard Martin claims, regarding the poet's political opinions, "Although certainly curious, he never gave much of his mind to the subject." It has come to seem that Tennyson's views were little understood, at least by him. Elevated in 1884 to the peerage by Gladstone, liberal prime minister, and affiliated with the Liberals by no less an authoritative guide than Debrett's Peerage, Tennyson has nevertheless long been considered conservative, by vague instinct if not by specific profession. Martin maintains, "His instincts were deeply conservative, but otherwise he tended to confuse political thought with a xenophobic patriotism."[62] Tucker calls the poet "conservative in most respects," remarking in particular a "psychological conservatism," inescapable because internalized.[63] Among the most comprehensive discussions of Tennyson's politics is that of his grandson Charles Tennyson, but even he introduces his essay on the subject with a disclaimer as to its fundamental relevance for the poet: "As he was, before everything, a creative artist, his interest was likely to be instinctive, not giving allegiance to any single political creed or party."[64]

Tennyson thus appears to be either an unconvincing liberal or an unconscious conservative. Either because or in spite of this dichotomy, he seems to have enjoyed support among a variety of governments. Placed on the civil lists in 1842 by the Tory Robert Peel (largely on the basis of the prime minister's appreciation of "Ulysses"), which gave him a measure of recognition and financial support as a young poet, Tennyson was elevated over four decades later to the House of Lords under Gladstone's liberal leadership at Gladstone's instigation, an event I revisit in the conclusion. Though he held himself apart from political parties, themselves very much in flux throughout the nineteenth century, Tennyson is nevertheless closely and clearly allied with a very specific political position, albeit a long obsolescent one, and this position has a great deal to do with the processes of transformation that consistently engage his poetry. Understanding his political affiliations requires reviewing the history of a party that has moved into obscurity, one, indeed, with close if strained connections both to nineteenth-century conservative ideologies and to what was to become, in the course of the century, the Liberal Party. The apparent contradictions in Tennyson's allegiances closely reflect the fissures within the ancient, once powerful, but now disappeared political party of the Whigs. Between 1830 and 1852 the Whigs were in government for seventeen years, ultimately overseeing a range of social reforms, and yet by midcentury the party had come to seem increasingly anachronistic, and in 1936 G. M. Young could declare, "The great Whig name has not been heard for fifty years."[65] Although there are differences as to when it finally passed into other incarnations, some consider that the party was "dispersed after 1852." The Whig ideological position nevertheless remained congenial to Tennyson, and not to him alone; as historian Peter Mandler notes, "Whiggism, and the high aristocratic style that went with it, . . . kept its presence and meaning deep into the heart of Victoria's reign."[66]

Ironically, given what I hope to show was his own profound ideological influence on the poet, it was Arthur Henry Hallam who originated the reading of Tennyson, so long prevalent, as removed from contemporary political or social contexts. In his important essay "On Some of the Characteristics of Modern Poetry, and on the Lyrical Poems of Alfred Tennyson," published in *Englishman's Magazine* in August 1831, Hallam sought to establish the terms by which this new poet was to be apprehended. He assures prospective readers, "He comes before the public unconnected with any political party, or peculiar system of opinions" (*Letters*, 191). In dissociating Tennyson from any party or ideology, Hallam may have been trying to shield his friend from the openly political partisanship that characterized early nineteenth-century reviewing, a tactic that failed, given that Tennyson's early work was championed by Benthamite reviewers such as W. J. Fox and J. S. Mill and savaged by Tory reviewers such as John Wilson Croker.[67]

This resistance to endorsing openly any particular party or position is one the poet himself maintained throughout his life; his son reports his reply when "asked what politics he held": "I am of the same politics as Shakespeare, Bacon, and every sane man."[68] When elevated to a peerage in 1884, Tennyson sat on the cross benches in the House of Lords to show that he was unaffiliated with either party. His intermediate placement marks an attempt to appear neutral, but it also points to the fact that the poet's deepest ideological allegiance was to a party no longer formally in existence, itself known for straddling ideological divides, whose influence on Tennyson's politics and poetry was formative and inescapable.

Becoming a Democracy

Tennyson's grandson Charles tells us that "the Tennyson family were Whigs by tradition."[69] The Whigs rose to prominence in the seventeenth century as a party of aristocrats who resisted the possibility that their property and liberties could be compromised by the arbitrary powers of the monarchy. Aristocratic rebels, they were opposed to both despotism and full democracy, assiduously protecting their oligarchical privileges against the incursions of either the crown or the crowd. Because they operated as a check against the king, they had defiantly served as "a permanent party of opposition" before themselves taking power in 1830.[70] The Whigs were committed to protecting the closely held interests of England's ruling families; it can seem incongruous, then, that it was they who managed to propose and pass, after successive attempts, the "Great" Reform Bill of 1832 (also called the Whig Reform Bill and eventually termed the First), which ushered in limited electoral and social reforms and profoundly altered British society. That the Whig Party should spearhead these measures was one of its most contested aspects, since the party rested so solidly on aristocratic foundations. Benjamin Disraeli, like Gladstone a rising conservative politician at the time of the passage of the Whig Reform Bill, called the Whigs "pretended advocates of popular rights" and claimed that though the measures of the bill were "apparently of a very democratic character," they actually "veil an oligarchical project."[71] This widespread suspicion of the aims of the Whigs in advancing a cause that all called at points "democratic" may have had something to do with what seemed an internal contradiction in the aims and allegiances of the party itself; they presented what T. A. Jenkins terms a "characteristically Whig blend of reformism and conservatism."[72] Disraeli sums up the confusion and the skepticism they aroused: "A Tory and a Radical, I understand; a Whig—a democratic aristocrat, I cannot comprehend."[73]

Upon the news of the passage of the Whig Reform Bill, Tennyson, then at home at his father's rectory in Somersby, broke into the church with several of his siblings "to ring the church bells madly." The horrified parson, a Tory, rushed in; the poet's son Hallam reports, "More than once my father thought of turning this scene into verse as an interesting picture of the times" (*Memoir*, 1:93). The poet's uncle Charles Tennyson was a Whig member of Parliament from Grimsby, who in the few years previous to the bill's passage had been, according to the poet's grandson and biographer Charles Tennyson, "one of the leaders of the movement for Electoral Reform," even holding a minor position in the reform government.[74] In 1833 Charles Tennyson, a member of the "extreme left wing of the Party," sponsored a resolution that found strong support, though it did not carry, to require that general elections be called every three years instead of seven, a resolution that Hallam mentions in a letter to Tennyson.[75] And yet the clanging of the Somersby church bells did not ring in radical alterations, only those deemed sufficient to appease public opinion, such as limited extension of the franchise. Armstrong valuably reminds us that no Victorian poems were "written in a full democracy," a crucial fact that tends to be overlooked.[76] The Reform Bill's attainment of highly circumscribed political alteration was the stated goal of the leading Whig orator on the subject, Thomas Babington Macaulay, whose "parliamentary speeches in the grand crisis of the first Reform Bill," as Gladstone recalled, "achieved for him . . . immense distinction."[77] Macaulay's speech of March 2, 1831, in particular is widely considered one of the greatest oratorical events in the history of the British Parliament. In it, he argues that without some extension of the electorate, "great and terrible calamities will befall us." Insisting that limited reform was the only way to avert "the wreck of laws, the confusion of ranks, the spoliation of property, and the dissolution of social order," Macaulay urged, "Turn where we may, within, around, the voice of great events is proclaiming to us, Reform, that you may preserve."[78]

Tennyson's powerful bond with Hallam, so critical to the dramatic monologues I consider in depth, was cemented in part by their shared commitment to Whig political positions. Whiggism was Hallam's longest standing and most abiding ideological and even practical commitment. For years his correspondence constantly recurs to questions of Whig history and contemporary Whig politics, reviewing parliamentary debates, bills, and cabinets in minute and impassioned detail. (Chapter 3 looks at a sampling of these letters, focusing on an epistolary argument Hallam had with Gladstone concerning the "character" of Ulysses.) His father, Henry Hallam, was a prominent Whig historian with close ties to party leaders, whose great work at this time was his four-volume *Constitutional History of England* (1827). While he also authored an influential history of the Middle Ages, Henry Hallam's *Constitutional History* constituted the "first work on modern England of national and international importance," a text cited often in parliamentary debate and studied by the young Victoria and Albert "as a guide," according to G. P. Gooch, who calls Hallam "the first authoritative exponent of Whig historical philosophy."[79] Constitutional history was an especially dear Whig topic.

Since the 1688 Restoration, Whigs had sought to protect aristocratic privilege against monarchical rule; they fiercely protected the Constitution as the central means by which they could hold the crown in check and maintain liberty, as they conceived it, against tyranny. The 1830 journey of Hallam and Tennyson in aid of the insurgency in Spain may have been partly inspired by what one historian calls the "popular Whig sympathy for peoples fighting for national independence and constitutional liberty."[80] According to Charles Tennyson, Henry Hallam was "one of the leading historical and literary scholars of the day...known in all the great Whig houses and the best literary society."[81] It was impossible for Arthur Hallam's friends not to be aware of his father's stature; as Gladstone, Hallam's close friend at Eton, reminisced, "To be the son of Mr. Hallam, the historian, was in itself a great distinction."[82]

Tennyson "had a peculiar horror of revolutions, and all sudden and violent change in the established social order," an early twentieth-century critic observed.[83] This horror can be seen as specifically antidemocratic. Defining "democracy" in *Keywords*, Raymond Williams notes that the investment of a positive valence in the word is a phenomenon of the late nineteenth and early twentieth centuries; previously it was in general "a strongly unfavourable term." He explains in *Culture and Society* that in the early nineteenth century democrats "were seen, commonly, as dangerous and subversive mob agitators."[84] Tennyson's fear of what he took to be a revolutionary stance was far from singular, and indeed was reflective of a political party in ascendance in the period of his political maturation; Macaulay also felt that universal suffrage would "produce a destructive revolution."[85]

A resistance to all but the most gradual introduction of democracy characterized Tennyson's political opinions throughout his life; he declared in 1887, "I do not in the least mind if England, when the people are less ignorant and more experienced in self-government, eventually *becomes* a democracy" (*Memoir*, 2:338). "He had never shaken off the disappointment," his grandson Charles Tennyson explains, "shared by so many of the old Whigs, at the social and economic results of the extension of the franchise, and he feared the effects of further extensions, if unaccompanied by a real improvement on the education of the people."[86] Tennyson's stress on *becoming*, a process of transition slowed still further by the adverb "eventually," does not imagine that democracy delayed is democracy denied. Perhaps most revealing in his wording, however, is the opening clause, "I do not in the least mind," not simply because the qualifier "in the least" is, at the least, unconvincing, but because its tone might be termed aristocratic, suggesting that the approval of a few might weigh more than the direct representation of the many.

Tennyson's wary attitude toward the oratorical basis of some aspect of Victorian democratic practice, articulated in complex ways in his dramatic monologues, is itself a major consideration of this book. In his 1886 poem "Locksley Hall Sixty

Years After," which infuriated Gladstone, Tennyson mocks what he sees as the illusion and illogic of a high-flown rhetoric of equality:

> Equal-born? O yes, if yonder hill be level with the flat.
> Charm us, Orator, till the Lion look no larger than the Cat,
>
> Till the Cat through that mirage of overheated language loom
> Larger than the Lion,—Demos end in working its own doom. (111–14)

The antidemocratic fervor of these lines struck Walt Whitman forcibly. In "A Word about Tennyson" in the January 1, 1887, issue of *The Critic*, Whitman quotes them and then observes, good-naturedly, "The course of progressive politics (democracy) is so certain and resistless, not only in America but in Europe, that we can well afford the warning calls, threats, checks, neutralizings, in imaginative literature, or any department, of such deep-sounding and high-soaring voices as Carlyle's and Tennyson's." He considers it, indeed, "a signal instance of democratic humanity's luck that it has such enemies to contend with—so candid, so fervid, so heroic," and adds, reflectively, "But why do I say enemy? Upon the whole is not Tennyson...the true friend of our age?"[87]

Tennyson's speaker in "Locksley Hall Sixty Years After" (who, as Tennyson always insisted, did not necessarily represent his own views) excoriates the creeping disproportion of the ratio of the Cat to the Lion—as the cat, like the grinning feline in Alice's Wonderland, grows from a smaller, to a similar, to a greater size than the lion (itself an emblem for the British monarchy). But this image is not antidemocratic in any simple sense, since it concludes by claiming that it is democratic oratory itself that puts democracy at risk. The threat *of* democracy is that all differences are leveled, but this leveling also constitutes a threat *to* democracy, because democracy "dooms" itself by its adherence to the orator's overheated language. Tennyson's own overheated language voices skepticism regarding oratorical mirages, as well as anxiety over the increasing potential for the orator's discursive power to overtake the poet's.

In spite of the awed pride Tennyson felt in Hallam's "rapt oration," the undisputed oratorical gifts that I noted in the introduction, he was profoundly distrustful of public eloquence, as was Hallam. We hear this skepticism manifested at a number of points in his dramatic monologues and in his conversation. In the course of an exchange in the late 1870s that was recorded by the poet's son, Thomas Carlyle called Gladstone "the man with the immeasurable power of vocables," to which Tennyson replied, "I love the man, but no Prime Minister ought to be an orator" (*Memoir*, 2:236). Gladstone came to preside over what is regarded by some as a "golden age of parliamentary oratory." The arenas of such performances extended beyond Parliament, with the growth of what H. C. G. Matthew calls "the phenomenon of late Victorian extra-parliamentary rhetoric,"[88] which is inseparable from the growth of democracy over the course of the nineteenth century. Gladstone is credited with inaugurating the practice of mass speeches made directly to the electorate (with his orations in 1867–77 on Bulgaria and his 1879–80 Midlothian campaigns), and he came routinely to address crowds in the tens of thousands, his own "rapt oration" serving to enrapture not a college coterie but a radically altering nation.

I read Tennyson's dramatic monologists as fascinated by processes of change, and Gladstone's career is itself notable for his dramatic self-transformations. Reviewing Gladstone's rise as the period's foremost popular orator, his contemporary R. H. Hutton concludes, "Truly such a career as Mr. Gladstone's is amongst the most remarkable phenomena of a century full of remarkable phenomena."[89] Beginning his career, in Eugenio Biagini's succinct summary, as a "son of a wealthy Liverpool merchant and slaveowner, High-Churchman educated at Eton and Oxford, then a Tory MP for a rotten borough," and serving initially, in Macaulay's famous description as the "rising hope of those stern and unbending Tories," Gladstone became in later decades "the People's William," and "the Grand Old Man," the greatest force for mass democracy in the century.[90] In chapter 3 I look at his views of Homeric characters and history, as well as his early and fierce conservative stances, articulated in fervent letters to his Eton classmate, the equally partisan Whig Arthur Henry Hallam. During the Crimean war (1854–56), Gladstone was chancellor of the exchequer under the conservative Aberdeen, but it was in this decade that he shifted his allegiances to the Whigs, officially decamping in 1859.[91] G. M. Young observed of Gladstone that he became "the greatest liberal of all time" and yet "never for a moment abated his reverence for monarchy, aristocracy, and the Church."[92] "The process by which Gladstone's political career...evolved towards Liberalism," according to Jenkins, "was tortuous, often tormented, and never wholly complete." In this straddling of ideological positions he was perhaps representative of his adoptive party itself, in which was apparent, according to Jenkins, the "survival of the Whig tradition of aristocratic leadership."[93]

Though Tennyson's ambivalence regarding oratorical power ran deep, Arthur Henry Hallam, himself so gifted a public speaker, took particular pride in the oratorical skills of the Whig Party. In a short biography he wrote of Edmund Burke (published by the Society for the Diffusion of Useful Knowledge, a Whig organization of which his father was a director) he called the Whig statesman "an orator in all his thoughts, and a sage in all his eloquence." Chronicling the historical growth of the party, Hallam described how the Whigs "by a continued display of powers the most accomplished...gained an ultimate victory, first over popular prepossessions, and then over royal obstinacy. The court party were so inferior in eloquence and genius, that their arguments are little remembered, while the speeches of the Whigs are in everybody's hands" (*Writings*, 299, 295).

Ever vigilant for the promotion of Tennyson's work, Hallam suggested that the great contemporary Whig orator Macaulay (who had written a detailed and largely favorable notice of his father's *Constitutional History*) would be an appropriate reviewer of Tennyson's poems. Referring to Macaulay in a shorthand way, he ended a letter to Tennyson in April 1832, "I think Mac has some poetic taste, and would appreciate you" (*Letters*, 550). Some months later, as he oversaw the publication of Tennyson's 1832 *Poems*, Hallam wrote, "I have begun a sort of article upon you" (*Letters*, 690). This article has not been found, but an earlier essay, "On Some of the Characteristics of Modern Poetry, and on the Lyrical Poems of Alfred Tennyson" (1831), emphasized and theorized the beauty of his friend's poetry, inaugurating a major critical approach that I address in chapter 5. Perhaps Macaulay might have been similarly inspired. When he was shown some of Tennyson's poetry some twenty-five years later, he responded, repeatedly, "'Oh, it is very beautiful—very beautiful indeed'" (quoted in *Memoir*, 2:515–16). Hallam's critical writings, including his surviving essay on Tennyson, figure prominently in this study and offer clear signs of what he might have gone on to produce had he lived. But he had been ready to leave off writing a second essay on Tennyson, telling him, "If however Macaulay would review you favourably it would be much better" (*Letters*, 690).[94]

"We must not forget," the poet's friend Arthur Sidgwick admonishes, "that the years covered by young Tennyson's residence at Cambridge were precisely the period of the keenest intellectual stir and the stormiest political warfare that preceded the great Reform Bill."[95] A great many readers have felt that this great storm did not rain down upon Tennyson, however. Tennyson biographer R. B. Martin draws a highly representative conclusion: "Under the influence of his politically minded friends he talked a great deal about Reform, tyranny, and revolution, but his interest was never profound, for he lacked the theoretical mind that makes politics more than personal emotions writ large."[96] I am not certain that Tennyson lacked a theoretical mind, though I am certain that his revered friend Hallam possessed one of the highest order. And while Hallam's political views were historically informed and theoretically sophisticated, they were also passionately engaged; one lesson he taught the poet was that politics might always be constituted of personal emotions writ large.

Becoming a Poem

The Whig Earl Grey, prime minister of the first government after the passage of the Great Reform Bill, declared that the government should "promote and…encourage a quiet and moderate course of conduct" while avoiding "extreme and violent changes."[97] In this leading call for moderate reform, we can hear that Tennyson's similar calls for political and social moderation, consistent throughout his works, correspond closely to an official party position. A stance that has been taken as particular to Tennyson was well defined and widely shared, as was readily acknowledged by Victorian critics, who recognized, not always approvingly, the vigor of Tennyson's party affiliation and its direct bearing on his poetry. Stopford Brooke, in his 1894 study of the poet, is lucid in his identification of Tennyson's ideology and his suspicion regarding its potential cost for his poetry: "His was the view of the common-sense, well ordered Englishman—of Whiggism in her carriage with a very gracious smile and salute for Conservatism in hers—and he tried, unhappily, as I think, to get this view into poetry."[98] Brooke is entirely right to suggest that Tennyson's ideology is manifested in his poetry, but we need to go much further than we have in tracing its operations, both thematically and structurally, and in assessing the causes and the consequences of a Whig poetics.

Subsequent chapters trace the nuanced relation of Whig ideology to Tennyson's dramatic monologues, but it is useful here to review Tennyson's outright political pronouncements. In the context of a discussion of "Ulysses," Culler elucidates Tennyson's "philosophy of gradualism."[99] He sees this as characteristic of the poems of 1833–34, but Tennyson's favoring of the notion of a very gradual civic improvement, accomplished always and only, as he phrases it in a number of poems in this period, "by degrees," "by still degrees," "by just degrees," "by degrees to fullness wrought," is consistent throughout his career. Tennyson's "gradualism" has long been recognized; though the descriptive term often differed, this tendency to champion deferral, especially in matters of social or political change, was remarked frequently by his contemporaries. What has been obscured in subsequent criticism is the fact that this tendency reflects the ideological basis of the period's dominant political party. Recent studies of Tennyson's political leanings do not stress, or even identify, his significant Whig affiliations. Armstrong, for example, gives a compelling account of what she calls Tennyson's "subversive conservatism," hearing rightly in his early poems a "peculiarly radical conservatism, which dreads change and sees its necessity," but does not identify this as a traditional Whig position.[100]

Historians agree that moderation was, as Jenkins puts it, "the true Whig principle,"[101] and this principle was articulated in Tennyson's poems throughout his career. Tennyson's political poems of the early 1830s, written during the years of debate over Whig reform initiatives, propound with particular clarity the conviction that civic transformation should unfold with due and indeed lingering deliberation. "Hail Briton!" (c. 1833) imagines an ideal leader who cares "to shape, to settle, to repair / With seasonable changes fair / And innovation grade by grade" (150–52). "You ask me, why" (c. 1833) imagines the ideal polity:

> A land of settled government,
>   A land of just and old renown,
>   Where Freedom slowly broadens down
> From precedent to precedent. (9–12)

The poet wants freedom, a value historically associated with the Whigs (challengers of royal authority), to edge "from precedent to precedent," with each development tested before the next is attempted. We might note that precedent itself is dependent on likeness: the poet wants the present to differ from the past, but not very much or very soon, maintaining always such clear likeness that each precedent, as we can hear in his own repetition of the word, differs from yet may appear almost indistinct from the one before. Freedom itself is personified in "Of old sat Freedom on the heights" (c. 1833), which concludes by admonishing "the falsehood of extremes!" (24). And "Love thou thy land" (c. 1832–34) establishes moderation as a quality defined less by what it offers than what it negates: "Not clinging to some ancient saw; / Not mastered by some modern term; / Not swift nor slow to change" (29–31).

These poems were written during the years of wild agitation over the Whig Reform Bill, as well as during the period of Tennyson's intimacy with Hallam. All were written in the distinctive verse form that he turned to immediately as he began the long composition of *In Memoriam*, his elegy for his friend: iambic tetrameter with an *abba* rhyme scheme. That the poems that articulate his politics most directly are written in what was subsequently termed the "*In Memoriam* stanza," a form Tennyson and others believed he had originated, only cements the association between this friend, this ideological position, and this poet's innovations in lyric practice, an association my readings of his dramatic monologues, also conceived in this period, pursue. These early political poems are written in one form, and (in their attempts not only to describe but aggressively to promote the ideas of his party) in one voice: that of a Whig orator.

Tennyson's promotion of a political moderation indelibly associated in his lifetime with the Whigs outlasted by decades the existence of the party itself. In the poem "Freedom," published in *Macmillan's Magazine* in December 1884, the month he attained the barony, Tennyson upbraids demagogues for "Expecting all things in an hour" (39). In the 1889 poem "Politics," one of several addressed to Gladstone, he warns the prime minister not to "lend an ear to random cries" but instead to maintain a constantly monitored and moderated progress: "Up hill 'Too-slow' will need the whip, / Down hill 'Too-quick,' the chain" (7, 11–12). These late political poems continue in the tradition of those written a half-century earlier, advocating what we might call Tennyson's committed ambivalence toward transformation, which is at once anticipated and resisted. In this he is essentially following a course set for him by Hallam. In his 1831 essay on Tennyson, Hallam asserts, "In the old times the poetic impulse went along with the general impulse of the nation; in these it is a reaction against it, a check acting for conservation against a propulsion towards change" (*Writings*, 190). Whig poetics were precisely what the age not only required, but dictated.

The idea that political transformation is inevitably taking place, and yet at a rate so slow that one may not notice it in one's own generation, was forwarded by Victorians in discourses that extended beyond the realm of contemporary partisan politics. Tennyson's attraction to a theory of political reform that views change as necessary and even salutary but ideally occurring over a highly protracted span of time, accords with his attraction to emergent theories of evolution. In *In Memoriam* he marvels, "O earth, what changes hast thou seen! / There where the long street roars, hath been / The stillness of the central sea" (23.2–4). Gesturing to the crowded city street, he hears in its long advancing roar the glacial pace of evolution. In "Freedom," he addresses a personified figure that "like Nature, wouldst not mar / By changes all too fierce and fast" (21–22), thus naturalizing, through a simile, his political position. "So many a million of ages have gone to the making of man" (1.135), the speaker of the 1855 monodrama *Maud* exclaims, looking back into remote history. "Man as yet is being made," he declares in the 1892 poem "The Making of Man," looking ahead to the passing of "aeon after aeon" (3, 4) before completion. "The Dawn" (1892) ends with a question, not really hypothetical for Tennyson: "Ah, what will *our* children be, / The men of a hundred thousand, a million summers away?"

Tennyson's 1832 volume *Poems* was shepherded through publication by Hallam, who in a letter to Tennyson in late fall of that year writes that the editor "says the volume must make a great sensation. He & your friends are anxious it should be out before the storm of politics is abroad." Hallam elaborates on various international events likely to take place "before your last revise is ready" ("The French Fleet has got the start of you"), concluding, "But still you may be beforehand with the Elections which is more important" (*Letters*, 678). He is referring to the elections that were to take place in mid-December for the first reformed Parliament after the passage of the Whig Reform Act. Though Hallam is teasing Tennyson for what he took to be a preoccupation with the revision of poems he himself considered eminently publishable, he nevertheless places his friend's work centrally within the orbit of contemporary political life, and reform politics in particular.

Hallam positions Tennyson's poems in their immediate political context, but we can also see the poet's Whig tendencies reflected formally in this predilection for revision itself. Tennyson often resisted publishing his work; as Hallam wrote to a friend in July 1831, "He is terribly fastidious about publication, as you know" (*Letters*, 443). ("Do not publish too early," Tennyson advised an admirer in 1848, "you cannot retract" [*Memoir*, 1:278].) Without multiplying examples, we might look just to the major Hellenic monologues that will occupy this book, "Ulysses," "Tithonus," and "Tiresias." All were conceived together in 1833 and published in significantly revised form in, respectively, 1842, 1860, and 1883. Revision is a retrospective act, requiring looking back at past labors, and at the same time a progressive one, seeking improvements through often minute alterations; it therefore stands as a quintessential Whig activity. Intellectual labor especially requires postponement, according to Tennyson, so that "the strength of some diffusive thought / Hath time and space to work and spread" ("You ask me, why," 15–16). My discussion of a number of Tennyson's poems will attend to his revisions, not all of which were felicitous, but it is important to note that the very process of revision, of modifying by way of perpetual reform, producing sometimes minor adjustments, sometimes major reorganization, to accumulated effect, exemplifies Tennyson's Whig poetics. What he says of a progressive conservatism in politics can apply to a revisionary, reformist poetics: "That man's the true Conservative / Who lops the mouldered branch away" ("Hands All Round," 7–8). Certainly, for a poet who rarely hastened into print, preferring instead to publish revised versions of such poems as "Tithonus" and "Tiresias" decades after their inception, gradualist reform is only another term for revision. To borrow from Macaulay, the poet reforms, that he may preserve.

For all that his ideological stance was shared by a wide range of theoretically sophisticated yet eminently practical political leaders, Tennyson might be considered in his Whig poetics to have taken moderation to immoderate lengths. He consistently imagines personal and social transformation so gradual as to extend over a virtual infinitude. If the pace of evolutionary change is unhurried, the pace of divine change is imperceptible; as he declares in *In Memoriam*, "I can but trust that good shall fall / At last—far off—at last, to all" (54.14–15). Imagining the descent of the "good" produces the stuttering "at last... at last," as the repetition elongates a postponement whose assurance ("I can but trust") itself provides great solace. This telos, vouchsafed democratically "to all," could not be more "far off." "The words 'far, far away' had always a strange charm for me" (*Poems*, 3.197), Tennyson mused, recalling his childhood absorption in a phrase that evokes both temporal and geographical remoteness. The famous concluding lines of *In Memoriam*, anticipating "one far-off divine event, / To which the whole creation moves" (Epilogue, 143–44), look to an inclusive "far off" future we can understand as a deeply held Whig fantasy of infinitely unfolding but also infinitely delayed transformation.

The political implications of this delay were not lost on Victorian readers. Stopford Brooke quotes a line from Tennyson's late poem "The Dawn," "We are far from the noon of man, there is time for the race to grow" (20), and responds, "Time! when half the world and more are in torture! It ought not to be in a poet to take things so easily." Tennyson's far-sightedness can look ethically myopic, offering a sharply narrowed rather than expansive moral or political vision. "He represented the political and social opinions of [his] time very fairly, but not as a poet who had much prophetic fire and pity in him would be expected to write," Brooke concludes,[102] a view that has been long echoed. In *Alfred Tennyson: How to Know Him*, a 1917 publication in an American educational series, Raymond Macdonald Alden discusses Tennyson's moderate political leanings, then asks the pertinent question: "What is the significance of all this for Tennyson as a poet?" He offers this answer: "Chiefly, one must admit, a negative significance." This negative significance is due less to this particular poet's particular beliefs (which Alden identifies as a commitment to political gradualism, though he does not identify this as a specifically Whig ideology) than to what this critic considers a fundamental incongruity between a certain kind of politics and a certain kind of poetry. Alden argues, "It is as difficult for conservatism to take up its abode in the soul of poetry as it is easy for radicalism to do so, and this is quite without reference to the absolute merits of the two temperaments." He gives as his example of the lyrical effects of radicalism the poet Shelley "piercing the very heavens for a vision of that which shall make all things new."[103]

"Through the whole of Tennyson's poetry about the problem of man's progress, this view of his does damage to the poetry; lowers the note of beauty, of aspiration, of fire, of passion; and lessens the use of his poetry in the cause of freedom," Brooke claims. Making direct the relation of a poet's politics and poetics, Brooke argues that Tennyson's was an "unfortunate position," not for a person to happen to hold, but specifically "unfortunate for a poet."[104] Arthur Sidgwick recognizes the challenge of his friend's Whig poetics: "It is easy to idealize freedom, revolution, or war: and the ancients found it easy to compose lyrics on kings, athletes, warriors, or other powerful persons. . . . But the praise of ordered liberty, of settled government, of political moderation, is far harder to idealize in poetry."[105] Readers of Tennyson have variously articulated what we might term the twin problematic of the unquestioned magnificence of his style and the ostensible narrowness of his social or political vision. G. K. Chesterton contends, "Tennyson suffers by that very Virgilian loveliness and dignity of diction which he put to the service of such a small and anomalous national scheme."[106] But the majesty of his lyric and the moderation of his political vision may be consonant; Tennyson's unwavering, even obsessive commitment to order and gradualism stands at the center of his poetic practice.

Whiggism cannot but appear to be a distinctly unimpassioned and indeed unrapturous ideology. Freedom, for example, the surpassing Whig value, requires exemption from external or physical compulsion, and is thus a wholly dissimilar condition from the submission to external power suggested by rapture. The Whig commitment to gradualism similarly runs counter to the sudden seizure that is at the heart of most narratives of rapture. Thus the overwhelming, unexpected, and unstoppable forces productive of states of rapture would seem in every way unwelcome or antithetical to Whig sensibilities. William Butler Yeats in "The Seven Sages" (1933) asks, "But what is Whiggery?" and his answer suggests that it is a position that disallows human emotional extremes: "A leveling, rancorous, rational sort of mind / That never looked out of the eye of a saint / Or out of a drunkard's eye" (10–13).[107] Tennyson's Whig vision, however, as developed in his dramatic monologues, does look out of the eye of the elevated and the fallen, of the inspired and the inexplicable. And Whiggery itself was associated by Tennyson with profoundly passionate feeling, given that its tenets were passionately espoused by his passionately loved friend Hallam. It is possible, moreover, to conceive of what we might term Whig rapture. In Tennyson, rapture is a discursive experience, brought about and represented by suasive speech. Rapture thus unfolds consecutively, proceeding word by word, or "point by point," as Tennyson puts it when describing Hallam's rapt oration. That this mode of attaining rapture derives from and appeals to a "rational sort of mind" might also point to a democratizing element, itself potentially radical. Appealing to individual reason, even choice, Whig rapture counters what could in this light look like the authoritarian implications of a more traditional rapture, which demands an individual's powerless submission to overwhelming external force. As we shall trace in a series of dramatic monologues, rapture in Tennyson is a condition attained by deliberative degrees.

Tennyson's Whiggism is not only thematically recurrent, then, but formally resonant in his poetry. It is foundational to poems not overtly concerned with political questions, evident not only in the content but also in the form his poems took, and even in the ways the poems took form. The poems that refer directly to politics invariably advocate any kind of change arriving by judicious steps, carefully measured and therefore of necessity prolonged. A cadenced measure, a kind of lingering advance, has been observed from his earliest poems, and recognized, it might be fair to say, by virtually every careful reader of this poet, as perhaps the most characteristic aspect of his poetics. To cite just one of a multitude of possible examples, Walter Bagehot observes of Tennyson, "His genius gives the notion of a slow depositing instinct; day by day, as the hours pass, the delicate sand falls into beautiful forms—in stillness, in peace, in brooding."[108] Tennysonian lyric attenuates transformation, shifting almost imperceptibly from one beautiful form into another, advancing by way of restraint. J. F. A. Pyre, an early twentieth-century critic given to calculating percentages of syllables and caesurae in the verse, observes of Tennyson's style, "Having set narrow limits to variation, he is prepared to develop within those limits every capability of manipulation which the prescribed form will permit." These tightly controlled lyric variations may constitute the heart of this poet's appeal: "An intensive cultivation of a limited and yet sufficient range of minute variations is the secret of Tennyson's metrical charm so far as such a quality can be analyzed and measured."[109] Whig values structure the poems themselves: the poet's abiding commitment is to imperceptibly shifting and intricately mutable hierarchies of words and sounds. Tennyson's claim in "Love thou thy land," "We all are changed by still degrees" (43), encompasses personal, political, and poetic transformation, delineating the ambitions of his Whig poetics.

2

VICTORIAN RAPTURE

For the Lord himself shall descend from heaven with a shout, with the voice
of the archangel, and with the trump of God: and the dead in Christ shall rise first:
Then we which are alive and remain shall be caught up together with them
in the clouds, to meet the Lord in the air: and so shall we ever be with the Lord.
Wherefore comfort one another with these words.

—1 Thessalonians 4.16–18

Both Alfred Tennyson and Emily Brontë were struck by the hirsute wind-
blown figure of St. Simeon Stylites each happened upon—he in his father's
Lincolnshire parish home, she in her father's Yorkshire one—in William Hone's
1825 *Every-Day Book*, a calendar with anecdotes and illustrations for each day of
the year.[1] Brontë was inspired to copy the engraving by S. Williams accompanying
the textual entry for January 5 (Simeon's saint's day), and Tennyson was inspired
to write his dramatic monologue "St. Simeon Stylites." An early Christian ascetic
at Telanissos in Syria, Simeon (c. 388–458) is the first and most famous of the
stylitae, hermits who sought penance by enduring long habitation at the top of
a pillar (*stylos*). Simeon lived for some four decades (accounts vary) at the top of
columns of increasing heights, starting at nine feet, gradually rising to some sixty
feet, drawing great crowds to marvel and seek healing. Brontë's pencil drawing
(figure 2.1) is dated March 4, 1833; Tennyson drafted his poem in fall 1833 (by
early November, when he read it to friends). That two of the Victorian period's
most towering literary figures were separately drawn to produce their own representations of this pillar hermit must stand as a first sign of the monumentality
of a character we have yet to take full measure of. "People do not generally care
for pillar-saints," George Saintsbury dryly observed, commenting in his *History
of English Prosody* on the relative inattention accorded to Tennyson's "St. Simeon
Stylites,"[2] but in the same year Tennyson and Brontë found him fit subject for
scrupulous delineation.

In its way, Brontë's depiction of Simeon is as painstaking as Tennyson's dramatic
monologue; both answer to Leigh Hunt's 1842 description of the poem as "powerfully graphic."[3] Brontë often copied illustrations meticulously from journals and

FIGURE 2.1 Emily Brontë, "St. Simeon Stylites" (4 March 1833).
Copyright © The Brontë Society.

books, a pastime that served to train her eye and hand, and her drawing is a close approximation of the original in Hone's *Every-Day Book*. Both show Simeon in animal skins, with flowing hair and beard, kneeling on his right knee, holding high in his left hand a cross made of sticks. Both show two of the cubit-length segments of the narrow pillar on which the anchorite perches, and both show the clouds billowing behind his body and the people assembled below the pillar, in the distance. In Brontë's copy, the background is less distinct; in the version Tennyson knew, the people are clear and even individuated. Some raise their arms to hail Simeon, while others kneel, and it is possible to make out the crude features of a few faces. Brontë obscures these worshippers to some degree but brings Simeon forward, so that his body looks far more substantial than in Hone, and nearer. Her Simeon is darker in his shading and more muscular; Hone's looks bent and compact (the angle of his back is more bowed). Brontë's looks vigorous, a Romantic striver, almost defiant: a brooding figure, both in his relation to the environment over which he looms and in the contemplative cast of his expression.

Brontë emphasizes the strong verticality of this image, as the dark striated lines of Simeon's cross draw down to the strained muscles of his arm, bearing its burden high in the air, past the long filaments of his beard and the sharp angle of his raised knee, to the deeply etched planks and wood grains of the pillar. She calls attention to the geometry of the image's horizontal lines as well, from the arms of the cross to the arms of Simeon, both at right angles, to the triangle's base of his bent kneeling calf to the demarcation between the two top cylinders of wood supporting his knee. Brontë thus accentuates the image's linear composition, from the intersecting lines of the cross through the lineaments of Simeon's visibly taut body to the material foundation of the pillar, itself composed of nearly intersecting vertical and horizontal lines.

This chapter attempts to scale the heights of Tennyson's Simeon, who is, like Brontë's, a figure of sharp delineation, etched deeply and with breathtaking precision into the poet's blank verse lines. Tennyson's speaker is keen to embody a particular homophonic alliance between spatial and discursive measure, well aware that he can calculate both his height and his words by way of meters. We shall study Simeon from several angles. In the first section I contextualize his prophetic drive toward "the end," an obsession he shares with a cohort of early Victorian divines whose theological positions align in striking ways with those of Tennyson's pillar saint: the Reverend Charles Simeon of Cambridge, of whom Tennyson critics have taken brief notice, and the still more relevant evangelists Edward Irving and John Nelson Darby. The latter two have gone entirely unmentioned in studies of the poet, but their highly controversial views (Irving's in particular) attracted the close attention of a number of Tennyson's Cambridge friends. In the second section I take the literal and figurative measure of the speaker, attending closely to his intricate discursive calculations, manifest in the rhythms of his speech and in his stunningly ambitious rhetorical goals. His central aims—to arrive at the end and to attain a divine similitude—are for him as much discursive as they are spiritual. This chapter begins by attending to Simeon's placement among British evangelicals of the early 1830s; it ends in the equally germane, if equally surprising, company of a present-day American ecological evangelist, the "tree-sitter" Julia

Butterfly Hill. Like Tennyson's Simeon, Hill seeks to accomplish transformation (of herself, of the world) by positioning herself high in the air for an extended period of time to attain very specific ends: in his case, that end is salvation through rapture; in her case, it is salvation through a redwood.

Upon the publication of Tennyson's 1842 *Poems*, Robert Browning singled out in a letter to a friend "'St. Simeon of the Pillar,' which I think perfect."[4] The praise for "St. Simeon Stylites" is of course especially resonant coming from the poet whose own name was to become so closely associated with the genre of the dramatic monologue, of which this poem of Tennyson's is considered the first Victorian instance. Browning, though, was the first to enter into print; by the time he had read Tennyson's poem he had published his own major prototypes of this unnamed genre, "Porphyria's Lover" and "Johannes Agricola in Meditation." These appeared in the *Monthly Repository* in January 1836 and were reprinted under the combined heading "Madhouse Cells" in his 1842 *Dramatic Lyrics*, a volume published some six months after Tennyson's.

That the status of "St. Simeon Stylites" as the first Victorian dramatic monologue is in itself a contested position makes it an especially fitting one for Simeon to hold, master as he is of controversial self-positioning. What was clear, even to those who were not drawn to this highly experimental ascetic, was the poem's astonishing generic inventiveness, displaying a talent of Tennyson's especially prized by Hallam. In his 1831 essay on Tennyson, Hallam had observed that his friend's recently published poems featuring female characters were "like summaries of mighty dramas." He sees in these "expressions of character," which he calls "brief and coherent," "a new species of poetry, a graft of the lyric on the dramatic," and concludes, "Mr. Tennyson deserves the laurel of an inventor" (*Writings*, 197). Tennyson's formal originality corresponds to Simeon's invention of heightened forms of self-punishment. In *The Decline and Fall of the Roman Empire*, Tennyson's other major source for the poem, Edward Gibbon writes that among the "heroes of the monastic life, the name and genius of Simeon Stylites have been immortalized by the singular invention of an aërial penance."[5] As Victorian poetry's first dramatic monologue, "St. Simeon Stylites" sets a crucial precedent in his voicing of an ambitiousness that preoccupies every major dramatic monologist conceived by Tennyson (and Browning as well). James Spedding, fellow Cambridge Apostle and an early reviewer of the poem, remarked that the speaker "is bent on qualifying himself for the best place."[6] Spedding nicely characterizes the speaker's contradictory placement, since Simeon *is* bent, doubled over in his aerial overreaching, enjoying a self-crippling posture that is simultaneously self-vaunting.

In a genre of explicitly ambitious speakers, Simeon may well be the utmost, seeking as he does nothing less than to become "whole, and clean, and meet for Heaven" (210). And yet whole, or holy, perfection would seem to be entirely unattainable for Simeon, who insists repeatedly on the wild range of his imperfections, on his stature as the vilest of sinners and "the basest of mankind." Spedding notes the speaker's attainment of this position, itself a superlative, in his observation that Simeon "represents the pride of asceticism in its basest."[7] Disapproval of this subject position could shift easily into disapproval of this subject. John Sterling, another Cambridge Apostle of this era, concluded in his review of the 1842 *Poems*, "This is no topic for Poetry: she has better tasks than to wrap her mantle round a sordid, greedy lunatic."[8] But it is only, indeed, by becoming a "topic for Poetry," a figure quite distinctly of and for blank verse, that Simeon can attain the perfect—that is, be made regular and whole—not only in the adjectival sense of becoming complete or faultless, but in the verbal sense. "To perfect" is to perform or accomplish, and this consummation will be possible for him in and through the performance of his monologue.

Spedding and Sterling were not alone among Tennyson's Cambridge associates in feeling mystified by this "topic for Poetry." Tennyson read Simeon's monologue to a group of friends in November 1833. This record of an early performance makes the dramatic monologue one of the few literary genres whose first instance we can date, but the date is striking for reasons more personal to the poet. Tennyson had learned, from a letter dated October 1, 1833, of Hallam's death on September 15 in Vienna, and this gathering of fellow Cambridge Apostles was one of the first following this shattering news. Christopher Ricks notes that it is "unlikely" (*Poems*, 1:593) that the poem was written in October, but it was clearly a new work of this period and one that struck his friends as a surprising poem to hear at this time. On November 11, 1833, W. H. Thompson wrote to J. W. Blakesley (also both Cambridge Apostles) of a visit from Tennyson, "He seemed less overcome than one would have expected: though, when he first arrived, he was very low—He left among us some magnificent poems and fragments of poems. Among the rest a monologue or soliloquy of one Simeon Stylites: or as he calls himself Simeon of the Pillar."[9] Among other "magnificent poems and fragments of poems" (perhaps parts of "Ulysses," "Tithonus," "Tiresias," or *In Memoriam*, since we know that Tennyson began composing fragments of each of these in the immediate aftermath of learning of Hallam's death), what stands out is Simeon's monologue, already jostling for first place.

Tennyson's earliest audiences had no term for the kind of poem this was: his friend W. H. Thompson in this letter classifies it "a monologue or soliloquy"; John Sterling called it in his review "a kind of monological personation."[10] And though this grasping after appropriate terminology inaugurated some fifty years of experimental naming until the term "dramatic monologue" became established, what "St. Simeon Stylites" seems to have been chiefly for Tennyson himself was a joke. Thompson's first report of Tennyson, "He seemed less overcome than one would have expected," is entirely connected to his friend's introduction of the indefinable poem that appeared an inexplicable initial lyric response to Hallam's death. And Tennyson's reading of the monologue seemed, according to another early auditor, almost raucous. Describing his performance of "St. Simeon Stylites," another

Cambridge friend, Edward FitzGerald, recalled that Tennyson "would read with grotesque Grimness, especially at such passages as 'Coughs, Aches, Stitches, etc.,' laughing aloud at times" (*Poems*, 1:594). Readers have long felt that they joined in the joke on Simeon (and in turn in a joke on Tennyson's own comical behavior), but taking the poet's laughter seriously can suggest an alternative way to read this speaker. Simeon himself laughs in his monologue ("Ha! ha!" [123]), making it reasonable for Tucker to ask, "Are Simeon and his poetic creator not laughing together at the same bittersweet blend of humbuggery and aspiration...?"[11] But we might question still further: What if Simeon is not the object or audience of the joke, but its performer? If the joke is not on him, but his, it would mean that the speaker is deliberately wielding an extreme comic language to some effect, the first of which might be laughter. If so, what might his own performance attain for the speaker of this dramatic monologue?

Simeon is a speaker who is far more elusive, and allusive, high up on his pillar, than he may initially seem. As he says to his primary interlocutor early in his monologue, "O take the meaning, Lord" (21). Simeon makes the task of interpretive contemplation less his than God's: it is Simeon whom even God must wrestle to understand. He raises a clear challenge to interpretation, especially given that his words can have so many meanings. Take "take." He employs this verb again with reference to another of his audiences: "The silly people take me for a saint" (125). By this does he mean accept, understand, or violently appropriate? This is one of Simeon's numerous puns (some of which are themselves numerical, relating to units of measure), and in order to take up the challenge of taking their meaning we must first entertain the possibility that these puns (and thus the multiplications of his meanings) are the speaker's own.

Quintilian in *Institutio Oratoria* defines puns (Greek *paronomasia*, Latin *adnominatio*) as a "class of *figures* which attracts the ear of the audience and excites their attention by some resemblance, equality or contrast with words."[12] Turning from the attraction and excitement of punning wordplay for auditors to the labors of speakers, we might note Jonathan Culler's observation that puns "show speakers intently or playfully working to reveal the structures of language, motivating linguistic signs, allowing signifiers to affect meaning by generating new connections."[13] Especially striking in Culler's representation of this linguistic practice is his sense not only of what puns may reveal in the language, but what they may reveal in speakers, who, whether "intently" or "playfully," work with deliberation to generate new meanings. Punning seems, in these definitions, an exceptionally social linguistic exercise, drawing for its effects on an interlocutor's close perceptions of a speaker who in all likelihood intends these effects—an ideal "class of *figures*," then, for the genre of the dramatic monologue.

Homophonic words—having the same sound, but different meanings, such as rite, write, right, wright—serve as building blocks of the pun and also of Simeon's dramatic monologue. According to the *New Princeton Encyclopedia of Poetry and Poetics*, a pun or homophone "can be a powerful instrument of poetic language when it reveals that two things which bear the same name, i.e. the same phonic sequence, also share deeper affinities."[14] Homophonic resemblance can appear etymologically determined or random and accidental; in either case the challenge to a reader or auditor of "poetic language" is to try to identify the "deeper affinities" it may suggest. One homophonic series in "St. Simeon Stylites" begins when the speaker hails God: "O Lord, Lord, / Thou knowest I bore this better at the first, / For I was strong and hale of body then" (26–28). His "hale" body is compromised, however, by lashings of the weather, including hail: "Rain, wind, frost, heat, hail, damp" (16). The healthy body is undermined as well by his haling or hauling up from the depths a chosen means of self-torture: "For many weeks about my loins I wore / The rope that haled the buckets from the well / Twisted as tight as I could knot the noose" (62–64). W. E. H. Lecky reports, "[Tennyson] once confessed to me that when he wrote his *Simeon Stylites* he did not know that the story was a Syrian one, and had accordingly given it a Northern colouring which he now perceived to be wrong" (*Poems*, 1:594). "The tolerance of cold" is Simeon's "peculiar forte," Tucker comments,[15] but whether the climate of fifth-century Syria included frost and hail is less at issue than the uses to which this speaker could put this chain of homonyms (hale, hale) and homophones (hale, hail). He ceases to be hale because of the hail and the haling, but this associative chain can also suggest the possible outcomes of these instruments of his penance: whether, for example, he shall end up with a halo or in hell. Hale is etymologically linked to "heal" and thus brings him full circle, because by way of these severe penances inflicted by the hail and his haling, his body has itself acquired the power to heal; he recalls "those that came / To touch my body and be healed" (77–78). "Yes, I can heal," he concludes. "They say that they are healed" (143, 144). The *Oxford English Dictionary* defines "heal" as "to make whole and sound in bodily condition," and I argue that he greets or hails this condition of wholeness by the end of his monologue, as he declares he does: "I trust / That I am whole, and clean, and meet for Heaven" (209–10). His monologue opens with his assertion that he is "scarce meet / For troops of devils, mad with blasphemy" (3–4); he becomes meet for Heaven in the course of the monologue, by way of the monologue.

"The pun constitutes a forced contiguity between two or more words": Umberto Eco's conception of *forced contiguity* (a phrase he later italicizes) can help us begin to track the aggressive intentionality of Tennyson's first monologic speaker. Aside from words rooted in the same etymological ground, most homophones share only specious equivalence; there is no necessary connection, for example, between hale and hail, only random homophonic likeness. But Simeon forces a connection, as we shall see in still more striking examples, which exists because he has forced their contiguity. Eco continues, "The resemblance becomes necessary only after the contiguity is realized."[16] Homophonic contiguity makes us believe there is a logical and indeed necessary continuity among these terms, as Simeon's haling will lead either to health or to hell. His puns structure his speech: his monologue is as carefully wrought and incremental an edifice as his pillar.

Writing of puns, Eco suggests, "It is enough to find the means of rendering two terms phonetically contiguous for the resemblance to impose itself,"[17] and the imposition of resemblance is precisely Simeon's ambition. Tennyson's speaker loudly proclaims that he can find no similitude for himself among men, saints, or devils, but Simeon is obsessed with the challenges of forcing likeness between himself and men, saints, or devils. His homonymic and homophonic discursive acts highlight the issue of resemblance, which becomes not only a phonemic and generic matter, but a theological one as well. Simeon's is a poetics based on likeness, but his puns constitute a formal manifestation of a theology wholly, and heretically, based on resemblance as well, rendering him a remarkably appropriate inaugural speaker of a genre everywhere fascinated by the problem of likeness, that is, with both what and whom the monologue sounds like.

VICTORIAN END-TIMES

Tennyson himself, on the conscious level of the man who talks to reporters and poses for photographers, to judge from remarks made in conversation and recorded in his son's Memoir, consistently asserted a convinced, if somewhat sketchy, Christian belief. And he was a friend of Frederick Denison Maurice—nothing seems odder about that age than the respect which its eminent people felt for each other.

—T. S. Eliot, "*In Memoriam*"

Alfred Tennyson and Arthur Henry Hallam met at Trinity College, Cambridge, probably in 1829; the former left without a degree in early 1831, the latter graduated in January 1832. They became friends initially in the course of the competition for the Chancellor's Gold Medal in English Verse. Both entered a poem on the assigned topic, "Timbuctoo" (Tennyson reluctantly); Tennyson won the prize, but each won a friend whose admiration was virtually boundless. Both were elected in 1830 to the Cambridge Conversazione Society, more commonly called the Apostles, an undergraduate group at this time centered at Trinity that met to debate a wide and challenging range of literary, metaphysical, philosophical, political, scientific, and religious subjects. Hallam had come to college from Eton, where his closest friend had been William Ewart Gladstone, at this time a student at Christ Church, Oxford. The Apostles who preceded them were already legendary, especially John Sterling (of whom Carlyle would write an admiring biography) and Frederick Denison Maurice (whom Tennyson years later would name godfather to his eldest son, Hallam). Recommending Maurice to Gladstone's attention, Hallam wrote in a letter of June 24, 1830, "[The] effect which he has produced on the minds of many at Cambridge by the single creation of that society, the Apostles (for the spirit though not the form *was* created by him), is far greater than I can dare to calculate, & will be felt both directly & indirectly in the age that is before us" (*Letters*, 372). Eschewing the requirements of formal presentation and debate, Tennyson resigned from the Apostles in February 1830 (remaining informally connected), but Hallam from the start distinguished himself brilliantly. He soon became "the intellectual center of the society," as R. B. Martin notes; "he seemed the natural successor to Maurice."[18]

When Tennyson and Hallam joined, the Cambridge Apostles had been in existence scarcely a decade. Founded in 1820, the society was so named in part because there were a dozen founding members, and the group attempted to restrict itself to this number, though Edward FitzGerald (at Cambridge in this period but not a member) suggested this term was instead a reference to the collegiate nickname for the dozen students with the weakest academic performance. FitzGerald's wry suggestion is in keeping with the ironic tone that came to characterize some aspects of Apostolic discourse, but the origins of the society's name seem to have been considerably more earnest. According to John Punnett, one of the founding members, "'The Apostles' was the name we gave ourselves in secrecy, but I think it would be more becoming to describe ourselves as Apostolicans in that we were all evangelists. We were concerned to propagate and explain the Gospels and in doing this honestly and sincerely to revolve all doubts concerning our respective interpretations by debating them in secret." A historian of the society claims, "There seems little doubt that the members... in the early 1820s regarded themselves as theological apologists and natural successors to the Apostolic Fathers of the second century A.D."[19]

So portentous an identification can seem far removed from a group that prided itself on probing intellectual and metaphysical inquiry, often with an ironic or skeptical bent. The original mission, however, to enter into thoughtful debate regarding "our respective interpretations," removed by secrecy from the potential censors and censures of the university, does presage the spirit of open investigation that at its best typified the organization in Tennyson's time. Intellectual inquisitiveness was certainly a chief characteristic of Hallam, as all who knew him frequently noted. One of his fellow Apostles wrote in a testimonial included in the volume *Remains, in Verse and Prose, of Arthur Henry Hallam*, posthumously published by his father a year after his death, that Hallam's "chief pleasure and strength lay certainly in metaphysical analysis....I never knew him decline a metaphysical discussion. He would always pursue the argument eagerly to the end, and follow his antagonist into the most difficult places."[20] Although the Apostles soon ceased to be explicitly evangelical in their disposition, an often overlooked aspect of the organization was its predilection for theological deliberation. Hallam's own essay of spiritual inquiry, "Theodicæa Novissima," which I discuss in relation to

"St. Simeon Stylites," was first presented to the group on October 29, 1831. The author of the most comprehensive history of the society writes, "The relation of the Apostles to religion" is "complex,"[21] and part of my aim in this chapter is sustained engagement with an intellectual tendency of this society that has direct bearing on a range of Tennyson's poems, including and especially the era's first dramatic monologue. The foundation of Tennyson's poetic achievement is partly built on works produced in response to his friend's death, but one of the poems he wrote about poetry itself was written jointly with Hallam, perhaps in 1829 but certainly in their college years, and it opens with a clear proclamation of the relevance of theology to poetry. Their sonnet "To Poesy" opens with this injunction to the entity they personify and address: "Religion be thy sword" (1).

Simeon of Cambridge

"It was fortunate for Tennyson that the theological controversies of his age were restricted, if not simplified, for him by the fact that he had gone to Cambridge," Harold Nicolson declares. "He escaped the Oxford Movement."[22] Though he did not wade into the particular waters of controversy that engulfed Arnold, Clough, and many others, Tennyson nevertheless entered into an intellectual community powerfully occupied by a range of religious questions that were far from simple. The most prominent divine at Cambridge during Tennyson's years was Sir Charles Simeon, vicar of Holy Trinity Church for fifty-three years, until his death in 1836. Known in his later years as "the old Apostle of Cambridge," Simeon over-saw a large and highly influential Evangelical ministry.[23] Jerome Buckley writes, "Simeon had succeeded long before Tennyson's time in making Cambridge the principal training ground for the Evangelical clergy and the strongest force in the procurement of church patronage for those of Evangelical views."[24] So long was his tenure and so wide his reach that it included Patrick Brontë, father of Charlotte, Emily, and Anne, as well as W. Carus Wilson, the son of Simeon's first convert and founder of the Clergy Daughters' School at Cowan Bridge. Simeon served as one of several distinguished Evangelical patrons of this institution, which was attended by four of Brontë's daughters (two of whom died as a result of the insalubrious conditions there), and unfavorably immortalized as Lowood School in Charlotte Brontë's *Jane Eyre*.

An impassioned, forceful preacher, Simeon drew great crowds to his sermons, and his biographer surmises that Tennyson "no doubt attended Holy Trinity Church from time to time when he was at college."[25] At the least, as Buckley asserts, Tennyson "could not have been unaware of the active and vociferous Evangelical party...making its impression even upon Cambridge."[26] Not only personally magnetic but prolific, Simeon published a twenty-one-volume work, *Horae Homileticae*, consisting of 2,536 sermon outlines spanning from Genesis to Revelation. In an article in 1821, he advised other Evangelical preachers, "Screw the word into the minds of your hearers. A screw is the strongest of all mechanical powers...when it has been turned a few times scarcely any power can pull it out."[27] His oratorical fervor could confound as well as convert; as Tennyson and Hallam's friend Richard Monckton Milnes wrote to his mother in November 1827 after hearing one of Simeon's orations, "His action is absurd in the extreme. He brandishes his spectacles when he talks of the terrible, and smirks and smiles when he offers consolation."[28]

"The starting point of Evangelical theology," according to Ian Bradley, "was the doctrine of the total depravity of man," which required regular indulgence in "an orgy of self-criticism."[29] This Simeon excelled at; as Buckley reports, "On his deathbed, he solemnly described himself as 'the chief of sinners and the greatest monument of God's mercy.'" Buckley concludes, "We may, not too fancifully, suspect a parallel with Simeon not only in the saint's name but also to some degree in his manner of speech."[30] Culler goes beyond suspicion to certainty: "St. Simeon is undoubtedly a wicked allusion to the Rev. Charles Simeon."[31] Indeed, Simeon of Cambridge does appear to resemble the earlier Simeon, the pillar hermit who, as Hone's *Every-Day Book* put it, "treated himself as the outcast of the world, and the worst of sinners."[32] In a sermon of 1831 Simeon reminded his audience never to forget not only "the mere existence of sin, for nobody can be ignorant of that," but "the *extent* and *heinousness* of our transgressions."[33] We can easily track this conviction of personal sinfulness to Tennyson's Simeon, who begins by introducing himself as "the basest of mankind, / From scalp to sole one slough and crust of sin" (1–2). The speaker in Tennyson's "Supposed Confessions of a Second-Rate Sensitive Mind," published in his 1830 *Poems* while he was still at Cambridge, may also owe something to the prevailing Evangelical temper, in his opening cry, "O God, my God! have mercy now. / I faint, I fall. Men say that Thou / Didst die for me, for such as *me*" (1–3). This rhetoric of concurrent self-abasement and self-aggrandizement, by which the worst sinner is ultimately the greatest, interested Tennyson before he came to Trinity. In "Remorse" (published in 1827), the speaker imagines his crimes being read out; the poem concludes, "How shall I bear the withering look / Of men and angels, who will turn / Their dreadful gaze on me alone?" (81–83).

Despite these resemblances, I would argue that Charles Simeon is not the model for Tennyson's Simeon (to the extent there is one model), but is notable instead for having offered a rousing *critique* of the model. In November 1831 Charles Simeon preached a series of four sermons at Holy Trinity that were timely enough to be published immediately, titled *The Offices of the Holy Spirit: Four Sermons preached before The University of Cambridge, in the month of November, 1831*. According to Simeon's biographer, "They were listened to we are told 'with mute attention' by a vast congregation."[34] Part of what the congregation heard was the usual thrust of Simeon's sermons: "Beg of God, especially, that you may be impressed with a deep sense of your exceeding sinfulness. . . . And do not rest in a mere outward acknowledgement of your guilt and helplessness, but cry mightily to God, and 'give him no rest' till he bestow his Holy Spirit upon you."[35] "I will not cease.../...to clamour, mourn and sob, / Battering the gates of heaven with storms of prayer" (5, 6–7) is Tennyson's Simeon's articulation of this ambition to weary God by his mighty cries, exemplified by his repetition "cease I not to clamour and to cry" (41).

Simeon's series of sermons in November 1831 was meant specifically to attack a new and fast-growing movement that directly threatened his own, and it is to this movement, millenarianism, which anticipates Christ's imminent return to rule a kingdom of a thousand years, that Tennyson's Simeon most closely owes his inspiration. Millenarian debate centered less on whether the event was imminent than how it would occur; some believed that "Christ would come and set up his reign on earth for a thousand years" (called the premillennialists), whereas others "looked for his coming at the final end of all human history without an earthly millennium intervening."[36] Culler doesn't use the term millenarianism, but gives a succinct account of the phenomenon: during the Evangelical revival "it was widely believed that the world was rapidly approaching its end, that a last terrible battle between the forces of good and evil was impending, that the Second Coming of Christ was at hand, and that when he came he would judge all men and set up his Kingdom on earth, which would last for a thousand years."[37] "Millenarianism won hundreds of converts in a sudden rush of notoriety between 1825–30," according to Ernest R. Sandeen in *The Roots of Fundamentalism*.[38] This phenomenon was particularly associated with what came to be called the Catholic Apostolic Church, under Edward Irving, and the Plymouth Brethren, under John Nelson Darby. In October 1831 congregants in Irving's London church began to speak in tongues, and it is to this occurrence that Charles Simeon's sermons the next month so forcefully responded. Simeon demanded of his audience, "Are we all to possess the power of 'working miracles, and speaking divers kinds of tongues'? No; the time for such things is long since passed...no such power exists at this day, except in the conceit of a few brain-sick enthusiasts."[39] One such enthusiast was the Cambridge Apostle Richard Chenevix Trench, a close friend of Hallam's, who wrote dismissively to his cousin and fiancée, Frances Mary Trench, on May 1, 1832, "Simeon is worn out, and, moreover, spoiled by being at the head of a set who have fed him with...religious adulation....Besides, his doctrine is low, compared with that of men who have recovered so much from oblivion that goes to the fullness and completion of the Church."[40]

Simeon had reason, then, to be "particularly worried," as one of his biographers puts it, that Irving's teaching was "beginning to affect evangelical congregations."[41] Charismatic manifestations, or "speaking in tongues," he characterized in his November 1831 sermons as "a delusion, a desperate and fatal delusion."[42] It is reasonable to surmise that some Apostles were among the great audiences for these sermons, but in any case they cannot have been deaf to their reverberations, particularly as many of them were themselves powerfully drawn to Irving's church. In a letter dated November 17, 1831, the middle of the month of Simeon's sermons, Trench wrote to his brother Francis Trench, "I have some purpose of going up to London for a day with Hallam, for we are both very anxious to hear the tongues at Irving's church." He wonders, "Are they going on every day?" (Trench, *Letters*, 1:102). His brother was in a position to know, having been in recent attendance at the church, noting in a letter to their father, "The subject, as you know, is much talked of." His letter from London of November 1, 1831, describes Irving's prayers being interrupted by a woman's "loud outcries" ("The chief noise consisted in sounds of Oh! Oh! variously modulated from high to low"). By the end of the month, Francis Trench had made a trip to Cambridge to visit his brother, informing their father, in another letter, dated November 26, 1831, that he had met Hallam there and "dined in company with Tennyson, a real poet, rare as such personages are now." The remainder of the letter reviews his impressions of the sermons of Irving's he had recently heard, some lasting nearly three hours, in which he "dwells a great deal on the future coming of the Lord in his glory."[43]

Anticipating his foray into London with Hallam to hear "the tongues at Irving's church," Trench observes to his brother, "At any other time than this it would have made a mighty stir, but cholera and reform do not leave people much time to attend to spiritual goings on" (Trench, *Letters*, 1:102). His plan with Arthur Hallam to attend a service confirms Reverend Simeon's fears. Irving's church was indeed making "a mighty stir," aided, in fact, by anxieties over such matters as the fatal spread of the nation's first major cholera epidemic and the contentious debate over the First Reform Bill, both of which were taken as signs presaging a highly specific vision of the rapture. It was not what Simeon of Cambridge preached, then, but what he preached *against* that has the most bearing on "St. Simeon Stylites."

The Catholic Apostolic Church and the Cambridge Apostles

"If early nineteenth-century millenarianism had produced a hero," Sandeen declares in his history of British and American fundamentalism, "he would have been Edward Irving"[44] A Scot, Irving was an intimate friend of Thomas Carlyle and Jane Welsh Carlyle, whom he had introduced to one another. He met Thomas Carlyle in 1815 when both were schoolteachers in Kirkcaldy, and he met Jane Welsh in 1810 when she was nine, having been engaged as her Latin tutor. A decade later, he sought to marry her, but the father of the woman to whom he was already betrothed would not release him from his bond; he remained her ardent admirer and her husband's close friend. Ordained as a minister of the Church of Scotland, Irving moved in 1822 to the Caledonian Chapel in Hatton Garden, London. Due to his powerful oratorical style at the pulpit, his congregation, drawn generally from the upper ranks of society, expanded rapidly. The chapel was soon overwhelmed by the "flood of noble and fashionable hearers who poured in," a Catholic vicar, Edward Miller, author of the two-volume study *Irvingism* (1878), reports. "All the approaches to Hatton Garden were crammed with carriages and vehicles of all sorts and journeyers thither on foot."[45] Most could not even enter the church; tickets were required, and there were fifteen hundred applicants for six hundred seats. Carlyle, who frequently stayed with the Irvings when visiting London in these early years of his own career, recalled Irving's "immense popularity" in a memorial essay written more than thirty years after his death, bemoaning "the crowd of people flocking around him" in "superabundant quantity and vivacity."[46]

To accommodate this demand, Irving built a new church in Regent Square in 1828. In this period Carlyle was again lodging with Irving. In the company of Charles Buller, whom Carlyle had tutored years before in Scotland (a post Irving had acquired for him) and who had been a student at Trinity from 1826 to 1828 and a Cambridge Apostle, Carlyle visited Regent Square as the foundation was being laid for the new Caledonian Chapel. Carlyle and Buller came upon "Irving and a great company," before whom, Carlyle describes, "Irving of course had to deliver an address." "Of the address," he recounts, "which was going on when we arrived, I could hear nothing, such the confusing crowd and the unfavourable locality (a muddy chaos of rubbish and excavations...); but I well remember Irving's glowing face, streaming hair, and deeply moved tones as he spoke."[47]

The Regent Square church was also strained beyond capacity, and the crowds streaming in swelled further when, on April 30, 1831, in a church prayer meeting at the home of a congregant, a governess who was a member of the church began to manifest what were considered the "gifts" of glossolalia and prophesied the second advent of Christ and the end of the world. Speaking in tongues erupted at the church's morning prayer meetings in May 1831 and then on October 16, 1831, at the morning and afternoon services. "The news of the scene in church in the morning...ran rapidly...through London," Miller writes, and the evening service was mobbed by both detractors and potential believers. The morning services alone, which met at 6:30 throughout the winter, were attended by almost a thousand people daily.[48] Many were attracted; others were appalled. Another historian of this phenomenon reports that at Regent Square a "tumultuous, angry crowd assembled in the evening," and "newspapers and periodicals now rose against Irving," the *Times* being especially active in the "frequency and intensity" of its strictures.[49] "The 'Gift of Tongues' had fairly broken out among the crazed and weakliest of his wholly rather dim and weakly flock," Carlyle commented. "Sorrow and disgust were naturally my own feeling."[50] In 1832 Irving was forced from the church he had built and was excommunicated by the Presbytery of Annan in 1833. Harassed but unswerving, he founded the Catholic Apostolic Church and continued to hold meetings in London until his death in 1834 at the age of forty-two. Although considering Irving prey to a fatal delusion, Carlyle always revered his lost friend's integrity and brilliance. Coleridge, who had also known Irving well, thereafter referred to him as "honoured Irving."[51]

Irving's imminent death was of course unforeseen by Tennyson at the time he drafted "St. Simeon Stylites" in 1833. He was nevertheless well aware of Irving's final tumultuous years, in part because these events were intensively reported, but still more because among the people who crowded into Irving's services, both before and after congregants began speaking in tongues, were a number of the poet's friends, all Cambridge Apostles, whose close attention to and even involvement in these events I chronicle, in particular Hallam, Milnes, and Trench. This period witnessed wide-ranging religious foment, including the development of the Tractarians and the Plymouth Brethren, and what Reverend Simeon's biographer characterizes as "a marked revival of interest in eschatology...on top of [which] came the impact of Irving and his views on the second coming of Christ."[52] This phenomenon is widely considered a response to the French Revolution, the horror of which threads its way through many Irvingite texts. Contemporary events intensifying millennial anxiety included Catholic Emancipation in 1829, the arrival of cholera in 1831, and agitation over the Reform Bill, passed in 1832. As Miller put it in 1878, "Naturally they began to wonder what was preparing in the womb of Time." Many began to believe that gestating in the womb of Time was the end of time as they knew it. According to Miller, many "were filled with the idea that the period in which they were living would prove to be the critical turning-point in the commencement of the end,"[53] among which we may include some persons especially close to Tennyson.

Among the millenarians in this period, Irving and his followers had the greatest immediate impact, in part because of Irving's own rhetorical powers. He attained fame in 1823 when George Canning, in a speech in the House of Commons, described his preaching as the most eloquent he had ever heard. Thomas De Quincey called Irving "the greatest orator of our time."[54] His physical performance was highly mannered, even awkward; Carlyle describes "a something of strained and aggravated, of elaborately intentional, which kept jarring on the mind." Affirming Irving's "violent and ungraceful, but impressive gesticulation," Miller nevertheless notes, "His 'orations,' as he appropriately loved to call them, were true rhetorical efforts of a high order."[55] Spedding expressed reservations in a letter to Blakesley after a visit to Irving's church in 1830: Irving "is a splendid declaimer," he writes, "but his eloquence is too little allied to logic for my taste."[56] But other Apostles were attracted; also in 1830, a year in which he was frequently in the company of Tennyson and Hallam, Milnes was "a regular attendant at the church of Edward Irving."[57] In a letter to his parents dated January 4, 1830, Milnes describes having heard "a most beautiful and effective sermon from Irving in town—he is indeed the apostle of the age" (quoted in *Letters*, 405, n3).

Irving had notable oratorical skills, but his church became notorious for speech that was emphatically not his own. Although he himself never spoke in tongues, he believed in the charismatic manifestations among his congregants, which were considered the return of apostolic gifts described in the New Testament. When the Apostles gathered in Jerusalem after Christ's resurrection on the date of the Jewish Pentacost, "they were all filled with the holy Spirit and began to speak in other tongues, as the Spirit gave them utterance" (Acts 2:4). This descent of the spirit was manifested in spontaneous healings, speaking in tongues, and prophesying. While the prophetic mode is recurrent throughout "St. Simeon Stylites" and, indeed, Tennyson's other early dramatic monologues, we might note a few more surprising points of comparison between the genre and the discursive phenomenon of speaking in tongues, or glossolalia. Robert Baxter, for a time in the early 1830s a devout Irvingite and the author of *Narrative of Facts Characterizing the Supernatural Manifestations in Members of Mr. Irving's Congregation*, an 1833 book that decried the phenomenon, describes glossolalia as "no language whatever." He considers it, rather, "a mere collection of words and sentences; and, in the lengthened discourses…much of it, a jargon of sounds," though it may appear "when the power is very great, that it will assume much of the form of a connected oration."[58]

Tennyson's monologists can hardly be considered to speak in an unknown tongue, but they nevertheless also depend for a part of their effect on a radical disjunction between a speaker and his or her speech (and it is important that both men and women manifested these apostolic discursive gifts): a voice issues from a person that is not the voice of the person. Glossolalia also constitutes a dramatic utterance that was by all accounts emphatically public speech, since the outbursts seem always to have taken place in the company of an audience. As such, one might posit that this speech seeks to be persuasive, whether one takes the speech to be that of the Holy Spirit or the human speaker, with an ambition to draw an audience to repentance and redemption. Thus these might be seen as performances of performative speech, constituting acts, effective theatrically because believed by many to be efficacious, and thus supreme instances of what Austin over a century later would term doing things with words. Among the transformations believed to be occasioned by this speech was spontaneous healing: Miller reports, "It is asserted…that…there have been numerous cures wrought amongst the Irvingites: so much so, indeed, that the number of reported instances is said to have reached in one year the total of forty-six in England alone, being only such as were sufficiently important to be reported." Finally, these episodes appear to have been occasions of rapt oration. According to Miller, "To many a mysterious power seemed to bear along the speaker almost without his or her origination, or even connivance." Being thus discursively carried away, the speakers in turn elicited "rapt attention."[59]

Though not necessarily enraptured, "much of London was excited and alarmed" by the apostolic gift of tongues at Irving's church in October 1831.[60] The alarm was shared by the Carlyles, who, while paying a call on Irving, heard in a nearby room, according to Carlyle's later account, "there burst forth a shrieky hysterical 'Lah lall lall!'" Irving commented to them, "There, hear you, there are the Tongues," about which Carlyle reflected, "Why was there not a bucket of cold water to fling on that *lahlalling* hysterical madwoman?"[61] Gladstone, then a student at Oxford, was initially less skeptical, sharing, according to his biographer H. C. G. Matthew, "like many of his generation...at certain moments and especially in 1831–2, a millenarian feeling that European society stood on the brink of revolution and moral disaster." Gladstone also made a pilgrimage to Irving's Catholic Apostolic Church, but when he visited found what he described as "a scene pregnant with melancholy instruction" and Irving "little short of madness."[62] Interest in Irving was high among many of Tennyson's cohort of Cambridge Apostles even before the advent of these charismatic episodes, and this fascination only deepened for some in the wake of them, a striking phenomenon chronicled in a thick network of epistolary references that has garnered no attention from Tennyson's biographers and critics.

Tennyson left Cambridge in February 1831, the month of Hallam's first reference to Irving (in a letter to fellow Apostle W. B. Donne on the thirteenth). Seamlessly connecting theological and literary discussion, Hallam shifts in his letter from Irving's theology to Tennyson's poetry, both clearly being objects of Cambridge Apostolic enthusiasm. Hallam contrasts the "Churchmen...whom we may hear for our sins most Sundays in the year," with "Irving and his Millenarians," with their "living and spiritual faith." He moves immediately into a lengthy paragraph beginning, "I rejoice exceedingly at the admiration you express for Alfred Tennyson." Providing an example of "Alfred's peculiar power," he copies out all of what came to be titled "Mariana in the South," a poem inspired by his travels with Tennyson in southern France (*Letters*, 400–402). In the spring Hallam accompanied Milnes to Irving's church. Apostolic interest continued into the fall; Trench wrote from Trinity to Maurice on October 10, 1831, "I have been reading many of Irving's books, which drive one into new worlds of thought" (Trench, *Letters*, 1:101).

Within a week, on October 16, 1831, as I have noted, the governess began to speak in tongues in the morning service at Irving's Regent Square church. The London *Times* of October 26, 1831, describes the chaos that ensued among the congregation a few days later when, at Irving's invitation, a woman began speaking in tongues, in "the most discordant yells." During this, Irving "stood up in his pulpit, with his eyes fixed towards Heaven, as if in a state of mental aberration, and seemingly unconscious of the scene which was acting around him, he looked, or pretended to look, as if were in deep converse with his God."[63] We might note the questions of inauthenticity and dramatic intent raised by speaking in tongues, as well as by Irving's own "seemingly unconscious" performance, as he "looked, or pretended to look" as if his attention was fixed not on the words of the woman but on the words of God. This month, October 1831, when Trench was intensively reading Irving's works and Reverend Simeon was fervently preparing to denounce them in his series of November sermons, is also significant because it is when Hallam delivered to the Apostles, on the twenty-ninth, his essay "Theodicæa Novissima." Subtitled "Hints for an Effectual Construction of the Higher Philosophy on the Basis of Revelation," the essay has bearing on several of Tennyson's poems of the early 1830s, particularly the dramatic monologue "St. Simeon Stylites." Some version of what the *Times* journalist reported is what Hallam and Trench may have seen when they visited Irving's church, as they planned to do in mid-November, a month after the first manifestation of the tongues. Although the London press and others were skeptical, these Pentacostal performances became an obsessive interest of Trench, the friend with whom, in Tennyson's absence from Cambridge, Hallam spent much of his time.

Spedding wrote to W. B. Donne on October 30, 1831, that Trench's "only hope is in a speedy millennium, of which he hails the newly given gift of unknown tongues as a forerunner and assurance."[64] But Donne would have gathered his friend's burgeoning belief in rapture theology from letters from Trench himself. On December 6, 1831, in a letter written from Trinity, Trench begins by passing along to Donne a message from Hallam, then immediately asks, "Do you share in the general despondency of wise and good men at the present aspect of the world? . . . I live in the faith of a new dispensation, which I am very confident is at hand—but what fearful times shall we have to endure ere that!" (Trench, *Letters*, 1:103). Less than a week later, in another letter to Donne, again from Cambridge, Trench writes, "We are now . . . on the eve of the mightiest change, which the world has ever known." After various warnings about the destruction of institutions and the coming of a false Prophet, he adds, perhaps unnecessarily, "You see that I am a believer in the approaching Millennium and personal coming of Christ, but I know that before it, the nations will endure such things as never have been endured." More warnings ensue, regarding "revolution on revolution, and war on war," before he concludes, "Have you read any of Irving's later works? if not pray do it. I feel sure that he is *the* man of the Times, the man who sees most clearly, on whom rests most of the Spirit of Prophecy: for his *vision* has almost arrived at that."[65]

Given his preoccupation with Irving's works and evident expectation of the approach of the Second Coming, Trench might seem likely to hold a marginal relation to the Apostles or any group of searching but skeptical undergraduates. But Trench was at the bosom of the Apostles, a figure arguably more central in this period even than Hallam, because he connected so many of them to one another. In particular, he constitutes a primary link between Hallam's cohort and the earlier members Sterling and Maurice, to whom he was even closer. At the turn of the new year, in a letter of January 9, 1832, from Trinity, Trench conveys to Donne this community's pleasure in one another's company, at once doleful and delightful: "Hallam, Blakesley and myself and one or two others sit like a congregation of ravens, a hideous conclave, and croak despair, which however does not prevent us from smoking a multitude of cigars and drinking whatever liquor falls in our way."[66] Hallam had a particular appreciation for Trench; about a month later Hallam wrote him a letter (dated February 12, 1832) with a fervor comparable to some of his letters to Tennyson: "I thank God that at so critical a moment in my life He has brought me into daily intercourse with you. I feel more benefit from it than I fear I ever can repay." Trench's friendship seems to Hallam God-given, providential, but it is crucial to remember that to be friends with Trench was to anticipate another, harsher future, also providential, to which Hallam in this letter appears to allude, in his expectation that the two friends will go on "exhorting one another, and so much the more as we see the day approaching" (*Letters*, 523).

Tennyson was considerably more resistant to the appeal of Trench and his millenarianism; in turn Trench, who also wrote poetry ("He was first and before all things a poet," according to his daughter [Trench, *Letters*, 1:55]), seems to have been resistant to the appeal of Tennyson. This may be attributable partly to jealousy over Hallam's affections, perhaps on both sides. In mid-March 1832 Hallam visited the Tennyson home at Somersby, from which he wrote a letter to Trench, and Tennyson wrote a letter about Trench, who was clearly on both of their minds. In a letter to W. H. Brookfield, Tennyson declares, "It is impossible to look upon Trench and not to love him," but then goes on to describe traits not particularly loveable. Trench, comments Tennyson, is "always strung to the highest pitch, and the earnestness which burns within him so flashes through all his words and actions, that when one is not in a mood of sympathetic elevation, it is difficult to prevent a sense of one's own inferiority and lack of all high, and holy feeling. Trench is a bold truehearted Idoloclast—yet have I no faith in any one of his opinions."[67] The *Oxford English Dictionary* (which Trench, decades later, was instrumental in founding) defines "idoloclast" as "a breaker or demolisher of idols, an iconoclast," and lists its first instance as a publication of J. C. Hare's in 1843, eleven years after its appearance in Tennyson's letter. In chapter 3 I discuss the influence of Hare on the Apostles; apparently the word had a particular currency at this time at Cambridge. In any case, contemplating Trench calls faith itself into question for Tennyson: in the face of his burning earnestness, the poet feels insufficient "high, and holy feeling." It is not faith in God, however, that is compromised as much as faith in Trench. Tennyson could not be more dismissive, or decisive: "Yet have I no faith in any one of his opinions."

Having denounced Trench's opinions, the chief among which in this period was the rapidly approaching coming of the end, Tennyson continues, "Hallam got a letter from [Trench] the other day."[68] Henry Hallam destroyed much of his son's correspondence after his death, and Trench's letter has not been recovered, but we have the letter Hallam wrote to Trench from Somersby on March 20, 1832, probably written within days of Tennyson's stinging rejection of Trench's views.

Hallam's letter ends by referring to the rural isolation of the Tennyson home: "I see a newspaper very rarely.... I am most impartially ignorant respecting Irving.... Pray write again soon, and tell me what news you can about the stirring world out of which I live" (*Letters*, 539). The letter begins, though, by reporting on Tennyson's state: "Alfred I was most glad to find better than I had apprehended." The letter is concerned with the current conditions of the Somersby poet and the London preacher. Reporting on Tennyson, as if in payment for an expected report on Irving, Hallam writes:

> His mind is what it always was, or rather brighter, and more vigorous. I regret, with you, that you have never had the opportunity of knowing more of him. His nervous temperament and habits of solitude give an appearance of affectation to his manner, which is no true interpreter of the man, and wears off on further knowledge. Perhaps you could never become very intimate, for certainly your bents of mind are not the same, and at some points they intersect; yet I think you could hardly fail to see much for love, as well as for admiration. I have persuaded him, I think, to publish without further delay.

Hallam appears to be joining Trench in a previously expressed regret ("I regret, with you") that Trench knows little of Tennyson, and perhaps also to respond, in his explanation of the poet's "appearance of affectation," to some earlier characterization of Trench's. In the course of making an argument for intimacy between these two friends, Hallam comes to realize its impossibility because of their dissimilarity ("your bents of mind are not the same") and perhaps also their similarity ("at some points they intersect").

Trench thought the "love" and "admiration" Hallam and others bestowed upon Tennyson, apparently a condition as well as a result of knowing the poet, was excessive. He had already voiced his disapproval in a letter to Donne of June 23, 1830, which expresses a dire, and in the end mistaken, view of the effect of Apostolic encouragement of Tennyson's poetry, warning that his "friends at Cambridge will materially injure him if he does not beware; no young man under any circumstances should believe that he *has* done anything, but still be forward looking" (Trench, *Letters*, 1:74).[69] We can hear Trench's censoriousness in Tennyson's report of Trench's pronouncement in the Eversley edition of his poems, "Trench (afterwards Archbishop of Dublin) said, when we were at Trinity (Cambridge) together, 'Tennyson, we cannot live in Art,'" which the poet gives as the origin for his poem "The Palace of Art."[70] There is some question as to when or in what spirit this dictum was uttered, but Culler notes that the result was "peculiarly an 'Apostolic' poem" passed from friend to friend, several of whom made suggestions that Tennyson attempted to incorporate.[71] It is prefaced with a dedicatory poem to Trench, "To ——. With the Following Poem," which ends with its own stark warning, "And he that shuts Love out, in turn shall be / Shut out from Love, and on her threshold lie / Howling in outer darkness" (14–16).[72]

By April 1832, "The Palace of Art" had been drafted; in the next month, it was Irving himself who had been cast out, if not into outer darkness then at least into the streets of London. Trench, and Hallam through him, was a direct witness to these momentous events. Likely of greater moment to Tennyson was a sharply critical review of his 1830 *Poems* by "Christopher North" (John Wilson), which had appeared in the May 1832 *Edinburgh Magazine*. Writing to Tennyson in a letter of late April or early May 1832 that must have been especially significant to the poet, Hallam (whose own published essay on Tennyson had also been lambasted in Wilson's review) reassures his friend, "I think the Review will assist rather than hinder the march of your reputation" (*Letters*, 562). In the next paragraph, he announces that Trench is "in town now for a few days, a great comfort to me," though he notes the millenarian gloom of Trench's sense of the future of the world. Trench's conviction of the coming rapture, strangely cheering to Hallam, may have been due in part to the fact that he was in daily attendance at Irving's church during the most tumultuous period in its history. Writing to his fiancée, Frances Mary Trench, on May 1, 1832, Trench reports, "This morning I attended Irving's chapel, and with such advantage to myself, that I shall not be absent any day during my stay here.... I bore away with me a renewed conviction of his holy earnestness" (Trench, *Letters*, 1:113–14). Trench seems to have divided his time between Irving and Hallam, writing from London on May 4, 1832, to Frances, "I have dined with the Hallams once, and passed an evening with the Kembles, which is all my going out." According to his own correspondence with Tennyson and his sister Emily, Hallam also attended this dinner with the Kembles, and attended a performance of the actress Fanny Kemble on May 3.

In a letter written to Frances the next day, Trench voices concern that he may have offended the Kembles by not attending Fanny's performance, "which took place last night" (Trench, *Letters*, 1:114). But the events of May 4 provided sufficient drama. Trench appeared as usual at Irving's church, to find "the doors of the Church closed against" its minister. As it was widely reported (another congregant noted in a letter that his correspondent "will have seen" what occurred "by the newspapers"), Trench would have witnessed something like the scene described by this other member: "Our dear pastor bare-headed [stood] before the gates of that building where for so many years he had been minister. He was engaged in prayer, with a few of his flock around him."[73] Trench writes to his betrothed, "You have probably seen in the papers the decision of the Presbytery against Irving." Even at the moment of this decision, Trench was present; while Irving met with the Presbytery, a prayer meeting was held "at which I was present.... I felt that it was good to be there" (Trench, *Letters*, 1:115).

Hallam reports in a letter of May 8, 1832, to Milnes, then in Rome, on the doings of "all our common friends"—Sterling, Maurice, and other Cambridge Apostles—including Tennyson, who "is much as usual, except that, methinks, his genius grows brighter and more vigorous every day." He echoes the terms for

Tennyson he had used when writing of him in March to Trench, when he had found his mind "brighter, and more vigorous." And Trench was no doubt on his mind when he wrote to Milnes, who had been a regular at Irving's church, at least once in Hallam's company, details about Irving: "Irving is turned out of his church: he preaches in the environs of London, waiting until some of his faithful flock shall build him a chapel" (*Letters*, 572–73).

Trench and Frances Mary Trench were married on May 31, 1832; a week later Hallam wrote to him from London, on June 6, 1832: "I find daily how much I miss the assistance and support of your conversation and example" (*Letters*, 590). But marriage and removal from London did not remove Trench from Irving's sphere. While again visiting the Tennysons at Somersby, Hallam reports to Brookfield, "I heard the other day from Trench," writing from his family home, where he was "mild and happy—bless him! and thinking about the Church & the Morning Watch still" (August 12–14, 1832; *Letters*, 619). Mildness and happiness would not be states normally occasioned by reading the *Morning Watch*, a prophetic journal founded by Irving in 1829, and indeed in the fall of 1832 Trench was back in London among the Irvingites. He wrote to reassure his wife that though he had attended a sermon of Irving's "held in the open space under Cold-Bath Fields prison" and was to be introduced to Irving the next day, "you must not think that your apprehensions are realized, and that I am altogether given over into the hands of Irving and his friends." She cannot have found consolatory the news that Trench had heard a woman speaking in tongues, expounding the "far more exceeding terribleness of the judgments coming on the earth than it has entered into the hearts even of the denouncers of coming woe to conceive" (Trench, *Letters*, 1:124).

Trench refers to his wife's "apprehensions," and it was the case that his friends were also increasingly remonstrating with him about his attachment to Irving's teachings. He reports to his wife in his October 10, 1832, letter, "I have had a long interview with Coleridge, who speaks of 'poor dear Mr. Irving,' and says it makes his heart break every time he thinks of him," admitting that Coleridge "altogether dissents from the scheme of prophetic interpretation which I have adopted" (Trench, *Letters*, 1:123–24). The Apostles with whom he was most closely associated were equally clear in their rejection of Irving's views. After describing a morning service with several prophetic exclamations ("It was exceedingly appalling, and shook my whole being through and through"), he informs her, "Sterling and Maurice, with whom I have spoken much and earnestly on the subject, are decidedly opposed to the belief in these gifts" (Trench, *Letters*, 1:125). These discussions were beginning to have an effect. Though Trench wrote to his wife a few days later, on October 15, "I have not failed any day since I arrived here in attending Mr. Irving's church one or more times" and had been "invited to private meetings at...Mr. Irving's" (invitations he declined), he nevertheless asserts, "I am not at all convinced." The incidents he witnessed daily left him "staggered"

and "perplexed," but "circumstances...induce me much to question these goings on" (Trench, *Letters*, 1:126). By March 27 of the following year, he could
write to Maurice that though not yet unconvinced, he was also not yet convinced:
"I have not yet been able to acquiesce in the powers manifested in the midst of
Mr. Irving's Church, though, if at any time I should do so, I trust I may have the
grace to follow out my convictions faithfully" (Trench, *Letters*, 1:135).

In his May 8, 1832, letter to Milnes, Hallam mentions another mounting
scandal for Irving: "Two of his principal speakers in the tongue have put forth
recantations, avowing direct imposition, as I am told, but I have not yet seen them."
Like Carlyle, Coleridge, and others, he is personally sympathetic to Irving, commenting, "This will grieve poor Irving much, and I suppose, will diminish considerably his followers," though he notes that it may instead have the opposite effect:
"Latterly the sect has spread much in London" (*Letters*, 573). The governess who
had been among the first to speak tongues in the church had admitted that some
of her prophetic utterances had been premeditated, and Robert Baxter, an attorney
who had attended Irving's Regent Square church beginning in 1831 and intensively in January and February 1832, by April had begun to doubt whether the
tongues he not only witnessed but repeatedly spoke through were not gifts of the
Holy Spirit but manifestations of diabolical possession. His book *Narrative of Facts
Characterizing the Supernatural Manifestations in Members of Mr. Irving's Congregation*
was published in early 1833 (followed by *Irvingism* in 1836). Baxter recounted in
detail his growing faith, then disillusionment, but his tone throughout is respectful, even mournful, rather than denunciatory. His own utterances were powerful,
unfeigned, and fundamentally inexplicable to him, and he knew this to be true of
other congregants, who "really believe," while Irving, though deluded, was "sincerely searching after truth" (Baxter, *Narrative*, 130, 129). Carlyle held to another
view; having breakfasted with some of these associates in Irving's company, he
described them as "a strange set of ignorant conceited fanatics."[74]

Baxter's book regarding Irving's Apostles, as his church's highest members
were termed, was of immediate and profound interest to a number of Cambridge
Apostles. Sterling exhorted Trench in a letter of February 27, 1833, "The printed
book I have read of late that has interested me most is Baxter's memoirs of his
own life, which I hope you will look at as soon as it falls in your way" (Trench,
Letters, 1:134). Hallam also pressed the memoir on Trench's attention in a letter of
April 3, 1833, asking, "Have you seen Baxter's book? It is one of the most curious
I ever read. Pray get it, if you have it not" (Hallam, *Letters*, 744). Trench's initial
response to Baxter's account seems to have been divided, even contradictory. In a
letter from London to his wife of May 1, 1833, he writes, "I have read Baxter's
book, which is passing strange." It seems not to have diminished his interest in
the church, however, as he mentions Baxter's book after announcing that he and
his brother "are going this afternoon to hear Irving" (Trench, *Letters*, 1:142).
Gladstone, who read Baxter in mid-March 1833, described it in his diary as "very

remarkable and interesting" and "*convincing*" (quoted in Hallam, *Letters*, 745 n6). As it happens, in another example of Hallam's capacity to weave his friends together, that month Gladstone, recently elected to his first seat in Parliament, was addressing himself to the future of Trench, recently ordained in the Church of England. Hallam wrote to Trench on March 25, 1833, to suggest that "a friend of mine, Gladstone, the new member of Newark," might be able to use his influence to get Trench "a small living in Buckinghamshire" (Trench, *Letters*, 1:134), a position Trench expressed an interest in, until hearing from Hallam a week later that it was no longer available, in the letter recommending Baxter's book.

Tennyson, too, would have been fully aware of the developments with Irving's church and the nascent careers of both Gladstone and Trench, especially given that the career Hallam was most actively involved in advancing was Tennyson's own. In the days when Hallam was reading Baxter and ardently recommending it to Trench, he was in the constant company of Tennyson and his sister Mary, who were visiting London. A letter to Trench from Blakesley of April 1, 1833, reports, "Alfred Tennyson is in town.... He has a sister with him... of a noble countenance and magnificent eyes" (Trench, *Letters*, 1:136). A few days after recommending Baxter to Trench, Hallam wrote to Emily Tennyson, to whom he was now openly betrothed, describing a foray on April 4 with Alfred and Mary to the Zoological Gardens and other London sights (including an oxy-hydrogen microscope). Hallam writes joyfully on April 5 that the two Tennysons paid a call on Hallam's mother, who received her sister, an emissary for Emily herself, especially warmly, so much so that Hallam could take her brother "up into my room" while leaving Mary "to chat" with his mother and sister (*Letters*, 746).

That fall, Hallam traveled to the continent with his father; in Vienna, on September 15, 1833, he died suddenly of a hemorrhage in his brain caused by an aneurism. Even without Hallam's ongoing career ministrations, Tennyson became the era's leading poet and Gladstone its leading politician. Trench became dean of Westminster, then archbishop of Dublin. Starting in 1830 and throughout the vicissitudes of its existence, Trench had been deeply occupied with Irving's church, an involvement that intrigued and eventually troubled his Apostolic friends; by the spring following Hallam's death, he had withdrawn his sharpest attention. Sterling could write to Blakesley on May 16, 1834, about a reassuring conversation with Trench: "We had of course much talk about Coleridge, Irving and so forth—and I was rejoiced to find him as little inclined as you or I to believe in the divine origin of gibberish."[75] Trench had moved from the "gibberish" of glossolalia to the judiciousness of glossography, one result of which was his 1851 collection of five lectures, *The Study of Words*, which reached twenty-seven editions by 1904.[76] Trench became an active member of the Philological Society (one of whose founding members was William Whewell, master of Trinity College and tutor to Hallam and Tennyson). It was Trench's call for a new kind of dictionary in a highly influential 1857 address to the Philological Society (an inscribed copy of which he sent to Tennyson) that led to the founding of the monumental *Oxford English Dictionary*.[77]

Trench writes on July 8, 1834, to Donne that Hallam's father "has sent me a volume of the remains of our departed friend, which is, indeed, a precious gift." Trench especially remarks in *Remains* verses addressed to Emily Tennyson, "some later poems, not before printed, of exquisite beauty, but very painful to read, when one remembers of whom and to whom they were written. I should be glad to know whether she has been quite smitten down by the blow" (Trench, *Letters*, 1:160). He himself sounds smitten down by words, in the abstract: "I am becoming every day more conscious of the imperfect machinery of words, more weary of word-fighting." He feels acutely the need, one his *Study of Words* explicitly attempts to meet, "to discipline one's mind for the detection of all the mischievous fallacies which lie in equivocal terms." Though he does not refer to what many felt were the dangerous fallacies of Irving's church, he does suggest that at this point for him theological disputes might best be settled by increased linguistic precision: "most theological controversies want rather right stating than debating" (Trench, *Letters*, 1:160).

Their circle of Cambridge friends all recognized the primacy of Tennyson's reaction to Hallam's death, including Francis Garden, who wrote to Tennyson, "My dear Alfred...yours is not a sorrow that will soon die," adding that he had received a letter "from one who dearly loved Hallam, and who takes a deep interest in all of you, dear Trench. You may be assured that you will not want his prayers and we read that the prayer of such an one as him 'availeth much.'"[78] Whether Trench's "deep interest" or his prayers provided solace to Tennyson we cannot say; like Trench, though, in the wake of Hallam's death he rededicated himself to the "machinery of words." In a letter dated October 25, 1833, a little more than a month after Hallam's death, FitzGerald wrote to Donne that Tennyson "has been making fresh poems, which are finer, they say, than any he has done."[79] Among these fresh poems were early drafts of what would over ensuing decades become the dramatic monologues "St. Simeon Stylites," "Ulysses," "Tithonus," and "Tiresias." I have noted that to his friends the first of these seemed an unlikely response from Tennyson, as Thompson had written to Blakesley on November 11, 1833, in a letter I have previously quoted, "He seemed less overcome than one would have expected: though, when he first arrived, he was very low—He left among us some magnificent poems and fragments of poems. Among the rest a monologue or soliloquy of one Simeon Stylites." In the same letter, Thompson described another powerful discursive performance, that of Trench delivering a sermon during which his congregation had "some difficulty in swallowing the gobbets of strong meat flung among them with so vigorous a hand." "Trench's manner in the pulpit astonished churchmen and laymen," W. C. Lubenow comments in his history of the Cambridge Apostles, so much so that his friend Donne, after witnessing an 1833 sermon, compared him to Elijah.[80] In the remainder of this chapter, I show how clear was the intersection, drawn by the friend who had deeply loved and admired both men, of Tennyson's poems and Trench's prophecies. These intersecting discursive lines form the critical undergirding of the pillar of Simeon Stylites, the erection of which, in this millenarian context, is not unexpected, but rather has the inevitability of the rapture Trench had been convinced would overtake them all.

Theories of Rapture

To understand the centrality of a vision of rapture to the theological and discursive ambitions of Tennyson's St. Simeon Stylites, we must first understand the concept as it was defined in the period of this poem's, and this genre's, inception. In his *Narrative of Facts Characterizing the Supernatural Manifestations in Members of Mr. Irving's Congregation*, Robert Baxter recounts of the doctrine of the coming of Christ to rapture his church, "This was the leading theme of the utterances. The nearness of it, its suddenness, and the fearful judgments which would accompany it, were the continual arguments which were used to excite our minds...and to induce us to lay all other things aside to further the work" (142). This belief in the nearness of the coming rapture was based "most particularly of all," as Edward Irving writes in his two-volume prophetic work, *Babylon and Infidelity Foredoomed of God* (1826), "in the 4th of the 1st Thessalonians," the most relevant verse of which reads, "Then we which are alive and remain shall be caught up together...in the clouds, to meet the Lord in the air: and so shall we ever be with the Lord" (1 Thessalonians 4.17). Irving comments that in this verse concerning what came to be called the rapture "not only is the fact revealed, but in some sort the very manner of it is also revealed."[81]

Baxter's own most consequential occasion of speaking in tongues gave critical weight to this expectation of the imminence of the rapture. In an interpretation of the significance of the number 1,260, specified in Revelation 11:3, Irving claimed that the years from 533 to 1792, beginning with the Justinian recognition of the papacy and ending with the French Revolution, constituted a cataclysmic 1,260 years. During the evening service at Irving's church on January 14, 1832, Baxter, speaking not through his own voice but through what he took to be the offices of the Holy Spirit, offered another interpretation of this consequential number: that they were "commanded to 'count the days one thousand three score and two hundred'—1260—the days appointed for testimony, at the end of which the saints of the Lord should go up to meet the Lord in the air, and evermore be with the Lord" (Baxter, *Narrative*, 17). He explains, "The prophecy of the 1260 days testimony and going up of the saints, set forth a period of three years and a half, from the time of its delivery, up to the translation of the saints." "The words of the prophecy were most distinct," he recollects, and also most insistent: "On innumerable other occasions, by exposition and by prophecy, was the same thing again and again declared" (Baxter, *Narrative*, 18–19).

Although there was some debate among church members as to which days were to be counted, calculations determined that the rapture would take place on Sunday, July 14, 1835. This event did not occur on that day, although July 14 is significant in the annals of Victorian theological history as the date in 1833 of John Keble's famous Assize sermon, "A National Apostasy." This is considered to have inaugurated the Oxford Movement, and John Henry Newman always held the date of July 14 especially dear. For members of Irving's Catholic Apostolic Church, although "the Lord did not come," "the date was momentous in the movement," and the "Fourteenth of July" was thereafter commemorated annually.[82] Irving himself, however, came to disavow this prophetic date, writing in a letter to Baxter quoted in his *Narrative of Facts*, "concerning the time which you have been made so often to put forth." Irving informs Baxter that, through another prophetic speaker, "the Lord hath sent me a very wonderful and wonderfully gracious message," namely, "that the day is not known, and that it is a mystery, and that you, as well as myself had erred in repeating in the flesh, this matter of the time" (Baxter, *Narrative*, 92).

Just as Irving retreated from fixing a date for the rapture, however, another Protestant sect intensified its expectations of its imminence. Established in the same years as the Catholic Apostolic Church, the Plymouth Brethren, as they came to be called, also prophesied the coming rapture. As the former church was often termed "Irvingite," so the "exclusive" branch of the Plymouth Brethren was often termed Darbyite, after its charismatic leader, John Nelson Darby. An ordained Anglican minister, Darby left the established church in 1827; with a powerful personality and preaching style, he attracted numerous adherents, the more so because of extensive proselytizing not only throughout Britain but in Switzerland and America. His appeal was intensified by the severity of his style and message; as one historian of the Darbyite movement puts it, "Some have called him a saint, but if he was he belongs to the hermit saints."[83] Darby recounts that in 1830 he "went to Cambridge and Oxford." "In this latter place some shared my convictions," he reports, though he does not seem to have found much fellowship in the former place, where in this year Charles Simeon was still powerfully influential and at least one group of students, as we have seen, was looking with interest toward Irving's church.[84] Darby propounded a theory of dispensationalism, which held that there are seven eras, or dispensations, spanning from creation to judgment, in each of which humans are tested according to God's plan. Although it may not have excited much interest at Cambridge in 1830, dispensationalism would eventually become, in Peter Prosser's words, "the key-stone of the eschatological system of many millions of charismatics and pentecostalists, to say nothing of the tens of millions of (U.S.) fundamentalists."[85]

Darby's dispensational eschatology was bound together with the belief that the church will be raptured to meet Christ in the air, which event he distinguished from Armageddon, the day of judgment. The rapture was to occur first, with Christ coming *for* the saints; after the period of Tribulation Christ would come again *with* the saints to fight the battle of Armageddon and thus usher in the millennial kingdom. James Scofield, author of the *Scofield Reference Bible* (1909) and a widely influential American proponent of dispensationalism, clarifies that with the rapture, the coming "is not *to the earth*, but into 'the air'; it does not establish anything on the earth, but takes a people away from the earth."[86] This pre-Tribulation rapture was one of the distinctions of Darby's theological system.

According to Larry Crutchfield, a historian of dispensationalism, Darby's theory of Christ coming for the saints in the rapture was without clear precedent: "That Darby himself claimed no source for the doctrine, other than Scripture, is beyond question."[87] Another religious historian, Timothy P. Weber, writes, "Historians are still trying to determine how or where Darby got it."[88] Darby claimed he conceived this doctrine around 1827, but others argue that "the doctrine originated in one of the outbursts of tongues in Edward Irving's church about 1832," a charge Ernest Sandeen considers "groundless and pernicious."[89] Darby promulgated his theory of the secret rapture of the church at conferences hosted by Lady Theodosia Powerscourt in Wicklow, Ireland, in the early 1830s, although it may have been developed earlier.[90] Debate may continue regarding whether this concept originated with Irving or with Darby, but it is certain that the theory of the rapture as we know it—one now espoused by millions—dates from these years and these spiritual communities.

Sandeen acknowledges that among the glossolalic utterances in Edward Irving's church in January 1832 was the prophecy that after 1,260 days "the saints of the Lord should go up to meet the Lord in the air," but he distinguishes this from Darby's doctrine of a *secret* rapture, also called the doctrine of "any-moment coming," or "maybe tonight."[91] This doctrine holds that the rapture could come at any moment, to be witnessed only by raptured Christians; all others will be left behind, bewildered and terrified by the sudden disappearance of the blessed. That the date of the rapture must necessarily be unexpected means that believers must always be at the ready. A secret rapture also avoids the potential embarrassment of the failure of a prophetic schedule or the disappointment presumably felt by some of Irving's congregants when they awoke on July 15, 1835, to a largely unchanged world.

Whether Irving or Darby originated the enormously influential doctrine of the rapture, Darby accurately declared, "The rapture of the saints to meet the lord in the air...is happily attracting the attention of Christians."[92] It continues to do so; the fundamentalist tendency to "predict the speedy end of the world" has shown, in Sandeen's words, "an unexpected vitality and appeal" in the contemporary American context.[93] According to a 2002 poll, 70 million Americans are

Evangelicals (25 percent), and over half the population (59 percent) believes that the predictions in Revelation will be fulfilled. Tim LaHaye's apocalyptic thriller (written with Jerry B. Jenkins) *Left Behind: A Novel of the Earth's Last Days* (1995) and the series of related novels it engendered have sold more than 63 million copies, making LaHaye "one of the best-selling authors in all of American history," according to a profile of the movement in *Vanity Fair*.[94] An editorial in the *New York Times* calls the book and its sequels "the best-selling American novels of our age," and the movement is further advanced by a plethora of popular end-time Web sites.[95] These include, to list only a sampling, leftbehind.com, endtime.com, and raptureready.com (which features the Rapture Index, a calculus of the nearness of the coming rapture based on current international news events).

Tennyson's interest in the coming end-times as a subject for his poetry seems to have predated the establishment of the doctrines of rapture developed by Darby or Irving. In "The Fall of Jerusalem" (1827), published before he went to Cambridge, he envisions the destruction of the city: "Signs on earth and signs on high / Prophesied thy destiny; / A trumpet's voice above thee rung," as "flaming chariots, fiercely dashing, / Swept along the peopled air, / In magnificent array" (65–67, 72–74). "Babylon," another poem published in 1827, draws on Isaiah's prophecy of this city's destruction, a vision Irving was also attracted to, as witnessed by his two-volume *Babylon and Infidelity Foredoomed*, published in the previous year. Tennyson's poem depicts the foredoom more succinctly, as the Lord declares in a forceful dactylic tetrameter couplet, "I will sweep ye away in destruction and death, / As the whirlwind that scatters the chaff with its breath" (37–38).

Also written before entering the orbit of Cambridge or its Apostles, Tennyson's long poem "Armageddon" was, according to Charles Tennyson, "evidently very early work." The draft seems to have been written "when the poet was not more than fifteen," and perhaps younger. Yet the poem, in an altered version, served in some sense as his entrance into this circle of college friends. I have noted that Tennyson and Hallam came to know each other in the course of the competition for the Chancellor's Gold Medal in English Verse, for which all entrants had to produce a poem on Timbuctoo. Tennyson's submission drew some 120 lines, "roughly half," as Ricks calculates, "almost verbatim from *Armageddon*" (*Poems*, 1:188). In a letter to Gladstone in September 1829, Arthur Hallam exalted over Tennyson's prizewinning "Timbuctoo," so much of which came from the adolescent boy's vision of the destruction of the world: "The splendid imaginative power that pervades it will be seen through all hindrances. I consider Tennyson as promising fair to be the greatest poet of our generation, perhaps of our century" (*Letters*, 319). A poem with a central vision borrowed from images of Armageddon thus stands as the origin of the profound literary intimacy of Hallam and Tennyson.

In some 270 lines of visionary blank verse divided into four parts, "Armageddon" imagines the vast destruction of the last battle at the Day of Judgment. In the poem, a "Hebrew prophet or seer," as Culler puts it, is "granted an apocalyptic vision comparable to that of St. John so that he can prophesy of the latter times."[96] The poem opens with an apostrophe to the "Spirit of Prophecy whose mighty grasp / Enfoldeth all things," declaring, "I thank thy power," which has "removed / The cloud that from my mortal faculties / Barred out the knowledge of the Latter Times" (1:1–2, 9, 11–13). Part 1 describes the stirrings of destruction, recounting the horrifying sights and sounds he sees, standing "upon the mountain which o'erlooks / The valley of destruction" (1:14–15). Part 2 begins, "A rustling of white wings! The bright descent / Of a young seraph!" (2:1–2). The speaker's vision is magnified so expansively as to encompass infinitude, so that he announces, "I felt my soul grow godlike" (2:21). In part 3 the angel speaks, prophesying, after which the poet sees again "living things" in a strangely silent scene. The poem ends in part 4 with a vision of a ruined and yet potentially promising world:

> The clear stars
> Shone out with keen but fixed intensity,
> All-silence, looking steadfast consciousness
> Upon the dark and windy waste of Earth.
> There was a beating in the atmosphere,
> An indefinable pulsation
> Inaudible to outward sense, but felt
> Through the deep heart of every living thing,
> As if the great soul of the Universe
> Heaved with tumultuous throbbings on the vast
> Suspense of some grand issue. (4:24–34)

Although occurring amid "All-silence," and itself "Inaudible," this conclusion— of the world and of the poem—with its steadfast "beating," "pulsation," and "throbbings," constitutes an overwhelming sonic advent. In the pivotal scene of his reunion with the deceased Hallam in *In Memoriam*, Tennyson describes how he is "caught up" into the air, and there can feel "the deep pulsations of the world" (95.40), affirming the association of his friend with the physical sensations of lyric rapture. But we can hear already in the postapocalyptic world of "Armageddon" that, although the Earth is a "dark and windy waste," for Tennyson rapture is above all a rhythmic state, and what remains even after the end of the world is poetry.

THE RAPTURE OF ST. SIMEON STYLITES

Late in his life, Tennyson reminisced, "Archbishop Trench (not then archbishop) was the only critic who said of my first volume, 'What a singular absence of the 's'!" (*Memoir*, 2:286). If he remembered half a century later the singularity of this comment regarding his 1830 *Poems, Chiefly Lyrical* (Trench was the "only critic" who mentioned it), then he must surely have recalled it in 1833, as he conceived a character with a name marked by a singular presence of the *s*: St. Simeon Stylites. While the very title of this poem might be heard as a defiant rejoinder to Trench's comment, the poet himself consistently revised lines containing too many sibilants due to what Eric Griffiths describes as the "harshness of the sound to Tennyson's ears."[97] Indeed, Simeon, although he cites the name he has been christened by the crowd ("they shout / 'St. Simeon Stylites'" [144–45]), is also acutely aware of the effects of any sound, whether consonant or vowel, he produces. "I drowned the whoopings of the owl with sound / Of pious hymns and psalms" (32–33), he announces, thereby revealing, as Linda K. Hughes comments, that the "'hymns' and 'psalms' are important for their physical sound, not their sense." She adds, "Ironically, through the assonance of 'owl' and 'sound' Tennyson lets us hear the owl rather than the hymns."[98] Her reading affirms T. S. Eliot's observation, "I do not think any poet in English has ever had a finer ear for vowel sound."[99] In a memoir published in Hallam's *Remains*, one of his friends recalled that Hallam considered "metrical harshness to indicate a defect rather in the soul than the ear of the poet."[100] Given that Simeon's vowel sounds overwhelm the owl's sounds through the discordance of what can only have been superior whooping, his soul, not to mention his ear, must be especially defective. And yet Robert Browning declared Simeon's dramatic monologue "perfect" in 1842, and twenty years later Gerard Manley Hopkins wrote of the poem, "It is indeed magnificent."[101] More recently, William E. Fredeman, one of the poem's most thoroughgoing critics, has called it "a perfectly conceived and structured poem."[102] Simeon's aim is indeed to be made perfect, to prove through the precision of his monologue's sound the perfection of his soul as well as his ear.

Hughes notes that this speaker is "obsessed with quantities rather than qualities," and Fredeman observes that he views his mortifications "in a purely *quantitative* way."[103] James Kincaid remarks in Simeon "an absurd dependence on numbers."[104] This preoccupation is taken by some critics to be a moral failing, and possibly a rhetorical failing as well. Certainly, it can seem an antithetical emphasis for Tennyson, who left Cambridge without a degree essentially because he would not even attempt what Martin calls "the apparently unscalable wall of mathematics."[105] Arthur Hallam did meet this requirement for his degree, but without enthusiasm or distinction. In Gladstone's reminiscences of Hallam sixty-five years after his death, he recalls his friend's "complaints, which are really touching, of the difficulties, almost the agony" of learning trigonometry. Under the bold-faced subtitle "His Distaste for Mathematics," Gladstone argues that this is one of several reasons Hallam should have attended Oxford (his own alma mater, which had no mathematics requirement). The only argument against what Gladstone calls his "case" is that Hallam would not then "have known Tennyson; and the world might not have been in possession of *In Memoriam*," although there is a suggestion that nevertheless his case still stands.[106]

Henry Hallam, who had desired his son to attend Cambridge in part because of its mathematics requirement, lamented in his preface to his son's *Remains*, "It was however to be regretted, that he never paid the least attention to mathematical studies." The father considers that it may have helped counteract the quality of mind that his son's friends particularly revered: "A little more practice in the strict logic of geometry...would possibly have repressed the tendency to vague and mystical speculation which he was too fond of indulging."[107] For Simeon, though, "the strict logic of geometry" provides the basis for his mystical speculation; he must quantify if he is to qualify for sainthood.

This chapter takes Simeon's measure, scanning the height of his pillar, the number of his bows, the minute of his death, and also the iambic pentameter of his blank verse. He calculates:

> Three years I lived upon a pillar, high
> Six cubits, and three years on one of twelve;
> And twice three years I crouched on one that rose
> Twenty by measure; last of all, I grew
> Twice ten long weary weary years to this,
> That numbers forty cubits from the soil. (84–90)

Simeon's enjambed words ("high," "rose," "grew") reenact his strenuous extensions beyond prescribed limits of space and time. An ancient unit of measure, the cubit is based on the body, constituting a forearm's length, roughly eighteen inches. Computing a geometrical equation between length of time and height of pillar, he multiplies increasing years by increasing cubits (three by six; three by twelve; twice three by twenty; twice ten by forty), his magnitude in space and time seeming by these equations to increase almost exponentially. The pillar becomes not only a unit of measure but an instrument of it, precisely gauging not only spatial length (height) but temporal length (time), since it serves as a sun dial: he figures that he has "borne as much as this— /...—and for so long a time, / If I may measure time by yon slow light, / And this high dial, which my sorrow crowns" (91–94). James Spedding defined metrical quantity as "length measured in time,"[108] and Simeon's dramatic monologue exploits the fact that a meter may be a unit of sight or sound, and measure may be gauged by a ruler or a rhythm. In Emily Brontë's depiction of Simeon, we can trace the articulation of the divisions of his pillar, and Tennyson's speaker utilizes all the structural devices of articulation available to him, architectural and rhetorical: his engineering feat is a function of his engineering feet.

Simeon begins his monologue with a pun based on comparative measure:

> Although I be the basest of mankind,
> From scalp to sole one slough and crust of sin,
> Unfit for earth, unfit for heaven, scarce meet

For troops of devils, mad with blasphemy,
I will not cease to grasp the hope I hold
Of saintdom, and to clamour, mourn and sob,
Battering the gates of heaven with storms of prayer,
Have mercy, Lord, and take away my sin. (1–8)

Every part of him is sinful, from the top of his head to the bottom of his feet, inside and out, from each sole to his soul, a homophonic association and also an anagrammatic one, in the densely punning phrase "sole one *slough*." Though insisting that puns constitute "an exemplary product of language or mind," Jonathan Culler acknowledges that they may be considered "the lowest form of wit," but debased language is itself appealing for a speaker so fascinated with material debasement.[109] At the pinnacle topping what he calls later "the column's base" (38), he is the basest. The pillar serves as a kind of headquarters or center of activity and can provide for us, in modern terms, a base line, or reference for further measurements or computations. His monologue begins "Although," but he could more accurately state "Because," since this base is itself the basis of his hope for sainthood and his qualification as the basis of mankind's potential salvation, as what he in the end of the monologue terms "an example to mankind."

This opening declaration makes clear his massive ambition: "I will not cease to grasp the hope I hold / Of saintdom," since, as Ricks observes, "'Grasp' is what the poem both possesses and is about."[110] Campbell nevertheless reasonably asks, "Need one 'grasp' something one already holds?" The apparent redundancy of the action of grasping what one holds can seem an immediate sign that Simeon's reach exceeds his grasp. "Surely repeated grasping, if it is to be seen as a series of single acts, and not a continuous one, relaxes the hold at successive moments," Campbell observes, but what can seem a contradictory motion boldly introduces the speaker's central activity throughout the monologue. For Campbell, the overall effect of the opening lines is to expose Simeon's unintentional self-revelation: "We can sense the unstable personality through the uncontrolled words of which he is barely conscious." Simeon does produce a series of single acts, but the successive actions of release, grasp, release, grasp establish the highly stable iambic rhythm of a controlled blank verse that is to help him not only articulate his goals but attain them. And this primary goal, or "hope," is to be raptured, which, as we shall see, is what he means by saintdom. Campbell claims of Simeon in these lines, "As we imagine, or recreate, his intentions, we can see areas where his grammar confuses what he wishes to say, his rhetoric overstates it," but he also alerts us to "a pun in 'cease,' seize," and this pun can help to show how wholly controlled, and indeed intentional, are the words of this monologue from its outset.[111]

Fredeman notes of lines 5–7, "The aggressiveness of Simeon's diction makes unequivocal the militancy of his campaign for sainthood,"[112] and we might say that what he demands ceaselessly is his own seizure. Campbell hears the enjambment in the assertion, "I will not cease to grasp the hope I hold / Of sainthood, and to clamour, mourn and sob," as an example of "thought spilling beyond the bounds of the language chosen to accommodate it."[113] I would argue, however, that the enjambment itself announces the sure-handedness of Simeon's rhetorical hold. The line that announces his ceaselessness cannot cease itself, battering the gates of the subsequent line. He essentially repeats this claim several dozen lines later: "Yet cease I not to clamour and to cry, / While my stiff spine can hold my weary head, / Till all my limbs drop piecemeal from the stone" (41–43). This reveling in the separation of his limbs can help us understand more fully the ambition of his earlier enjambment, itself a separation of limbs, in its etymological source in the French *jambe*, or leg. This extended process of his mortification—his penance as well as his death—is what Simeon believes distinguishes him from the other saints, since "I die here / Today, and whole years long, a life of death" (52–53), whereas, he demands of God, "did not all thy martyrs die one death?" (49). In dying one death, the other saints are in a sense end-stopped, unlike the ceaseless Simeon, who knows that he must obtain sainthood specifically through the extended and extenuating rhythm of rapt oration. He is ceaseless in his ambition for seizure, which is to be attained through the lineation of his pillar and also of his dramatic monologue.

Simeon compares himself to angels who "Enjoy themselves in heaven" (104) and to "men on earth" under "comfortable roofs" eating "wholesome food" (104, 105, 106), complaining, "and even beasts have stalls" (107). All beings, from the highest to the lowest, are comfortably placed, but Simeon labors in relentless self-positioning: "I 'tween the spring and downfall of the light, / Bow down one thousand and two hundred times, / To Christ, the Virgin Mother, and the saints" (108–10). Gibbon, one of Tennyson's sources, reports of Simeon, "His most familiar practice was that of bending his meager skeleton from the forehead to the feet; and a curious spectator, after numbering twelve hundred and forty-four repetitions, at length desisted from the endless account."[114] Although it is Simeon bowing incessantly on the pillar, it is his witness who falls away exhausted, perhaps not only from the duration of this exercise but also from its unvaryingly repetitious nature. Hone, Tennyson's primary source, also records the number of times Simeon "bowed his body in prayer": "A certain person...counted one thousand two hundred and forty-four reverences in one day, which if he began at four o'clock in the morning and finished at eight o'clock at night, gives a bow to every three-quarters of a minute; besides which he exhorted the people twice a day."[115] Hone extends the mathematical labors of Simeon's spectator, himself calculating the numbers of bows per minute. This suggests that Simeon's numerical obsession can be contagious, but also that the periodicity of this movement in time is central to Simeon's discourse. His twice daily exhortations, of which this dramatic monologue is, he believes, the final installment, must be heard to take place while he rocks, seemingly ceaselessly, down up, down up, down up, down up, down up.

This action takes place "'tween the spring and downfall of the light," that is, in between another temporal patterning of cosmic dimension, the sun's rise (spring) and fall (downfall) that begin and end each day. We may therefore understand his bowing down and rising up as the visual analogue to the sound patterning, the release and grasp, of his speech. His body physically enacts his monologue's iambic rhythm: ∪/ ∪/ ∪/ ∪/ ∪/.

The most frequently used metrical foot in English, the iamb consists of an unaccented syllable followed by an accented syllable. This duple metrical foot is often called a *rising meter* or *rising foot* because of the strong stress on its second syllable, as in Horace's definition: "A short and then a long is called an iambus, / Light on its feet" (*Syllaba longa brevi subiecta vocatur iambus, / pes citus*).[116] Paul Fussell observes that rising rhythm is so called because "the reader is presumed to feel, in each foot, an 'ascent' from a relatively unstressed syllable to a relatively stressed one," but he cautions, "The term is useful only if we keep in mind that it has no metaphoric or symbolic value: ascending rhythm does not, in itself, transmit a feeling of aspiration."[117] But it does for Tennyson's speaker, whose aspirations are at once in measure and immeasurable. In a discussion of recurring podiatric puns in Swinburne, Yopie Prins observes that the foot became "the fetish of Victorian metrical theory,"[118] and we can hear in Simeon's monologue an early articulation, and embodiment, of a pun that structures his identity. Reviewing his situation, and his self, Simeon asks, "Am I to blame for this, / That here come those that worship me? Ha! ha! / They think that I am somewhat. What am I?" (122–24). The rising rhythm even of his laughter (Hă! há!) can alert us to the shock of the pun he suggests. In attempting to position himself, he has compared himself to angels, men, and beasts, but here the allusion, stressed through a chiasmus (I am ... what / What am I) is to the identity of God himself, who "said unto Moses, 'I AM THAT I AM'" (Exodus 3:14). Later in this chapter I explore the audacity of Simeon's claims for divine resemblance, but here we should note that his identity is established not only in the course of but by way of a pun on his temporal rhythm: *iamb that iamb*.

"It is to be feared however that the men of this generation will hold it to be somewhat too unwholesome; the description of his sufferings being too minute for any but those whom the knowledge of the Art holds above the subject," W. H. Thompson posited, after hearing Tennyson chortle his way through the reading in November 1833 of an early version of this poem.[119] His caution was not unwarranted; indeed, the descriptions of his sufferings seemed unwholesome to men of a later generation. Langbaum remarks of Simeon, "His hallucinations, self-loathing and insatiable lust for self-punishment suggest a psyche as diseased (we should nowadays call it sado-masochistic) as the ulcerous flesh he boasts of." He considers Tennyson interested in "pursuing the saint's passion to its obscurely sexual recesses."[120] In *Victorian Sappho*, Prins illuminates Swinburne's association of the pleasures of being beaten with the production of metrical beats. Although

Swinburne exalted that even Tennyson envied him his submission to, and mastery of, the "rule of rhythm and rhyme,"[121] the dramatic monologist Simeon had mastered this rule some decades before Swinburne's poetic career began. Langbaum argues that this monologue serves as "a conventional liberal Protestant attack upon asceticism,"[122] but Simeon is a highly sensuous ascetic: not a drift of air passes without his shuddering at its force. Starvation and exposure would seem means to suppress the needs, let alone the desires of the body, yet in Simeon's practice these serve to intensify his sensations and also his discourse. A draft of the monologue of another early Tennysonian martyr, St. Lawrence, from Trinity Notebook 15 (1833) can help show the homology established between pain and prosody: "Slow fire! inch by inch to die—to creep / Step by step down to death—able to count / Measured successive pangs" (*Poems*, 3:576). In the measure of successive pangs we can hear the measure of his iambic cadence, itself a reminder that the term "iamb" derives from the Greek *iambos*, a verb meaning "to assail."

What Thompson might have written instead in his letter to Blakesley is that, for this poem, "knowledge of the Art" *is* the subject. "God hath now / Sponged and made blank of crimeful record all / My mortal archives" (155–57), Simeon comes to exult, and what he celebrates is the rendering, through his dramatic monologue, of his mortal archives into a blank record, that is, a blank verse record. The unrhymed iambic pentameter lines of blank verse, introduced by Milton to nondramatic English verse, is one of the most common forms of poetry in English. Considered to convey the rhythms of English speech, it is well suited to the genre of the dramatic monologue in ways that are exploited by each of the generic examples this book treats. "Timbuctoo" was believed to be the first winner of the Chancellor's Gold Medal written in blank verse rather than heroic couplets, and thus for his friends the form had immediate associations with Tennyson. And blank verse is associated with Tennyson by many others; George Saintsbury, naming the Victorian poet's two great precursors in this form, refers to "the great Tennysonian blank—a descendent and representative, but in no way a copy, at once of the Shakespearian and the Miltonic."[123] It is a legacy of which his friends were well aware. In a published review in 1832 (a copy of which he sent to Tennyson) of an Italian translation of *Paradise Lost*, Arthur Henry Hallam appreciates the efforts of the translator but remarks the metrical challenges posed by translating blank verse: "It is above all in this point that we feel the utter hopelessness of seeing a real translation of Milton." Regarding Miltonic blank verse, Hallam observes, "Not the metre merely, nor the pauses, nor the balanced numbers; but every word, every syllable, every combination of vowels and consonants, appears the offspring of consummate art." He appreciates in Milton's prosody in particular "that flexure, and, as it were, that muscularity of sound" (*Writings*, 236–37), and this muscularity of sound is a quality that Tennyson, in his first blank verse dramatic monologue, attempts to represent in the strenuous physicality of Simeon's words.

"There is no end to his belief in the power of arithmetic," Kincaid observes skeptically,[124] but this belief is justified, in several senses. Simeon seeks to accomplish his own rapture, and that of the world, in the monologue, by way of the monologue. This speaker attempts to attain his ends through the suasive efforts of the rising meters of his pillar and the rising of his meter: these serve as his battering ram against the gates of heaven. In its intensively self-conscious attention not only to measurements but to its own measure, this dramatic monologue forwards an extraordinarily elaborate joke, but one regarding the suasive effects of metrics as much as mortification, of prosody as much as penance. When his "weather-beaten limbs" (19) could endure it no longer, Simeon "died bowing,"[125] an end attained in the midst of but also through the offices of his discursive measure. If Simeon is to attain rapture, conceived of by Tennyson as a rhythmic state, it will not be through the beating of his limbs but through the beating of his iambs.

SIMEON'S END-TIMES

Early in November 1833, Tennyson read "St. Simeon Stylites" to fellow Cambridge Apostles; later that month, in an undated letter (but before November 27), John M. Kemble wrote to Tennyson in anticipation of a reunion dinner for members, regretting that Tennyson would be absent. He turns to Tennyson's dramatic monologue, clearly an ongoing subject of conversation among his friends, reporting:

> Simeon Stylites is said by the prophane [*sic*], that is the mathematicians [Stephen] Spring Rice and [John] Heath, to be not the watcher on the pillar to the end, but to the *n*th; and I think this is an improvement; the more so as it shows your universality off, and marks that you have a touch of mathematics in you: O Alfred! could you only have made the height of the pillar a geometrical progression! (*Memoir*, 1:130)

The *nth degree*, referring to the mathematical concept of the number n in a series, where n is an unspecified or variable number, signifies the utmost part, the highest level or degree. Simeon desires to take everything to extremes, of course, and if he could raise the height of his pillar exponentially, he would. Tennyson's friends make a pun of the *n*th and the end, but it is one that Simeon has already established, because in seeking his "end" he is seeking not finitude but infinitude, not death but rapture.

Critics have long held that Simeon wants to die; as Tucker puts it, "A desire to be a saint, to have had oneself sanctified, is a desire, in short, to be dead."[126] But Simeon does not desire death; although all are thought to, none of Tennyson's early dramatic monologists does. When Simeon uses the words "death" or "die" in reference to himself, he is referring to an ongoing process that is inseparable from life as he presently experiences it; he speaks as if he were already dead. The other saints were merely stoned, crucified, burned, or boiled to death, but, in Simeon's contrast, "I die here / Today, and whole years long, a life of death" (52–53). He imagines the eventual disarticulation of his body into "my relics," "my dust," "my bones" (191, 192, 193), but he also demonstrates consistently that in his case further decay will be redundant, since he has already successfully labored to produce his own bodily corruption. "Feeble grown" (35), "almost blind" (38), with both thighs "rotted with the dew" (40), he is in a state of advanced decay, as even his teeth "now are dropt away" (29), presumably falling on the watchers below. "Half deaf" (36), Simeon calls himself, the assonance of his phrasing suggesting that his aural sensibilities are nevertheless sound, but also that he is already half dead.

What this speaker seeks is the "end," a word he repeats six times, which for him is neither a euphemism nor a synonym for death. Indeed, for him the "end" signifies rapture, and thus a desire in some sense to evade death, to be "caught up," or, as he puts it, "gathered to the glorious saints" (194) like Enoch and Elijah. In his memoir *Father and Son* (1907), Edmund Gosse recounts how his father, a devout member of the Plymouth Brethren, saw the end "as absolutely imminent, and sometimes, when we parted for the night, he would say with a sparkling rapture in his eyes, 'Who knows? We may meet next in the air, with all the cohorts of God's saints!'" "This conviction I shared, without a doubt," Gosse recalls, though he admits to "a touch of slyness" in offering this as an excuse not to return to school after the end of summer, suggesting instead, "Let me be with you when we rise to meet the Lord in the air!"[127] Simeon's pillar, "a sign betwixt meadow and the cloud," is a sign of Simeon's own ambition to meet God's saints in the air; like Gosse's father, he speaks "with a sparkling rapture" in his sight.

I began this chapter with Emily Brontë's illustration of Simeon, drawn, like Tennyson's depiction, from Hone's *Every-Day Book*. Tennyson's lyric depiction of the same scene reads:

> I wear an undressed goatskin on my back;
> A grazing iron collar grinds my neck;
> And in my weak, lean arms I lift the cross,
> And strive and wrestle with thee till I die:
> O mercy, mercy! wash away my sin. (114–18)

According to Hone, "His garments were the skins of beasts, he wore an iron collar round his neck, and had a horrible ulcer in his foot."[128] We shall look at Simeon's ulcerated foot below, but we may note here that in his monologue, this sartorial description is a joke in itself, as Simeon attires himself in an "undressed goatskin," rendering his dress a state of undress, merely covering his own skin with another. His resemblance to the beast on his back is compounded by the "grazing iron collar" around his neck.

The more shocking comparison, however, is the one suggested by Simeon's plan to "strive and wrestle with thee till I die," an allusion to Jacob wrestling with the angel. Having wrestled together until the break of day, the angel declared, "Let me go," to which Jacob responded, "I will not let thee go, except thou bless me" (Genesis 32:26). Tennyson had alluded to this struggle at the end of a poem dedicated to J. W. Blakesley, "To —— [Clear-headed friend]" (1830), that ends by predicting that his friend will give strength to "Weak Truth":

> Like that strange angel which of old,
> Until the breaking of the light,
> Wrestled with wandering Israel,
> Past Yabbok brook the livelong night,
> And heaven's mazèd signs stood still
> In the dim tract of Penuel. (24–29)

Whereas Blakesley is compared to the angel, Simeon takes on Jacob's audacity, eagerly asking toward the end of his monologue, "Is that the angel there / That holds a crown?" (200–201). As Fredeman notes, Simeon "snatches the crown from the hands of the reluctant angel and crowns himself saint."[129] In the climax of the monologue, to which I shall return, Simeon wrestles with an angel who vacillates between coming forward and moving back with the crown. Simeon grasps it, even as Jacob grasps the angel, exulting, "So I clutch it" (204). The struggle over the crown continues ("'Tis gone: 'tis here again"), until Simeon emerges victorious, announcing, "So now 'tis fitted on and grows to me" (206), demonstrating how ceaselessly he grasps the hope he holds, as he had promised at the outset of his monologue.

Simeon announces his intention to engage in this strenuous effort "till I die." The most consistent critical claim concerning Tennyson's Ulysses, Tithonus, and Tiresias is that each desires death, and yet for all of them, as for their precursor Simeon, death is neither the aim nor the attainment of the dramatic monologue. Tennyson's Ulysses echoes Simeon's phrase "till I die" in his declaration, "my purpose holds / To sail beyond the sunset, and the baths / Of all the western stars, until I die" (59–61). Rather than anticipating death, each speaker is anticipating a state of tremendous ongoing exertion. Emphasizing "*till* I die" or "un*til* I die," rather than calling down death, the phrase postpones it, stressing action rather than its cessation. With its span of *i*'s, the phrase "till I die" might be heard less as an assertion than a hypothetical, since each speaker suspects or knows that he never will die, in any conventional sense.

This phrase is echoed in Tennyson's "Enoch Arden" (1864), in which the title character, resolving to keep the secret of his existence from his wife (who, believing him dead, has remarried), declares, "let me hold my purpose till I die" (871). In entering a state of death in life, Enoch evades life, but also evades death, like his biblical namesake. Enoch, and Elijah after him, Old Testament patriarchs who had direct passage to heaven, are figures of unmediated ascension. According to Genesis, "Enoch walked with God: and he was not; for God took him" (Genesis 5:24), an assumption recounted this way in Hebrews: "By faith Enoch was translated that he should not see death; and was not found, because God had translated him" (Hebrews 11:5). Elijah is taken more dramatically: "There appeared a chariot of fire, and horses of fire, and parted them both asunder; and Elijah went up by a whirlwind into heaven" (2 Kings 2:11).

Enoch and Elijah were figures of particular significance for Edward Irving and his followers. In *The Last Days: A Discourse on the Evil Character of these our Times* (1828), Irving argues, "As Enoch 'was translated that he should not see death, and he was not found, because God had translated him,' so in the Church, the mystery of God shall be finished." This completion is described in the foundational verse in 1 Thessalonians, which Irving here quotes, namely, that the Church "shall be caught up together with them in the clouds, to meet the Lord in the air."[130] In his *Narrative of Facts*, Robert Baxter explicates this claim, pausing in his narrative

> to explain what was meant by the going up of the saints, as it was afterwards more at large opened. An opinion had been advanced in some of Mr. Irving's writings, that before the second coming of Christ, and before the setting in upon the world of the "days of vengeance,"...the saints would be caught up to heaven like Enoch and Elijah; and would be thus saved from the destruction of this world. (17)

In the course of his ongoing revisions of "The Palace of Art," Tennyson removed two statues from its premises, one of Olympias, mother of Alexander the Great, and the other of Elijah. The omitted passage describes the sculpture of the patriarch as "Tall, eager, lean and strong, his cloak windborne / Behind,... / Lit as with inner light" (*Poems*, 1:443). Describing a considerably less hale Simeon, Hone refers to "a horrible ulcer in his foot," an infirmity Gibbon places in the saint's thigh: "The progress of an ulcer in his thigh might shorten, but it could not disturb, this *celestial* life; and the patient Hermit expired without descending from his column." Gibbon's phrasing can seem to suggest that Simeon's expiration did not disturb the "celestial life" he was already experiencing, especially since in this account he appears to have ascended to heaven without "descending from his column." An allusion to Elijah is made explicit in a footnote regarding Simeon's diseased limb: "I must not conceal a piece of ancient scandal concerning the origin of this ulcer. It has been reported that the Devil, assuming an angelic form, invited him to ascend, like Elijah, into a fiery chariot. The saint too hastily raised his foot, and Satan seized the moment of inflicting this chastisement on his vanity."[131] The ulcerated appendage is therefore a sign of Simeon's vaulting ambition to resemble Enoch and Elijah, and like them to be caught up directly to heaven.

If we can see the resemblance Simeon seeks to establish between himself and his precursors Enoch and Elijah, to whom he makes implicit comparison, then we can begin to see the breathtaking aspiration of his monologue. This ambition is voiced early, although it is initially articulated as disappointment:

> And I had hoped that ere this period closed
> Thou wouldst have caught me up into thy rest,
> Denying not these weather-beaten limbs
> The meed of saints, the white robe and the palm. (17–20)

Roger S. Platizky comments on these lines, "The desire for communion with God conveys the image of a dependent child wanting to be 'caught up' in the arms of a loving and powerful but distant parent."[132] Rather than holding a familial character, being "caught up" had by 1833 a highly specific biblical and contemporary theological context, as the act at the center of rapture, during which the saved shall be "caught up together with them in the clouds to meet the Lord in the air" (1 Thessalonians 4:17), or, as Baxter and the Irvingites glossed the scripture, "caught up to heaven like Enoch and Elijah."

Simeon conveys a sense of disappointed expectation necessarily common to some rapturists, since he had hoped for this event "Ere this period closed." The closing of one period and its replacement by another is the cornerstone of dispensationalism, a theological doctrine most closely associated with Darby, and in currency, it appears, among some Cambridge Apostles, notably Trench and Sterling. A letter from Trench to Donne written from Cambridge on December 31, 1831, begins by conveying several messages from Hallam ("Hallam desires me to thank you for the letter"), then goes on to ask, "Do you share in the general despondency of wise and good men at the present aspect of the world? I live in the faith of a new dispensation, which I am very confident is at hand—but what fearful times shall we have to endure ere that! We must pray earnestly not to be swept away by the great torrent." More than a year later, a letter from Sterling to Trench of February 19, 1832, indicates Trench's ongoing belief in the coming end to the present period, and the skepticism toward this held by some of his friends: "As to your view of our nearness to the end of this dispensation, I have often been inclined to entertain it; but I know that this belief is a ready means to self-delusion" (Trench, *Letters*, 1:109–10).

A "period" can refer to a length of time (the Victorian period, for example) but also to an end or conclusion. And of course it can refer to the grammatical unit indicating a full stop, and Simeon makes use of this association as well, in this formal articulation of his hopes. Simeon's "period" makes a pun of the most common concluding punctuation mark, though his own monologue is animated by a frequency of exclamation and question marks. Pyre has helpfully calculated the number of end-stopped lines in the poem, concluding, "The verse-end is firmly emphasized; only 21 per cent of the verses run-on."[133] Most of his lines are end-stopped, so that the sense and the syntax reach their close with each period. The majority tend aggressively toward a terminal point, as the speaker again and again undergoes his self-appointed sentence. The beginning and definitive end points of end-stopped lines emphasize linearity; these lines serve as yet another of his units of measurement, structuring the poem and its rhythmic lengths. T. V. F. Brogan in the *New Princeton Encyclopedia of Poetry and Poetics* notes the common though controversial view that "verse must be measured in order to be verse," then adds, "In any event, it is incontrovertible that measuring is a fundamental principle of verse-structure, and that such measure in verse realizes itself in and through the line; measurement seems to inhere in the very concept of lineation." The definition concludes, "The line itself measures out language in ways that are essential and unique to verse,"[134] and certainly it can sound in "St. Simeon Stylites" as if Tennyson is asserting his early and complete mastery over this essential building block of traditional versification.

Simeon conceptualizes his column as having a base and a crown, a beginning and a definitive end, like an upended line, and the pillar's measurement itself enforces Simeon's own linear relation to it. As Hone reports, "This pillar did not exceed three feet in diameter at the top, so that he could not lie extended on it: he had no seat with him."[135] In a footnote Gibbon quibbles with the ancient report of these dimensions: "The narrow circumference of two cubits, or three feet" assigned for "the summit of the column, is inconsistent with reason, with facts, and with the rules of architecture. The people who saw it from below might be easily deceived."[136] It would all have been a matter of perspective, of course, but let us assume the accuracy of those who watched the watcher on the column. We know he spends much of his time on his knees, as in Hone's (and Brontë's) illustration, bowing and rising, and that he stands as his weak body and ulcerated foot might allow, given that, according to Hone, "one of his thighs rotted a whole year, during which time he stood on one leg only,"[137] and according to Tennyson, "*both*" his "thighs are rotted with the dew" (40, emphasis added). It seems Simeon cannot be imagined ever to have sat with his legs dangling over the edge, as he might conceivably have had to by dint of the available space, and in resisting throwing his leg over the line of the ledge, he resists becoming a figure of enjambment. Prior to his decades-long mounting of pillars of increasing height, however, he had lived exposed for "Three winters" "up there on yonder mountain side. / My right leg chained into the crag, I lay / Pent in a roofless close of ragged stones" (70, 71–73). He had been chained by one leg to a crag, while his other leg crossed over the mountain's edge. "I lay / Pent," he recollects in one of his relatively rare enjambments, as if momentarily resisting being pent in his own pentameter. That Simeon puns deliberately is borne out by another pun on enjambment, in his references to previous martyrs having been "sawn / In twain" (51–52). By this point in his career, however, Simeon fits himself to the full point of his narrow stage. It would be impossible to be more end-stopped than this figure at the crest of the pillar's line, "The watcher on the column till the end" (160): the watcher at or till the end of the column, till the end-time.

Simeon's commitment to the recurrent metrical unit of the end-stopped line formalizes his radical commitment to the end-times. The linearity of his pillar and the linearity of his monologue show him always pushing himself to a terminal point, to the closure of the period. His impulsion toward the end is powerful even at the beginning of his monologue, in which he announces, "Now I am feeble grown; my end draws nigh; / I hope my end draws nigh" (35–36). He repeats his prophecy that his "end draws nigh" even as he undermines it with the enfeebling "I hope." The monologue works to precipitate the end, until this hope is fulfilled with his cry, "The end! the end! / Surely the end!" (198–99). He spots the angel and describes his struggle to grasp the hope the angel holds (in the form of a crown) this way: "What! deny it now? / Nay, draw, draw, draw nigh. So I clutch it. Christ!" (203–4). The alliteration and array of vowels, "now / nay / nigh," represent a compact version of his struggle with the angel, in its temporal urgency ("now"), its denial ("nay"), and its near capture ("nigh"), as does his homophonic question and reply, "deny…? / draw nigh." The line urging the angel to "draw, draw, draw" closer contains three commas, two periods, and an exclamation point. As he is inviting the angel closer, he is also extending, with this range of caesurae, the time it takes to arrive, drawing out the drawing nigh. Denying the beat of his iambs with a spondee (dráw, dráw), this contradictory invitation aggressively shifts the weight of his syllables in a kind of lyric enactment of wrestling with an angel.

Prophecy

Disavowing the teachings of Irving's church in which his friend had become so entrenched, Sterling wrote to Trench on February 19, 1832:

> Every man's life is to him the latter times, and every man's death-hour to him the dawning of the day of judgment. Moreover I cannot see my way to any such certainty as Irving derives from the prophecies; and I have scarcely the trace of doubt that the unknown tongues are the familiar and easily intelligible language of mere human vanity and superstition.…But I do not see that the line is yet outwardly so plain and broad between the white and the impure, the faithful and the rebel spirits, as to warrant us in looking for any speedy and final manifestation of the Person of Christ. (Trench, *Letters*, 1:109–10)

Seeing less cause than Trench for the imminent onrush of awesome divine judgment, Sterling questions whether theirs are indeed the times of the end-times and wisely suggests that an overwhelming intimation of divine judgment may be a matter of individual more than communal urgency. Simeon's monologue raises a similar question: his aggressive propulsion toward the end might seem to draw his own closer, but how might his claim that *his* end is nigh signify that *the* end is nigh, universally? Just prior to his clutching the crown, Simeon prophesies the advent of the latter times:

> Yet I do not say
> But that a time may come—yea, even now,
> Now, now, his footsteps smite the threshold stairs
> Of life—I say, that time is at the doors
> When you may worship me without reproach. (186–90)

Simeon's words herald, indeed are calculated to provoke, an imminent change. He has forced the moment to a crisis by his insistent "now, / Now, now," the trochee announcing the footsteps that return to the rising iambs as they ascend the line's stairs. Across the threshold of the dash, the speaker moves from the prophecy of a coming time ("a time may come"), which he disavows ("I do not say"), to an announcement of its arrival at the threshold ("that time is at the doors") that he assuredly avows ("I say"). He describes Christ climbing the "threshold stairs," but we hear in the recovered iambic of the line the smiting of Simeon's own ulcerated feet.

"It may be rational or irrational to balance yourself on pillars of increasing cubital height," George Saintsbury sensibly observes, taking the measure of St. Simeon Stylites. "I think we had better not be too sure about that either way." Whatever skepticism we may hold regarding the structure of the column, however, he insists that we may be certain of the soundness of the structure of the poem: "But there is no possible dubiety—for any one who has ears to hear—about such verses as 'The watcher on the column to the end,' and the splendid paragraph of pure Tennysonian structure and symphony which closes the poem. I have indeed known people to laugh at 'A quarter before twelve.' Let them."[138] At the end of his monologue, Simeon moves into full prophetic mode, apparently no laughing matter: "For by the warning of the Holy Ghost, / I prophesy that I shall die tonight, / A quarter before twelve" (216–18). Saintsbury recognizes how mature Simeon's representation of "pure Tennysonian structure" is and suggests that though the speaker's precision sounds risible it is itself a measure of the extraordinary precision of the poem's measure. This prophecy, which does not appear in Tennyson's sources, nevertheless marks Simeon's keenest moment of sounding like a Pentacostal speaker, especially given his direct reference to the Holy Ghost, among whose gifts is prophetic language. Simeon's assertion "I prophesy" binds him still more closely to other charismatic speakers, since prophecy was the central discursive activity of the evangelicals whose efforts so occupied some of the poet's friends. It is a term particularly associated at this time with the Irvingites, "prophet" being a ministerial rank in the Catholic Apostolic Church. For Carlyle, Irving's downfall began when he started "listening to certain interpreters of prophecy, thinking to cast his own great faculty into that hopeless quagmire along with them."[139] Irving is cited in three entries under the word "prophet" in the *Oxford English Dictionary*, twice from books concerning him (from 1854 and 1883) and once from an 1832 pronouncement of his, quoted in Margaret Oliphant's two-volume *Life of Edward Irving* (1862). Especially striking to many was Irving's policy of accommodating prophetic outbursts during services, about which he made this statement (quoted in the *OED*): "After I have preached, I will pause a little, so that then the prophets may have an opportunity of prophesying if the Spirit should come upon them; but I never said that the prophets should not prophesy at any other time." These "arrangements," according to Oliphant, "had been largely commented on" because of the striking implication that the Holy Spirit seemed willing to keep to an appointed schedule in order not to interrupt Irving's notoriously long sermons.[140] The overt references to prophetic speaking indicate how confidently Simeon, in rendering Pentecostal utterance into pentameter, is looking toward rapture, since the dominant prophecy in this period was the imminence of the rapture.

Trench asked fellow Cambridge Apostle W. B. Donne in a letter in the beginning of 1833, "Do you not think that the roll of prophecy is unfolding very fast, and the vision that at the end will speak and not lie?" (January 8; Trench, *Letters*, 1:131). His question conveys at once prophetic urgency and a hint of prophetic failure, and indeed the nature of the more detailed end-time prophecies is always—at least to date—to fall short. As Sandeen writes of this period, "There was scarcely a year that passed without one or another millenarian expectation being disappointed."[141] In his *Narrative of Facts*, Baxter records one of his own revelations while in the country with a companion, "a most emphatic declaration, that on the day after the morrow we should both be baptized with fire": "We were overjoyed with these communications, and, in fullness of hope and confidence, awaited the day of fulfillment.... The day named arrived.... Nothing, however, ensued. Again and again we knelt, and again and again we prayed, but still no fulfillment." He marvels in retrospect, "Surprising as it may seem, my faith was not shaken" but continued "day by day, for a long time" (90–91). This recovery from disappointment does not shake a faith that the end remains nigh; rather, as Frank Kermode observes, disconfirmation tends to be "quickly followed by the invention of new end-fictions and new calculations." Eschatalogical visions "can be disconfirmed without being discredited," he notes; indeed, disconfirmation is "the inevitable fate of detailed eschatological predictions," or so Kermode predicts.[142]

One of Darby's innovations was to avoid the revisionary challenges posed by disconfirmation, himself prophesying of the expected rapture, "It may be tonight, but this is known only to the Lord."[143] But Simeon knows what God knows, as he repeatedly reminds God: "Thou knowest I bore this better at the first" (27); "More than this / I bore, whereof, O God, thou knowest all" (68–69); "Thou, O God, / Knowest alone whether this was or no" (81–82); "O Lord, thou knowest what a man I am" (119). Simeon also knows the time of the end—"tonight / A quarter before twelve"—although any auditor might question whether this is a prophecy destined to be disconfirmed.

Is the monologue repeated daily, indeed, twice daily, as Hone reports, or with this specific monologue does Simeon reach some end, or even *the* end? Langbaum argues that no dramatic monologue is conclusive: "The whole point of the dramatic monologue is to present not the Aristotelian complete action but habitual action." As an example of this claim he invokes St. Simeon Stylites, whom he believes will "go on pleading his case with God" because every dramatic monologist "will talk this way again with the same result."[144] My claim, however, is that every Victorian dramatic monologue marks, indeed provokes, a definitive end, enabling its speaker to perform a stated goal, and Simeon establishes this pattern. Tennyson's Ulysses does not appear on the shore to speak these same words daily; rather, his monologue changes the situation it describes, as do the monologues of Tithonus and Tiresias. Simeon is not daily setting dates that keep requiring delay; instead, this dramatic monologue is a singular enunciation (as are all dramatic monologues), and through it Simeon reaches a certain end, now.

Healing

The speaker in Tennyson's early "Supposed Confessions of a Second-Rate Sensitive Mind" (1830), a forerunner to Simeon's dramatic monologue, laments, "That even now, / In this extremest misery / Of ignorance, I should require / A sign!" (7–10). Belief often expects a sign for its confirmation, and prophetic voices in particular require a sign for their authority, as J. F. C. Harrison explains in *The Second Coming*: "Proof of his gift of the spirit is required from the prophet, and he provides this by divination, healing, counseling and raising the dead. Through such 'signs' he first attracts and then holds his followers."[145] Baxter's *Narrative of Facts* recounts the troubling absence of confirmatory signs in Irving's church: "They are now avowedly exercising apostolic functions, upon the mere command of the voice, without pretending to have the signs of an apostle, 'In signs and wonders, and mighty deeds.'" He singles out one particularly desperate Irving follower who had risen in the church's ranks, who "prays, in their meetings, in the following strain: 'Lord, am I not thine apostle?—yet where are the signs of my apostleship?—where are the wonders and mighty deeds?'" (84–85).

Simeon initially considers himself to be the evidence that he seeks, identifying his person as "A sign betwixt the meadow and the cloud," but he also repeatedly offers proof that appears incontestable. He has the power to heal, one confirmed again and again by his followers before, during, and after his sojourn on the pillar. After his death, according to Hone, "his corpse was carried to Antioch attended by the bishops and the whole country, and worked miracles on its way," indeed, "more miracles were worked at and after Simeon's sepulture, than he had wrought all his life."[146] Simeon's healing powers increase after his death, but the ability to heal by way of his battered body is established early in his monologue. He recalls lying chained by his right leg "into the crag" (72) and being visited by "those that came / To touch my body and be healed, and live" (77–78). Recalling the effects of his immobilized body, he reminisces, "And they say then that I worked miracles, / Whereof my fame is loud amongst mankind, / Cured lameness, palsies, cancers" (79–81). "For all his expressed hatred of his body," Hughes observes, "he has come to see it as a source of power."[147] His ability to heal constitutes his clearest sign, but it is crucial to note that early in his martyrdom, Simeon's body is the source of healing; words seem either unnecessary or impossible when he is in the monastery or chained to the crag. Why, then, might Simeon require language at all, let alone prophetic speech? His body itself appears his greatest, and at this point his only, instrument of persuasion.

Throughout his monologue, efficacious prophetic language is consistently attributed not to Simeon's voice but to that of the people whom his monologue addresses. Fredeman divides "St. Simeon Stylites" into two parts, the first part ending at line 130, which he considers "unmistakably *intended* as a prayer," and the second part beginning "Good people," which "marks a radical shift in emphasis within the monologue" because it shifts its address to the people at the base of his column.[148] Both parts, I would agree, are "unmistakably *intended*" to be heard (rather than overheard), and Simeon attends closely to his auditors, whether human or divine, with every word he utters. And yet it is not what Simeon says but what he hears that has transformative effects and serves as the clearest sign of his prophetic capacity, as he suggests in his call for their speech: "Speak! is there any of you halt or maimed? / I think you know I have some power with Heaven / From my long penance: let him speak his wish" (140–42). Speak!: the injunction demands speech that must necessarily resemble his own because its prior condition is identical to his own, namely, whether and to what extent one is "halt or maimed."

His halt and maimed auditors have been enjoined to speak by this halt and maimed speaker, and what they announce when they speak is his sanctification, a condition they create through the miracle of their performative utterance. Simeon reviews this rhetorical process:

> Yes, I can heal him. Power goes forth from me.
> They say that they are healed. Ah, hark! they shout
> "St Simeon Stylites." Why, if so,
> God reaps a harvest in me. O my soul,
> God reaps a harvest in thee. If this be,
> Can I work miracles and not be saved?
> This is not told of any. They were saints.
> It cannot be but that I shall be saved;
> Yea, crowned a saint. They shout, "Behold a saint!"

And lower voices saint me from above.
Courage, St. Simeon! (143–53)

Simeon declares definitively that he "can heal," but the authority for this claim resides with the people; they are healed if "They say" they are. Simeon moves from what "They say" to what "they shout," as this amplification makes audible their transition from declarative to performative speech. With their shouts ("they shout / 'St. Simeon Stylites'"; "They shout, 'Behold a saint!'"), power goes forth *to* him, and he is twice nominated for sainthood. Lower voices saint him from above, but these seem lesser voices, since higher (because shouting) voices have already sainted him from below. His annunciation occurs as a simultaneous result of their enunciation: at the moment they call him a saint, he becomes one. Inspired by his performance, it is his audience whose language is performative.

Simeon's sanctification is accomplished in the course of his monologue, occurring in the utterance of these speech acts. It is crucial to understand that this moment of sanctification is neither a past action nor a recurring one. He is describing events in the present tense, as they are occurring "here / Today" (52–53). Early in his monologue he eagerly asked, "Who may be saved? who is it may be saved? / Who may be made a saint, if I fail here?" (46–47), and now, after having spoken another hundred lines, he has arrived at the reassuring answer that it is he who may be saved and sanctified, here and now. Their first nomination follows the exclamation "Ah, hark!" indicating that Simeon has suddenly heard a new sound; their second nomination is preceded by the shout "Behold...!" indicating that his audience has suddenly seen him transformed ("hark" and "behold" being exclamations traditionally heralding sanctified beings). Simeon at this moment accepts his nomination, now exclaiming to himself, "Courage, St. Simeon!" To confirm that he takes his full title from his human auditors, Simeon next calls himself "I, Simeon of the pillar, by surname / Stylites, among men" (158–59).

"It cannot be but that I shall be saved; / Yea, crowned a saint" (150–51): critics have been virtually unanimous in doubting Simeon's apotheosis, finding his expectations of salvation and sanctification at the least unlikely, and at the most insane. His dramatic monologue insists, however, that these expectations are fulfilled in the course of his speaking, as when he describes his attainment of the crown at the end of his monologue: "So now 'tis fitted on and grows on me, / And from it melt the dews of Paradise, / Sweet! sweet! Spikenard, and balm, and frankincense" (206–8). Platizky identifies this as "the climactic part of the poem" but suggests that "the whole vision may be the product of a delirium"; Fredeman also considers that at this point "he becomes increasingly the victim of hallucination and madness." Tucker comments, "Simeon's prodigious lust for the crown of sanctity, which is also a craving for the benediction of 'the end'... gives us an earnest of his not conclusively attaining it."[149] There may be no reason to disbelieve him, however, especially as Simeon's claim here is consonant with ecclesiastical history, however distinct this may be from verifiable fact. After his death, a "precious odour" was reported to have emanated from his dead body,[150] presumably composed of such pleasing ("Sweet! Sweet!") aromas as spikenard, balm, and frankincense. Simeon considers sweetness an attribute of saintliness; in the line following his appreciation of the air's fragrance, he turns to address the "sweet saints" (209), whose perfumed ranks he considers himself, based on the evidence of his olfactory sense, now to have joined.

The crowd below already calls him "St. Simeon Stylites," a title he has accepted, and yet critics have strongly doubted his canonization, although it is the least contestable of his claims. There is no question that Simeon has joined the ranks of the "many just and holy men, whose names / Are registered and calendared for saints" (129–30); indeed, knowledge of this is the precondition of Tennyson's dramatic monologue. Simeon's saint's day is calendared on January 5 in Hone's *Every-Day Book*; perhaps one reason both Tennyson and Brontë took particular notice of the narrative and its accompanying image is because it is one of the first entries. Ricks acknowledges, "'St. Simeon Stylites' does not bear the title 'Simeon Stylites,'" and yet he understands the poem as "heading away from saintdom" for all the logical reasons, including simply that this speaker is "loathsome," as Sterling (quoted by Ricks in his discussion) put it. In the face of what can look like a discrepancy, Ricks asks the crucial question: "And yet can the poem simply contradict its own known outcome?"[151]

Fredeman proposes that "the Simeon of this poem is not the historical Saint Simeon,"[152] a solution with which I disagree but that can help clarify one aspect of the fledgling genre in which Tennyson's monologist speaks. As with Browning poems based on readily identifiable historical personages (the painters Fra Lippo Lippi and Andrea del Sarto, for example), the historical referent specified in the title is clear and incontestable, and cannot be disavowed. Indeed, the details each poet draws on from sources we too may consult require us to make full use of the available range of literary and historical contexts available to flesh out the speaker's representation. Tennyson could have conceived a fictional saint, but instead he produced a monologue in the *likeness* of an authentic one, thus establishing a crucial precedent for all other Victorian dramatic monologues based on known figures. Simeon speaks as a Syrian pillar saint.

Simeon's prophetic language has seemed to provide the surest proof of its own disconfirmation. "With his...sanctimonious careerism," Tucker writes, "Simeon chiefly offers up exercises in autohagiography, a peculiarly doomed genre that can but estrange him from the sainthood he hopes his words may underwrite."[153] Simeon's words fail at their task because the genre in which he speaks is a "peculiarly doomed" one, but of course the genre in which Simeon speaks is that of the dramatic monologue, which he calls into being as he calls his transformed self into being. That this speaker can produce a saint's life for himself is what makes it possible for him to produce a saint of himself. Simeon is made a saint in the course, and not only for the course, of this extraordinarily efficacious monologue; concurrent with his speaking is his sanctification. In achieving his rhetorical goal simultaneously with its utterance, a move we are to see again and again in Tennyson's dramatic monologues, Simeon's monologue does not "contradict its known outcome," but causes it.

We may question whether Tennyson's Simeon merits canonization, but not whether he attains it, and the same is true of Simeon's ambition to attain "the end." Noting the rhyme of the declaration "I shall die tonight" and the last line of the monologue, "lead them to thy light" (220), Ricks comments that this "sounds like a firm ending." Nevertheless, he claims, the poem "ends before Simeon's end," thus setting up "a tension between its existing moment and its unmentioned outcome."[154] Fredeman also hears the poem as exploring "not the end, but...the penultimate moment before the end, which is unrevealed."[155] I would argue instead that Simeon does reach the end, and his auditors (or readers of the monologue) are witness to this eschatological achievement. Simeon is not hallucinating the end, but dictating it; when his monologue ends, so does he.

In what Fredeman calls "the most amazing shift in the poem," Simeon "assures his fellow saints of his trust that he is 'whole, and clean, and meet for Heaven,'" a conclusion far removed from his opening "claim that he was 'Unfit for earth, unfit for heaven, scarce meet / For troops of devils, mad with blasphemy.'"[156] This shift represents a transformation rather than a contradiction, however, indicating definitively that something has happened in the course of the monologue, because of the monologue. Simeon's sanctification does not occur because of the measure of years and cubits, although these are contributing factors, in that they are the basis—and the base—of the monologue. In the performative act of naming him a saint, his auditors give the speaker a model for his own performative language, which he uses to provoke the end. I have noted the radical efficacy of the words of his auditors in the two enunciations of his new title: "they shout / 'St. Simeon Stylites'" and "They shout, 'Behold a saint!'" In between these sanctifying cries, Simeon muses, "Why, if so, / God reaps a harvest in me. O my soul, / God reaps a harvest in thee. If this be." Framed within conditionals ("if so," "If this be"), the repeated phrase they encircle is one of stunning confidence that, he declares twice, "God reaps a harvest" in him. He posits that God gathers the ripened Simeon, but "reap" derives etymologically from the Latin *raptus*, suggesting that in his understanding he is not cut down but caught up. If he is made a saint by being named one, then he is, with his nomination, raptured. This rapture is predicated on discursive suasion: his rapt oration has persuaded his auditors of his sanctity, and now their words have persuaded him of it.

Simeon had earlier enjoined the sick to "Speak," that he might heal them; requiring again the benediction of external speech, he now enjoins any "priest, a man of God / Among you there" to "Speak": "climbing up into my airy home, /

Deliver me the blessèd sacrament" (211–12, 214–15). No longer inhabiting what early in his monologue he characterized as "this home / Of sin, my flesh, which I despise and hate" (56–57), he now inhabits an aerial abode, an acknowledgment that he has been caught up to meet the Lord in the air. Simeon is raptured because he has himself enraptured his auditors through his performance of rapture in the sense of an inspired vision spoken by a prophet. His ambition has been not to die but to be translated, as he is—certainly, to the air, but even more certainly into the medium of the dramatic monologue, which Simeon creates, and perfects, as he speaks. Already with the saints in the air, he is caught up discursively, inhabiting a rapt state to which his own speech has brought him. The monologue itself not only precipitates and represents this experience: it constitutes the rapture.

Simeon is not referring to some future end, then, but one to which we are witness: as he speaks, he is in a state of rapture, and the rapture is occurring because he speaks. That the rapture is discursive only intensifies its experience for him. Langbaum argues that dramatic monologues are superfluous, but Simeon could not attain his end without having made himself so apparent to his auditors. In this he resembles the mythical sea creature of Tennyson's "The Kraken" (1830), slumbering deep in the sea while "above him swell / Huge sponges of millennial growth and height" (5–6), his immeasurable depth making him a counterweight to Simeon's measured heights. There he lies, "Until the latter fire shall heat the deep; / Then once by man and angels to be seen, / In roaring he shall rise and on the surface die" (13–15). The revelation the Kraken anticipates "then," Simeon provokes "Today," as he rises to his end in the sight of audiences both human and divine. His dramatic monologue is a sign we may take for a wonder.

The Sin of Similitude

When Simeon turns to address the "Good people" over whom he towers, he insists that he is not like them:

> I am a sinner viler than you all.
> It may be I have wrought some miracles,
> And cured some halt and maimed; but what of that?
> It may be, no one, even among the saints,
> May match his pains with mine; but what of that? (133–37)

At the conclusion of another of Tennyson's early dramatic monologues, Ulysses also twice repeats the phrase "It may be": "It may be that the gulfs will wash us down: / It may be we shall touch the Happy Isles" (62–63). Each speaker employs the same phrase signifying the hypothetical or uncertain nature of what he at this moment speaks, and in each case it is a rhetorical ploy, for what each claims merely to conjecture is what each certainly believes. Simeon frames these words with the repetition of a rhetorical question: "but what of that?" If we set aside these oratorical flourishes we can hear his clear and outright assertions, namely, that he has worked miracles and cured the sick. We have seen already "what" he expects "of that," which is nothing less than sanctification and the end-time. The claim he moves to is, remarkably, still more ambitious: "no one, even among the saints, / May match his pains with mine." We might say that he has cured the halt and maimed by competing with them: no matter the severity of his audience's afflictions, none are like his, a claim he extends to the saints. No one may best him in a match (and we know he goes on to win the wrestling match with the angel), and no one may match him, that is, either equal or even resemble him.

Simeon is wholly absorbed in questions of resemblance: Who is like him? Who is he like? At this moment he compares himself first to the good people, then to the truly good people, now saints. His monologue mounts a range of more shocking and consequential comparisons, however, to devils, to Christ, to God. He commences his monologue declaring himself "unfit" for earth or heaven, barely fit for the unredeemable, "scarce meet / For troops of devils, mad with blasphemy" (3–4), and this association announces from the start that he will enter into blasphemous comparisons. It also raises the question of whether the comparison, or the trope of divine similitude, is itself heretical, a question with which Edward Irving and his followers, and Arthur Henry Hallam as well, mightily wrestled.

Claiming that his spirit has been "crushed…flat" by "tons" of it, Simeon calls sin "lead-like" (25–26), and what must weigh on us is less the tonnage than the trope of likeness. Simeon likens sin to lead and likens himself to the vilest of sinners:

> I, Simeon of the pillar, by surname
> Stylites, among men; I, Simeon,
> The watcher on the column to the end;
> I, Simeon, whose brain the sunshine bakes;
> I, whose bald brows in silent hours become
> Unnaturally hoar with rime, do now
> From my high nest of penance here proclaim
> That Pontius and Iscariot by my side
> Showed like fair seraphs. (158–66)

The "silent hours" grow hoar with rime, though without rhyme, in the extreme deliberation of his blank verse. Just after having been proclaimed a saint as well as one of the stylitae, he makes his own proclamation ("I… / do now / …here proclaim") of identification with Pontius and Iscariot. Placed "by my side," as Simeon says, the two sound as physically near as the angel with whom he later wrestles, though of course he also means "compared to me." Pontius and Iscariot are inherently comparable to one another in this formulation; when compared to

Simeon, they are comparable to ("like") seraphs; their proximity therefore suggests a dizzying range of likenesses.

Having felt his brain being baked, Simeon now recounts his sensation of having been roasted ("On the coals I lay" [166]) and boiled ("all hell beneath / Made me boil over" [167–68]). While in this furnace he encounters Abaddon, an "angel of the bottomless pit" (Revelation 9:11), and the murderous spirit Asmodeus, held responsible for killing the seven husbands of Sarah, daughter of Raguel (Tobit 3:8): "Devils plucked my sleeve, / Abaddon and Asmodeus caught at me. / I smote them with the cross; they swarmed again" (168–70). Caught to these depths rather than into the air, he is crushed by *their* leadlike tons of sin: "In bed like monstrous apes they crushed my chest"; "With colt-like whinny and with hoggish whine / They burst my prayer" (171, 174–75). What they oppress Simeon with is likeness. In their resemblance to animals—they are like apes, colts, and hogs—the devils torment him with debased nonhuman similitude, but in doing so they suggest his means of escape, which will also be accomplished through nonhuman likeness.

Simeon says his sin is greater than that of Judas Iscariot (disciple and betrayer of Jesus) and Pontius Pilate (Roman governor and executioner of Jesus). But Simeon's real point of comparison is not to those considered to bear the greatest responsibility for the suffering and death of Christ, but, more scandalously, to Christ himself. He explains his transition from sinners to saints:

> Yet this way was left,
> And by this way I 'scaped them. Mortify
> Your flesh, like me, with scourges and with thorns;
> Smite, shrink not, spare not. (175–78)

Simeon moves from asserting similitude with the damned to asserting similitude with the savior, a resemblance he urges upon his audience, who should mortify their flesh "like me," which is to say like Jesus. 'Scaping by way of the alliteration of scourges, smiting, sparing not, and the assonance of scourges and thorns, Simeon alludes to Jesus' crown of thorns, perhaps the crown he so eagerly snatches. When he exclaims, "So I clutch it. Christ!" (204), we may hear less a cry for divine intervention than a curse, but his reference to Christ at this moment is an assertion of the identity he grasps as eagerly as the crown. The line in an earlier version read "So I have it—God!" but the revision makes it clear that he is not addressing God here, though he does so elsewhere in the monologue, but the figure to whom he is comparing himself, Jesus. In suggesting this resemblance, considered by many to be outrageous, even sinful, the monologue enters into a major theological controversy explored by Hallam, Trench, and others. It is not that Simeon's sins resemble those of Pilate and Judas, but that he sins in claiming to resemble Christ.

According to Ian Bradley's history of evangelicalism, the "doctrine of sanctification, or striving gradually to attain behavior nearer and nearer to that of

Christian perfection," is central to the movement's theology.[157] But this took what many felt was a heretical turn in a doctrinal position of Edward Irving's considered more disturbing than the glossolalia of some of his congregants. In a number of sermons, and most fully in his treatise *The Orthodox and Catholic Doctrine of Christ's Human Nature* (1830), Irving expounded on the sinful human nature of Jesus, arguing that Jesus serves as an example because he was like humans in all respects. Jesus was saved by the Holy Ghost rather than by innate divinity; therefore, every believer can achieve the holiness he attained. These were the central heretical views that led to Irving's excommunication from the Church of Scotland in 1833.[158]

Trench and his circle were well aware of Irving's beliefs and their implications. Trench wrote to his wife from London on May 1, 1833:

> At the present moment Irving seems to me certainly to have erred much on the matter of our Lord's Nature, though not more than many of his opponents; and, after all, I know not how much of high imagination which needs casting down there may not be in all that he has written concerning holiness in the flesh; and there are some dangers that we shall bring Christ's holiness down to that which we can attain, instead of raising up ourselves to His height. (Trench, *Letters*, 1:142)

This was also a key issue Baxter wrestled with as a follower of Irving, a struggle he recounts in his *Narrative of Facts*. Baxter quotes in his book from a letter to him from Irving of April 21, 1832: "Concerning the flesh of Christ, we will discourse when we meet. I believe it to have been no better than other flesh, as to its passive qualities or properties, as a creature thing." But Christ "did for his obedience... receive such a measure of the Holy Ghost as sufficed to resist its own proclivity to the world and to Satan." Because Christ was like us, we can become like him: Baxter considers this claim "fearfully erroneous" and comments, "Dark, indeed, must be our state, if we do not instantly see how Christ is first abased towards our sinful condition, and we next exalted to be put on an equality with him" (Baxter, *Narrative*, 109).

It is his disagreement with what he terms Irving's "heresies most fearful and appalling" that brings Baxter to doubt the authenticity of the tongues: "I was then, of necessity, compelled to conclude the utterances which supported those views were not of the Spirit of God" (Baxter, *Narrative*, 109, 116). Perhaps his own resistance to the notion of likeness between Christ and humankind contributed to Trench's "especial interest" in recognizing keen distinctions among words, whether in his work with the Philological Society that would lead to the production of the *Oxford English Dictionary* or in his own philological writings.[159] In *On the Study of Words*, Trench specifically propounds the "desynonymizing" of words, commenting, "How large a part of true wisdom it is to be able to distinguish between things that differ, things seemingly, but not really, alike."[160]

Both Baxter and Trench are agitated by the claim that Christ was like human beings, and still more by its corollary, that humans are like Christ. Arthur Henry Hallam had pursued just this analogy in his most ambitious essay for the Cambridge Apostles, a composition of which Tennyson had especially intimate knowledge. Hallam read his "Theodicæa Novissima" on October 29, 1831, in response to the proposition "That there is ground for believing that the existence of moral evil is absolutely necessary to the fulfillment of God's essential love for Christ." This was the end of the month during which Trench was immersed in Irving's writings, and he and Hallam planned to visit Irving's church, where congregants had begun speaking in tongues. Tennyson's influence on the composition of the essay (through conversation or comments) is unknown, as is whether he attended the meeting at which it was delivered, but afterward Hallam sent Tennyson the notebook in which it was written (and had to appeal to the poet's sister Emily to get it returned). It was printed after his death by his father in Arthur Hallam's 1834 *Remains* at Tennyson's express request, though his father chose not to publish it in subsequent editions and his prefatory remarks indicate his reluctance to publish it at all:

> A few expressions in it want his usual precision; and there are ideas which he might have seen cause, in the lapse of time, to modify, independently of what his very acute mind would probably have perceived.... It is here printed, not as a solution of the greatest mystery of the universe, but as most characteristic of the author's mind, original and sublime, uniting, what is very rare except in youth, a fearless and unblenching spirit of inquiry into the highest objects of speculation with the most humble and reverential piety.[161]

T. H. Vail Motter, the twentieth-century editor of Hallam's writings, is right to call the essay "a kind of summation of Hallam's belief and practice" and to observe, "There is no question but that Tennyson was strongly affected by the essay and felt for it associations not wholly philosophical" (*Writings*, 199).

"Theodicæa Novissima" directly engages the theological implications of similitude, establishing as its premise, "Similarity, it has been said, is an essential condition of love, and it is equally true that reciprocity is implied in its idea," since "it is impossible to love without desiring such a return" (*Writings*, 204). Hallam characterizes Christ as "subordinate" to God: "Elevate and magnify the Son, as you will: he is the Son still, and not in all points or in all senses equal to the Father. A personality derived must be wonderfully different from one self-existent and original." This subordination makes reciprocal love impossible; Hallam asks, "How then will the requisite similarity be possible, since the nature of God is Infinite, Absolute, Perfect? And how will reciprocity be possible, since the attributes of God are all infinite" and his love "must be altogether illimitable?" In answer to the proposed topic, defending the proposition of the necessity of evil for the "fulfillment" of God's love for Christ, Hallam now asserts that the only way the Son may prove his reciprocal love, and thus attain similitude with God, is by entering into "a contest with evil." Evil may exist as "the necessary and only condition of Christ's being enabled to exert the highest acts of love" (*Writings*, 205–6).

The relation between the Son and the Father is predicated on the challenges posed by similitude. God's "great feeling for Christ," according to Hallam, "arose from the idea of complete similarity and union actually to be realized in him." Christ "imitated" this by "a full return of God's love for him," and also by "a manifestation of exalted love towards inferior spirits," or his sacrifice for human-kind (*Writings*, 208). Hallam posits a triangulated and conditional love: if we are to love God, we must love the object of his love, Christ, and in turn we shall gain the love of God. Why, though, Hallam asks, should we love Christ? The answer he gives is because Christ has proven that he loves us: "Now that Christ has excited our love for him by shewing unutterable love for us; now that we know him as an Elder Brother, a being of like thoughts, feelings, sensations, sufferings, with our-selves, it has become possible to love as God loves, that is, to love Christ and thus to become united in heart to God." Because we perceive a likeness between ourselves and Christ ("a being of like thoughts, feelings, sensations, sufferings"), we may perceive a likeness between ourselves and God (it becomes "possible to love as God loves"). This network of similitude develops still further: "Nor is this all: the tendency of love is towards a union so intimate, as virtually to amount to identi-fication; when then by affection towards Christ we have become blended with his being" until our "personality" "has become confused with his, and so shall we be one with Christ and through Christ with God" (*Writings*, 210). In seeking to move from a relation of resemblance to a relation of identification, Hallam's ambi-tion, we might say, is to move from the trope of simile to the trope of metaphor. As we come to be united, even "confused" with Christ, and therefore with God, with whom Christ is united, God becomes confused with us.

Hallam admits that a critic "may assert that a God animated by emotions resembling our own, and for whatever reason, mixing himself up with our pas-sions, and caring for our love, is a figment of presumptuous imagination" (*Writings*, 212). His idea of the processes of similitude, especially between God or Christ and human beings, demonstrates his own "presumptuous imagination." This theologi-cal equation, which bears resemblance to Irving's doctrinal heresy, has implications less for Tennyson's religious belief than for a poetical practice that interests itself deeply in the processes and problems of similitude and identification. "I believe," Hallam declares at the outset of "Theodicæa Novissima," "that the Godhead of the Son has not been a fixed, invariable thing from the beginning: he is more God now than he was once; and will be perfectly united to God hereafter, when he has put all enemies under his feet." Invoking the image of Christ's victory at Armageddon, Hallam nevertheless considers Christ to have been imperfect while in his human form and, indeed, still in the process of transformation, still moving toward perfect union, which is to say identification, with God. "Is this heterodox?" Hallam asks, answering, "Yet the Scriptures say it plainly; 'He is made perfect through sufferings.' That which is already perfect hath no need to be made so" (*Writings*, 204).

Some two years later, in response to Irving's highly publicized beliefs rather than to Hallam's private essay for a coterie of metaphysically inquisitive friends, Baxter insists, "Our calling is 'Be ye perfect, even as your Father which is in heaven is perfect.' This is our mark at which we aim, the standard high and lifted up, to which we desire to conform. This, however, we shall never fully attain" (Baxter, *Narrative*, 112). Simeon, however, has this hope, asserting toward the end of his monologue, "Ah! let me not be fooled, sweet saints: I trust / That I am whole, and clean, and meet for Heaven" (209–10). Though his concern not to be "fooled" can suggest that his faith may be insecure, he nevertheless insists on his ultimate integrity and wholeness, his "trust" that he has been made perfect through sufferings.

In Baxter's view, this idea of attaining resemblance to Christ is not merely wrongheaded but sinful: "And certain is it that if the arch-enemy can seduce us to take our eye off that perfect and ineffable holiness which is found in Jesus, and persuade us to look for a perfect holiness in ourselves, whilst we are compassed with flesh and blood, he will soon teach us to debase the standard of holiness, and to call darkness light, and light darkness." The arch-enemy seduces with a temptation of likeness so radical as to alter the facts of the universe, so that darkness and light resemble each other so fully that they are indistinguishable. Jesus' holiness was "perfect and ineffable" even when he too was "compassed with flesh and blood," but such holiness is impossible for "ourselves." "And certain is it," Baxter continues, "that nothing but the continual view of the ineffable and perfect holiness of Jesus can teach us when we offend, and keep us humble followers of him" (Baxter, *Narrative*, 116). Christ is by this argument an example continually before us of a likeness we shall never attain but must nevertheless humbly, continually, and fruitlessly pursue.

For Tennyson's Simeon, however, Christ's example inspires an almost Whiggish ambition for future perfection, attainable by slow degrees, as he rises over the years to what Trench termed, regarding Christ, "His height." And through his rising, Simeon himself becomes a Christ-like example:

God only through his bounty hath thought fit,
Among the powers and the princes of this world,
To make me an example to mankind,
Which few can reach to. (183–86)

"Few can reach to" Simeon's heights because he has literalized them, and to reach him would require an arduous climb up his pillar, but his joke underscores his standing more abstractly as an example to which few may aspire. He has definitively established his likeness to those held most responsible for Christ's suffering and death, and now, in establishing himself as an example to mankind, he establishes his likeness to Christ, that is, as an inspiration for other far-reaching human attempts at similitude.

In setting himself up, literally and metaphorically, as an example, Simeon establishes himself as a figure of exemplum, the rhetorical term that Quintilian classified "under simile, which bears the nonfigurative sense of 'resemblance,' 'similarity.'"[162] The exemplum is a central component of oratory; as Cicero puts it in *de Inventione*, "An example supports or weakens a case by appeal to precedent or experience, citing some person or historical event."[163] An example is intended as a persuasive device, although it may not always serve as such, as Cicero suggests. Many have felt that in offering himself as an example Tennyson's Simeon weakens his case, but we know, as Tennyson did, that his swaying figure did serve as a figure of suasion. Platizky cites a biographical dictionary of the saints in acknowledging that the historical Simeon was followed "by a succession of pillar-saints extending over many centuries," and concludes, "We cannot regard his cultural influence or exemplification as negligible."[164] Tennyson writes in the knowledge of the potency of Simeon's example, as if scanning a horizon ranged across with pillar saints in succession.

The significance of his exemplariness is so great to this speaker that he ends his monologue invoking it, just after he prophesies his death "tonight," concluding, "But thou, O Lord, / Aid all this foolish people; let them take / Example, pattern: lead them to thy light" (218–20). Early in the monologue Simeon instructed God to "take" his meaning; now he instructs God to instruct the people to take his example. In calling them "foolish" he implies that they may already have done so, since he has just previously prayed, "Ah! let me not be fooled, sweet saints" (210), suggesting that the people aspire to be like him in this trait as well. But the likeness that Simeon forwards in his conclusion is far more ambitious, as Fredeman observes: "Not content with mere sainthood, he aspires toward personification in the Trinity itself." In the final lines of the poem, according to Fredeman, "Simeon, now assured of his own celestial identity, assumes the prophetic role of Christ in announcing his impending death to the disciples." "His temptation demonstrably parallels that of Christ's," Fredeman writes, and Simeon thus offers himself "as the kind of supreme exemplar and ultimately the means through which 'foolish people' attain salvation."[165] Although, as we have seen, Simeon's most characteristic activity was rhythmical bowing, Gibbon reports of the historical saint, "He sometimes prayed in an erect attitude, with his outstretched arms in the figure of a cross."[166]

Fredeman considers Simeon's claim of resemblance to Christ an example of "delusion" on "a grand scale."[167] Baxter considers the belief in any human likeness to Christ, or access to prophetic utterance, dangerously delusional because outrageously imitative: "The whole work is a mimicry of the gifts of the Spirit—the utterance, in tongues, a mimicry of the gift of tongues—and so of the prophesyings, and all the other works of the power. It is Satan, as an angel of light, imitating, as far as permitted, the Holy Spirit of God" (Baxter, *Narrative*,

135). Rather than constituting divine examples of prophetic speech, these utterances constituted diabolical imitation; the claim of likeness to Christ itself proves a likeness to Satan. In performing an utterance that is an imitation of utterance, however, Tennyson's Simeon establishes the original example of a literary genre posited on the imitation of powerful suasive effects. Even the metrical pattern of his iambic pentameter becomes the dominant (though by no means the exclusive) rhythm of dramatic monologists.

Referring to "The Palace of Art," Jack Kolb, editor of Hallam's letters, argues, "Trench inspired the poem," and Ricks notes in addition that the poem was "probably not begun before October 1831, the date of Arthur Hallam's 'Theodicæa Novissima'" (*Letters*, 550 n2; Ricks, 1:436). After quoting Trench's admonition, "Tennyson, we cannot live in art," in his own annotations to the poem in the Eversley edition (one of which cites Hallam's essay directly), Tennyson comments, "This poem is the embodiment of my own belief that the Godlike life is with man and for man."[168] With the possessive declaration of "my own belief" in this highly compact statement, he contends that he does not consider himself or anyone else to live in art, but rather in "the Godlike life," which sounds like an assertion of humankind's capacity for some measure of divine similitude. Tennyson in "St. Simeon Stylites" returns to the controversy of resemblance to God or Christ articulated in "Theodicæa Novissima," indicating how some of even the most outrageous notions of this speaker derive their intellectual and aesthetic force from debates in which Hallam and Trench were closely concerned. Simeon's pillar is rooted firmly in the ground of Apostolic (whether Cambridge Apostolic or Catholic Apostolic) speculation.

Despite speculative similarities, however, it is critical to resist forcing any claims of direct resemblance between Tennyson's St. Simeon Stylites and Irving, Trench, Hallam, or any other contemporary; the dramatic monologue is far more subtle in the operation of its references and reflections, playing always with likeness rather than identification. Certainly, in spite of his heterodox ideas regarding human and divine similitude, Hallam himself would have stood aghast at any claim of his own perfection, or even perfectibility—personal modesty being among his most remarked-upon traits. But his friends were less resistant to this idea. On October 6, 1833, the day he learned of Hallam's death, Gladstone wrote in his diary that he mourned "for myself, my earliest near friend," and "for my fellow creatures, one who would have adorned his age and country." Grieving for the loss of Hallam to humankind, he recalls of his friend "a mind full of beauty and of power, attaining almost to that ideal standard, of which it is presumption to expect an example in natural life." Hallam stood as an "example," attaining an "ideal standard" ("almost," Gladstone qualifies) beyond what human ("natural") life can be expected to offer. He laments, "When shall I see his like?"[169]

Anne Thackeray Ritchie records a conversation in which "a lady" commented to Tennyson regarding Hallam, "I think he was perfect." Tennyson replied,

"As near perfection as a mortal man can be."[170] The poet does not agree with the lady, but rather corrects or at least refines her claim, indicating how closely he had followed the logic of Hallam's argument regarding mortal perfectibility and how deeply he had made it his own. The lady may herself have been following the logic of Tennyson's own representation of Hallam, however. Section 51 of *In Memoriam* voices Tennyson's anxiety that in the increased intimacy with the poet occasioned by his death, Hallam ("he for whose applause I strove") would now "See with clear eye some hidden shame" of Tennyson's and his "love" consequently would be diminished (51.5, 7, 8). He comforts himself by asserting the direct resemblance of Hallam's loving forgiveness to God's, addressing the friend who had mused deeply over the relation between human love and divine similitude: "Ye watch, like God, the rolling hours, / With larger other eyes than ours, / To make allowance for us all" (51.14–16). Simeon's suggestion of his own "perfect holiness" (to use Baxter's term) by way of divine likeness is one that Tennyson explores rather than endorses, though Browning had no hesitation in hailing this dramatic monologue as "perfect." As the "supreme exemplar" of the Victorian period's most distinctive genre, Simeon articulates and embodies a complex of similarities that can dizzy us, as if we too were balanced precariously on that high, narrow column, like him.

SIMEON'S AFTERLIFE: THE MESSAGE OF THE BUTTERFLY

A simile, in the standard definition, yokes together unlike things, and so does a pun. "The pun constitutes a *forced contiguity* between two or more words," Eco writes, with its "force" deriving from the unexpectedness of the resemblance.[171] In making a claim for the efficacy of Simeon's speech, I want to force contiguity between Simeon and a far more recent example of someone climbing to a great height, and remaining there, for a higher purpose. On December 10, 1997, twenty-three-year-old Julia Butterfly Hill climbed a thousand-year-old, two-hundred-foot-tall redwood tree in northern California named Luna, where she lived for 738 days, until the Pacific Lumber Company agreed not to cut it down. Tennyson's monologist can seem a ragged and risible figure, as can Hill (as she admits, although when not dwelling aloft she has occasionally worked as a model). But the contemporary environmental activist can help us to see that the platform Simeon mounts is ideological as well as architectural. Hill's memoir of her tree-sit and St. Simeon Stylites's dramatic monologue both stand as oratorical performances in which the ascension to lofty physical heights makes possible the more ambitious ascension to rhetorical heights.

In her book, *The Legacy of Luna: The Story of a Tree, a Woman, and the Struggle to Save the Redwoods* (2000), Julia Butterfly Hill likens herself to the creature of her adopted middle name, who must move from its confining casement, "breaking through the barrier of self in which it has wrapped itself" in order to enter its "final transformation," until it becomes "beautiful and free."[172] Tennyson's Simeon, who makes so much of his own dramatic nomination, also uses figurative language concerning a winged insect to envision his own alterations: "This dull chrysalis / Cracks into shining wings" (153–54). Both images stress transformation of the self through a process of "breaking" or "cracking," and this violent emergence of the self instigates a process of not only personal but public transformation. The ideological goals of the contemporary environmentalist are clearly discernible and, in this case, attainable: while Hill continues her ecological activism through other venues, once Luna the tree was to be spared by legal agreement with the lumber company, she climbed down. Simeon's ideological aims are more difficult to discern, and potentially to attain; certainly, there will be no descent until his ascension.

Writing of "St. Simeon Stylites" in his 1842 essay on Tennyson's poems in the *Church of England Quarterly Review*, Leigh Hunt refers to "the poor phantom-like person of the almost incredible Saint of the Pillar—the almost solitary Christian counterpart of the Yogees of the Hindoos, who let birds build in their hair, and the nails of their fingers grow through the palms of their hands."[173] Hunt forges a resemblance between the Christian saint and the Hindu Yogi, and I want also to set Simeon beside someone with whom he can initially seem to bear little similarity, who might herself have been willing to let birds nest in her hair, in the hope that the resemblance will come to seem "necessary," as Eco puts it, "after the contiguity is realized."[174] Simeon's monologue and Hill's memoir chronicle the inspiration to ascend, the endurance of extreme physical hardship, the manner and modes of communication with people below, an awareness of appearing insane, and a conviction of personal spiritual transformation that has far-reaching social and political implications. Hill, aptly named even without her assumed moniker "Butterfly," reaches physical heights Simeon could only dream of. She initially roosts on a six-by-eight-foot platform rigged with tarpaulins, 180 feet high (with a supplementary four-by-eight-foot platform for food and supplies); she eventually moves to a hundred-foot-high platform originally built for the press. After a year and a half, she can "hardly imagine living anywhere else," partly because, like Simeon, who seems an extension of his pillar, she takes on a dendritic resemblance to her residence. The weathered cracks on her muscular hands remind her of "Luna's swirling patterns," her fingers are "stained brown from the bark and green from the lichen," and, though she washes infrequently and in a limited manner, she reports, "People even said I smelled sweet, like a redwood" (227).

For all their dependence on the irrefutable authority gained by putting their bodies into extreme and nearly untenable positions, suffering unusual pains (Hill chronicles physical torments that rival Simeon's) to carry their arguments, these two speakers are still more dependent on the suasive effects of their monologic narratives. For Simeon, only his monologue can attain for him the position he feels is his by right; his oratorical performance instigates and constitutes the rapture he seeks. Hill also recognizes that merely inhabiting the redwood will accomplish little without a voice that is both literally and figuratively raised by the fact of her physical position. From her perch in Luna's branches (comparable to what Simeon terms his "high nest of penance"), she talked tirelessly on her cell phone, sometimes for close to ten hours a day, she estimates, "doing outreach, speaking to churches, conferences, organizations, schools," not to mention writing "between 100 to 150" letters a week and speaking to numerous reporters.[175]

"Patient on this tall pillar I have borne / Rain, wind, frost, heat, hail, damp, and sleet, and snow" (15–16), Simeon recounts, and Hill, who endured what she calls "the worst storms in recorded California history," demonstrates that no dweller at the heights exaggerates her or his defenselessness in the face of inclement weather.[176] Hill is not infrequently hanging on for her life, and she too remarks the particular effects of hail, which "in Luna was intense—like throwing pebbles on somebody's roof or the side of their house, *tadatadatadatada*, but magnified" (187). The hail's iambic tetrameter is but one of the auditory assaults she endures, as when, during an especially ferocious storm, "the wind howled. It sounded like wild banshees, *rrahhh*, while the tarps added to the crazy cacophony of noise, *flap, flap, flap, bap, bap, flap, bap!*" (113). Simeon's vulnerability is exacerbated by his ulcerated foot, and Hill faces a similar impediment. She eschews shoes because "I couldn't stand the feeling of separation from the tree": "But barefoot in winter in a tree on a hill in the freezing wind," she admits, "is not always a great idea" (95). Her feet hurt "all the time," turning red then white then blue then finally black and purple with frostbite. With the pain already "excruciating," she then broke the little toe on her right foot, "but my foot was so cold I didn't realize I had broken it." "The pain was agonizing" (96), though ameliorated by the application of Tiger Balm, a splint of cardboard and duct tape, and, eventually, thermal booties she purchases from a reporter.

Throughout Hill's childhood, her father had been "an itinerant preacher," who, with his family in tow, "traveled the country's heartland preaching from town to town and church to church" (3), and in many ways she can seem a latter-day daughter to the evangelical Simeon as well. She prays every morning and every night, and, though less vehement than the monologist "Battering the gates of heaven with storms of prayer," she attributes her survival of storms *to* prayer. In particularly challenging circumstances, as when helicopters are circling overhead to try to root her out, her response is to "fast and pray" (130). Often under siege by loggers from Pacific Lumber, who felled trees close to hers and threatened repeatedly to chop Luna down, Hill remarks a resemblance between herself and Christ, with Luna as the cross to which she is nailed: "To make a tree fall in a certain direction, they drive a wedge into it. Since I was raised in a Christian background, driving that wedge into the tree reminded me of the crucifixion. Jesus, an amazing prophet of love, was crucified by others driving spikes through him into a fallen tree" (63).

Although theological resemblances between the New Age ecologist and the Catholic anchorite can seem groundless, each reports a conviction of having been chosen by God to serve as an instrument of public instruction. Simeon explains:

> But yield not me the praise:
> God only through his bounty hath thought fit,
> Among the powers and princes of this world,
> To make me an example to mankind,
> Which few can reach to. (182–86)

This claim has more merit than critics have acknowledged: he is certainly accurate on a literal level—his height makes him unreachable except by a few—and he is accurate on a metaphysical level as well. In the previous section I discussed his status as an exemplum, but I want here to focus on his exemplary relation specifically to "this world," that is, not merely to the stylitae who succeed him, but "to mankind." Hill's narrative can help us understand the political effects of Simeon's discourse, his bearing in the civic rather than celestial sphere. Simeon accurately, as we shall see, notes his influence "Among the powers and princes," as well as the "good people," while Hill is especially proud of the example she sets for dispirited striking members of the United Steelworkers of America, who would tell each other, according to a union leader who visits her in Luna, "'Think about that woman up in the tree. If she can live up in a tree for over a year, you can keep on with the strike and help make the world a better place, too.' And then the grumbling stopped." Such public effect seems to her God-given, as it felt to Tennyson's Simeon: "I felt blessed and honored," she writes, "to be able to give strength to someone" (220).

Simeon's pride in his popular appeal is especially striking given that "St. Simeon Stylites" was written soon after the passage of the 1832 Reform Bill. I have read this first Victorian dramatic monologue in the context of millenarian debates of the early 1830s, and the political positions of the most closely engaged evangelical communities merits noting. In his *Narrative of Facts*, Baxter recalls his own prophecy "that the Reform Bill would not pass—that the people thought they had it, but it should not pass." Due to his and other prophetic utterances in Irving's church, he continues, "the certainty of the rejection of the Reform Bill was looked to by all [Irvingites]." Disconfirmation of this political prophecy further confirms his present distrust in prophetic utterance: "When the Bill was finally passed, which was after I had abandoned the work, it was not slight additional proof of the falseness of this Spirit of prophecy" (Baxter, *Narrative*, 61). Millenarians in this period tended to be politically conservative; as Sandeen writes, "Catholic emancipation, the Reform Bill, democracy, industrialization—the millenarian opposed them all, but with a sense of resignation born of the knowledge that the world must grow more evil day after day."[177] Carlyle elegantly counterbalances Irving's political views with his own: Irving "found *Democracy* a thing forbidden, leading down to utter darkness; I a thing inevitable, and obliged to lead whithersoever it could."[178] And yet, although prophetic convictions were bound together with political conservatism, millenarianism was in some sense a radical movement, as Harrison explains: "In a society dominated by an aristocratic and Anglican establishment any movement outside its paternalistic control was a radical departure, a potential threat to that deference, respect and subordination which was held to be necessary for social stability." The official positions of millenarians in this period might be highly conservative, even reactionary, but the revolutionary nature of this theological vision allied them in unexpected ways with popular radicalism. After examining psychological and social explanations for this religious movement, Harrison concludes, "Basically millenarianism was an ideology of change: it focused attention on the great changes which were currently taking place in these last days, and promised a vast transformation of the social order when all things would be made new."[179] Even though prophets of the end-time might see this coming cataclysm as retribution for the evil tendencies of an increasingly liberal society, rapture itself can be seen in some sense as a progressive event.

It might appear that the only organization of the polity St. Simeon Stylites can consider is a virtually monarchical one, in which the populace kneels as he clutches "the crown! the crown!" (205). It is true that he is a believer in hierarchies among men and angels. It is also true that the innovation of the pillar was the result of a powerful antisocial impulse. He ascends his first pillar, he informs God in the dramatic monologue, "that I might be more alone with thee" (84), and Tennyson reflects his sources in making clear that it was also to remove himself from the physical reach of "those that came / To touch my body and be healed" (77–78). Hone recounts of the period when Simeon was chained to a mountainside, "Multitudes thronged to the mountain to receive his benediction, and many of the sick recovered their health. But as some were not satisfied unless they touched him…and Simeon desired retirement from the daily concourse, he projected a new and unprecedented manner of life."[180] Gibbon suggests that Simeon's removal is due less to a desire for retirement than to a cruel indifference to the people and their needs. He refers to Simeon as the Syrian Anachoret, having characterized Anachorets as indulging in "unsocial, independent fanaticism." In this Simeon stands, as Gibbon puts it derisively, as one of the "heroes of monastic life": "A cruel, unfeeling temper has distinguished the monks of every age and country." In his insistence on the "stern indifference" and "merciless zeal" of the monastic saints, we may merely hear a Protestant pillorying of a Catholic pillar saint, but Gibbon is perceptive regarding the political implications of Simeon's self-mortification: "A prince, who should capriciously inflict such tortures, would be deemed a tyrant; but it would surpass the power of a tyrant to impose a long and miserable existence on the reluctant victims of his cruelty." Simeon is seen to embody a cruelly despotic mode of self-government, one Gibbon takes as expressive of similarly pitiless detachment from the people. He continues, "Nor can it be presumed that the fanatics who torment themselves are susceptible of any lively affection for the rest of mankind."[181]

Fredeman considers Tennyson's "St. Simeon Stylites" to present "a study in isolation and concomitant dehumanization,"[182] but I would argue instead that Simeon, both in Tennyson's sources and in his dramatic monologue, is always seeking and attaining community. Continually fascinated by the vulnerability of his body to natural, temporal, and self-inflicted assault, Simeon turns in his monologue, finally, to his most painful obsession: his place among men. For all his elaborate alienation, Simeon craves society, though he claims it is the society of saints he seeks. But this ambition puts him at the center of all this sick humanity and all its desperate worship. As Theodoret (Gibbon's primary source), the fifth-century Syrian bishop and theologian who wrote a life of Simeon, whom he knew personally, put it, followers poured around his pillar's base "like a river along the roads, and formed an ocean of men about it."[183] The extremities of his physical position, palsied atop a pillar, conversely work to join Simeon to the community from which he has so literally distanced himself. In moving to the pillar, moreover, he moves from a faith that the touch of his body might work miracles to a radical dependence on the power of his benediction, and theirs.

Julia Butterfly Hill serves as an example, perhaps to all humankind but at least to striking steelworkers; in spite of his apparent ability to heal his followers, Simeon can seem to have no such immediate effects on the political life of his time. And yet it is significant that Hone begins with the report, "St. Simeon Stylites astonished the whole Roman empire by his mortifications."[184] Gibbon details his broad civic impact:

> The monastic saints, who excite only the contempt and pity of a philosopher, were respected and almost adored by the prince and people. Successive crowds of pilgrims from Gaul and India saluted the divine pillar of Simeon; the tribes of Saracens disputed in arms the honour of his benediction; the queens of Arabia and Persia gratefully confessed his supernatural virtue; and the angelic Hermit was consulted by the younger Theodosius in the most important concerns of the church and state.

Although Gibbon is mocking, we might nevertheless take Simeon more seriously when we see how seriously he was taken: his asociality has far-reaching social impact. And with death he extends his power, as Tennyson's Simeon exalts: "For I will leave my relics in your land, / And you may carve a shrine about my dust, / And burn a fragrant lamp before my bones" (191–93). Gibbon recounts, "His remains were transported from the mountain of Telenissa, by a solemn procession of the patriarch, the master-general of the East, six bishops, twenty-one counts or tribunes, and six thousand soldiers; and Antioch revered his bones as her glorious ornament and impregnable defence." Borne to Antioch by civil as well as ecclesiastic authorities, Simeon is supported by soldiers and in turn supports them, as his relics contribute to the defense of the nation. Concluding his account of the "servile and pusillanimous reign of the monks," Gibbon writes, "If it be possible to measure the interval between the philosophic writings of Cicero and the sacred legend of Theodoret, between the character of Cato and that of Simeon, we may appreciate the memorable revolution which was accomplished in the Roman empire within a period of five hundred years."[185] In comparing Cicero's philosophy to Theodoret's legends, and Cato's severe self-discipline to Simeon's, Gibbon suggests that Simeon is himself one of the most striking avatars of the decline of the Roman Empire.

When a young monk, Simeon had tightly bound his body with the rope from the well for several weeks, telling not "a single soul," until exposed by an ulcer "eating through my skin," at which point, "all / My brethren marvell'd greatly" (65, 66, 67–68). Fredeman hears in Simeon's reminiscence a "naïve revelation that always he has played to an audience";[186] he is right to remark Simeon's unwavering attention to his public, though too quick to assume that Simeon's revelation is naïve. Rather, Simeon calculates his revelations as closely as he calculates the events of Revelation. We must understand him as playing to an audience just as deliberately now that, as a result of the curative power of his columnar position, he can accurately report, "My fame is loud amongst mankind" (80). Although, like Simeon, Hill may be particularly suited to the solitude of her aerie ("She did well in the tree because she wanted to be alone and felt personally comfortable being alone," according to the producer of a documentary of her tree-sit),[187] she also might be understood to seek public attention aggressively.

Hill plays to an audience at every opportunity, which she justifies as a way to save both her tree and herself. After recovering from a car accident, she had happened upon ecological activism, and this tree-sit in particular, as an answer for what to do with the life she had been spared. When facing various difficulties in the tree, she fasts and prays, then realizes that the solution is to be found in intensified press exposure: "The resulting media interest gave me an expanded purpose and a new life in Luna" (131). She retreats into the thicket of leaves and branches in Luna, the better to be seen ("Because of my peculiar visibility, the media interest in me only continued to increase" [181]) and heard, aided by the latest technological devices: "a radio phone powered by solar panels that are connected to two motorcycle batteries, an emergency cell phone, a hand-powered radio, a tape recorder, a digital camera, a video camera, walkie-talkies, and a pager that functions as my answering machine and controls my life" (131). While enjoying the few days of quiet that come after she accidentally drops her pager and it shatters from the 180-foot fall, Hill marvels at the amplified voice she has attained by her withdrawal to this tree, which itself takes on a technological cast: "Up in Luna, I was living on the world's most amazing radio tower, which receives and transmits all the beautiful and powerful truths of our universe, and I had been blessed to be at the microphone on that tower" (132). The heights of tree and pillar can seem to distance Hill and Simeon from humanity, and yet they also draw them closer, as they transmit a higher vision to those below. Simeon "scarce can hear the people hum / About the column's base" (37–38), and yet he is heard rather than overheard, as they can hear his twice-daily broadcast to them, and of course his monologue, as if the humming he hears is feedback from his own radio frequency.

"Frankly, I think she enjoys the cult that's building up around her," a fellow environmentalist complains of Hill.[188] She is accused of selling out, of self-promotion, of not sharing credit with fellow activists. She is also accused of hypocrisy, specifically for publishing books, which are produced from wood pulp. *The Legacy of Luna* is printed on 70 percent FSC (Forestry Stewardship Council) certified and 30 percent postconsumer recycled paper with soy-based ink and chlorine-free processing, with proceeds donated to causes such as her own foundation, but her publisher is owned by Rupert Murdoch's media empire. "A life of hypocritical selfishness" is the verdict passed on Simeon by Fredeman, an insightful and even admiring reader.[189] Variations on this claim come from the majority of this poem's critics; in contradiction to Langbaum's well-established formula regarding the dramatic monologue, Simeon has received plenty of judgment, but little sympathy.[190] "The receiving ear, whether God's or the reader's," argues Fredeman, "can conclude only the unconscious hypocrisy implicit in Simeon's words; and the irony is intensified by their being but the articulation of a misspent life."[191] Given the rigors of his daily self-mortifications, Simeon describes frequent episodes of physical unconsciousness, but he is, we have seen, entirely conscious, and indeed calculating, in all he speaks in this dramatic monologue. The judgment of hypocrisy leveled at Simeon seems inapposite: he speaks what he believes, and what he intends to persuade his auditors to believe as well.

Qualified admiration for his authenticity seems to have been the conclusion reached by Trench's circle on the matter of Edward Irving. Frederick Denison Maurice and John Sterling voice an appreciation for Irving and his followers that is, though ambivalent, also genuine. In a letter of October 1, 1832, concerning "the advocates of gifts," Maurice writes to Trench, "I have a respect approaching to reverence for some of the believers." "I do not say these gifts are of the devil," he states, accepting the logical consequences of refusing to demonize this congregation; "and if not of the devil, they are of the Spirit, sent, as I conceive, in answer to prayer; neither wholly faithless, nor yet right in themselves." Although Baxter in his *Narrative of Facts* determines that the source for these gifts is indeed diabolical, Maurice reads Baxter as offering "striking confirmation" of his own exculpatory opinion. In extending toleration and the benefit of the doubt to the Irvingites, Maurice offers himself almost as a sacrifice, stating that, if he is shown to be wrong, he would "cheerfully bear all the contempt which the world, infidel and religious, bestows upon Irving and his followers" (Trench, *Letters*, 1:121–22). In a letter to Trench of August 31, 1832, Sterling writes that he feels he owes "the deepest gratitude" to Edward Irving: "Although his unceasing vehemence makes me dizzy, his polemical violence repels me, and I see much rashness and presumption and (as I think) some positive error, I yet feel throughout the love, faith, and hope, the life, though not always the light, of a richly gifted and regenerate man" (Trench, *Letters*, 1:119).

Hill is similarly exonerated. She marvels, "In August 1998, *Good Housekeeping* nominated me as one of the most admired women in America. Me—the same person who had been called crazy, wacko, extremist, far left, terrorist, idiot. That proved to me that social consciousness regarding direct action and civil disobedience was beginning to shift" (163). This equivalent of a *Good Housekeeping* Seal of Approval indicates for Hill that she was not "this insane radical," but instead simply one of those "who have opted to put their lives on the line for their beliefs" (163). Even Tennyson's Simeon has been read as exemplary, just as his dramatic monologue anticipates. In his entry on Simeon Stylites in his 1872 *Lives of the Saints*, S. Baring-Gould quotes the passage from Tennyson's poem (though he does not identify its title or author) in which Simeon describes his three winters chained to "yonder mountain side," thirsty, fasting, and blackened by "branding thunder." This Victorian reader comments, "It was worth all this, if souls could be added to the Lord, as they were, by the hundreds and thousands." Baring-Gould asks that readers suspend contemporary judgment and instead accept ecclesiastical judgment: "It is not for us to condemn a mode of life which there is no need for men to follow now. It was needed then, and he is rightly numbered with the Saints."[192]

The reasons to suspend skepticism for Hill are many, as they are, perhaps more surprisingly, for Tennyson's Simeon: each produces a range of effects that are not merely self-serving, but in many lights estimable. Hone opens his narrative with a quotation from Alban Butler's eighteenth-century *Lives of the Saints*; in his full account, Butler concludes of Simeon, "God is sometimes pleased to conduct certain souls through extraordinary paths, in which others would find only danger of illusion and self-will."[193] As Hill observes of "frontline activism," presumably for evangelicals as well as ecologists, "its intense nature makes it extremely hard to sustain" (174)—though she sustained her efforts for over two years, and Simeon for forty. Both are accused of delusion and self-will, yet both were effective in converting others to their causes: Simeon converted numerous Persians, Iberians, and Armenians who made pilgrimages to him, and Hill powerfully affected admirers such as Woody Harrelson, Joan Baez, and Reba MacIntyre, who made pilgrimages to her, themselves mounting to her platforms (and staying overnight, in Harrelson's case). Hill saved a thousand-year-old redwood and the two-mile buffer zone surrounding it. Luna still stands, though its trunk was attacked by someone wielding a chainsaw in 2000. Simeon's pillar, or that of one of his descendent (so to speak) stylitae, also still stands in Syria. Indeed, Simeon's site remains a pilgrimage destination. An article in the *New York Times* about population growth in long-abandoned Syrian villages that are now archaeological sites reports, "Qal'at Semaan, where St. Simeon stayed atop a pillar for some 42 years as a show of faith, already has been declared off limits for development. It is a major site for tourists."[194]

Tucker claims that Simeon's dramatic monologue "finds its theme in the evasion of responsibility,"[195] but what Tennyson's first major dramatic monologist articulates ceaselessly is his staggering assumption of responsibility—for himself, for humanity, for the end. In his physical and rhetorical ardor, Simeon is an activist, demonstrating, as Harold Nicolson wrote of this character, "that the truly religious man was the man of action."[196] The fact that he speaks a dramatic monologue, however, renders his speech inherently ineffectual, according to Langbaum's theory of the genre: "The motive for speaking is inadequate to the utterance.... The utterance is in other words largely gratuitous—it need never have occurred."[197] And yet Hill's and Simeon's speech is no more gratuitous than their ascent to the topmost heights of pillar or tree: the quest for extreme solitude makes possible, indeed necessitates greater and more direct involvement in the lives of the communities they would appear to have spurned. For both Simeon and Hill, it is imperative that they speak, and they ascend these high platforms so that their voices will carry. As Hill comments, "A tree-sit is about more than just protecting a tree; it's a form of public outreach" (61). For Simeon and for Hill, the platforms for which they stand derive their authority from the platforms on which they stand. These speakers desire to achieve transformation, a goal they not only describe in the course of their monologues, but labor to achieve through the media of his monologue and her memoir.

In "Theodicæa Novissima" Hallam observes, "Pain is a component part of all desire" (*Writings*, 206). The tremendous pain undergone and described by these figures seems an inevitable component of a desire for profound personal and public transformation. Enduring an especially violent storm, Hill sounds caught up by events beyond her physical or discursive control: "I howled. I laughed. I whooped and cried and screamed and raged. I hollered and I jibbered and I jabbered" (114). Overwhelmed by this experience, she concludes, "That's the message of the butterfly. I had come through darkness and storms and had been transformed. I was living proof of the power of metamorphosis" (115). She describes an experience of being rapt and transported, akin to Simeon's eager welcome of the approaching "end," but we learn another lesson from Hill about Simeon's far longer tenure at the topmost point, namely, that the experience of living aloft is itself a rapturous one. Though each experiences sensations of being caught up in the air by some external force, each has also gone to considerable lengths to climb up into the air and remain there, thus gaining by their own efforts and by progressive degrees of ascent an ongoing sensation of rapture's dizzying heights.

Although each of these aerial speakers is exceedingly ambitious and remarkably efficacious, for each there is also something about the height, precariousness, solitude, and exposure of his or her platform that is in itself transformative. Hill recounts her desire to climb the brittle branches to the very top of the tree: "I felt a constant calling to go to the top," positing that all seek "that feeling of making it to the highest place possible, the inner urge to find our higher self" (122–23). Eyeing the "lightning-hardened pinnacle" of Luna, she writes, "I just felt compelled to reach it" (123), and this too can illuminate the compulsions voiced in Tennyson's dramatic monologue. "She didn't simply articulate a narrow political agenda," an attorney who helped provide logistical support for Hill reflects. "It was poetic."[198] Supremely poetic as well, Tennyson's "St Simeon Stylites" inaugurates a literary form with ongoing vitality not only for its Victorian successors but also for twentieth- and twenty-first-century poets; in the literary as well as the theological sphere, Simeon has attained canonicity. In his speaking, because of his speaking, his pillar becomes a pen. To conclude with a pun Simeon might approve, since it is one he embodies: by way of his transformative dramatic monologue, the *stylos* becomes a *stylus*.

PART II

Unreal City

Victorians in Troy

There was, I well remember, a sixpenny encyclopedia of great service to young schoolboys on the eve of examinations," G. M. Young reminisces in his 1939 essay, "The Age of Tennyson," "which contained, with other useful matter, a list of the Hundred Greatest Men: 'to know their deeds is to know the history of civilization'; it began of course with Homer, and ended, not less of course, with Tennyson."[1] The cheap encyclopedia that Young describes lists Tennyson at the culmination of "the history of civilization," and conveys (through his "not less of course") the absolute predictability at the time of such a placement. Young reminds us how quickly and thoroughly Tennyson became requisite for schoolboys, or canonical. "One thing is certain," John Churton Collins proclaimed a year before the laureate's death: "The poetry of Lord Tennyson has become classical, and is therefore becoming, and will become more and more, a subject of serious study wherever the English language is spoken."[2] Tennyson himself recognized the perils of becoming a subject of serious study, an example for schoolchildren. "He would lament," his son Hallam recalled, "'They use *me* as a lesson-book at schools, and they will call me 'that horrible Tennyson'" (*Memoir*, 1:16). The affiliation of Tennyson with Homer was not confined to study manuals; Robert F. Horton in *Alfred Tennyson: A Saintly Life* recounts the poet Sydney Dobell's description of Tennyson: "If he were pointed out to you as the man who had written the *Iliad* you would answer, I can well believe it."[3]

The similitude imagined between Homer and Tennyson went deeper than their sharing, like two bookends, their assignment to the beginning and end of a list of the Hundred Greatest Men; Tennyson mused over Homer's poetry, as well as his stature in literary history, throughout his life. More particularly, he recurs consistently throughout his poetry to Ilion or Troy, Homer's city built to music and doomed to destruction, a city whose disappearance from historical record must have appeared to the Victorian poet inextricable from its origins in ephemeral song. The poet in his youth accumulated an empire of lost cities—Troy, Timbuctoo, Atlantis, Eldorado, Camelot—and for him in each instance the city's imaginative creation appeared simultaneously to engineer its devastation.

Before concentrating in chapter 4 on the dramatic monologue "Ulysses," I want first establish in chapter 3 the multiple and intricate contexts of Tennyson's major contribution to the genre. "Ulysses" is known to have been among Tennyson's first poetic responses to the news of the death of Arthur Henry Hallam, but criticism, while exploring suggestively the emotional bonds between these two men, has given less attention to the spiritual ones I suggested in the previous chapter, or the intellectual ones I explore here. Though rightly emphasizing that this period was the most formative of Tennyson's life, R. B. Martin, one of the poet's most probing biographers, dismisses the relevance of the academic enterprise for Tennyson: "Since he was a poet and not a scholar, most of the traditions about his Cambridge career are naturally unconcerned with what he was meant to be learning."[4] We ought to be concerned, however, with what Tennyson was learning, and therefore chapter 3 revisits Tennyson's experiences at Trinity College, Cambridge, a critical site of his education, not only in humanity but in the humanities. I then tour briefly Tennyson's "mystick" cities, before focusing on Homeric Troy both in the Tennysonian and the larger Victorian imagination.

Victorian dramatic monologues attempt to represent and to constitute efficacious language. In parts 2 and 3 I examine the relation of "Ulysses," "Tithonus," and affiliated poems to the greatest example Western literary history offers us of poetic efficacy, of a poet's song inducing monumental effects: Apollo's musical raising of the walls of Troy. To explore the profound manner in which this myth underwrites some of Tennyson's most representative works, I first establish the Victorian debate over whether indeed Troy was a mythic city or, conversely, a historically verifiable one. This debate points to conflicting notions of the poet's power: for Tennyson and such influential scholars as the Benthamite George Grote, the epic city is understood to be the creation of the poet's imagination.[5] An opposing view held by such proponents as William Gladstone, the most prolific writer on Homer of his age, and Heinrich Schliemann, the discoverer of a putative Troy, was that the poet is a divinely gifted historian, reporting his version of verifiable fact. In the second section of chapter 3 I review this consequential debate, which fundamentally concerns whether a poet's relation to his or her culture is productive or descriptive, in order to foreground readings of Tennyson's Hellenic dramatic monologues. I read these monologues in the context of Tennyson's other early lyrics based on classical material; in part 2 I concentrate on the speaker Ulysses, situating him amid a community of other poems and speakers.

I pursue in what follows the centrality of the figure of Troy for this poet, scrutinizing a pattern that some critics have briefly noted, yet which has remained largely unexamined.[6] Long and intense speculation on the topic of Troy was, however, far from exclusive to Tennyson. As a matter of course educated men (and some women) in the nineteenth century were thoroughly versed in ancient Greek and Latin, and although his father's erratic behavior rendered the conditions of Tennyson's childhood at times alarming, the poet's tutelage at the hands of this highly literate man seems to have been in many ways not unusual.[7] Certainly, he acquired an impressive command of ancient literatures, one long acknowledged by his contemporaries. Herbert Paul's 1893 commemorative essay on Tennyson focused on his poems on classical subjects, remarking, "The boy who loves Homer and Virgil makes friends for life.... They remained with Tennyson till his death. They remain with Mr. Gladstone still. They come unbidden to the lips of the great orator. They moulded and coloured the verse of the great poet."[8]

In restoring to Tennyson's classical poems the fullness and intricacy of their contexts, we must bear in mind situations not only literary but social. We must situate Tennyson's monologists within a community of figures drawn from classical sources and situate Tennyson himself among a community of nineteenth-century classicists, both amateur and professional. As the author of the 1880 *Troy: Its Legend, History and Literature* (a book intended for a popular audience, which reviewed the legend as well as its critical history in Germany and England) wrote, "To-day...the Homeric legend and literature actually receive more attention and possess more importance than ever before; the vitality of the Homeric question is the most remarkable phenomenon in secular history."[9] Herbert Paul, in reviewing Tennyson's "love" for this material, singles out Gladstone for comparison, and I too will make particular use of this pairing, frequently suggested by their contemporaries, of the poet and the orator, following their relations over the course of a half century. Although the "friendships" these men formed with the ancients differed in instructive ways, for each the attachment to the ancients can be seen to have been causative of aspects of his discursive achievements. Tennyson spent his first sustained visit with Gladstone in May 1863, after which he wrote to their mutual friend the Duke of Argyll regarding Gladstone, "Very pleasant, and very interesting he was, even when he discoursed on Homer, where most people think him a little hobby-horsical: let him be. His hobby-horse is of the intellect and with a grace" (*Memoir*, 1:493). Tennyson here is himself gracious (some would say uncharacteristically so), but in fact he differed with Gladstone, as we shall see, profoundly and revealingly on numerous matters of Homeric scholarship.

In his *Memoir*, Hallam Tennyson appears to foreclose the topic of his father's classicism at the same moment that he introduces it:

> I need not dwell on my father's love for the perfection of classical literary art, on his sympathy with the temper of the old world, on his love of the old metres, and on his views as to how the classical subject ought to be treated in English poetry.

He purposely chose those classical subjects from mythology and legend, which had been before but imperfectly treated, or of which the stories were slight, so that he might have free scope for his imagination, "The Lotos-Eaters," "Ulysses," "Tithonus," "Oenone," "The Death of Oenone," "Tiresias," "Demeter and Persephone," "Lucretius." A modern feeling was to some extent introduced into the themes, but they were dealt with according to the canons of antique art. The blank verse was often intentionally restrained. (*Memoir*, 2:13–14)

Tennyson's "love" for this literary art is so self-evident it eschews articulation, and yet its terms, as outlined here, merit dwelling on. The "canons of antique art" are defined in an abbreviated fashion, but it is clear that a central requirement is restraint. This quality is specified in the matter of form, but this restraint would necessarily also attend his treatment of the "classical subject"—fitting especially for a poet who wrote an early unpublished "Ode to Reticence" ("I would shrine her in my verse!" [8]). And yet Hallam's summary makes clear that this restraint is coupled with freedom even unto license, in a liberation of the "free scope of the imagination" in its contemplation of antique material. Tennyson's poems on the "classical subject"—which go so far as to imagine classical subjectivities— therefore enact a dialectic of liberty and limits, one with which every dramatic monologue is concerned.

Gerhard Joseph rightly observes, "Although some of Tennyson's finest poems are on classical subjects, we are not accustomed to weave 'The Hesperides,' 'Oenone,' 'The Lotos-Eaters,' 'Ulysses,' 'Tithonus,' 'Tiresias,' 'Lucretius' and 'Demeter and Persephone' (to name the major works) into a single textual pattern."[10] Over the course of parts 2 and 3, I discuss each of the poems listed by Hallam Tennyson, demonstrating that none stand alone; for example, I read "Ulysses" specifically in the context of "The Lotos-Eaters," and "Tithonus" in the context of the Oenone poems. The affiliations among these speakers are deep and intense: while Tennyson's sources are widely varied (including Homer, Anacreon, Callimachus, Horace, Ovid, Virgil, and Lucretius), from their constellation he engineers the re-creation of a very specific community. Tennyson's early step into the genre of the classical dramatic monologue is toward the figure of a Ulysses who in turn articulates his own yearning toward Achilles, necessarily a yearning toward the underworld, what Gladstone calls the "weird scenery of the Eleventh Odyssey."[11] The Homeric underworld introduces a host of characters taken up in eponymous Tennysonian monologues named in Tennyson's son's list: "Ulysses," "Tiresias," Persephone (of "Demeter and Persephone"), and even "Tithonus," whose beautiful son Memnon (considered in detail in part 3) is referred to by Achilles and Ulysses in their underworldly conversation. Although among the shades Ulysses encounters in the underworld is that of the great Achilles, who figures so prominently in several of Tennyson's dramatic monologues, the hero has actually descended, he informs Achilles, in Chapman's translation, "To visite wise Tiresias" (11:628).[12] Horace, "drummed into" the young Tennyson by his father (*Memoir*, 1:16), directly contrasts Achilles' short life with Tithonus's long one: *abstulit clarum cita mors Achillem, / longa Tithonum minuit senectus* (*Ode* 2.16.29–23). A verse translation by Christopher Smart in his father's library renders these lines, "A sudden death Achilles seiz'd, / A tedious age Tithonus wore."[13] Although Tennyson's Tiresias is not yet dispensing counsel among the shades, the Thebes he is so desperate to save shares a crucial similarity to Troy, in that both are fabled to have been built from song, an origin I discuss in part 3. The underworld Tiresias remains possessed of knowledge of the world, lost to most shades, by the grace of the Persephone whose loss Tennyson's Demeter so laments. Gladstone reminds us of Persephone, "It is she...who endows Tiresias with the functions of a Seer,"[14] and the Queen of Hades' "imperial dis-impassioned eyes" ("Demeter and Persephone," 23), which awe even her mother, rule all this demesne.

An exception on many grounds would appear to be the monologue "Lucretius," concerned with the death of the Roman poet of the first century BCE. As Douglas Bush summarizes, "*Lucretius* is of course very different from Tennyson's other poems of antique inspiration. The subject is 'historical,' and not mythological, it is Roman and not Greek."[15] One crucial aspect of the relations among these poems, however, has less to do with Hellenic sources than with the manner in which each of these speakers has entered Ilion's orbit, and here Lucretius circles with the rest. In his dementia, Tennyson's speaker has a dream, borrowed from the *Iliad*, of "the breasts, / The breasts of Helen" threatened by a sword, which, rather than piercing, "sank down shamed / At all that beauty." He continues, "as I stared, a fire, / The fire that left a roofless Ilion, / Shot out of them, and scorched me that I woke" (60–61, 63–66). The dreamer, punished for a voyeurism that is as much historical as it is sexual, is scorched by jets of Ilion's fire, and so joins with other subjects, including those speakers in "The Lotos-Eaters" and "Oenone," who also stand marked by Ilion's flames. In these poems on classical subjects, Tennyson takes up imaginative residence in accounts of Ilion, placing himself among the doomed and displaced, allying himself with the creators, citizens, or destroyers of melody-born civilizations.

Hallam Tennyson's list of his father's classical poems gives some slight indication of the many genres Tennyson employed in exploring this material, including lyric, choric, and soliloquizing modes. The distinction between such early poems as "The Lotos-Eaters" and "Oenone" (which predate the death of Arthur Hallam) and the classical dramatic monologues is an important one: the latter are very much an extension or continuation, formally and thematically, of the former, and yet one would want to avoid positing an evolutionary scale whereby powerful early works are considered developmentally lesser. The classical poems, however varied generically, join in a kind of discursive community, bound together by their representations of arduous personal histories and grim prognoses of their imagined futures. Yet each speaker of a dramatic monologue addresses an audience that he or she hopes to influence, and in this dramatized determination to have an effect on auditors lies a central distinction. Speakers such as the early and the late Oenone, for example, and the chorus of the Lotos-Eaters foreground the powerlessness of their own words and a certain passivity toward their own circumstances—what we might call, following Tucker, a submission to the measure of doom. Tennyson's dramatic monologists, however, resemble orators (Arthur Henry Hallam's definition of this term, derived from his study of Cicero, will have bearing on my reading of "Ulysses") and are a significant exception to the pattern Tucker identifies. These speakers cleave forcefully to ambitions as fast held as they are seemingly nebulous, as private as they are necessarily public, articulating their desire, widely conceived, for varieties of transformation.

The poems listed by Hallam Tennyson in his comment on his father's classical subjects—"The Lotos-Eaters," "Ulysses," "Tithonus," "Oenone," "The Death of Oenone," "Tiresias," "Demeter and Persephone," "Lucretius"—eddy out like concentric circles from narratives of Troy's spectacular creation and dissolution. The figurations of Troy to which Tennyson returns again and again link, slenderly but securely, all of the classical monologues, and in tracing this specter of Ilion, we can track to the center of Tennyson's poetics. Anne Thackeray Ritchie's memoir of Tennyson records an anecdote of his Cambridge friend Edward FitzGerald, the translator of *The Rubaiyat of Omar Khayyam*, who feels the story illustrates the "definition of a poet." Reminiscing about Tennyson, "the only living—and like to live—poet I have known," FitzGerald recalls, "During a pretty long and intimate intercourse I had never seen [tears] glistening in his eyes but once, when reading Virgil—'dear old Virgil,' as he called him—together; and then—oh, not of Queen Dido, nor of young Marcellus even, but of the burning of Troy, in the second Aeneid—whether moved by the catastrophe itself, or the majesty of the verse it is told in, or...scarce knowing why."[16] The definition of the poet, by the account of a friend whose confidence in Tennyson was so great that he subsidized him financially for some years, consists of someone whose eyes fill with tears over Aeneas's chronicle of the rapture of Troy in book 2 of the *Aeneid*.

Tennyson's attraction to Virgil's account of "the burning of Troy" was of long standing, as a marginal comment indicates in an 1817 edition of Virgil he heavily annotated in childhood (next to his signature on the flyleaf is recorded his receipt of the volume from his father at the age of nine: "A. Tennyson Aetat 9"). At the start of book 2, Tennyson has written, *"Liber pulcherrimus in tota Æniade!* [sic]," his appreciation for lyric beauty already pronounced.[17] Attempting to arrive at some understanding almost less of Tennyson than of the concept of poetic immortality (a poet "like to live"), FitzGerald suggests that the subject, the Trojan "catastrophe," or the form, the "majesty of the verse," may account for Tennyson's tears, and in this he is looking to the traditional pairing of form and content for an explanation of this poetry's effects on this poet. Invoking "Tears, Idle Tears," that richest of evocations of unspecifiable sorrow, FitzGerald leaves open another explanation, namely, that the poet's eyes glisten with tears "scarce knowing why."

One of Tennyson's own meditations on the qualities that define a revered poet—indeed, Virgil himself—is his homage "To Virgil" (1882, 1885). He begins his hymn of praise:

> Roman Virgil, thou that singest
>   Ilion's lofty temples robed in fire,
> Ilion falling, Rome arising,
>   wars, and filial faith, and Dido's pyre. (1–4)

Addressing Virgil, he calls him by a name thereafter attached by Victorian readers to Tennyson himself, "lord of language" (5), but here he honors foremost Virgil's position as the singer of Troy's colossal destruction, of what in "Lucretius" he calls "the fire that left a roofless Ilion." In "Ulysses" and a host of related poems, "Ilion's lofty temples," the topless towers and well-built walls of a city called in Homer and in Virgil sacred, holy, again rise and fall.[18]

3

LOCATING TROY

In the late poem "Development" (1889), one of his rare openly autobiographical works, Robert Browning recounts the joys and vexations of the history of his knowledge of Troy. Significantly, the poem begins not with his own knowledge, but with an assertion regarding that of his father: "My father was a scholar and knew Greek" (1). As a five-year-old, he asks his father what he is reading about, and the answer is "The siege of Troy," which prompts another question from the child: "What is a siege and what is Troy?" (3–4). In answer, his father sets up a make-believe siege of Troy, with a housecat as Helen, their dogs as Menelaus and Agamemnon, and the pony in the stable as the sulking Achilles. A few years later, his father comes upon the young Browning and some friends "playing at Troy's Siege" (25) and suggests that he read Pope's translation, until such time as "by dint of scholarship" he might hear the tale "from Homer's very mouth" (31–32). (In the chapters to follow I frequently employ Pope's translation, because it was a text so intimately known to this generation of poets.)[1] Tennyson reported to his son that when he was around ten or eleven, "Pope's *Homer's Iliad* became a favourite of mine and I wrote hundreds and hundreds of lines in the regular Popeian metre, nay even could improvise them." Tennyson kenned not only Homer's poem from Pope, but also the discipline of his couplets. While his recollection elucidates the early training of his ear, it tells us as much about a familial precursor as a literary one. Metrical command seems itself to have been seen as a family trait, one entailed, apparently, by his father. Recalling his ability to improvise great quantities of lines in Pope's style, the laureate continues, "So could my two elder brothers, for my father was a poet and could write regular metre very skillfully" (*Memoir*, 1:11). The poet holds his father's influence as causal, explaining his own astonishing metrical precocity in this way: "for my father was a poet."

In "Development," Browning next describes how he "ran through Pope" (38) and labored away at his Greek primer. After he had progressed sufficiently, his father gave him C. G. Heyne's 1801 edition of the *Iliad* in Greek, the same one

Tennyson used as a child. (As an adult Tennyson recorded on the flyleaf of the first volume of his family's copy of Heyne, "My father who taught us Greek made us . . . write the substance of Heyne's notes in the margin to show that we had read them.")[2] Browning also worked intensively, "till I learned / Who was who, what was what, from Homer's tongue, / And there an end to learning" (48–50). With all the certainty of an "all-accomplished scholar, twelve years old," Browning was shocked next to learn the theories of the German philologist F. A. Wolf's *Prolegomena in Homerum* (1795), which holds that the Homeric text derived not from a single author but from an accumulated oral tradition. He complains of Wolf and the critics who followed, "It's unpleasant work / Their chop and change, unsettling one's belief" (64–65):

> And, after Wolf, a dozen of his like
> Proved there was never any Troy at all,
> Neither Besiegers nor Besieged,—nay, worse,—
> No actual Homer, no authentic text,
> No warrant for the fiction I, as fact,
> Had treasured in my heart and soul so long—
> Ay, mark you! and as fact held still, still hold,
> Spite of new knowledge, in my heart of hearts
> And soul of souls. (68–76)

Lamenting "ah, Wolf! / Why must he needs come doubting, spoil a dream?" (82–83), Browning describes how hard, indeed impossible it was to abandon his initial knowledge, his belief in an "actual Homer" and an "authentic text," to accept that there "was never any Troy at all."

Browning's "Development" records a son's profound gratitude for this paternal pedagogical method, for his father "by such slow and sure degrees / Permitting me to sift the grain from chaff" (89–90). Considering the many lessons—ethical as well as academic—that he learned, he asks, "Could not I have excogitated this / Without believing such men really were?" (103–4). His answer is clearly that he could not have, that his development, carefully managed by his father, the amateur but wholly dedicated scholar, depended on his believing, as he felt when reading Pope's version, "what history so true?" (39). Yet even this progressive introduction to a range of Homeric questions cannot prepare him for the fundamental epistemological challenge posed by a text that may have no author and no foundation in fact. Yopie Prins nicely articulates the period's struggles with the Homeric Question, which "haunted nineteenth-century Classical philologists, obsessively disassembling and reassembling Greek texts in the name of a poet who never quite existed in the authorial form they imagined."[3] Browning conveys the sense that reading Homer was a process, an activity that never ended, because the text and the author were as liable to transformation as the reader who first encountered Homer in childhood and is still questing after the Homeric text in his old age. "Development" thus also chronicles, finally, a failure of learning, a refusal to absorb or accept this "new knowledge."

Browning's anecdote tells a story not uncommon in the education of boys in the period, one in which any account of one's childhood, and more, one's "development" or transformation over time, is an account of Homeric instruction. Perhaps no one since Wolf did more to "unsettle" beliefs about the historical Troy than Heinrich Schliemann, and he too gives a detailed account of a classical education that determined, as Browning tacitly indicates regarding his own recollection, the future course of his life. Schliemann also begins with a summary of his father's education, in this case a somewhat inadequate one: "My father did not know Greek, but he knew Latin, and availed himself of every spare moment to teach it to me." Describing his childhood in Ankershagen, Germany, he continues, "Though my father was neither a scholar nor an archaeologist, he had a passion for ancient history.... He related to me with admiration the great deeds of the Homeric heroes and the events of the Trojan war, always finding in me a warm defender of the Trojan cause."[4]

Schliemann's father's lessons take as their starting point the absence of any record of a historical Troy. "With great grief I heard from him," he records, "that Troy had been so completely destroyed that it had disappeared without leaving any traces of its existence." His father's own insufficient education prevents him from proposing such increasingly scholarly assignments as those of Browning's father, who oversaw a progression from child's play to Pope to "Homer's mouth" to Wolf's treatise. (Indeed, Browning himself produced a controversial translation of Aeschylus.) What the senior Schliemann gives his son instead is a picture book:

> My joy may be imagined therefore, when, being nearly eight years old, I received from him, in 1829, as a Christmas gift, Dr. Georg Ludwig Jerrer's *Universal History*, with an engraving representing Troy in flames, with its huge walls and the Scaean gate, from which Aeneas is escaping, carrying his father Anchises on his back and holding his son Ascanius by the hand. I cried out, "Father, you were mistaken: Jerrer must have seen Troy, otherwise he could not have represented it here." "My son," he replied, "that is merely a fanciful picture."

While the scene that especially affects the young Schliemann is one representing filial piety (I discuss in chapter 4 the impact on Tennyson as well of the escape of Aeneas from raptured Troy), his account also suggests a struggle between father and son, played out under the elusive walls of Troy itself. Schliemann concludes this account of his formative education, one associated with frustration over various inadequacies, both in his father and in the historical record:

> But to my question, whether ancient Troy had such huge walls as those depicted
> in the book, he answered in the affirmative. "Father," retorted I, "if such walls

once existed, they cannot possibly have been completely destroyed: vast ruins of them must still remain, but they are hidden away beneath the dust of ages." He maintained the contrary, whilst I remained firm in my opinion, and at last we both agreed that I should one day excavate Troy.[5]

The contest between father and son over Trojan architectural remains is re-solved in the imagining by both of a future excavation. Certain even as a child of the existence of Trojan walls, Schliemann in his defiance of his father sets up a pattern for his later dealings with those (and there were many) who were skeptical of his archaeological discoveries. And the skepticism now extends to Schliemann's autobiographical account. One of his twentieth-century biographers, David Traill, holds that although this childhood exchange is "one of the best-known biographical 'facts'" about Schliemann, it is "entirely fictitious," "devised" to "foreshadow" his later achievements.[6] For my purposes, however, the issue is less the veracity of the anecdote than the necessity of having such an account at all.

Schliemann's British publisher, John Murray, opposed the inclusion of this autobiographical essay in the English translation of *Ilios*, but Schliemann felt it to be "as interesting as [it is] instructive; nay, for ages to come the book will be bought by thousands merely for the lessons in the autobiography."[7] Ever perceptive in matters of marketing (he made his fortune as a salesman), Schliemann found approbation in his anecdote from no less a connoisseur of the genre than Sigmund Freud. At the end of the century Freud wrote to a friend, "I gave myself a present, Schliemann's *Ilios*, and greatly enjoyed the account of his childhood. The man was happy when he found Priam's treasure, because happiness comes only with the fulfillment of a childhood wish."[8] According to Freud biographer Peter Gay, "The man in whose life history Freud took the greatest pleasure, and whom he probably envied more than any other, [was] Heinrich Schliemann." This had much to do with Freud's own predilections; he said of himself that his "partiality for the prehistoric" was "an addiction second in intensity only to his nicotine addiction." He owned so many ancient sculptures, friezes, and the like in his office that one patient, the Wolf Man, recalled that it seemed not like "a doctor's office but rather...an archaeolo-gist's study." Collecting antiquities, themselves the fruits of the nineteenth-century hunger for acquiring remnants of the past, was for Freud "a lifelong avocation."[9]

Freud told Stefan Zweig that he had, in his life, "read more archaeology than psychology," a claim that Gay suggests should be treated skeptically. But of course archaeology is akin to psychology, at least metaphorically. Or so Freud told the Wolf Man: "The psychoanalyst, like the archaeologist in his excavations, must un-cover layer after layer of the patient's psyche, before coming to the deepest, most valuable treasures." According to Gay, archaeological excavation was employed by Freud as his "master metaphor." Writing to a colleague about a patient's uncover-ing of a primal experience, Freud exulted, "I still scarcely dare to believe it properly. It is as if Schliemann had dug up Troy, considered legendary, once again."[10]

Browning's and Schliemann's narratives regarding their childhood apprehensions of a legendary Troy are offered as scenes of primal or originary experience. Their anecdotes differ in telling ways, but both reveal how teasing was the legend of Troy, how passionate was the desire to attain intimate knowledge of the place and its epic destruction. The rapture of Troy was, as they tell it, the central event in their education, a story seen by both as causative not only for their childhood development but for their adult projects and ambitions. The historical authenticity of the Trojan War, so pressing a concern for these boys, is still debated; one more recent chronicler of the city's fate notes, "To this day, no one can say with certainty what happened at Troy, or whether there was a Trojan War at all."[11] In the second section of this chapter I address the ways in which the fall of Troy, because of its very remoteness and indeterminacy, had direct and ongoing repercussions for the Victorians, as they came to produce a Troy as much invented as it was discovered. But in assessing Tennyson's knowledge of Troy, we need first to elucidate the poet's understanding of the challenges generally of attaining knowledge about remote historical periods and persons. I have noted some aspects of Tennyson's childhood education in classical materials; I turn now to his years at Cambridge to scan the range less of Tennyson's particular knowledge than the social and institutional conditions of its acquisition and articulation.

FEEDING THE HEART: EDUCATING TENNYSON

Eventually to be enrolled, according to G. M. Young, among the Hundred Greatest Men, Tennyson began meditating on the vexed benefits of legendary standing long before he was a candidate for any such roll call. His dramatic monologues, especially those begun in October 1833, immediately after news reached him of the death of his friend Arthur Henry Hallam, interest themselves in various ways in a speaker's relation to a song-built city (Troy or Thebes), threatened or disappeared at the time of the monologist's speaking. "Ulysses," "Tithonus," and "Tiresias," all old men, muse on personal and social devastations passed, passing, and to come, and it is this that renders them especially appropriate as versions of Tennyson's larger elegiac response to his friend's death. Critics have long probed the problematic of a young poet's retreat into the personae of old men who contemplate the attractions of death, generally offering versions of the argument that these speakers demonstrate, in the wake of the death of Hallam at twenty-two, the idea, according to Ricks, that "immortality would not simply in itself be a blessing" (*Poems*, 2:606). Culler is representative in declaring, "Arthur Hallam died in Vienna on September 15, 1833, and Tennyson immediately felt like an old man."[12] I hope to show, however, that Tennyson's personae might be seen to reflect most keenly less upon the appeal of mortality than upon the youthful scholarly enterprise and ambition of Hallam and his circle.

A letter from James Spedding, Tennyson's closest friend in college after Hallam, to W. H. Thompson indicates the tides that swept together Tennyson and various currents of thought. Writing from Cambridge, Spedding heads his letter with a fragment of Tennyson's "Palace of Art." He writes, "Only think of an 'Apostolic' dinner next Friday" and lists the names of those who will attend, including Hallam. He continues, "Only think of Heath's essay on Niebuhr the day after! Only think of the 'Palace of Art,' of which you may see part of a stanza, horribly misquoted, at...the beginning of this sheet! Only think of all these things!" (*Memoir*, 1:85). "All these things"—the gifted company of the Cambridge Apostles, the historical criticism of Barthold Georg Niebuhr, the poetry of Alfred Tennyson—wash together in their associations. These friends are immersed too in debates over utilitarian philosophy and political reform, since part of what Tennyson learned in the company of his colleagues at Trinity was how indivisible were social issues, classical scholarship, oratorical exhibitions, and his own poetry.

Spedding addresses his letter to Thompson, who was one day to become Regius professor of classics and master of Trinity. The bonds among these friends were forged through links of classical study, which was then at Cambridge of a "higher" standard than at Oxford and "very much centred at Trinity."[13] This preeminence was in part due to the influence of the scholars J. H. Monk and C. J. Blomfield, whose short-lived periodical of classical philology, the two-volume 1826 *Museum Criticum*, was in the library of Tennyson's father. In the years during which Tennyson and Hallam were students, however, classical instruction was dominated by two of the most noted classicists of the period, Julius C. Hare and Connop Thirlwall, who served as tutors at Trinity from 1822 to 1832 and 1827 to 1834, respectively. These were especially intense years for classical study at Trinity. Charles Merivale, a Cambridge Apostle who later wrote an eight-volume *History of the Roman Empire* and who at the shy poet's insistence recited Tennyson's prizewinning "Timbuctoo" (winner, we recall, of the Chancellor's Gold Medal in English Verse) at the awards assembly, recollected that the "fame" of the tutors Thirlwall and Hare "had animated the most ardent aspirants for classical distinctions...to acquire the most accurate appreciation of the ancient languages."[14] Tennyson's academic and social life was dominated by contemplation and debate over the classical world, especially Greek and Latin philology, innovatively conceived.

Hare and Thirlwall exerted a particular sway over the Apostles. Hare was tutor to John Sterling and Frederick Denison Maurice, the most influential of the early Apostles, while Tennyson and Hallam felt, according to fellow Apostle Richard Monckton Milnes, a "profound affection" for Thirlwall. Late in his life Milnes (by then Lord Houghton), a man renowned for his remarkably wide circle of impressive friends (we shall look at just one of his private parties, a dinner attended by Tennyson, Gladstone, and Henry James, in honor of Heinrich Schliemann), was asked "to name the most remarkable man whom he had known in his long experience." He replied "without a moment's hesitation": "Thirlwall." At Cambridge, Thirlwall's lectures were "crowded with the rising young classics of the time."[15] Both tutors valued the company of students, sometimes entertaining them in their rooms with such visitors as Coleridge or Wordsworth, whose work they were influential in promoting. Thirlwall was so close to many of the Apostles that he was considered an honorary member.[16] In an 1834 letter to Tennyson, R. J. Tennant called Thirlwall "subtle and quick" and proudly reported, "Thirlwall pays high compliments to the Apostles."[17] The phenomenon of this tuition was short-lived; Hare left to take a living at Hurstmonceaux in Sussex, and Thirlwall lost his position at Cambridge in 1834 because of his opposition to compulsory chapel and advocacy on the part of Dissenters who sought to take degrees.

Of Tennyson's and his own years at Cambridge, Edward FitzGerald recalled, "The German School, with Coleridge, Julius Hare, etc. to expound, came to reform all our notions" (*Memoir*, 1:36). Hare and Thirlwall published the first volume in 1828 of a translation of G. B. Niebuhr's *History of Rome*; the second volume followed in 1831 (Tennyson owned both volumes). This translation of Niebuhr revolutionized the discipline of historiography in England, marking, according to Leslie Stephen, "an epoch in English scholarship."[18] In a letter to Niebuhr's secretary, Thirlwall explains that philology had heretofore been brought into "disrepute" in Britain because "an infinitely minute branch of the subject has been severed from the rest and treated as the whole."[19] What Niebuhr championed was a "new philology," one that investigated multiple sources with searching, even skeptical critical attention, in order to develop an understanding of the totality of an ancient culture.[20] Philology, according to Niebuhr, maintains an "unbroken" relation to "the noblest and greatest nations of the ancient world, by familiarizing us, through the medium of grammar and history, with the works of their minds, and the cause of their destinies, as if there were no gulph dividing us from them."[21] Niebuhr attempted to gain an intimacy with the past by way of more minutely questioning and analyzing historical information, subjecting all evidence, however long established, to what was termed the "critical method." His methodology, introduced to England by way of Hare and Thirlwall, was not only significant for the Apostles ("Niebuhr for them was a god, who for a lengthy period formed all their sentiments," according to Frances Brookfield, relative of Tennyson's Cambridge friend William Brookfield), but was highly influential for nineteenth-century historians.[22] And indeed this method of "palingenesis," defined by Hayden White as "the pious reconstruction of the past in its integrity," has, White notes, "continued to dominate nostalgic historiography down to the present."[23]

Aside from its larger sphere of influence, the translation of Niebuhr held a significant local status; according to Thirlwall's biographer, it "became a revered text at both Oxford and Cambridge."[24] Under Thirlwall's influence, Milnes was one of several Apostles to study in Germany; in an 1829 letter to his father, written while Hallam sat with him reading "in my great-chair," he suggested to his father the possibility of going to Germany, as "a few months with such men as Niebuhr...must be of deep mental advantage."[25] The Niebuhr translation immediately aroused controversy, prompting a negative notice in the Tory *Quarterly Review*, to which Hare responded with a sixty-page pamphlet, the *Vindication of Niebuhr*, while Thirlwall appended a brief and withering retort. A letter of Hallam's to his father, the prominent Whig historian, indicates the closeness with which the Apostles attended to this reception: "Hare's pamphlet on Niebuhr seems to have been liked here; I thought it much too long, and declamatory. Thirlwall's concluding page was the sharpest, and perhaps the best part" (*Letters*, 288). Tennyson also attended closely to these scholarly controversies; Benjamin Jowett recalled the poet years later making "a very striking remark, namely, that 'the true origin of modern Biblical Criticism was to be ascribed not to Strauss, but to Niebuhr, who lived a generation earlier'" (*Memoir*, 2:463).

The influence of Hare and Thirlwall's translation of Niebuhr was expressed more publicly by Hallam in his undergraduate "Essay on the Philosophical Writings of Cicero," which won a Trinity College essay award in 1831, in which he refers in a footnote to the "wise impartiality" of this "philosophic historian" (*Writings*, 147n). I shall return to Hallam's essay on Ciceronian oratory in my discussion of Tennyson's "Ulysses," but it is crucial to stress how broad was the influence of these teachers and their historical method. A number of the Apostles of Tennyson's generation went on to produce works in classical history or philological research, very much in the vein of their tutors. Indeed, it is remarkable how many books in the aggregate they produced on the subject of either philology or classical history. Thirlwall himself, who eventually become bishop of St. David's in Wales, within a few years of his forced resignation from Cambridge produced an eight-volume *History of Greece* (1835–45). This work, though monumental, was soon eclipsed by the publication of his old school friend George Grote's twelve-volume *History of Greece* (1846–56). (As if to showcase how compatible was their scholarly overlap, Thirlwall and Grote are buried together in Westminster Abbey.) Thirlwall came also to preside over the founding in 1842 of the Philological Society of London, the majority of whose members had some connection to Trinity; this association would eventually produce (in answer to an exhortation from Trench, as I noted in the previous chapter) what became the *Oxford English Dictionary*.[26] It is possible, I believe, to see Tennyson's own turn to the monologic representation of such speakers as Ulysses, Tithonus, and Tiresias as a version of this larger attempt to attain and articulate an unmediated form of knowledge of ancient figures, inspired by a new philology that seeks, as Hare and Thirlwall's translation of Niebuhr has it, to recover "the cause of their destinies, as if there were no gulph dividing us from them." This sort of "classicality," as Carlyle termed it in his 1851 biography of the Apostle John Sterling, was not a matter of "mere gerundgrinding" but of "the practical conception, or attempt to conceive, what human life was in the epoch called classical."[27]

The translation, defense, and explication of Niebuhr's *History of Rome* constituted only part of the work Hare and Thirlwall undertook in the years they were tutors at Trinity. They produced translations of other German scholars and also founded a periodical as short-lived as its predecessor, the 1826 *Museum Criticum*, that their own teachers Monk and Blomfield had produced. Hare and Thirlwall's periodical, the *Philological Museum*, published in 1832–33, saw itself as a milestone in classical studies in Britain. The preface to the first volume deplored "the mite which England has contributed during the five years from 1825 to 1830 toward the increase of knowledge concerning classical antiquity" and remonstrated, "It is not well that we should import all our knowledge from abroad." Although its focus held to matters philological, the "main object" of the *Philological Museum*, according to Hare's preface, was "to illustrate the language, the literature, the philosophy, the history, the manners, the institutions, the mythology, and the religion of Greece and Rome"—in short, to pursue Niebuhr's philological method.[28] Thirlwall outnumbered any other contributor, with essays on such subjects as irony in Sophocles, vase painting, Attic Dionysia, and the figures of Ancaeus and Memnon; I draw from some of his writing in my discussion of "Tithonus." The periodical also included translations of Virgil by William Wordsworth and two "imaginary conversations," themselves possible precursors to the genre of the dramatic monologue, by Walter Savage Landor, a former student of Hare's.

In his first semester at Cambridge, Arthur Hallam wrote a letter to Gladstone expressing his initial unhappiness, calling Trinity "this odious place." After describing his tutors Hare ("the translator of *Niebuhr's Rome*") and William Whewell, also Tennyson's tutor, he complains of the Cambridge Union Debating Society, "What I have seen I dislike. The ascendant politics are *Utilitarian*."[29] Hallam came to revise many of his initial impressions, as he suspected he would (he describes himself here as one "not competent to say *much* from experience"), and he was to find colleagues greatly antagonistic toward utilitarianism (*Letters*, 243–44). Whewell, Thirlwall, and other faculty at Trinity were known for their fierce opposition to this philosophy, which they found morally bankrupt. As one historian of the college summarizes, "Hare and Thirlwall...and Whewell, foremost in England in German scholarship, led the attack on utilitarian thinking"; their students, among whom he singles out Tennyson and Hallam, "were in deep sympathy."[30]

The "ascendant politics" of Cambridge in these years came to be defined to a small degree by Hallam himself, influential as he was in debate and in friendship. Isobel Armstrong, in noting that Apostolic politics were anti-utilitarian and favored institutions such as the church and the monarchy, suggests, "It was a redefined conservatism of considerable sophistication; it required radical transformation at the same time as it required continuous and non-revolutionary change."[31]

For reasons discussed in chapter 1, I would term their affiliations Whig rather than conservative, but agree with Armstrong's characterization of the Apostolic commitment to continuous yet restrained change. In describing the poet's experience at Trinity, Tennyson's son draws together poetic, scholarly, and political interests: "He worked on at his poems, read his classics and history and natural science. He also took a lively interest in politics" (*Memoir*, 1:41). Subsequent readers have discounted this "lively interest," but his attentiveness to the tumult of reform politics has important consequences for a reading of the poems produced in and after this period.

Tennyson certainly followed events concerning the Great Reform Act, references to which run throughout Hallam's correspondence, at the least because his closest friends did so avidly; the poet himself was, according to his grandson, "an ardent supporter of Reform."[32] Indeed, it is important to recall how consequential this matter was generally and in what a fever pitch the bill was developed and passed; as Hallam Tennyson points out in his father's biography, "England was in a state of ferment with the hope or dread of the Reform Bill" (*Memoir*, 1:41). E. P. Thompson observes that England was "within an ace of revolution" for the first time since the seventeenth century.[33] The first version of the bill was rejected by the House of Lords, and this led to widespread and violent rioting. When local farmhouses were set ablaze, Tennyson went with Cambridge friends to help operate a fire engine. Spedding wrote to a friend, "Poets are not always living out of the world: for Alfred Tennyson, when we came within sight of the flames, was struck with the truth of the case: and declared that it was really time that these things should be put a stop to."[34]

Although Hallam was not initially impressed with the Cambridge Union Debating Society, he was to distinguish himself in its arena. The Apostles were impassioned discursive combatants, and many of them sought and attained distinction in the universitywide debates of the Cambridge Union. Their letters reverberate with descriptions of their oratorical victories, and in these rhetorical arts their tutors also led by example. Thirlwall was especially impressive in debate. John Stuart Mill, whose utilitarian beliefs were deeply antipathetic to the classicist, recalled debating Thirlwall in London in 1825. Mill disagreed strongly with his opponent, but he nevertheless recalls in his *Autobiography*, "Before [Thirlwall] had uttered ten sentences, I set him down as the best speaker I had ever heard, and I have never since heard any one whom I placed above him."[35] Thirlwall and Whewell had themselves been early members of the Cambridge Union, which was formed in 1815, when they were undergraduates; Thirlwall had served as secretary, Whewell as president. Although it was the university's "only organized diversion" and a central part of their activities and conversation, the organization was suspended in 1817. It was permitted to resume in 1822 provided that debates did not address contemporary subjects; discussion could not refer to events or questions unless they were twenty years past.[36] Hallam was accustomed to such restrictions, since they obtained at Eton, where he and Gladstone had been the foremost orators of the Eton Debating Society. Gladstone recalled, "We were excluded by a rule of needless...rigidity from touching any matter which had occurred within the last preceding fifty years. We were thus a great deal stinted in our choice of subjects, and occasionally obliged to seek out unusual paths."[37]

One of the "unusual paths" for the Etonians led to the private apartment of classmate James Milnes Gaskell, where, Gladstone recalls, "four or five of us would meet and debate without restraint the questions of modern politics." We might see in this retreat of a small band of informed and impassioned students into private rooms to discuss openly the issues that most interested them a foretaste of the gatherings of the Apostles.[38] Another "unusual path" was discursive. Although the Cambridge Union did not permit debates over current political questions, political issues such as reform found articulation in roundabout or subverted ways. Approved debating topics, seemingly remote historically, could often become veiled political ones. My readings of Tennyson's dramatic monologues featuring classical and contemporary speakers show that they forward political arguments and positions—not necessarily Tennyson's own, I would stress—even when they may not appear to, and that they too are exercises in oratorical prowess. In all of these debating organizations, the abiding purpose was the development of oratorical skills. *In Memoriam* recalls the Apostolic past, "Where once we held debate, a band / Of youthful friends" (87.21–22), and we know that Hallam was preeminent in these meetings. In a letter to his brother from this period, James Spedding referred to "Hallam's natural skill in the dazzling fence of rhetoric."[39] Hallam's essay on Ciceronian oratory won a college award, but he was as adept in the practice of oratory as in its theory, winning also in 1831 the college prize for declamation.

After the December 1832 elections following the passage of the Reform Bill, Hallam wrote a letter to James Milnes Gaskell congratulating him and Gladstone (Hallam's two closest friends at Eton) for having been elected to seats in Parliament. He ends the letter noting that he is also glad to see that Macaulay had won election: "One naturally wishes eminent men to hold their seats...especially in a Reformed House, where oratory and genius are likely to be at a discount." Hallam notes that, as a result of the election, Gaskell will soon be coming to London, and warns, "When you do I shall make you buy Alfred Tennyson's book, which may serve by way of recreation after hot stormy debates" (*Writings,* 704). Hallam reported the attainments of friends pursuing poetry to those pursuing politics, and vice versa. In a letter to Tennyson describing the opening of the reformed Parliament, Hallam invokes not only Macaulay, but also these intimate friends and former sparring partners in fervent political debate.

Hallam's oratorical ear was finely tuned. His "Essay on the Philosophical Writings of Cicero" centers in part on what he calls a "characteristic of Cicero's disposition": "Whatever he thought, whatever he experienced, assumed with him an oratorical form" (*Writings*, 150). Hallam defines the term "oratory," and his description will have a bearing on my reading of "Ulysses":

> It is the bringing of one man's mind to bear upon another man's will. We call up our scattered knowledge, we arrange our various powers of feeling, we select and marshal the objects of our observation, and then we combine them under the command of one strong impulse, and concentre their operations upon one point. That point is in every instance some change in the views, and some corresponding assent in the will of the person, or persons, whom we address. (*Writings* 151)

Hallam's investment in this definition can be marked in the slippage from describing an orator to describing *himself* as an orator ("we call up...we arrange...we select and marshal"). Two aspects of Hallam's argument about oratory are especially pertinent to my claims regarding the aims of the dramatic monologue. First, in both, the speech is instigated and sustained by its intention to convince another. The ambition for discursive efficacy, which is patent in oratory, less obvious in dramatic monologues, is paramount. Second, and closely related, oratory and the dramatic monologue are similar in their keen desire to provoke transformation; the "one point" on which all efforts are concentrated is to attain "some change in the views, and some corresponding assent in the will" of the auditor. In each case the speaker attempts to alter circumstances by altering persons, to effect social metamorphoses by inciting personal ones.[40]

Tennyson himself observed of the Apostles, "They used to make speeches—I never did,"[41] but we may hear in the dramatic monologues that followed upon Hallam's death an exploration of a politically and socially consequential experimentation with rhetorical dexterity. Unable, it appears, to enter into formal debate or presentation of his work (he had to resign from the Apostles because he would not make presentations, and he refused even to read his prizewinning "Timbuctoo" in college assembly), Tennyson performs his own manner of public articulation in his dramatic monologues, in which a speaker addresses an audience he or she hopes to move by speech. The ancient art of rhetoric and the new philology expounded by their tutors and exalted by these friends inform the dramatic monologues. It is from this educational experience that we must read Tennyson's classical monologues as graduating.

I have reviewed some dominant issues at Trinity College during Tennyson's years of affiliation, including reform politics, utilitarianism, and the new philology, all of which were debated intensively by colleagues who cared deeply about the art of the public articulation of ideas. Too often the subjects that so absorbed, indeed obsessed his friends are seen to have been scarcely apprehended by the young poet whom so many of them revered and whose poetry in turn fed the intellectual ferment of their time at Trinity. We are accustomed to seeing these years from the viewpoint of Tennyson's complex emotional attachment to Hallam, as indeed we must, but these emotional bonds are not separable from the intellectual ones. And chief among their academic interests was Greek literature. In a letter written at the end of his first term at Trinity, Hallam exclaims, "The Greek language I have worshipped and will worship with an unblenching loyalty—I love it for the swell and the majesty and interminable melody of its diction. I love it too for the grandeur of the associations that cluster and play round it" (*Letters*, 256). Early in *In Memoriam*, Tennyson recalls the conversations he and Hallam lingered over, when they not only discussed Greek philosophy and poetry but felt themselves wholly surrounded by it: "And many an old philosophy / On Argive heights divinely sang, / And round us all the thicket rang / To many a flute of Arcady" (23.21–24). The phenomenon of intense male homosocial bonding around shared intellectual pursuits, especially classical study, is well established, as academic passions can come to substitute or stand for erotic ones. In *Hellenism and Homosexuality in Victorian Oxford*, Linda Dowling investigates some of the ways "Greek studies operated as a 'homosexual code.'" She examines this intimacy between academic and affective pursuits later in the century, focusing on Walter Pater, John Addington Symonds, and Oscar Wilde, but her observations are instructive for this earlier period. In the Old Mortality Society at Oxford in the 1860s, which counted among its members Pater and Symonds, classical study provided, she notes, "masculine comradeship, a window or halcyon interval of particularly intense male homosociality."[42] Among the most compelling recent discussions of Tennyson are those that explore the way his evident passion for Hallam finds its own articulation in *In Memoriam*. These discussions have not addressed these questions sufficiently to the dramatic monologues, however, which, as I discuss in part 3, also articulate a range of nonnormative sexual identities.

Like Hallam, Tennyson was initially unhappy at Cambridge and wrote a bitter poem that he later regretted, titled "Lines on Cambridge in 1830." He complains about the college's isolation from national issues ("your manner sorts / Not with this age wherefrom ye stand apart") and concludes with the condemnation, issued to the institution as a whole, against "you that do profess to teach / And teach us nothing, feeding not the heart." Tennyson's poem calls for the academy to involve itself in the pressing political and social questions of the day, and yet, as he came to see, in their conversations and actions neither the students nor their most influential teachers stood apart from the age and its turmoil (Thirlwall, for example, lost his position four years later as a result of his principled advocacy of Dissenters). We also know that this intense atmosphere did, quite specifically, feed the poet's heart. In the years that Tennyson and Hallam spent there, Trinity College was the epicenter of a classicism at once radical and familiar, that is, epoch making, and yet part of their everyday lives and relations to one another; part also of the political foment of these years heady with reform debate. Tennyson's classical monologues stand as memorials to an intensely shared intellectual life that held Hallam at its center. Richard Monckton Milnes wrote in a letter to his father from Trinity on December 8, 1828, referring to Hallam, "Thirlwall is actually captivated with him. He really seems to know everything, from metaphysics to cookery. I dine with him, Thirlwall, and Hare (think what a *parti carré* we shall be!) on Wednesday." In another letter, dated October 22, 1829, he tells his father that Hallam is "in full force; his marvelous mind has been gleaning in wisdom from every tract of knowledge."[43] So impressive was Hallam that when Trench's brother Francis met him at Cambridge in November 1831, he grouped him, in a letter to his father, not with his fellow students but with his tutors: "I met Thirlwall, Whewell, and Hallam, all men of firstrate abilities."[44]

Tennyson had already produced, to the passionate approbation of Hallam, such poems as "The Lotos-Eaters" and "Oenone," and we may now see that his turn after his friend's sudden death to other characters in Greek literature and mythology, including Ulysses, Tithonus, and Tiresias, was a spontaneous and wholesale return to the scholarly absorptions of Hallam and his circle, just as his development of the monologue of St. Simeon Stylites had represented their theological speculations. Indeed, Thirlwall himself was a particular admirer of Tennyson's anchorite, according to Aubrey de Vere: "Carlyle says that it was 'Ulysses' which first convinced him that 'Tennyson was a true poet.' I remember hearing that Bishop Thirlwall made the same statement respecting 'St. Simeon Stylites'" (*Memoir*, 1:505). These dramatic monologues mark the poet's return to the complex network of classical and theoretical texts these friends shared and his turn, fitting emotionally and intellectually, to the Trojan diaspora, which is to say, to the aftermath of epic catastrophe. This condition of Homeric dispossession, powerfully shaped by the seismic destruction of a well-loved community, was now, after the death of the friend at the apex of that intellectual and social circle, Tennyson's own.

LOCATING VICTORIAN TROY

Tennyson had a particular affinity for Troy, but throughout his life he was preoccupied with the illusory creation of a number of other cities and, as powerfully, their destruction.[45] Repeatedly, a Tennysonian city's prosperity is lavish and fleeting, dispersing into the smoke and mist out of which it drew form. The epigram at the head of Tennyson's prizewinning collegiate effort, "Timbuctoo," so admired by Hallam, reads, "Deep in that lion-haunted inland lies / A mystick city, goal of high emprise." The couplet is attributed by Tennyson to Chapman (the great translator of Homer), but its source has never been located, and many suspect that Tennyson wrote it himself. What seems to me to be certain about the epigram is that it goes to the heart of Tennyson's own "goal of high emprise," to the aim of his own highest ambitions and enterprise. For Tennyson seeks repeatedly, especially in his early poetry (though the project is also at the center of *Idylls of the King*), to locate mystick cities. He is recurrently drawn to these communities, with their fantastical origins and ends: Timbuctoo, Thebes, Troy, Atalantis, Eldorado,

"Old Memphis" ("Old Memphis hath gone down: / The Pharaohs are no more" ["A Fragment," 27–28]), Camelot. These are cities of mythical or historically remote origin, each in its prime a glittering, lofty, often many-towered metropolis. This dynamic shimmers at the center, of course, of *Idylls of the King*, and that epic provides another example of a story concerned with the forces that will break apart idealized civic institutions.

In "Timbuctoo," the speaker, musing on "legends quaint and old" (16), apostrophizes:

> Divinest Atalantis, whom the waves
> Have buried deep, and thou of later name
> Imperial Eldorado roofed with gold:
> Shadows to which
>
> . . .
>
> Men clung with yearning Hope which would not die. (22–25, 27)

He links this "yearning" to that of a "pale Priestess," desperately clasping the "marble knees" of her idol, staring into its lightless eyes, even as her "great City" is riven by earthquake. The speaker identifies the belief in these mystick, legendary cities as foundationless, even as he continues in his own search of them, asking the continent of "Wide Afric" if it contains such a place as those found in the "elder World": "'Or is the rumour of thy Timbuctoo / A dream as frail as those of ancient Time?'" (56–61). Suggesting that the pale priestess is perhaps answered by her unyielding idol, the speaker's question is answered by a Seraph, who appears in a flash of light, bearing still more brilliant insight. He is shown a place that looks like so many of Tennyson's cities:

> methought I saw
> A wilderness of spires, and chrystal pile
> Of rampart upon rampart, dome on dome,
> Illimitable range of battlement
> On battlement, and the Imperial height
> Of Canopy o'ercanopied. (158–63)

These spires, ramparts, domes, battlements, and canopies seem to multiply exponentially upon themselves, fronted by "the glory of the place," a "pillared front of burnished gold, / Interminably high" (171–72). He falls before this vision, but the vision vouchsafes for him his own discursive puissance: the Seraph announces, "I have filled thy lips with power" (211).

The "young Seraph" gives the speaker a vision of the city, and the poem becomes a hymn to myth itself, to the "great vine of *Fable*" (218). What he views is possessed by being seen, even as the speaker is possessed by his vision; Timbuctoo becomes "my City" (235). And yet as soon as it is apprehended or known, its doom is sealed. After the apostrophe "Oh City! oh latest Throne!" (236), the speaker announces, "the time is well-nigh come / When I must render up the glorious name / To keen *Discovery*" (238–40). With the speaker's vision of it, *Fable* yields wholly to *Discovery*, and it is clear that the two cannot coexist, that discovery brings fable literally to earth. Timbuctoo is culled from the poet's earlier "Armageddon," yet it is not divine Revelation that destroys this city but prosaic *Discovery*. Due to a failure in himself rather than in the place, the discoverer will find not "brilliant towers" (240) but mud huts.

Tennyson regretted "Timbuctoo" ever afterward as a poem he was compelled to write, calling it in a letter to Hallam's father after his friend's death a "wild and unmethodized performance,"[46] but its concerns haunt other poems of the late 1820s. "In Deep and Solemn Dreams," written in this period, also concerns dream visions of a city, with a civic architecture not unlike that of Timbuctoo or the later Camelot, boasting "pinnacles, and airy halls / With fairy fretwork on the walls, / And rows of pillars high and light" (7–9). Here too the inhabitants of the city are spectral; the speaker visiting the dream city is greeted by "sunny faces of lost days, / Long to mouldering dust consigned" (14–15). This is the luminous home of the long dead who live, like the city, "but in the mind." Though he calls the dreams deep and solemn, the terms do not accord with these airy heights and bright inhabitants. Rather, he wakes to the deep and solemn, the "hollow dark I dread" (59).

A pattern whereby the poetic subjectivity must make its grim return from the imaginative realm to the disappointingly pedestrian was established in boyhood. While on childhood visits to the seashore at Mablethorpe with his family, Tennyson imaginatively enacted the battles of the *Iliad*, as Browning when a child had in his parlor with his pets. In his "Lines: Manchester Athenaeum Album, 1850," which Ricks dates to 1833 (noting that Tennyson visited there in March of that year), the poet recalls:

> Here often, when a child, I lay reclined,
>   I took delight in this locality.
> Here stood the infant Ilion of the mind,
>   And here the Grecian ships did seem to be.
>
> And here again I come, and only find
>   The drain-cut levels of the marshy lea,—
> Grey sandbanks, and pale sunsets,—dreary wind,
>   Dim shores, dense rains, and heavy-clouded sea! (1–8)

Tennyson's infant Ilion is destroyed by his adult perceptions. The thrilling shore, ranged with "Grecian ships" massed around a besieged town, is reduced to a "grey," "pale," "dreary," "dim," "dense," "heavy-clouded" marshland, described by him in an 1833 letter as "a miserable bathing place on our bleak, flat Lincolnshire coast" (Tennyson, *Letters*, 1:88). Published during what has been called Tennyson's *annus mirabilis*, the year in which he published *In Memoriam*, married, and assumed the laureateship, this poem describes less the diminishment of the landscape than the failure of the mind any longer to transform it. The poem appears to provide one possible answer to the question he asks in the late and highly personal poem "The Ancient Sage" (1885): "What had he loved, what had he lost, the boy?" (227). But in spite of the poem's own focus on the stark alterations he finds upon his return, the reduced nature of the place and the self that beholds it, I would like to dwell on the former scene of delight, since his other figurations of Ilion show us that the infant mind vividly beheld the city, and its besiegers and the place can never lose that former glory. As Tennyson himself determines, "Yet though perchance no tract of earth have more / Unlikeness to the fair Ionian plain, / I love the place that I have loved before" (9–11). "Mablethorpe" articulates a consistent pattern, most elaborately developed in *Idylls of the King*, whereby a dream city, magnificent, pillared, lofty, splendid, is devastated, and so joins a poetic empire of great and disappeared cities, glorious and irretrievable.

In these early poems, Tennyson establishes a dichotomy between the escape to visionary cities and the return to the dark, dull, utterly diminished realm of actual experience. This divide between the lush worlds of poetic imagination and the disappointing world of prosaic fact is certainly one of Tennyson's most traceable links to his Romantic predecessors, especially Keats and Shelley; it is also a dichotomy that may be seen to characterize the question, for the Victorians, of Troy itself. The debate over the existence of Troy was one to which Victorian Britain returned incessantly, one that intensified in the wake of the claims of Heinrich Schliemann, who in 1870 offered to the world a Troy of exceedingly small scale, without particular architectural distinction, a Troy welcomed by some, reviled by others. Those claiming that the *Iliad* recorded historic fact found a notable advocate in Gladstone, whose credo is summarized in the introduction of his 1876 *Homeric Synchronism*. He insists that "the poems of Homer are in the highest sense historical," and that "there was a solid nucleus of fact in [Homer's] account of the Trojan war."[47] Previous to this, Grote had articulated the claim that the tale of Troy divine, however compelling, is nevertheless a myth: "Taken as a special legendary event, [the Trojan War] is indeed of wider and larger interest than any other [legend], but it is a mistake to single it out from the rest as if it rested upon a different and more trustworthy basis."[48]

What all certainly knew was that the myth of Ilion is a myth also of its poet. Gladstone's reverence for Homer was as deep and abiding as Tennyson's, but Gladstone's conception of the poet's inspiration and ambition differed. At points in the course of the century a debate ensued over whether Homer's Troy was a product solely of the poet's imagination or a place that had existed historically, about which the poet left a sometimes faithful, sometimes fabulous record. These two views came to be espoused respectively by Tennyson and Gladstone, and it is important to understand their positions, as they have significant bearing on

Tennyson's poetics and contributed to the larger question of how the role of poetry was itself to be understood. For Gladstone, the *Iliad* provided a historical record based on facts that were recoverable, and this historical fidelity offered an example of the poet's supreme art. It should be noted that Tennyson's teachers held something of a wary compromise position; writing a few years earlier than Grote, Thirlwall in his *History of Greece* pronounced, "We...conceive it necessary to admit the reality of the Trojan war as a general fact; but beyond this we scarcely venture to proceed a single step. Its cause and its issue, the manner in which it was conducted, and the parties engaged in it, are all involved in an obscurity which we cannot pretend to penetrate." In this Thirlwall follows Niebuhr, who declares in his *History of Rome*, "Mythical the Trojan war certainly is, so that not a single point among its incidents can be distinguished as more or less probable than the rest: yet it has an undeniable historical foundation."[49] On some level Tennyson may have subscribed to this commonsensical dialectic, but he clearly held in a larger sense to the primacy of the poet's imagination in fashioning both the city and its narratives.

In the early 1830s, when Tennyson was writing many of his poems on Hellenic characters and situations, the state of the Victorian study of mythology was in its infancy; one reviewer noted in 1831, "Ancient mythology seems to be considered as a licensed field for the wildest conjectures and the most farfetched combinations and etymologies; and there are few books on the subject which can be safely consulted by the general reader."[50] Among the more flamboyant writers on the subject was Jacob Bryant, who in the late eighteenth century, Turner notes, "started a brief pamphlet war by suggesting on geographical premises that the *Iliad* was historical fantasy," providing what Paden calls "a reasoned denial that Troy had ever existed."[51] It is likely that Bryant's arguments regarding Troy, which continued to be a subject of debate through midcentury, in part due to the vociferous attacks and counterattacks it spawned, would have been known to Tennyson, since his father owned a still more outlandish work of Bryant's, the three-volume *A New System*, which I consider briefly in relation to "Tithonus."[52] Excited by recent geographical studies based on the arguments of J. B. Le Chevalier, who claimed to have located Troy, Bryant's Trojan pamphlets enter chiefly into details about the topography of the *Iliad*. Skeptical of any exploration yielding a location for Troy, he declared, "I believe that I am the first of the moderns who have thus ventured to entertain these doubts," and his conclusions about Troy are forthright: "I am confident it never existed." The volumes of polemic produced by Bryant and others are in many ways absurd; for example, he painstakingly computes Helen's age, to show that she would have been almost seventy when abducted by Paris, and is met with arguments in kind. But in spite of his obsession with the dates and calibrations pertinent to the story of Troy, he is insistent on a conclusion opposed by his own extremely literal methodology, one so wedded to what facts he can glean: "The whole is a figment, and every step that we take is upon fairy ground."

Fairy ground is the same ethereal matter that underpins many of Tennyson's early poems, the ground also upon which his epic Camelot rises. Bryant's conclusion is stated in more absolute terms than those later employed by Niebuhr, Thirlwall, Grote, Ruskin, Pater, or Symonds, each of whom, among many others, also weighed the evidence at hand. While these comparatively measured critics generally allowed for the possibility of some nucleus of fact at the center of the fable, they nevertheless emphasized the primacy of the poetic imagination in the construction of the city of Troy, a position put most baldly by Bryant: "With the poet it began and ended."[53]

It is certain that Tennyson was acquainted with the work of Thomas Keightley, whose 1831 *Fairy Mythology* quickly became, according to Armstrong, "almost a cult book for the Apostles."[54] In Hare's 1832 preface to the *Philological Museum*, he singles out Keightley's 1831 *The Mythology of Ancient Greece and Italy* as proof that "the spirit of philological criticism, if it has been dormant, is reawakening amongst us."[55] Thirlwall wrote to Keightley the same year, "Your book is one of those which encourage me to hope that the next generation will be much wiser than our own."[56] Keightley saw his work as ordering the chaos of Greek and Latin mythology, but he extends his claims still further, exhibiting a faith in destiny perhaps acquired in the course of his studies: "I was destined to be the introducer of mythology into our literature." In the preface to the 1866 third edition, Keightley claims that his work was a novel conception: "I count it no vanity to state the simple truth, that [this book]...stands alone in European literature. Previous to its appearance mythology lay, as I may say, in a chaotic state.... I gave order to the whole, and my original discoveries were not few."[57]

In his 1831 edition of *The Mythology of Ancient Greece and Italy*, Keightley uses Troy to define mythology itself; he writes in a footnote at the start of his study, "The Trojan war, for example, is what we term mythic; not that it was not in all probability a real event, but because so much fable manifestly enters into it, that it is impossible to fix on any one circumstance which can be decidedly taken for truth." Here he seems to hedge between two conceptions of the Trojan War, which he feels must have been a "real event," and yet cannot have been, since it is "impossible" to identify even "one circumstance" as factual or true. The influential Keightley uses this inbuilt ambiguity, this straddling between patent fact and still more patent fiction, to establish the defining quality of "mythology itself."[58]

Keightley's reasonable surmises, and even the far-fetched and improbable claims of Bryant, anticipate the school of reading that sees Homeric Troy as, in Grote's terms, "a past which never was present." The first two volumes of Grote's *History of Greece* provided a highly influential account of myth's foundation in the imagination. Of the Trojan War he writes:

It is in the eyes of modern inquiry essentially a legend and nothing more. If we are asked whether it be not a legend embodying portions of historical matter,

and raised upon a basis of truth,—whether there may not really have occurred
at the foot of the hill of Ilium a war purely human and political, without gods,
without heroes, without Helen, ... without Ethiopians under the beautiful son
of Eos [Memnon, son of Eos and Tithonus], ... if we are asked whether there was
not really some such historical Trojan war as this, our answer must be, that as the
possibility of it cannot be denied, so neither can the reality of it be affirmed.

He concedes that it is not impossible that Troy existed, yet neither is it inevitable.
Indeed, for a historian especially Troy is the province of the poet's imagination:
"History recognizes neither Troy the city, nor Trojans, as actually existing." And he
warns historians against overestimating their own analytic capacities, commenting, "Whoever therefore ventures to dissect Homer...and to pick out certain
portions as matters of fact, while he sets aside the rest as fiction, must do so in full
reliance on his own powers of historical divination, without any means either of
proving or verifying his conclusions."[59] Grote may have been more skeptical than
those he influenced; writing decades later John Addington Symonds stresses the
realistic impression given by the details of the story: "The wanderings of Odysseus, the Trojan War" have "the appearance of dimly-preserved or poetised history." Symonds posits, "A nucleus of fact may...have formed the basis of certain
myths."[60] Turner, in claiming that Grote's work "constituted the most extensive
and learned discussion of Greek myth and mythic thought generally to appear
in English," shows that his "concept of myth as the product of the imagination
became a major factor in the aesthetic criticism of Greek myths by John Ruskin,
Walter Pater, and J. A. Symonds."[61]

Such temporizing views found vigorous and voluminous opposition from
Gladstone. Drawing from his own experience with public oratory, Gladstone felt
that, according to Turner, "the speeches and orations rang true to life." This led
him "to reject Grote's mythical view of Troy" and to anticipate the claims of
Schliemann and other archaeologists regarding the existence of a historic Troy.[62]
"In his mind," remarks Jenkyns, "Homer and politics were intertwined."[63] Gladstone promulgated a variety of controversial positions throughout his Homeric
writings, perhaps foremost being his theory that Homer's works constituted
a divine revelation corresponding to that of Hebrew scripture. His arguments
often had other applications as well, such as the promotion of his political theories
and of expanding Homeric study in the universities. Gladstone's claims merit our
brief attention, as they help to illuminate Tennyson's views on Troy, not least because of their clear differences from one another, but also because when Gladstone
writes of Homer, what he often comes to define more generally is the role of the
poet in civic life.

In *Juventus Mundi* (1869), at once a condensation and revision of arguments
forwarded in his three-volume *Studies on Homer and the Homeric Age* (1858),
Gladstone insists, "It cannot be too strongly affirmed, that the song of Homer
is historic song. Indeed he has probably told us more about the world and its

inhabitants at his own epoch, than any historian that ever lived."[64] Homer's work unequivocally comprises "historic song" (which we might contrast with what Symonds called "poeticized history"), and indeed is so closely bound to historical fact and verifiable accuracy that it exceeds the work of any historian in the history of that discipline. The poet, "it cannot be too strongly affirmed," is not merely indistinguishable from the historian, but immeasurably superior. Moreover, the poet forwards a distinct, almost statesmanly cause: for Homer, Gladstone argues in the 1890 *Landmarks of Homeric Study*, "it appears that nationality, or patriotism, supplies his governing aim." This leads to a generalized definition of the central aim of poetry itself: "The Poet seeks to fashion his country, to glorify his country."[65] The poet comes to bear a striking resemblance to the prime minister.

Perhaps also reflecting his own political experience, in which all good men come to the aid of their party, Gladstone reads Homer as wholly promoting the interests of the Greeks, or Achaeans. Debate over whether Homer is impartial in his depiction of the Trojans is of long standing, and Gladstone is hardly alone in detecting a bias on Homer's part in favor of the fleet at Troy's shores, but he seems to go further than the poet in excoriating the residents of that sad city. The Trojans he deems inferior in every possible respect: "There is not a single Trojan chieftain who has the true Achaian fibre." Troy itself, although credited as a historic reality, is virtually inconsequential, since its system of government and residents are so unappealing. Indeed, the inferiority of the Trojans is itself proof of the historical reality of the *Iliad*, as he had declared in his 1858 *Studies on Homer*: "Nowhere do the signs of historic aim in Homer seem to me more evident, than in his very distinct delineations of national character on the Greek and Trojan part respectively" (*SH*, 3:190). "In the 'Tale of Troy Divine,'" Gladstone insists, "Troy is wholly subservient. For Troy, and for the war of Troy, the Poem has no beginning, and no ending. Not so for the glory and character of the 'man' whose 'wrath' the Poet sang."[66] Unlike Tennyson, who wept at Virgil's representation of the rapture of the city he always held as divine, Gladstone seems to revel in its destruction, or perhaps even to go further and count it insignificant. Gladstone's own partisanship, as so often, is palpable—again, as surely befits so vigorous a politician. Indeed, he links the poet's patriotism to his own: "We may trace with reasonable pleasure an original similitude between the Homeric picture and the best ideas of our European and our British ancestry."[67] Gladstone joins with Grote and many others in viewing an ancient Greek culture they consider proto-democratic as ancestor to the burgeoning democratic culture of Victorian Britain.[68] In turning his back so fully on Troy, however, Gladstone is casting away without a backward glance the tradition, spanning centuries, of London itself as Troynovant, through a line of succession from Troy to imperial Rome to London.

The differences between Gladstone and Tennyson on the strangely pressing matter of Homeric Ilion came to be directly contested in the course of an evening in 1865 recognized as so "memorable" as to require a lengthy narrative by one of its participants or, more specifically, witnesses, the young John Addington Symonds. Symonds, recently graduated and, as his proud father tells Tennyson, "an Oxford first class man," was not yet decided on the career that was to include his own major study of Greek poetry.[69] As the son of another guest, the Bristol physician Dr. John Symonds, he was invited to join the dinner party at the sculptor Thomas Woolner's for postprandials. The guests included William Holman Hunt and Gladstone, but the draw for Symonds, as presumably for any promising young man eyeing a career in letters, was Tennyson. Symonds's account revels in specificity; he knew already, presaging his later writing of learned and in some ways personal and impressionistic multivolume studies of Greek literature and Renaissance art, the value of details.

The younger Symonds arrived while the party, or rather Tennyson and Gladstone (as Symonds calls them, "the two great people" [1:594]), were arguing over Governor Eyre's recent violent suppressive acts in Jamaica. Tennyson supported Eyre, along with Carlyle and others who did not share Gladstone's growing opposition toward colonial governance. Symonds, in attempting to "fix the difference between the two men," compares their modes of debate ("Gladstone arguing, Tennyson putting in a prejudice,... Gladstone full of facts, Tennyson relying on impressions"). In his desire to arrive at what essential differences mark the poet as opposed to the statesman, the young man strikes at details physical and even physiognomic, coming to contrast not only their conversation and political viewpoints, but also the timbre of their voices, the size of their hands, the shape of their heads. Tennyson's "head is domed, quite the reverse of G[ladstone]'s...strong in the coronal, narrow in the frontal regions, but very finely moulded," Symonds observes, whereas Gladstone has a forehead that is "broad and massive" (1:593, 592).

Gladstone, skilled in debating opponents of far greater experience and aptitude than Tennyson, easily had the upper hand. Symonds reports, "Gladstone is in some sort a man of the world, Tennyson a child & treated by him like a child" (1:593–94). As the party moved from the dining room to join the women in the drawing room, Tennyson became still more infantile. Put out by Woolner, in Tennyson's brief absence, having given Gladstone a notebook with some of his translations from the *Iliad*, Tennyson refused to read it to the group, "standing in the room with a pettish voice & jerking his arms & body from the hips. 'No, I shan't read it: it's only a little thing—must be judged by comparison with the Greek— can only be appreciated by the difficulties overcome'" (1:594). Robert Bernard Martin and Gerhard Joseph, in discussions of this scene, note that it is Gladstone's reading of the translation that upsets Tennyson, but it seems finally that, far from wanting to keep the translation from Gladstone, he wants only Gladstone, along with Dr. Symonds, to hear it. Dr. Symonds, exhibiting what must have been a considerable talent with distraught patients, begins to soothe Tennyson, assuring him of an understanding audience. His request for a reading is answered ("Yes, you & Gladstone—but the rest don't understand it"), and Tennyson returns to the dining room accompanied by Gladstone and the doctor, with the young Symonds following surreptitiously.[70]

If Tennyson was a "pettish" and grudging reader, Gladstone was an equally pettish and grudging audience: "It was always to air some theory of his own that he broke Tennyson's recital; & he seemed listening only in order to catch something up." Symonds observes that Gladstone's discursive mode, though gaining the upper hand in discussions of political matters, was less engaging when discussing literary ones: "Gladstone continually interrupted him with small points about words. He has a combative House of Commons mannerism." While Gladstone's stress on the verifiability of the Homeric story predated the fact-finding efforts of Schliemann and other archaeologists (which he largely welcomed), Tennyson clearly was confounded by the dramatic shifts in the understanding of Homer that had already occurred in his lifetime. Symonds, fresh from attaining his first at Oxford, cannot help but sound condescending: "Tennyson was sorely puzzled about the variations in Homeric readings & interpretations. 'They change year after year. What we used to think right in my days, I am now told is all wrong. What is a poor translator to do?'" (1:595–96).

The laureate's complaint about alterations in the theories of Homer and Homeric translation in the course of his lifetime is sincere, although it seems not to have interfered with his satisfaction in his own production. Symonds continues, "But he piqued himself very much on his exact renderings: 'These lines are word for word. You could not have a closer translation: one poet could not express another better. There, those are good lines'" (1:596). Tennyson frequently complimented his own verse; some admirers found this justifiable or endearing, while others, like Symonds, found their own admiration waning as such words were uttered. And yet Tennyson's self-satisfaction points to a contradiction in his position that may have been insurmountable, between the desire to produce an exact, almost schoolboy rendering and the desire, as a poet, to "express another" poet. Indeed, aside from two brief passages and a few other fragments, Tennyson never did formally translate more than a few passages from Homer. It is in his dilations on Homer in his dramatic monologues, conceived long before this awkward dinner party, that he succeeds, not as a direct translator, but as a poet expressing his original rendition of another poet's work.

That evening Tennyson understandably "invited criticism," since he was not in fact giving exact renderings; thus Gladstone in effect kept catching him out at being a poet. Symonds records their bickering: "Gladstone w[oul]d object; 'but you will say Jove & Greeks: can't we have Zeus & Achaeans?' 'But the sound of Jove! Jove is much softer than Zeus—Zeus—Zeus.'... Much was said about the proper means of getting a certain pause, how to give equivalent suggestive sounds & so on" (1:596). Tennyson repeats "Zeus" over and over to demonstrate the harshness of its monosyllable; his attention is to sound, his profoundest lyric commitment. Gladstone declares a few years later, in his 1868 *Juventus Mundi*, his preference for

Greek words, averring, "I have felt great embarrassment, in common I suppose with many more, in consequence of the unsettled and transitory state of our rules and practice with respect to Greek names, and to the Latin forms of them." He continues, "I follow many high authorities in adopting generally the names of the Greek deities and mythological personages, instead of the Latin ones." In this he follows Keightley, who wrote, "I must...claim the credit of having been the first who ventured to use the Greek names of the Grecian deities in our language—a practice now grown so common."[71] This practice is alluded to by Tennyson in his 1868 dramatic monologue "Lucretius," in which the speaker's confusion over the matter of nomenclature is a sign of his more general disorientation. Lucretius, having reflected on Venus, moves to "another of our Gods, the Sun, / Apollo, Delius, or of older use / All-seeing Hyperion—what you will—" (124–26). The speaker's search for the appropriate name follows immediately after his recognition "my mind / Stumbles, and all my faculties are lamed" (122–23). While the Latin version might make sense in the monologue of a Roman poet, so might the Greek, and thus this passage is representative of the Victorian poet's defensive attempt to evade criticism on this linguistic point.

At Woolner's dinner party, Gladstone holds his position regarding his preference for Greek words, citing Philip Stanhope Worsley's recent translations of Homer into Spenserian stanza: "Well, Mr. Worsley gave us Achaeans." "Mr. Worsley has chosen a convenient long metre," retorts Tennyson, "he can give you Achaeans, & a good deal else" (1:596). Tennyson maintained that the most suitable form in English for Homeric translation was blank verse, feeling that English hexameters were unacceptable. In "On Translations of Homer: Hexameters and Pentameters" (1863), he denounces "Barbarous experiment, barbarous hexameters," and asks, "When was a harsher sound ever heard, ye Muses, in England?" (6, 3).[72] Herbert Paul in 1893 recalled of Tennyson, "Hexameters, especially in rendering Homer, were his soul's abhorrence."[73]

Jenkyns notes that over a twenty-year period in the middle of the nineteenth century a dozen translations of the *Iliad* were published: "It was somehow assumed that translating Homer was a worthwhile activity, like doing charitable works."[74] Determining the meter appropriate for rendering Homer into English was one of the period's high debates, as Matthew Arnold's controversial lectures (*On Translating Homer: Three Lectures* [1861] and *On Translating Homer: Last Words* [1862]) demonstrate. Arthur Coleridge reports Tennyson commenting, "Since Matthew Arnold's lectures on Homer, a new translation has appeared annually in [America]. It would take me ten years to translate the *Iliad* into Bible English," while Tennyson told H. D. Rawnsley that he would not produce a full translation of Homer, "although perhaps none but a poet could do it."[75] Herbert Paul lamented after the poet's death, "It is a commonplace and a platitude to lament that we have not more of Tennyson's Homeric translation."[76] Gladstone apparently would have welcomed more translations from Tennyson, to whom he wrote, in a postscript in a letter of December 19, 1873, "I wonder whether you have ever tried the last line of the *Iliad*."[77]

In debate with Tennyson at Woolner's 1865 dinner, Gladstone displayed a fairly technical knowledge not only of Homeric language but of persons and customs, explaining at one point, in reference to the description in book 6 of the "women of Troy with their trailing garments" (*Iliad* 6:441) that "a long trailing dress was not Achaean but Ionion." Tennyson's understanding of the same garment is far less academic; Symonds continues, "Tennyson did not heed this super-subtle rendering, but said 'Ah! there's nothing more romantic than the image of those women floating along the streets of Troy with their long dresses flying out behind them—windy Troy—I daresay it was not windier than other places, but it stood high, open to the air. As a schoolboy I used to see them. A boy of course imagines something like a modern town'" (1:596). Gladstone's super-subtlety forwards an ideal of scholarly accuracy (although many have questioned whether his own work came near to attaining it); his pedantry is a mark of a lifetime's obsessive delineations among these words and these various peoples, down to their local costume. We have no record comparable to Symonds's for Tennyson's elaboration on the garments of Troy, one that cares nothing for "exact renderings" but instead follows an image of the women of Troy, than which "there's nothing more romantic," floating along the streets of a city that Tennyson feels himself to have beheld. As a schoolboy, he "used to see them," as if he had floated alongside those beautiful and ethereal figures. Indeed, he attributes the shape and strange lift of their clothing to the city that is indistinguishable from its epithet: "windy Troy" is the train his thought follows as his eyes followed the floating trains of their dresses. And though Schliemann had not yet located what he claimed were the streets of Troy or calibrated its dimensions, Tennyson knows already how it towered over the plain, knows "it stood high, open to the air," and, beyond this, knows the slightest effects of that troubled air on its residents.

Robert Bernard Martin's and Gerhard Joseph's discussions of this evening both agree that there existed, in the adult interactions of the poet laureate and the prime minister, what Martin calls "a curious, unstated rivalry that had sprung up years before when Tennyson displaced Gladstone in Hallam's regard"; Joseph aptly labels it a "Homeric competition."[78] Hallam had been Gladstone's closest friend at Eton but transferred his attentions to Tennyson soon after meeting him at Cambridge, and both critics consider the many subsequent decades of interaction between Gladstone and Tennyson as continuing an indirect but nonetheless active competition for the primacy of Hallam's memory. Tennyson and Gladstone's relationship was at once distant and intimate, and certainly of long standing. Circumstances, in the form of a shared friend, brought them early into one another's ken, and, as they grew in stature, concurrently but separately, circumstances kept them tethered. In battling over the minutiae of translation these eminent men were indeed wrestling over their friend's memory, but it is important to recognize that the match occurred in the ring of classical study, an arena associated for both with Hallam. Tennyson and Gladstone, flanked by Symonds *père et fils*, were in fact genuinely discussing Troy, its appearance and its inhabitants. And in considering Troy each felt, with some justification, that the other was trespassing on territory he considered his own; this might echo or run parallel to another, deeper sense of territorialism with regard to their mutual friend, but it is also a separable debate, one it is vital to read on its own terms.

In discussing Troy, Tennyson and Gladstone were tacitly avoiding volatile contemporary issues on which they disagreed, and yet few topics could have been as politically charged as that of Homeric poetry. "Debate over the classics could in a more or less exclusive manner," remarks Turner, "explore potentially disruptive modern public topics that were carefully concealed in the garb of the ancients."[79] Gladstone's own tendency to look to Homer to establish precedents for contemporary political behavior was remarked by many of his contemporaries. Writing of Gladstone's analyses of ethics in Homer, Benjamin posits, "We have a suspicion that the elevated sentiments and character he attributes to Homer are of post-Homeric origin; that they are suggested by a culture of far later age or spring from the natural goodness of heart of the critic himself."[80] In his copious writings Gladstone tirelessly forwards the idea that Homer's Greeks were proto-Christian and also proto-democratic. He reads Ulysses, skilled in addressing assemblies of men, as an exemplum of the liberal politician. Tennyson's reading of the same figure differs sharply, and yet his is a representation, I argue, as politically resonant as the prime minister's. Gladstone was unimpressed by Troy's aristocratic system of rule, dominated by one family, headed in the generation of the Trojan War by Priam, brother of Tithonus; I show in part 3 how deep ran Tennyson's sympathy for this dynastic line. For Gladstone, the city of Troy and the events narrated in the *Iliad* have a factual basis; he therefore seeks information about the daily lives of living people who were not solely, or merely, the poet's creations. The polis holds primacy over the poet. For Tennyson, priority rests with the poet; for him the profound appeal of Troy, its representational attraction, is its origin in poetic imagination. The statesman believes in historical communities with real individuals with real concerns, a reading of epic that accords with his advancing liberalism. The poet believes in the efficacious creativity of the individual poet, and in his classical monologues we are witness to a dovetailing of his aesthetics and his politics.

Unlike other readers of Symonds's narrative, I hold that Tennyson and Gladstone really were arguing about what they appeared to be arguing about, and that the tensions so absorbing to their young witness were caused by profound differences in the ways they read, or even heard, Homer. But beyond this, their arguments may show us less about the territory they attempt to mark around Hallam than the delineations marked by Hallam himself: they help illuminate why he may have come to privilege one friend over the other. Gladstone dramatized the facts, as any effective orator will do, but in the main he stuck to them; his corrections and arguments about the words of the Homeric text attempt (whether they succeed in this or not) to attain historical and linguistic fidelity. Tennyson, however, displays a fundamental resistance to facts in themselves, whether regarding the Eyre incident in Jamaica or the translation of Homer. "Poetry is truer than fact," Tennyson's son records him saying on several occasions (*Memoir*, 2:129). In transferring his keenest attention from his Eton classmate Gladstone to his Trinity College classmate Tennyson, Hallam (who helped arrange the first English publication of Shelley's "Adonais" in 1829) appears to have cast his lot percipiently with one of the unacknowledged legislators of the world, rather than a someday-to-be-acknowledged one. As if in affirmation of the Latin proverb *Orator fit, poeta nascitur*, he was dazzled finally more by the born poet than by the practiced orator. We may trace in Hallam's correspondence the shifts in these allegiances; he wrote to a friend in 1830, "Friendship certainly plays sad pranks with one's judgement in these matters; yet I think if I hated Alfred Tennyson as much as I love him, I could hardly help revering his imagination with just the same reverence" (*Letters*, 363). He allied himself with the man whose lyric imagination he revered with a fervor almost religious, venerating the friend who seemed to see Troy itself.

John Addington Symonds's account of the Woolner dinner party trails off into fragmentary comments on particular Greek words, itself seemingly distracted by the minutiae of translation so occupying the "great ones" whose exchange it chronicles. It is as if the party did not end so much as break up into super-subtle linguistic distinctions. Woolner's dinner took place in December 1865; in 1870, Schliemann discovered what he took to be the city of Troy. These findings (the English translation of *Troy and Its Remains* appeared in 1875) altered still more dramatically the Homeric interpretations that Tennyson had already complained "changed year after year." This presented problems for all Hellenists, whether professional or amateur, as all had to incorporate this excavation into their conceptions of Troy or defend their rejection of Schliemann's findings. Walter Pater, for example, seems to have accepted the usefulness of and even to have entered into the excitement aroused by the excavations. Writing in 1880 about ancient Greek aesthetic sensibilities, he refers to "the recent extraordinary discoveries at Troy and Mycenae." He warns, however, that "the aesthetic critic needs always to be on his guard against the confusion of mere curiosity or antiquity with beauty in art," and specifies only two objects, of the great number illustrated in Schliemann's volumes, that qualify as art under his aesthetic criteria, that rise above the status of "mere curiosity," including "the so-called royal cup of Priam." Pater is more skeptical about Schliemann's subsequent adventure: "The story of the excavations at Mycenae reads more like some well-devised chapter of fiction than a record of sober facts."[81]

The reactions of Gladstone and Tennyson were opposed, with Gladstone largely accepting the importance of the finds and Tennyson largely resisting. According to Jenkyns, Schliemann's excavations in Troy "had seemed to confirm

all that [Gladstone] had always believed; his decision to withdraw from the leadership [of the Liberal Party, in 1875] was perhaps influenced by the importance of
these new discoveries."[82] Somewhat against his will, Gladstone later wrote a preface for Schliemann's book on his related excavations at Mycenae, which opens,
"It is with much reluctance that, at the persevering request of Dr. Schliemann, I
have undertaken to write a preface to his Mycenean volume."[83] Schliemann's gift
of salesmanship, as well as his shrewd reading of Gladstone's own motives, inspired
his persistent requests. In a letter to his publisher John Murray, he wrote, "The
idea has struck me that we will be able to sell five times more copies of the book
on Mycenae if Mr. Gladstone writes the preface to it. I have no doubt he will
do it in acknowledgement of the extraordinary services I have done in proving
by my disinterested labours that his theories are correct."[84] Gladstone was able to
resist, however, the invitation to become godfather to Schliemann's son in March
1878, and to name him, as he was also invited to do. (The boy, joining his sister
Andromache, was named Agamemnon.)

The differences in the reactions of Gladstone and Tennyson to Schliemann's
findings came to the fore at another dinner party, hosted by Lord Houghton (formerly Richard Monckton Milnes, Cambridge friend of Tennyson and Hallam)
at Almond's Hotel on March 28, 1877. Among the guests assembled in honor of
Schliemann's visit to London were Tennyson, Gladstone, and Henry James, himself a no less awed and amused recorder than Symonds. In a letter written the
next day to his brother William James, he also contrasts, though more indirectly,
these "men of 'high culture.'" During the dinner he "sat but one to the Bard," and
later exclaims, "Behold me after dinner conversing affably with Mr. Gladstone."
He is struck by Tennyson's "simplicity," his "strange rustic accent," and extends
this association of the poet with primitiveness until Tennyson comes to seem
neither contemporary nor even fully human, but instead "altogether like a creature
of some primordial English stock." Gladstone's "urbanity," on the other hand, is
"extreme," and James was "glad of a chance to feel the 'personality' of a great
political leader." Like Symonds, James reads physiognomies, observing that Tennyson, despite being "very swarthy and scraggy," nevertheless owns a "face of
genius," while observing of Gladstone, "His eye [is] that of a man of genius."[85]

Gladstone "made a great impression" on James, who found him "fascinating"
and admired "his apparent self-surrender to what he is talking of." Tennyson's
conversation was notably less engaging. James reports that he heard "most of
his talk, which was all about port wine and tobacco: he seems to know much
about them, and can drink a whole bottle of port at a sitting with no incommod-
ity." Such subjects genuinely interested a man whose appetite for pipes and port
seemed to his friends virtually limitless, and Martin, considering Tennyson's table
talk, posits additionally the poet's social awkwardness and defensiveness. Recalling
a conversation in the late 1840s with an admirer, Tennyson recognized that his
interlocutor "wished to pluck the heart from my mystery; so for the life of me

from pure nervousness I could talk of nothing but beer" (*Memoir*, 1:264). Yet for all his attentiveness, James seems to have missed any discussion of Troy, or at least did not find that conversation worth recording. In overlooking any references to the site of Troy, surely a central subject at a dinner honoring its renowned excavator and attended by many with profound intellectual and emotional stakes in the validity of the findings, the American James may have missed the invisible thread that bound what he calls "men of 'high culture.'"[86] Virginia Woolf seems to have suspected as much; reviewing Percy Lubbock's 1920 collection of James's letters, she cites this description of James's evening at Almond's Hotel with Tennyson and Gladstone as an example of what disappoints her in many of his letters: "While he writes charmingly, intelligently and adequately of this, that and the other, we begin by guessing and end by resenting the fact that his mind was elsewhere."[87]

Hallam Tennyson, the poet's son, also left an account of the evening with Schliemann, which, though lacking James's descriptive powers, does record an important fragment of the exchange between the poet and the archaeologist:

> On March 28th [1877] my father and I dined with Lord Houghton at Almond's Hotel to meet Schliemann. In the course of the conversation Schliemann said: "Hissarlik, the ancient Troy, is no bigger than the courtyard of Burlington House." "I can never believe that," my father replied. As we were leaving the room after dinner, Schliemann, duly impressed with the splendour of the entertainment, remarked to us of our host: "Our lord is a very glorious lord, is he not?" (*Memoir*, 2:217–18)

London's courtyards, its "glorious" lords, the splendor of its entertainments, overshadow Schliemann's Troy. Tennyson finds such comparisons ludicrous and rejects them absolutely, even though such correspondences might implicitly raise England's poet laureate to an eminence at least as high as Homer. He meets this relativizing assertion with flat denial, and his emphatic "I can never believe that" rings as a rejection of Schliemann's historical Troy.

Schliemann seems to have done a good deal of sightseeing around London; in *Homeric Synchronism*, Gladstone writes of the excavator, "He has himself, in communication with me, compared [Troy] to Trafalgar Square."[88] These local comparisons point to an anxiety raised by the site of Troy for Schliemann and his supporters, one based less on its placement in Hissarlik than on its modest dimensions. Schliemann writes:

> I am extremely disappointed at being obliged to give so small a plan of Troy; nay, I had wished to be able to make it a thousand times larger, but I value truth above everything, and I rejoice that my three years' excavations have laid open the Homeric Troy, even though on a diminished scale, and that I have proved the *Iliad* to be based upon real facts.
>
> Homer is an epic poet, and not an historian: so it is quite natural that he should have exaggerated everything with poetic license.

Schliemann sets the archaeologist or historian, who values "truth above everything," against the dissimulation of the poet. The Troy he has unearthed, despite its disappointingly "diminished scale," is nevertheless superior to the former conceptions of the city, which stood as "a mere invention of the poet's fancy." While acknowledging that many will be "disappointed that the city of Priam has shown itself to be scarcely a twentieth part as large as was to be expected from the statements of the *Iliad*," he shifts the burden for disappointment from the "truthful" archaeologist to the "exaggerating" poet.[89]

One of the fiercest critics of Schliemann's findings was Richard Claverhouse Jebb, the distinguished classical scholar and friend of Tennyson, to whom the poet dedicated his late dramatic monologue "Demeter and Persephone" (1889). Jebb's acrimonious exchanges with Schliemann merit our brief attention for several reasons. They indicate how violently the battle over Troy's existence could rage, and also illustrate a divide between philological study and the developing discipline of archaeology. These notorious published attacks and counterattacks, moreover, spanned the early 1880s, and we might understand Tennyson's dedication to Jebb later in the decade of a monologue on classical material as an open endorsement of his friend's position. Jebb's ferocity toward Schliemann might have been especially striking to his friends, since he was in person, according to another friend of Tennyson's, "intensely shy and intensely refined."[90] His vehemence is also noteworthy given his own wider academic commitments. As Traill notes, "Ironically, Jebb himself was a leading advocate of establishing British Schools of Archaeology in Athens and Rome so that the training of young classicists could be broadened through exposure to the monuments and material remains of antiquity," and Jebb himself visited Schliemann's site at Hissarlik in September 1882.[91] Schliemann claimed nevertheless that Jebb's resistance was based on ignorance of archaeological principles, and indeed Turner understands Jebb to have been more resistant to the study of archaeology than Traill suggests, calling Jebb "the British literary scholar most disturbed by the implications of archaeology."[92]

In response to several review articles of Jebb's, Schliemann in his 1884 *Troja* describes him as "my persistently bitter critic," and fulminates, "If in Professor Jebb's whole tone, in [his] discussions of my discoveries, I trace an animus of which I might with good right complain, I will certainly be no party to bringing down this great scientific question to the level of a personal dispute." Claiming to rise above Jebb's level of personal invective, Schliemann continues, "But no courtesy on my part can save Professor Jebb from the fate on which an eminent classical scholar rushes when he mingles in an archaeological debate in ignorance of the first principles of archaeology." After providing detailed refutations of Jebb's criticisms, calling them absurdities and "wild theories," he concludes, "I shall say no more on the subject; and be content to add, that it is no part of the duty of a discoverer to waste his time in giving his critics elementary lessons in archaeological science."[93] Jebb responded with his own pointed rejoinders. A collaborator of Schliemann's, A. H. Sayce, professor of Assyriology at Oxford, wrote to him that Jebb, in his 1884 response, "is so angry that he has shown his readers that he is in a passion." Sayce's letter also reports that Jebb enjoyed a measure of public support, an indication of the wider public interest in these debates. Sayce informs Schliemann, "The ignorant newspapers have been speaking of this article as the 'convincing criticism' of 'the greatest of living English Hellenic scholars,'" and he concludes, "We did not trample upon Jebb sufficiently in *Troja*."[94]

In spite of his support for some archaeological programs, Jebb was indeed contemptuous of the authority of physical evidence so celebrated by Schliemann and his supporters; for him it is no compliment to declare of the archaeologist, "His appeal is to the spade." In his 1881 review of Schliemann in *Edinburgh Review*, he rejects categorically such evidence as the study offers and insists vigorously that Troy is entirely "a city of the poet's fancy." Denying outright "the historical character of the Trojan war, or of any persons connected with it," he declares that the excavation of a city that never was is preposterous: "If it is once allowed that the Troy of the *Iliad* is an imaginary city, created by the poet in the likeness of later cities which he had seen, the attempt to recognize it in remains found at Hissarlik becomes futile."[95] Turner posits that the resistance of Jebb and others owed its vehemence to their disbelief that such cities as were being brought to light "could have fostered a culture" consistent with the values of "English humanistic critics."[96] It seems, however, that the fervent tone of their rejections, the absolute and uncompromising dismissal of even the possibility of a discovered Troy, may also have something to do with how the *Iliad* was read and how the poet's relation to his culture was conceived. While Schliemann anticipated the controversy so small a site would provoke, for critics like Jebb the statistics relating to this plot of ground in Asia Minor were less problematic than the very idea of looking to land surveys for insight into poetry: "Reasonings of this kind start from the assumption that an epic poem is constructed on the principles of an Ordnance Survey."[97] As Jebb declared in his 1887 book *Homer: An Introduction* (which Turner calls "probably the most widely read late-century guide to the poet"), "The tale of Troy, as we have it in Homer, is essentially a poetic creation; and the poet is the sole witness."[98]

Jebb and others sought not only to refute Schliemann's specific claims but also to deny the possibility that the city of Troy could ever be found. Sigmund Freud's brief essay "A Disturbance of Memory on the Acropolis" (1936) can help to explain this disbelief in the existence of a historical site. In the essay, Freud recounts a journey to the Acropolis with his younger brother in 1904, during which he experienced a sense of depression and unease. He attributes these emotions to a disbelief in the very existence of the site. Even as he stands before its ruins, he experiences "a momentary feeling: *What I see here is not real.*" He attributes this initially to a sense that perhaps, even as a schoolboy studying this structure, he had never believed in its existence—but soon recalls that this was not in fact the case. Viewing the Acropolis appears to make Freud misremember his childhood apprehension of the Acropolis, so that he believes in retrospect his former disbelief, a disbelief in the place in fact occasioned only by witnessing the place directly: "By the evidence of my senses I am now standing on the Acropolis, but I cannot believe it." He asks, "But why should such incredulity arise in something which, on the contrary, promises to bring a high degree of pleasure? Truly paradoxical behavior!" What Freud comes to realize is that it is not that he had disbelieved in the Acropolis, but that he had doubted that he would ever see it, so that what was unreal as he stood in Athens looking at the Acropolis was not that it was there, but that he was: "It is not true that in my schooldays I ever doubted the real existence of Athens. I only doubted whether I should ever see Athens." He terms this a "feeling of derealization," and admits the situation is "confused and...difficult to describe"; experiencing this phenomenon, "the subject feels either that a piece of reality or that a piece of his own self is strange to him."[99]

Freud traces his own sensation of disbelief to guilt over his traveling to places his father could not have visited and, lacking secondary education, would not have cared to visit. Considering this account, Gay concludes, "It is as perilous to win one's oedipal battles as it is to lose them."[100] It might be more difficult, though no less intriguing, to advance the explanation of filial guilt for Jebb, Tennyson, and others who in various ways nursed doubts less about Schliemann's being the historical Troy than that any excavation pit might reveal the fabled city. The analogy to Freud's disturbance of memory breaks down, because precisely what strikes him is that he could have ever doubted the existence of a place about which there had never been any doubt. The disbelief of the opponents of Schliemann's conclusions seems far less perverse. But Freud calls his own incredulity regarding a storied classical site a "fending off of what is distressing or unbearable,"[101] and this can take us a little further toward understanding a resistance that went deeper than legitimate skepticism regarding Schliemann's methods and claims. For Tennyson, his childhood memory is not that of a schoolboy learning about Troy, but is far more direct. His is a memory specifically of viewing Troy itself: as he declared at the Woolner dinner party, recalling the women of Troy, "As a boy I used to see them." His experience may indeed provide an exact antithesis to that described by Freud; Tennyson's anxiety may be that he no longer can see a city to which he had former easy access, playing on the sand on the bleak coast of Lincolnshire. The excavation at Hissarlik seemed to threaten (rather than to secure, as it did for Schliemann, Gladstone, and others) a solidly held, ontologically vivid knowledge of a place. When told details of Troy by its discoverer himself, Tennyson can only reply, with perfect truth, "I can never believe that."

This disbelief in a historic and geographically locatable Troy seems most often to have been bound to a belief in the existence of a single historical poet, named Homer. As I noted in the beginning of this chapter, Wolf's *Prolegomena*, published in 1795, had posited instead an *Iliad* less composed than accumulated, representing the combined work of a number of rhapsodists. Although many accepted the idea that the text may have had several contributors, nevertheless the negation of a single poet's predominant composition remained for many hard to fathom. John Addington Symonds insisted in his 1873 *Studies of the Greek Poets*, "That...there never was a Homer...appears to the spirit of sound criticism...ridiculous."[102] For some, there had been a Homeric poet, but no Troy; now, many believed that there had been a Troy, but the poet had vanished.

Other friends of Tennyson's gave virtually wholesale support to the idea that Troy had been discovered, and, because they also subscribed to Wolf's theory, it may have seemed that the discovery of Troy was connected to the loss of its poet. Such may have been the case for Walter Leaf, a translator of the *Iliad* and author of numerous books on Homer and Troy, who by the end of the century was "probably the most distinguished Homeric scholar in Great Britain," according to Turner.[103] Leaf was sufficiently close to Tennyson to have been a member of his funeral procession, and he was married to a daughter of John Addington Symonds. Leaf was for the most part a "separatist," believing in many poets (as opposed to the "unitarians," who believed in only one), and so convinced of the authenticity of Schliemann's findings that he traveled to the site of Troy three times. In his 1912 *Troy: A Study in Homeric Geography*, Leaf provides photographs, detailed maps, and lengthy discussions of archaeological strata in order to trace correspondences to the landscape of the *Iliad*. For Leaf, the small scale of the site seemed to confirm its authenticity, since Hector's extraordinary triple course around Troy, running for his life with Achilles in hot pursuit, is therefore shown to be a logical possibility: "The triple course round the city is easy even now...it is not superhuman." Leaf adds in a footnote, "It took me less than eleven minutes to walk round."[104]

Hallam Tennyson records a visit to Tennyson from Walter Leaf (who arrived in the company of Bram Stoker, among others) in the last year of the poet's life: "[Tennyson] was sitting with an *Iliad* on his knee and the talk naturally turned on Homer. 'You know,' he said to Leaf, 'I never liked that theory of yours about the many poets.'" (In this conviction, at least, Tennyson would have found accord with Gladstone, who held to a unitarian line.) Leaf, the noted translator of the *Iliad*, complimented Tennyson on his own "splendid translation" of a simile from book 8, then inquired whether Tennyson thought that the repetition of the simile in a later book pointed to a discrepancy. Tennyson acceded, but one can hear in his response the same defensiveness he brought to bear on textual matters at the Woolner dinner party some twenty-five years before: "Yes, I have always felt that, I must say." In spite of the concession, Tennyson appears to have easily gained the upper hand in this Homeric competition, which is to say that probably Leaf politely demurred. Hallam continues, "[Tennyson] then enlarged for some time upon the greatness of Homer, quoting many lines from both the *Iliad* and *Odyssey*" (*Memoir*, 2:419). Having ceded a specific textual point, Tennyson nevertheless proceeds to glorify the author Homer, the first of the list of the Hundred Greatest Men, of which Tennyson was to become, according to G. M. Young's reminiscence, the last. Wolf's theory of a text produced over time by rhapsodists, espoused by Leaf, diverged significantly from Tennyson's understanding of authorship, his profound imaginative fidelity to the notion of an individual poet producing a range of discursive effects. At a dinner decades earlier, Tennyson had complained about the constant shifts in Homeric study, but this conversation in the year of his death indicates that none of them had significantly altered his understanding of the poet or the unity of his work.

Another conversation in Tennyson's last year confirms his rejection of Schliemann's Troy. In her account "A Visit to Farringford, January 1892," Agnata Frances Butler, a distinguished classicist and the wife of Henry Montagu Butler, then master of Trinity College, Cambridge, describes a conversation she had with the poet that ranged from Horace's Alcaics to Sappho. "Then we spoke of Schliemann," she recalls, "of whom I had just been reading in Schuchardt's book, and [Tennyson] said he had no faith in him. 'How could a great city have been built on a little ridge like that (meaning Hissarlik)? Where would have been the room for Priam's fifty sons and fifty daughters?'" Tennyson owned Schuchardt's book, but his questions concerning the size of the site at Hissarlik and his distrust of its topographical position echo Jebb's more detailed objections. His dismissal of this supposed Troy is founded still more, however, in his own imaginative projection into the city itself, one that persists from his childhood after all. In worrying about the accommodations for Priam's offspring, Tennyson considers room assignments like the host of a weekend house party. Agnata Butler's account continues: "He also thought the supposed identifications of topography absurd, and preferred to believe that Homer's descriptions were entirely imaginary. When I said that I thought that was a disappointing view, he called me 'a wretched localizer.' 'They try to localize me too,' he said. 'There is one man wants to make out that I describe nothing I have not seen.'"[105] Tennyson throws his support fully in the direction of those who would deny that there existed a geographical Troy that could ever be discovered. He also extends his imaginative identification from the ruler of the sacred city to its creator, stating that he too knows what it is to have poetic imagination reduced by critics to mere reportage.

"My excavations have reduced the Homeric Ilium to its real proportions": Jebb quotes this claim of Schliemann's with bemused astonishment. In Jebb's view, the findings at Hissarlik were, precisely, reductive, and any comparison between the text he knew so intimately and the gritty strata of the excavation site was bathetic:

> The Ilium of the "Iliad" is a city with a lofty acropolis, with spacious streets, with temples and palaces of wrought stone. The prehistoric Ilium recognized by Dr. Schliemann in the fifth of his strata at Hissarlik was a town with no acropolis, with an area about as large as that of Trafalgar Square, and with houses of which the largest—the presumed dwelling of royalty—contained four small store-rooms on the ground floor.[106]

For Jebb it is unimaginable that the imperious Trojans lived among such squalid conditions; for Schliemann and his supporters, it was enough to think that they had lived at all. Writing early versions of "Ulysses" and "Tithonus," dramatic monologues featuring characters drawn from narratives of Troy, Tennyson could not have imagined the discoveries and theories, indeed the major epistemological shifts, that were to threaten to overtake the Troy of his youth. Yet he does appear to have imagined, repeatedly, that such investigations might generally steal away more than they yield, replacing the poet's proud and gorgeous city with the explorer's muddy site. Schliemann claimed to have "reduced" the city he discovered, and Tennyson would no doubt have found accord with such an assessment. In one of Tennyson's childhood translations of the odes of Horace, Juno exalts over the city she has schemed to vanquish: "Ilion, Ilion, thou art thrust / Down to earth" (30–31). Schliemann's claims might seem to reverberate with this cry.

In a letter to Gladstone in September 1829, Arthur Hallam exalted over Tennyson's prizewinning "Timbuctoo": "The splendid imaginative power that pervades it will be seen through all hindrances. I consider Tennyson as promising fair to be the greatest poet of our generation, perhaps of our century" (*Letters*, 319). A month later he visited Gladstone at Oxford and brought a copy of the poem; Gladstone wrote in his diary, "Read the Cambridge Prize Poems at n[igh]t—Tennyson's sundry times in order if possible to understand it." In spite of the difficulty of the poem, the enthusiasm of Hallam was contagious; Gladstone adds, "Liked it exceedingly."[107] In a debate in a college society at Oxford founded by Gladstone and others on the model of the Apostles, Tennyson himself was the subject; in his biography of Gladstone, John Morley records, "By four to three, Mr. Tennyson's poems were affirmed to show considerable genius, Gladstone happily in the too slender majority."[108] Under Hallam's influence, Gladstone had begun the championing of Tennyson that, for all their many differences, would culminate half a century later in his obtaining for the poet a hereditary peerage.

Perhaps in later years Gladstone did not recall a poem he had not entirely understood, but the terms surrounding the discovery of Troy eerily echo Tennyson's description of the fate of this other fabled city. Timbuctoo, with its dazzling "wilderness of spires," its "interminably high" pillars, the "blinding brilliance" of its doors, and its city's "argent streets" (159, 172, 174, 227), was reduced to mud. The Seraph tells the poem's speaker that this "glorious home" must soon be rendered up "To keen *Discovery*," and predicts, pointing to "yon brilliant towers," that they shall soon "Darken, and shrink and shiver into huts, / Black specks amid a waste of dreary sand, / Low-built, mud-walled, Barbarian settlements" (239, 240, 242–44). "Timbuctoo" had anticipated by some four decades what the incursions of exploration would yield; mud walls were precisely what *Discovery* unearthed at Schliemann's Hissarlik, in what can only have seemed to many a second Fall of Troy.

4

ULYSSES AND THE RAPTURE OF TROY

In book 2 of the *Aeneid* (the part of the epic Edward FitzGerald tells us Tennyson wept as he read), as the Trojans gather around the inexplicable wooden horse and hear Sinon's false account of it and himself, Laocoön rushes down from Troy's heights and implores his people, "*sic notus Ulixes?*" (2:44), which Dryden translates: "And are Ulysses' arts no better known?" (2:57). A more literal translation perhaps better captures the stark simplicity of Laocoön's question: "Is it thus ye know Ulysses?" though Dryden is right to stress Ulysses' artfulness.[1] Knowing Ulysses, as Laocoön's and Troy's fates indicate, is appallingly difficult and vitally necessary; it is this task that Tennyson's dramatic monologue, with its persistent stress on the knowledge of and about Ulysses, undertakes. Part of my argument in what follows is that to know Ulysses is to know that he is the destroyer of cities, responsible more than any other hero, even Achilles, for the downfall of Troy's lofty towers (one of his epithets, an honorific, is *ptoliporthos*, sacker of cities). The ways in which Tennyson's "Ulysses" is an exploration of civic responsibilities have frequently been discussed in terms of his abnegation of responsibility for Ithaca, which he stands eager to abandon. I address here, however, what is never considered in discussions of Tennyson's monologue: the responsibility, greater by far, that he bears toward Ilion.

In the *Odyssey*, Ulysses is recognized upon his return by his aged dog, who thereafter expires, and that other faithful retainer, his nurse. The nurse fingers a childhood scar and thus comes to be among the few Ithacans to whom he is known. Tennyson in this poem also takes account of Ulysses' return by fingering his scar, the psychic wound acquired later than the physical one, but that makes itself felt, like an arthritic joint or a battle injury, in certain climates and under certain conditions, as when the lights begin to twinkle from the rocks. My argument, however, addresses less the psychological subconscious of Ulysses than the literary one, the depths of which must be plumbed in Homer, Virgil, and Dante.

To know Ulysses is to know that his arts seek to cause that largest of effects, the annihilation of a city and a people. I hope to show in this the grim inevitability of Tennyson's turning, in October 1833, in what can only have been a kind of appalled shock at the news of Hallam's death, to the figure of Ulysses, chief architect of ruined Troy.

My discussion of this dramatic monologue begins by reviewing Ulysses' first major appearance in Tennyson's poetry, in the opening of "The Lotos-Eaters." This will help to establish some early generic features of the monologic form, which stood, at its inception in Tennyson's practice, distinct from other related forms. I move next to a telling example of the contemporary debate regarding the character of Ulysses, as conducted in an exchange of letters between William Gladstone and Arthur Henry Hallam in 1826–27. These letters, themselves informed by impassioned readings of the figure of Ulysses, bring us closer to the complex of associations animating Tennyson's foremost monologic speaker, and thus enable us to draw on some early nineteenth-century theories regarding the arts of Ulysses. Laocoön urges the Trojans to recognize Ulysses, to consult their knowledge of him in order to resist the effects of his guile. In this, the Trojans fail, and Ulysses consequently levels their fabled city. In the second half of this chapter I show how the incendiary figure of a burning Troy ignites all of Ulysses' monologic representations.

THE CHARACTER OF THE HOMERIC STATESMAN

In locating a Ulysses in Tennyson of whom we might gain knowledge, it is useful to begin with Tennyson's representation of him prior to the eponymous dramatic monologue. "The Lotos-Eaters," powerful in its own right and of course an entirely autonomous work, must interest us here largely because of the appearance in it of Ulysses and because of the distinctions it can help us to sketch between its choric voice and that of the dramatic monologist. The poem opens with Ulysses' bold and definitive pronouncement, "Courage" (1), itself a succinct preamble, introducing an emotion his later monologue will enlarge upon. His is the only utterance in the poem that seeks to be efficacious, that intends to convince auditors, and the first irony among many in this work is that this opening cheer marks the termination of this kind of speech. When the "mild-eyed melancholy Lotos-Eaters" (27) come, they do so in eerie silence, dispensing the enchanted stems without explanation or encouragement. But there exists another speaker, whom we hear just before the commencement of the choric song, who is the catalyst for the communal chant that follows. Lounging on the shore, "between the sun and moon" as between consciousness and this newly experienced "dream of Fatherland" (38, 39), the chorus sings of the weariness that overwhelms not themselves but the sea, the medium they have counted on to buoy them. The prologue continues:

> Then some one said, "We will return no more";
> And all at once they sang, "Our island home
> Is far beyond the wave; we will no longer roam." (43–45)

"Then" marks the moment of turning, the break between prior and future existence, a moment of sheer decisiveness for men who are concurrently foreswearing all future decisions. "Some one," unnamed, unnamable, might point to a separable individual, related discursively to the "he," Ulysses, whose opening command compels his auditors. Here, though, the some one is unindividuated, indistinguishable from the others even before his statement, and merging wholly into the group immediately following it, like the pitch pipe of an a cappella group. "All at once" (the phrase conveying both the immediate nature of the response and the assembled persons who make it) the chorus forms, merging and emerging as a common entity, as "one said" transforms seamlessly into "they sang," as monologic speaking is enveloped in choric song.

This moment of group formation, with the assembly's ceding of individual voices, is possible partly because all are in immediate agreement. There is no need for efficacious or convincing speech, as the "some one" only instigates what all in accord will sing. In Ulysses' monologue, the speaker sets out to convince auditors whom we must understand to be resistant; they can enter such discursive accord with him only if they accede to his representations. His resolutions, however, can only with difficulty attain such full accession, partly because of their content, partly because of his stature. What Ulysses tasks his auditors with can never be what they themselves were also considering, and when he speaks it is never as a vague and unnamed "some one," but as a prominent and well-known "some one" (the phrase in the first case stresses the indeterminate "some"; in the second, the individuated "one"). These pronominal shifts from the singular to the plural will be seen, later in this chapter, to assume vital political implications.

Ricks notes that the major revisions for "The Lotos-Eaters" in the 1842 *Poems* were the addition of section VI and the rewriting of the final twenty-three lines of the poem. These revisions are the essential points in the poem for my argument, as a brief consideration of them will help us understand more fully the representation of Troy in these poems generally, but also the extent of that city's suppression in the revised 1842 "Ulysses." Section VI is crucial to the poem, as necessary as the substantial 1842 verse paragraph addition in "Ulysses," the introduction of Telemachus (lines 33–43). In both cases, these additions supply to a large extent the speakers' justifications for their rejection of Ithaca, even as both additions focus specifically on the sons who will assume the burdens the Lotos-Eaters are unshouldering:

> Dear is the memory of our wedded lives,
> And dear the last embraces of our wives
> And their warm tears: but all hath suffered change:
> For surely now our household hearths are cold:
> Our sons inherit us: our looks are strange:
> And we should come like ghosts to trouble joy. (114–19)

The Lotos-Eaters posit several scenarios of return. If the island is prospering, they will return as if from the dead, "like ghosts," and intrude upon an inheritance already taken up by their heirs. Even as the mariners here and Ulysses in his monologue resoundingly reject an Ithaca they find wholly unappealing, they at key points attempt to make it sound as if the gift they are bestowing might be worth the taking. "Or else," they continue, apparently rejecting the possibility that there could be joy in Ithaca as an unsustainable fiction, positing what is more likely to be the situation they would return to:

> Or else the island princes over-bold
> Have eat our substance, and the minstrel sings
> Before them of the ten years' war in Troy,
> And our great deeds, as half-forgotten things.
> Is there confusion in the little isle?
> Let what is broken so remain. (120–25)

There is some small irony in the fact that men whose sole remaining activity is to eat the lotos are disturbed at the idea of others eating their substance, as if they now understand all communities as gustatory. What the singers expand on, however, is the idea of being the subject of the minstrel's song. Why does the epic song, which is being composed even as they now repose, itself make impossible their return? The minstrel's song of their "great deeds" inspires in them only inertia. Part of being made redundant, becoming "half-forgotten," is being the subject of such a song. In a dynamic that is also to trouble Ulysses, they seem to know that to become legendary is concurrently to become half-forgotten. Becoming a name in these cases is tantamount to becoming a memory, to attaining a cultural significance even as one is losing it. With the minstrel's song, the mariners seem to have ceded their name and their right to self-representation. The Lotos-Eaters cannot imagine return, then, because it is in fact the minstrel who has inherited them, who has dispossessed them of their "substance."

The misery of homecoming that we hear the chorus anticipating is not that the island of Ithaca has suffered change, but that they have. This can take us a little distance in understanding the revision of the final section of the poem. Later in the chapter I address the extended representation of the gods that brings the poem to its close; here I focus on the Lotos-Eaters' representation of themselves, since that is ultimately what the choric song attempts: the acquisition of a new identity for these weary vegetarians. In the 1832 version, they call themselves "Men of Ithaca" (*1832* 11), and the poem in its early incarnation concludes, "Oh! islanders of Ithaca, we will not wander more.... / Oh! islanders of Ithaca, we will return no more" (*1832* 37, 40). The name of "the little isle of Ithaca" is erased entirely in the 1842 revision; the only place-name given beyond that where they presently live and recline is that of Troy. But more crucially, with the revision their self-definition is radically altered. In 1842, the song ends, "Oh rest ye, brother mariners, we will not wander more" (173). In calling themselves "brother mariners," they redefine not only themselves but also their familial context. They are now defined less by the place where they were born than the place where they fought, less by their families than by their comrades in arms. No longer tied to wife and son, they band with their brothers. Having long ceased being "men of Ithaca," they are now "men of the ten years' war in Troy," and therefore wholly part of a scattered and disoriented community for which they have few adequate terms.

As brother mariners, they name themselves by the labor they have shared, the toil at war and sea that they would abandon. At least, that is the name they assign themselves; the poem's title, however, shows the supremacy of the minstrel's song. They take their name finally not from the land of their origin, the land of their great deeds, or the sea that ferries them from one to the other; rather, their designation is now based on their degustation. With their song, they effect their own transformation from brother mariners to *lotophagi*; now they are only what they eat. But who would nevertheless deny them the right to compose their own choric song in opposition to the minstrel's? Apparently not Tennyson, who, unlike the singer of the *Odyssey*, leaves these men where they lie. We know that in the *Odyssey* Ulysses (perhaps their auditor here) gets them back on board, and thus on to assorted miserable deaths. And yet, as resistant as presumably he is to their song, Ulysses' monologue takes up many of its notes.

Oratorical Ulysses

The question about Tennyson's Ulysses that has most exercised critics in the twentieth century is whether Ulysses is admirable or reprehensible, and to what degree he is either or both. Some critics contend that Ulysses is irresponsible and possibly even insane. Others find in him a model for statesmen and other citizens, as witnessed by the use of this poem in generations of British schooling to shore up notions of an intrepid national spirit. But we should look to other debates than our own in assessing the character of this hero. I propose that one of the many converging points of origin for Tennyson's "Ulysses" is a debate that involved Hallam and Gladstone, and as a consequence closely touched Tennyson. In the winter of 1826–27, the Eton classmates had an epistolary argument regarding the qualities of Ulysses. In a letter Hallam compared Gladstone to Ulysses, intending a compliment, and Gladstone instead took quite strong offense, in a manner that rather startled—and perhaps amused—Hallam. The debate helps frame Tennyson's own conception of the hero; a sounding of the textual depths of this epistolary exchange will bring us closer to an understanding of the echoes, contemporary and classical, to which the poet himself attended.

The correspondence between Hallam and Gladstone while both were still students at Eton and for a time thereafter was thick with argument over contemporary politics, deliberating the minutiae of controversial policies, reviewing numerous examples of historical precedent, and analyzing the characters and actions of ministers and cabinet members. The significance for Gladstone of these letters is made apparent in a diary entry recording a visit to Cambridge to hear Hallam deliver the Prize Declamation at Trinity. He writes that Hallam indicated a desire to revive their lapsed correspondence, "to my *very* great joy."[2] Embedded in their dense debates (which are credited with helping the young Gladstone hone his argumentative skills) is an argument over the character of Homer's Ulysses. For Hallam and Gladstone—and, I argue, for a Tennyson so often not seen to be concerned with political questions—the character of Ulysses resonates with political significance. It seems entirely likely, in the years during which he and Tennyson were so constantly together, when Tennyson was already writing poems drawn from Hellenic material, that Hallam might have shared the substance of an extended disagreement regarding Homer, one with implications personal, political, and poetical. *In Memoriam* stresses how continuous their conversations were and how widely they ranged (from literature to politics to Socratic philosophy): "We glanced from theme to theme, / Discussed the books to love or hate, / Or touched the changes of the state, / Or threaded some Socratic dream." Characterizing their outings, Tennyson writes, "We talked: the stream beneath us ran, / The wine flask lying couched in moss" (89:33–36, 43–44). Later in the elegy he describes Hallam's "Heart-affluence in discursive talk / From household fountains never dry" (109:1–2).

While I examine here the implications of Hallam's comparison of Gladstone to Ulysses, it is germane to note that in one of Hallam's letters Tennyson was also compared (more subtly) to a Homeric character. In a letter of February 1833, he addresses Tennyson, by way of a quotation from the *Iliad*, as Patroclus, that desperately loved friend of Achilles. As it happens, Hallam is defending himself regarding the intensity of his letter writing to other friends in the past (Gladstone had been among his chief correspondents), which the two had clearly discussed and which seems to have bothered Tennyson. Immediately after quoting an exclamation of Achilles to Patroclus, he expostulates against what must have been petulant accusations on the poet's part, telling him, "You are very impertinent about my talent of letterwriting." Hallam asks, "Why should I blush to acknowledge, that in my young days I used to work for hours at a letter?" He had apparently shared with Tennyson information about his former epistolary passions (and presumably their content), and his tone, usually warmly indulgent in his letters to Tennyson, is here at once defensive and pleading, insisting that in earlier years something of his life was in his letters. He tells Tennyson, "I don't care to joke about it. That labour if labour it was, was one of love. . . . I composed a letter as I composed a poem." Hallam's letters constitute, he suggests, juvenilia as telling as Tennyson's own early efforts. He continues, "Heart & mind went into it, & why?—because I couldn't help it. I was full of ardent thoughts so new to me that I was afraid of losing them . . . so dear too that I could not rest till those I loved were familiar with them" (*Letters*, 721).

This letter ends with a political report. Hallam had just attended the speech of William IV at the first opening of Parliament after the passage of the momentous 1832 Reform Bill. Among other details, he informs Tennyson that his uncle Charles Tennyson spoke in favor of ongoing reform. It was clearly a memorable letter for Tennyson, as decades later Arthur Coleridge recalled the poet telling him, "Arthur Hallam said to me in 1832: 'To-day I have seen the last English King going in State to the last English Parliament,'" a direct quotation from this particular dispatch.[3] Hallam concludes his report to Tennyson with a prediction regarding the newly seated Parliament: "There will be some fine spectacles of intellectual combat" (*Letters*, 722). In the intense youthful correspondences that had so provoked Tennyson, Hallam had himself engaged in such "spectacles," pursuing most ardently "intellectual combat" with his Eton classmate Gladstone.

The epistolary exchange between Hallam and Gladstone (one side of which must be inferred from internal evidence, since Hallam's father destroyed the letters his son had received) was in many ways a continuation of their long-standing debate regarding the politics of reform. Hallam, the son of the prominent Whig historian Henry Hallam, was in favor of Whig causes, the chief of which in these years was the formation and eventual passage of the Reform Bill, which sought limited but nevertheless significant political changes. Gladstone, although he was later in his life to become the standard-bearer for the Liberal Party, itself an outgrowth of the Whigs, was in these early years intensely conservative and "hostile to Whiggish and radical causes." "If we look at his letters, writings, and speeches in the late 1820s and early 1830s," observes Gladstone biographer Matthew, "it is not difficult to portray him as a very hard-nosed Tory indeed." Hallam, however, was "like his father, a steadfast Whig"; although Hallam put the case to Gladstone in arguments of "astonishing maturity," according to Matthew, "he did not convince him."[4] "It is difficult for me now to conceive how during these years he bore with me," Gladstone reflected in 1898. "Not only was I inferior to him in knowledge and dialectical ability, but my mind was 'cabined, cribbed, confined,' by . . . intolerance."[5] Gladstone was so violently opposed to the reform momentum that he was the prime author of an antireform petition in 1831 at Christ Church, his college at Oxford, and so obsessed with the matter that at points his health was threatened.

The disagreement between Hallam and Gladstone over the character of Homer's Ulysses laces its way through a correspondence of enormous significance to them both. In a letter written late in December 1826, Hallam offers a detailed examination of the opinions of the late eighteenth-century figures Pitt, Fox, and Burke regarding the French Revolution. At the end of the letter, he calls Gladstone "divine Ulysses," telling him, "You speak with modesty about your own future government: I am forming no Utopias on the subject; I only hope for what is practicable. I have also another hope: it is that you may sometimes support me with your eloquence, & fight the battles of freedom & justice in union with myself. Few things would give me more pleasure" (*Letters*, 105–6). As Hallam had accurately predicted Tennyson's topmost placement among the poets of their age, here he speaks with certainty and a kind of clear-eyed practicality ("forming no Utopias upon the subject") of his expectations for Gladstone's "future government." And Hallam may have been suggesting that their political positions were closer to one another than Gladstone suspects. As Bruce Coleman reminds us, "Even the Whigs, a vital component in the future Liberal party, were hardly radical reformists outside a narrow range of constitutional issues." In spite of heated debate between Whigs and Tories, "much of nineteenth-century politics concerned shades of difference—perhaps dispute about means rather than ends—within a relatively cohesive and predominantly conservative elite."[6]

After proposing to Gladstone their future political union, Hallam then quotes in Greek four lines from book 10 of the *Iliad* (10:242–45). The passage is taken from the moment when Diomedes, having conceived a plan for a night raid among the Trojans, is asked by Agamemnon who, among all the assembled Achaean heroes, he would choose as a companion. Diomedes immediately, without any hesitation, elects Ulysses. Pope's translation runs:

> "My choice declares the impulse of my mind.
> How can I doubt, while great Ulysses stands
> To lend his counsels, and assist our hands?
> A Chief, whose safety is Minerva's care:
> So famed, so dreadful in the works of war." (10:284–88)

Hallam thus compares himself to Diomedes, who would choose Gladstone without hesitation as his fellow warrior in noble causes, in fighting "the battles of freedom & justice." With these lines and his interpretive introduction, Hallam tells Gladstone that he is his chosen comrade (we have seen the turn Hallam's favor took and some of its consequences for dinner parties later in the century), citing as explanation Gladstone's already apparently well-developed discursive skills, his "eloquence."

The lines that follow directly upon Diomedes' choice of Ulysses read, in Pope's translation, "Bless'd in his conduct, I no aid require. / Wisdom like his might pass thro' flames of fire" (10:289–90). Pope's "wisdom" may not be the best term; shrewdness and tactical skill seem to be more specifically what Diomedes presently honors in Ulysses (Lattimore translates these lines, "Were he to go with me, both of us could come back from the blazing / of fire itself, since his mind is best at devices" [10:246–47]). We recall that when Dante and Virgil come upon Ulysses in the *Inferno*, he is bound with Diomedes perpetually in a fire—transmogrified into flame—from which even the great tactician cannot extricate them. This is the image of the conjoined Ulysses and Diomedes that Dante and his guide Virgil discover:

> The guide, who marked
> How I did gaze attentive, thus began:
> "Within these ardours are the spirits, each
> Swath'd in confining fire." (*Inferno* 26:46–49, trans. Cary)

In answer to Dante's question as to how these two come to be so hotly confined, Virgil offers this explanation, each facet of which, I hope to show, is taken up in Tennyson's dramatic monologue:

> "These in the flame with ceaseless groans deplore
> The ambush of the horse, that open'd wide
> A portal for that goodly seed to pass,
> Which sow'd imperial Rome; nor less the guile
> Lament they, whence of her Achilles 'reft
> Deidamia yet in death complains.
> And there is rued the stratagem, that Troy
> Of her Palladium spoil'd." (*Inferno* 26:59–66, trans. Cary)

Criticism of "Ulysses," for all its awareness of the poem's source in Dante, seems largely to have overlooked the significance to the poem of the full range of causes for Ulysses' immersion in flame. The punishment of Ulysses and Diomedes is based not only on Ulysses' false counsel to his men upon his return to Ithaca, which I examine later, but also on his wily destruction of Troy, brought about in large measure through his false dealings with the Trojans and Achilles. Three wrongs for which the spirits suffer are catalogued: the ambush of the city made possible by the ruse of the Trojan horse; the ambush, in a sense, of Achilles from his lover Deidamia; and the ambush, in the night raid, of Troy's Palladium (the sacred throne of Athena, which guarded the city). Each of these constitutes an instance of guile, of convincing others to do what they do not want to do or had best not do (and these examples anticipate Ulysses' later address to his mariners, in both Dante and Tennyson).

In the first instance, the Trojans initially are suspicious of the massive horse but are tricked into accepting it by Sinon, the mouthpiece of Ulysses (who waits in the structure's interior), whose story to them is at every point preoccupied with narratives of the cruel cunning of Ulysses. Aeneas tells Dido in book 2 of the *Aeneid* (the set piece we have established was of special significance to Tennyson):

> "With such deceits he gained their easy hearts,
> Too prone to credit his perfidious arts.
> What Diomede, nor Thetis's greater son,
> A thousand ships, nor ten years' siege had done,
> False tears and fawning words the city won." (2:259–63, trans. Dryden)

Stronger in its effects than the arms of Diomedes or Thetis's son Achilles, this perfidy leads directly—indeed, by that night—to the firing of Troy's citadels.

Achilles initially refused to join the Achaean forces, although Ulysses' ruse compels him to do so. The guile wrought against Achilles is placed in Dante's list between the bookends of Ulysses' two major assaults on Troy, which were together far more the direct cause of Troy's fall, in this account, than even Achilles' exceeding strength in combat. (Achilles seems thus exempted from moral responsibility for Troy's destruction.) In introducing the figure of Achilles' lover Deidamia, who in the underworld "yet in death complains," we see on a more local level the way that Ulysses' ruses are the cause of mourning in others. But Ulysses also absorbs, takes on, this perpetual ache for Achilles; it is Achilles' absence that Ulysses too laments, in Dante and especially in Tennyson. In placing the example of Ulysses' guile toward Achilles in the context of his guile toward Troy, Dante forges a link between the two fallen eminences, human and civic, which Tennyson is to perpetuate. The Achaean hero and the Trojan city are thus inextricably linked as objects of Ulysses' guilt. As we shall see, seeking the great Achilles is for Tennyson's Ulysses bound wholly in its associations, as adumbrated here in Tennyson's chief literary source, with seeking the great raptured Ilion.

The final cause that Virgil names for Dante in explaining the accursedness of Diomedes and Ulysses is their joint role in an adventure so pivotal as to have, more than any other "great deed" among the Achaeans, caused the destruction of the city. In book 2 of the *Aeneid*, Aeneas credits the ultimate destruction of Ilion to the foray in which Diomedes and Ulysses took by "stratagem" the Palladium, or statue of Pallas Athena, which assured the city's safety, from its shrine:

> But from the time when impious Diomede
> And false Ulysses, that inventive head,
> Her fatal image from the temple drew...
> From thence the tide of fortune left their shore. (2:218–20, 224, trans. Dryden)

Aeneas calls Ulysses the "contrivor of crime" (*sclerum inventor Ulixes* [2:164]; Dryden's "inventive head"), and it is clear from his accounts that there is no one whom he holds more responsible for the ruin of the lofty city, brought low by low schemes. To destroy a civilization is a massive undertaking, but it was in this case accomplished, according to both Virgil and Dante, with the aid of qualities less than heroic. Ulysses' eloquence is the cause of a victory indistinguishable to some from damnation.

Hallam in his final years became a promising Dante scholar, preparing an edition of *Vita Nuova* with full translation and commentary; among the last communications Tennyson received from him were two articles he had written, one lengthy, on recent controversies in Dante scholarship. Nevertheless, Gladstone may in 1826 have had a sharper memory for the crimes of the night raid as well as the ultimate literary fate of these two warriors. Certainly, he took exception to the comparison Hallam had made. A letter from Hallam a little more than a week later (the majority of which probes the breadth of Gladstone's Tory allegiances, then reviews the "tyrannical rule" of Charles I) makes it clear that Gladstone's response was one of stiff rejection of the conceit. Hallam begins the letter, "You 'do not consider yourself much complimented' by the 'formidable quotation'!... Surely as the lines stand (& to anything else relating to Ulysses I never alluded), few higher compliments... can be found. Since however you force me to look to other points of the character of the Homeric statesman, you may perhaps make the application of the following passage with more pleasure" (*Letters*, 108). Hallam then provides another quotation in Greek from the *Iliad* (3:221–23), again regarding the unequaled eloquence of the "Homeric statesman." In a moment taken from early in the epic, Priam is calling upon Helen's expertise in identifying the Achaeans whom he can see from his citadel. Immediately after Helen's identification of Ulysses, the Trojan Antenor shares his own knowledge of Ulysses, who had come to Troy with Menelaus long years before to lobby for the return of Helen.

The three lines quoted by Hallam are spoken by Antenor, and rendered thus by Lattimore:

> But when he let the great voice go from his chest, and the words came
> drifting down like the winter snows, then no other mortal
> man beside could stand up against Ulysses. (3:221–23)

As in the earlier instance of his comparison of Gladstone to Ulysses, Hallam omits crucial points of context. Here, Antenor's comments concerning the way Ulysses' eloquence is unmatched in its effects on his auditors follow immediately lines that describe Ulysses' awkward, almost risible demeanor; the line directly preceding the three Hallam quotes, in Lattimore's translation is, "Yes, you would call him a sullen man, and a fool likewise" (3:220). Having remembered Menelaus as succinct and plainspoken, Antenor in his account turns to the more complex spectacle of Ulysses. Pope renders the full scene Antenor recalls thus:

> But when Ulysses rose, in thought profound,
> His modest eyes he fix'd upon the ground;

As one unskill'd or dumb, he seem'd to stand,
Nor rais'd his head, nor stretch'd his sceptred hand.
But when he speaks, what elocution flows!
Soft as the fleeces of descending snows,
The copious accents fall, with easy art;
Melting they fall, and sink into the heart!
Wond'ring we hear, and, fix'd in deep surprise,
Our ears refute the censure of our eyes. (3:279–88, trans. Pope)

A measure of Ulysses' unequaled oratorical ability is his seeming inability; part of his skill in speech derives from his appearing unskilled, speechless, a phenomenon we can observe in other speakers of the dramatic monologue, in Robert Browning as well as Tennyson. The Trojan marvels at the dissonance between Ulysses' awkward demeanor and his smooth speech. This is of course Laocoön's point: *sic notus Ulixes?* Ulysses is always promoting illusions, what for him is "easy art"; his appearance, whenever Trojans are concerned, is deceiving. At this moment, he proleptically impersonates the Trojan horse, with an exterior that belies nothing of its interior.

Gladstone knew well the context of the three lines Hallam so carefully extracts, which point to a foolishness in Ulysses or, alternatively, in his ever-susceptible auditors, and he was still more infuriated by the "application" of this set of lines to himself. Hallam's final letter on the subject indicates that Gladstone's feelings on this matter were unappeasable: "'*Obstupui, steteruntque comoe!*' What a tremendous thunderbolt have I called down on my devoted head!…How my Whiggism must flutter within me to hear that Ulysses had all *the bad qualities* of the set? Now, how remarkably kind, & liberal this is of you! Craft, I suppose, dissimulation, low cunning, cruelty, & such like little items are to be marked off as the Whig qualities of Ulysses" (*Letters*, 113). Apparently, Gladstone turned the tables on Hallam, as Hallam's own political leanings come to be compared to the unappealing qualities in Ulysses that led to his rejection as an exemplary figure. The exclamation of Aeneas's that Hallam quotes ("I was appalled, my hair stood up"), also from book 2 of the *Aeneid*, is uttered at the moment when the ghost of his wife Creusa rises up before him, immediately after he has seen Ulysses guarding the Trojan booty. While Hallam uses it to express his shock and even dismay at Gladstone's continued rejection of his comparison, the quotation would seem to show that Gladstone has a point, as there are desperate consequences to Ulysses' machinations.

That the character of Ulysses could be employed to represent a political position was patent to both young men; Hallam in later letters desisted from a comparison the young Gladstone found odious, and he turns from this particular epistolary debate by insisting to Gladstone, "If the Whigs are to be cried down, let it be in the broad glare of day, by fair argument, & not by covert insinuation" (*Letters*, 113). The letter goes on to discuss the regicide of Charles I, before concluding, "I hope this little controversy therefore has brought us to as good an understanding as our mutual prejudices will allow us to entertain." Their "mutual prejudices" had of course fostered for them the joy of sustained intellectual combat. Close to thirty years later Gladstone in *Studies on Homer* describes the pleasure of intensive rhetorical exchange: "If the power of oratory is remarkable in Homer, so likewise is the faculty of what in England is called debate. Here the orator is a wrestler, holding his ground from moment to moment; adjusting his poise, and delivering his force, in exact proportion to the varying pressure of his antagonist" (*SH*, 3:111). These friends clearly felt themselves well matched in the virtually physical sport of debate; Hallam ends by offering Gladstone "many thanks for the pleasure your letters (or packets shall I call them?), always afford me," asking only for more: "The longer the epistle is the better" (*Letters*, 116). For his part, Gladstone returned and perhaps even exceeded this admiration, extending the ambition for a future political career to Hallam. Doodling in a notebook as a student at Oxford in 1829, Gladstone elevated himself and a handful of his closest friends to the status of members of Parliament, including Hallam, whose name he wrote out twice (once immediately above his own) as "Rt. Hon. A. H. Hallam."[7] Tennyson had also imagined, he says in *In Memoriam*, that Hallam would become "A potent voice of Parliament, / A pillar steadfast in the storm, / Should licensed boldness gather force." The same section of the elegy contains a line that echoes, in its cadence and content, the final line of "Ulysses." The poet notes that Hallam was "keen / In intellect, with force and skill / To strive, to fashion, to fulfil—" (113:11–13, 5–7). In the 1850s, F. T. Palgrave asked Tennyson whether he genuinely held to these lines, and reports, "Tennyson's earnest look is still before me as he gave the assurance that he truly and fully believed that, in no form or way, had he exaggerated Arthur's wonderful promise" (*Memoir*, 2:496).

His friends' predictions regarding Hallam's future took an unexpected turn, since his name would be elevated ultimately not in political league with Gladstone but through poetic memorialization in Tennyson's 1850 *In Memoriam*. But Hallam's predictions were again remarkably accurate. In his initial comparison of Gladstone to Ulysses, he imagines his friend as a charismatic speaker advocating something vaguely like Whig causes, pursuing "battles of freedom & justice" with his unrivaled eloquence. Such a vision comports less with the sharp conservatism of the early years of Gladstone's political career than with the liberalism he came to espouse decades later. So associated did Gladstone become with liberal politics that one historian notes, "Popular support for Liberalism took the form almost of a personal devotion to Gladstone, rather than to his party or government." Gladstone's mass popularity was achieved in no small measure by way of his "rhetorical magnetism," a suasive power so extreme it has been likened to hypnotism; its effect was called "being Gladstonized."[8]

In his youthful letters to Gladstone, Hallam reads Ulysses the way critics of Tennyson's poem have often desired to read the speaker of "Ulysses," namely, as an inspiring leader of worthy causes of a vaguely progressive sort. Gladstone for his part reads the character of this Homeric statesman as many have come to read Tennyson's version by way of Dante's: as untrustworthy, manipulative, beguiling, cruel, even a liar.[9] Clearly, for Gladstone and Hallam in these years, Ulysses is to be admired selectively and invoked carefully, since he is, for readers such as these, a figure whose implications must always be controversial. Both use him to experiment with and illustrate political stances, to shore up their definitions, for example, of Whiggism, and we need to see more than we have that Tennyson also addresses his own Ulysses to such concerns. The reasons for Gladstone's resistance to being compared to this character appear to be supported by Tennyson's poem. For Tennyson, Ulysses is the destroyer of Troy, consigned to the inferno for this sin more than for his oratorical manipulations, though his sins and his skills are inseparable. Although we must take seriously Hallam's amused refusal in his adolescence to consider this figure altogether reprehensible, we must also bear in mind that it was in the years Tennyson knew him best that Hallam began working closely with Dante's texts. *In Memoriam* recalls Hallam reading Italian poetry on his visits to Somersby: "O bliss, when all in circle drawn / About him, heart and ear were fed / To hear him, as he lay and read / The Tuscan poets on the lawn" (89. 21–24). "It is worthy of remark, because it was a remark made by himself," recalled Benjamin Jowett, "that the description of Ulysses in the poem bearing that name is derived not from Homer, but from Dante" (*Memoir*, 2:464). Tennyson's turn to Dante in the acuteness of his mourning must be seen as a turn to Hallam's projected intellectual labor.

In January 1832, Hallam wrote to a friend, "Towards the end of the year, I may have ready for the Public (alas, most incurious of such things!) a translation of Dante's *Vita Nuova*, prefaced by some biographical chatter, & wound up by some philosophical balderdash about poetry & morality & metre & everything" (*Letters*, 512). We can hear a note of the breezy self-mockery that was one of Hallam's charms in the terms he applies to his introduction: "chatter," "balderdash." But more significant is Hallam's sense of the complexity of the critical enterprise, the conviction that to understand this poem he will need less to separate than to yoke together "poetry & morality & metre & everything." And for guidance in this enterprise, he turned respectfully to Tennyson. In a letter from about the same time (undated; probably January or February 1832), Hallam wrote to Tennyson concerning his Dante volume, "I expect to glean a good deal of knowledge from you concerning metres which may be serviceable, as well for my philosophy in the notes as for my actual handiwork in the text. I propose to discuss considerably about poetry in general and about the ethical character of Dante's poetry" (*Letters*, 502). Tennyson was given his friend's copy of Dante (inscribed "A. H. Hallam, 1828") after his death, but his own treatment of a character who spans Hallam's commitments both to Homer and to Dante might be seen as a reciprocal offering, one that employs the astonishing new generic mode of one possessed of so sophisticated a knowledge of "metres" and "poetry in general" that his brilliant friend deferred wholly to him in these matters. We are reminded that in Tennyson's dramatic monologues the technical precocity of the poems is inseparable from questions, in Hallam's terms, of morality and ethics. As we turn now to "Ulysses," we must press upon the relations among "poetry & morality & metre & everything."

"ULYSSES" AND THE RAPTURE OF TROY

In his 1859 review essay on Tennyson, Gladstone had little to say about "Ulysses," an uncharacteristic reserve that he explains by noting that the poems of Tennyson's 1842 volume were by this point so familiar to the public that it would be "superfluous" to comment in detail. My discussion considers the manner in which "Ulysses" came to resonate in the British culture at large, but one might note in a preliminary way that the early canonicity of "Ulysses" should in itself pique our curiosity. The densely allusive dramatic monologue of a character out of remote literary history, expressing misanthropic opinions in his characterization of his own people, urging members of his audience on to their certain deaths: the broad appeal of the poem might in this light seem unlikely. Gladstone notes, somewhat curtly, that Tennyson's "Ulysses" is "a highly finished poem," and it is certainly the case that its breathtaking mastery of steady but audacious blank verse can help to account for the effects the poem can have on a reader; already in 1844 "Ulysses" was being called "one of the most exquisite... poems in the language."[10] The year before publishing his essay on Tennyson, Gladstone had published his own three-volume *Studies on Homer*, a commentary weighing in at well over fifteen hundred pages; thus, he cannot resist adding of the poem, "It is open to the remark that it exhibits (so to speak) a corner-view of a character which was in itself a *cosmos*."[11] Here, Gladstone prevaricates. The monologue proffers in its seventy lines not only a manifold, if concentrated, representation of its speaker, but a cosmos: "Ulysses" does indeed "exhibit (so to speak)" a politically consequential, and potentially troubling, vision of a cosmos, a harmonious and well-ordered universe.

"Ulysses" opens with the speaker edging his way out of a community not unlike that which the Lotos-Eaters have also rejected, one made up of the men described derisively in Tennyson's earlier dramatic monologue "St. Simeon Stylites," who "House in the shade of comfortable roofs, / Sit with their wives by fires, eat wholesome food, / And wear warm clothes" (105–7). For Ulysses, as for Tennyson's Simeon, these benefits and even luxuries of civilized life are untenable. The life to which Ulysses has made his difficult return prompts his opening observation:

> It little profits that an idle king,
> By this still hearth, among these barren crags,
> Matched with an agèd wife, I mete and dole

Unequal laws unto a savage race,
That hoard, and sleep, and feed, and know not me. (1–5)

The speaker's adjectives would appear to bear the burden of his disaffection: he is "idle," his home is "still," his wife is "agèd" (and, one surmises, by metonymy, "barren"), the laws "unequal," and the people "savage." He is not alone in remarking the disjunction between his own majestic nature and the decidedly pedestrian nature of this place. In Pope's translation of the *Iliad*, Helen says of Ulysses, whom she is identifying for Priam, "A barren island boasts his glorious birth" (3:263); Ulysses' use of the word "barren" echoes her description. The environmental desolation of Ithaca is overwhelmed, of course, by its social isolation. While his adjectives convey immediately and unmistakably Ulysses' grim impression of his island, I would argue that his nouns ("king," "hearth," "wife," "laws," "race"), themselves seemingly without tonal valence, are what provoke so decided a shudder in this speaker. These lines, apparently rejecting the experience not only of domesticity but also of hierarchy, give already a glimpse of Ulysses' revisionary theories of government.

The despicable monotony of the lives of those he oversees (including that of his wife) has required him to husband himself, in order still more metaphorically to save himself, or, as he puts it, "For some three suns to store and hoard myself" (29). Among this population, Ulysses feels wholly solitary; the inhabitants' chief affront, in the phrase weighted at the stanza's end, is that they "know not me." Since Ulysses is renowned, presumably even among the Ithacans, it cannot be mere recognition he seeks. Rather, he yearns for a more profound intimacy, some ideal of community that Ithaca, with its strict hierarchies and domestic routines, cannot provide. The term "unequal," a pivotal word to which I shall return, is significant in light of the mission he proposes, namely, to re-create for himself a life among "peers," to be known among other names, to be reunited, in his most specific example, with "the great Achilles, whom we knew" (64). He seeks voyage not to escape the confines of sociality, but to draw still closer to its ideal. If some among this audience can be made to know him, then he will have re-created the selves whom he knew, including his own. The dramatic monologue in some sense thus serves as his introduction, as a primer to knowing Ulysses.

Many readers contend that the opening thirty-two lines of the poem, roughly the first half, constitute an interior monologue.[12] In contrast, I view the entire poem as performing what we now call a dramatic monologue: Ulysses is always addressing an audience. I hold this not only because I hold to the unity of the poem, as do others (I see this as an intensively crafted, highly composed, and internally consistent work, one consistent, moreover, with others of its generic kind). I would also argue, on a more thematic basis, that part of what this poem establishes is that its speaker is socially constructed to such an extreme degree—what hero isn't?—that it would be virtually impossible to separate him from his (in Ulysses' case) various audiences and social contexts. My claim regarding him, one I would extend to all of Tennyson's dramatic monologists, is that there is no private self beyond or unavailable to this representation, although there certainly is a complex of implied though unspoken ambitions and intentions. This is why, indeed, he is addressing the mariners at all: he needs them not just to man the ship, but to establish the identity of the speaker—in a sense, to man Ulysses.

I am claiming, moreover, that a key aspect of the genre from its inception is that it seeks to represent suasive speech, and these early lines must work to convince auditors that the speaker is in the wrong place, and so are they. Part of the fiction of the poem is that he is overheard, but Ulysses contrives, like Simeon Stylites and so many other speakers in dramatic monologues, to be thus overheard. As for his wielding of such insulting phrases as "savage race" and "rugged people," we might bear in mind, first, that this character has always displayed a robust talent for insult (we remember his punishing mockery of the common soldier Thersites in book 2 of the *Iliad*), and second, that he is presumably hoping to enlist some members of this citizenry, to turn them from rugged people to brother mariners, and he must establish a reason for their differentiating themselves, as his friends and comrades, from the mass of Ithacans. A third point in favor of his being entirely aware of his audience from the outset of his oration has bearing on the genre itself, in a dynamic we shall see again in other dramatic monologues. We learned from Antenor's description about the initially unprepossessing nature of Ulysses' speech; when he first begins, you would think him unskilled or a fool. Only such a speaker would insult his own auditors.

Part of the brilliance of Ulysses' rhetorical strategy, moreover, in the early lines of the monologue, the reason indeed that once he stands to speak no man can vie with him, stand up either against or to him, is that he makes his audience believe that what is at stake is his judgment of *them*. He usurps the power of judgment, so concealing the true nature of assessment at stake in the monologue—namely, how the speaker himself will be judged, his evaluation by his listeners, who may or may not be willing to accept his exhortations. In these opening lines, however, when he speaks of his auditors with distanced and clinical objectivity, he renders this populace the object of severe scrutiny and judgment, not himself. This is the Ulysses, we must remember from Tennyson's precursor Dante, who speaks from the position of having been definitively judged, indeed damned. Yet in the *Inferno*, Virgil silences Dante, disallowing his speech, for fear of the Greek's damning judgment of his inquisitor: "do thou / Thy tongue refrain... / For they were Greeks, [and] might shun discourse with thee" (26:73–74, 76, trans. Cary). Even Virgil and Dante lose sight of the fact that they are not the objects of judgment; the condemned Ulysses and Diomedes are. So too in Tennyson's monologue: Ulysses from the outset deftly shifts the burden of being evaluated onto his auditors. A dramatic monologist is always entering an arena of assessment and reflecting on, even as he or she manipulates, the complexities of public evaluation.

In an early manuscript of the poem, now at Harvard, the lines that follow his introductory outburst read:

Much have I suffered both on shore and when
Through scudding drifts the rainy Hyades
Vext the dim sea: I am become a name. (6–8)[13]

In revision, Tennyson seems to have attempted to give Ulysses greater motives for movement. I want to dwell for a moment on the difference this makes, because it anticipates the difference made by other revisions in the poem. In this earlier version, Ulysses is definitive in stressing that the significance of his past is in the consistency of its agony: "Much have I suffered" sums up his experience. With the revision, Ulysses becomes the future-oriented, forward-looking quester we have come to know:

I cannot rest from travel: I will drink
Life to the lees: all times I have enjoyed
Greatly, have suffered greatly, both with those
That loved me, and alone; on shore, and when
Through scudding drifts the rainy Hyades
Vext the dim sea: I am become a name. (6–11)

A past marked exclusively by singular suffering has been altered; to the original antinomies of the shore and the sea are added those of enjoyment and suffering, and of solitude tempered with loving companionship. The revision marks an advance poetically, with its intensification of the propulsive enjambment, which conveys how unstoppable he is until halted by recognition of what he has become. Every enjambed line marks another stride beyond customary limits. The revision also marks an advance rhetorically on Ulysses' part, since he must make the journey more appealing than on its merits it is; the Lotos-Eaters have taught us how unremitting is the labor of Ulysses' crew. His solipsism is evident in remembering "those that loved me," but so too is his calculation, as he now is attempting to re-create and so replace such fervent admirers, to join his auditors to the larger community of those that loved him.

But the revised version, for all that it now reveals about Ulysses' past, blunts the sharpness of one of its central elements. Suffering is clearly a leitmotif among Tennyson's monologists, especially suffering greatly, beyond the common sorrows of men and women. "Show me the man hath suffered more than I" (48), asks the self-mutilating Simeon, reasonably. Tithonus and Tiresias are among those who would attempt to meet this challenge, and the monologues of Demeter and Rizpah extend excess of suffering to the female sex. The invocation to the *Odyssey* gives us a Ulysses who is a person of infinite pains, like his monologist peers. Chapman's rendering of the invocation to the *Odyssey* introduces him as one who "at Sea felt many woes, / Much care sustaind" (1:7–8, trans. Chapman). Part of the burden of Tennyson's monologic speakers is to show that their suffering marks them as distinct from, and indeed superior to, what Tithonus calls "the kindly race of men" (29).

Both versions culminate in the clause "I am become a name." This pronouncement does not necessarily follow from either version, although the string of colons that structures a sentence of nearly a dozen lines appears to set up each clause as following rationally from the previous one, as indeed most do. But the construction of this lament is itself curious: why is it phrased "I am become a name," instead of, for example, "I have become a name" (one of many other now inconceivable options)? The lines that precede this vary from present tense ("I cannot cease") to future tense ("I will drink") to past tense ("I have enjoyed"): "I am become a name" seems to encompass each tense, so comprising a grammatical survey of the man before us, himself an amalgam of past achievements, future possibilities, and, above all, present rhetorical predicaments. To become a name is to have become a name, but also to be always becoming a name, always in formation of a public self. In the distinctive phrasing, certainly, inheres the idea that in all of these experiential antinomies and oppositions, he became the renowned hero, the great Ulysses who now speaks. But its uneasy dramatic present tense seems also to suggest that this process of becoming is ongoing, and is occurring even as he speaks, as he seeks to become a name, again, for auditors who have not known him. Part of the transformation this monologue must effect, then, is that the speaker must become, as he speaks, the name he has become. His ironic predicament is precisely that anticipated by the Lotos-Eaters: his "great deeds," which have caused him to suffer and enjoy "greatly," have rendered him legendary, and yet therefore unrecognizable, unknown, "half-forgotten." The dramatic monologue seeks his transformation into infinite denomination, as he seeks becoming a name perpetually and in perpetuity.

In reminiscing about his heady former days, Ulysses recalls for his audience what it is to know and be known, to enjoy social context and "civilized" engagement:

> For always roaming with a hungry heart
> Much have I seen and known; cities of men
> And manners, climates, councils, governments,
> Myself not least, but honoured of them all;
> And drunk delight of battle with my peers,
> Far on the ringing plains of windy Troy.
> I am a part of all that I have met. (12–18)

Placing "myself" securely among "them all," Ulysses is "honoured," a point he makes in order to assess for his audience his placement, his prior evaluations, so as to dictate his current one. But there has been and still is no viable existence for him that is removed from the architecture of social hierarchy. For Ulysses, there is also little distinction between smooth governments and battlefields, as he drinks delight from any cup of communal interaction. To have "drunk delight of battle with my peers" refers both to his allies and his enemies, as the honor was in battling worthy opponents. In a sense, these lines provide an example of his enjoying greatly and suffering greatly concurrently, since delight and the rigors of battle are allied. Declaring "I am a part of all that I have met," Ulysses lists not the topography of land or sea, nor the fantastical beings that make up the details of much of his story, but only the types of society through which he has so fluidly moved. And in this he is similar to the hero of the *Odyssey*; as Chapman's translation of the invocation puts it, "The cities of a world of nations, / With all their manners, mindes and fashions, / He saw and knew" (1:5–7, trans. Chapman). Ulysses does not list the individuals who inhabit these cities, the rulers and villains he has known. He has positioned himself not among people, but among social organizations, as if in implicit recognition that he is himself less a man than an institution.

But critics have not had much to say about Ulysses' catalogue of what he has seen and known, as if he lists disjointed, imprecise impressions. Tucker, for example, largely dismisses the summary of experience that Ulysses offers:

> The "Much" he has seen and known boils down to little enough. The jingle of "men / And manners" takes each of its terms a step away from referentiality toward mere sound; "councils" and "governments" seem identical; and if these curiosities do not suffice, the impatient, time-keeping insertion of "climates" into Ulysses' catalogue of the social and political achievements of mankind gives the game away.[14]

Although Tucker's skepticism justifiably resists the manipulations of this speaker, I propose that we take Ulysses' catalogue more literally. It is true that "men / And manners" as a phrase reflects Tennyson's overly developed alliterative tendencies, a problem the poet recognized in himself; his signature predilection for producing "mere sound" is a question I take up in chapter 5. It seems to me nevertheless that Ulysses' referentiality is highly specific. "Cities of men / And manners" contrasts Troy's sophisticated urban aristocracy (which I consider more closely in part 3) with the savage people among whom he now resides. "Councils" points to one form of government; Ulysses is surely referring to the councils of the Achaeans in the *Iliad*, in which he as orator especially shone. The monarchy of Troy might stand as a contrasting form of "government." Some decades after the publication of "Ulysses," Gladstone in *Juventus Mundi* would make a similar point, writing of the "political society" of Troy: "We have every sign that the Trojan elders did not act collectively as a Council. This is an important defect in such a body with reference to the means of moral influence."[15] The term "climate," rather than being "time-keeping," may be the most specific invocation of all that he has seen and known. By "climate," he intends environments social as well as meteorological; in both categories he has experienced heavy weather. Helen was perhaps inexact in placing the seat of his "glorious birth" on Ithaca's rocky shores; she witnessed that emergence as she looked out on the Achaean encampment. Now his peers can only be the members, comrades as well as enemies, of the Trojan theater ("men of the ten years' war in Troy," as the Lotos-Eaters put it), including, I hope to show, the Trojans Aeneas and Tithonus. Ulysses is a part of all who were defined and formed by the events in and around that windy city.

Tucker observes that in this summary of experience, "Ulysses appears to have traced his itinerary backward through the world of the *Odyssey* to that of the *Iliad*,"[16] and we can see that Ulysses' monologue does move him steadily back from Ithaca to Troy. Jerome Buckley praises "Far on the ringing plains of windy Troy" as a "spacious line,"[17] and it is indeed capacious not only in its evocations but also in the range of its allusions. Troy's remoteness is recalled ("Far"), as is the way that battle is inscribed in its topographical features ("ringing plains"); one line encompasses that city's geography, geology, and a climate that is indistinguishable, in the familiarity of its epithet, from the place it engulfs, "windy Troy." In ending this catalogue by inviting the ghost of that city to linger about a place that has little other record of its existence, Ulysses is of course borrowing the minstrel's own phrase. This poem, as demonstrated by Ricks's notes and the exhausting if not wholly exhaustive excavation of classical sources provided by such nineteenth- and early twentieth-century cataloguers of Tennyson's allusions as John Churton Collins and Wilfred P. Mustard, is in many ways a pastiche of phrases drawn, consciously or not (the poet was defensive on this point), from Tennyson's classical literary background.

"Windy Troy," an especially evocative phrase for Tennyson, as we saw in the previous chapter, is recognizable even without the good offices of editors and critics, but he ensures, in a note provided in the Eversley edition of his works, that we do not miss the allusion in the next line. Tennyson attributes Ulysses' conclusive declaration, "I am a part of all that I have met," to a phrase from the proem to book 2 of the *Aeneid*: *quorum pars magna fui* (Eversley ed., 2:339). Dido has just requested that Aeneas recount the story of Troy's fall, and he tells her how sorrowful the sights were:

> All that I saw, and part of which I was,
> Not ev'n the hardest of our foes could hear,
> Nor stern Ulysses tell without a tear. (2:8–10, trans. Dryden)

In recalling the event "of which I was a great part," Tennyson's Victorian Ulysses evokes Aeneas's version of events, a linkage to the Dardanian prince that is consequential for my reading of the rest of the monologue. But Virgil's Aeneas himself links what he saw to Ulysses, and this should signal that Ulysses is returning us to the scene of Troy's destruction. We know from the *Odyssey* that Ulysses weeps when he hears the minstrel Demodocus sing of "the town sacked by Akhaians / pouring down from the horse's hollow cave, / this way and that raping the steep city" (8:518–20, trans. Fitzgerald). The narrative of Troy's rapture, accomplished through Ulysses' equine ruse, is one that even Ulysses appears pained to hear. But Aeneas imagines the burden Troy's destroyers might feel in *telling* the story, and we must attend to the ways in which Ulysses, embarking here on his own recollection of the rapture of Troy, cannot evade tears.

Ulysses' catalogue of his experiences constitutes the poet's summation not of what can be known of Ulysses, but of what Ulysses has known, and it does seem in retrospect that his adventures have provided civic lessons, lessons in cities, in citizenry, in *civitas*. Why this stress on governing bodies and social organizations? Partly because, as he moves to the subject of the governance he imagines under the regime of his son, the choices he is making and is attempting to compel others to make are social and political in nature. In the case of "Ulysses," how is it that a speaker so drawn to the abstract notion of society is so loath to remain in the society where he now finds himself? The monologue has specified Ulysses' attraction to "cities of men / And manners," but the speaker's turn to Telemachus dramatizes the inaptness of such terms for this place and this people:

> This is my son, mine own Telemachus,
> To whom I leave the sceptre and the isle—
> Well-loved of me, discerning to fulfil
> This labour, by slow prudence to make mild
> A rugged people, and through soft degrees
> Subdue them to the useful and the good.
> Most blameless is he, centred in the sphere
> Of common duties, decent not to fail
> In offices of tenderness, and pay
> Meet adoration to my household gods,
> When I am gone. He works his work, I mine. (33–43)

I have compared the addition of this verse paragraph to the version of "Ulysses" published in Tennyson's 1842 *Poems* to his addition of the verse paragraph that is section 6 in "The Lotos-Eaters," in which the speakers also pass on their property as well as their responsibilities to their sons. The Lotos-Eaters, however, are more ambivalent about the transfer than Ulysses, who here insists on his son inheriting him: "to whom I leave the sceptre and the isle" is contractual, indeed performative language. Ulysses in more ways than one states his will.

He is also subjecting to his will his auditors; with the introduction of Telemachus comes the overt recognition, and perhaps also the public positioning, of the speaker's audience, and thus the invention for this hero and king of a corporate "we." The deictics that begin the penultimate and final verses ("This is my son"; "There lies the port") establish for the speaker a social and physical context that the preceding lines do not. Immediately before introducing Telemachus, Ulysses has declared his ambition "To follow knowledge like a sinking star / Beyond the utmost bound of human thought" (31–32). That geographical and conceptual boundlessness narrows precipitously to his knowledge of this son and this place, as the speaker's vision shifts from the farsightedness of one who has long scanned the horizon to the myopia of one who squints even upon what is near.

According to Ricks, this moment constitutes for Tennyson a poetic failing: "The crucial passage is that in which Ulysses hands over the mundane responsibilities to his son Telemachus. But at this point something goes wrong in terms of the poem's addressees. 'This is my son, mine own Telemachus'; too staged, this invites a demeaning 'How do you do.'" Although I agree with Ricks's sense of the tonal alteration of these lines, I see this staged transition serving as a fitting rhetorical move for the monologist, who intends this abrupt shift to the local. In describing his son as "Well-loved of me," Ulysses intends to will not only his title and property but also his quality of being loved by others, as if to say, Let him be well-loved *like* me. But it is evident that Telemachus is nothing like Ulysses, and this patrilineal dissonance is so patent that it has long provoked debate over the nature not only of the terms of Ulysses' introduction of his son, but more elusively, of his tone, since the poem was first published. Mermin comments, "The praise is so unconvincing that many readers quite reasonably suspect the presence of irony,"[18] and certainly the great warrior's description of his civilized son can sound ambivalent. Many read Ulysses' introduction as a scornful, and ultimately dismissive, assessment; others argue that for Ulysses Telemachus is exemplary. Culler offers a representative positive reading, based on Tennyson's own commitment to gradualism: "Ulysses could hardly be more affectionate or approving."[19]

To understand Ulysses' representation of his son we must consider more deeply the ways in which Telemachus bears a strong resemblance to another epic hero, one noted also for being prudent, decent, discerning, blameless, one skilled in civilizing others, subduing them to his mild yoke, a hero noted especially for his filial devotion, his tenderness and meet adoration for his household gods, one to whom Ulysses has already alluded: *pius* Aeneas. Perhaps few since Dido have found that hero especially riveting, yet no one could gainsay his ability to establish an empire, to subdue into civilization any population he finds himself ruling. The powerful similarity, in Ulysses' representation of him, of Telemachus to Aeneas has been insufficiently examined, although certainly it has always been clear that Aeneas is a far more Tennysonian hero than the wayward Ulysses, strongly resembling the Arthur of *Idylls of the King* in his mildness and capacity to found a society its chroniclers perceive as ideal. More to the point for this dramatic monologue, it is clear that the figure of Aeneas, and especially his piety with regard to his father's household gods, pressed as closely upon Tennyson in his mourning as the figure of Ulysses.

Tennyson's two major statements about "Ulysses" overlap, and both pertain not only to "Ulysses" but also to the poem "On a Mourner" (1833, 1865), which ends with an image of Aeneas. In both statements the poet claims "Ulysses" was a response of mourning: it "was written soon after Arthur Hallam's death," the *Memoir* records; it "was written under the sense of loss and that all had gone by," he told James Knowles. "On a Mourner" was written "immediately" (*Poems*, 1:610) after Tennyson learned of the death of his friend. Tennyson also told Knowles regarding "Ulysses" that "there is more about myself in it" than in most of *In Memoriam*, although any reader of the poem knows that the poet's self is not of easy access. "On a Mourner" was initially directly self-referential, speaking openly of the sensations of an "I" who is the poet himself, but in extensive revision he omitted more personal stanzas, altered "my" to "thy," and supplied a title that makes claims to objective rather than subjective observation in an attempt to render it nearly as oblique in its self-referentiality as "Ulysses." Tennyson's two statements on "Ulysses" make the same point regarding that poem's interest in propulsion: "It gave my feeling about the need of going forward and braving the struggle of life more simply than anything in *In Memoriam*" (*Memoir*, 1:196) and expressed the "sense" "that still life must be fought out to the end."[20] "Going forward" is the central impulse represented in "On a Mourner" as well. Though not generally discussed together, these poems parallel one another in their origins and aims, and "On a Mourner" sheds particular light on Ulysses' injunctions to his son.[21]

"On a Mourner" ends with the story of Aeneas rising to make sacrifice, having resolved to lead his people from the disastrous shores of Crete, where they are perishing, and on to the further shores of Hesperia, or Italy. This is a crucial moment for Aeneas, one in which he resolves quite literally to trust his "feeling about the need of going forward and braving the struggle of life," not to rest on this shore but to proceed to the necessary trials ahead. Tennyson imagines the conditions whereby will come "Faith" and "Virtue," and what the arrival of those personified abstractions (in some sense, two of the names Tennyson gives to Aeneas's household gods; others are Hope and Memory) will effect:

> VI
> And when no mortal motion jars
>   The blackness round the tombing sod,
> Through silence and the trembling stars
>   Comes Faith from tracts no feet have trod,
>   And Virtue, like a household god
>
> VII
> Promising empire; such as those
>   Once heard at dead of night to greet
> Troy's wandering prince, so that he rose
>   With sacrifice, while all the fleet
>   Had rest by stony hills of Crete. (26–35)

These closing lines of "On a Mourner" refer to the story Aeneas tells Dido in book 3 of the *Aeneid*, in which the wandering Trojans have attempted to settle in Crete, mistakenly believed by Aeneas's father, Anchises, to be the original seat of "the race and lineage of the Trojan kind" (3:138, trans. Dryden).[22] The Trojans begin to build one of their failed serial Troys, a city with lofty towers of similar design to the original, and are overjoyed when Aeneas calls it by the old name of Pergamum. While Aeneas is going about civilizing the place and the people ("I myself new marriages promote, / Give laws, and dwellings" [3:188–89, trans. Dryden]), plague and scorching sun begin to destroy both. That night, Aeneas has a dream in which his household gods appear to him; they "spoke and eased my troubled mind" (3:207, trans. Dryden). Reminding him that they "from the burning town by thee were brought" (3:211, trans. Dryden), they do indeed, and quite specifically, promise empire. Because of this dream, "Troy's wandering prince" at once recommences his journey and ends his wandering. In this transitional moment the terms Tennyson uses for Aeneas cease to designate his identity, as the household gods essentially tell him that he will become an empire's established king. In awe at these visitants, he, as Tennyson with brevity puts it, "rose with sacrifice." But in ending the poem Tennyson suspends Aeneas here, thus making his posture perpetual, as if in effect accepting and denying the future the household gods have just vouchsafed him. Directly upon Virgil's Aeneas telling his father the dream, the fleet quits Crete's shore, but Tennyson's Aeneas can never leave, standing as fixed to the rocky shore as is Tennyson's Ulysses at the start of his monologue.

Ulysses' turn to Ithaca's household gods is a turn, then, to those of Troy, since the Victorian Ulysses cannot but speak in intimate knowledge of the *Aeneid*. Even the landscape of "stony" Crete resembles that of Ithaca; Fitzgerald's translation has Helen characterizing Ithaca (in place of Pope's "barren"), as a "bare and stony island" (3:240). The household gods animate Virgil's account of the fall of Troy. Aeneas had in effect a previous dream to that represented in "On a Mourner" involving the household gods, early in the night when Ulysses and his men had already been disgorged from the horse's interior and were setting the city alight. Hector returns to him in ghastly form, but does not answer Aeneas's many questions regarding himself, instead announcing Troy's fall from its great height: *ruit alto a culmine Troia* (2:290; Dryden's version has "Troy nods from high and totters to her fall"). Hector thereupon gives to Aeneas's safekeeping the household gods. The announcement of the fall of Troy's towers and the bequeathing of the household gods are thus aligned along the keen geometry of sorrow's logic. This is what Troy's greatest hero, appearing to Aeneas in the physical state to which his awesome opponent Achilles had reduced him, does in the moment of a return that is in fact a farewell: attend to the household gods. His words (*sacra suosque tibi commendat Troia Penates* [2:291]), committing Troy's sacred things and household gods (*Penates*) to Aeneas, will haunt Aeneas's future dreams, as they do in Crete. It is the hero's chief responsibility before his leave-taking (in Hector's case, his vanishing) to place these sacred objects in the hands of the future ruler.

This moment of the assumption of responsibility for the household gods is one that Tennyson holds, in a poem written directly upon his becoming one of literature's most prominent mourners, as most analogous to the mourner's situation. In the chaos and despair of the Trojan aftermath, Aeneas's rising in sacrifice displays heroism as subtle as it is immense. It connotes the resuscitation not only of an individual but of the Trojan line, the perpetuation of a people now decimated and dispersed. And it points to the ultimate triumphing of the Trojans, or Romans, over the Greeks, of Aeneas over the Ulysses who has tricked and exterminated his people.

Aeneas's qualities of decency, piety, and filial obedience render him the architect of a civilization, along lines Ulysses is now commanding that Telemachus draw; Ulysses sees in Telemachus both the harbinger and the product of a certain social ideal. But the contrast between Aeneas's legacy and his own must be striking to Tennyson's Ulysses, the product as much of Virgil and Dante as of Homer. From Troy's ashes rises a greater empire; this realm, when contrasted with Ulysses' savage people on a barren island, constitutes vengeance indeed. Dante makes this clear when he notes, even as he is listing Ulysses' infractions, that the "ambush of the horse, ... opened wide / A portal for that goodly seed to pass / Which sow'd imperial Rome." Surely that knowledge is itself more painful than the flame that engulfs him and the punishment that he and Diomedes "with ceaseless groans deplore." Aeneas himself curses Ithaca as the Trojan ships pass it in their journey toward Hesperia; in Aeneas's account, "We fly from Ithaca's detested shore, / And curse the land that dire Ulysses bore" (3:353–54, trans. Dryden). And it is indeed as if Ulysses recognizes that his island is cursed by the escaped seed of Troy.

Out of Troy's flames, Aeneas bore his father and his household gods on his back, clutching his young son by the hand; when Ulysses turns to Telemachus, he speaks as if he had borne furious (unrecorded) witness to Aeneas's burdensome retreat. (Aeneas himself sees his enemy when he returns to try to find his errant, unlucky wife, Creusa: he spots Ulysses guarding the plundered treasures of Troy, some of which was later unearthed, ostensibly, by Schliemann.) In charging the son he acknowledges as "mine own" to pay "Meet adoration to my household gods," Ulysses is yielding possession of each to each, in the hope that his abdication is an annunciation.

Ulysses' injunctions to and about his son are in earnest; he wants a son like his enemy Aeneas, which can help account for the fact that the qualities of Telemachus are at once detestable in their associations and desired in their effects. The Trojan's are the skills that build a city and an empire, while Ulysses' more aggressive talents decimate them. In a sense, he is offering praise for qualities he never desired to have and detailing a project he has no interest in undertaking—therefore both his praise and his condescension are, we might say, authentic. And yet Telemachus is a part of what Ulysses is desperate to leave, as unacceptable to his father ultimately as the scepter and the isle that by the direct will of his father, here stated and thus enacted, he at this moment assumes and represents. In characterizing his son's qualities, it becomes clear, Ulysses is characterizing a political position, a theory of social organization, but we must bear in mind that it is finally a position he finds personally uncongenial. With what would the resourceful Ulysses replace it?

In making so dramatic and elaborate a public introduction of a son who is already known, Ulysses is enacting a ceremonial installation of his son into public life, handing him the scepter that represents rule over the isle. This ceremony of introducing a young man into the polis points to Telemachus's own status as an ephebe, as in the Telemachiad (the first four books of the *Odyssey*), as an adolescent in search of his father, he was. But in introducing an ephebe, Ulysses produces a king. The critical fact for the speaker regarding his son is that Telemachus will not merely make a capable bureaucrat; rather, he is a ruler, now holding this sceptered isle in his power. Ulysses begins his monologue despairing of his own status as an "idle king," and the sting in this for him is not an insupportable idleness (the tasks he sets Telemachus indicate there is much to be done), but his own position as the monarch of Ithaca. The laws of Ithaca are "unequal" because they do not legislate a society that would recognize or value equality. The verse paragraph assigning Telemachus his tasks is less concerned, finally, with the new king than with the "savage race" he is charged with ruling: "rugged," in need of being subdued to "the useful and the good," subjugated into unaccustomed states of usefulness and virtue. Telemachus must be their king, not their "peer," while Ulysses turns away to search out more viable companions among the audience he addresses. Ulysses contends that, unlike his son, he would not be a king but a comrade.

With his words of introduction and evaluation, Ulysses has transformed the status of his son; he has created a ruler and a system of rule by the performance of his words. When he turns in the next stanza to his audience, he transforms it too by his address, by way of the dramatic monologue itself. Given the connection I have been exploring between Telemachus and Aeneas, and especially the moment when Aeneas turns again to his ships on Crete's stony shore, it is not surprising that Ulysses also would now turn, having made his own provisions for household gods that he still acknowledges to be his own, to his own ship and stony shore. This is the moment of Ulysses' clear transition to a mode of direct address, although I have contended that he has been aware of, and indeed indirectly but deliberately addressing, this audience all along. It is nevertheless certainly the case that a major shift occurs, as he draws them fully and directly into the discursive world he would have them inhabit:

> There lies the port; the vessel puffs her sail;
> There gloom the dark broad seas. My mariners,
> Souls that have toiled, and wrought, and thought with me—
> That ever with a frolic welcome took
> The thunder and the sunshine, and opposed
> Free hearts, free foreheads—you and I are old;
> Old age hath yet his honour and his toil,

> Death closes all: but something ere the end,
> Some work of noble note, may yet be done,
> Not unbecoming men that strove with Gods. (44–53)

"Frolic welcome" is hardly the attitude toward voyage characterized by the Lotos-Eaters, who tell us that life with Ulysses "all labor" was ("Lotos-Eaters," 87). But the speaker represents the ongoing renewal of apparently uncontainable joy: "ever" did they offer eager willingness to face, indeed oppose the elements. In this somber, incantatory evening piece, this note of glad abandon seems inapposite, and yet he is attempting quite directly to dictate their reception of his current proposal. Referring to their "free hearts, free foreheads" even as he works to enthrall them, he invokes these body parts to serve metonymically. He suggests to them that their desire, their frolic welcome of the scheme he proposes, is at once emotional and intellectual.

In considering Telemachus, Ulysses does allow, within limits, for the autonomy of another person; whether dismissive or respectful, Ulysses' "He works his works, I mine" allows and indeed insists upon his son's distinction from himself. He shifts, however, to the focus of his address, the mariners, and the work of the monologue takes a sharp turn when he calls them "My mariners, / Souls that have toiled, and wrought, and thought with me." These all work their work together with Ulysses, and, he implies, the "utmost bound of human thought" take its broad measure in part from these fellow souls. I have argued that Ulysses has been indirectly addressing these auditors all along; here, he transforms them into mariners, a metamorphosis he accomplishes in the monologue, by way of the monologue. He creates them by naming them, as he has created a king in his son by decree. This moment of direct address, when the dramatic monologue most fully announces itself, constitutes the creation by the speaker of an audience directly affected and indeed transformed by his speech.

Ulysses' shift to the direct address of his mariners is represented in Dante's account, as his speaker in effect describes in retrospect what Tennyson's Ulysses now says. In the *Inferno*, Ulysses repeats to Dante his counsel to the mariners:

> "O brothers!" I began, "who to the west
> Through perils without numbers now have reach'd,
> To this the short remaining watch that yet
> Our senses have to wake, refuse it proof
> Of the unpeopled world, following the track
> Of Phoebus. Call to mind from whence ye sprang:
> Ye were not form'd to live the life of brutes,
> But virtue to pursue and knowledge high."
> With these few words I sharpen'd for the voyage
> The mind of my associates, that I then
> Could scarcely have withheld them. (26:111–22, trans. Cary)

Dante's Ulysses quotes his own disastrously convincing "few words," and Tennyson extends this speech into what would become a prototype of the dramatic monologue.[23] Although he has prefaced this exhortation by stressing their age ("Tardy with age / Were I and my companions" [104–5]), in following the track of Phoebus, these ancient mariners become again literally ephebes, followers of Apollo. As Ulysses has made his son inherit him prematurely, so he has himself usurped the role of ephebe, becoming again a figure marginal to his own society, with much to prove. Dante's Ulysses urges his men toward "the unpeopled world," though the voyage is testimony to Ulysses' need for people, and especially these "brothers" and "associates." Tennyson renders the "brutes" to which Dante's Ulysses alludes into the inhabitants of the speaker's own Ithaca, a. "savage race," and elaborates on Ulysses' desire not only for exploration but also for "companions." Tennyson's Ulysses desires to embark on a journey both as a radical rejection of civic life and in profound espousal of those whom he may call brothers, associates, companions, peers.

But what would a world without people (*mondo sanza gente* in Dante), a depopulated country, look like? I think Ulysses will know it when he sees it, because he knew it when he left it. With the rapture of Troy, its population was slaughtered, enslaved, or fled into exile and its towers decimated, "A peopled city made a desert place," as Aeneas tells Dido (2:7, trans. Dryden). In Tennyson's translation of Horace's *Ode* III.iii, we hear Juno insist, regarding that city, that what is broken so remain, vowing that if ever another Troy rose, she would devastate it anew. In a review of Schliemann's findings, Jebb, forwarding an insight more useful regarding the nature of Victorian Homeric emotion than the nature of archaeological excavation, underscores the import of these lines from Horace. Jebb insists that had a place called Troy existed, its destruction would have been so complete as to leave no trace behind, not even the quadrant Schliemann claimed to have unearthed:

> The Greek belief that Homeric Troy had been utterly destroyed is an inseparable part of the Trojan legend.... That the conquerors, when the long-deferred day of vengeance came, should have destroyed part of the town, but left one quarter of it standing for the use of any Trojans who might prefer to go on quietly living there, would have seemed to ancient Greeks not merely an absurd anticlimax, an inexplicable weakness, but a positive impiety towards the gods.[24]

To refuse proof of the unpeopled world to his own vigilant eye, Ulysses would have to avoid the Trojan plain (perhaps this is one reason his "purpose" is to sail beyond the western stars, moving ever westward to avoid the eastern realms that were Troy's). After having been awakened by the ghostly Hector and entrusted with the household gods, or Penates, Aeneas races toward the burning center of Troy, and on his way encounters the priest Panthus, himself carrying household gods. The words of this minor figure, burdened with a cargo similar to that Aeneas will also carry from the flames of the city, are stark and overwhelming, and perhaps the keenest statement of what Ulysses has accomplished. Tennyson's Ulysses knows the substance of what Aeneas is told by Panthus because he wrought it, rendering a city and a people into past tense: *fuimus Troes, fuit Ilium* (2:325; "We have been Trojans, Ilium has been"). In Chapman's translation, Ulysses describes the city in the aftermath of the war as "High Troy depopulate," and his rendering of a verb into an adjective itself shows how the place is now marked by its unpeopled state. Benjamin, in his popular 1880 book *Troy*, composes a kind of elegy for this holocaust: "When the gray light of dawn appeared, unsightly heaps of ashes, and smouldering embers, intermingled with calcinated bones, and piles of blackened ruins, and lurid volumes of smoke rolling up to the skies, alone remained to indicate where Troy had been. A city and a nation had passed out of existence."[25]

But what of Ulysses' relation to the people he now addresses? Tennyson's monologue is interposed in the moment of the *Inferno* when Ulysses quotes the convincing arguments he made to his men. He extrapolates from this example of "false counsel," and his own poetics are so successful that readers ever since have been roused by its call, as if illustrating how it is that anyone could be. I propose, however, that the counsel is "false" not because the speaker is deliberately leading his auditors to their deaths, but because he is leading them to a dream of being his peer. In hinting at the possibility of social equality, Tennyson's Ulysses dangerously pursues that alternative of political organization still at the margins of Victorian political culture in the years of the poem's composition and revision: democracy. That the idea of democracy, a definitive word for the nebulous terms of Ulysses' proposal to his auditors, is a subtext of the poem can help to account for its appropriation for the ends of progressive politicians. We might look, for example, to the use of the poem in the United States: the 1984 Democratic Convention speech of Senator Edward Kennedy closed with a selection from the final lines of "Ulysses," which he described as having been one of the favorite poems of his brother, President John F. Kennedy. By the end of the nineteenth century, a critic in Britain could note that quoting from the poem is almost superfluous, so widely and intimately is it known: "There is no need to quote what everyone knows by heart; but I cannot imagine an age which should be indifferent to 'Ulysses.' Ulysses puts into imperishable words an aspiration as old as man, and growing stronger with every century of his development." The same critic also insists, and in this view found ample company, "A better expression of the best English spirit than breathes in 'Ulysses' cannot be found."[26]

In midcentury Victorian Britain, Gladstone claimed that the oratory employed by Homer's Greeks was "essentially an instrument addressing itself to reason and free will, and acknowledging their authority" (*SH*, 3:111). Considering the Achaean assembly, Gladstone surmises in *Studies on Homer*, "All ranks apparently went to the Assemblies as freemen, and were treated there by their superiors with respect" (*SH*, 3:92). The debate occasioned by Agamemnon's question as to whether to end the war, for example, according to Turner, "suggested to Gladstone that the soldiers were accustomed to hearing policy debated and then reaching some collective decision."[27] In this light, Ulysses' address to the mariners appeals to what he calls their "free hearts, free foreheads"; the decision to stay or leave is ostensibly theirs. Gladstone's description of the oratorical methods of the Greeks raises important questions for our reading of this dramatic monologue. His reading of Homeric orators as exemplifying proto-democratic ideals can be useful in reading Tennyson's earlier dramatic monologue, in which Ulysses claims that, in contrast to relations on this stony island, with its savages and kings, the community they will form in moving "beyond the sunset" will be one of free men. In an ideological flirtation, the poem experiments with the viability of something like democracy, but finds it an unsustainable notion. Ulysses is no (living) man's comrade, or equal, or peer, or even friend, nor is he a democrat thwarted by his ruling status. He cannot therefore sustain this fantasy of future democratic interaction.

In his capacity for subduing a rugged people into usefulness by "slow de-grees," we might see in Telemachus's rule the implementation of the Whig ideal of gradualism, a concept with profound appeal for Tennyson. Indeed, Kozicki al-lies this character so closely with the poet that, though he warns us that Tennyson "'is' neither Ulysses nor Telemachus," he declares, "If we must choose, the poet is certainly Telemachus."[28] Under Telemachus, a savage people will be made mild by offices of slow prudence, undergoing unhurried but ongoing amelioration, overseen and orchestrated by a benevolent system of rule. This sluggish pace of transformation cannot suit Ulysses, though, and while Telemachus's project may be congenial to Tennyson, it is Ulysses' stance, his bold consideration of what looks like "unbounded" progress, social more than nautical, that the monologue explores.

Ulysses appears to offer a more accelerated, even revolutionary, pace of change. But would the community he seeks now to form, by way of his monologue, in the end differ so greatly from that he seeks to abandon? Readers have always felt Ulysses to be offering, whether to his credit or discredit, an alternative to the civic organization he leaves in Telemachus's capable hands, but we might see these ap-parently contrasting systems of governance, both ostensibly progressive, as finally the same. He is to join with his auditors, he says at the end of the monologue, in "one equal temper of heroic hearts," engaging in the shared opposition of all obstacles with "free hearts, free foreheads," and yet his dramatic monologue nevertheless patently maintains the prerogatives of his own position, the sense of a certain inborn priority. Such an attitude does answer to one definition of the word "democratic." According to Raymond Williams, "To be democratic, to have democratic manners or feelings, is to be unconscious of class distinctions, or consciously to disregard or overcome them in everyday behaviour: acting *as if* all people were equal, and deserved equal respect, whether this is really so or not."

A person might, he continues, "believe in free speech and free assembly," and yet "could for example oppose universal suffrage, let alone government directed solely to the interests of the majority."[29]

The conservative young Gladstone's representation of Ulysses as a Whig in his correspondence with Hallam may not, in some sense, be too far different from Tennyson's representation here. Any reductive, retroactive assignment of the complex character of Ulysses to a political party in ascendancy at the time of this poem's composition is of course to be strenuously avoided. But criticism should not avoid, as it largely has, the richly significant social and political context of this poem. It is crucial, in considering this dramatic monologue or any other, to avoid fixing overly direct correspondences or identifications between the world of the monologist and that of the poet. Achilles does not stand in any simple sense for Hallam, any more than Ulysses or Telemachus flatly represents Tennyson, Hallam, or Gladstone. Gladstone's aversion to Hallam's attempt to forward any direct comparison between himself and a Homeric character was a sound impulse. But Gladstone also found that attaching contemporary significance to Homeric material was unavoidable, and indeed desirable.

"How my Whiggism must flutter within me," Hallam teasingly wrote to Gladstone in the 1820s, "to hear that Ulysses had all *the bad qualities* of the set? . . . Craft, I suppose, dissimulation, low cunning, cruelty, & such like little items are to be marked off as the Whig qualities of Ulysses." I have reviewed the suspicions aroused by the Whigs for both conservatives and liberals. The suspected duplicity of the Whigs was much remarked upon by Benjamin Disraeli, as I have noted, who called them "pretended advocates of popular rights." At the same time, radicals were also skeptical: the trade union orator in George Eliot's *Felix Holt, the Radical* pronounces, "I say, the Reform Bill is a trick," a ruse serving "to keep the aristocrats safe in their monopoly." The extension of the franchise is the surest sign of Whiggish dissimulation: "It's bribing some of the people with votes to make them hold their tongues about the rest." Just as Disraeli asserted he could not "comprehend" such an entity as a "democratic aristocrat," so the trade union orator concludes, "I don't believe much in Liberal aristocrats."[30]

While "Ulysses" has been used to forward progressive agendas, it has also been used for more conservative ones. One of the poem's most fervent initial admirers was Thomas Carlyle, whose 1843 *Past and Present* makes direct use of the recently published 1842 "Ulysses" to exemplify the concept of "hero-worship," which he calls "the soul of all social business among men." The final pages of book 1 of *Past and Present*, titled "Hero-Worship," derive their figurative ferocity from a reading of "Ulysses" that is unconditionally political. Carlyle urges his readers to cease revolutions in favor of reverence:

> Yes, friends: Hero-kings, and a whole world not unheroic,—there lies the port and happy haven, towards which, through all these stormtossed seas, French

Revolutions, Chartisms, Manchester Insurrections, that make the heart sick in
these bad days, the Supreme Powers are driving us...Towards that haven will
we, O friends; let all true men, with what of faculty is in them, bend valiantly,
incessantly, with thousandfold endeavor, thither, thither! There, or else in the
Ocean-abysses, it is very clear to me, we shall arrive.

Echoing Tennyson's Ulysses ("there lies the port") and finally referring to the
"Happy Isles" where, in his slight misquotation, "there dwells the great Achilles
whom we knew," Carlyle advances an interpretation of "Ulysses" that suits his
rhetorical purposes.[31] The "Hero-king" charts an aggressive course through the
popular revolutions and insurrections of those who seek to replace this ruling
force with a more diverse and representative leadership. Offering evidence that
Ulysses' supreme oratorical gifts, as skillfully represented by Tennyson, are so flex-
ible as to succeed with any audience, the poem has impressed not only Democratic
presidents in our day, but conservative prime ministers in the poet's own. Richard
Monckton Milnes, later Lord Houghton, described how, following the orders of
Carlyle, he obtained for Tennyson a civic pension in the 1840s. Sir Robert Peel,
then Tory prime minister, "knew nothing" of Tennyson when his name was
suggested; his son Hallam records, "Houghton said that he then made Peel read
'Ulysses,' whereupon the pension was granted to Tennyson" (*Memoir*, 1:225).

I would like to avoid endorsing either Carlyle's reading of this poem or that
of the Kennedys. It does appear, nevertheless, that Ulysses' ability to appeal to
conservative and progressive views alike indicates that he has somehow given the
ideological straddling associated in the 1830s with Whigs a wider appeal. It seems
likely, at any rate, that the audience he is specifically addressing might be turning
their faces already toward the beckoning sea in answer to his invitation:

> Come, my friends,
> 'Tis not too late to seek a newer world.
> Push off, and sitting well in order smite
> The sounding furrows; for my purpose holds
> To sail beyond the sunset, and the baths
> Of all the western stars, until I die. (56–61)

In effect, Ulysses is reiterating for these men what we heard him declare in the
opening of "The Lotos-Eaters": "Courage." We might note that the Lotos-
Eaters did enjoy something like discursive and presumably social equality, which
may have been another of the attractions of that fruit and that place; in their las-
situde, they were leaderless, exempted from the orders of a "Hero-king." Ulysses
seeks to effect the transformation of his auditors into mariners by way of his
words, to convince them that they must join him, and surely they will. That he
is here commanding a similar audience to those ashore in Lotosland is borne out
by his direct echo of a line repeated several times in the *Odyssey*, including at the

very end of the episode of the Lotos-Eaters (and provided in Greek in the notes to "Ulysses" in Tennyson's Eversley edition). In urging them "Push off, and sitting well in order smite / The sounding furrows," Ulysses links them to that earlier crew, uniting them discursively to their brother mariners. But the line also indicates the ways hierarchy will be wholly preserved, as the instruction "well in order" suggests careful and specific placement, with one commander at the helm. Decades after publishing "Ulysses," Tennyson would urge this formation on Gladstone in "'Captain, Guide!'" (c. 1885), a political poem that promotes the idea of singular leadership, lest the ship run aground: "List no longer to the crew! / Captain, guide!" (5–6).

Roused by Tennyson's Ulysses' call to heroic action, Carlyle asks his readers to imagine a division, in his view necessarily a hierarchy, of labor: "How will each true man stand truly to *his* work in the ship?"[32] I began my discussion of "Ulysses" citing Gladstone's suspicion that Tennyson's monologue exhibits "a corner-view of a character which was in itself a *cosmos*." We can see instead how extraordinarily multifaceted is Tennyson's depiction of this character, and as the speaker moves toward his conclusion we can see also the harmonious, well-ordered universe that he attempts to define and attain. "Sitting well in order," the mariners will take appointed positions, there to smite, literally to strike or inflict heavy blows upon the "sounding furrows," in a powerful display of uniformity, regularity, and steady progress. Taking their places, they will subordinate the sea's furrows even as they subordinate any individuality to the unity of the whole.

Ulysses seeks to make his audience yearn for the sea because they yearn for the order they will take once out there. What he offers them is not only a visual image of symmetry as they take to their oars, but an aural impression of symmetry, of well-ordered *sounding*. In this, the dramatic monologue's majestic blank verse, the rhythm that it steadily keeps to, may be the speaker's greatest rhetorical tool. His monologue mimics and thus evokes that resonance, one directly echoing Homer, although he translates Homer's hexameter into his own iambic pentameter. Pyre characterizes the meter of "Ulysses" as "masculine and austere," and after enumerating its formal elements concludes, "'Ulysses' is extraordinarily regular and solidly syllabled."[33] Ulysses seeks less the exertion of the expedition than the exertion of the oratory; his concern is less to make one last voyage than to make one last speech, to test whether his language is still equal to the ardors of persuasion. If the speaker can get the mariners to *hear* the "extraordinary" regularity—not to mention the masculinity and austerity—of their labor, he can get them to voice their assent by imitating his voice, by way of the rhythmic beats of their orderly rowing. Ulysses' oratory finally addresses itself less to an auditor's logic than to his ear; as Douglas Bush notes of this poem, "In our ears is the sound of the waves, for Tennyson, who can be so satiny, so weak and tame, is nevertheless the greatest English poet of the sea."[34] We might also hear in these lines the potential for future democratic engagement. Elaine Scarry reminds us that the "alliance between poetic meter and rowing has endured over many centuries." She also notes that "rhythmic striking of the water, in time with the pipeman's flute," is connected by both political scientists and historians to the development of democracy in a later period in Greek history: "Out of the spectacle of the trireme ship, Athenian democracy was born."[35] The "sounding" of Ulysses' voice must fill their ears with the sound of the waves, and thus make these men he has named mariners doubt whether they are indeed even still on shore; his words alone must put them at sea.

Swathing Troy in Flame

Ulysses draws his monologue to a close with lines many readers have found power-fully affecting. Thomas Carlyle, notoriously resistant to the lure of poetry, admitted to Tennyson, "These lines do not make me weep, but there is in me what would fill whole Lachrymatories as I read" (Eversley ed., 2:338). Criticism has not had much to say about why these lines have the kind of effect they have, but surely one reason they are so moving is that they create an illusion of communal enterprise:

> It may be that the gulfs will wash us down:
> It may be that we shall touch the Happy Isles,
> And see the great Achilles, whom we knew.
> Though much is taken, much abides; and though
> We are not now that strength which in old days
> Moved earth and heaven; that which we are, we are;
> One equal temper of heroic hearts,
> Made weak by time and fate, but strong in will
> To strive, to seek, to find, and not to yield. (62–70)

The monologue closes with a choke of sonorous repetitions ("It may be... / It may be"; "Though...though"), words that would appear to express hesitancy but for the confidence such rhetorical maneuvers demand. The apparent reservation of these terms is belied by the certainty with which Ulysses asserts equilibrium ("Though much is taken, much abides"). The authoritarian nature of this speaker is most exposed when it least appears to be; he has ceased from the pronouns "I" and "me" and committed to the inclusive and frequently repeated "we," and yet he steadfastly maintains his singular prerogative: "my purpose holds." The mono-syllables of the final line, where verbiage is broken down to its constituent verbs, bring this end around to the monologue's beginning, contrasting aurally these seafaring citizens with his earlier monosyllabic characterization of the Ithacans "That hoard and sleep and feed and know not me."

Ulysses' most resonant repetition, however, as he discursively smites the sounding furrows, must be his almost existential tautology, "that which we are, we are," which marks an end to the divisive individuating of his earlier dismissal, "He works his works, I mine." The balance these lines sustain between loss and gain results in the parallel equation "we are, we are." He tells them they are the sum of their losses, which is to say that what is taken *is* what abides. In so doing, he has transformed his monologue into a solitary performance of the choric song heard on the shores of the land of the Lotos. "One equal temper" of what Ulysses has previously termed "free hearts, free foreheads" (49), these mariners are about to fall prey to the dream Ulysses proffers of radical equality. And the lines must have this effect, not only on these Ithacans but on readers, whether in Victorian Britain or in other times and places; this way the poem performs what it represents. One can hear the efficacy of the lines, because one may—many do—experience its effects directly. The mariners will climb the gangway, as who would not?

What might stay the mariners' feet, of course, would be confusion regarding who precisely is being addressed, since none of Ulysses' original mariners made it home to Ithaca. Addressing what has from the start been perceived as a discrepancy, Hallam Tennyson suggests what can seem to be two contradictory solutions: "The comrades he addresses are of the same heroic mould as his old comrades," an explanation he potentially undercuts by adding, in a note, "Perhaps the *Odyssey* has not been strictly adhered to, and some of the old comrades may be still left" (*Poems*, 1:613, 614). In thus raising the question of whether Ulysses' auditors are *like* old comrades ("of the same heroic mould") or *are* actual old comrades, Hallam neatly summarizes one of the most remarkable discursive accomplishments of this monologue. Ulysses inspires in his auditors the ambition to be identical to his earlier crew, rather than similar to them. The idea of their wholesale identification with his "old" (in this case meaning former, rather than agèd) comrades is not a discrepancy, then, but a necessity for the monologue, and presages a still more extraordinary ambition fostered in auditors by the monologue, namely, for wholesale identification with its speaker.

Ulysses' extraordinary assertion of communal identity, "we are, we are," is an assertion of identification as well, in that he here attempts to persuade his auditors of their metaphoric relation to himself. Elizabeth Sewell defines metaphor as "a unity where everything in the cosmos runs into everything else in one enormous oneness, and in place of succession and similarity there only remain simultaneity in space-time, and identification."[36] Himself a cosmos, as Gladstone put it, Ulysses seeks through his monologue to convince his auditors of their enormous oneness with himself. They are not only equal, but united, indivisible; they too are now a part of all that he has met. And yet we know him to have been *only* a part of all he has met, which is to say fundamentally apart *from* all he has met, on this shore as on any other. In becoming his mariners, they are in essence to join him in becoming his name, to be transformed by the dramatic monologue into wholesale identification with, rather than resemblance to, his previous mariners and also himself. This oneness can foster the illusion of democratic unity, but marks instead the silencing of a potential multiplicity of voices, identities, or interests. The mariners are silenced by the univocality of the dramatic monologue itself.

Perhaps the most plangent line in the poem is the bait Ulysses throws to his seamen, the offer to "see the great Achilles, whom we knew." This name, he knows, resonates like his own, but in a different register: while Ulysses is a figure whose deceiving self-representations render him difficult to know, as the Trojans Antenor and Laocoön each in his own way counsels, one may gain full cognizance of Achilles. Ulysses is known not, Achilles "we knew." The speaker wants to re-constitute a community containing such men, and this line indicates that he will not find it here on earth. And yet it is Achilles who tells Ulysses in the underworld that he would rather be alive, even as a servant to a lowly master, than lord among the dead, so teaching his visitor the value of every breath. Achilles tells Ulysses, "I rather wish to live in Earth a Swaine / Or serve a Swaine for hire, that scarce can gaine / Bread to sustaine him, than (that life once gone) / Of all the dead sway the Imperiall throne" (11:643–46, trans. Chapman). It is this lesson learned from Achilles' shade that Ulysses essentially repeats in complaining, "life piled on life / Were all too little." Perhaps Achilles' words, which associate kingship with death, partly inspire Ulysses' present embrace of the illusion of life-assuring equal-ity between himself and these mariners. The line reminds us, too, of this poem's status as an elegy. As the mourning Tennyson well knew, community may repose symbolically in one figure, an Achilles, say, or a Hallam.

I have taken into account in this discussion the revisions Tennyson made prior to his publication of the 1842 *Poems*. In "The Lotos-Eaters," he added specific references to Troy, as the chorus comes to identify their memories of that place with their resistance to returning home. Having reached Ithaca, Ulysses voices a similar sense of displacement. In revising "Ulysses," however, Tennyson deleted a crucial reference to Troy, a decision leading to alterations in the final lines of the poem that radically alter the poem's implications. The final lines in the Harvard manuscript read:

> Though much is taken, much abides; and though
> We are not now that strength that in one night[37]
> Swathed Troy with flame; that which we are, we are;
> Made weak by time and fate, but strong in will
> To strive, to seek, to find, and not to yield. (*H. MS*)

The entire weight of these final lines, the great example and indeed lodestar of the journey Ulysses now proposes, is the night for which every terrible detail is chronicled in book 2 of the *Aeneid*. (Lemprière, basing his date on the Arundelian marbles, suggests in his *Classical Dictionary* [1788] that this attack occurred "on the night between the 11th and 12th of June.")[38] The events over which Tenny-son (and Ulysses, as we have seen) could not but weep are those that this speaker originally invoked in concluding his monologue (with the same kind of brevity that marked Aeneas's rising with sacrifice in "On a Mourner"). The rapture of Troy constitutes his chief example of his old strength of will, which was mighty indeed. Part of Ulysses' sorrow here is apparently in no longer having the strength to reduce a god-built city to char and ash, a regret whose corollary is that he is so far from repentance as to lament that there is (in Yeats's phrase) no second Troy for him to burn.

A "swathed" Troy suggests a city engulfed, surrounded, confined, but also perhaps decorated, embellished, brought down by an enveloping substance as ethereal as the god's song that raised it. This image retained its force for Tennyson, as his 1882 "To Virgil" attests, in its homage to the singer of "Ilion's lofty temples robed in fire." What Apollo's aspiration raised, Ulysses' flame brought down, as only linguistic guile could breach the breath-built walls. This flaming Troy is another visually and climatologically kinetic image of the place, like the "windy Troy" whose image appears early in the monologue. At Troy, the elements themselves cannot rest, as indeed the fire was surely fanned by the city's endemic wind. The revision's "old days" replaces this recollection of "one night," obfuscating the monologue's origin in a single nocturnal event. This earlier identification of so specific and local a memory helps us to identify other vaguely stated ambitions. "Something more" (27), "something ere the end" (51), "some work of noble note" (52) is what he seeks; we may better understand to what these refer, since he names in these lines his work of noblest note. His aim, though, is necessarily elusive. Seeking always to move "beyond" prescribed limits, he imagines a destination made of fading margins and sinking stars and also, as these lines in the Harvard manuscript show, burning cities. All of these are of course destinations that must recede as one advances, whose point as goals is that they are ultimately unapproachable.

The revised version of "Ulysses" replaced "that strength that in one night / Swathed Troy with flame" with "that strength which in old days / Moved earth and heaven"; the original claim is incontestable, while in Tucker's term the later claim seems "hyperbolic."[39] But the Harvard and Heath manuscripts show why Ulysses is accurate even in his revised claim, since a specific scene stands behind his abstract boast. That night in Troy, he did in fact help to "move" earth and heaven in at least two ways. He literally displaced, or moved, divine Troy, ruined its sacred walls, thereby causing, however inadvertently, another version of that city with a better chance of longevity to be transplanted to Hesperia. And in this devastation, wrought almost as agonizingly on the victors as on the vanquished, he moved gods and men to pathos, sorrow, and suffering, himself not least. Like the expansion of lines earlier in the poem characterizing his past, this revision broadens the monologue's reach. But the alterations are also akin to those of "On a Mourner" and certain sections of *In Memoriam*, in that the poet works to lessen the acuteness and specificity of the individual's burden of the past.

In omitting the name of Troy, Tennyson generalizes the literary history he knows so well and diminishes our association of Ulysses as *ptoliporthos*, sacker of cities, our memory that it is he, as Chapman's translation puts it, who "the towne /

Of sacred Troy had sackt and shiverd downe" (*Odyssey* 1:3–4). This earlier version reveals that the speaker considers his crowning achievement the events of the night Aeneas gives so harrowing an account of (it is that horrific strength to which he compares this current strength "in will"): Troy's rapture was also his. But with the revision, he veils the event that would recall to his present audience devastations earlier wrought by his skill in speech. *Sic notus Ulixes?* Like the serpents that strangle Laocoön and his sons, these revisions work to suppress our knowledge of Ulysses. With these alterations, the poem is thus still more strikingly mimetic of Ulysses' own rhetorical methods.

Since what Tennyson's Ulysses is trying to accomplish with his monologue is the recapture of a particular community, and even a particular moment of rapture, that of the night of Troy's destruction, is he successful? Does Ulysses, a character whom Arthur Hallam held up in his letters to Gladstone as an unrivaled orator, attain in Tennyson's dramatic monologue the "assent in the will" of his auditors that Hallam's university essay on Cicero anticipates for all practitioners of this art? Do his words attain some end, as I have claimed is the ambition of every dramatic monologue? In a sense, yes; with his monologue he becomes again a man of discursive guile and resourcefulness, a man whose words sway auditors. The Trojans came to do willingly, eagerly, speedily what was wholly against their interests, what in fact brought on their destruction, and so will these putative mariners. When he tells them not to yield, he means except to him.

The monologue does not, however, attain for Ulysses all that he seeks. The community he would assemble cannot reconvene, because he himself destroyed the place around which that community formed; all have now undergone the devastations of holocaust and diaspora. And what of the community gathered around him presently on the shore? With the disappearance in Tennyson's revision of a burning Troy comes the appearance of the line "One equal temper of heroic hearts," underscoring Ulysses' proffered illusion of democratic engagement, of an impossible equality between himself and his auditors. In appealing to the "heroic hearts" of these men, he is addressing brother mariners who bear relation to those earlier *lotophagi* who owned "hearts worn out by many wars" ("Lotos-Eaters," 131). These present auditors will attend to him, but the vision of equality that the monologue extends (in contrast to its opening disparagement of "unequal laws") is withheld by the genre itself. Ulysses seeks equality among his peers, to know and be known, but his monologue exposes the impossibility of his entering any community as anything but in a position of command, militarily and discursively. The monologue's climax, the seemingly resigned but also utterly triumphant "we are, we are," seeks to forge a bond between speaker and auditor, between ruler and ruled. He has replaced the earlier repetitions, "I am...I am," with "we are, we are," revising his own identity in the course of representing it. But no such union is possible to the speaker of a dramatic monologue; the structure of Ulysses' democracy is as evanescent as that of Apollo's towers, to which I turn in the following chapter.

What Tennyson forwards in "Ulysses," then, is a knowledge of Troy as a site of vigorous and ongoing contestation, a topic pervaded, as Gladstone later claimed of Homer's epics, by an "intense political spirit" (*SH*, 3:3). No single subject can account for the complex articulations of this speaker, but in this dense poem, challenging start to what proved to be a vigorous Victorian genre, the monologue raises pointed questions about political and discursive representation. Tennyson also locates in the site of Troy a sense of loss so acute that the speaking subject recoils from its memory, even as he cleaves to it. And indeed, what is at stake for all Victorian explorers of Troy's mysteries appears to be personal as much as historical knowledge. We might now understand more fully, in the light cast by Troy's flames, the elaborate exertions, less finally in excavation pits in Asia Minor than in drawing rooms in Europe, of Schliemann and his adherents. This light also illuminates Gladstone's tireless insistence—as if he could carry his points through the sheer mass and vigor of his writings—on an "acknowledgement, which some are still indisposed to make, of the broad vein of historical reality, that runs through the delineations of the *Iliad* and *Odyssey*."[40] For Gladstone, to establish the reality of Troy's history, and especially its Achaean heroes, is to reify his own most urgent political, religious, and cultural enterprises. We have seen how his readings of Homer correspond to his movement from intense youthful conservatism to equally intense and profoundly influential liberalism. For others, from such dubious theorists as Bryant to such unimpeachable scholars as Grote and Jebb, the light of Troy burned brighter because stoked by poetic invention. Troy can be known, for these inquirers, only through the poet, and in turn, what the fable of that sacred city teaches are lessons about the poet's foundational relation to the fictions of any national history.

For Tennyson, the knowledge of Troy is indivisible from his knowledge of his own poetic practices and aims. Troy is the poet's province, and in it this poet always found sanctuary. "Oenone," greatly admired by Hallam and published in the 1832 collection of Tennyson's poems that he was instrumental in arranging, begins and ends with the female speaker being drawn—visually, in the first lines of the poem, and physically, in the last—to Troy's walled city. In the final lines of the poem she rises from Mount Ida to "go / Down into Troy," seeking that most interior and incomprehensible of subjectivities, "wild Cassandra":

> for she says
> A fire dances before her, and a sound
> Rings ever in her ears of armèd men.
> What this may be I know not, but I know
> That, wheresoe'er I am by night and day,
> All earth and air seem only burning fire. (259–64)

Cassandra's deranged prophecy finds its cognate in Oenone's own desperate consciousness. "The Death of Oenone" (1892), Tennyson's late return to this character, ends with the nymph leaping into Paris's funeral pyre, where, presumably, she will find that her sensations were as vivid as Cassandra's ("She leapt upon the funeral pile, / And mixt herself with *him* and past in fire" [105–6]).[41]

Cassandra's is the chief prophetic voice Oenone hears in the 1842 revision of the poem, but in the 1832 version she hears a strangely similar prediction from Cassandra's sibling Paris, who recognizes how consequential his day of judgment on Mount Ida is to be. In the 1832 version, as Paris first shows Oenone the golden fruit he is to bestow upon a goddess, he says that it "in afterlife may breed / Deep evilwilledness of heaven and sere / Heartburning toward hallowèd Ilion" (*1832* 71–73). The excision of these lines in the 1842 revision marks another erasure of the city whose presence, we have seen, becomes increasingly shadowy, mystified, in Tennyson's poems based on events at Troy. But the Trojan Paris accurately foretells the consequences of his yielding to the temptation that is to bring about the rapture of Troy. For these speakers of Tennyson's the heart itself burns toward holy Ilion: all are "on fire within," as the feminized Soul howls at the end of "The Palace of Art" (285). Each identifies the self searingly with the city that never was.

This immersion in flames, into an existence that is "only burning fire," must remind us of the fate suffered by Dante's Ulysses, a figure at the heart of Hallam and Gladstone's youthful epistolary debates, whose influence is felt throughout Tennyson's dramatic monologue. We have seen that the direct subtext of Ulysses' monologue is the rapture of Troy. If that night is the ideal "old day" to which he would return, does the monologue bring him closer to its experience? If he reached the Happy Isles, would he fire them too? Ulysses seeks in a newer world another Troy, like so many of its refugees. In a sense, his is a mistake similar to Aeneas's on the island of Crete, but he desires to recapture not only a place but a sensation of a place: Aeneas attempts to re-create Troy's towers, its Pergamum, Ulysses its wind and fire. But the monologist knows Troy is as inimitable and irreplaceable as the Achilles whom he beguiled into going there. The city and the warrior are irrecoverable, and as Dante's canto tells us, Ulysses is essentially responsible for their joint destruction. And yet Dante also teaches us that Tennyson's Ulysses will return to the sensations of that glorious night; the "something" he seeks and strives for he will find. We know from Dante's account, which Tennyson renders antecedent to his own, the outcome of this dramatic monologue. Ulysses will return to Troy's flames, and know the place for the first time. Ilion's inferno is Ulysses' destination: he is to be robed in Trojan flame, an eternal igneous citizen of the city legendary because he has rendered it as unknowable as he. *Sic nota Troia?* He is to be a part of all that he has destroyed, the literal keeper of the city's flame, swathed even as he speaks in his own far-shining fire.

PART III

The Rapture of the Song-built City

The speaker of "The Palace of Art" begs, even while taking leave of that place, "Yet pull not down my palace towers, that are / So lightly, beautifully built" (293–94). Tennyson's civic towers are so light they should merely evaporate, return to the air out of which they are formed. So it is with Camelot: recounting his arrival with two servants to the city, Gareth in Tennyson's *Idylls of the King* describes the spires and turrets they see as they approach. One of his disbelieving companions insists, "Lord, there is no such city anywhere, / But all a vision" (203–4), and Gareth also doubts the evidence of city walls that appear and disappear before a traveler's eyes. But Tennyson sees these visionary cities everywhere, trusting to their evanescent presence, endorsing Merlin's teasing explanation:

> "For an ye heard a music, like enow
> They are building still, seeing the city is built
> To music, therefore never built at all,
> And therefore built forever." ("Gareth and Lynette," 271–74)

Tennyson's cities reflect the airy gorgeousness of towers built to music, Apollonian in their origin, and therefore lyrical in their insubstantiality. This may be not unconnected to the association, forged enthusiastically by the Apostles, of Tennyson with Apollo. Entertaining college friends at Somersby, Tennyson carried a small pony around the yard, causing W. H. Brookfield to exclaim, "Come now, you mustn't be wanting me to believe that you are both Hercules and Apollo in one."[1] Arthur Henry Hallam went so far as to declare in a letter to Leigh Hunt, whom he was asking to review a volume of Tennyson's poetry, that his friend was "the legitimate heir to Keats," and as such the "last lineal descendant of Apollo" (*Letters*, 31). I have looked at the shifting appearance of Troy in relation to its pulling down, the rapture of the lofty towers of a city "never built at all." I turn now from Troy's ends to its origins, to monologists whose keenest identification is with walls "lightly, beautifully built," whose own strange songs are nothing less than conjuring acts.

I began with "Ulysses," which is to say with a lost Troy, because Tennyson himself assigned to "Ulysses" priority. And indeed any Victorian reader would begin with the knowledge of Troy's decimation; the razing and the raising of Troy would appear in some sense synchronous events. The poems on which I focus in part 3, although they were also conceived and drafted in 1833 in the aftermath of the death of Arthur Henry Hallam, were always figured as secondary. Tennyson completed "Tithonus" (1860) over a quarter-century and "Tiresias" (1883) a half-century after their conception. They were held by him, however, as poetic companions to "Ulysses." Calling "Tithonus" "pendent" to "Ulysses" upon its publication in William Makepeace Thackeray's *Cornhill Magazine* in 1860, Tennyson stresses their affiliation, and in doing so he also assigns to them an intimate generic relationship. In conceiving of one in relation to the other and affirming their connection nearly thirty years later, he announces their like relation; they provide for one another essential contextualization. Part 3 deals chiefly with the dramatic monologue "Tithonus," but "pendent" status was also assigned by Tennyson to "Tiresias," the subject of the final section of chapter 6. "Partly written at the same time" as "Ulysses," according to his son Hallam (*Poems*, 1:622), "Tiresias" at once reflects similar concerns as its fellows and alterations in poetic practice marked by fifty years. This cluster of dramatic monologues heralds Tennyson's entry into generic consciousness, as he tells us that each poem must be understood in relation to others of its kind.

Both of these deferred monologues are preoccupied with the notion of "kind," of categories both familial and social. I place Tithonus within a definition of his kind that is at once narrowly focused (he is a member of the Trojan royal family, a lineage I trace in some detail) and, in terms of the poet's conception of his own poetic practice, broadly suggestive. Tiresias, like Tithonus in initially appearing woefully solitary, straddling communities human and divine, resembles him too in his monologic bid for some clearer and better placement. The speakers Tithonus and Tiresias have been linked primarily by gerontology, by each speaker's dismayed sense of his physical decrepitude, as if the most significant aspect of their identities were their geriatric status. Certainly, both speakers are ardently aware of being very old men, and it has long been remarked that their excessive seniority is in some sense mystifying in light of their conception by so young a poet, mourning the death of a friend who died at twenty-two, since when a young person dies what disturbs particularly is the very fact of his or her youth. I argue, though, that it is not from a vantage point of extreme age that each monologist speaks, but of extreme youth; each mounts in his monologue an elegy for ephebism.

The similarities between these wizened speakers, however, are more than skin-deep. Both speakers have been resident in the two legendary ancient cities built of song. Stephen Scully in *Homer and the Sacred City* reminds us, "Only two cities are said to have sacred walls, Troy and Boiotian Thebes."[2] Troy, ruled by Tithonus's brother Priam, boasted walls constructed of the music of Apollo, and Thebes, whose walls Tiresias is desperate to save, rose to the music of Amphion. Each speaker is sharply aware of the architectural origins of his city, so much so, I argue, that each conceives of himself as indistinguishable from his city's walls and ramparts, its pavements and towers, and in turn each crafts a monologue that itself seeks architectonic effects. Both of Tennyson's "pendent" speakers, moreover, lament physical intimacies with goddesses. Tithonus, lover of the goddess of the dawn, is cursed by his alliance with her with an immortality he would shed, and Tiresias, viewer of the naked Athena, is cursed by her with prophetic gifts he would gainsay. Both desire in their monologues release in some manner from the punishing gifts of the gods, and, due to the transformative nature of the dramatic monologue itself, both will attain a transformation as spectral and as solid as the song-built walls each invokes.

To establish Tennyson's early imaginative residence in cities built to music, this introduction opens by looking at two early poems drawing from mythology, "Ilion, Ilion" and "Amphion." I then pursue, across the next two chapters, the nature and the ambition of the monologists Tithonus and (to a lesser extent) Tiresias. In chapter 5 I examine Tennyson's complex allegiances to Troy's ruling family, a clan whose legendary beauty is perhaps its most notable inherited trait. I examine some of Tithonus's familial, social, and literary contexts and their implications for Tennyson's own poetic practice. I then work more intensively with the dramatic monologue "Tithonus." Following the logic of the speaker's dangerous, we might even say fatal, slippage from identifying himself as beautiful to identifying himself as godlike, my reading interrogates the intricate processes generally of Tithonus's sympathetic affiliations. In the context of studying the phenomenon of masculine beauty in a cluster of related poems of Tennyson's (including "Oenone"), I study the aesthetics more generally of Tennyson's poetics, which, in its perceived excess of beauty, has been accused from the start of ineffectuality and vacuity.

In chapter 6 I explore, in contrast, attempts of the speakers Tithonus and Tiresias to attain rhetorical, and potentially political, power, to produce efficacious speech and attain its rewards. In seeking to understand the kinds of polity each speaker describes or idealizes, I examine in particular their aristocratic allegiances. I first look at the range of transformations that Tithonus undergoes by way of his monologue and their consequences for a wider reading of the poet's own labors. I then look to Tiresias, Tennyson's other speaking citizen of a song-built city, questioning the depth of his attachment to the city walls he labors to uphold. Both monologists seek to accomplish a set of complexly conceived and perhaps parallel goals, notably, to be rapt from their present locations and to effect rapturous transformations of their situations and of their selves.

MELODY BORN

While a student at Trinity, Tennyson composed "Ilion, Ilion," a lyric in experimental quantitative measure about the creation of Troy's lofty walls and pillars. The poem seems built up from a massing of epithets, as if the language that composed the city composed the poem as well. But the music that builds the city already sings of the end of the city, and by the close of the poem, even as the walls are raised, they are razed "To a music sadly flowing, slowly falling." This progression, or perhaps more accurately, regression, is revealing, and this little-known work merits quotation in its entirety:

> Ilion, Ilion, dreamy Ilion, pillared Ilion, holy Ilion,
> City of Ilion when wilt thou be melody born?
> Blue Scamander, yellowing Simois from the heart of piny Ida
> Everwhirling from the molten snows upon the mountainthrone,
> Roll Scamander, ripple Simois, ever onward to a melody
> Manycircled, overflowing thorough and thorough the flowery level
>   of unbuilt Ilion,
> City of Ilion, pillared Ilion, shadowy Ilion, holy Ilion,
>   To a music merrily flowing, merrily echoing
>   When wilt thou be melody born?
>
> Manygated, heavywallèd, manytowered city of Ilion,
> From the silver, lilyflowering meadowlevel
>   When wilt thou be melody born?
> Ripple onward, echoing Simois,
> Ripple ever with a melancholy moaning,
>   In the rushes to the dark blue brimmèd Ocean, yellowing Simois,
> To a music from the golden twanging harpwire heavily drawn.
> Manygated, heavywallèd, manytowered city of Ilion,
>   To a music sadly flowing, slowly falling,
>   When wilt thou be melody born?

"Ilion, Ilion" is glutted with the compound words that enchanted Tennyson in this period, and as Douglas Bush notes, "Like most English poems in quantity, it has the air of a cat picking its way along the top of a fence, yet it does deserve the threadbare adjective 'haunting.'"[3] Based on evidence from the 1830 pocket-notebook in which this lyric appears, Charles Tennyson and Christopher Ricks have each called this poem a fragment (*Poems*, 1:282), but as it stands, it seems to me to have the scope and closure of a completed poem.

In opening, the poem addresses a city not yet existent: "unbuilt" is only one of Ilion's adjectives. The city is conjured from the ground, called the "meadowlevel" or "flowery level," the fecund plain that it supplants. We see the way the epithets of the city construct what they characterize: the impatient question

"When wilt thou be melody born?" is (after the opening repetition "Ilion, Ilion") always preceded by the epithets for the city whose contours the melody anticipates. As Ricks points out, this repetition of the place-name echoes an early translation of Tennyson's from Horace's *Odes* (3:3), in which Juno utters "welcome words: Ilium Ilium" (*Poems*, 1:282). Juno's words in Horace lay further curses on the ravaged Ilion, however, whereas the speaker's words here do in fact greet, or welcome, the imminent appearance of the city. After this repetition, which echoes Horace but in which the place-name also echoes or repeats itself, "Ilion" is never without its adjectival modifiers. And the epithets for Ilion are never unaccompanied by the question that is the refrain, as these four moments establish the structure not only of the poem but also of the city. The first stanza both opens and ends asking of a city already taking vague ("dreamy," "shadowy") but definitive ("pillared") shape, "When wilt thou be melody born?" The second stanza repeats this question: "Manygated, heavywallèd, manytowered city of Ilion, / ... When wilt thou be melody born?" What rises with each question is the holy city of Ilion, first its pillars, then its many gates and towers, its heavy walls. "Everwhirling," "overflowing," "manycircled," gushing with alliteration ("Roll Scamander, ripple Simois") and internal rhymes (their source is "piny Ida"), the rivers pulse in time to a music that they accompany but are not alone in producing. Culler feels that it is "not formally the lyre of Apollo but the two rivers" that build the city.[4] I agree that the poem's own flow, its forward propulsion, seems bound to the two rivers that roll and ripple ever "onward," but I read them as answering to the same music that constructs the city they come to girdle.

The first stanza represents the "unbuilt Ilion." The tumbling rivers encircle an Ilion still "shadowy," "dreamy," imagining the moments before the erection of its famed walls, as these forces gather and accrete in fervid anticipation. There is an urgency, an almost frantic impatience marked by the question that grows more insistent and even imploring with each repetition. Although the question closes the poem, giving it a circularity that echoes the sound of the manycircled rivers, I think we can see how the city begins to take shape in the second stanza. The edifices, the gates, walls, and towers, rise not only in profusion ("many") but also in weight and substantiality ("heavy"), leaving the shadows to acquire a clear mass and solidity. The alteration in the place is witnessed especially by one of its contributors, the river Simois. Still rippling ever and onward, its echo has turned melancholic, and it has flowed from the oxymoronic "molten snows" of its source to the "dark" Ocean that will one day bring the Achaean fleet. The poem closes with an echo, or repetition, of the image of Ilion that opens the stanza, with its many gates and heavy walls, but heralds too a distinct and sorrowful change in the melody itself. The question has metamorphosed from being merrily anticipatory to sounding sorrowfully prophetic; the notes have changed to tragic.

The poem ends with a turn to describe the music, the strange song that is changing even as it is becoming more directly specified. The clause "To a music" begins the penultimate line of "Ilion, Ilion," and it describes a merrily flowing, merrily echoing sound. We now hear of the source of the music, to which the rippling rivers lent their accompaniment. In closing the melody, both the instrument and the player's style are figured: the harpwire is itself heavily drawn and the weight of walls impregnable to assault seems itself a function of the heavy-handed playing. But the echo of the second stanza is no echo but a dying fall, as the "merrily flowing" music is now "sadly flowing," as the repetitions that structured this song will now also undo it. Inbuilt in the unbuilt wall are dismal notes. Even as the towers commence to rise, they slowly fall; how sad, how strange this melody grows, now twanging the melancholy moaning it will induce. In the music of its inception is the music of its fall, because as Ilion is rising before our eyes so is the specter of its ruination. Towers so "lightly, beautifully built" (like those in "The Palace of Art") may be most beautiful in their certain falling. The question "When wilt thou be melody born?" reflects both the insistence of the player and the imploring of an auditor that is altering with each note, as surely as is this lily-flowering meadowlevel. The music by which the rising shadows of the city affix themselves to the plain transfixes its listeners; Apollo's song conjures both a city and an audience. Tennyson's Oenone and Tithonus, each witness to this moment, we learn from Tennyson, can never forget its "strange music," and we shall hear in their voices its doleful echoes.

In representing the performance that builds the city of Ilion, Tennyson enters a debate regarding the chief engineer of this mythical construction. According to Lemprière, the late eighteenth-century producer of the *Classical Dictionary*, the walls of Troy were built jointly by Apollo and Poseidon, who were indentured to Laomedon, ruler of Troy (and father of Tithonus); indeed, greater responsibility for the construction is ceded to Poseidon, who labored mightily as Apollo tended flocks nearby.[5] "In the later tradition," however, as one classicist points out, "Apollo is more frequently identified with the constructing or remaking of city walls than is Poseidon,"[6] and Tennyson's poem endorses this tradition. For those who upheld that a historical Troy had existed, encased in walls as heavy as those Tennyson describes but less airily constructed, the myth was problematic. Gladstone, in his preface to Schliemann's book on his findings at Mycenae, employs the new archaeological discoveries to endorse his own view of Poseidon's more crucial role, explaining, "The walls of Troy were built by Poseidon; that is, by a race who practised the worship of the god." The myth of Poseidon's powerful civic construction in turn provides a solid foundation for crediting that the walls recently unearthed in Turkey were in fact those of Troy: "If [Dr. Schliemann] is right, as seems probable, in placing Troy at Hissarlik, it is important to notice that this work of Poseidon had a solidity, which bore it unharmed through the rage of fire, and kept it well together amidst all the changes which have buried it in a hill of rubbish and promiscuous remains." Gladstone continues, "I am tempted, at least until a better name can be found, to call this manner of building Poseidonian;

at any rate, whatever it be called, to note it as a point of correspondence between the Poems and the discoveries."[7] Gladstone was adamant, that a god's celestial song had no part in the erection of the walls, insisting in *Juventus Mundi*, "Whilst Poseidon built...Apollo fed oxen."[8]

Tennyson allied himself with the Trojans and their god Apollo—whom Gladstone called "a Trojan deity"—aesthetically (as I argue in chapter 5) and also politically (as I argue in chapter 6). Not only did Tennyson credit the god's song with the raising of a mythical city, but "Ilion, Ilion" surely echoes Apollo's song itself. Its command of these forces and elements to assemble themselves, its call to the natural world to compose a place, is after all the call described in Tennyson's "Amphion" (c. 1837–38, published 1842), a poem about Apollo's fellow builder of song-built walls. Amphion, son of Orpheus, moved stones by the music of his lyre and thereby constructed Boiotian Thebes, the city that obsesses and torments Tiresias in Tennyson's eponymous dramatic monologue. In "Amphion," the modern-day speaker, bequeathed a plot of land by his father, finds his patrimony "wild and barren" and desires an easier method than physical labor to, in a sense, reclaim his inheritance. His repeated lament runs, "O had I lived when song was great / In days of old Amphion" (9–10). The poem imagines a kind of promenade of trees and twining vines, as across successive stanzas the oak, ash, beech, briony, ivy, linden, woodbine, poplar, cypress, willow, alder, yew, elm, and pine all "Ran forward to his rhyming" (30), each in a manner distinctive to its kind. The urbane male speaker details the music's effect on a manipulable feminized nature ("You moved her at your pleasure" [60]), but by the end the speaker accepts the horticultural challenge of "years of cultivation," combined with reduced ambition: "Enough if at the end of all / A little garden blossom" (103–4). In reconciling himself to his limitations the speaker is recognizing the absence not just of so gifted a singer but also of so compliant a natural world.

In a move that came more and more to attend Tennyson's publications, moral lessons were drawn from even so apparently frivolous a poem as "Amphion." The poet's wife, Emily Tennyson, in a note on the poem in the Eversley edition, interpreted the poem thus: "Genius must not deem itself exempt from labour" (2:347). This can sound like a spousal admonition to her laureate husband, but her implicit point about the labor subtending even melodic construction is an important one. The poet's wife discredits the sense of autocratic ease whereby Apollo or Amphion accomplishes his civic effects. Their descendents, Tithonus and Tiresias, seek also to perform monumental transformations, and in chapter 6 I look at the labors of these ostensibly impotent old men. Both stand as previously failed speakers whose words have never attained for them the results they sought; this accounts for the predicaments in which their monologues find them. At the moment each monologue commences, each speaker's words appear to have gone badly awry. On the one hand, an eager outburst of Tithonus's has been taken literally; he has been granted the "immortality" he asked for, instead of the "eternal youth" that would have vouchsafed for him certain ongoing pleasures. On the other hand, Tiresias's words of counsel and warning to his fellow citizens have never in the slightest way been heeded, but instead fall only on deaf ears. These would appear to be converse phenomena, since one speaker has been heard all too well and the other not at all, but each details in his monologue what appear to be catastrophic discursive failures. My readings question this assumption of failure by probing the past and present rhetorical intentions of these monologists. These two speakers radically transform themselves even as their monologues forward Whiggish, or aristocratic, ideals. Identifying themselves with the walls of their song-built cities, each seeks to be gathered into some other, better future of communal existence. These monologues attempt to provoke civic transformations, like the songs that shaped their cities, but also personal ones, as each importunes a burgeoning identity: When wilt thou be melody born?

5

TITHONUS AND THE PERFORMANCE
OF MASCULINE BEAUTY

[Tennyson] reflects the upper-crust of his time, its pale cast of thought—even its
ennui. . . . He shows how one can be a royal laureate, quite elegant and "aristocratic," and a little queer and affected, and at the same time perfectly manly and
natural. As to his non-democracy, it fits him well, and I like him the better for it.

—Walt Whitman, "A Word about Tennyson" (1887)

Among the murals in the Jefferson Building of the Library of Congress in
Washington, DC, is a series produced in the 1890s by American painter
Henry Oliver Walker depicting scenes from English literature. The images appear
below the names of poets. The majority of the figures are prepubescent boys: slim,
lithe, beardless ephebes. Under "Keats" appears Endymion, stretched out, asleep, a
cloth barely covering his loins, a thin crescent moon in the distance behind him.
In another mural, Adonis, just killed by a wild boar, also lies supine, backward,
head toward us, limbs stretched out, torso arching up, his genitals scarcely covered
by a diaphanous swatch of material. Figured similarly as boys on the edge of pu-
berty (though arrayed in more fabric), are the Boy of Winander in a cloak and
Comus in an animal skin, each in a separate arch under the names "Wordsworth"
and "Milton." Under the arch for "Tennyson" appears another naked ephebe,
barely adolescent and again barely covered across his groin, in a waft of fabric that
stretches around and floats behind him as he is carried aloft into the sky on the
wings of Jupiter, appearing in the form of an eagle: Ganymede (figure 5.1).

According to Aeneas's account in the *Iliad*, Ganymede, called "godlike" even
before his ascension, was "The loveliest born of the race of mortals, and therefore /
the gods caught him away to themselves, to be Zeus' wine-pourer, / for the sake of
his beauty, so that he might be among immortals" (20:232–35, trans. Lattimore).
One would search in vain for a poem of Tennyson's featuring the figure of Ganymede in any central way; in this, the figure is unlike the young men representing the
other English poets named in these murals. There are a few scattered references to
Ganymede in Tennyson's work, including the apparent source for Walker's mural,

FIGURE 5.1 Henry Oliver Walker, "Lyric Poetry: Ganymede." Tennyson arch mural, Jefferson Building, Library of Congress, Washington, DC. Prints and Photographs Division, LOT 5183, Library of Congress, c. 1899.

the fleeting appearance in "The Palace of Art" of "flushed Ganymede, his rosy thigh / Half-buried in the Eagle's down" (121–22). In "Will Waterproof's Lyrical Monologue" (1837, 1842), the "plump head-waiter" at the Cock Tavern in Fleet Street, a favorite watering place of Tennyson and his friends in this period, is declared to be "like Ganymede" (1, 119). In a parody of the myth, the poet imagines the waiter as "A something-pottle-bodied boy, / That knuckled at the taw," abducted not by an eagle but by a Cock, who "stooped and clutched" the child and carried him over many shires, depositing him at this tavern, where instead of the nectar of the gods he serves pints of stout (131–32, 133). Edward Moxon's 1859 illustrated edition of Tennyson features with this poem an engraving by William Mulready of the headwaiter delivering a platter to a man sitting in a bustling tavern who pauses while writing a poem, in rapt contemplation of a vision (hovering in the background) of the waiter, naked, astride an enormous flying rooster (figure 5.2).[1]

Despite the rarity of appearances in Tennyson's poetry, and the predilections of an American muralist who appears to have searched for boys, rather than poems, to illustrate, Ganymede is a curiously appropriate figure to represent Tennyson and his work. Like his relative Tithonus, Ganymede was a beautiful youth, a member of Troy's ruling family, who was rapt away by an immortal. I consider in depth this multifarious status, one shared by other Trojans, exploring the ramifications of Tithonus's aristocratic lineage, his beauty, and his relation to his immortal lover. All of these categories, involving Tithonus's class position, his ambivalent gender roles, and his swerve away from his own people and the human race generally,

FIGURE 5.2 W. Mulready, "Will Waterproof's Lyrical Monologue." Illustration in Alfred Tennyson, *Poems* (London: Edward Moxon and Co., 1859), p. 330.

have direct if complex implications for Tennyson's poetic practice. In "Tithonus," Tennyson uses the story of the beautiful Trojan who coupled with the goddess of the dawn for a radical imagining of the processes of identification and transformation and a searching examination of the most extreme perils and pleasures of imperative, efficacious speech.

Ganymede's rapture by Jupiter (or Zeus), his translation into a realm of perpetual pleasure, establishes important patterns for a line of Trojan men. In his 1858 *Studies in Homer*, Gladstone observes that beauty is ascribed to Achilles and other Achaeans, but "of the Trojan royal family it is the eminent and peculiar characteristic" (*SH*, 3:40). He concedes, "The great Greek heroes are also called beautiful," but maintains, "Their mere beauty, particularly in the *Iliad*, is for the most part kept carefully in the shade" (*SH*, 3:216). In *Juventus Mundi*, Gladstone further remarks, "Among the bodily qualities of the Kings, one is personal beauty. This attaches peculiarly to the Trojan royal family, and is recorded even of the aged Priam in his grief." Forwarding a genealogy of morals, Gladstone everywhere feminizes this patriarchal line, insisting on "a more base and less manly morality among the

Trojans."[2] Walter Pater notes a similar pattern, calling the Trojans "superior in all culture to their kinsmen on the Western shore, and perhaps proportionally weaker on the practical or moral side, and with an element of languid Ionian voluptuousness in them, typified by the cedar and gold of the chamber of Paris."[3] (The Trojan love of beautiful objects was apparently confirmed by Schliemann's finds, which included what were called "Helen's jewels," modeled in a famous photograph of Schliemann's wife, Sophie.) What Gladstone calls "peculiar" Pater calls "superior," yet the voluptuous sensuality of the inhabitants of Troy is seen by both critics to carry a proportional weakness in practical or moral sense. What is the significance for Tennyson of this line of extraordinary male beauty, one "peculiar" in its consistency? Male beauty for these men appears to reduce them to a condition of torpor, rendering them indifferent to and incompetent in the civic arena. Though referring more to his poetics than his person, Tennyson exclaimed to Hallam, "Alas for me! I have more of the Beautiful than the Good!" In responding to Tennyson's comment, Hallam endorsed the idea of the likelihood of a divide between beauty and morality, reassuring his friend, "Remember to your comfort that God has given you to see the difference" (*Letters*, 446). In "Tithonus" we may trace some of the associations in Tennyson's poetics of this Trojan genetic trait of both possessing and inciting the desire for beauty.

Toward the end of his life, during an illness that his family feared might be fatal, Tennyson woke from a dream to announce to his son Hallam, "Priam has appeared to me in the night."[4] But in some ways Tennyson's consciousness had long been visited by members of the Trojan royal family, headed by Tithonus's brother Priam during the Trojan War; we have seen how Tennyson saw himself to some degree resident, or at least guest, in their imagined city. While I develop an argument concerning Tennyson's monologic poetics on the grounds of his larger aesthetic and political alliances, I must acknowledge also what anyone familiar with Tennyson's own appearance as a young man, or familiar with Samuel Laurence's portrait, will recall, namely, Tennyson's own remarkable "physical beauty" (figure 5.3).[5] When the poet's son Hallam gifted the Laurence portrait in his will to the National Portrait Gallery, he described it as "beautiful."[6] The poet himself recognized the significance of the portrait for his public (and perhaps even self-) perception, drawing attention to the eventual distinction between his appearance in youth and in old age. Late in his life, according to an anecdote of F. T. Palgrave, "laughingly he pointed out how, though unable then to boast of the luxuriance of locks conspicuous in that excellent [portrait], through which he was first made familiar to everyone, yet there was not a single white hair on his head" (*Memoir*, 2:510). Tennyson's pride may rest less in his appearance than in his longevity, a Tennyson family trait. As his sister Emily, who had been betrothed to Arthur Hallam, wrote to the poet after Hallam's death, "If I die (which the Tennysons never do)" (*Memoir*, 1:135).

In a letter to Ralph Waldo Emerson, Thomas Carlyle called the young Tennyson "one of the finest looking men in the world"; his is only one of many

FIGURE 5.3 Samuel Laurence, "Alfred Tennyson" (c. 1840). Courtesy of the National Portrait Gallery, London.

contemporary accounts of the young Tennyson's often stunning visual impact.[7] And, indeed, he was of a beautiful line; virtually all the members of the poet's large family were renowned for being "exceptionally handsome."[8] Arthur Henry Hallam (himself "thought stunningly beautiful" and, according to Gladstone, possessed in addition of "a character profoundly beautiful"), became engaged to Tennyson's striking sister Emily.[9] The family's effects on viewers were individual and collective; Hallam wrote to Alfred that his mother said of another of his sisters, "Nobody could see Mary [Tennyson] come into the room without being struck by her beauty" (*Letters*, 766). In his biography of the poet, Martin elaborates on the effect of seeing the young Tennyson: "To some his withdrawn manner could seem both arrogant and affected. With a beautifully modeled nose and sensuous mouth, he was so startlingly handsome that Edward FitzGerald, who did not know him for some years after, always remembered him walking the tortuous streets of Cambridge looking 'something like the Hyperion shorn of his Beams in Keats' Poem: with a Pipe in his mouth.'"[10]

Hartley Coleridge told Tennyson upon meeting him in 1835 that he "was far too handsome to be a poet."[11] Yet Tennyson had already articulated in the unpublished 1833 dramatic monologue "Tithon" an intimacy between beauty and poetics, one that followed closely not only the line of Trojan kings, but also the line of Apollo, beautiful god of poetry and composer of Troy's walls. In this chapter I trace Tithonus's self-construction partly by way of Tennyson's related representations of Paris in "Oenone" and of Tithonus's son, Memnon, who figures in a number of Tennyson's early poems. Tithonus forwards in his monologue not only an argument about his own history and position but an intricate aesthetics of identification and inversion. Tennyson in his early poetry and in this monologue recurs to these examples of masculine beauty, closely and elaborately identified with representations of femininity and effeminacy. The images of these beautiful young men at once enchant and trouble perception, and it is important to follow their contours, tracing them partly through the writings of Arthur Henry Hallam. These men are for Tennyson, I argue, figures of incarnate poetics.

Ganymede, Tithonus, Paris, Memnon, and other Trojan men can all be charged with a superflux of beauty, but the accusation of perhaps possessing too much beauty has long been addressed to Tennyson's poetry more generally. Casting a bemused eye on the "white-breasted" Paris advancing "like a star" toward his lover Oenone, Douglas Bush notes, "Beautiful as the picture of Paris is, one may wish for something less refined." Remarking the contrast between the rings of tobacco smoke inevitably encircling Tennyson and the arabesques of his verse, he asks, "We wonder how many pipes he smoked over these delicately contrived embroideries of phrase and rhythm." Tennyson's lines, Bush continues, "constantly call attention to their beauty," and it is their apparent self-consciousness that renders them dubious.[12] Such exhibitionism appears to be characteristic of the Trojans, as conceived of by the Victorians; Gladstone explains, regarding Paris, "One solicitude only he cherished: it is to decorate his person, to exhibit his beauty."[13] Even Priam, called genial and kindly by Gladstone, is prone, he claims, to "overindulgence." While Gladstone must admit the "capacity of the Homeric Greeks for acquisition," he sees in them nevertheless "a remarkable temperance, and even detestation of excess, in all the enjoyments of the senses" (*SH*, 3:211, 80). Tennyson's great profusion of images and the density of what Bush calls his "beauty of verbal ornament"[14] correspond to the attraction to gorgeous display that we might label a Trojan aesthetic. The Trojans were renowned for their love of luxurious decoration, of embellishment, and here too this culture provides a relevant and surprisingly far-reaching context for the reading of a poet whose works were from the start either valued or dismissed on the grounds of their aesthetic richness. This tendency to prodigious, even prodigal spectacle came early to be attributed to the poet, and although it was encouraged by Hallam, as we shall see, Tennyson came to be dissuaded from exhibiting too much beauty, indeed, too much lyricism, in his poetry. Discussing the revisions that differentiate the poems of 1832 from the 1842 versions, Hallam Tennyson argues that the alterations "wrought a marvelous abatement of my father's real fault." He identifies the defect in his father's work by quoting from Spedding's 1833 review, in which his friend deplored the poet's tendency toward "an over-indulgence in the luxuries of the senses, a profusion of splendours, harmonies, perfumes, gorgeous apparel, luscious meats and drinks and 'creature comforts' which rather pall the sense" (*Memoir*, 1:97).

I have argued that Tennyson's return to the Trojan plain is a return, in this period of keenest mourning for his friend Hallam, to their intensely shared intellectual and political interests. We might extend the focus of those interests still further, from classical subjects to the more abstract philosophy of beauty. Hallam himself linked his theories of poetry to Tennyson's practice by way of an essay on aesthetics; in his 1831 essay on his friend, Hallam stresses from the start the centrality of "beauty" to poetics. Writing more than a century later, T. S. Eliot observes, "It is an advantage to mankind in general to live in a beautiful world; that no one can doubt," then asks, "But for the poet is it so important?" Eliot arrives at a bleak modernist conclusion: "We mean all sorts of things, I know, by Beauty. But the essential advantage for a poet is not to have a beautiful world with which to deal."[15] For Hallam, however, beauty was paramount for poetics, so much so that its apprehension and manufacture was the prerogative and the obligation of the poet. This idea was already forming in his mind when he visited Gladstone at Oxford, bringing with him a copy of Tennyson's "Timbuctoo." Gladstone's diary entry for October 17, 1829, describes having tea with Hallam and a few other Eton friends, during which they had "a long conversation on the nature of Poetry & of beauty." Hallam came to "define poetry, after much discussion[, as] 'the attempt to produce the impression of the beautiful by the mental faculties.'" This Gladstone found overly complex, commenting, "To me it seemed better 'the image of the beautiful' or simply 'beauty' or 'the beautiful,'"[16] but Hallam was to continue to develop his terms in more formal venues.

At the outset of his 1831 review essay on Tennyson, "On Some of the Characteristics of Modern Poetry, and on the Lyrical Poems of Alfred Tennyson," Hallam insists that the "predominate motive" of the artist must be "the desire for beauty" (*Writings*, 184). The intense perception of beauty is itself a quality of the poets Hallam most vehemently admires, Shelley and Keats: "Susceptible of the slightest impulse from external nature, their fine organs trembled into emotion at colors, and sounds, and movements, unperceived or unregarded by duller temperaments." He notes with approval of these "poets of sensation" that their perception of beauty extended from their writing to their own reading: "They would hardly have been affected by what is called the pathetic parts of a book; but the *merely beautiful* passages ... would have melted them to tears" (*Writings*, 186). When the essay turns to introduce Tennyson as a poet of sensation, Hallam notes of his friend the "strange earnestness in his worship of beauty," which is accompanied by an ability to "communicate the love of beauty to the heart." This communication is accomplished by way of a kind of rhetorical luxuriance, even excess: "He lavishes images of exquisite accuracy and elaborate splendour, as a common writer throws about metaphorical truisms and exhausted tropes" (*Writings*, 193). Hallam's readings of Tennyson's poetry are suffused with a sense, specifically, of what he again and again terms its beauty; after quoting Tennyson's poem "Adeline," he asks, "Is not this beautiful?" (*Writings*, 197). In promoting his friend's poetry to Leigh Hunt, Hallam had delineated a genealogy for Tennyson, whom he calls "heir" to Keats and the "last lineal descendent" of Apollo. He traces what amounts to an aesthetic birthright, but this is an ominous legacy: in standing as the "last" in the line, Tennyson is its most recent member, but also perhaps the final exemplum of a fated kind. This position of representing a line at once exalted and exhausted is one Tennyson's Tithonus knows all too well.

TROJAN AESTHETICS

"Why should a man desire in any way / To vary from the kindly race of men ... ?" (28–29) surely stands as Tithonus's most trenchant question, in a monologue propelled by the speaker's pleading interrogation of a silent auditor. "Why should a man desire in any shape / To vary from his kind ...?" (20–21), the speaker inquired in "Tithon," the 1833 version of a poem revised and published as "Tithonus" in 1860. The revision is telling in many ways, most especially in its characterization of what exactly a man, as he once was, might desire to vary from: "the kindly race of men," or "his kind." For there is no Tennysonian speaker who appears, literally, to have varied from the kindly race of men more than Tithonus, and yet I hope to demonstrate that he is a speaker who, as Tennyson's revision indicates, varies not at all from his kind. This claim necessitates establishing the nature of Tithonus's kind, which in turn requires a return to the Trojan plain. What he may indeed desire is more fully to join his kind, which, as for Ulysses, is a group defined by events at Troy. And, as with Ulysses, to understand Tithonus's position among his kind requires probing the depths of Tennyson's literary sources, which are varied, as Tucker notes, and obscure.[17] Tithonus's kin are the generations of the Trojan royal family, a context that criticism of this poem has widely overlooked.[18] His brother is Priam, ruler over Troy throughout the war and, perhaps more important for Tennyson, one of a line of beautiful Trojan men, godlike in their beauty and desired by the gods; this is part of his complex patrimony. Tithonus, beautiful human lover of the dawn, asked the gods for immortality, which, to his eternal regret, he was granted. According to myth, what he meant to say was "Give me eternal youth"; instead, Tithonus's lot is to age, to increase in decrepitude hour by hour for all time, unlike his eternally youthful lover. But it is another, less obvious but more appalling irony that the dramatic monologue explores: the speaker, now doomed to a solitary status at variance, in his infinitude of aging, both from gods and men, in asking to be more literally godlike only desired a condition most characteristic of his kind. More even than Ulysses, Tithonus is deeply embedded in narratives of Ilion, of which he is the most shadowy and yet most definitive representative.

In establishing the intricacies of Tithonus's embeddedness among his kind, we shall look first at Tennyson's own schemata for the genealogy of Troy's ruling family, then focus on those male members known for their beauty (Ganymede, Tithonus, Anchises, Paris, Memnon), and those who mate with goddesses, two categories that rivet "Tithonus" to the earlier "Oenone." As the Trojan Tithonus addresses a divinity he finds perfidious, so the nymph Oenone reviews the wretched history of her entanglement with the Trojan Paris. Gladstone notes of the line of Trojan rulers, "The family appears to have had personal beauty for an almost entailed inheritance" (*SH*, 3:398). Gladstone's word "entail" is significant; he uses a legal term more often reserved for the inheritance of property. For the Trojans beauty is not only a kind of property, but linked *to* property, as if this characteristic, like the city, were an outgrowth of the plain. The gods themselves call these beautiful Trojan men "godlike," and in considering this crucial aspect of Tithonus's kind, we can enrich our understanding of this dramatic monologue's generic kind. I have read "Ulysses" in conjunction with "The Lotos- Eaters" because of the depth and the significance of the dramatic monologue's departure from a poem it holds as an ancestor. "Oenone" offers a similar opportunity, bearing heavily in its concerns upon the later "Tithonus," and yet, in its differences of method and aim, helping to teach us about the "kind" that is the dramatic monologue. "Tithonus" demonstrates the centrality of genealogy—familial on the speaker's part, literary on the poet's—at this moment of Tennyson's poetic imagination. The Tithonus who speaks is not only disfigured but is displaced from his kind, and part of the monologue's task is to attain for its speaker both a dramatically altered position and a new figurative identity.

A comprehensive review of Tithonus's kind can follow lines literally drawn by Tennyson. In *H. Ilias Graece et Latine*, an edition of Homer's *Iliad* in Greek and Latin owned by the poet's father and used by Alfred for his lessons, are many marginal notes and, on the front boards and flyleaves, drawings.[19] The inside cover is signed first "E. libris G. C. Tennyson," the poet's father, and below, "Alfred Tennyson." This vertical set of names constitutes its own highly abbreviated genealogy. As a child, he (and perhaps his brothers) doodled a number of genealogical diagrams, some extensive, some brief. Among the latter are abbreviated lines showing simply that the union of Anchises and Venus yielded Aeneas and illustrating ancestral lines culminating in such figures as Ulysses and Achilles (this twice). Dominating are several sketches of the genealogy of the Trojan royal family. On the most extensive of these, Tennyson appended a title: "Line of Illion [*sic*] kings" (figure 5.4). This diagram begins with Saturn,

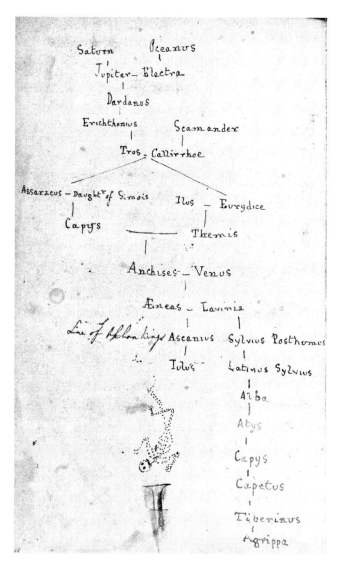

FIGURE 5.4 Alfred Tennyson, "Line of Illion kings," front flyleaf verso of *Homeri Ilias,* ed. Samuel Clarke (London, 1806). Reproduced by permission of Lincolnshire County Council, Tennyson Research Centre (TRC no. 157).

moves through the early members of the male line, then centers on Anchises (father of Aeneas). The longest chart even has a lengthy column parallel to that of Ascanius, son of Aeneas, which runs from Sylvius Posthumus down seven further generations to Agrippa. The central line of this most extensive chart, spanning from the union of Tros and Callirrhoe to Aeneas's grandson Iulus, is rendered in two other diagrams. Tros married the daughter of the Scamander, his son Assaracus married the daughter of the river Simois; thus various generations have intermarried with the daughters of the rivers that embrace the city. The generations that follow are therefore descended in part from the rivers whose rippling and rolling helped structure the walls of Troy in "Ilion, Ilion."

Tennyson also separately diagrammed the line centering on Ilus, whose son Laomedon (father of Priam and Tithonus) caused the walls of Ilion to be constructed by contracting the services of Apollo and Poseidon. I wish to dilate on this branch of the family, following the generations of Ilus and Assaracus:

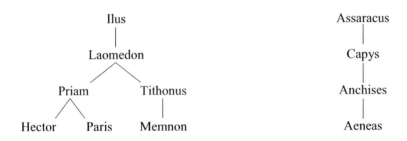

The diagram is based largely on Aeneas's account of his lineage and near relations, which he provides in answer to a taunt of Achilles' in book 20 of the *Iliad* (20:215ff), a genealogical account that Gladstone notes is "the longest and most detailed in Homer."[20] Aeneas first reminds his opponent of the similarities of their genealogies ("Each from illustrious fathers draws his line, / Each goddess-born; half human, half divine" [20:246–47, trans. Pope]), reminding him that whichever of them dies in this combat, "tears shall trickle from celestial eyes" (20:246–47, trans. Pope). Nevertheless, Aeneas recounts the "glorious origin" of his line, from Dardanus's rule over a rural community to the increased wealth of Ericthonius, to the "sacred Tros, of whom the Trojan name," whose offspring were Ilus, Assaracus, and Ganymede. He then continues through the line of Ilus, who begat Laomedon, who begat Priam and Tithonus. Finally, he delineates his own parallel descent. "Such is our race," he concludes; "'tis Fortune gave us birth" (20:290, trans. Pope).

Aeneas terms Laomedon, father of Priam and Tithonus, "blameless" (20:236, trans. Lattimore); Loeb has "peerless," Lang, Leaf, and Myers have "noble," and

Pope omits an adjective.[21] This is a polemical claim on Aeneas's part, since it is Laomedon who contracted with Apollo and Neptune to build his city walls, then cheated them of payment. (In relation to the events of the *Iliad*, Troy's wall is of fairly recent vintage; the speaker in Tennyson's "Tithonus" witnessed its building because it was at his father's behest.) Laomedon's bold impiety is seen to predate Paris's abduction of Helen as the beginning of the troubles at Troy. This incident is recorded in one of the Horatian odes for which we have Tennyson's childhood translation. The passage follows a few lines after Juno's invocation, "Ilion, Ilion"; she dates her fury toward the Trojans from this incident of Laomedon's cozening the gods:

> Ever since that fatal day
> > When thy monarch broke his faith
> When he falsely took away
> > The fixed reward he vowed to bring.
> > Pallas and I condemned to death
> > > Thy people and thy perjured King. (3.3:34–39, trans. Tennyson)

"Long enough have we paid in our blood for the promise Laomedon broke at Troy," proclaims an exasperated Virgil in the *Georgics*.[22] But whatever the ill effects experienced by later collateral generations, the direct line of Laomedon is blotted out by the end of the Trojan War, with the sole exception of Tithonus, who stands as the last of the major representatives of that particular line.

Aeneas presumably would prefer in answer to the taunt of Achilles to dwell on the qualities of military and moral leadership exhibited by his family, stressing in particular the fact that Priam was "blest with Hector, brave and bold" (20:285, trans. Pope). Yet even he is apparently distracted by the figure of Ganymede, the uncle of Laomedon. While listing the three sons of Tros, he lingers over

> The matchless Ganymede, divinely fair
> Whom Heav'n, enamour'd, snatch'd to upper air,
> To bear the cup of Jove (ethereal guest
> The grace and glory of th'ambrosial feast). (20:278–81, trans. Pope)

The gods feast their eyes on the ethereal, matchless Ganymede, "divinely fair," that is, godlike in his beauty. Pope generalizes the divine desire (of "Heav'n") for this Trojan, snatched up by Jupiter. Although Victorian mythological dictionaries could be evasive about the nature of this relationship, Lemprière is not. In his *Classical Dictionary* he describes Ganymede as "a beautiful youth of Phrygia, son of Tros, and brother of Ilus and Assaracus," who was "taken up to heaven by Jupiter as he was hunting, or rather tending his father's flocks on Mount Ida." He adds, "Some say that he was carried away by an eagle, to satisfy the shameful and unnatural desires of Jupiter."[23]

Tennyson's primary source for "Tithonus" is the *Homeric Hymn to Aphrodite*, which recounts the seduction of Anchises by that goddess. His use of the *Hymn* is marked both by direct echoes and dramatic deviations. The monologue "Tithonus" finds the speaker "at the quiet limit of the world" (7), while in the *Homeric Hymn* he dwells "at the world's end" (Lang), "at the ends of the earth" (Athanassakis and Loeb). In the larger story recounted in the *Hymn*, Zeus causes Aphrodite to desire the beautiful herdsman Anchises so that she can never boast that she, unlike other gods, had never lain with a mortal or begot a mortal child. After their lovemaking, she reveals her true identity to Anchises, informing him that they will have a son, Aeneas. Perhaps with an eye to their son's genetic inheritance, Aphrodite links Anchises with his kind, telling him, "Of all mortal men these who spring from thy race are always nearest to the immortal gods in beauty and stature." She gives as an example "golden-haired" Ganymede, carried away "for his beauty's sake." He remains, she reports, "a marvelous thing to behold, a mortal honoured among all the Immortals."[24]

Aphrodite's next example is that of Tithonus. Tennyson's chief literary source for this dramatic monologue thus wholly integrates the story of Tithonus within a network of direct familial association: "So too," continues Aphrodite, "did Dawn of the Golden Throne carry off Tithonus, a man of your lineage, one like unto Immortals." It is vital to note that these are, as Aphrodite suggests, parallel raptures; however much he may come to desire her ravishment, as his monologue suggests, Tithonus had initially been taken forcibly. K. J. Dover describes ancient representations of this seizure of Tithonus, pointing to images showing that Dawn "lays violent hands" on Tithonus. Some images of the "rape," as Dover calls it, show Tithonus "brandishing a lyre" in his struggle against her.[25] In the *Homeric Hymn*, Aphrodite cites the hideous example of Tithonus's perpetual aging to explain why she will not attempt to make Anchises immortal: "Therefore I would not have thee to be immortal and live forever in such fashion among the deathless Gods."[26] Tennyson in his dramatic monologue pursues the story embedded within two other stories of Trojan male beauty, those of the more fortunate Ganymede and Anchises, the first who retains eternal youth, the second who is graced with the honorable death we see depicted in the *Aeneid*. Tithonus in the *Hymn to Aphrodite* straddles the possibilities available to his kind.

Gladstone can only look with disapproval at so licentious a lineage. He insists that the story of Ganymede was "afterwards perverted to the purposes of depravity" but is "in Homer, perfectly pure." But he then follows what he calls the "downward course" of these legends: "Two generations after Ganymede, Tithonos, of the same family, is appropriated by the goddess Eos as a husband. One generation more gives us the lawless love of Aphrodite and Anchises, and the same goddess, in the next generation, promises to Paris a beautiful wife, whom he was to obtain by treachery and violence as well as adultery."[27] While he lists some of the specific vices of Paris, Gladstone's disapprobation points more vehemently to the larger, more complex issue of a kind of mythic miscegenation. It is clear, from the "appropriation" of Tithonus to the "lawless love" of Aphrodite and Anchises to the ongoing special relationship between that goddess and Paris that the Trojans are errant in consorting, in one manner or another, with divinities, from generation unto degenerate generation. Tennyson seems to have followed this course of Trojan intermingling with goddesses still more closely, and earlier, than Gladstone: aside from the 1833 "Tithon," he explored more thoroughly the perfidy of Paris in the 1830 "Oenone." Indeed, he had long before followed the line to its conclusion in the extraordinarily beautiful son of Tithonus and Eos. Their offspring, Memnon (killed in the Trojan War), is figured curiously, as we shall see, in a number of Tennyson's early poems, predating his arrival at Cambridge. While Tennyson would hardly have endorsed the promiscuity Gladstone remarked in this family, he appears to have found it rich territory for poetic exploration.

"Oenone" and the Judgment of Paris

To determine more exactly the profundity of Tennyson's representation of what I have labeled a Trojan aesthetic, and its political valences, we must understand his wider portrayal of Troy's princes, especially in the godlike beauty of their persons and in their own desire for beautiful objects. One poetic site for witnessing such luxuriance, in terms of its verbal and visual abundance, is "Oenone," a poem in which the eponymous speaker, a nymph of the Troas (the environs of Troy), describes the judgment of Paris and laments her abandonment by her lover Paris in favor of Helen. The earliest versions of the poem were written virtually at Hallam's side. Oenone's Troas was modeled after the countryside of the Pyrenees, where the two men traveled together in 1830, which Tennyson ever afterward associated (both in conversation and in poems such as the elegiac "In the Valley of Cauteretz" [1861, 1864]) with his friend. Tennyson's overt likening of this countryside to the Homeric landscape further indicates the significance of his imaginative returns to a Trojan culture ruined and dispersed.

"Oenone" was first published in 1832. In the revised version, published in 1842, the opening lines, which establish the context for the narrative that follows, describe how "The swimming vapour slopes athwart the glen... / And loiters, slowly drawn" (3, 5), moving alongside hanging flowers and waterfalls. In the revision, Oenone's description of the vale she inhabits is absorbed in the natural aspects of the place, with its cataracts and creeping vapors. It is only at the end of the first verse paragraph that the city of Troy is spotted in the distance: "The gorges, opening wide apart, reveal / Troas and Ilion's columned citadel, / The crown of Troas" (12–14). The revision makes Ilion difficult of scopic access and, once seen, less visually complex than the vale of Mount Ida. Troy is veiled, seemingly enveloped and obscured by the glen's swimming vapor, and rendered more a part of the natural landscape, as if it were an extension of the gorges. This change continues in the vein of a general excising of visions of Troy in his revisions, as we saw in "Ulysses."

In its earlier 1832 appearance, however, the city is far more highly wrought, more reflective of the Trojans' legendary love of rich personal and civic ornament. In the earlier version, the description of the dale moves more immediately to the sighting of an elaborated city:

> Far-seen, high over all the Godbuilt wall
> And many a snowycolumned range divine,
> Mounted with awful sculptures—men and Gods,
> The work of Gods—bright on the darkblue sky
> The windy citadel of Ilion
> Shone, like the crown of Troas. (*1832* 9–14)

Ilion's glistening range of white columns and the height and majesty of its "windy citadel" more fully substantiate its claim, retained in the 1842 version, to be the "crown of Troas." This excised passage of "Oenone" is one of Tennyson's fullest accounts of the city as seen from afar, and what is most striking is his stress on the "divine" nature of its decoration. The young Tennyson surmounts the "Godbuilt wall" with "awful sculptures," and we must attend to their awesome representations of "men and Gods, / The work of Gods." The city's architecture is structured by the peculiar relation between its ruling family and the gods; they are a people known for consorting with divinities, and its sculptural embellishment, crafted by Apollo and Poseidon, reenacts the terrible commingling of gods and mortals. As if he too had seen these representations, or suspected them, Gladstone remarked:

> A tendency...to sensual excess appears to run in the royal line of Troy, under much less of restraint than we find in the Greek houses. This is especially remarkable in the mythology. Aphrodite and Eos, goddesses markedly Trojan, and Demeter...condescended to irregular relations with men. So it is with the Naiad nymphs of Troas. But with the goddesses recognized by the Homeric Greeks, Pallas, Artemis, Persephone, and even Hera, we hear nothing of the kind.[28]

Tithonus sees himself as both beneficiary and victim of this tendency of his kind toward "irregular relations" with gods and goddesses, and it is important to look at its precedent in "Oenone" in order to contextualize his intercourse with his auditor, the goddess Eos (Greek) or Aurora (Latin).[29] These speakers, Oenone and Tithonus, are not generally read in direct relation to each other, presumably because their generic kinds differ, although the ways they differ can help bring us to a keener understanding of the form of the dramatic monologue. "Oenone," moreover, is patterned closely after the epistle of Oenone to Paris in Ovid's *Heroides*, a precursor to the genre of the Victorian dramatic monologue, so it is a poem whose resemblance to the form that concerns us is not only stylistic but generational, deriving as it does from one of Tennyson's classical prototypes. And while part of the project of this and the following chapter is to tease out the intricacies of the connections among "Tithonus," "Ulysses," and "Tiresias," the resemblance between Tithonus and Oenone as mythic characters is far more direct. I have established genealogy as important to these poems, and it is worth noting that both are descendents of river deities. Tithonus's mother was Strymo, daughter of the Scamander, and Oenone is the daughter of the river Cebrenus in Phrygia: as she pronounces, "I am the daughter of a River-God" (37). Both speakers address former lovers who have abandoned them. And both record in their monologues their viewing of the rising of Troy's wall to Apollo's song. Each bore witness to that song's architectonic effect along the lines recorded in Tennyson's early "Ilion, Ilion," and for both that experience is bound together with her or his own lyric articulations.

And yet Tithonus, for all his similarities to Oenone, bears a still more striking resemblance to her lover Paris. As two generations of the descendents of Laomedon, Tithonus and Paris are members of the Trojan royal family renowned not only for their beauty but for their poor judgment. It is necessary therefore to look briefly at Oenone's representations of the figure of Paris, who, though he is the nephew of Tithonus, is nevertheless in Tennyson's canon his precursor. Oenone's recollection of her first sighting of Paris points to another, deeper bond between him and Tithonus, a lineage traced not through Laomedon, but through his contracted (and bilked) builder, Apollo. She describes the approach of "Beautiful Paris" (49):

> white-breasted like a star
> Fronting the dawn he moved; a leopard skin
> Drooped from his shoulder, but his sunny hair
> Clustered about his temples like a God's. (56–59)

In "fronting the dawn," he comes in advance of that light-bearing goddess mated to Tithonus, but he also follows Apollo in the details of his appearance. The leopard skin is his distinctive garment in the *Iliad*, and Tennyson drew from this representation in Homer (by way of Pope): "beauteous Paris came: / In form a God! the panther's speckled hide / Flow'd over his armour with an easy pride" (3:26–28, trans. Pope). Tennyson himself translated the simile in *Iliad* 6:503–14 comparing Paris to a stallion, "glorying in himself / And galloping to the meadows of the mares" (8–9). He rendered the passage into both prose and blank verse; the latter version, probably produced in 1863–64, begins, "Nor lingered Paris in the lofty house" (1) and ends, "So ran the son of Priam from the height / Of Ilion, Paris, sunlike all in arms / Glittering" (10–12).[30] Tennyson calls Paris "sunlike," Pope calls him godlike ("In form a God"), and both comparisons indicate that the god he is ineluctably "like" is Apollo.

The description of Paris's appearance for which I have given Pope's version occurs in the early turning point in the *Iliad*, when he strides forward, implicitly challenging the Greeks, only to withdraw ignominiously when Menelaus leaps to meet his challenge. Hector scolds Paris for his retreat, saying that had he stood against his opponent (in Lattimore's closer translation), "The lyre would not help you then, nor the favours of Aphrodite, / nor your locks, when you rolled in the dust, nor all your beauty" (3:54–55). Pope's translation elaborates on the curling hair and lyre commonly associated with Apollo:

> Thy graceful form instilling soft desire,
> Thy curling tresses, and thy silver lyre,
> Beauty and youth, in vain to these you trust,
> When youth and beauty shall be laid in the dust (3:79–82)

In his 1831 *Mythology of Ancient Greece and Italy*, Thomas Keightley describes the appearance of Apollo: "His long curling hair hangs loose," and "his brows are wreathed with bay; in his hands he bears a bow or lyre."[31] Paris's aureole of "sunny curls" and the lyre with which he is associated render him representationally akin to Apollo.

In insisting, by way of what Pope renders as the chiastic "beauty and youth," "youth and beauty," upon the ineluctably doomed nature of this pairing, Hector gives Paris a warning that it is too late for Tithonus to heed. At this moment for Paris, his youthfulness is as preternatural as his beauty; he is represented repeatedly as an ephebe, in particular in his most disastrous puissance, at the time of his judgment of goddesses. Tennyson's dramatic monologist Lucretius, reviewing the beautiful men (Anchises, Adonis, and Paris) favored by Venus, the same goddess he sees as tormenting himself, calls Paris "the beardless apple arbiter." In this too Paris resembles Apollo; Lemprière writes of the god, "He is always represented as a tall beardless young man, with a handsome shape, holding in his hand a bow, and sometimes a lyre; his head is generally surrounded with beams of light."[32] If such Trojans as Paris and Tithonus are like gods, they are like sun gods, like the Apollo who built their city and whom they overtly resemble: bright, radiant, "sunlike" (as Tennyson's translation fragment has it), associated with "youth and dawn." This mark of ephebism seems especially prized by these handsome men, and its loss is part of the complex punishment endured by Tithonus.

So striking is the likeness between Paris and the god whose music built Troy that Tennyson's Oenone, on seeing the glowing Paris coming to meet her, remembers having "called out, / 'Welcome Apollo, welcome home Apollo, / Apollo, my Apollo, loved Apollo'" (*1832* 61–62). These lines were questioned by Tennyson's Cambridge friend J. M. Kemble, writing early in 1833, who, looking from his

Ovid to his Tennyson, queried, "Let me ask whether Ovid or you are in the right? You seem to know something about Oenone; was it the strength of character that made her burn Troy which enabled her to call Paris 'her Apollo'? he knowing all things."[33] In Ovid's *Heroides* Oenone says that Apollo was her first lover, from whom she obtained the secret art of healing. In lines of questionable provenance that have exercised Ovid's commentators as well as Tennyson's friends, she declares, *me fide conspicuus Troiae munitor amavit, / admisitque meas ad sua dona manus* (*Heroides* V, 145–46; Loeb trans.: "Me, the builder of Troy, well known for keeping faith, loved, and let my hands into the secret of his gifts").[34] Her outburst may reflect her amatory history, but it is also in accord with the terms of her description of Paris, in which his physical resemblance to Apollo is wholesale. Though Tennyson in his 1842 revision omitted these lines, the construction of this outburst remained a key element of this narrative and the relation between these lovers, and late in his life he returned to them. In "The Death of Oenone," published in 1892 in his final volume of poems, Tennyson revisited this place and this speaker. The narrative centers around her possession of the knowledge of Apollo's healing arts (learned "of a God"), and, as if in answer to her 1832 supplication (some sixty years earlier), "Apollo, my Apollo," Paris is twice heard to cry out, "Oenone, my Oenone" (29, 81).

Oenone's description of the Apollonian Paris culminates in his proud brandishing of the Hesperian golden apple, his announcement that, in the terms of Tennyson's Lucretius, he has been made "apple-arbiter," judge of the most beautiful of three naked goddesses. (This nakedness Tennyson stresses: "Then to the bower they came, / Naked they came to that smooth-swarded bower" [92–93]). It is of course the case that, in determining the question of comparative beauty, Paris judged well, if not wisely, in declaring Aphrodite fairest. But I want to look briefly at another element of the contest, namely, the terms of the offers of the goddesses, to deepen our sense of why Paris decided as he did, because these terms come to dictate his own and Tithonus's predicaments. Hera offers Paris "royal power, ample rule / Unquestioned" (109–10), explaining, at the close of her offer, that "men, in power / Only, are likest gods" (127–28), a condition she defines as attaining "undying bliss / In knowledge of their own supremacy" (130–31). Although Pallas Athena, speaking next, claims she will not bribe him, she makes him an offer that bears a covert resemblance to the terms of Hera's proposition. She promises Paris, "my vigour, wedded to thy blood, / Shall strike within thy pulse, like a God's" (158–59). Pallas's superadded vigor will propel Paris to a life of "deeds" and "action" (161, 162), offering to the languid, passive Trojan, called by Gladstone "effeminate and apathetic,"[35] her own version of muscular polytheism.

Only Aphrodite does not offer Paris a promise gilded with the simile "like a God." She laughingly utters instead a straightforward and economical sentence: "I promise thee / The fairest and most loving wife in Greece" (182–83). We know of course that this is not the first time she has descended upon Mount Ida with an offer no Trojan could refuse. Tennyson's Lucretius says of her seduction of Anchises (recounted, as we have noted, in the *Hymn to Aphrodite* that is the chief source of "Tithonus") that "all the pines of Ida shook to see [the goddess] / Slide from that quiet heaven of hers, and tempt / The Trojan" ("Lucretius," 86–88). In the *Hymn*, Aphrodite specifically withholds from Anchises any offer of immortality, of becoming godlike, even as here she makes no such offer to Paris. (Aphrodite, or Venus, broods over "Tithonus" as well. He can see, he tells Aurora, that "the silver star, thy guide, / Shines in [your] tremulous eyes" [25–26]; in the Eversley edition, Tennyson glossed the "silver star" as "Venus" [2:340]). Why does Paris forgo the two offers of divine similitude? Oenone's own description of Paris, ascending Mount Ida, golden fruit in hand, tells us: he is already "like a God," a status he attains here not by way of imperial power or heroic action, but by way of his beauty.

Paris therefore does not eschew being godlike; he just makes the mistake of thinking that he is in sufficient possession of that resemblance. But what does it mean to be "like a god," a condition that early and long interested Tennyson? The simile of course appears repeatedly in the *Iliad*, to describe both Trojans and Achaeans; "godlike" is a not uncommon epithet. To be "like a god" means, as in the example of Ganymede that Aphrodite provides to Anchises in the *Homeric Hymn*, to be deathless and unaging. But we have also the definitions of two other goddesses, known to hold wider interests than Aphrodite, with her unwavering dedication to physical pleasure: the Hera and Pallas who speak in "Oenone." What Pallas offers, "Self-reverence, self-knowledge, self-control," "Paris pondered," as if trying to understand the appeal of what she describes. G. K. Chesterton responded to this virtuous trinity as Paris might have done: "These three alone will make a man a prig."[36] Oenone's endorsement (and presumably the poet's, according to many readers), "O Paris, / Give it to Pallas!" falls on ears as indifferent to the counsel as to the offer ("Oenone," 142, 165–66). Paris hesitates over the words of Hera, however, and even briefly extends the Hesperian fruit toward the goddess whose offer of kingship "Flattered his spirit" ("Oenone," 135).

While Aphrodite's temptation is bound to the fates of both Paris and Tithonus, the appeal of being godlike for the Trojans has larger social and political dimensions, which I consider further in chapter 6. At present we may note that the status of being "like gods" consists for them of holding and exercising an arbitrary and indeed willful power, enjoying what Hera calls "ample rule / Unquestioned" ("Oenone," 109–10). Promising an avoidance of the civic discord that will occupy the monologue "Tiresias," Hera describes the result of such a position as being "likest gods," enjoying "Rest in a happy place and quiet seats, / Above the thunder" ("Oenone," 128, 129–30). Tennyson was profoundly drawn to this paradigm, characterizing this state repeatedly in similar terms.[37] In "The Lotos-Eaters," the chief desire of the chorus, finally, is "to live and lie reclined / On the hills like Gods together, careless of mankind" ("The Lotos-Eaters," 154–55), while the speaker of "Lucretius" struggles with his knowledge that "The Gods are careless" (150), repeating, in fruitless address, "O ye Gods, / I know you careless" (207–8). Being "godlike," then, is defined repeatedly by Tennyson as an elevated removal from the chaos as well as the banality of human existence.

Prior to Paris's decision regarding the beauty of the goddesses he regards, Oenone renders her own judgment of Paris. Comparing him to the assembled goddesses, she exclaims, "How beautiful they were, too beautiful / To look upon! but Paris was to me / More lovelier than all the world beside" (*1832* 103–5). These lines were omitted in the 1842 revision of the poem, but they give a critical sense of the kind of beauty this man—and all of the beautiful men of his line—enjoys. His looks are in the league of Apollo and Aphrodite, and, more, he can compete, and win, in a contest of female beauty. In a sense such Trojans as Paris and Tithonus are tempted less by the goddesses' beauty than their own, and in the next section I consider further the ramifications of this desirous self-regard both for a reading of Tithonus's monologue and for Tennyson's poetry.

So indivisible are the Trojans from the Troas that Paris's beauty is described by Oenone in terms identical to those she uses to describe Mount Ida itself, the landscape in which these events occur. The 1832 version of the poem begins, "There is a dale in Ida, lovelier / Than any in old Ionia, beautiful" (*1832* 1–2). "Lovelier," "beautiful": these are precisely the terms Oenone one hundred lines later applies to Paris. The Trojan resembles the landscape of the Troas as closely as he resembles those gods who favor it; this striking corporeal identification of person with place is also to characterize Tithonus's relation to the city of Troy and Tiresias's to Thebes. And Paris is associated not just with the Trojan outskirts but also, like Tithonus, with the city itself; his poor judgment is seen as a chief cause of Troy's ruination. In the Horatian ode we have already looked at, translated by Tennyson in 1822, the blame for Troy's end is placed by Hera on Paris (and the Spartan Helen) as well as Laomedon. Tennyson's translation reads, "Ilion, Ilion . . . / . . . the beauteous maid / Of Sparta, and her spouse have laid / Thy gorgeous temples in the dust" (30, 31–33).[38] Tennyson seems to have endorsed this judgment seventy years later, since in "The Death of Oenone" (1892) Paris is called the man "Whose crime had half unpeopled Ilion" (61). Yet even Gladstone, usually unsympathetic to the Trojans, concedes, "The offense of Paris is regarded in Homer as arising from want of self-control rather than from hardened wickedness."[39] Paris lacks the wisdom or even practicality to make a decision of such magnitude—and yet, who better to judge beauty than its possessor, who seeks only the pleasure of another's beauty as reward?

Early in this discussion I noted that Oenone's lament can help to define the generic category of Tithonus's monologue. Its thematic, emotional, and discursive proximity to "Tithonus" demands that we ask an almost impertinent question: Why is "Oenone" not a dramatic monologue? The poem is multivocal, as Paris and the three goddesses whom he judges all speak, but of course other dramatic monologues, especially in Browning, report internal conversations. It does appear, nevertheless, that Oenone's lack of an audience beyond the generalized nature she hails as "Mother Ida" renders her song more a Romantic crisis lyric than a Victorian dramatic monologue. Oenone "sang to the stillness" (20), and in doing so disavows any ambition to have an effect with her words, to alter her condition by way of her speech, as Ulysses and Tithonus attempt. Indeed, her monologue records her rhetorical inefficacy, the powerlessness of her words. Discussing Oenone's complex generic standing, Tucker justly remarks "her pathetic enervation as a speaker, the incapacity of her discourse to break away either from her surroundings or from its own inertial patterns."[40] "Paris choose Pallas!" her unheeded cry, sounds "pathetic" because unlike the language of Ulysses or Tithonus, it is so wholly rejected as not even to have been considered. Her words may find accord among some readers, but like the Lotos-Eaters who preach to the converted chorus they themselves comprise, they cannot attain their overt objective. The speaker resolves at the end of "Oenone" to "rise and go / Down into Troy," there to "Talk with the wild Cassandra" (257–58, 259). Oenone here acknowledges her sorority with the woman whose gift of prophecy, like her own healing arts, comes from the amorous Apollo; as Tucker observes, the "Apollonian connection these two women share discloses a network of classical allusions that is exceptionally rich even for Tennyson."[41] Oenone's resolve to search for Cassandra acknowledges, moreover, a yearning toward a rhetorical inefficacy that is wholly familiar to her. Cassandra and Oenone both prophesy disaster and are unheard, or, more accurately, heard only in retrospect. Anchises on the shore of Crete marvels to an Aeneas newly resolved to find Hesperia (as chronicled in "On a Mourner"), remembering that such a destination had been prophesied before the destruction of Troy, "But who could think the Trojans would migrate / To evening lands? Or whom then could Cassandra / Move by foresight?" (3:199–201, trans. Fitzgerald). Tennyson seems also to have returned to Oenone's fruitless words: his "Death of Oenone," published half a century after "Oenone," marks his own retroactive attention to her rhetorical predicament.

Lyric Construction

Tennyson returned to Oenone's description of Paris's arrival, fruit in hand, in the sequel or conclusion, "The Death of Oenone," published the year of his death. So crucial was this incident that the nymph repeats it, as she remembers

> Him, climbing toward her with the golden fruit,
> Him, happy to be chosen Judge of Gods,
> Her husband in the flush of youth and dawn,
> Paris, himself as beauteous as a God. (15–18)

And yet in this continuation of the story, the Paris whom she soon sees approaching, pleading with her to apply her healing arts learned of the Apollo whom he had uncannily resembled, is changed utterly: "on a sudden he, / Paris, no longer beauteous as a God, / ... through the mist / Rose, like the wraith of his dead self" (24–25, 27–28). So physically altered is Paris that he seems already dead; in being unlike a god, he is no longer like himself. After Oenone, in the fury of a woman scorned, rejects his pleas, "He groaned, he turned, and in the mist at once / Became a shadow, sank and disappeared" (49–50). His resemblance to Apollo has ceased, yet he now resembles another, albeit newly minted, immortal: Tithonus. A shadow, "no longer beauteous as a God," engulfed in far-folded mists, is how Tithonus represents himself at the start of his monologue, and we may now turn to that poem with a keener sense of its mythical and literary echoes and portents.

Before turning in the next section to the withered Tithonus whom we meet in Tennyson's dramatic monologue, let us linger with him in his earlier, still beautiful incarnation, at the moment of his own commingling with an immortal. In "Tithonus," the speaker recalls his own past, lingering himself over the memory of dawns when he

<blockquote>
lay
Mouth, forehead, eyelids, growing dewy-warm
With kisses balmier than half-opening buds
Of April, and could hear the lips that kissed
Whispering I knew not what of wild and sweet,
Like that strange song I heard Apollo sing,
While Ilion like a mist rose into towers. (57–63)
</blockquote>

Just as, in Tennyson's monologue, the definitive moment in Ulysses' life is the destruction of windy Troy, Tithonus's definitive moment is its creation. In the extremity of his endlessly ongoing old age, he turns, by an ineluctable inner logic, to Troy's creation, as if its origin and his eternity are coincident. This comparison indicates that he has come to understand the profound ways in which he is implicated in these wild and airy songs. In his train of associative recollections Tithonus connects seduction with construction. Given his regional history, this is not surprising; we recall that when Oenone boasts of having been the lover of Apollo she identifies him as the builder of Troy (me ... Troiae munitor amavit). Both Aurora's lovemaking and Troy's creation are moments of erection; by way of this analogy, Tithonus suggests that he himself, like the city, might be characterized as god-built, having been also transformed and elevated by divine song.

Tithonus's likeness not only to other members of the ruling family of Ilion, but to the walls and towers of the city itself, is a matter of architectural history. In Dante's Inferno, several cantos after that featuring Ulysses engulfed in flames, Dante describes the overwhelming grief of Hecuba at the fall of Troy, when "the pride / Of all-presuming Troy fell from its height, / By fortune overwhelm'd, and the old king / With his realm perish'd" (30:13–22, trans. Cary). Tithonus is known for his pride and hauteur (a trait we shall consider in depth), and we can see its source here in the Trojan culture itself. He is connected by his hauteur, his "all-presuming" pride, to the high and haughty city ruled by his brother Priam, the "old king." And indeed in his rash ambition he takes liberties with the gods, thus resembling his father, Laomedon, who refused Apollo payment for constructing the walls of the city he ruled. Juno, in Tennyson's translation from Horace, also links the presumptuousness of the Trojans to the walls themselves, threatening that if ever descendents have the temerity to raise the walls again, she will pull them down. She warns, "Thrice should that god-built wall arise / And proudly threat the vaulted skies, / Thrice should that high and haughty wall / Beneath my fearless Argives fall" (92–95).

Virgil extends the connection between the walls of Troy and members of its ruling family to the Trojans' progenitor Dardanus. In book 2 of the *Aeneid*, at the precise moment when he is describing the entrance of the enemy horse, surrounded and pulled by eager, celebratory, uncomprehending Trojans into the midst of the city, Aeneas exclaims, "*o divum domus Ilium et incluta bello / moenia Dardanidum!*" (2:241–42; "O Ilium, home of gods, and Dardan battlements, famed in war!"). *Moenia Dardanidum* refers to the Dardan bulwarks, defensive walls or ramparts, although *moenia* can also refer more generally to a walled city. Aeneas exalts what is being breached, crediting the Dardanian walls themselves with military skills. Dryden translates this exclamation, "O sacred city, built by hands divine! / O valiant heroes of the Trojan line" (2:316–17), and his version reminds us how homologous are the god-built walls and the "Trojan line." The walls and the family that rules within them are connected not merely by contiguity, but also by consanguinity. The walls of Dardanus and the line of Dardanus are inseparable; they rise or fall together.

Tithonus therefore yet again defines his kind, connected by his hauteur and "all-presuming" nature to the lofty ramparts and towers commanded by his brother, bound wholly to a city that is home of the gods (*divum domus*) and the godlike. Jacob Bryant (the eighteenth-century mythologist whose three-volume *A New System of Ancient Mythology* was in Tennyson's father's library) specifically linked Tithonus, by way of idiosyncratic etymology, to the structural formation of towers. Ricks tells us that Bryant wrote of "towers" in his *New System*, "Tithonus, whose longevity is so much celebrated, was nothing more than one of these structures, a Pharos, sacred to the sun, as the name plainly shews" (*Poems*, 2:612). While Bryant's etymologies are invariably strained, his identification of this character with this architectural element is not without foundation. As Tennyson represents him here, Tithonus is inseparable from the towers whose formation he witnessed; by way of what Tucker terms "sublimated phallicism," he links his sexual seduction to the erection of those structures, to the moment when Ilion "rose into towers."[42]

Tithonus, moreover, not only bears a striking resemblance to the towers created by Apollo's song, but he now attempts to establish kinship with the singer himself. By way of his present monologue Tithonus seeks another way to resemble a god; he would confirm by his speaking his identity as both god-built and godlike. This connection between the "song" of the monologist and that of the god is articulated explicitly by Oenone:

> Hear me, for I will speak, and build up all
> My sorrow with my song, as yonder walls
> Rose slowly to a music slowly breathed,
> A cloud that gathered shape: for it may be
> That, while I speak of it, a little while
> My heart may wander from its deeper woe. ("Oenone," 38–43)

Oenone and Tithonus are bound together by sharing a fundamental, literally foundational experience as witnesses to the rising of Troy (an event each attributes wholly to Apollo's aspiration). As auditors, they so attach themselves to this experience that their own speech is ever after haunted by that "strange music." Oenone hopes for a direct personal effect from her speech, namely, that it may distract her from "deeper woe." She imagines her speech itself as architectonic. Something (however abstract; in this case, sorrow) will rise from it, take structure from it, as Ilion's walls took shape from so nebulous a source as the slowly breathed music, as the exhalations of Apollo's laboring breath formed "a cloud that gathered shape." Hallam Tennyson compared these lines to a promise given in Ovid's *Heroides*, in the epistle from Paris to Helen, urging her to join him: "*Ilion adspicies firmataque turribus altis / moenia, Phoebeae structa canore lyrae*" ("Ilion you will look upon, and its walls made strong with lofty towers, reared to the tunefulness of Phoebus' lyre" [16.181–82; Loeb ed.]). Paris, like Tithonus, associates these walls with seduction, using the very ramparts their union will destroy to tempt Helen to abscond with him to Troy.

In turn, Oenone comes to confuse Paris's body with the city's structure. In "The Death of Oenone," the nymph falls asleep after "The sunset blazed along the wall of Troy" (77), waking to question an eerie light in the darkness: "What star could burn so low? not Ilion yet. / What light was there?" (83–84). Yeats in "The Gyres" also fastened on the moment of this ominous sign of Troy's final conflagration, pronouncing, "Hector is dead, and there's a light in Troy" (7). But Tennyson postpones the fiery destruction, as the light Oenone describes is "not Ilion yet." Dismissing her own drowsy prophecy (her "yet" indicates that at least she, unlike the Trojans, has evidently believed the ravings of Cassandra, which end the earlier "Oenone"), she briefly confuses the burning of Paris's funeral pyre with the burning of the city. But this error is in its way accurate. Though Troy's heroes Hector and Aeneas labor most to preserve its household gods and royal line, to some degree no one represents this city in its destruction more absolutely than

Paris and Tithonus. Tithonus cements his association with Troy's towers not only in their rising, but in their incineration: reflecting on his own ruined beauty, his monologue comes to lament, "all I was, in ashes" (23).

We have established the architectonic association Tithonus holds to Troy, in his own beauty and imperiousness resembling both its towers and the singer that summoned them into being by his song. In concluding this genealogy of Trojan aesthetics, whereby masculine beauty is a component of Troy's civic structure, inseparable too from an illusion of godlike power, it behooves us to follow through to the conclusion of this ancestral line in another marvelous edifice, one that stands as a monument to Tithonus's son Memnon. It is a construction itself built of the aspirations of Aurora's strange song. Part of what both Oenone and Tithonus note in their recollections of the creation of Troy is the climate of the city that rose "like a mist," like a "cloud that gathered shape." The moist atmosphere of Ilion's creation saturates these accounts, and to follow the trail of the "Far-folded mists" (10) within which Tithonus now speaks is to discern more of the cause and the status of his speech. From her earlier balmy kisses that leave his "mouth, forehead, eyelids, growing dewy-warm" (58) to her present tears on his cheek (45), Aurora bathes the speaker in moisture. He imagines himself in a passive relation to her, prostrate before this reverse succubus that, rather than draining his fluids, drenches him in dew and balm. This celestial moisture is a noted characteristic of the goddess, who, according to Lemprière's *Classical Dictionary*, is "generally represented by the poets...opening with her rosy fingers the gates of the east, pouring the dew upon the earth."[43]

Tennyson was also well aware of another aspect of Aurora's balmy kisses: they draw forth music from those they touch. In concluding this section I wish to examine this legend in some detail, since it is a crucial association of the monologist with his auditor. The legend of Memnon (an elusive figure, unpursued in Tennyson criticism) is one that Tennyson adverted to in several poems that predate the dramatic monologues, such as "A Fragment" (1830), "The Palace of Art" (1831), and to some extent "The Hesperides" (1830). These early poems inform Tithonus's monologue. In Grote's words, Memnon was the "son of Tithonus and Eos, the most stately of living men," who came "after the death of Hector... with a powerful band of black Ethiopians, to the assistance of Troy."[44] In his role as king of the Ethiopians, Memnon intersects with the Hesperian fruit, guarded "warily" (15, 39, 95, 113, 114) but unsuccessfully, as described in Tennyson's "The Hesperides" (1832). Oskar Seyffert's late Victorian *Dictionary of Classical Antiquities* recounts, "[Memnon's] brother...had ousted him from the throne, but Heracles, on his expedition for obtaining the apples of the Hesperides, murdered the usurper, and reinstated Memnon."[45] The chief defense of Troy after Hector's death, Memnon killed Antilochos, Nestor's son and Achilles' favorite after Patroclus. Lemprière, who observes that Memnon, in assisting "his uncle Priam," "behaved with great courage," says of his end, "The aged father challenged the

Ethiopian monarch, but Memnon refused it on account of the venerable age of Nestor, and accepted that of Achilles. He was killed in the combat in the sight of the Grecian and Trojan armies."[46] Not long after Achilles kills Memnon, Paris kills Achilles, so these deaths bring us closer to the end of Troy. Memnon appears in the vivid depiction of the Trojan War over which Aeneas marvels in Carthage, and Dido specifically names him in her request to hear the story of Troy's fall (*Aeneid* 1:464, 723). The Greeks also associate Memnon with their own losses in the Trojan War. In book 4 of the *Odyssey*, Ulysses' son, Telemachus, presents himself at the court of Menelaus, and as all recall the events at and after Troy, "Even Argive Helen wept...; / Ulysses' sonne wept; Atreus' sonne did weepe." The son of Nestor, Pisistratus, also "his eyes in teeres did steepe," but his tears "flowd / From brave Antilochus' rememberd due, / Whom the renowmed [*sic*] Sonne of the Morning slue" (4:243–45, 247–49, trans. Chapman).

Grote's description of Memnon as "the most stately of living men" is an apt phrase to describe the appearance of one who is in some ways the last of a central line of extraordinarily beautiful Trojan men. So handsome is he that Achilles and Ulysses use his beauty as a point of comparison when they are reunited in the underworld in book 11 of the *Odyssey*. Achilles asks for news of his son Neoptolemus, and in assuring Achilles of his son's skills in speech and battle, Odysseus does not neglect to mention his comeliness, noting that it was comparable only to Memnon's: "past all doubt his beauties had no peere / Of all that mine eies noted, next to one, / And that was Memnon, Tithon's Sun-like sonne" (11:698–700, trans. Chapman). The answer he receives of his son's role in the sack of Troy so satisfies him that he strides off in joyful silence through the fields of asphodel, an image Tennyson invokes at the end of his dramatic monologue "Demeter and Persephone."

Although the *Homeric Hymn* attaches the blame for Tithonus's predicament to Aurora's careless phrasing in her pleas to Jupiter, her mistake seems not to have prevented her from returning to him with a tearful request regarding her son Memnon. Some accounts maintain she begged for immortality for Memnon; according to Seyffert's *Dictionary of Classical Antiquities*, "Eos entreated Zeus to grant her son the boon of immortality."[47] Lemprière claims, however, that "Aurora...flew to Jupiter, all bathed in tears, and begged the god to grant her son such honours as might distinguish him from other mortals."[48] Whether or not she specifically sought immortality for her son, she did attain for him ongoing distinction, or what his father, in Tennyson's dramatic monologue, calls variance from the kindly race of men. Memnon's distinction is to be associated with ongoing transformations after his death. The smoke from his funeral pyre shaped itself into flocks of birds called *memnonides*, which return every year to sprinkle drops of water from the Aesepus River, into which they have dipped their wings (see Ovid, *Metamorphoses*, 13:576–622). He is also associated with the creation of a renowned statue. According to the editorial notes of Hallam Tennyson for the Eversley edition of Tennyson's works, glossing a line from "The Palace of Art,"

"The statue of Memnon near Thebes was said to give forth music when the rays of the rising sun struck it" (2:369). Tennyson's own gloss to a reference he makes in *The Princess* defines "A Memnon" as "the statue in Egypt which gave forth a musical note when 'smitten with the morning sun'" (*Poems*, 3:100n). Lemprière says that Strabo, the geographer who claimed to have located Troy, testified to this effect, and added, "Its ruins still astonish modern travellers by their grandeur and beauty."[49]

Memnon's monumental afterlife was represented at several points in Tennyson's poems prior to the dramatic monologues, and in each case "the lips that kissed" Tithonus stroke the statue, drawing from it its own "strange song." In the poem "A Fragment [Where is that Giant]," published in October 1830 in *The Gem* and not reprinted by Tennyson, Aurora's labial influence makes itself heard. "A Fragment" is steeped in sources such as Jacob Bryant's *A New System* and describes massive figures that lie in ruined fragments across Eastern landscapes, imagined as

> shadowing Idols in the solitudes,
> Awful Memnonian countenances calm
> Looking athwart the burning flats, far off
> Seen by the highnecked camel on the verge
> Journeying southward. (15–19)

"Awful Memnonian countenances calm," once representing flourishing societies, stare fixedly across a depopulated landscape, turning their serenely beautiful ruined faces toward distant travelers. These abandoned Memnonian physiognomies share clear kinship with Shelley's "Ozymandias" (1817), that "shattered visage" (4) reported by "a traveller from an antique land" (1), majestic also in its awful solitude: "Round the decay / Of that colossal wreck, boundless and bare / The lone and level sands stretch far away" (12–14).[50]

Colossal wrecks are the subjects of Tennyson's "A Fragment," from the Colossus of Rhodes to Sphinxes to mummified pharaohs, and among these he elaborates on the silencing of the legendary Theban Colossus of Memnon, itself a kind of aeolian harp:

> Memnon when his peaceful lips are kist
> With earliest rays, that from his mother's eyes
> Flow over the Arabian bay, no more
> Breathes low into the charmèd ears of morn
> Clear melody flattering the crispèd Nile
> By columned Thebes. (22–27)

Memnon no longer "Breathes low" his "Clear melody" into his mother's "charmèd ears." His "peaceful lips" evincing the same serenity as his "countenance calm," Memnon's song, itself resembling the "Music slowly breathed" that Oenone describes building Ilion, had been effortless, indistinguishable from unlabored breath or aspiration. In "The Palace of Art" this melodiousness comes to characterize the Soul, as "the lights... / Flushed in her temples and her eyes, / And from her lips, as morn from Memnon, drew / Rivers of melodies" (169–72). Rousing those it touches into streams of discourse, Aurora's kissing is inextricable from the production of melody, as her own wild and sweet whisperings draw forth from her son, as well as in her husband's compensatory memory, slowly breathed, unearthly music.

Tennyson was not alone at Trinity in fixing on the figure of Memnon. Connop Thirlwall, tutor and friend to the Cambridge Apostles, also mused over the beautiful son of Tithonus. Tennyson arrived at Cambridge having already fastened on Memnon as a significant figure for inspired song, but Thirlwall in the early 1830s examined the legend from a more sustained academic viewpoint. In an article titled "Memnon," published in the second volume of the *Philological Museum* in 1833 (the year of Hallam's death, when "Tithon" was drafted), Thirlwall devotes close to forty pages, dense with reference to classical authors and German critics, to the question "Who is this rosy son of the morning?" He begins his inquiry, "Among the celebrated names which strike the attention of every one who has been led to stray in the twilight of mythical history, few perhaps rouse a livelier curiosity, or present a more enticing and perplexing problem, than that of Memnon."[51]

Thirlwall reviews in detail the legends of Memnon, drawing from myriad ancient sources, and sets out to refute point by point recent explanations posited in the periodical of the Royal Academy of Munich for the multiplicity of memorials to Memnon. He then forwards his own hypothesis (that Memnon was "a hero who had come from the East, and had achieved many glorious exploits," and not "imaginary") by way of "analyzing the legend and successively examining its elements," which he enumerates as "the parentage of Memnon, his extraordinary beauty, his premature death, his funeral honours." Thirlwall specifically compares him to Achilles, who, like Memnon, is renowned for his beauty and valor (he "surpasses all the other Greeks equally in both") and is "cut off in his prime."[52] Indeed, while Odysseus compares Neoptolemus to Memnon, the cases of Memnon and Achilles, both the offspring of immortal mothers and mortal fathers, bear a similarity. As Gregory Nagy observes, "Mortal genes, as it were, are dominant, while immortal ones are recessive, in that any element of mortality in a lineage produces mortal offspring."[53] Thirlwall stresses that Achilles (as he argues is also the case for Memnon) was "a historical person," but he nevertheless adds, "Still it will be certain that it could be only by the choice and design of the poet, that the hero's untimely death is represented as the price which he has to pay for his glory." The fates of such beautiful doomed heroes as Achilles and Memnon are specifically linked to the elegiac mode, being "the appropriate epical expression for the same feeling which afterwards breaks out in the plaintive strains of the lyric muse, the feeling of sadness produced by the shortness and uncertainty of life."[54]

Gladstone, writing on Memnon decades later, is not inspired by this figure to reflections on the sorrows of mortality. In his 1876 *Homeric Synchronism: An Enquiry into the Time and Place of Homer*, he discusses Schliemann's findings at length in the first two chapters and attempts to connect "internal evidence" from Homeric poems to "other sources," chiefly archaeological and historical. Reviewing his earlier works, Gladstone cites the first tenets of his credo "that the poems of Homer are in the highest sense historical" and "that there was a solid nucleus of fact in his account of the Trojan War." But he begins his chapter on Memnon (titled "The Legend of Memnon, and the Keteians of the Eleventh Odyssey") with an outright and immediate dismissal of legend: "Nothing, I make bold to say, can be more improbable than the common tradition respecting Memnon, that he came from Egypt to take part in the war against Troy."[55]

Gladstone mounts a vigorous argument as to the national, historical, and geographical origins of the hero, providing evidence on many points, including what he calls the "ethnical": "Memnon was associated by Homer with the East, and the East with dark skin: and he did what no properly Trojan chief is ever related to have done; he killed a leading Greek warrior, seemingly in fair fight." Noting the "tribute . . . paid to Memnon for his personal beauty" by his comparison to the son of Achilles in the *Odyssey*, Gladstone writes, "When Homer compares men on this ground [beauty], it seems to be always within the limits of some race. He does not compare the beauty of a Greek with that of a Trojan, but with that of other Greeks." Since these two are compared, "analogy clearly leads us to suppose" that they are "of the same race, that is to say that both were Asiatics"; indeed, he concludes, the "presumption thus arises that both were Keteians." Gladstone is not much interested in the legend of heroism followed by lyricism that so haunts Tennyson's early poems, and indeed is sharply dismissive of the individual character, declaring, "With [Memnon's] personality we need not be greatly troubled." Rather, the legend functions to confirm Gladstone's larger argument regarding Homeric facticity. Having placed the figure of Memnon in what he takes to be an explicable context, he concludes, "We thus find Homer, with respect to the Memnonian tradition, in contact and full consistency, upon a reasonable and probable interpretation of his text, with the facts of real history."[56]

Tennyson is less concerned with the facts of the case than the resonance of mellifluous statues built to the early dead. Memnon's song, according to "A Fragment," Tennyson's dense, youthful elegy for the shattered visages that litter ancient landscapes, is "no more," but in Tithonus's dramatic monologue we are witness to its final articulation. Especially in his early career as a poet, the music of Memnon stood for Tennyson for those powers of articulation beyond the common range: in *The Princess*, the eponymous heroine's admirer notes that in her speech she is "A

Memnon smitten with the morning sun" (3.100). Tithonus compares the song he heard his lover sing, which attained for her his seduction, to that of Apollo, which created not only the city of Ilion but, by analogy, the transformed identity of the auditor Tithonus. We can hear in these analogous songs also the strain of the elegiac song associated with sculptural representations of his son, renowned also for "dazzling beauty" not less than for a fate antithetical to his father's, namely, "premature death."[57] Thirlwall reports of legends concerning Memnon's melody, "He answers the greeting of his worshippers with a joyful strain when he is touched by the first rays of the rising sun, but in the evening his voice is plaintive like the tone of a broken chord."[58] Yet even as Tithonus echoes the plaintive tone of the monumental representation of a valorous son he has outlived, it is his own multiply toned vocalization that he now hopes will achieve some highly specific effect. Our task is to discern more precisely the range of transformations that Tithonus's Memnonian melody, also inspired by Aurora's presence, seeks to perform.

THE RAPTURE OF TITHONUS

Looking backward at the successive versions of "Tithonus," we may glimpse a regressive transit appropriate to a monologic speaker whose assimilation of present to past and future selves is infinitely complex. Behind the 1860 "Tithonus" lies the 1833 "Tithon," and behind that poem stand still other versions that gesture toward the perfected form this dramatic monologue ultimately would take. Indeed, these earlier forms, available to us in Trinity College *MSS A* and *B*, raise directly the specter of form or shape, or, more precisely, the horror of uncertain forms. The speaker in *T. MS A* invokes this specter as a threat, insisting to his auditor, "Release me," lest he "rise, go forth and call / ... the uncertain shadow feared / Of Gods and men," termed in another fragmented version "the uncertain shape / Not loved of Gods." Tennyson omitted this threat of a fearfully indeterminate shape of death, to which we might compare Milton's figure of Death in *Paradise Lost*, that "shape, / If shape it might be call'd that shape had none" (2:666–67).[59] Perhaps he recognized that this threat was as empty as Aurora's courts, since the withered and enervated Tithonus is powerless to rise and go forth beyond his present limits. Tithonus, moreover, need not summon this dreadful shape because he already embodies it: a "shadow," involved in perpetual shape-shifting because in a material state of unending decay, Tithonus himself takes grotesquely "uncertain" form. My discussion of this speaker seeks to trace his endlessly variable lineaments, whose radical metastasis predates and may even have caused his present predicament and may point to the solution he hopes his monologue to attain. In *T. MS A* he endeavors to intimidate Aurora by searching out "The Shape I seek," but that ambivalent form, one whose presence he would summon as a figure of suasion (to convince her to release him), can only be his own.

Tithonus's ambition is to obtain a more definitive form for himself, to secure himself again to some kind, and this will be accomplished through the form of his dramatic monologue itself. As he now speaks Tithonus is involved in an infinitude of deformation—because what else is unending aging?—but he has always been attracted to intense and immense experiences of bodily alterations. Indeed, he persistently involves himself in a range of ambivalences. His monologue makes us question whether his identification is with mortals or immortals, with men or women, with the living or the dead, and the monologue therefore requires that we enter with him into the very nature of identification. To understand his complex affiliations, we shall begin with Arthur Henry Hallam's 1830 reflections on the temporal aspects of identification, what he terms "sympathy." Then we shall turn to the processes at work in Tithonus's monologue, drawing from a range of mid- to late Victorian aesthetic, poetic, and psychosexual theories, in order to grasp the shapes that Tithonus describes having taken and the form into which his monologue seeks to transform, or more precisely, transport him.

Hallam's Sympathy

We have established the extreme particularity of Tithonus's line, comprising not only Troy's royalty but also its beautiful men who are like gods and desired by gods. When Tithonus begins his monologue, though, he expresses nostalgia for a broader sense of his former kind:

> The woods decay, the woods decay and fall,
> The vapours weep their burthen to the ground,
> Man comes and tills the field and lies beneath,
> And after many a summer dies the swan. (1–4)

Tithonus marks his radical dissociation from the natural world with his abrupt, enjambed lines, "Me only cruel immortality / Consumes" (5–6). As has long been noticed, the "decaying woods" are evocative of Wordsworth's description of the Gondo Gorge in book 6 of *The Prelude*, with its "immeasurable height / Of woods decaying." Wordsworth's line continues, "never to be decayed" (6:624–25),[60] but this clause would not suit Tithonus, who at the start of the monologue conceives of himself as unaccompanied in perpetual, and perpetually incomplete, decay. He especially separates himself here from generic "man," whose life is summarized in a line that runs swiftly from birth to death, culminating in burial beneath the fields over which he toiled. This is the brief and dismissible narrative that St. Simeon Stylites, Ulysses, Demeter, and other Tennysonian speakers also make of the lives of the mass of mankind, which are undistinguished and indistinguishable. Indistinguishable, even, from the natural world, as all, woods, vapors, and men, sink eventually into the soil. Indeed, it is the soil with which Tithonus claims also finally to seek union, closing his monologue with the fantasy of becoming "earth in earth" (75).

Although it appears that death for Tithonus is a communal endeavor, his clearest identification may have less to do at this point with buried mortals than with vapors whose movement also tends always downward. In weeping "their burthen to the ground," they anticipate not only the desire Tithonus articulates at the end of the monologue—to be restored "to the ground" (72)—but the tone of his own speech. Pursuing the diaphanous track of this vapor is thus crucial for establishing what Tithonus identifies as a central problem with his current situation. The line originally read, in an 1833 manuscript of "Tithon," "The vapours weep their substance to the ground." This notion of the vapor's burdensome cargo ("burthen") supplants that of the more abstract fact of its fundamental materiality ("substance"), thereby establishing a dialectic that is to continue throughout the monologue, namely, that between corporeality and ethereality, between the substance and the shadow. The line originally underscored the problem of Tithonus's own contradictory physicality, inherent in the opening idea of the infinite decay of the woods. Burdened by his own inescapable though ever diminishing corporeality, he nevertheless at the monologue's commencement twice refers to himself as a shadow ("white-haired shadow," "gray shadow" [8, 11])—even as the opening lines regarding decay admit at the outset that Tithonus's concern is that he is all too material. "A white-haired shadow roaming like a dream," he identifies himself as a shade, not inhabiting a dream but dreamlike himself.

In an opening stanza that stresses his unlikeness to anything, any claim of similitude is significant. We shall examine more closely his affinity for the trope of similitude, but here the simile stresses his increasing insubstantiality, as the shadow's movements are compared to an entity still less substantial than the speaker, even unreal: a shadow like a dream. His monologue, however, has already marked him as cursedly corporeal, housed within as physically rent and sensate a body as Tennyson's St. Simeon Stylites. In keeping not only with his Trojan kind but also with his generic precursor Simeon, he is intensely sensational. Moreover, as with Simeon, Tithonus's physical agony renders him unmeet for human or divine company or communities. And yet he may be attempting here to render himself into the vaporous nonbeing that his words conjure, to become ethereal by consistently associating himself with, because he is continuously swathed in, vapor, mist, steam, dew.

In these opening lines, Tithonus raises the question of finality, of the mortal ends to which all these other entities turn, but the pattern he seems equally if not more fascinated with is that of the processes they are undergoing. All move through successive stages: the woods decay, and then further decay; the vapors drift, moving ever downward; man labors toward death; and the swan floats from one summer to another and "many" another. Tithonus seeks an analogue for his own transformations in these fellow beings, being both attracted to and troubled by these examples of progressive alteration. In seeking a category of *being* with which he might identify, in any state, Tithonus enters into the knotty subject of what Hallam called "sympathy."

Arthur Hallam delivered his essay "On Sympathy" to the assembled Apostles in Cambridge on December 4, 1830; it was printed after his death and in all subsequent editions of *Remains, in Verse and Prose, of Arthur Henry Hallam* (1834). One can hear in the essay debts to the philosophical and literary traditions of which Hallam was such a gifted student (he refers to "some recent philosophers" [*Writings*, 140] by name, and he directly echoes Romantic sources), yet this is nevertheless an accomplished and even profound performance for a youth of nineteen. He begins by noting that the definition of "sympathy" is necessarily a "fluctuating" one, and focuses initially on "that precise moment" when the soul (feminized throughout the essay) "has become aware of another individual subject, capable of thoughts and feelings like her own," and thus subsequently undergoes an increased ability to be "pleased with another's pleasure and pained with another's pain, immediately and for their own sakes." But he ultimately finds this standard account of "the machinery of sympathy" inadequate to explain "the peculiar force of sympathy itself" (*Writings*, 133–34, 135).

In developing his theory, Hallam admits, "Some of you, perhaps, may be disposed to set me down as a mystic, for what I am about to say":

> It is an ultimate fact of consciousness, that the soul exists as one subject in various successive states.... Far back as memory can carry us, or far forward as anticipation can travel unrestrained, the remembered state in the one case, and the imagined one in the other, are forms of self.... At length the discovery of another being is made. Another being, another subject, conscious, having a world of feelings like the soul's own world! How, how can the soul imagine feeling which is not its own?... She realizes this conception only by considering the other being as a separate part of self, a state of her own consciousness existing apart from the present, just as imagined states exist in the future. (*Writings*, 136)

Hallam marvels at the experience of the "discovery" of another being, conscious, having a world of feeling that is not one's own, and yet that somehow is not another being but part of oneself. He suggests that one can only conceive of this discovered subjectivity by appropriating it, but such an acquisition is necessarily incomplete: the "other being" becomes a "part of self," but a part "apart." Addressing Hallam's broadly relevant essay to Tennyson's "The Palace of Art," Armstrong explains, "The act of empathy, or sympathy, can never be an appropriation of the other by a total self, for the divided self will always recognize difference."[61] The self or soul thus "absorbs" the other being "into" her own nature, Hallam continues, as if that other person were the equivalent of her own past or future experience. The other consciousness is thus absorbed into the self as a temporal figure, as one of the self's own successive states.

Hallam's "notion," as he calls it, attempts to account for the "difficulty attending the structure of our consciousness; a difficulty of conceiving any existence, except in the way of matter, external to the conceiving mind." It is difficult to conceive of another's subjectivity, but it is as difficult to apprehend one's own, since the problem with existing in "innumerable successive states" (*Writings*, 137) is that one cannot constitute a unified self; with each transition in time, the self alters. Hallam says again that he fears these arguments "will be thought to border on mysticism." But he maintains that his listeners must all have felt moments "in which he has felt it miserable to exist, as it were, piece-meal, and in the continual flux of a stream; in which he has wondered, as at a new thing, how we can be, and have been, and not be that which we have been." "So also," he continues, is the soul disturbed "in its eager rushings towards the future, its desire of that mysterious something which now is not" (*Writings*, 138), by the knowledge that she cannot maintain her past, present, and future states as one coherent and singular entity.

"But were these impossibilities removed," he insists, "were it conceivable that the soul in one state could coexist with the soul in another, how impetuous would be the desire of reunion, which even the awful laws of time cannot entirely forbid!" It is something akin to a reunion of the self with itself that "sympathy" in its deepest form makes possible, however complex and even unlikely the process:

> The cause, you will say, is inconceivable. Not so; it is the very case before us. The soul, we have seen, contemplates a separate being as a separate state of itself, the only being it can conceive. But the two exist simultaneously. Therefore that impetuous desire arises. Therefore, in her anxiety to break down all obstacles, and to amalgamate two portions of her divided substance, she will hasten to blend emotions and desires with those apparent in the kindred spirit. (*Writings*, 138)

Sympathy with another allows one to reunite the divided facets of a self always undergoing alteration, which in any given moment is different from what it has previously been and what it will momentarily be. Rather than constituting the contemplation of a separable person, sympathy makes possible the soul's "identifying the perceived being with herself" (*Writings*, 139). It is this *identification*, in which another being becomes inseparable from a temporal state in one's own ever-shifting consciousness, that Hallam marks.

Hallam recognizes that this "amalgamation," in which two separate entities mix into simultaneous rather than successive states of one perceiving consciousness, can seem inconceivable, but it is just such a state that Tithonus in his monologue both remembers and desires, seeking vainly for analogues to himself with his opening words and finding none. Tennyson, who felt mystic and ongoing connections with Hallam, living and dead (as recorded most dramatically in *In Memoriam* 95) had opportunity to study this essay, which Hallam sent to him. This vision of a union that draws on but exceeds similitude between two entities has wide repercussions for a reading of Tennyson's poetics, at the level not only of theme but also of prosody. In what follows I work closely with the terms Tithonus uses to describe the states of the union between himself and his lover Aurora, which are based on and yet confound conceptions of identity or identification.

"Impetuous" is the word Hallam uses several times to characterize the desire for simultaneity of states—within and between selves—which the "awful laws of time" "forbid" but cannot entirely prevent. And certainly Tithonus describes his request for immortality in terms that suggest the headlong; presumably a moment's hesitation or reflection would have enabled him to ask for eternal youth rather than eternal life. Yet Hallam's essay helps us to understand that Tennyson's Tithonus asked for precisely what he desired. Here is his account of the progression of thought that led to his apparently heedless outburst:

> Alas! for this gray shadow, once a man—
> So glorious in his beauty and thy choice,
> Who madest him thy chosen, that he seemed
> To his great heart none other than a God!
> I asked thee, "Give me immortality."
> Then didst thou grant mine asking with a smile,
> Like wealthy men who care not how they give. (11–17)

The second stanza of "Tithonus" begins with the same antithesis between the present shadowy nature of a Trojan and his former godlike physicality that Oenone, near her own death, remarks in Paris. Doomed to bear perpetual witness to his body's ruination, Tithonus claims here to be bodiless, now only a "gray shadow." As he reveals, however, he has always been entirely absorbed in his own materiality. He implicitly insists that, although he was "once a man," he is one no longer. Indeed, so far is he from that status at this moment that he is divorced too from any previous experience of subjectivity; recalling of himself "his beauty," he can judge his former appearance only objectively. Tithonus's moment of most acute self-perception, then, is the moment of his sharpest self-destruction, because as he perceives his own beauty he destroys it.

Tithonus's identity as he remembers it has always been based on a theatrical passivity. He knew himself, he tells Aurora, only as "thy choice" and "thy chosen," referring diplomatically to her (by some accounts, violent) sexual aggression, as if rapture by another were a self-defining act. For all his own passivity, moreover, he felt divinely empowered when ravished by this divinity; it is through this transportation that he came to seem to himself, as a beautiful man, "none other than a God!" My review in the previous section of a line of Trojan men who are godlike in their beauty shows how reasonable is the progression of association that he follows: so like a god already in his beauty, he requires only immortality to render the resemblance into complete identification. Tithonus does not describe himself, however, as "like a god" or godlike, the simile so frequent, with minor variations, in Tennyson and the Western tradition. Considering the long tradition of interpreting the Delphic injunction *gnothi sauton* ("Know thyself"), Michel Foucault notes that among its primary meanings is "Do not suppose yourself to be a god."[62] But Tithonus's comparison reveals his dangerous assumption, not of similitude but of identification.

Tithonus ends his explanation of how he reached his present condition with another observation of similitude, this one regarding Aurora, not himself. Although he has wrought his fate with his own words (an act of deliberate, efficacious speech I examine in chapter 6), he attempts to shift the blame to the auditor who acceded to his demand to the letter: "Then didst thou grant mine asking with a smile, / Like wealthy men who care not how they give" (16–17).[63] In truth, his asking was granted not only with a smile but also with a *simile*, an enormously revealing and appropriate figure of speech at this moment. In the course of this simile, he becomes a feminized figure. It is here that his break with having been "once a man" is twofold: he was once a mortal and also once a member of the male sex. At the moment of becoming still more like a god, he becomes feminized, since at precisely that point she becomes indifferent to her effects on others, like a wealthy man, as he (as a Trojan aristocrat) once was; they have neatly reversed their positions. In so doing, they have brought to fruition the prediction that culminates *The Princess*, which defines men and women as "Not like to like, but like in difference," and prophecies, "Yet in the long years liker must they grow; / The man be more of woman, she of man" (7:262–64). By this argument, gender distinction appears fundamentally a question of the timing of likeness (who is like whom, and when?), as evolution steadily promotes resemblance. The way this has operated with Aurora and Tithonus, who have shared many "long years," is not that they grow identical to each other, but that each comes to resemble the former sex of the other: he has become like her ("more of woman"), while she has become like him (more "of man"). Time has not led to a blending of gender identities, but an exchange of them.

Tithonus is unsexed by Aurora's desire. He also shifts from being a consumer (a trait of the luxuriating Trojans), demanding gifts from wealthy patrons, to being consumed precisely by that which his words purchased: "cruel immortality / Consumes me." For Tithonus as for his kind, in rendering them "like gods," and indeed the lovers of gods, their beauty unmans them. We have seen already that the structuring of Tithonus's identity was founded on a similitude, indeed, on a double trope, as Aurora's song was "like" Apollo's, which in turn led to walls that rose "like a mist." The simile that Tithonus invokes in order to understand what happened at the precise moment when he was granted his request, and so set into motion a range of transformations, points also to a wide network of tropological identifications. The equivalencies his simile suggests are themselves a product of the history of this speaker's simultaneous successive states.

Effeminacy and Eonism

In observing how "Homer has overspread the Dardanid family, at the epoch of the war as well as in former times, with redundance of personal beauty," Gladstone in *Studies on Homer* concludes, "With this was apparently connected, in many of them, effeminacy, as well as insolence and falseness of character" (*SH*, 3:216). Reviewing the history of the word "effeminacy," which he calls "a misogynist but powerful term," Alan Sinfield observes, "Certain manners and behaviors are stigmatized by associating them with 'the feminine'—which is perceived as weak, ineffectual and unsuited for the world of affairs." The *Oxford English Dictionary* gives definitions of effeminate that include, as Sinfield summarizes, "womanish, unmanly, enervated, feeble; self-indulgent, voluptuous; unbecomingly delicate or over-refined." He reminds us, "Up to the time of the Wilde trials—far later than is widely supposed—it is unsafe to interpret effeminacy as defining, or as a signal of, same-sex passion. Mostly, it meant being emotional and spending too much time with women," indeed, "often it involved excessive cross-sexual attachment."[64] Joseph Bristow has examined the issue of effeminacy in the late nineteenth and early twentieth centuries and its relation to national character, and he notes that in the 1850s Tennyson's use of the word could signify "a man's intense heterosexuality." Bristow gives as an example the "indulgent wife-loving" exhibited in "The Marriage of Geraint" (1859). Geraint's wife, Enid, becomes concerned for the "slur" on her husband, as she worries that it is said that "all his force / Is melted into mere effeminacy."[65] Although Enid belittles this state, I hope to show that it is precisely this deliquescence that Tithonus intensely recalls and would revive through his monologue.

In the context of their discussions both Sinfield and Bristow address Tennyson's 1889 poem "On One Who Affected an Effeminate Manner," which reads in its entirety:

> While man and woman still are incomplete,
> I prize that soul where man and woman meet,
> Which types all Nature's male and female plan,
> But, friend, man-woman is not woman-man.

Sinfield reads this late poem as "a nasty little squab, qualifying his earlier flirtations with gender-bending," noting for example that decades earlier in *In Memoriam*, "the poet goes out of his way to draw cross-sex analogues" both for himself and for a Hallam who is memorably praised for exhibiting "manhood fused with female grace" (109.17).[66] Calling Tennyson "always responsive to the difficulties involved in making distinctions between masculinity and femininity," for reasons that he rightly notes "require much greater exploration," Bristow sees "On One Who Affected an Effeminate Manner" as not necessarily negative in its address, and yet nevertheless responding to a late-century hardening of gender binarism. He explains, "An effeminate manner expresses for Tennyson an admirable desire for a change in—if not a unification of—masculinity and femininity, only to witness the immediate reinscription of gender difference itself."[67] It is significant that Tennyson revised the poem's title to add the word "Affected," as if to indicate that this trait was not fixed but performative, a manner one might adopt or feign. Contemporary queer theory characterizes sexual identity as constructed, and always under construction, in its vast permutations resistant to categorical language. Tennyson's "squab" was published late in the nineteenth century, during a period when, in a well-documented phenomenon, sexual categories were taking fixed form. Jeffrey Weeks notes, for example, that from 1898 to 1908 the publications "on homosexuality alone" numbered more than one thousand.[68] Tennyson's poem responds to this larger context, but his earlier representations of sex assignments were, as Sinfield and Bristow suggest, far more elastic.

Tennyson's Oenone compares Paris to three beautiful goddesses and says he is more beautiful than they. This judgment risks feminizing him, but may more accurately effeminize him, acknowledging as it does that Paris is drawn to and most understood in the company of women. The beauty of Trojan men is so rich as to put into question the categories of masculine and feminine, as it does distinctions between goddesses and mortal men. The pattern of seduction and rapture of these Trojan princes I have traced points also to what Gladstone in *Studies on Homer* considers their disconcerting "sensuality": "Whereas in Greece we are told occasionally of some beautiful woman who is seduced or ravished by a deity, in Troas we find the princes of the line are those to whose names the legends are attached." Gladstone gives as examples Tithonus, Anchises, and Paris, and claims by way of contrast that Ulysses' "detention" by Calypso was in his case "not a glory, but a calamity" (*SH*, 3:210). Tithonus's own relation to "masculinity" is vexed; as Michael Greene notes, the "words 'man' and 'men' appear six times in the poem, but he does not use them of himself, except to recall that he was 'once a man.'"[69] Indeed, it is Aurora who Tithonus most often associates with manliness. His similes compare her repeatedly to male figures: she is "like a wealthy man," and her whispers are like the song of the male sun god, Apollo. But the categories of sex and gender identification get confounded deliberately by Tithonus, whom we know already to be impetuous in his blurring of other divisions, such as that between gods and mortals. It may be that the speaker sees himself not only as being like or none other than a god, but also as being like or none other than a goddess.

In Tennyson's first dramatic monologue, St. Simeon Stylites catalogues the alterations that nature and self-torture have made to his body, and we know that Ulysses acknowledges himself to have been "made weak by time and fate." The depredations that time has wrought on Tithonus's form are still more harrowing, and promise to be continually so. We gain some sense of the spectacle that

brings the tears (to which Tithonus twice refers) to Aurora's eyes when we look
to Oenone's vision of the dying Paris in "The Death of Oenone." The nymph
envisions "a face / *His* face, deformed by lurid blotch and blain" (71–72). Aeneas,
dreaming of a wounded Hector as the Achaeans overtake Troy, exclaims regarding
his cousin, "*quantum mutatus*" (*Aeneid* 2:274): "how changed." Yet Tithonus did
not always lament change, but rather found in the sensations of physical transformation his most extreme pleasure. He recalls:

> Ay me! ay me! with what another heart
> In days far-off, and with what other eyes
> I used to watch—if I be he that watched—
> The lucid outline forming round thee; saw
> The dim curls kindle into sunny rings;
> Changed with thy mystic change, and felt my blood
> Glow with the glow that slowly crimsoned all
> Thy presence and thy portals. (50–57)

In other days, with another heart and other eyes, another self watched Aurora's
daily alterations and, he tells her, "Changed with thy mystic change." He oscil-
lates in his memory from watching her extraordinary transformation to watching
himself, marveling, "if I be he that watched." Describing his conjugal pleasure,
he speaks as one wholly divorced from his former beautiful self, as earlier he
acknowledged an identity articulated in the third person. This objectifying self-
regard tells us that his beauty has long played havoc with his subjectivity.

This temporal division of himself from himself is the state on which Hallam
premises his argument in "On Sympathy." The process Tithonus describes moves
from his watching of his own watchfulness of her to his incorporation within
her, in a union that another of Hallam's essays, his 1831 "Theodicæa Novissima,"
which I discussed in the context of "St. Simeon Stylites," can illuminate. In this
essay, he remarks, "Philosophers who have fallen in love, and lovers who have
acquired philosophy by reflecting on their peculiar states of consciousness, tell
us that the passion is grounded on a conviction, true or false, of similarity, and
consequent irresistible desire of union or rather identification" (*Writings*, 203). Although Tithonus now feels disunited from his former self, he recalls the intensity
of union with Aurora, as he merged with her altering form: changing with her
mystic change, glowing with her glow, feeling his own blood alter with her crimsoning. What so overwhelms him, of course, are not only her numinous changes
but also his concurrent participation in them. In the intensity of their lovemaking,
he felt what it was like to become her, which is to say, to become her becoming, to
change with her, a change in himself that is also a change of and into her. This simultaneity of successive states is the impossible sensation he seeks to regain. Earlier
he complains, "Ever thus thou growest beautiful" (43), but here we see that he has

known what this growth felt like, since when he "lay, / . . .growing dewy-warm," basking in the dew that is Aurora's calling card, he not only felt it on his skin, but in it, as if he were inseparable from her expansive aesthetic development.

In "Theodicæa Novissima," Hallam defines love as "direct, immediate, absorbing affection for one object, on the ground of similarity perceived, and with a view to more complete union" (*Writings*, 204). He uses this human experience in an attempt to understand God's love, since part of his argument is that we can come to apprehend the totality of divine love only by understanding the passion of human love. Armstrong, discussing this essay's figurations of sexual union in the context of "The Palace of Art," notes that in his revisions to the 1832 version of that poem Tennyson "deleted the passages concerning the Soul's capacity for empathy."[70] He also deleted some telling lines regarding a feminized capacity for identification in the revisions that led from the 1833 "Tithon" to the 1860 "Tithonus," and these deletions describe precisely the union that the speaker vividly recalls and would recapture. In both *T. MS B* and "Tithon" the speaker describes the sensation of their humid fusion. In "Tithon," the speaker claims that he can no longer "know / Enjoyment save through memory" (*1833* 14–15), and in the deleted passages in which Tithonus conveys the experience of being lover of the dawn we witness more fully the enjoyment with which his memory taunts him. Their union is represented in *T. MS B* and "Tithon" as a wholesale melding: "my mortal frame / Molten in thine immortal, I lay wooed." In an insight that elucidates the attraction of divine and human commingling, Tennyson makes clear that Tithon was a mortal at their intensest merging. Engulfed, encircled, enraptured, molten, Tithonus suggests that the pleasure they took in their integration was itself dependent on the dissonance between being mortal and immortal, a division in this moment at once breached and affirmed.

Tithonus forged himself, his earlier avatar Tithon tells us, in the smithy of Aurora's molten embraces. In *T. MS B* he describes how he was "By thy divine embraces circumfused," as her embrace becomes indistinguishable from what it encircles. *T. MS B* also describes his mortal heart as "Drowned deep in rapturous trances, beating fast." Called "rapturous" in the *Homeric Hymn to Aphrodite*, their lovemaking is a process of transportation, as his bodily sensations take him out of his body but also house him more certainly there. Referring to the amorous philosophers he mentioned earlier in "Theodicæa Novissima," Hallam notes that these persons have been "strenuous maintainers of the doctrine that this erotic feeling is of origin peculiarly divine, and raises the soul to heights of existence, which no other passion is permitted to attain" (*Writings*, 203). Given that Tithonus's dramatic monologue is informed, given form, by one of the most intense descriptions of sensation ever produced by a poet who had been introduced in Hallam's groundbreaking essay as a "Poet of Sensation," we are obliged to specify still further the nature and kind of these sensations. To review: it is not only that Tithonus feels the effects of Aurora's rising; he too rises, not in tandem but in unison, becoming her becoming. If we can understand the process Tithonus describes, then we will be in a position to understand that his request for immortality expressed a specific desire to prolong this transformative state, that is, to further his similitude to her.

Tithonus, we recall, suggests that Aurora granted his request for immortality—a request to continue in a simultaneity of successive states—with a simile. This simile, "Like wealthy men who care not how they give," inverted their sexes, since it feminized him and masculinized her, in an inversion that his later simile regarding Apollo (which culminates his description of their commingling) echoes. And certainly their lovemaking itself put him in the traditionally feminized role as recumbent recipient of her "wooing" (a word Tennyson omitted in revision: "I lay wooed," he recalls in *T. MS B* and "Tithon"). "Abduction (like the fulfill-ment of sexual desire) is the prerogative of the more powerful over the weaker: Olympian over nymph, immortal over mortal, older over younger, and male over female, to the Greek way of thinking," Jennifer Larson observes. The abductions of mortals by nymphs or goddesses "fit the expected pattern in one way (immor-tal over mortal) and reverse it in another (female over male)." She singles out the abduction "of Tithonos by Eos" to argue, "The tension produced by the reversal of 'normal' power relationships between the sexes is reflected in the outcomes of these myths. Tithonos suffers a terrible fate when he is given immortality without eternal youth," thus crediting his "terrible fate" to sex reversal.[71]

It is possible, indeed it is virtually unavoidable, to read Tithonus and Aurora in terms of roles characterized most commonly as masculine or feminine. But I would like to take their circumfusion literally, and to take seriously the blurring of binaries (mortal/immortal, male/female) that Tithonus reports as having been the highlight of their luminous union. He has sought, loving well if not wisely, to overgo the temporal distinction between them, taking on the experiences of the dawn, itself necessarily an event of successive stages. The dawn is indisputably a figure of time, and the time that she keeps becomes a measure of the successive stages of his altering self. This is why he asked her so specifically, in demand-ing immortality, for still *more* of her time. As he seeks to dissolve their temporal dissonance, he seeks similarly, I believe, to collapse the gender divisions between them.

"Why should a man desire in any way / To vary from the kindly race of men" (28–29), Tithonus asks, and though his question is generally assumed to refer to mankind or humankind, it is also sex-specific: Why *should* a man desire to vary from men? But this is the monologist's desire, namely, to vary from masculinity itself. As we have seen, in his essay "On Sympathy" Hallam referred to the soul as "she," a traditional pronominal identification of that entity, based in the feminized Greek *psyche*. Describing the Soul in Tennyson's "The Palace of Art," Armstrong posits, "The Soul is gendered as feminine because of Hallam's belief in the capac-ity of women to transgress fixed forms, though in Tennyson's poem it is sometimes androgynous."[72] I would like to expand on this notion of transgressing fixed forms because it nicely captures the range of Tithonus's desires, as it characterizes too the ways he will attain for himself release from Aurora's courts. We have seen some ways in which the exceeding beauty of some Trojan princes was associated with a torpid voluptuousness that seemed to emasculate them, to remove them from the sphere of masculine action. This is a state whose implications Tithonus explores, and from which, paradoxically, he derives potency.

Focusing chiefly on such poems as *The Princess* and *In Memoriam*, some of the most compelling recent critical work on Tennyson has explored his representations of homosocial or homoerotic desire.[73] The definition of another, little known term, "Eonism," coined by Havelock Ellis at the end of the nineteenth century (like the term "sexual inversion"), however, enables us to tease out the complexity of Tithonus's highly particularized representations of gender and sexuality. Ellis stresses in the course of his study that persons answering to the description of the pathology of Eonism are numerous, yet he observes that there has existed no term for them, stating with evident relief, "Toward the end of the nineteenth century they at last began to come under psychological observation."[74] Before looking at the condition that Ellis so self-consciously categorizes, it is important to sound a warning against setting up too restrictive or limited an explanation of the predilections of so sensational a figure as this speaker. I hope, indeed, that my reading of him militates against any singular explanation or approach to so fluid, even slippery a monologist.

Tithonus—no less than Tennyson—seems to offer himself up to psychological readings. In both cases we may want to avoid pathological categorizations less because they are inapplicable than because the terms can multiply all too quickly. Tithonus's algolagnia has been much remarked, whether in his masochistic or sadistic tendencies in his relations with Aurora. And perhaps the label of narcissist, a term drawn from the mishap of another legendary male beauty, goes without saying. As it happens, Ellis tells us that the condition that he identifies can manifest itself through these other categories; for example, Eonism "resembles, in some of its features, the kind of auto-eroticism called Narcissism or erotic self-admiration" (28). My aim is not to categorize Tithonus, still less to pathologize him, but to find ways to articulate the processes that he has undergone and seeks to continue undergoing.

Ellis claims the anomaly he identifies, which he labels Eonism or "sexo-aesthetic inversion," is widespread among all cultures, contemporary and historical, because it is based in "a deeply rooted natural instinct" (32). Though common, however, it is also unacceptable:

> Although this psychic peculiarity is so difficult both to name and to define, it is, strange as that may seem, the commonest of all sexual anomalies to attain prominence in the public newspapers. There are several reasons why that

should be. There is not only the real frequency of the condition, but the fact
that it is so striking and so intriguing a violation of our most conventional rules
and regulations of social life. There is the further consideration that, since in
its simple uncomplicated form it constitutes no violation of our moral feelings
and laws, it is easily possible to discuss it plainly in the most reputable public
prints. (29–30)

The condition is at once general ("a real frequency") and anomalous, a violation
and yet no violation, a peculiarity that has escaped our notice and yet has never
been far from the public's sight. Ellis explains this pervasive anomaly by way of a
raft of case studies, beginning with that of Chevalier d'Eon, whose name he hopes
to adapt in the manner of the appropriations for clinical purposes of the names
Leopold Sacher-Masoch and the Marquis de Sade. Although he begins with some
scattered examples of the disorder in women, he largely concentrates on the extensive first-person narratives of a number of men, who detail in their accounts a
desire to make love to women as women *themselves*. They imitate the feminine, in
terms not only of their garments (he includes many descriptions of the acquisition and employment of lingerie), but in their experiences of their own physical
pleasure, as they fantasize about and attempt to attain, for example, the sensations
of female breasts. The men whom Ellis reveals in his study seek to imitate their
female lovers in appearance, action, and, as they can, sensation.

Ellis insists that the phenomenon he describes is distinct from what Magnus
Hirschfeld had recently termed "transvestism." Hirschfeld subtitled his book on
the topic "An Investigation into the Erotic Impulse of Disguise," but Ellis argues
that in his view the cross-dresser is not in disguise, but "feels on the contrary that
he has thereby become emancipated from disguise and is at last really himself"
(12). Also, the sartorial element in Eonism is subsidiary: "The inversion here,"
explains Ellis, "is in the affective and emotional sphere." Ellis finds his own coinage also wanting, however, admitting that he has experienced "great difficulty
in naming this anomaly." He has, in particular, aesthetic objections to his term
"sexo-aesthetic inversion," since it wavers uneasily between philological identities:
"Even if acceptable as a descriptive term, [it] still remains one of those hybrid
Graeco-Latin compounds which it is best if possible to avoid" (28). The term
"inversion," moreover, although one he himself was instrumental in coining, he
finds problematic in this case. Ellis stresses throughout his study that these persons
(male and female) whose experiences he chronicles were "not sexually inverted;
that is, their sexual feelings were not directed towards persons of their own sex"
(1). Eonism is not, Ellis insists, "aesthetic homosexuality." He also considered the
term "psychical hermaphroditism" but decided that it was "not accurate," since
Eonists "are not always conscious of possessing the psychic disposition of both
sexes, but sometimes only of one, the opposite sex, the sex to which they are attracted." Ellis suggests that any logical inconsistencies are the fault of the anomaly

rather than the scientist who identifies it: "This impulse springs out of admiration and affection for the opposite sex, therefore the subject of it is not usually tempted to carry the inner imitation so far as to imitate the sexual desires of that sex and so to become unlike it by being homosexual; that is how it is that, to superficial view, he seems less logical, less thorough-going, than the sexual invert" (28).

The word "inversion," Ellis argues, is "too apt to arouse suggestions of homosexuality, which may be quite absent, though it remains true that the phenomenon we are concerned with is one of erotic empathy." Indeed, he insists that the pathology he has classified may be the mean rather than the deviation from "normal" sexuality: "We must regard sexo-aesthetic inversion as really a modification of normal hetero-sexuality" because at its base, and apparently in contradistinction from inverted and other deviating sexual drives, Eonism manifests a "desire for union" (103). Eonism consists of "usually heterosexual inner imitation, which frequently tends to manifest itself in the assumption of the habits and garments of the desired sex," but it manifests itself finally less in the outward trappings of imitation than in the attraction toward mimetic eroticism itself. Ellis explains that the person experiencing aesthetic inversion "achieves a completely emotional identification which is sexually abnormal but aesthetically correct" (108). The Eonist, while confounding the logic of sexual binarism, answers directly to an established logic of aesthetic theory: "The main characteristic of these people—the impulse to project themselves by sympathetic feeling into the object to which they are attracted, or the impulse of inner imitation—is precisely the tendency which various recent philosophers of aesthetics have regarded as the essence of all aesthetic feeling" (27).

Ellis does not specify the "recent" aesthetic theorists he has in mind, but this is so established a concept that there may be no need to do so. Edmund Burke, for example, in the eighteenth century defined "sympathy" as "a sort of substitution, by which we are put into the place of another man, and affected in many respects as he is affected."[75] Such a definition would have been a starting point for Arthur Henry Hallam (for whom Burke was politically congenial) in his inquiry into the mechanics and force of sympathy; Hallam also stresses the centrality of imitation to any intimate relationship: "To repeat desires, volitions, actions, is the unquestionable tendency of conscious beings." Hallam's analysis of this imitative tendency, one he universalizes, continues: "Novelty is in itself an evident source of pleasure. To become something new, to add a mode of being to those we have experienced, is a temptation alike to the lisping infant in the cradle and the old man on the verge of the grave." Extreme youth and extreme age are indistinguishable in this regard: both seek the transformative pleasures of mimesis. Hallam continues, "To become this new thing, to imitate, in a word, the discovered agent, no less in the internal than the outward elements of action, will naturally be the endeavor of faculties already accustomed in their own development to numberless courses of imitation" (Writings, 136). "To become something new" indicates a change in state that imitates another state, by entering into its internal and external courses of action and sharing what Hallam calls "a coalition of pleasures and pains."

This endeavor to become a "new thing" by way of imitation recognizes the self as historically variable, even capricious. Tithonus sought just such an infinitude of variation when he asked not to stay as he was (eternally youthful), but to continue to change, to enter into further and further transformations, which in turn constantly challenge fixed identities, and especially fixed gender identities. This is the cause for what can sound like annoyed recognition on his part, in his description of Aurora at the end of his monologue as always "returning" on her "silver wheels." Her returns seem a betrayal not because they indicate that she is continuing to go about her business, but because they reveal that her changes were cyclical rather than infinitely ongoing, as he had mistakenly, in his rapture, taken their mutual metamorphoses to be. Rather than continuing herself to change in any ongoing way, as he now is, she has become a repetition lacking complexity, revolving around, in some sense, in imitation of herself. Havelock Ellis's theory of sexo-aesthetic inversion, or Eonism, can take us further in our comprehension of Tithonus's complex, indeed queer sexuality. And yet, so inventive and irreducible are his formulations of gender and pleasure that we might coin other terms to catch his desire in a word: rather than Eonism, perhaps *Eosism*, after the Greek name for the lover with whose transformations he so identifies as to desire them for his own; or *Aeonism*, after the eternity, the state of unending successive stages, which he also sought to imitate.

The final verse paragraph of "Tithonus" begins with another of the speaker's questions, like his others far from rhetorical: "Yet hold me not forever in thine East: / How can my nature longer mix with thine?" (64–65). "Hold me not" can refer, of course, to a wish for escape both from her embrace and from her clutches. The urgency of his command, its suasive imperative, indicates that Tithonus is still withering in her arms at the moment of his speaking: they have not yet shifted position from their places at the start of his monologue.[76] While she holds his shrinking form, however, they are far from growing incorporate. They inhabit, he tells her, "thine East"; hers is a separate sphere now, not a shared one. Tithonus has experienced divine rapture, or seizure, by this goddess, but his current predicament is that her hold on him is now tenuous at best. Rather than being enclosed within her "slowly crimsoning" presence, he "withers slowly" in her arms, in a travesty of their earlier protracted circumfusion; they are now only contiguous rather than commensurate. Now himself immortal, he dwells in her "presence" but is not part of her immanence; his age places him "beside" her youth (his misery is "To dwell in presence of immortal youth, / Immortal age beside immortal youth" [21–22]). Describing her undergoing her now customary alterations "once more," as her eyes brighten "slowly close to mine," he indicates that her optical influence is now external to him, condensing into the tears she leaves on his cheek, abandoning them as she abandons him.

Early in *In Memoriam* Tennyson describes entering into a confusion of sympathetic association. Seeing the yew whose roots are "wrapt about the bones" of the dead, grown incorporate into the corpse, he addresses the "sullen tree": "I seem to fail from out my blood / And grow incorporate into thee" (2:15–16). The mourner thus enters into identification with the tree in order to gain through it a subsidiary commingling with the corpse. This desire for merging with decay by way of a mediating sympathy with a living object elucidates the ways Tithonus's turn at the end of his monologue from Aurora to the earth is a return to the woods, vapors, men, and swan of his opening, as well as to the kind of merging of corporal identity that we know this speaker craves.

In light of the reading I have forwarded of Tithonus's desire for wholesale absorption into Aurora's being and becoming, his question "How can my nature longer mix with thine?" can be interpreted literally. With this phrasing, he acknowledges that their relationship has been founded entirely on his dialectical "mixing" with her, on an implicit subordination of his "nature" (mortal, male) to hers (immortal, female). And his rejection of that synthesis, or mix (a word that connotes both a thoroughgoing amalgamation and a mix-up), signals this dramatic monologue's major turning point. What the gods have joined, Tithonus would now put asunder. He claims to be experiencing a reversal from enjoying the infusion of dewy warmth to suffering the equivalent of a cold bath, and he turns from the capital body parts he focused on in describing their mingling (mouth, forehead, eyelids) to their antipodes, his "wrinkled feet." Himself a "shadow" at the start of the monologue, he describes her now as associated with "rosy shadows." In closing he makes clear that he is shifting from merging with her to emerging from her.

In his decisive leave-taking, Tithonus enjoins his auditor:

> Release me, and restore me to the ground;
> Thou seëst all things, thou wilt see my grave:
> Thou wilt renew thy beauty morn by morn;
> I earth in earth forget these empty courts,
> And thee returning on thy silver wheels. (72–76)

These lines have invariably been read not as Tithonus's farewell to her arms, as they are, but as a claim that he will persist in attempting to die,[77] in spite of his clear recognition, in a line he recites by rote, that "The Gods themselves cannot recall their gifts" (49). Tennyson's Tithonus is in command of what he asks for at all points. His demand for immortality, for instance, was a specific bid for rapture, defined by him as an unending experience of simultaneous states of successive identity, not a misstatement. This final command, "Release me, and restore me to the ground," is as specific, serious—we should say, as intentional—and as possible to fulfill as the earlier one. Indeed, what he wants is for Aurora to see not only his grave but also his gravitas.

In closing, Tithonus expresses his desire to become particulate. The expansive Ulysses desires too to be "a part" of all he has met, but for Ulysses this will enable the appropriation of the world by the self, whereas for Tithonus, to become a part is to dissolve the self, to merge the *I* with soil. Tennyson names his source for "earth in earth" as Dante's *terra in terra*; Tithonus envisions an afterlife of compost. This merging of self is not predicated on death, however. As we saw in his opening lines, Tithonus refers more to a process than to a destination, and it is a process that resembles the experience of lovemaking that his monologue records. With the phrase "earth in earth," he invokes the process of one entity ("earth") being incorporated, merging wholly into another, virtually identical one ("in earth"). With Dante's help, Tennyson's Tithonus is able to view this relocation as a restoration, not to human mortality, but to intense identificatory mixing. And if he is restored to an infinitude of simultaneous successive states (the eternity of decay that his monologue evokes in its opening lines), then he will indeed be spared bearing witness to Aurora's daily transformation, while she will have to carry the burden of witnessing *his* daily alterations, or at least their location: "Thou wilt see my grave." Decay, too, can be conceived of as a dialectical process, and in his monologue's closing Tithonus hints that perhaps the rapture of their lovemaking was not for him, in retrospect, unlike being decayed. Both experiences involve for him the slow and staggered diffusion of the self into another entity, a submission of personal agency and bodily control, a receptivity to forces external to the body or the self's own motivations, an enveloping synthesis.

Rich and Rare Similitudes

Describing Eonism, Ellis notes that the exercise by which one person enters sympathetically into the sex of another "corresponds to the impulse which various modern philosophers of aesthetics regard as of the essence of the aesthetic attitude, an inner sympathy and imitation, an emotional identification with the beautiful object" (104–5). This procedure is especially complicated in Tithonus's case, because one might see, in his stress on Aurora's aggressive, masculinized desire for him, presumably also an example of Eonism, in that she seeks to subsume his beauty to her own aesthetic no less than sexual purposes and pleasures. The couple undergoes, in these terms, a double inversion, wherein each is each and neither; as the simile accompanying the granting of his wish indicates, just as he sought to become more like her, she became more like him.

Elaborating on the wider relevance of sexo-aesthetic inversion, Ellis explains, "The philosophic students of aesthetics have frequently shown a tendency to regard a subjective identification with the beautiful object as the clue to aesthetic emotion. They hold that we imaginatively imitate the beauty we see, and sympathetically place ourselves in it. Our emotions, as it were, beat time to its rhythm" (106–7). His description of sympathetic placement, in which an admirer enters the subjectivity of the beautiful object, may resonate in our reading of what is by wide consensus one of Tennyson's most beautiful poems, a literary status I interrogate in the remainder of this chapter. Entering into "subjective identification with the beautiful object," our emotions "beat time to its rhythm." Tithonus describes himself as being literally beaten by time, as his lover's "strong Hours / indignant" "beat" him "down," even as her "wild team," equally mastered by her ("yearning" for her yoke), "beat the twilight into flakes of fire" (18, 19, 39, 40, 42). In an indication, however, of how time might also be understood as offering an experience of embrace that resembles his lover's engulfing of him, the speaker of the 1833 "Tithon" requested, "let me call thy ministers, the hours, / To take me up, to wind me in their arms, /. . . And lap me deep within the lonely west" (24–25, 27). He had, we know, commenced his own sympathetic transformations as he witnesses what he used to join, her "bosom beating with a heart renewed" (36). That bosom, called "throbbing" in *T. MS B* and "Tithon," beats out a rhythm that her other subjects (her beating Hours and rhythmically galloping horses) can follow. Tithonus's measure, however, is checked by his own infinitude: he calls repeated attention to the tempo of his temporality, brought about, he knows, by his intemperance. Tithon had asked, "Why should a man desire in any shape / To vary from his kind, or beat the roads / Of life?" ("Tithon," *T. MSS*), but this variance is what led to his ecstatic syncopation with her, to his own mortal heart "Drowned deep in rapturous trances, beating fast" (*T. MS B*). As we are reminded by E. S. Dallas, the Victorian poetic theorist, "Keats, making mention of what is in plain English the rapture of a kiss, says that the lips *poesied* with each other."[78]

I have maintained that Tithonus's request for immortality was not the blunder it is generally taken to be, but rather, like his closing demand, an articulation of a desire to extend a particular array of pleasures, based closely on his association of sympathy with the mutual coordination of simultaneous successive states. And yet this speaker is taunted, as he knows, by his own figurative language (always unavoidable, as Dallas demonstrates, in his "plain English" evoking the metaphoric "rapture of a kiss"). Tithonus is still confused, even circumfused, by that responsive smile of Aurora's that accompanied a simile all too representative, and reductive, of their relations. If I have been right to stress the totality of Tithonus's identification with Aurora, one based on an extreme notion of similitude, then my argument necessitates following still more closely his logic of mimesis. In the verse paragraph describing his responsibility for his immortality, in which he asked for and received precisely what he desired, he also utters the self-description "none other than a god," which I have said confused the precise fact of his existence, namely, that he was *only* like, rather than the same as, a god.

The simile "like a god" would have acknowledged that Tithonus's relation to immortality was one of similitude, not identification. As a figure of speech, simile is, as M. H. Abrams defines it, "a comparison between two distinctly different things," generally indicated by the words "like" or "as."[79] The simile "like a god" recognizes the distinction between humans and gods; it acknowledges that they are essentially unlike. Generally, simile is considered a simpler kind of figurative language than metaphor; certainly it is less theorized. In his chapter "Metaphor," for example, John R. Searle notes that simile constitutes a "statement of similarity" (pointing out that many metaphors are implied similes, just omitting "like" or "as"). But he discusses similes chiefly as a way to distinguish and more precisely define metaphor, declaring, "Similarity is a vacuous predicate: any two things are similar in some respect or another."[80] E. S. Dallas's 1852 *Poetics*, an exploration of poetic theory and practice, is less dismissive of the structure and aims of simile, and his analysis can help us adumbrate the all too consequential comparative language of Tithonus.

Dallas calls simile a "lower form" than metaphor. But he states succinctly the problem with standard theories of simile and metaphor: "A simile is distinguished from a metaphor by the accident of having certain words to herald the comparison formally. Rely upon it, unless in our hearts we felt that between the two there lies a difference less trifling than this of having, or not having, a kind of usher, the distinction would long ere now have been forgotten" (200–201). He opposes the distinction between the two being left to "the verbal test" of the comparative conjunctions like, as, so: "Better no test whatever, than such a bad one. . . . The ordeal of words can no more detect metaphor from simile than the ordeal of drowning could detect a witch" (202). Dallas proposes an improved test in distinguishing simile from metaphor: "The difference between them must lie in their very nature, and in the feeling which gives them utterance, not in the mode of that utterance, which, of course, must depend upon the accidents of language, the metaphors of one tongue being often the similes of another" (202).

Hoping that we may "arrive at something like the truth," Dallas clarifies what he takes to be the difference between simile and metaphor: "Simile is the comparison of like with like, not forgetting that they are only like; metaphor is the employment of like for like, not doubting that they are one and the same" (203–4). Simile is not lesser because of the minor matter of conjunctions, but in fact because it illustrates conjunction rather than amalgamation. With metaphor, "the likeness will be more or less blended with that which it reflects, so that in many cases one may not be able at once to tell the substance from the shadow." Two ideas are "matched" with simile, Dallas argues, whereas with metaphor, they become "one flesh." Simile expresses "Assimilation," whereas metaphor expresses "Identification" (206). According to this logic, Tithonus mistakes his relation to the gods as being a matter of metaphor, or identification, when it was instead one of simile, or assimilation. This confusion is one Hallam in "On Sympathy" guards against, maintaining always the fundamental distinction even between two beings in sympathy with one another. The other person can seem to constitute a successive stage of the self, but that stage is itself a measure of one's own self-division. Tithonus, however, appears to have felt that he and Aurora were so "mixed" as to have become indistinguishable from each other, to have merged into "one flesh." But their relationship, and its keenest pleasure, was predicated instead on the rhetorical trope of simile, on the yoking together of unlike things, on the breaching of binaries (male/female, mortal/immortal) that, by breaching, confirmed them.

Describing the general category of figurative language, M. H. Abrams notes its use "in order to achieve some special meaning or effect." "Such figures," he continues, "were long described as primarily poetic 'ornaments,' but they are integral to the functioning of language."[81] Similes are especially likely, according to Dallas, to be looked on "merely as an embellishment" (214). Dallas himself betrays a suspicion toward figurative language, commenting, "By imagery many seem especially to understand similitude; and it would seem to be a common opinion that rich and rare similitudes form the peculiar device of poesy. They form indeed a splendid ornament" (190). He goes so far as to conclude that "comparison is not essential any more than a staff is essential for walking," objecting strenuously to the assumption, which he believes is common, that "the mere tracing of resemblances, whether clearly as in simile, or confusedly as in metaphor, is poesy above everything else." As a consequence, he laments, "a poem is often judged by the novelty and the number of such comparisons" (196).

Contemplation of inessential and ornamental figurative language leads Dallas into his own threads of figuration: "These partial beauties, a ribbon here and a trinket so, are very dandilike. We want a more manly poesy; rich in ornament if you will, so it help out the idea, and do not encumber the poem" (198). Constituting so many trinkets and ribbons, comparative language can not only feminize but also trivialize poetry, since such ornaments, he argues, are stray and valueless additions to any sartorial effort. And it makes impossible a manly poetics, leading to a kind of prosodic transvestism, in which the masculine is tricked out in female trappings.

"We want a more manly poesy," declares Dallas in 1852, his verb conveying both a lack and a desire that he was not alone in remarking. "How much I love this writer's manly style!" (1) we hear Tennyson exclaim the same year in his poem "Suggested by Reading an Article in a Newspaper" (1852). Sinfield notes, "Literature, and poetry especially, has, since the time of the Romantics, been in a state of conflict around imputations that there is something intrinsically feminine in its constitution."[82] This assignment of a gender to an artistic mode has its corollary in the attachment of gender binaries to artistic pursuits generally.[83] Havelock Ellis, classifying the Eonist, again and again insists on this association between Eonism and aesthetics: "The aesthetic tendencies of this impulse cannot be ignored. They help to explain, moreover, why … it so often happens that the Eonist is an artist or a man of letters" (105). So likely is the link that certain behavioral traits themselves constitute signs, and perhaps even symptoms, of one of the "peculiarities of Eonism." He reveals, "It tends to occur among people who are often educated, refined, sensitive, and reserved." Ellis attaches a sexual to a social type, and stresses this connection repeatedly: "The Eonist is frequently refined, sensitive, and highly intelligent" (104).

Ellis teases us with unnamed exemplars of Eonism, stating at the essay's opening that "it is on record that various prominent people, some of high ability, have shown this peculiarity" (1). One of his cases, R. M. (who says of his wife, with whom he shared an "idyllic" thirty years of marriage, "Nothing would have pleased me better than for us to have gone to sleep, and to have waked up in each other's bodies" [95]), was a "man of science and letters" (91). "The subject was a man of exceptional intellectual culture and of exceptional sympathetic sensitiveness," Ellis insists. "He possessed marked feminine affectability" (100). "Affectability" is a central concept for Ellis, who in his *Man and Woman*, a popular study that went through numerous editions after its initial 1894 publication, defines this trait as a capacity for greater responsiveness to stimuli, one that he considers far more prevalent in women than in men.[84] Another subject was "a distinguished musical composer" whose "bisexual constitution involved by the anomaly [of transvestism] aided him to reach his highest musical possibilities" (27). Musicality itself is symptomatic, Ellis suggests: "We may even agree with Dr. Pudor that a feminine element is of special importance for the artist as musician, since 'music implies embodied receptivity'" (106).

The Eonist, that person so desirous of "embodied receptivity," may be identified as much by behavior and accomplishments—his or her "sensitive impressionable artist's temperament" (106)—as by his or her sexual predilections. Although Ellis does attempt to preserve the anonymity of his subjects, he mentions two Victorian authors by name in the cause of exempting them from the possible imputation of Eonism: "Ruskin and Rossetti cannot be regarded as Eonists, although both of them, even on the physical side, may have presented female traits" (106). But it is Tennyson whose work, no less than his person, seems elsewhere to have excited an astonishing array of suppositions and declarations regarding the presence of "female traits." His "affectability," for example, was remarked, in different terms, by Benjamin Jowett, who recalled of the poet, "He had the susceptibility of a child, or of a woman." (He adds that his friend presented "a strange combination," however, since he also had "the strength of a giant, or of a God.")[85]

I have drawn from Ellis's category of Eonism in my discussion of Tithonus less to pigeonhole this majestic figure into either a sexuality or an aesthetics than to toy with Victorian fusions and confusions of gender and aesthetics more generally, since the erotic sympathy into which the monologist enters cannot by its "nature," to use Tithonus's word, be contained. I would avoid still more strenuously the attachment of any such term to Tennyson: Ellis's mention of Ruskin and Rossetti shows how bathetic such a clinical assignment can be. I am interested, though, in probing the implications of a significant pattern in Tennyson's reception (and, indeed, his imputed receptivity or affectability), whereby from the publication of his earliest volumes, his poetry was classed as feminine and ornamental, troublingly arrayed in trinkets and ribbons.

Extolling Tennyson's poetry of sensation, Hallam declared in his 1832 review of his friend, "There is a strange earnestness in his worship of beauty, which throws a charm over his impassioned song." Of the poem "Adeline," one of the clutch of poems that included such related works as "Madeline," "Lilian," "Isabel," "Claribel" (for which Tennyson was widely mocked and which surely helped to inspire Bulwer-Lytton's galling 1830s sobriquet, "School-Miss Alfred"), Hallam had written, "Is not this beautiful?... How original is the imagery, how delicate" (*Writings*, 191, 197). In his 1844 volume regarding up-and-coming poets titled *A New Spirit of the Age*, R. H. Horne also noted, "There are no qualities in Tennyson more characteristic than those of delicacy and refinement."[86] Whether a critic was favoring or castigating Tennyson, the same terms were applied; all that shifted was their valuation. John Heywood, in an 1877 essay titled "Tennyson: An Over-Rated Poet," claimed, "In refined, delicate, attenuated expression, or rather indication, of indistinct, somewhat melancholy, and very sentimental longings, Mr. Tennyson is at his best." Tennyson, with his indistinct indications ("expression" clearly being too forceful a word) and "sentimental longings," can be said almost to be sighing more than writing. The critic here insists on the poet's passivity even in the production of his own work. Heywood makes explicit both the identification of Tennyson as feminine and the identification of that gender with passive receptivity: "He is generally passive, rarely active; his function is to take in, not to give out. He is like the moon more than like the sun; he receives and reflects, and if spoken of figuratively should grammatically be mentioned as she. His most contented mood is a state of idle voluptuousness."[87] In a critical assessment characterizing the person rather than the poetry, Tennyson appears to be in a swoon or stupor that comes to unsex him, to transform his sexual identity, to metamorphose him fully into a "she." And to be a "she" is to be voluptuously passive. According to this critic, it is Tennyson's own poetry that, to use the poet's later title, "Affected an Effeminate Manner," in a way that, he suspects, goes beyond mere affectation.

The Uses of Redundant Beauty

Summing up Tennyson's career, George Saintsbury remarked, "He was accused of a somewhat excessive prettiness, a sort of dandyism and coquetry in form, and of a certain want of profundity in his manner."[88] Saintsbury doesn't acknowledge that these two accusations are intimately related, indeed, that the first charge, of prettiness, of the lack of manliness apparently represented by both dandyism and coquetry, is what leads inexorably to the second charge, the lack of substantiality. This "want of profundity" is represented by Saintsbury's comparison to the dandy and the coquette, as Tennyson is transformed into both male and female incarnations of social creatures whose self-representation has largely to do with sartorial and discursive surfaces. We have looked at some of the rhetorical manifestations of what Havelock Ellis uneasily termed the sexo-aesthetic; in moving to the conclusion of this discussion, we need now to consider the relation, for the Trojan monologist Tithonus and the poet Tennyson, between aesthetics and discursive efficacy. Can an excess or, in Gladstone's terms, a redundancy of beauty, like so many trinkets and ribbons, have its uses?

Tennyson himself considered ornamentation a divine attribute. Plucking a daisy as he walked with a friend, he looked closely at its "crimson-tipt leaves" and asked, "Does not this look like a thinking Artificer, one who wishes to ornament?" (quoted in *Memoir*, 1:313 n1). For many of Tennyson's contemporaries, however, the sheer exquisiteness of much of his verse began to point to a vacuity in the author rather than to evidence of intelligent design. One critic in 1899 averred of Tennyson, "Take from [him his] intricate perfection of style, [his] sense of...beauty..., and you [leave him] devoid of almost everything," although this same critic also concedes, referring specifically to "Tithonus," "Beauty is not so common that we need ask it always to be more than beauty."[89] This image of beautiful vacuity in Tennyson was raised early in his career; writing in 1844 R. H. Horne could praise Tennyson for producing a "poem with nothing in it except music," which "will charm your soul." As if in recognition that this is not necessarily a compliment, Horne continues, "Be this said, not in reproach,—but in honour of him and of the English language, for the learned sweetness of his numbers."[90]

"O for a Life of Sensations rather than of Thoughts," Keats wrote to Benjamin Bailey in 1817.[91] A. S. Byatt has observed that it is a characteristic of Tennyson's poetry to be "concerned with aesthetic *sensation* both as technique and as subject-matter."[92] In this he had been encouraged by Arthur Hallam, whose admiration of his friend's "desire for beauty" must have come to seem an assignment to continue in that desire. But while Hallam, following Keats, contrasted sensation with thought, he did not see the beautiful in poetry as wholly emptying itself of meaning or becoming either merely or excessively decorative. Indeed, Hallam insisted on beauty being a prerequisite for poetry, constituting both its etiology and its end point.

Tithonus's sensibilities are of so exquisite a turn that he is transfixed by the way the light moves across his lover's face and haunted by a strange song heard long ago. Chilled in the dawning sunlight, electrified by whispered sound, he is one from whom, though trapped himself, nothing escapes, and in the keenness of his sensational life he resembles the poet Hallam celebrates. Describing Keats and Shelley in his essay on Tennyson, Hallam claimed, "Susceptible of the slightest impulse from external nature, their fine organs trembled into emotion at colours, and sounds, and movements, unperceived or unregarded by duller temperaments." In the intensity of his physical apprehension and the apparent heedlessness of his request for immortality, Tithonus surely seems, to employ Hallam's dichotomy, a poet of sensation rather than of thought, but he seeks nevertheless to accomplish specified goals and to attain them by way of this monologue. Hallam's theory also accounts for this ambition for efficacious engagement, since he does not see sensation as finally separable, for these poets, from reflection: "exertions of eye and ear" become for them "mingled more and more with their trains of active thought" (*Writings*, 186).

The commitment to beauty that Hallam saw as a necessity for poetry others saw as largely dispensable. Writing roughly at the midpoint of Tennyson's career, Walter Bagehot labeled Tennyson's most characteristic style "ornate," and explained, "Even in the highest cases, ornate art leaves upon a cultured and delicate taste the conviction that it is not the highest art, that it is somehow excessive and overrich, . . . that it is in an unexplained manner unsatisfactory." For all its excess of surface, the ornamental is insufficient, even inadequate; for all its plenitude, it is insubstantial. "The gorgeous additions and ornaments with which Mr. Tennyson distracts us" create "an atmosphere of indistinct illusion and of moving shadow." His is a style "which as you are scrutinizing, disappears." Discussing the laureate's most recent publication, the 1864 *Enoch Arden*, Bagehot writes that it presents the fairly straightforward story of a simple sailor, a narrative not necessarily well served by the "splendid accumulation of impossible accessories" in which Tennyson has outfitted it. These accessories, for all their elaboration of detail, complicate and confuse rather than clarify, leaving one lost, in Bagehot's own splendidly rich language, in "a mist of beauty, an excess of fascination, a complication of charm."[93]

Behind Bagehot's description of his frustration with ornate poetic style, in which so much is offered but so little can be grasped, we can hear a frustration with figurative language itself. With ornate art, he complains, "nothing is described as it is, everything has about it an atmosphere of *something else*." He continues, "A simple thing . . . is never left by itself, something else is put with it; something not connected with it." When looking at one object, the reader is being made to contemplate another, different object, one perhaps inexplicably connected or at least whose connection is not explained. A "simple" object is not left "by itself," but rather complicated by being "put with" something else, which it does not clearly resemble. Bagehot's problem with ornate art is that it yokes together unlike things; this is of course the standard definition of the trope of simile. Bagehot's analysis, though dismissive, is penetrating, because its argument is not that Tennyson employs too many comparisons, but that his prosody is in some way *structured* on the logic of the correlation of unlike things. Tennyson's ornate art, because composed chiefly of figuration, according to Bagehot, represents "illusions" rather than "what is as it is," providing not substance but "condiments," or accessories, like the trinkets and ribbons Dallas holds up for display. Rather than "helping out the idea," in Dallas's terms, Tennyson's elaborations instead embellish and finally encumber it. Employing what Bagehot calls "undue disguises and unreal enhancements," ornate art deals in misrepresentations (the "unreal"), but it deals as well in superfluities (the "undue").[94]

Bagehot casts Tennyson's ornate art as a decline from Wordsworth's "pure" art. Matthew Arnold, writing also in the 1860s, makes a similar point in his comparison of Tennyson to Homer. Arnold's "Last Words" contrasts Homer's "grand style," his "plainness" and "simplicity," to Tennyson's "heightened and elaborate air." "Mr. Tennyson is a most distinguished and charming poet," Arnold concedes, "but the very essential characteristic of his poetry is, it seems to me, an extreme subtlety and curious elaborateness of thought, and extreme subtlety and curious elaborateness of expression." After quoting snippets from several of Tennyson's poems, Arnold declares, "This way of speaking is the least *plain*, the most *un-Homeric*, which can possibly be conceived."[95] Arnold quotes from "Ulysses" at several points in *On Translating Homer*, employing again variations on the words "curious" and "subtle," words associated with the peculiar and recondite. Curiously wrought, indeed overwrought and abstruse, Tennyson's poetry is perhaps least Homeric when it addresses Homeric subjects.

Tennyson's friends and supporters leapt to his defense, igniting a flurry of response, but Arnold was perspicacious in his characterization of Tennyson as un-Homeric. Arnold defines Homer by his understanding of an aesthetic of restraint and lack of adornment that he calls Greek. Setting aside the merits of Arnold's claims regarding either the ancient or the contemporary poet, we might pursue the notion that Tennyson's poetry reflects instead what I have called a Trojan aesthetic. Gladstone and others charge the Trojans with a "redundancy" of beauty: they possess more than is necessary, more than is of use. But Tithonus's beauty has been for him wholly necessary, virtually a condition of his existence. His overabundance of beauty is a privilege he was born to, and he knows no identity apart from this birthright. We have seen that Tennyson's poetics were met with a similar accusation of excess, and also that the charge of discursive superfluity, of speech being divorced from any discernible use, has been leveled at the genre of the dramatic monologue more generally in Langbaum's influential claim that this speech is "superfluous" and "need never have taken place."

Arthur Hallam contended that the "predominant motive" of the poet is the "desire for beauty," but I have reviewed a number of expressions of skepticism as to the necessity of the ornate and the beautiful. Bagehot knows his argument raises just this question: "It will be said, if ornate art be as you say, an inferior species of art, why should it ever be used?"[96] Ornate, curious, subtle, embellished: Tennyson's poetry has been felt to be *too* beautiful, to become dismissible *because* aesthetically overwhelming—but beauty tends to raise such questions about its own usefulness. In his 1754 essay "On the Sublime and the Beautiful," well known to Tennyson, Edmund Burke remarks, "It is said that the idea of utility, or of a part's being well adapted to answer its end, is the cause of beauty, or indeed beauty itself." He concludes, however, that "many things are very beautiful, in which it is impossible to discern any idea of use."[97] This very resistance to use can be held *as* its use. The beauty of much of Tennyson's poetry has been cast as serving an antiutilitarian purpose; as Sinfield puts it, "The delicacy of expression, cultivation of exquisite sensations and evocations of feminine experience in his early poetry bespoke a critique of a brutally purposeful ideology of utilitarianism, political economy, and machinery."[98] This is a compelling claim, especially in the context of the antiutilitarian fervor of the Apostles. My reading of "Tithonus" suggests a complementary critique on Tennyson's part of the standard of use, however, one that, rather than dismissing, transforms it. In this dramatic monologue, Tennyson demonstrates the utility of beauty and how much its possession accomplishes for this speaker.

Tithonus desires to enter into a mimetic relation to Aurora, to become "like" her in all the ways he can, structuring his identity and his figurative language on the logic of assimilation. In stressing their present difference, he laments, "ever thus thou growest beautiful, / In silence"; he now seeks to grow beautiful again himself, but to do so in and through speech. Oenone forwarded a narrative of efficacious music, yearning after sound that will "build" something, gather shape, even as she commends her own song only to the silence. Hearing the same Apollonic song, Tithonus first identifies himself with the wall the singer raises, and in retrospect with the singer himself; his only analogues are the walls of Troy and the melodious god who built them. Finally, however, we might say that Tithonus must come to resemble, be "like," the song itself. The monologue must enact his beauty, which thus becomes the product not of appearance but of articulation. His dramatic monologue is a performance, a return for this speaker to the state of being apprehended and honored on aesthetic grounds, a return to his prior joy in being taken as "glorious in his beauty." But the monologue is also performative: his words transform him in the course of their utterance.

The beauty of "Tithonus" has long stood as a matter of critical consensus; even critics who might not agree with each other on much else agree on this. Christopher Ricks writes of the "superbly mellifluous movements of the verse" and stresses in his reading the "fineness of musical verbalism that makes 'Tithonus' [Tennyson's] most assuredly successful poem."[99] Harold Bloom praises the "surpassingly beautiful opening passage" of the poem, and concludes his reading with its "glorious closing lines."[100] It is not happenstance that "Tithonus" is one of Tennyson's most aesthetically pleasing poems, that like Tithonus among the Trojans, it is one of the most beautiful among a beautiful kind. Matthew Rowlinson has written of the poem that "its metronomic regularity takes it nowhere,"[101] but it may be that if Tithonus is to get anywhere, it is to be by *way* of metronomic regularity and the generally mellifluous, fine, and beautiful prosody of his monologic voice. As Edgar Allen Poe, who held Tennyson to be the greatest poet of the age, wrote in his essay "The Poetic Principle," poetry is constituted of "The Rhythmical Creation of Beauty."[102]

Tithonus's words bear the tremendous burden of representing a beauty now discursive rather than visual, and part of what the dramatic monologue effects for him is the reconnection of the concept of beauty to his name. This accounts for his need of the monologic, as Aurora must be transformed from the viewer who chooses him into the auditor who releases him. In replacing physical with rhetorical beauty, he is becoming a figure of speech, renewing his beauty word by word.[103] If what he intends is for his words to accomplish his release from immortality, they must surely fail; this is no swan song. But if what he intends is his release from the spectacle of her beauty and, more, the recapturing of his own aesthetic predominance, then his aim is accomplished in the monologue, by way of the monologue. He is indeed, as ancient images depict him, defending himself against Aurora by brandishing the lyre. As with "Ulysses," this poem is illustrative of the way, in Tennyson's hands, the dramatic monologue as a genre is mimetic, since again the effect of this discourse on a reader imitates its design on the auditor the poem posits.

Tithonus's chief ambitions, then, are formal ones, just as form is his chief predicament. His once physically beautiful form is now degenerate, a corporeal mass losing all definition and even such agency as he, "chosen" and rapt away by an immortal, enjoyed. The form into which he would now metamorphose is that of the dramatic monologue; before our eyes he is transfigured from an ancient form to a new kind, from the mythical Tithonus to the monologic "Tithonus." Seeking to effect rapture, Tithonus's dramatic monologue has need of and makes use of its beauty; the speaker knows that its glorious form will attain for him release, or nothing can. He renews his physical perfection in the monologue, by way of the monologue, since while losing bodily form he takes poetic form. After reviewing the poem's metrical features, Pyre declares "Tithonus" "a singularly perfect specimen of Tennyson's mature artistry," a lyric exemplum "even more perfectly executed" than "Ulysses." And the monologue voices formally the willing submission of a feminized Tithonus to the "beating" of Aurora's hours. Calculating its ratio of even pauses and caesurae, Pyre discerns the poem's "dominant feminine rhythm" and concludes his discussion of these and related metrical effects, "That such a music is suited to the substance and atmosphere of the poem it is almost idle to remark."[104]

The poem's beauty, then, itself constitutes the speaker's rhetorical strategy. And though the only closure possible to this speaker is poetic closure, in the transfer of his beauty from his corpus to his monologue even his infinitude may be an advantage. In the 1841 essay "The Poet as Hero," Carlyle considers the distinction between "true Poetry and true Speech not poetical," noting that much had been written on this subject in recent years by "German Critics": "They say . . . that the Poet has an *infinitude* in him; communicates an *Unendlichkeit*, a certain character of 'infinitude,' to whatsoever he delineates."[105] In "The Use of Poetry and the Use of Criticism" T. S. Eliot also suggests that advanced age, regardless of one's term of years, might be a defining mark of a poet: "Hyperbolically one might say that the poet is *older* than other human beings."[106]

In his 1831 essay on Tennyson, Hallam contrasts the artist who, pursuing "the pleasure he has in knowing a thing to be true," will "pile his thoughts in a rhetorical battery, that they may convince," with the artist who takes "pleasure" in knowing a thing to be "beautiful" and so lets his thoughts "flow in a natural course of contemplation, that they may enrapture" (*Writings*, 184–85). Tithonus knows the futility in his case of battering the gates of Aurora's heaven with storms of argument (to paraphrase "St. Simeon Stylites") and so seeks rather to enrapture his auditor by way of his dramatic monologue, even as he was enraptured by the strange songs of Apollo and Aurora. Readers have recognized the aesthetic and rhetorical implications of this transport. Referring to the passage in which Tithonus is rapt by his lover (which begins "while I lay"), Ricks calls it a "moment of uttered audible beauty," and Bloom also remarks Tithonus's "heightened powers of aesthetic perceptiveness while being embraced."[107] Tithonus has been rapt in the sense of having been physically translated or removed to Aurora's courts, as Ganymede was rapt to the heavens and Persephone rapt to Hades. Tithonus was enraptured as well in the discursive sense of Hallam's use of the term, by both Apollo's song and Aurora's whispers. Hallam places this "beautiful" discursive excess, efficacious because overwhelming, in opposition to oratory, establishing it, in effect, as a substitute for oratory. Having experienced it in many forms, Tithonus makes rapture his own discursive aim: what Tithonus has experienced, his monologue now performs.

Aurora's seduction, we recall, was not only labial (her kissing) but also linguistic (her whispers). The monologist Tithonus reminds her that he once was her auditor, that he too once knew, as she does now, the experience of being silent and beautiful: in this also they have reversed their previous positions. Her whispers recall to him his earlier audition of Apollo's city-raising song, since both of these were efficacious performances, causing myriad transformations. Although he claims at the end to desire to be released into another situation of simultaneous successive states ("I earth in earth"), no one could gainsay the fact that the experience of decay is a poor substitute for the dawn's lovemaking. But he does have the ostensible satisfaction of claiming that his is a leave-taking of her rather than an abandonment by her; earlier in the monologue he bemoans that every day "thou departest," a desertion stressed in "Tithon" with the repetition of the phrase "thou partest" (*1832* 39, 40). In his valediction, we can hear that his earlier implicit *Don't leave me* has been replaced by an entreaty still more desperate in its combined resolution and resignation: *Don't let me leave you.* But though he may attain release through his monologue, he can attain her sympathy only in the narrow meaning of regret or pity, expressed in the form of the tears she leaves on his cheek. This sympathy he vehemently rejects as also a poor substitute for the sympathy he had earlier enjoyed, in his identification with the successive states of her transporting presence. This vaster sympathy she now bestows on another, turning her melodious lips to infuse with dawning warmth and music another form that also changes in, and only in, her advent. She moves even as he speaks toward the statue of their beautiful dead son, who, like his father, had been so like a god.

6

TITHONUS, TIRESIAS, AND THE POLITICAL COMPOSITION OF THE SONG-BUILT CITY

The strangest, though not the worst, of all in me is a rebellion (I know not what else to call it) against growing old.

—W. E. Gladstone, diary entry, 29 December 1861

Some beautiful persons *are* granted eternal youth: Oscar Wilde's Dorian Gray, for example. Like Tithonus, he makes his bid for a stay against transience at the moment of his first keen apprehension of his own beauty, when he sees himself as another sees him: "The sense of his own beauty came on him like a revelation."[1] And he is like Tithonus in his likeness to other beautiful youths; prior to painting Dorian's portrait, the artist Basil Hallward had drawn him "as Paris in dainty armour, and as Adonis with huntsman's cloak and polished boar-spear" (114). Dorian is urged on in his folly by Lord Henry Wotton, who informs him of the force of pulchritude: "You have a wonderfully beautiful face, Mr. Gray. Don't frown. You have. And Beauty is a form of Genius—is higher, indeed, than Genius, as it needs no explanation. It is one of the great facts of the world, like sunlight, or spring-time.... It cannot be questioned. It has its divine right of sovereignty. It makes princes of those who have it. You smile? Ah! when you have lost it you won't smile" (21–22). When complimented, according to his observer, Dorian frowns; when told that his beauty will attain for him power, he smiles. And in between the young man's reactive facial expressions, Lord Henry explains that beauty attains for its possessor hierarchical predominance because it defies language and reason (traditional means of suasion), gaining the immediate assent of its audience since it "needs no explanation" and "cannot be questioned." While in possession of his beauty, Dorian enjoys an unassailable sovereignty that seems his by "divine right." His beauty transforms and elevates his civic stature; it "makes" him a prince among men.

In the first section of this chapter I explore a range of social consequences of Tithonus's beauty, looking at the relevance especially of his aristocratic stand-

ing for a larger understanding of Tennyson's poetics. While Lord Henry's observation on the power associated with beauty turns us most immediately to
"Tithonus," it also relates to "Tiresias" in terms of its narrative structure, since
the latter monologue represents a speaker greatly experienced in the ways of the
world, now seeking actively to influence a young man. "There was something
terribly enthralling in the exercise of influence," Lord Henry reflects, musing over
the effect his words have on Dorian. "No other activity was like it" (35). Lord
Henry's influence might be considered fatal for Dorian; Tiresias's certainly is for
Menœceus, the youth, a scion of Thebes's ruling family, whom Tiresias persuades
to sacrifice his life to save his city. Here is Lord Henry's advice to Dorian:

> Ah! realize your youth while you have it. Don't squander the gold of your days,
> listening to the tedious, trying to improve the hopeless failure, or giving away
> your life to the ignorant, the common, and the vulgar. These are the sickly
> aims, the false ideals, of our age. Live! Live the wonderful life that is in you! Let
> nothing be lost upon you. Be always searching for new sensations. Be afraid of
> nothing. . . . A new Hedonism—that is what our century wants. You might be its
> visible symbol. (22)

"Visible symbol" of a very old hedonism, literally decadent (in a degenerate state
clearly the result of his desire for constantly renewed sensations): Tithonus might
appear to be a gothic caricature of aristocratic superannuation. Tennyson's Tiresias,
on the other hand, quite precisely counsels Menœceus to hurry to his death, to
"give away" his life for the benefit of those whom Lord Henry calls "the ignorant,
the common, and the vulgar." This chapter explores the aristocratic ideology of
these monologists, both of whom are fascinated by the power derived from efficacious speech. Lord Henry seeks to gain influence over Dorian by way of his own
discursive potency, as he reflects to himself that he has, "through certain words of
his, musical words said with musical utterance" (57). Tennyson's speakers also seek
to achieve suasive potency, whether addressing a youth, as does Tiresias, or addressing the matter of his own youth, as in a sense does each of these ancient men.

Menœceus's civic-minded self-sacrifice conforms as much as Tithonus's does
to a tradition of aristocratic representation; as one historian of English aristocracy
notes, "In contrast to the material values of the bourgeoisie, the aristocracy . . . believed fervently in honour, even in the willingness to die for this nebulous virtue."[2]
Giving up one's life for lesser mortals is the special mark, even privilege of the
aristocracy, as Carlyle declares in his 1843 *Past and Present*:

> In a valiant suffering for others, not in a slothful making others suffer for us,
> did nobleness ever lie. . . . In modern, as in ancient and all societies, the Aristoc-
> racy, they that assume the functions of an Aristocracy, doing them or not, have
> taken the post of honour; which is the post of difficulty, the post of danger,—of

death, if the difficulty be not overcome. *Il faut payer de sa vie*. Why was our life given us, if not that we should manfully give it? Descend, O Donothing Pomp; quit thy down-cushions; expose thyself to learn what wretches feel, and how to cure it![3]

Learning, let alone palliating, the pains of wretches hardly conforms to Lord Henry's notion of a life well lived ("Live! Live the wonderful life that is in you!"); indeed, these are the arduous and drab responsibilities from which he by his title and Dorian by his beauty are exempted. Beauty is like aristocratic privilege, in Lord Henry's analogy, in that neither have been, or in some fundamental sense even *can* be worked for; they simply come to one as a matter of inexplicable favor or good fortune. But the recipients can come nevertheless to believe that the fortune of *eugeneia* or "good birth" is merited, that such "divine" gifts are not arbitrary but appropriate and are themselves not the cause but the sign of a superiority finally believed to be intrinsic and deserved, a "right." Carlyle, forwarding another and not necessarily competing notion of aristocracy, insists that those who inherit their distinction rather than attain to it by personal efforts inherit not merely the increased responsibility but the greater *capability* of laboring mightily in the "post of difficulty, the post of danger." Whether aristocratic position provides its bearers with an exemption from or an expectation of labor is a debate derived for the Victorians from conflicting but complementary notions of inborn superiority. An inherited aristocracy (a word rooted in the Greek *aristos* [best]; the *aristokratia* being the rule by the best [citizens]) raises this question: Do its members enjoy distinction unmerited by the qualities of its current representatives, or are they, as a matter of heredity, intrinsically meritorious?

Edmund Burke argued that members of the aristocracy were especially qualified to do the work of governing through the fact of inheritance: "Some decent regulated pre-eminence, some preference (not exclusive appropriation) given to birth, is neither unnatural, nor unjust, nor impolitic."[4] Tennyson's representation of social organizations, no less than his conception of beauty, can be illuminated by some of the writings of Burke. Hallam Tennyson's *Memoir* recounts of the education of his father and uncles, "The boys had one great advantage, the run of their father's excellent library. Amongst the authors most read by them were Shakespeare, Milton, Burke" (*Memoir* 1:16). The list of authors continues, but Burke's placement in this immediate company may be telling (the poet's library contained an eight-volume 1801 edition of Burke's *Works*). Tennyson's early poem "On Sublimity" (1827) begins with an epigraph from Burke's *On the Sublime and Beautiful* ("The sublime always dwells on great objects and terrible") and proceeds to adumbrate examples of the great and terrible.

Burke was of still greater ongoing interest for Arthur Henry Hallam. As a gift after graduation from Eton, Gladstone sent Hallam a set of the works of Edmund Burke. Hallam was moved and grateful, and reciprocated by sending his father's three-volume *Constitutional History*, by which in turn Gladstone was moved and grateful. Some of Burke's most celebrated passages were echoed repeatedly by Hallam in his own correspondence. He employed Burke's famous recollection of the last time that he saw Marie Antoinette, from his 1790 *Reflections on the Revolution in France* ("I saw her just above the horizon, decorating and cheering the elevated sphere she moved in,—glittering like the morning-star, full of life, and splendour, and joy") as a staple for his love letters, first to a young Englishwoman in Italy, then for his wooing of Tennyson's sister Emily. The passage was well known, so it is likely Hallam was being deliberately allusive; he certainly was in numerous letters to Gladstone, as when he echoes in another context Burke's lament that no one saved the queen from execution: the "days of Chivalry are gone."[5] Hallam's letters to Gladstone are full of analyses of Burke's political philosophy, but his knowledge of Burke found a more public venue as well. Soon after leaving Cambridge, Hallam wrote a brief essay on Burke, one of three biographical sketches (the others were on Voltaire and Petrarch) that he contributed to a series of publications by the Society for the Diffusion of Useful Knowledge. Hallam declared at the outset of his educational biography of Burke, "We are still within the heated temperature of the same political agitations in which he lived and struggled" (*Writings*, 292).

I am less interested in tracking any direct influences of Burke in "Tithonus" or "Tiresias" than in looking to him to elucidate several questions raised by these two speakers, especially the issue of an inherited preeminence that may either decrease or increase one's social responsibilities. Burke's *A Philosophical Enquiry into the Origin of our Ideas of the Sublime and Beautiful* (1757), as well as his *Reflections on the Revolution in France*, though very different works, might be seen to intersect on a number of points, not least of which is the question of inheritance, an abiding concern for Tennyson's Tithonus and Tiresias. Tithonus's beauty has been understood to be an inherited trait since Aeneas reviewed his genealogy in *Iliad* 20. He speaks as a member of the Trojan ruling family, a status of which his monologue is always aware. Tiresias also stresses in numerous ways the significance of genealogy, especially that of the Theban ruling family, whose heir he addresses. In Burke's formulation, inheritance is an inherently conservative concept, since it honors the preservation of assets sparingly distributed, though Burke sets the maintenance of inherited prerogatives as a ballast for the society at large. He writes, "The power of perpetuating our property in our families is one of the most valuable and interesting circumstances belonging to it, and that which tends the most to the perpetuation of society itself." Calling the liberties asserted in the English Constitution themselves an *"entailed inheritance"* (italics his), Burke exalts, "Besides, the people of England well know, that the idea of inheritance furnishes a sure principle of conservation, and a sure principle of transmission; without at all excluding a principle of improvement."[6] In seeking to balance the conservation of inheritance, with its commitment to the perpetuation of resources within a particular social sphere, with a generalized and vague spirit of "improvement," Burke succinctly articulates the uneasy balance of a central Whig ideological position, one that, as we have seen, came to be held suspect both by those conservatives who sought protection and those liberals who sought improvement. Whigs exhibited, Gladstone observed, "a more close and marked preference for the claims of consanguinity and affinity than was to be found among other politicians."[7]

Burke also tethers the apprehension of beauty to "society itself," explaining, "I call beauty a social quality; for where women and men... give us a sense of joy and pleasure in beholding them... we like to have them near us, and we enter willingly into a kind of relation with them." Part of what Tithonus seeks to accomplish in his monologue is a return to a sociality connected to beauty in the abstract; the speaker desires, as we have seen, again to be perceived with pleasure. Under the heading "Society and Solitude," Burke's essay on the Sublime notes that "absolute and entire *solitude*, that is, the total and perpetual exclusion from all society, is as great a positive pain as can almost be conceived." It is this solitude (although they are literally in the company of auditors) in which we find both Tithonus and Tiresias at the commencements of their monologues. This exclusion from their kinds, variously defined and experienced, does seem to each a fate worse than the death he appears to seek, in apparent endorsement of the idea, articulated more directly by Burke, that "an entire life of solitude contradicts the purposes of our being, since death itself is scarcely an idea of more terror."[8] For Tithonus, beauty is "a social quality," binding him to his kind and his culture and propelling him into the community of gods. But entrance into that elevated community leaves him ultimately with the antithesis of sociality, placing him in an extreme isolation, like St. Simeon Stylites on his pillar and the reluctant ruler Ulysses at the start of his monologue. Tiresias, too, cursedly unheard amid the civic chaos of Thebes, seeks a place in either a human or a divine community. Each speaker addresses a single auditor, Aurora or Menœceus, whom he hopes to move, but, for each, his language has broader civic consequences.

In this chapter I consider aspects of aristocratic thinking, and speaking, in the two classical dramatic monologues "Tithonus" and "Tiresias" and explore the direct and indirect political representations in these generic examples. I have previously emphasized Tennyson's Whig affiliations, formal and ideological, and my readings of these poems again probe relevant aspects of this connection. In *Aristocratic Government in the Age of Reform*, Peter Mandler argues that England in the 1830s and 1840s "witnessed a reassertion of aristocratic power." He stresses throughout his study the cherished ideal not only of aristocratic responsiveness but also of aristocratic utility, demonstrating that the Foxite Whigs in particular held a "highly political understanding of the aristocrat's responsibility." This group constituted "a small minority," but in arguing that it "took on a disproportionate political importance in the age of Reform," Mandler counters the idea that Whigs were "anachronistic survivors, clinging to power for power's sake."[9]

Mandler admits that the Whig style of governing was "amateurish and cavalier," but insists that it was not necessarily incompetent, claiming that significant electoral, labor, and health reforms were set in motion by this "aggressively aristocratic party" in their years at the helm. Although we have come to believe, in a view rooted in the nineteenth century, that the Whigs' "aristocratic character is one of their least attractive and politically useful attributes," leading to what can look like "fecklessness," Mandler contends instead that the Whigs "proved practically unique among the landed classes in their willingness, even eagerness" to respond to external pressures. "Their responsiveness was not merely cynical or opportunistic," he argues, "but rather part of a coherent definition of what an aristocrat should be and do," in fulfillment of "a traditional tenet of whiggism that the aristocrat's responsibility was to serve the people."[10] By way of a logic that could well look duplicitous or at least contradictory, some Whig aristocrats maintained that they inherited with their estates a higher responsibility and capacity for representing the lower orders. Not all Whigs were aristocrats, by any means, just as not all aristocrats were Whigs, but Mandler's argument helps to show why the connection nevertheless held, and some of the ramifications of this association for Victorian political life.

Thomas Carlyle and Tennyson met in the late 1830s and began their habit of extended conversations; Carlyle wrote to Ralph Waldo Emerson in 1841, "I do not meet, in these late decades, such company over a pipe!"[11] Book 1 of Carlyle's 1843 *Past and Present* quotes extensively from Tennyson's 1842 "Ulysses," as I noted in chapter 4, and Carlyle's comments on aristocracy in this work can help to illuminate why Tithonus, in contrasting himself so starkly with toiling mortal men at the beginning and end of his monologue, represents not only himself but a class that seemed threatened with obsolescence, as Carlyle insists: "Such a class is transitory, exceptional, and, unless Nature's Laws fall dead, cannot continue." He calls the group shadowy, insubstantial: "Aristocracy has become Phantasm-Aristocracy, no longer able to *do* its work, not in the least conscious that it has any work longer to do." The central problem this class presents is that its existence now little profits its members or anyone else; he warns the "Idle Aristocracy," "Be counselled, ascertain if no work exist for thee on God's Earth; if thou find no commanded-duty there but that of going gracefully idle? Ask, inquire earnestly, with a half-frantic earnestness; for the answer means Existence or Annihilation to thee. We apprise thee of the world-old fact, becoming sternly disclosed again in these days, That he who cannot work in this Universe cannot get existed in it."[12] Carlyle urges the upper classes to defend themselves against the potential disasters of onrushing democracy. He is not trying to savage aristocracy but to salvage it, but he must do the first if he is to cause the second, and he thus furiously exhorts the aristocracy to turn from its leisure and frivolity to take up its time-honored position of leadership. Tithonus, enduring an existence that is worse than annihilation, cannot get existed in the universe (like so many Tennysonian speakers), but he looks to men who, due to their labor, "happily" can. Tiresias also seeks to get existed in the universe, which is to say to find a use for himself. He considers himself invisible and inaudible, and his dramatic monologue imagines how he might contrive to be both seen and heard.

By the mid-nineteenth century, according to Mandler, "the denomination of 'whig' had taken on a narrow and largely pejorative connotation. Socially, it evoked images of the upper reaches of high society.... Politically, it conveyed a high-minded idealism and good intentions dissipated by dreamy impracticality and amateurish execution." The term conveyed also to its opponents "a deliberate coloration of anachronism" and a "mid-Victorian caricature of cliquish irresponsibility."[13] In his 1869 *Culture and Anarchy*, Matthew Arnold refers to this incompetence, citing the aristocracy's "helplessness" in handling "our perturbed social condition." He makes much of the inherited traits of the aristocracy (whom he labels "Barbarians"), noting archly "the vigour, good looks, and fine complexion which they acquired and perpetuated in their families." But Arnold hardly celebrates these inherited external traits, seeing in them a corresponding weakness in qualities of intellect or sense. He observes in the aristocracy an inflexibility, even an immobility, castigating "their want of sense for the flux of things, for the inevitable transitoriness of all human institutions." They are left, he says, "bewildered and helpless" in times of change and expansion. The aristocracy is both confused by and resistant to change because they cannot understand it, due to the group's "impenetrability, its high spirit, its power of haughty resistance."[14]

According to Arnold, the inability of the aristocracy to apprehend, let alone welcome, change is a mark of a larger cognitive lack; he notes of aristocrats that they are "by the very nature of things inaccessible to ideas, unapt to see how the world is going." And it is precisely their ignorance, a kind of congenital stupidity, that Arnold sees as most characteristic of this class, not so much weakening its members as securing them more fully and easily to their positions. Unlike members of groups that are necessarily compelled, that is to say, goaded on by "powers of industry, powers of intelligence," "the serenity of aristocracies...appears to come from their never having had any ideas to trouble them."[15]

Arnold's opinion, expressed openly in letters and more subtly in his public writings, that Tennyson also was "impenetrable to ideas" is well known, and *Culture and Anarchy* identifies Tennyson as specifically representative of the aristocracy, or Barbarians. Arnold derides those who seek the political favor of aristocrats by saying "all the smooth things that can be said of them," and this "smooth" and reassuring rhetoric leads him to the poet laureate: "With Mr. Tennyson, they celebrate 'the great broad-shouldered genial Englishman,' with his 'sense of duty,' his 'reverence for the laws,' and his 'patient force,' who saves us from the 'revolts, republics, revolutions, most no graver than a schoolboy's barring out,' which upset other and less broad-shouldered nations."[16] The snippets of quotation are drawn from the conclusion of Tennyson's *The Princess*, which begins and ends with a description of a summer day when "Sir Walter Vivian" opened his "broad lawns" (Prologue, 2) to his tenants and the neighborhood for a kind of science fair of the Mechanics Institute. The poem's narrator is visiting the estate as a college friend of "the son / A Walter too." In the opening lines of the poem the narrator describes the contents of the house, with special attention to objects drawn from "every clime and age" as well as the "arms and armour" of the ancient Vivian forefathers (Prologue, 7–8, 16, 24). Sir Vivian himself, called "A great broad-shouldered genial Englishman" (his expanse of chest apparently mirroring his expanse of lawn), is seen among the grateful crowd and praised for his generosity in giving up his park several times a year "To let the people breathe" (Conclusion, 85, 104). Arnold's other slips of quotation are drawn from the words of another houseguest, who disdains the "blind hysterics" of the French Revolution and extols a Britain in which "the rulers and the ruled" enjoy "Some sense of duty,... / Some reverence for the laws ourselves have made, / Some patient force to change them when we will" (Conclusion, 54–56).

Arnold chooses to ignore, however, the fact that it is not Tennyson who speaks these words, nor the narrator who might be understood to represent the poet, but another college friend, "The Tory member's elder son" (50). While the ideals of reverence, duty, and patient movement toward change were certainly also held by the poet, it is useful to bear in mind the dramatic context of this poem's representation of the British ruling classes. G. K. Chesterton also reads this character's lines as directly representing the views of the poet himself and also takes this to show Tennyson's cognitive shortcomings, in an argument that sees Tennyson's poetry as adversely affected by his political views. Chesterton marvels, regarding Victorian poets generally, over the "abrupt abyss of the things they do not know" and takes Tennyson in particular to task for his views on democracy, views engaged directly in his dramatic monologues. Chesterton claims, "We feel it *is* a disgrace to a man like Tennyson when he talks of the French revolutions, the huge crusades that had recreated the whole of his civilization, as being 'no graver than a schoolboy's barring out.'" Chesterton hears in Tennyson an antidemocratic strain, but he locates its source less in political ideology than in mental ineptitude. The galling issue for him is not Tennyson's view of the French Revolution (whose wisdom the poet did indeed question, as an ideological heir to Burke and smoking companion of Carlyle) but the impression he has that Tennyson has no cognitive hold on its significance, dismissing that momentous event as a schoolyard scuffle. When writing of political matters, according to Chesterton, Tennyson "quite literally did not know one word of what he was talking about."[17] Tennyson's perceived intellectual deficiencies are allied to his perceived political stances, but I would stress here the way these are seen as attributes of a class that Tennyson's "smooth" words (Arnold's term) are taken to represent. By this logic, Tennyson is representative of the aristocracy because he is as impervious to understanding as it is and also as resistant to any notion of social transformation, less because of considered conservatism than because of a kind of imbecility.

"They keep no aristocratic state, apart from the sentiments of society at large; they speak to the hearts of all": so Arthur Henry Hallam wrote of Shakespeare, Dante, and Homer in his review essay on Tennyson. He attributes their accessibility less to qualities in their work than in their historical periods; each wrote, he argues, in "a more propitious era of a nation's literary development." "Since that day," he acknowledges, "we have undergone a period of degradation" (*Writings*, 189). Anticipating the varied and not altogether enthusiastic reception that would greet Tennyson's work, and reassuring his friend and any reader of the unimportance of popular success, Hallam looks to the poets of sensation whom he so admires and asks, "How should they be popular, whose senses told them a richer and ampler tale than most men could understand, and who constantly expressed, because they constantly felt, sentiments of exquisite pleasure or pain, which most men were not permitted to experience?" The very intensity of their sensations is necessarily incompatible with popular success, let alone comprehension; such poets are divided from others by "their mission as artists, which they possess by rare and exclusive privilege." Recognizing that this "rare and exclusive privilege" enjoyed by poets might well exclude readers, Hallam continues, "But it may be asked, does not this line of argument prove too much? Does it not prove that there is a barrier between these poets and all other persons?" The "decent regulated pre-eminence, some preference . . . given to birth" that Burke saw as appropriate to the civic sphere applies also, apparently, to the aesthetic one. Hallam assures his reader, "Undoubtedly the true poet addresses himself, in all his conceptions, to the common nature of us all," But he reminds us that to follow the poet's compositional "law of association," the processes of the poet's "complex emotions," is not for everyone to attempt; to do so "requires exertion" which is "not willingly made by the large majority of readers" (*Writings*, 186–87, 188).

Not only are the poets of sensation an exclusive assemblage; so too are their readers, since the exertion or labor required by the poems will bar the less willing or able from joining their privileged ranks. This notion of indolence and even incapacity came to be attached critically, however, not to a mass of inadequate readers, but to the poet himself. The languorous lines of his poetry seemed to announce the torpor of the poet. Chesterton called Tennyson a "poet of beauty and a certain magnificent idleness";[18] Thomas and Jane Carlyle called him downright lazy. In an 1845 letter to her husband, Jane Carlyle refers to Tennyson exhibiting "his normal state of indolence," and Thomas Carlyle in an 1846 letter exclaimed of the poet, "Surely no man has a right to be so lazy in this world;—and none that is so lazy will ever make much way in it, I think!" Carlyle wrote of Tennyson to Emerson in 1847, "He wants a *task*; and, alas, that of spinning rhymes, and naming it 'Art' and 'high Art,' in a time like ours, will never furnish him.["19] Tennyson's work habits, which were inarguably productive if also idiosyncratic, are not especially relevant here, because to some degree the Carlyles' impressions were founded less, ultimately, on their observations of a friend who did appear shiftless in the years they first knew him than on a conception of poetry itself as trifling and inutile. Having heard a version of Carlyle's complaint, Tennyson claimed, credibly, never to have uttered such terms as "Art" or "high Art." Carlyle's words appear again in his later essay "Shooting Niagara: And After?" (1867), which also extols the superior qualifications of the upper classes to lead: "'Art,' 'High Art' &c. are very fine and ornamental, but only to persons sitting at their ease: to persons still wrestling with deadly chaos, and still fighting for dubious existence, they are a mockery rather."[20] The pursuit of Art is a trivial pastime for the idle, he asserts, an interest that in present circumstances is not merely useless, but actually a dangerous diversion. In a letter to Lady Harriet Baring that includes a kind of book report, describing and assessing a number of recent publications, Carlyle gives her a brief description of *The Princess*, published the preceding month (December 1847), that sounds like a characterization of the poet rather than the poems: "*Alfred Tennyson* very gorgeous, fervid, luxuriant, but indolent, somnolent, almost imbecile."[21]

Benjamin Jowett declared in a late recollection of Tennyson, "He ought always to have lived among gentlemen only." Jowett does not define his terms, although it is possible to assume he meant by "gentlemen" men of honor and probity. It is impossible not to hear, nevertheless, also an assignment of Tennyson to the upper classes, especially because in these brief notes he twice uses the phrase "high-bred". [22] This is a view that attaches itself to influential mid- and late Victorian studies of the poet such as Hippolyte Taines's *A History of English Literature*, which ends with a notorious comparison of Tennyson to the French poet Alfred de Musset: "De Musset, in this wretched abode of filth and misery, rose higher. From the heights of his doubt and despair, he saw the infinite." Taine describes English country-house life at length, depicting a world of serene prosperity and lovely views, and demands, "Does any poet suit such a society better than Tennyson?" In arguing that Tennyson is a poet of leisure and luxury for the moneyed upper classes, Taine explains that his poetry "seems made expressly for these wealthy, cultivated, free business men, heirs of the ancient nobility, new leaders of a new England. It is part of their luxury as well as of their morality; it is an eloquent confirmation of their principles, and a precious article of their drawing-room furniture."[23]

In an 1875 review of Tennyson's plays, Henry James describes himself and others having "been so struck...with M. Taine's remarkable portrait of the poet" that "every one...is rather shy of making an explicit, or even a serious profession of admiration." James accedes to Taine's characterization, noting in Tennyson his "exquisite imagery, his refinement, his literary tone, his aroma of English lawns and English libraries," but he suggests that readers succumb to the poems' implicit invitations to untroubled leisure and "give himself up to idle enjoyment."[24] F. T. Palgrave reports that Taine had asked him (before Tennyson became poet laureate and settled into marriage and a fixed address) "whether Mr. Tennyson in his youth had not been given to luxurious living, and surrounded by things of costly beauty." Palgrave, having himself "lately visited [Tennyson] in the Camden Town Road second-floor lodgings" where he then lived, informed Taine of Tennyson's childhood in a rural parsonage and limited means in college. Palgrave asked what had given Taine so different an impression of the poet's financial standing, and Taine said he had gathered it from his "early poems" (quoted in *Memoir*, 2:497). Tennyson's poetry, in its ornate, luxurious style, seems to have classed the poet as luxuriant, idle, removed from the cares and what Carlyle calls the "chaos" of his time.

Referring to Farringford, one of the laureate's two homes, Taine writes, "We think of [the poet], away there in the Isle of Wight," and imagines, "How happy he is amongst his fine books, his friends, his honeysuckles, his roses!"[25] Tennyson would not have disagreed; as he observed to William Allingham, "The fine thing would be to have a good hereditary estate and a love of literature."[26] But Tennyson's property was not hereditary; Farringford and Aldworth (built in Surrey in the late 1860s) were both acquired through the poet's income from his publications. Tennyson's life had been troubled by problems with inheritance, as his father, an eldest son, had been passed over (and, his family felt, thus ruined psychologically as well as financially) in favor of his younger brother Charles, who inherited the majority of Tennyson's grandfather's estate. In his notes of recollection Jowett observed of Tennyson, "He mastered circumstances, but he was also partly mastered by them, e.g. the old calamity of the disinheritance of his father."[27] Tennyson's grandfather survives in Tennyson lore by way of this anecdote: when his wife died in 1825, he handed the adolescent Alfred ten shillings to write an elegy and pronounced, "There, that is the first money you have ever earned by your poetry, and, take my word for it, it will be the last."[28] Considering the livelihood, not to mention the stature, Tennyson acquired from his poetry, these shillings, with their incitement to labor, were worth more than the inheritance. The poet did come to preside over extensive lawns and libraries and to accept a hereditary lordship, but these were earned by his work, and works; as the poet's wife put it in her admonitory gloss on Tennyson's "Amphion," "Genius must not deem itself exempt from labor."

TITHONUS AND TROJAN ARISTOCRACY

In a review of Tennyson's drama that does not encourage the poet to continue to produce it, Henry James turns from what he feels Tennyson does not do well to what he feels he does. Quoting the last verse paragraph of "Tithonus," James surrenders himself to "the magic of such a passage as this":

In these beautiful lines from "Tithonus" there is a purity of tone, an inspiration, a something sublime and exquisite, which is easily within the compass of Mr. Tennyson's usual manner at its highest, but which is not easily achieved by any really dramatic verse. It is poised and stationary, like a bird whose wings have borne him high, but the beauty of whose movement is less in great ethereal sweeps and circles than in the way he hangs motionless in the blue air, with only a vague tremor of his pinions.

James sees "Tithonus" as tremulously still, immobile but for the nearly undetectable flutter of its wings. He explains that this inaction is a function not only of the poem's plot but of its phrasing or prosody: "Even if the idea with Tennyson were more largely dramatic than it usually is, the immobility, as we must call it, of his phrase would always defeat the dramatic intention."[29] Many readers have similarly noted what Ricks calls an "eternal immobility" in this speaker.[30] Daniel Harris in his monograph on "Tithonus" considers him "paralyzed in indecision," "lamenting his miserable state, but lacking the tragic will power to change or accept it."[31]

Later in the review, James quotes from a description of a sunrise in *Enoch Arden* and characterizes the movement of the lines as "taking place in that measured, majestic fashion which, at any given moment, seems identical with permanence." Tennyson's majestic measure not only appears permanent in itself, but can seem immobilizing, inhibiting the kind of transformative action on which drama depends. James concludes, "When he wishes to represent movement, the phrase always seems to me to pause and slowly pivot upon itself, or at most to move backward."[32] The poet's language turns on itself and can offer no forward momentum to its audience. In this tendency to limited mobility, or even retrogression, we might begin to see Tithonus as representative of the aristocracy, characterized by Arnold as unable to comprehend or join the "flux of things." In his infinite dissolution, Tithonus appears in some sense to be a figure of Whig nightmare. If Whiggery assumes constant steady measured progress, however slow, toward an ideal condition, then Tithonus's endless decomposition exhibits its terrifying antithesis, figuring as it does an incremental but inexorable decline into ever worsening states.

But in the stately and magisterial dramatic monologue that James describes so beautifully, Tithonus is, I would agree with Herbert Tucker, "bent...upon decisive change." He is specifically changing position in the course of the monologue, by way of the monologue. Tennyson's monologue inserts itself into the *Homeric Hymn* on which "Tithonus" is based at precisely the moment in the narrative when Tithonus is about to be moved by Aurora. His demand to her, "hold me not forever," is an attempt to take control of his own movements, to transform, in Tucker's phrase, "his withering into a whither-ing."[33] He is also changing form—his previous rapturous pleasure through identification with Aurora, as we have seen, but also his present ambition. I have described Tithonus's metaphoric transformation, his ambitious translation into a discursive mode consistently labeled "beautiful." But we must now turn to the familiar shape that Tennyson himself stated that Tithonus is changed into, namely, the grasshopper, sometimes called by Tennyson the cicada or cicala. Although these are different insects, the words seem for Tennyson to have been roughly interchangeable, a confusion less etymological than entomological.[34] In his editorial notes to this poem in the Eversley edition, Tennyson recounts that Tithonus was "beloved by Aurora, who gave him eternal life but not eternal youth. He grew old and infirm, and as he could not die, according to the legend, was turned into a grasshopper" (2:340). Describing this alteration as a "miraculous but unmagnificent diminution," "verging on the kindly ludicrous," Ricks calls this transformation "perplexing." Looking to the grasshopper and then to the "exquisite" (as James terms them) final lines of the monologue, he justly asks, "How can we accommodate such an outcome to such an ending?"[35] In this section we shall take this creature into hand, to see why Tennyson could be so definitive in stating, in the flat clarity of a gloss that does seem inadequate, even antithetical, to so breathtaking a poem, that this is the end to which his majestic speaker moves. Given Tennyson's resistance to explicating his work, we might understand the grasshopper as in some sense diversionary, but transmogrification into this insect, as we shall see when examining its rich literary history, constitutes an extraordinarily fitting end point for this speaker. Before pursuing the elusive figure of the grasshopper, however, we shall look toward the dark earth and to the mortals that Tithonus claims he seeks now to resemble, however unlikely the likeness—because Tithonus's monologue is finally less a study of his stasis than his status.

Trojan Oratory

Analyzing Homeric oratory, Gladstone cites a scene from book 8 of Homer's *Odyssey* in which Ulysses observes that one man might have little physical beauty but be gifted in speech, while another man may possess beauty like an immortal, but his "comeliness [is] not crowned with eloquence" (8:178, trans. Pope). Gladstone calls this the "most remarkable speech given in the Odyssey" and employs this scene to support his claim that "Homer makes beauty a title to distinguished notice on behalf of those who have no other claim," which rings as a dismissal of a chief Trojan characteristic (*SH*, 3:104, 405). Ulysses himself uses the distinction to hurl an insult at the handsome young man to whom he has described this dichotomy: "In outward show Heaven gives thee to excel, / But Heaven denies the praise of thinking well" (8:182–83, trans. Pope). Tithonus would appear to answer to this description: inspired as he was by his own beauty, he woefully, even stupidly misconceived himself and the language of his request to the gods. I have argued that Tithonus is more deliberate, and deliberative, in his speaking, and in what follows I pursue this claim more closely. At the end of the previous chapter we began to see how Tithonus shifts his exceptional beauty from his body to the body of his monologue, but we need now to attend more fully to his oratorical eloquence both in its origins and its effects.

Tithonus's mode of speech takes a measure of its majesty from the speaker's inbred sense of sovereignty, as his dramatic monologue at once records and constitutes an example of his aristocratic discursive mode. In this section, I consider the terms of his demand for immortality, reviewed in the monologue, and in the next section I turn to his subsequent demand, by way of the monologue, for a change of position. In his call for immortality and his call for release (both of which he attains), Tithonus again manifests not only personal but national traits. We have remarked in this character, and in the Trojan royal family more generally, the possession of a hauteur closely associated with the high elevation of Troy's walls and towers. (Laomedon's cozening of the gods who raised those walls was itself a sign of this family's lofty presumption.) Victorians tended to see modes of discourse as expressive of national character types (a habit of mind hardly exclusive to them). For a near example, we might look to Taine, who states in the introduction of his compendious *History of English Literature*, "I intend to write the history of a literature, and to seek in it for the psychology of a people."[36] Taine was far from singular in pursuing an understanding of national character through discursive history and practices; his methodology is itself indebted to the "new philology" transported from Germany and propounded by Tennyson's tutors and peers at Trinity College.[37]

Gladstone took an unequivocal position in his comparisons of Greek and Trojan traits, based on his reading of Homer as an unmediated historical source. He elaborates on these differences in his three-volume 1858 *Studies on Homer and the Homeric Age*, which Tennyson owned, having been gifted with it in the year of its publication. Gladstone insists throughout that the Greeks have "superior intelligence" and are "more masculine" than the "feeble" Trojans, who, being "Asiatic rather than European," are "given to the vices of sensuality and falsehood" (*SH*, 3:245, 206). He specifies that the weaknesses of the Trojans were not only "moral" but also "political," contending, "The Trojan race had a less developed capacity for political organization" and lacked "political order." "There was no balance of forces in the Trojan polity," he pronounces, "less security against precipitate action, more liability to high-handed insolence and oppression of the people, and, on the other hand, ... likewise in all likelihood to revolutionary change" (*SH*, 3:206, 217, 242). His description not only employs Homeric epic to articulate contemporary racial stereotypes, but it encapsulates Whig fears of either unrestrained despotic power ("insolence and oppression of the people") or unrestrained demotic power ("revolutionary change"). Tennyson's Tithonus and Tiresias articulate this dread of vulnerability either to tyranny or to mob rule (especially the latter, who addresses these opposing but complementary threats directly).

Gladstone saw the foundations of sound government as based in the practice of political oratory, and he claims that Homer wanted to "draw a very marked distinction" between Trojans and Greeks "in regard to the use of that powerful engine of oratory." He concedes that Trojan government was "not an absolute despotism": it "appears that monarchy was limited in Troy, as it was in Greece, and that public affairs were conducted in assemblies of the people." But Greek and Trojan polity nevertheless differed markedly in several aspects, not the least of which was that the Greeks "employed oratory as a main instrument of government; the Trojans did not" (SH, 3:234). "Their kings were followed with a more servile reverence by the people," he maintains, discounting the need for oratorical efforts; "that authority was of more avail, apart from rational persuasion" (SH, 3:206). After a summary that has already provided a flagrantly biased account of the differences he perceives, he concludes, "Nowhere, in short, among the Trojans have we any example, I do not say of multiplied or lengthened speeches, but of real reasoning and deliberation in the conduct of business" (SH, 3:240). Gladstone was himself renowned for the number and prolixity of his oratorical performances, but he claims here not to expect similar verbal stamina, only to require "real reasoning and deliberation" and efforts of "rational persuasion." While Gladstone is forwarding a highly biased reading, Hilary Mackie also argues that the Trojans have a distinctive manner of speaking. She hears Trojan forms of speech as more "poetic": "Trojans generally prefer words over warfare, and poetry to fighting."[38]

Describing "Tithonus," Henry James evokes not only a poem but a speaker suspended "motionless in the blue air, with only a vague tremor of his pinions," and this monologist might therefore be expected to manifest the inefficacious discursive febrility that Gladstone hears as common to the Trojans. Tithonus does describe himself as quivering, made to tremble over a definitive statement that he quotes back to Aurora. His monologic speech at this moment strains to accommodate the vibrations of other voices:

> Why wilt thou ever scare me with thy tears
> And make me tremble lest a saying learnt,
> In days far-off, on that dark earth, be true?
> "The Gods themselves cannot recall their gifts." (46–49)

But to which gifts does he refer? In context he is of course referring to his immortality. But Tithonus has received several gifts, which were bestowed upon him, as gifts ostensibly are, without demand for recompense: the gift of immortality that he would now return, but also a gift that made possible that later beneficence, namely, his beauty. When the speaker looks to "that dark world where I was born" (33) and to "that dark earth" where "in days far off" he heard the answer that Aurora now refuses to articulate, his gesturing to the city of Troy is as pointed as that of Ulysses in his monologue. And although Tithonus might have learned this "saying" from many sources, at one point a version of it is spoken in the *Iliad* by Paris to Hector, in an exchange that might have interested Tithonus. After agreeing to meet with Menelaus in direct combat, Paris reminds his scornful brother, who has mocked his beauty, that his "charms" (3:93, trans. Pope), bestowed upon him by the gods, can neither be demanded nor escaped: "Never to be cast away are the gifts of the gods, magnificent, / which they give of their own will, no man can have them for wanting them" (3:65–66, trans. Lattimore).

As we know from the example of Cassandra, Tithonus's niece, Apollo could not revoke his gift of prophecy after she refused him her favors; according to Keightley's 1831 *Mythology of Ancient Greece and Italy*, "the indignant deity" was "unable to recall what he had bestowed," though he was able to render the gift "useless."[39] In a sense, though, the gift of beauty that Tithonus so enjoyed has been rescinded, in what he may faintly hope can be a precedent in his disburdening himself of the necessarily eternal gift of immortality. The gift of beauty is a transient one, however, as Lord Henry informs Dorian Gray (just after assuring him that his beauty bestows sovereignty): "Yes, Mr. Gray, the gods have been good to you. But what the gods give they quickly take away. . . . Every month as it wanes brings you nearer to something dreadful. Time is jealous of you, and wars against your lilies and your roses. You will become sallow, and hollow-cheeked, and dull-eyed. You will suffer horribly."[40] But can the immortality of Tithonus, now suffering horribly, finally be considered a gift? I would argue that, in Tennyson's version of the myth, it was not so much bestowed upon him voluntarily by the gods (or, more specifically, by Aurora) "of their own will" but granted as an allowance, perhaps even a concession. Although Tithonus appears with fear and trembling to respect the dictum he quotes, his very predicament, as Tennyson represents it, is based on his defiance of it. His autocratic demand for the gift of immortality goes beyond the great gift he had already received, that of his beauty. The aristocrat is like a child, William Empson observed: "It is his business to make claims in advance of his immediate personal merits."[41]

Tithonus actively desired the immortality he now suffers; in spite of claims of being "chosen," and indeed the larger dramatization of his erotic passivity that follows in his monologue, he has directly orchestrated his present condition. The trajectory he posits, from being chosen to making a choice, is important for us to chart carefully, because he moves directly from exulting in his likeness to a god ("none other than a God!") to speaking like one ("Give me"). Although the goddess Aurora selects and seduces him, according to his monologue she bears responsibility neither for the speaker's immortality nor for his correspondent ugliness, and in this aspect of the story Tennyson deviates radically from his primary source, the *Homeric Hymn to Aphrodite*, to which in other regards he adheres fairly precisely. Explaining to her lover Anchises why she will not grant him immortality, Aphrodite turns from the example of Ganymede to that of Tithonus, and in Tennyson's source, the colossal error in the phrasing of the request is made by

Aurora (Eos). She tells Anchises, "So also golden-throned Eos rapt away Tithonus who was of your race and like the deathless gods. And she went to ask the dark-clouded Son of Cronos that he should be deathless and live eternally; and Zeus bowed his head to her prayer and fulfilled her desire. Too simple was queenly Eos: she thought not in her heart to ask youth for him and to strip him of the slough of deadly age."[42] In the *Homeric Hymn*, not only does she make the request alone, to fulfill "her desire," but she is explicitly chided for her error: "too simple was queenly Eos."

Tennyson, however, gives Tithonus full responsibility for his present predicament; in his monologue, the speaker reminds Aurora, "I asked thee, 'Give me immortality.'"[43] The speaker characterizes his statement as a request ("I asked"), but the words he quotes himself as having said sound more like a command. And the monologue continues to employ this imperative mode: "Let me go: take back thy gift"; "Release me, restore me to the ground." As I have argued, I do not hold with the widespread critical interpretation regarding Tennyson's Tithonus, by which he has, through a semantic accident, said one thing but meant another. Certainly, an irony of the monologist's fate consists in his requesting "Give me immortality" when he might more judiciously have said Give me eternal youth. But his actual statement, like Paris's judgment on Mount Ida, was deliberate and intentional— although both pronouncements may themselves point to what Arnold called the high-spirited impenetrability of aristocrats. Perhaps Aurora recognizes the dark humor of this directive, granting it "with a smile" (though the affect of her expression is as difficult for us to read as for Tithonus).[44] Tithonus has not arrived at this impasse because of a slip of the tongue; he has dictated this fate. As is the case with every instance of the dramatic monologue, this is a form in which there are no rhetorical accidents. There are self-exposures, whether comical or consequential, but even these revelations are part of the complex manipulations by speakers of their auditors. Here, Tithonus states outright his ambition for immortality as an aim in itself. Immortality is the state that he sought above all the other appurtenances of being godlike, the single term to which he not unreasonably reduced the entire condition of divinity.

In demanding "Give me immortality," Tithonus is seceding from the human community. It is a command that is profound in its separation and elevation of the pleasures of a private self, and as such a full abnegation of the "kindly race of men," and more particularly of his society; we hear it confirmed in his lament "Me only." Such presumption and sense of superiority, even arrogance, tradition holds as a characteristic trait of Tithonus, and Tennyson's representation of his general condescension is as nuanced as it is accurate. Tithonus makes an appearance in the *Iliad* prior to his listing in the genealogical record Aeneas recites for Achilles in book 20. At the beginning of book 11, Tithonus is still the beautiful lover of the dawn; the morning begins when she rises out of his bed. Andrew Lang's late Victorian prose translation renders the opening line, "Now dawn arose from her couch beside proud Tithonus." Tithonus's pride (Lattimore's translation has "haughty") seems inextricable from the proximity of his celestial lover; his hauteur seems at once a condition and a result of his erotic elevation. In Tennyson his contumelious character shows itself less in the impetuosity of the demand than in its imperiousness, in the extraordinary presumption of commanding an immortal, "Give me." Such autocratic expectation may be a privilege that attends his beauty; as Linda Dowling puts it, "high beauty" can endow "its possessor with an overweening sense of personal worth, authorizing in turn a demand for erotic servility from others."[45]

In his comparison of Greek and Trojan polity, Gladstone asks "whether the Trojans, like the Greeks, employed eloquence, detailed argument as furnishing, [with] the other parts of oratory, a main instrument of government." His definition of "eloquence" is instructive, since again he stresses an ideal relation between rational persuasion ("detailed argument"), public speaking, and governance. His claim that the Trojan assemblies were not deliberative bodies will not surprise us: "I think it plain, that the decisions of [Trojan] Assemblies were governed rather by simple authority." Decisions were made not as a result of "suasive speech" but by the general submission to "the simple declarations, of persons of weight" (*SH*, 3:239). In his monologue, Tithonus speaks at crucial points in the customary declarations of an aristocrat, one who early asserted and still holds a sense of sovereignty, secure in the assumption that his words or orders can cause immediate actions or effects. But in his linguistic habits, at once impetuous and imperious, eschewing suasive speech in favor of declaratives that require what Gladstone called the "servility" of auditors, Tithonus also sounds like none other than a god.

Imperiousness is a discursive mode associated with the upper classes, but it is also a quality of divinity. Tithonus therefore seems to himself "none other than a god" not only because of his beauty but also because of his indifference. He is like a wealthy man who cares not how he gives, or takes. To be deathless is perforce to be removed from the mire of mortal life, and for Tithonus to seek such a state is to seek to sever all connections to the human community. The goddess speaking in Tennyson's dramatic monologue "Demeter and Persephone" deplores humankind's vulnerability to "the thunderbolt, ... / the plague, the famine" (131–32). In this, she returns to a catalogue from decades earlier in "The Lotos-Eaters," in which the mariners' enumeration of what the gods bear smiling (159, 162) witness to ("Clanging fights, and flaming towns, and sinking ships, and praying hands" [161]) might be seen to summarize in one line the action of Homeric epic. His ambition for permanent removal to a realm of erotic pleasure also reflects an aesthetic impulse, although in Tennyson's poetry there is no division between aesthetic and political desire.

The gods of the Lotos-Eaters desire to "lie beside their nectar" (156), served presumably by the beautiful cupbearer Ganymede. The loss of Persephone poisons just such pleasures for Demeter, who says of her divine peers, "Their nectar smacked of hemlock on the lips, / Their rich ambrosia tasted aconite" (102–3). Demeter comes to find more noble "man, that only lives and loves an hour" (104), and Tithonus here claims kinship with men whose lives are as abbreviated as their loves, in an address to the lover who has infinitely prolonged his life sentence. Tithonus's godlike indifference to human suffering is, for a refugee from Troy's civic strife no less than from the tillers in its fields, political in its implications. Referring to the "idle aristocracy," Carlyle marveled, "To sit idle, aloft, like living statues, like absurd Epicurus'-gods, in pampered isolation, in exclusion from the glorious fateful battlefield of this God's-World: it is a poor life for a man." For Carlyle, the state of being a man, in terms both of masculinity and of humanity, is predicated on labor.[46]

Differing strikingly from such Trojan heroes as Hector and Aeneas, Tithonus has abnegated his civic and communal responsibilities, an abandonment of his culture's toil and turmoil of which his dramatic monologue is well aware. As Aphrodite reminds Anchises in the *Homeric Hymn* that is Tennyson's primary source, "Jupiter / Your Gold-lockt Ganymedes did transfer / (In rapture farr from men's depressed fates)" ("A Hymne to Venus," 336–38, trans. Chapman). Tithonus's rapture, like that of his precursor Ganymede, ostensibly removed him from "men's depressed fates," but it is a lowering into those depths that he now seeks.

In his nostalgia at the beginning and end of his monologue for mortality and its victims, Tithonus appears to regret his peremptory demand for removal from his kind. He issues further dictatorial statements whose tone echoes the imperative that brought him to this state: "Let me go: take back thy gift" (27), each postulate of which is more challenging than the last. But then he pauses to marvel at his own audacity. Let us look again, in this different context, at the question he poses to his auditor and himself:

> Why should a man desire in any way
> To vary from the kindly race of men,
> Or pass beyond the goal of ordinance
> Where all should pause, as is most meet for all? (28–31)

In describing what he has varied, and indeed isolated himself from, he uses the phrase "kindly race of men," which stands as a triple redundancy. "Kind," "race," and "men" are all phylogenetic in their significance, and all point to the speaker's sense (shared with other Tennysonian speakers, including Simeon, Ulysses, and Tiresias) that the human species is largely an indistinct mass. Surely the ambition of any of these monologists is to vary widely from this kind. But while his question has broad implications for the genre as a whole, it is also one that is highly specific to this speaker's caste and situation, as "the aristocrat's continual need," in the words of one historian of the upper classes, "is to distinguish himself from other social groups."[47] It is a hallmark of Tithonus's kind that they do tend to vary from humankind; their extreme beauty (which Gladstone labeled a kind of entailment), not less than their hierarchical position, puts them at variance.

Tennyson defined "goal of ordinance" in his Eversley edition notes as an "appointed limit" (2:340), underscoring the municipal cast of the phrase, since the term "ordinance" refers to a regulation or established custom. Tithonus rebels against such edicts; for him any border offers less demarcation than detention. We saw in chapter 5 that he represents his relationship with Aurora as being one without appointed limits or boundaries; in their merging, he claims, he was circumfused, not circumscribed. More entirely removed from any social organization than any other speaker Tennyson or Browning conceived (even St. Simeon Stylites seeks the company of the saved, and Browning's Childe Roland seeks his blasted brother knights), Tithonus voices most acutely the dilemma of an individual straining against limits that seem arbitrary or inexplicable. The defiance of limits is both the cause and the effect of his demand "Give me immortality." While his command marks his capacity for sensual abandon, it also typifies his aristocratic lineage, in what Arnold calls its "pride, defiance, turn for resistance."[48] In "Democracy" (1861), an essay published the year after "Tithonus" first saw print, Arnold argues that the hereditary aristocracy has shown itself unable to meet demands of increasingly equal representation, and muses about how society might be sustained without a hereditary upper class. In considering the ways in which the aristocracy may not be able to sustain itself as democracy advances, Arnold observes, "They have a temper of independence, and a habit of uncontrolled action, which makes them impatient of encountering…the machinery and regulations of a superior and peremptory power."[49] Tithonus's resistance to a machinery of higher power resembles the historical Whig resistance to monarchical power: according to James Boswell, Samuel Johnson said, "The first Whig was the Devil," which his chronicler took to mean, "He was the first who resisted power."[50] But in his resistance Tithonus seeks to sustain his own elevated hierarchical position, at variance from the kindly race of lesser men.

At the end of his monologue Tithonus does not consider any power that he, or even the gods, might hold, but rather the power he now sees as possessed by mortal men. In gesturing toward "the homes / Of happy men that have the power to die, / And grassy barrows of the happier dead" (68–71), he acknowledges that for him death has long been conceived as a power struggle. In asking Aurora how his nature can longer mix with hers, Tithonus appears to be shifting his allegiances, disavowing the divine mixing that marked their union and committing himself to what he calls in "Tithon" his own "mortal heart." In this he is staking out a greater difference between mortals and the gods than the latter's immortality, which he now shares. Rather, he contrasts having a heart with the heartlessness and indifference that can characterize the relation of the gods to humankind. With this question of the incompatibility of their elemental natures, he returns to the issue of his kind, but he does not leave the discursive realm of troubling similitude. As a man, he saw himself as none other than a god; as an immortal, he now intimates his abiding humanity, seeking for his mortal heart the human community he has spurned. He seeks like humans to become *humus*, earth in earth, a resemblance "Tithon" made still clearer in its version of the third line: "Man comes and tills the earth and lies beneath." And yet in yearning toward "happy men" and the "happier dead" he signals an ongoing unwillingness to characterize rightly the kindly race he earlier abandoned. The dim fields and residences he looks to mark the ruination of the towers whose erection he witnessed, while in the case of his immediate family, the barrows of the dead are not as restful as he suggests. The graves of his brother Priam and nephew Paris are trespassed upon and eternally dishonored, by the will of the gods. According to one of Horace's odes for which we have Tennyson's childhood translation, Juno promises to let Rome flourish "Long as above old Priam's tomb / The roebucks bound and stray, / Long as the lions roar and rave / And hide their whelps within the grave / Of Paris" (3.3:56–60).[51]

Tennyson, as we know, "gave 'Tithonus' the same position as 'Ulysses'" (*Memoir*, 2:70), and these "pendent" monologues unite in their grounding of the self in experiences of Troy: the day of its creation, for Tithonus; the night of its destruction, for Ulysses. Witness to the erection of Troy's song-built towers, Tithonus was witness also presumably to their demolition, and links his own rise and wished-for fall to that of a civilization notorious for both. Like Ulysses, Tithonus is speaking after Ilion's devastation: he is displaced not just from the grassy burrows of men powerful enough to die, but from the city his family ruled. He has cause therefore to mourn an entire culture he has abandoned and outlived. In this he is like Dante's Ulysses, doomed for all eternity to dwell on the subject of a city that is no more, and possibly never was. These two speakers are also united in that in their dramatic monologues each advances a narrative of his former efficacious speech. Although Tithonus is as notorious for having ostensibly misspoken as Ulysses is for skillful oratory, both know that the right words can yield tremendous, even staggering effects. For each, finally, his dramatic monologue is provoked by recognizing the self's occupation of an untenable position, one that the monologue at once explicates and labors to change. These axes of the self for both are temporal and geographical: while each seeks a future beyond the utmost bound of human thought, each is wholly bound to a past that was another country.

Having defined himself, like Ulysses, geographically but also, in his identification with Troy's towers, topographically, Tithonus seeks like his family's resourceful enemy to move from one place and condition to another. He stands as much at a turning point as Ulysses; that speaker beckons at the water's edge, this one straddles "glimmering thresholds." Shivering in Aurora's radiance, Tithonus warms himself at the steam wafting up from below, from fields still dim in spite of the dawn. His is a wholly vaporous world, saturated in moisture as, in a condensation of melancholy, vapors first "weep their burthen to the ground," only to meet the rising steam. All is wet and dark, dripping down from above or wafting up from below. As he has acknowledged, his rash original insistence on immortality cannot be countermanded. He is the victim of a discursive strategy—one based in aristocratic habit—that he himself cannot recall. In this too he is true to type, since the Trojans are devastated by Ulysses' discursive strategy; we recollect that the Trojan horse was introduced into the city not by force but by guile masterminded by Ulysses. Tithonus's linguistic miscalculation (like Paris's) is presumably inconceivable for so calculating a speaker as Ulysses, and yet Tithonus's words here share the potency of Troy's antagonist. This surprising similarity can take us some distance in establishing the goal of the monologue, the reason it is taking place at all, which is always a crucial question for Victorian instances of the genre. Tithonus becomes a monologist because he has already learned that the right combination of words can attain a wide set of effects. His dramatic monologue is a direct response to the imperative nature of his own former speech, which he now quotes in disbelief and yet continues to repeat. If his monologue is to succeed in attaining release for him, however, its task (to borrow from Shelley's *Prometheus Unbound*, which Tennyson acquired while a student at Trinity) is to unsay his own high language. His monologue records his imperatives, but it must also move beyond them, in a discursive transformation from sovereign commands to the persuasive rational discourse Gladstone associates with democratic engagement.

"It is important that nowhere does a sentiment escape the lips of a Trojan chieftain which indicates a consciousness of the political value of oratory," Gladstone states, dismissing the Trojans as lacking not only oratorical skills but a "consciousness" of the "political value" of performances of rational persuasion (*SH*, 3:241). And indeed, Tithonus does not persuade the gods to give him immortality; he demands it of them, in his ongoing confusion regarding his similitude to them. In its continued employment of imperatives, Tithonus's dramatic monologue can sound like a continuation of the autocratic discourse that Gladstone associates with Trojan polity. But we can also hear in Tithonus's monologue certain gifts of persuasion that even Gladstone concedes to the Trojans. These are crucial for him to draw on, since his demands ("Let me go," "Release me") must otherwise sound ineffectual, even pathetic. His "simple declaratives" will not attain for him release; only his labors in the suasive, highly deliberative mode of the dramatic monologue can accomplish that.

Gladstone profusely admires in Homer the orations, which stand for him as "specimens of transcendent eloquence which have never been surpassed," employing "all the resources of the art" (*SH*, 3:107). He argues that eloquence is not only a matter of public speech, but has its place in private conversation also, and his prime example of this is Priam's speech to Achilles at the end of the *Iliad*. Priam has gone to ransom with well-wrought Trojan treasures the body of his dead son from Achilles (who will soon thereafter kill Tithonus's son Memnon). While even

Ulysses' suasive gifts had been unable to sway Achilles (most notably in book 9, when he and others had tried to convince Achilles to rejoin the war), Priam succeeds in moving the slayer of so many of his sons. Although not an instance of "oratory properly so called," according to Gladstone, Priam's words use the arts of persuasion to sound "the depths of pathos," and thus exemplify the "direct instruments of influence on the mind and actions of man" (*SH*, 3:108). Not accustomed to moving assemblies of citizens, according to Gladstone, because not required by Troy's system of governance to do so, Priam nevertheless can persuade a single auditor, in a model that Tithonus might bear in mind as he addresses Aurora. Tennyson's speaker will attain his release from her court by shifting his shape into that of the grasshopper, a fitting transformation that he will have earned by his own discursive labors.

Oratory of the Grasshopper

Tennyson tells us that Tithonus "grew old and infirm, and as he could not die, according to the legend, was turned into a grasshopper." But how to accommodate, as Ricks asks, this monologue's outcome to its ending? How is it possible to imagine Tennyson's magisterial Tithonus transmogrified into a grasshopper? The insect has an august literary history, one that highlights its association not only with song but also with the pleasure-loving indolence and irresponsibility widely identified as aristocratic traits. Yet though one might quickly see the fitness of these associations for Tithonus, we have been exploring a more measured and majestic, indeed infinitely more mature Tithonus. This weightier figure also finds fit representation in the contours of the grasshopper's form and the sound of its thin but insistent voice. The figure of the grasshopper might appear to take Tithonus still further from the world of the kindly race of men, especially his Trojan roots, but taking the form of that insect actually constitutes his surest route home, since we can hear also in his dramatic monologue the civic resonance of this insect's distinctive sound.

In his early lyric "The Grasshopper" (published in 1830 and, after critical drubbing, not reprinted), Tennyson toyed with the legend, and even appears to reject it. The poem forwards a playful refutation of the myth, indicating for us yet again that in Tennyson's early poems lie the seeds of so many of the images and concerns of the dramatic monologues begun in 1833. "No Tithon thou as poets feign," he insists of the insect he describes and addresses, parenthetically castigating the poets: "(Shame fall 'em, / They are deaf and blind)" (5–6). Indeed, the insect would appear to be wholly unlike the speaker of the 1833 "Tithon" or the 1860 "Tithonus." The poem apostrophizes:

> Thou hast no sorrow or tears,
> Thou hast no compt of years,

No withered immortality,
But a short youth sunny and free. (26–29)

Attacking "The Grasshopper," the reviewer Christopher North accused Tennyson of plagiarizing Wordsworth, but he does not mention that poem's resemblance to Keats's sonnet, "On the Grasshopper and the Cricket" (1817).[52] Keats describes a sensuous creature who "takes the lead / In summer luxury, —he has never done / With his delights" (5–7),[53] and Tennyson's insect is also wholly of the summer season (reveling in the "summerwind," "summerplain," "summerhours" [1, 2, 3]), leading a brief life of abandonment to easy pleasure. Keats claims that the insect's giddy song is not inconsistent with idleness: "for when tired out with fun / He rests at ease beneath some pleasant weed" (7–8). For Keats, these insects illustrate that "The poetry of earth is ceasing never" (9). Although what Tennyson celebrates in the grasshopper is its insouciant mortality, he too sees it as "Ever leaping, ever singing" (43).

Depicting the grasshopper as lithe, strong, supple, "in youth and strength complete" (13), Tennyson opposes this creature's effortless power to the physical decrepitude of the "deaf and blind" poets, urging, "Prove their falsehood" (9). And yet the grasshopper is itself a figure for the poet, not only in Tennyson's lyric but also in his Classical, Renaissance, and Romantic sources. Ricks points to a primary source for "The Grasshopper" in Anacreon's Ode 34, which also proclaims this insect's freedom from debility. Tennyson had employed this poet's distinctive meter in "Anacreontics," published along with "A Fragment [Where is that Giant of the Sun]" (in which the figure of Memnon appears) in the October 1830 edition of *The Gem*, and like that poem not reprinted. Having celebrated the grasshopper's joyful presence in his opening apostrophe ("Oh thou, of all creation blest, / Sweet insect!" [1–2]), Anacreon catalogues all those who love its song as a harbinger of summer, and then continues:

The Muses love thy shrilly tone;
Apollo calls thee all his own;
'Twas he who gave that voice to thee,
'Tis he who tunes thy minstrelsy. (19–22)[54]

I have traced Tithonus's complex associations with the song of Apollo; here, the grasshopper's own song is traced to him, as a gift of that god. Anacreon's ode makes clear that in the form of this insect, Tithonus might gain the elusive reward of eternal youth that he did not ask for; the poet praises the insect, "Unworn by age's dim decline, / The fadeless blooms of youth are thine" (23–24). Indeed, it cannot age because it does not inhabit a corporal body, since the grasshopper is fleshless and bloodless, with "not a drop of blood" (29) in its veins. Moore has a tendency in his translation, which met with great success, to bright exclamations ("Melodious insect! child of earth!" [25]), but we can hear in his closing cheer, "Thou seem'st—a little deity!" (32), the sobering conclusion that Anacreon draws, namely, that the grasshopper is like a god. The state of the grasshopper's being "like the gods" in its pleasure-loving propensities is defined here, but so is the state of being loved by the gods: their favor is marked by the gift not only of immortality but of poetry.

Although representing the delights of the natural world, the grasshopper is in its way also a political animal. It is so supreme in its happiness, Anacreon tells it, that even "happiest kings may envy thee!" and yet sufficiently lowly to appeal to peasants, "To whom thy friendly notes are dear" (6, 12). The insect's political ramifications did not go unremarked in Richard Lovelace's poem "The Grasse-Hopper" (1649), written by the Cavalier poet after the execution of King Charles. Don Cameron Allen traces the grasshopper's ancestry not only in Anacreon but Plato, Thucydides, Hesiod, and Homer, and concludes from these various sources that the grasshopper stands as "a sign of the aristocrat, the symbol of the poet singer, and the man in political ill favor."[55] Allen is especially helpful in tracing the tradition of the "aristocratic pretensions" of grasshoppers that play merrily in the summer while the industrious ants prepare for winter.[56] Castigating just such idleness among the Victorian aristocracy, Carlyle asks, "Is there a man who pretends to live luxuriously housed up; screened from all work, from want, danger, hardship, the victory over which is what we name work;—he himself to sit serene...and have all his work and battling done by other men? And such a man calls himself a *noble*-man?"[57] Lovelace's cavalier grasshopper illustrates the moral that Carlyle advances, namely, that the class may be destroyed by its own assumption of easy pleasure. Unprepared for the oncoming winter, the grasshopper is overtaken by it: "Poore verdant foole!" commiserates Lovelace, "and now green Ice!" (17).

But surely the most important of the grasshopper's literary sources for Tennyson's "Tithonus" comes from book 3 of the *Iliad*, from a conversation on the walls of Troy that we have already seen proved controversial for Hallam and Gladstone in their epistolary exchange on the character of Homer's Ulysses. Before Antenor describes Ulysses' oratorical prowess, Homer compares this group of elderly Trojan noblemen to grasshoppers, in a simile that is revealing in terms of both Tithonus's discursive history and Ulysses'. The Trojan elders have gathered by the Skaian gates: "There sat the seniors of the Trojan race / (Old Priam's Chiefs, and most in Priam's grace)" (3:191–92, trans. Pope). Homer then names the aged Trojans, who, to continue with Pope's version:

> Lean'd on the walls, and bask'd before the sun.
> Chiefs, who no more in bloody fights engage,
> But, wise thro' time, and narrative with age,
> In summer-days like grasshoppers rejoice,
> And bloodless race, that send a feeble voice. (3:198–202)

At this moment Helen "approach'd the tower" (3:203), and the men liken her beauty to that of a goddess. Priam calls for her to join them, and as they look across the battlefields, asks her to identify various Greeks. One of these is Ulysses, and it is here that his oratorical skills are recollected by Antenor, in terms I have previously discussed. Ulysses' "great voice," drifting down upon his auditors like flakes of snow, sounds in deep contrast to the sweet delicacy of the Trojan oratorical mode.

Gladstone, whose own oratorical performances now sought the likeness to Homer's Ulysses that he had rejected in his correspondence with Hallam decades earlier, characterizes the similarity of the speech of Troy's elders to chirping grasshoppers as a sign of their "volubility and shrill small thread of voice" (*SH*, 3:105). In terms of Homeric systems of governance, he sees the "aggregation of aged men" as unusual. Gladstone admits that elder statesmen are respected among the Greeks, but maintains that they are not held as the leaders or "ordinary guides": "This grey-headed company, with apparently the principal statesmanship of Troy in their hands, forms a marked difference from Greek manners" (*SH*, 3:235, 236). Describing the old men at the wall, Gladstone characterizes the grasshopper's song, and therefore their oratorical mode, as "a clear trill or thread of voice, not only without any particular idea of length attached to it, but apparently meant to recall a sharp intermittent chirp" (*SH*, 3:241). Speech that is so undefined, sounding in intermittent or unexpected intervals, Gladstone finds disturbing. Priam is associated, he says, with "the imputation of favouring either too many or else too long orations," and is objurgated by Isis for encouraging "indiscriminate speaking" (*SH*, 3:241), speech that is not clearly directed toward some goal or end.

Walter Leaf's 1883 prose translation of these lines of Homer's description of Trojan orators reads, "These had now ceased from battle for old age, yet were they right good orators, like grasshoppers that in a forest sit upon a tree and utter their lily-like voice; even so sat the elders of the Trojans upon the tower." Pope calls their voices "feeble," while Leaf has "lily-like," which he glosses as "delicate," but most readers nevertheless acknowledge that Homer credits these men with being commendable orators ("Yet were they excellent speakers still," Lattimore has). These elders at the Skaian gate, looking over enemy troops that they are too old to battle themselves, establish a crucial context for the dramatic monologue of Tithonus. They are, to begin with, of his generation, since Priam is his brother; they help us to see where he would stand had he not been rapt to Aurora's court. They are also of his class, the "chief men of the Trojans" (3:153, trans. Lattimore), seated on the tower that Tithonus recalls having witnessed Apollo raising and with which he closely identifies himself. These lines also set up an indirect comparison between the oratorical modes of Ulysses and Tithonus, whose translation into a grasshopper makes tremendous sense in this context. And while they hold Trojan power in their feeble hands, these are not autocratic speakers, but sound instead almost self-effacing, delicate, beautiful. Tithonus's transformation into the insect their voices resemble is not, then, a frivolous diminishment, but a profound discursive return to his doomed peers and his kind.

We are now in a position to see how closely Tennyson associated the grasshopper with the Trojan people and plain; we have only, in drawing this discussion of "Tithonus" to a close, to connect the grasshopper's singing still more closely to the dramatic monologue's causes and effects, and this requires a final return to the landscape of the Troas. We first journeyed through the Trojan landscape as it had been detailed in the 1832 and 1842 versions of "Oenone," and Tennyson's intricately referential insect makes an appearance in these. In the 1842 opening lines, Oenone's speech rings out amid the "noonday quiet" (24), when "The grasshopper is silent in the grass" (25) and all else—lizard, wind, flower, bee—droops and slumbers.[58] In the 1832 version the grasshopper is silent but more vivid: Oenone describes how "the scarletwinged / Cicala in the noonday leapeth not / Along the water-rounded granite-rock" (*Poems*, 1:422). Tennyson's revision of the grasshopper was remarked in Gladstone's 1859 essay on the poet: "When he was young, and when 'Oenone' was first published, he almost boasted of putting a particular kind of grasshopper into Troas, which, as he told us in a note, was probably not to be found there. It is a small but yet an interesting and significant indication that when, some years after, he retouched the poem, he omitted the note, and generalized the grasshopper."[59] The "almost boastful" note Gladstone refers to reads, "In the Pyrenees, where part of this poem was written, I saw a very beautiful species of Cicala, which had scarlet wings spotted with black. Probably nothing of the kind exists in Mount Ida" (Eversley ed., 1:360). The young Tennyson here concedes his poetic license while taking it, seeming at once to admit his inaccuracy even as he tacitly asserts his right to it.

Understanding Tennyson's revision as "a sign of the movement of his mind," Gladstone attributes this to "a reverence for Nature."[60] He praises this increase in accuracy and fidelity to the facts, but was it in fact an advance to generalize the grasshopper? This highly particular grasshopper did not hail, indeed, from the countryside of the Troas, but from a countryside whose details assumed a similar significance for Tennyson, since the trip to the Pyrenees to which he refers was taken with Arthur Hallam in the summer of 1830. His poem "Mariana in the South," also directly inspired by this landscape, observes, "at eve a dry cicala sung" (85). Tennyson revisited the Pyrenees in 1861, the year after he published the revised "Tithonus." His poem "In the Valley of Cauteretz" recounts the powerful experience of his return to the landscape in which he had "walked with one I loved two and thirty years ago" (4). This was an inaccuracy on which Tennyson piqued himself, as it had been one and thirty years since the trip. According to his son, Tennyson wanted to revise this "as late as 1892...since he hated inaccuracy" (*Memoir*, 1:475). His son convinced him to let it stand, partly for the sake of euphony, thus providing one of many examples of Tennyson's privileging of sound over fact. Indeed, Tennyson noted in a letter that in the intervening years it had become "a rather odious watering-place," a fact that he also omits in the lyric (*Memoir*, 1:492). Odious or not, Arthur Hallam also apparently made the return, since for Tennyson his presence is palpable, and vocal: "all along the valley, by rock and cave and tree, / The voice of the dead was a living voice to me" (9–10).

If critics are right in attributing Gladstone's and Tennyson's opposed stances on myriad subjects to an ongoing struggle for primacy in Hallam's postmortem affections, then this mention of a distinctly remembered detail from a trip that Gladstone knew was taken in Hallam's company might sound, if only to ears sensitive on the subject, gloating. The note in which Gladstone felt Tennyson "almost boasted" is preceded by an earlier note of his son's describing the poet's 1830 trip to the Pyrenees with Hallam and its ongoing poetic and personal influence: "From this time forward the lonely Pyrenean peaks... were a continual source of inspiration" (Eversley ed., 1:358). And though Tennyson came years later to generalize a keenly observed grasshopper, he nevertheless held to the profound significance of this landscape: "Cauteretz, which I had visited with my friend before I was twenty, had always lived in my recollection as a sort of Paradise" (*Memoir*, 1:591–92). The place seems also to have lived on in his poetry more particularly as a sort of Troas, home of a scarlet-winged cicada. Eschewing imagination for accuracy, the poet's generalized grasshopper marks a concession that is greater than it might initially appear. With its specificity vanishes a countryside boundless in its imaginative potential. The generalized grasshopper indicates yet again why the dramatic monologues written just after the death of his traveling companion constitute a flight to an intimately loved landscape, a now wholly displaced Troy.

If Tithonus is to be transfigured, surely one form this man famed for his hereditary beauty might take is that of "a very beautiful species of Cicala," resplendent in scarlet wings spotted with black. But though Tennyson's footnote points us in the direction of a Trojan grasshopper, in the dramatic monologue itself he entirely omits naming any outcome for a monologue that I have claimed intends an outcome, uttered by a speaker desperate for release into some other condition. Significantly, the chief source for "Tithonus" dictates quite another end, and looking at this alternative conclusion will enable us to review the stages of Tithonus's experience. In the *Homeric Hymn to Aphrodite*, immediately after chastising Aurora (Eos) for the foolishness of her framing of her request, the goddess Aphrodite continues telling Anchises the story of Tithonus:

> So while he enjoyed the sweet flower of life he lived rapturously with golden-throned Eos, the early-born, by the streams of Ocean, at the ends of the earth; but when the first grey hairs began to ripple from his comely head and noble chin, queenly Eos kept away from his bed, though she cherished him in her house and nourished him with food and ambrosia and gave him rich clothing. But when loathsome old age pressed full upon him, and he could not move nor lift his

limbs, this seemed to her in her heart the best counsel: she laid him in a room and put to the shining doors. There he babbles endlessly, and no more has strength at all, such as once he had in his supple limbs.[61]

This marks the completion of the goddess's account, and its terms, too seldom considered in criticism of "Tithonus," are significant. According to Tennyson's primary source, Tithonus is locked away, not turned into a grasshopper, and the way we read not only this poem but also the genre to whose definition it contributes will have greatly to do with which fate the poem appears to endorse.

The narrative of the *Homeric Hymn* describes three stages in the interaction between the goddess and her now immortal lover. In the first, they live "rapturously," at the quiet limit of the earth; we have examined the monologue's account of this rapture. In the second, as he becomes gray-haired yet still "noble" and "comely," she "kept away from his bed," but she continued to treat him as a "cherished" member of her court, attired in exquisite raiment and fed ambrosia, the gods' own food. (His age here may correspond with that of the elders at the Skaian gate, his brother and peers, who are not equal to doing battle but are mobile and articulate.) Although the luxuries he enjoys cannot have been wholly adequate compensation for the loss of her lovemaking, as Tennyson's representation of that intense experience demonstrates, it is impossible to underestimate the pleasure Trojans take in any and all aesthetic experiences. Gladstone's characterization of Paris surely extends to Tithonus, who sees "the display of his personal beauty, the enjoyment of luxury, and the resort to sensuality as the best refuge from pain and care."[62] Youthful beauty he has already lost, and with it the capacity to enjoy celestial luxuries; his monologue is to help him attain refuge from the state of pain and care to which he seems now consigned.

The critics who have attended conscientiously to this primary source have felt that the alterations to the story are Tennyson's. Writing after the poet's death about his classical poems, Herbert Paul in *The Nineteenth Century* (1892) notes, "The *Hymn* describes almost prosaically how Tithonus is constantly babbling in a weak, tremulous voice, and how the vigour which was once in his well-knit limbs has forsaken them.... It is not a pleasant nor a romantic picture."[63] Paul feels that Tennyson avoids this unpleasantness, and Douglas Bush, who calls the *Hymn* Tennyson's "main source," concurs: "Tithonus grows senile and repulsive, and the vigorous young wife, with the realistic matter-of-factness of the early world, shuts him up as one might bottle an insect. Tennyson has a more exalted conception."[64] Also studying the poet's use of the classical tradition, Theodore Redpath arrives at the same conclusion: "In the Homeric *Hymn to Aphrodite*, from which the story is derived, Aurora actually locked Tithonus up when he grew unbearably old. This does not happen in Tennyson's poem."[65] Those critics who have most assiduously compared "Tithonus" to its source are in agreement: Tennyson's Tithonus does not suffer so unpleasant, unromantic, or unexalted an end. Tennyson's poem, however, does evince the outcome prescribed in his source, and, more, the terms of this exile are dictated in the dramatic monologue. Indeed, in terms both of his immortality and his endless babbling, there may be little difference in kind between banishment and entomological transmogrification: Bush's likening of the *Homeric Hymn*'s Tithonus to an insect in a bottle is apposite. He is ousted, according to Seyffert's Victorian classical dictionary, when he "became completely wrinkled and bent by age,...powerless to move without assistance, and merely chirped like a cicada."[66] His limitless discourse in any case surely seems to his celestial auditor like the "garrulous" cicala whose sound, as wonderfully described in another suppressed 1832 passage of "Oenone," is as "thick dry clamour chafed from griding wings" (*Poems*, 1:422).

As Tithonus witnessed Apollo's "strange music" build Troy's walls, we are witness to the no less unearthly, indeed godlike music of Tithonus, dictating his own banishment. With this monologue, he at once reclaims and disclaims his passivity, as if to make his destiny his choice. Tennyson's speaker continues tacitly to follow the *Homeric Hymn*, in that even as Aurora first chose him, she now has full control over moving and positioning him. His plea "Release me, and restore me to the ground" acknowledges that, though at the start of the monologue his shadow appears to be roaming "like a dream," this illusion is a trick of the dimly dawning light. Called "infirm" in Tennyson's Eversley note to the poem (2:340), Tithonus has no movement left to him; "not a lyneament of his was grac't / With power of Motion," in Chapman's version (386–87). At the period of his speaking this dramatic monologue, he cannot effect this physical shift alone, rendering him as physically passive in his leave-taking as he was in his lovemaking. And yet in the monologue, by way of speech characterized in the *Hymn* as endless babble ("His voice flows on endlessly," in Lang's translation),[67] he enacts for himself another metamorphosis, and thus effects his removal from her court. The beginning of "Tithonus" emphasizes the noiseless quality of Aurora's abode, which is "quiet" and "ever-silent"; this, along with her wordless tears, must alert us to the complexity of her attention to him. According to Tennyson's source, the speaker is locked away not because he presents a ghastly spectacle, but because of his interminable chatter. It is as if Aurora does not attend to the content of this speech, but only to the fact of continuous speech itself, so that it is not what he speaks but that he speaks unceasingly. This may suggest another reason for his description of her as an auditor whose eyes "fill with tears / To hear me" (26–27). His words, more even than his physical desiccation, render him intolerable to her; his chief affront is his commitment to the monologic. Tithonus's extraordinary feat of self-representation sounds to her appalled ears like the chirping of a pest.

The goddess of the dawn, as Tennyson reminds us, is notable for her commitment to eternal recurrence, for always "returning on [her] silver wheels." Tithonus seeks to escape her cycles of emergence even as she seeks respite from what she considers his unending chatter: he seeks release from her circadian rhythms even as she seeks release from his cicadian rhythms. His continuous decay is coeval with his endless discourse; his speech is synecdochic for his infinitude. Mythic in its proportions, his speech figures his infinitely decaying body, an endless composition of infinite decomposition. Yet with this monologue he is now breaking the cycle. According to the *Homeric Hymn*, discursive closure is no more attainable for him than physical death, and yet this monologue enjoys an especially finely honed Tennysonian brevity. More, the monologue is suasive, enabling him to escape the confrontational quality of his auditor's beauty. As in the cases of St. Simeon Stylites, Ulysses, and Tiresias, the speaker is poised between states, and each dramatic monologue not only chronicles precipitous change but also provokes it.

I have reviewed the reasonableness of Tithonus's identification with the grasshopper, but I want in drawing this discussion to a close to show that the speaker is not laboring to become insectile, but to become what the grasshopper, in Tennyson's own early, highly indebted formulation, is like: namely, the poet. Tennyson's own phrasing in the footnote recounting the story of Tithonus has it that "according to the legend," Tithonus "was turned into a grasshopper." Tithonus acknowledges an earlier passivity in which he was chosen, but he also insists on rhetorical responsibility, on his having made the demand whose fulfillment now stands more as punishment than gift. He intends now to dictate the terms of his next metamorphosis. Tennyson's "Tithonus" is not a retelling of the myth, any more than is his "Ulysses." Rather, these are fictive extensions to the myths, always imagining what might happen *next*, in the part of the story that no source supplies. Tennyson begins where Homer's epic and the *Homeric Hymn* leave off, and the story that he tells is of his own invention. What the monologue, as opposed to Tennyson's sources, tells us is that Tithonus seeks now precisely to escape iterating the ceaseless, inutile song of the grasshopper. Endless chirping, without meaning or purpose, is precisely not what Tithonus produces, in a monologue in which the speaker assiduously turns his own beauty to use. Langbaum claims that all dramatic monologues have "no *necessary* beginning and end but only arbitrary limits"—like the intermittent chirping, "without any particular idea of length attached to it," to which Gladstone likens the sound of Trojan orators.[68] Speaking "Here at the quiet limit of the world" (7), however, Tithonus sets himself clear discursive limits, beginning his speech at the critical moment of his transition—the release he demands and achieves—from Aurora's East, and his monologue's end is a cry of its own necessity. Because the dramatic monologue comes to a conclusion, its speaker also comes to a conclusion, becoming finite, free from the infinite discursive and diurnal cycles to which he had been consigned by Aurora's "returning wheels." The monologue performs his end, because it is as fleeting, and as efficacious, as that strange song he heard Apollo sing.

Idle, aristocratic, creator of delicate, exquisite, "lily-like" songs: representations of Tithonus and Tennyson bear many surface resemblances. But the dramatic monologue "Tithonus" is not ultimately the song of a grasshopper, if that song is understood to be merely frivolous and blithe-spirited. If it is understood as the rhetorical equivalent, however, of the oratory of the Trojan elders, seated on their god-built wall, fated to be slaughtered when it is breached, we begin to gain a sense of its profundity and gravity. The speaker must produce efficacious speech, as opposed to meaningless, intermittent chirps. The grasshopper's is not a song that can build a city or fabricate a self; it produces only beautiful sound. And the suspicion of inutility must attend Tithonus too; Ulysses seeks to perform "some work of noble note," but Tithonus appears to have sought immortality for the sake of ongoing pleasure, as an end divorced from any cause beyond his own exquisite desires. In looking toward the dark earth, his former home, he is searching for a place within the human culture he has disdained, although now he shares his keenest resemblance neither to gods nor to mortals, but to an insect. Coldly contemplating what he called the "Idle Aristocracy," Carlyle imagines that his "reflective readers" will proclaim to a member of that group, "Not welcome, O complex Anomaly...for who of mortals knows what to do with thee?"[69] A complex Anomaly if ever there was one, Tithonus labors in his dramatic monologue to "get existed" in the world. Betrayed by the incessant aging of his body, battered by the predations of his dismayed lover, Tithonus every day loses his resemblance either to men or to gods (who of mortals or immortals knows what to do with him?), although his bid for eternal life sought for distinction among both communities. But it is his painful, ill-gotten immortality that is, paradoxically, to win for him a place in the cultural life of his lost civilization. His immortality is not a gift of the gods he has importuned, but of the kindly race of men and women that chooses to incorporate him as a part of its ongoing knowledge of its own origins and ends. His design is to become, like the ruined towers of Ilion, ancient myth.

THE RAPTURE OF TIRESIAS

A chirping insect makes a fleeting appearance in T. S. Eliot's "The Waste Land," amid a barren landscape in which "the dead tree gives no shelter, the cricket no relief" (23), but Tiresias, Eliot's footnote informs us, is "the most important personage in the poem."[70] Eliot's Tiresias is based far more closely on Ovid's *Metamorphoses* than is Tennyson's, who takes him chiefly from Greek tragedy (Aeschylus and Euripides), which is to say that Eliot stresses the old man's experience of sex transformation, with Tiresias calling himself "Old man with wrinkled female breasts" (219).[71] Eliot's Tiresias defines himself in ways that can look like Tennyson's version, though, which is to say as a figure who moves easily between the quick and the dead, calling himself "I who have sat by Thebes below the wall /

And walked among the lowest of the dead" (245–46). Both Tennyson and Eliot consider it important that Tiresias prophesied in the marketplace in the shadow of the Theban wall, thus closely associating him with the walls of the city he would save, and both look to the prophet's future communal destination, moving among the shades. In Tennyson's dramatic monologue, Tiresias is "the most important personage in the poem," in spite of his suggestion that his auditor, Menœceus, holds this status, but he is also the most important personage in the polis, an ambition represented and attained by the performance of his monologue.

Tiresias resembles Tithonus in being older than anyone he knows of; Lemprière in his *Classical Dictionary* explains, "He lived to a great age, which some authors have called as long as seven generations of men, others six, and others nine."[72] He also resembles Cassandra, another of Tennyson's frustrated speakers. At the end of "Oenone," the nymph descends into Troy to visit "wild Cassandra," whose curse, dictated by a baulked Apollo, god not only of poetry but also of prophecy, is radically inefficacious speech. Unheeded, she bears the intolerable burden of useless knowledge, and her foresight condemns her to dwell in a burning city long before it is actually torched. In a sign of the sensuality of Troy's ruling family's relation to language (the words of Tithonus and Paris win for them great physical pleasure and pain), Apollo's sexual frustration is echoed in Cassandra's verbal frustration. Her predicament is the fearful antithesis of the superflux of lyric power that Apollo employed to craft the walls of her city.

Tennyson's Tiresias is himself bound to Apollo not only as a prophet but, as the eight-line fragment that Tennyson initially wrote indicates, as an ephebe. In studying the song-built city of Troy, we have seen the association by one of its princes, Tithonus, of that event with his own seduction, his transformation from seeming godlike to seeming god-built, his profound recognition of the homology between the walls of Troy and his own identity. We have also witnessed in Tithonus an imperious disregard for humanity, an inborn sense of distinction that his language, no less than the singularity of his lineaments (first in their rich beauty, then in their unending degeneration) announces. Tiresias, in his desperate attempts to influence and indeed save Thebes and its people, would appear wholly unlike the removed and high-handed Tithonus. Like Tithonus, however, his deepest identity is cemented within the walls of his own song-built city, and like him, Tiresias forwards a monologue that interrogates the civic ambition of its own discourse. Amphion raised his city, but it is Tiresias who would rule it.

In book 2 of the *Aeneid*, Aeneas recalls how, at the moment when the great wooden horse is being dragged by the eager Trojans through the city walls, "Cassandra cried and cursed the unhappy hour, / Foretold our fate, but by the god's decree / All heard and none believed the prophecy" (2:323–25, trans. Dryden; *tunc etiam fatis aperit Cassandra futuris / ora, dei iussu non umquam credita Teucris*). Cassandra is a figure for insurmountable discursive impotence, and in the classical dramatic monologue of Tiresias Tennyson shifts the burden of her curse onto

Tiresias. Tennyson goes far out of tradition in burdening Tiresias with verbal impotence; as Culler reminds us, "The condition that Tiresias's prophecies shall not be believed was not part of any classical version of the myth but was added by Tennyson, presumably from the story of Cassandra."[73] When Tennyson's Tiresias recalls his own curse from a goddess, that of prophetic power coupled with the disbelief of auditors, he laments a people "who heard / And heard not" (58–59). The idea of a torment based in oratorical incapacitation, of producing words that must fail because of faults either in a speaker or an audience, is an abiding perturbation of the Victorian dramatic monologue, a genre invariably concerned with the successes and failures of suasive speech. We must question so radical an innovation as that of Tiresias's useless vatic voice on the poet's part, however, especially since Tiresias does not ultimately share Cassandra's verbal impotence; instead, his verbal puissance is at once challenged and established by his dramatic monologue.

Blinded by Athena, whom he accidentally witnessed bathing, Tiresias is cursed with a prophetic gift that will not be credited. At the start of his mono-logue, Tiresias is intent on persuading Menœceus, a young prince of Thebes, to sacrifice his life in order to propitiate an angry god. If Menœceus does not agree to this, which is to say, if Tiresias fails, Thebes will be destroyed. The monologue sets this task for itself: a speaker who by deific decree can never speak convincingly must now become rhetorically efficacious, powerfully so. Tiresias begins his assay on the life of his young auditor with the story of his own life, recalling how in his youthful explorations he eventually discovered "One naked peak," which led to his peeking at another singular naked eminence, Pallas Athene, who decrees, "'Henceforth be blind, for thou hast seen too much, / And speak the truth that no man may believe'" (29, 48–49).

If Tiresias is to save the city, he must counteract the uncivil curse of this god-dess. His monologue, then, constitutes his defiance of his punishment, although he long enacted defiance by way of his very sightlessness. Athena blinds Tiresias because he has seen her naked body, but instead of removing this image from his mind, she has more absolutely fixed it there. She is now always before him; her form is all he is capable of seeing. Indeed, he revels in her perpetual naked pres-ence: "I behold her still, / Beyond all work of those who carve the stone, / Beyond all dreams of Godlike womanhood, / Ineffable beauty" (51–54). Moreover, as it is Tiresias's fate never to be believed, the suasive success of this monologue will constitute a defiance of his damnation. In closing he begs Menœceus, "blunt the curse / Of Pallas, hear, and though I speak the truth / Believe I speak it" (149–50). If his prophecies are predicated on their incredibility, then in this most crucial of his utterances, he must eschew prophecy, in favor of something more persuasive. In the course of the monologue, Tiresias elaborates on the disasters, natural and political, that his words have been unable to avert. His prophetic voice has doomed him to solitude, to complete separation from the community of men and women he works so frantically to aid. In repeatedly calling Menœceus "Son," he is seeking to establish some kind of social union, seeking access to the communal by way of the familial. But for him to convince Menœceus, and so forestall the certain destruction of Thebes, he must avoid the prophetic mode, which he knows must fail. Tiresias must find another kind of suasive speech; his dramatic monologue thus must labor to produce a substitutive oratory, what he himself comes to call a heroic hymn.

Tiresias's dramatic monologue explores the challenges for a speaker of attaining a popular language. He arrives at his monologue, unlike Ulysses and Tithonus, having already failed ever to accomplish anything by way of his speech. And yet his monologue appears to achieve its goals explicitly, in the monologue, by way of the monologue, therefore confirming the similar attainment of the more obliquely represented goals and outcomes of the dramatic monologues of his classical Tennysonian colleagues. Bearing in mind the range of ambitions voiced in other classical monologues, however, we may question whether the saving of his song-built city is indeed Tiresias's most comprehensive objective.

Song-built Sons

According to manuscript evidence, the longest draft of "Tiresias" was written about the same time as the earliest versions of "Ulysses" and "Tithon," that is, in October 1833, and consisted of five sections, "separated by gaps," as David Goslee puts it. While these fragments were substantially reordered in the final 1885 version, I agree with Goslee that the five sections in their original order "make up a more straightforward argument than the final text."[74] The logic of their earliest progression, which I follow here, constitutes a sustained meditation on the homology between the self and the structure of the song-built city. In the first of the five fragments of this poem written soon after Hallam's death, the speaker's concern is overtly that of the potency of his words, their suasive value. Tiresias's first words to his young auditor illuminate not only his own predicament but also that of the other speakers, Ulysses and Tithonus, to whom Tennyson fastened him:

> My Son,
> No sound is breathed so potent to coerce,
> And to conciliate, as their names who dare
> For that sweet mother land which gave them birth
> Nobly to do, nobly to die. Their names,
> Graven on memorial columns, are a song
> Heard in the future; few, but more than wall
> And rampart, their examples reach a hand
> Far through all years, and everywhere they meet

And kindle generous purpose, and the strength
To mould it into action pure as theirs. (115–25)

"The brave man has to give his life away," Carlyle insisted.[75] Throughout the monologue Tiresias emphasizes to Menœceus his patrilineal heritage, his direct descent from "the seed of Cadmus" (114), even suggesting that Cadmus himself, "out of whom thou art" (13), in a sense gave him birth, and thus it is his noble ancestry that dictates his early death. Now it seems that the land itself is the mother of all heroes; he is part of the soil and ground of this city. Tennyson's "to do" or "to die" construction is notably taken up in a poem written midway between the 1833 inception and the 1885 revision of "Tiresias," the 1854 "The Charge of the Light Brigade": "Their's not to reason why, / Their's but to do and die" (14–15). But Tiresias, while calling for the same kind of complete and unquestioning obedience as that exhibited by the British in Crimea, promises nothing like the geographically remote anonymity that may be the soldier's lot. Rather, he urges his auditor quite literally to become a name. The hero's graven name, itself a prophetic "song / Heard in the future," is a song that constructs a city. Raising as it does "memorial columns," it induces structural effects. It is the song that, "more than wall / And rampart" (themselves, in Boeotian Thebes, the product of a song heard in the past), upholds the city built to music, that is building still.

In the second of the early fragments of the poem, Tiresias next turns to one of Tennyson's most evocative descriptions of war. This fragment pursues the suggestion of the first, moving from the construction of civic walls to their destruction:

> Menœceus, thou hast eyes, and I can hear
> Too plainly what full tides of onset sap
> Our seven high gates, and what a weight of war
> Rides on those ringing axles! jingle of bits,
> Shouts, arrows, tramp of the hornfooted horse
> That grind the glebe to powder! Stony showers
> Of that ear-stunning hail of Arês crash
> Along the sounding walls. Above, below,
> Shock after shock, the song-built towers and gates
> Reel, bruised and butted with the shuddering
> War-thunder of iron rams. (88–98)

Tiresias goes on to insist that helpless Thebans cry out for salvation, telling the young man, "And they wail to thee!" (104). He begins with the conjunction of Menœceus's eyes and his own hearing, but his description has entirely to do with sound; thus it directs Menœceus precisely into the role of auditor. Tiresias's experience of attack consists of hearing the sound track of war: "ringing," "jingle," "shouts," "tramp," "grind," "crash." Goslee writes that Tiresias describes this "with apparent relish," and Tucker agrees: "These militant lines indulge a vicarious ju-bilation that ill suits their speaker's avowed role as peacemaker."[76] The speaker's identification is not with the military, however, but with its target; he experiences what the wall does. For him the experience of attack is an "ear-stunning hail," while the walls endure "shuddering / War-thunder of iron rams." The walls themselves are not only specified as "song-built" at the moment of the deafening attack on them, but are themselves productive of sound. Thebes's "sounding walls," built from the melodies of Amphion, now both suffer and emit noise, growing, in this hail of sound, unsound.

The bombarded walls and ramparts can be preserved only by the sacrifice of the hero, a procedure described in the third fragment as consisting of self-slaughter at the altar of the self-destroyed Sphinx. By way of this self-immolation, he promises Menœceus, "Thebes through thee shall stand / Firm-based" (137–38). Firm-based but also, again, song-built. The fourth fragment reiterates that the glory Tiresias sees for Menœceus is architectonic. Thebes is to establish its physical foundation upon his heroism:

> if thou dare—
> Thou, one of these, the race of Cadmus—then
> No stone is fitted in yon marble girth
> Whose echo shall not tongue thy glorious doom
> Nor in this pavement but shall ring thy name
> To every hoof that clangs it. (129–34)

Returning to the sound of the names graven on memorial columns, Tiresias in-vites Menœceus to hear what we might anachronistically term a rock concert, as stones and pavements "ring thy name." The stones comprise a memorial not only to Menœceus but also to the noise of war, their ringing and clanging echo-ing that military assault. Of course, his appeal to Menœceus is an appeal to fame, but cast always, in the 1833 version, in stony terms; Menœceus is not so much to be sacrificed as to be petrified. He will go to the "smooth rock" (141) that is the altar of the Sphinx, and there become one, turn into the stone on which his name is graven. Names are songs that continue to build and to uphold walls and ram-parts of civic spaces, and Tiresias, among the most literal-minded of Tennyson's monologic speakers, envisions a hero not only representing the political and social life of a city, but in fact becoming part of its physical structure. The hero's body will become not merely a civic statue, but part of the very "pavement" on which the citizens walk, the "stones" of the buildings through which they move, and the "ramparts" that defend them. In dying for his city, Menœceus will become more thoroughly a part of its structure, indistinguishable from the materials that undergird it.

Tiresias is proposing to Menœceus concrete union with the city. In the fifth and final of the initial fragments from the fall of 1833, it follows that Tiresias harbors a similar ambition:

> O therefore that the unfulfilled desire,
> The grief forever born from griefs to be,
> The boundless yearning of the Prophet's heart—
> Could *that* stand forth, and like a statue, reared
> To some great citizen, win all praise from all
> Who past it, saying 'That was he!"
>   In vain! (78–83)

Goslee calls this final section "a lapse into self-pity,"[77] and certainly the speaker appears to recognize the vanity of these human wishes. We might nevertheless hear these lines instead as a lapse into self-vaunting, since what the speaker imagines is his own architectonic distinction. What he would cast into stone is less any particular deed than the abstraction of his ambition, a finite representation of the vast measure of "unfulfilled desire" and eternal grief ("forever born from griefs to be") and "boundless yearning." Tiresias desires, as he now makes clear, to become an icon, "like a statue," winning "all praise from all who pass it." Moreover, the recognition of the multitude will confer identity on the statue's subject. In imagining the communal exclamation "That was he!" Tiresias promotes a shift in the expectations of representation, as the self is here not the source of the image; rather, the image is the bedrock of the self. The statue would stand as a likeness not of his person but of his yearning, and in the limitless expanse of his ambition we hear his unmistakable likeness to Simeon, Ulysses, and Tithonus. This speaker seeks to become a physical object in his culture; like the other speakers, he seeks to be "known," distinguished ("That was he!"), set apart from, and yet set at the center of his society. This final fragment of the original sequence reveals that his exhortations to Menœceus intend also this effect: he seeks through the monologue to become an architect of the self.

But in what form would Tiresias construct himself? I have reviewed, in their original order, the fragments composed soon after Tennyson learned of the death of Arthur Hallam, but to understand Tiresias's self-representation we must look at a still earlier form of this late dramatic monologue, which predates that cataclysmic event in Tennyson's poetic and personal life. The poem's foundational eight lines, ransacked first for "Ulysses" and half a century later for "Tiresias," may predate, some critics suggest, the nascent form of the dramatic monologue, although I think we can hear its early iteration:

> I wish I were as in the years of old
> Ere my smooth cheek darkened with youthful down,

> While yet the blessèd daylight made itself
> Ruddy within the eaves of sight, before
> I looked upon divinity unveiled
> And wisdom naked—when my mind was set
> To follow knowledge like a sinking star,
> Beyond the utmost bound of human thought. (*T. Nbk 15*)[78]

In the course of his monologue Tiresias repeatedly adverts to Menœceus's youth, reminding him of the brevity of "thy term / Of years" (32–33) and recalling himself hearing an influential tale "When but thine age" (18). But this account, and especially the crucial line, "Ere my smooth cheek darkened with youthful down" (which was excised in revision), tells us that what Tiresias initially seeks is a representational return to his own youth, one specifically figured as ephebic.

In my discussion in chapter 5 of Paris (another viewer of the naked Athena), I noted Apollo's possession of a smooth cheek undarkened by youthful down; in having shared this particular physical trait Tennyson's Tiresias recalls his source in Callimachus's *Fifth Hymn*. In Callimachus, the Tiresias who ascends the hill where he sees the naked Athena is described as one "on whose cheek the down was just darkening" (quoted in *Poems*, 2:625). This darkening would appear almost to travel from his cheek to his eyes, which, after she sees him see her, "grew dark" (46). Tiresias associates ephebism with sight, because the two were conjoined in his experience; he reminds the youthful Menœceus, "thou hast eyes" (88). Noting that Greek images of Apollo "represent the god as young, beardless, and long-haired," Darice Birge observes that the god "was associated with young men at various stages of late adolescence and their introduction into city-centered social maturity, an association that is well-recognized in ancient Greek art, literature, and civic and religious customs."[79] The ephebe's association, then, is with the entrance into "city-centered social maturity," a step that Tiresias urges Menœceus to take. But a subtext of the monologue, we learn from these early lines, is that this moment of transition is one to which Tiresias, cursed now with knowledge beyond the bound of human belief, wishes to return, a state prior to entering the civic responsibilities that he appears to have failed.

The speaker begins his monologue by recalling himself, as each speaker does, to some ideal of his own past. Tucker believes Menœceus appears "after the solo murmur of the first eight lines," but it is vital that Menœceus hear them, because they establish the closest point of contact between the speaker and his auditor.[80] The youth of Menœceus leads to Tiresias's recollection of his own youth, and even of a moment when he too received advice from an elder. This confusion over which is the ephebe, the speaker or the auditor, connects to a more general blurring of the boundaries between fathers and sons. Tiresias tells Menœceus his own family history, one he might be expected to know already, as well as his personal future: Menœceus's grandfather, Cadmus, killed the dragon son of the god

Ares. Now the god demands Menœceus in return, son for son. In the *Phoenissae* of Euripides, one of Tennyson's sources, it is Creon, son of Cadmus and father of Menœceus, and so biologically the middleman, whom Tiresias addresses.[81] In replacing Creon with Menœceus, the father with the son, Tennyson risks losing the patrilineal drama of a father requiring his son to requite the debt of his grandfather. But Tennyson's speaker craves direct access to this family drama; he must insert himself into this patriarchy if his monologue is to establish his suasive abilities. Tiresias is seeking, like Tennyson's earlier speakers, identification with his audience, although, unlike these speakers, Tiresias seeks an intimacy that is both civic and familial. But of course the two are wholly inextricable; it is to save the Thebans that Tiresias tacitly adopts, or appropriates, Menœceus. Like Ulysses and Tithonus, Tiresias entrusts the welfare of a community to a son. But pious Telemachus and the more splendid (if in his father's monologue more shadowy) Memnon, though vital to their fathers' self-identifications, are nevertheless not the primary audience for their fathers' discourses, whereas Tiresias has placed Menœceus more directly at the center of his own monologic self-determination.

Tiresias begins by explaining the tenacity of Ares' anger toward the descendents of Cadmus, "out of whom thou art," but Menœceus's eventual suffering at the hands of the gods has already been preempted by Tiresias's own. He mentions a "tale" told him when young by an old man (so drawing another masculine line of descent, as well as forcing another blatant parallel between himself and his auditor) that "amazed." This tale fixed Tiresias's personal doom, as he is now fixing Menœceus's. Tiresias must convince this auditor to give up his life, although his oratory has so far wrought no equivalent effect. Each word must tell, and Tiresias's strategy initially is to tell his own story. In monologic logic, it should be noted, every narrative is the speaker's, so even the death of his auditor will primarily constitute Tiresias's own story. A discrepancy from Tennyson's primary source, Callimachus's *Fifth Hymn*, further illuminates the paternal drama that Tiresias is establishing. Ricks explains, "In Callimachus, Athene is accompanied by the mother of Tiresias; it is for her sake that Athene gives him the power of prophecy. T[ennyson] altered what would have been a distraction" (*Poems*, 1:625). Why is there no benignly influential mother in Tennyson's version? In blotting out the mother, Tiresias's narrative remains one structured by the mutual debts and duties of fathers and sons.

Describing in a letter how Tennyson worked on the revision of "Tiresias," Tennyson's friend H. M. Butler (then master of Trinity) exclaimed in a letter in 1883 that Tennyson was "in rather anxious doubt as to the paternity of Creon! Just like his old passion for accuracy and detail!" (*Poems*, 1:623). While the poet's discernible anxiety no doubt reflected a pressure for an approximation of scholarly accuracy, it also points to an anxiety over the overdetermined nature of the relationship between this speaker and his auditor. We might find in "Tiresias" an overt Christian analogy, of course, especially relevant in a poem in which a son must sacrifice his life for the salvation of the multitude, although the poem holds this sacrifice as the barbarous demand of a dangerous and bloodthirsty god. It seems more promising to look to nearer comparisons in Tennyson's own work, since these three classical dramatic speakers, however covertly, acknowledge, seek, or withstand their own usurpation by sons (openly with Telemachus, symbolically with the heroic Memnon, and through a surrogate in the case of Menœceus) who will not inherit them so much as expiate them. "Tiresias," with his complex displacement of anxieties regarding paternity, was itself resuscitated by Tennyson's own son. The poet informed Edward FitzGerald in a dedication to "Tiresias" that his friend did not live to read, "my son, who dipt / In some forgotten book of mine / With sallow scraps of manuscript, / And dating many a year ago, / Has hit on this" ("To E. FitzGerald," 46–50).

Tiresias, then, for all his apparent similarity to Cassandra, seems to escape her fate: his words are almost scarily efficacious, and directly through them his city is saved. The curse of Pallas is "blunted" to the point of dullness, and before the end of the monologue his suasive abilities are unquestionably equal to his prophetic ones. It would appear that this late dramatic monologue has at once evoked and evaded the mimetic complexity enacted by its fellow monologues, since even this most dramatic of situations is marked by a surprising absence of dramatic tension. None of Tennyson's other monologists speaks at so specific a moment of civic crisis (the timing of their monologues is for them a matter of personal rather than general necessity). Although all of the speakers I have been considering require their auditors to perform something as a result of the monologue, no other forwards so patent a request for an auditor's self-immolation. For all this, and in spite of the deafness of previous audiences, Tennyson's Tiresias seems never to provoke skepticism or even resistance in this auditor. His monologue registers only moved acquiescence on the part of Menœceus, so furthering his defiance of a goddess who seems to have been right after all in finding him impertinent. His stated intent, to impel Menœceus to self-slaughter, is easily attained. What, then, does this monologue seek to perform?

The Discursive Tyranny of One

Tennyson's Tiresias claims to the end of his dramatic monologue to have failed in his suasive or didactic purpose, and with this, finally, a reader must concur, even as Menœceus speeds to his death. Tiresias's very influence over his auditor points to a larger failure of his Orphic voice, but this failure, I hope to show, is precisely what the speaker labors to perform. The city he labors to save was built by the work of Amphion's lyre, as Lemprière tells us: "The fable of Amphion's moving stones and raising the walls of Thebes at the sound of his lyre has been explained by supposing that he persuaded, by his eloquence, a wild and uncivilized people to unite together and build a town to protect themselves against the attacks of their enemies."[82] Quintilian, following Cicero, attributes "the origin of oratory to the founders of cities and the makers of laws, who must...have possessed the gift of eloquence."[83] The song-built walls, standing at the center of Tiresias's earliest argumentative efforts, are the product of similar oratorical exertions. Tiresias, although he will, through Menœceus's sacrifice, prevent the destruction of the walls, can have no similar effect on the Thebans they define and enclose. Amphion's "eloquence" was productive, subduing a rugged people and inspiring them to fabricate their city, whereas Tiresias's monologue is finally uninterested in reproducing Amphion's foundational public eloquence. For all his claims of discursive futility, Tiresias is as breathtakingly ambitious as any other Tennysonian classical monologist, seeking through the medium of his monologue to attain to nothing short of a tyrannical state, ruled by dictation rather than suasion.

Tiresias's prophecies all concern state governance, and his monologue is in many ways a catalogue of political disasters that, because he has been futile in preventing them, represent his own personal failures:

> for when the crowd would roar
> For blood, for war, whose issue was their doom,
> To cast wise words among the multitude
> Was flinging fruit to lions; nor, in hours
> Of civil outbreak, when I knew the twain
> Would each waste each, and bring on both the yoke
> Of stronger states, was mine the voice to curb
> The madness of our cities and their kings. (63–70)

His account of his life grows indistinguishable from a history of civic upheaval. He is at once wholly intimate with the multitude, knowing their future, and wholly disconnected from them. Not even challenged or debated, his wise words have been met with irritated indifference. He suggests that his "wise words" were insufficient to satiate the hunger of the ravenous multitude, fruit having no appeal for lions. But the comparison stands as an accusation against this bloodthirsty mass, which in its brutishness is beyond discursive reach, wise words having no appeal for lions. Capable only of producing a "roar," the inarticulate multitude cannot comprehend the articulations of others. Although he speaks of the past inability of his voice to "curb" this unruly population and its rulers, Tiresias now attempts ("mine the voice") to subdue them to its yoke.

In Tiresias's most dramatic statement of his discursive futility, a desperate sweep of questions, inheres his most dramatic statement of his discursive ambitions:

> Who ever turned upon his heel to hear
> My warning that the tyranny of one
> Was prelude to the tyranny of all?

My counsel that the tyranny of all
Led backward to the tyranny of one? (71–75)

The speaker phrases his powerlessness in terms of tyranny, a word he repeats four times in as many lines, and beyond this, connects this lack of rhetorical power to competing systems of tyrannical governance. Tiresias initiates the turning of his two circular questions on the turned heel of an absent audience: "Who ever." His questions, because unheeded, are rendered rhetorical by the unresponsiveness of the public: the implicit answer is "no one." This "civic outbreak" is linked to Tiresias's own prophetic incapacitation, as his own cursed state is affixed to the cursed state of Thebes.

Buckley writes of Tiresias's set of questions, "The mistrust of anarchy as prelude to dictatorship parallels his dread of an aggressive, ill-educated democracy."[84] But are these alternative tyrannies, set up rhetorically as equivalent, actually "parallel," or what Goslee terms "reciprocal oppressions"?[85] I would argue that the equivalence the turning of these lines suggests is uneasy and unsustainable, and in fact that in the end these threats to civic stability are not parallel but divergent and unequal. Although Tiresias claims that the tyranny of one is as devastating as its alternative, only imagined by him as mob rule, the monologue promotes singular rulers. A single individual is of course the specific desire of Ares, who announces, "I loathe / The seed of Cadmus—yet if one of these / By his own hand—if one of these—" (113–15). Tiresias not only conveys this message but deliberately echoes its emphasis on a single savior with a high-born pedigree, repeating both the god's demand and his theatrical staccato, telling Menœceus, "but if thou dare— / Thou, one of these, the race of Cadmus—" (129–30). (It is notable that Tiresias is also a descendent of a Theban ruling family, binding the speaker further to his auditor.)

At the moment of his self-sacrifice, Menœceus most represents the people's interest, and is least representative. He becomes in some sense akin to what Mandler, referring to Victorian society, calls "the people's aristocrat," since acute responsiveness to people's welfare was for the nineteenth-century "high whig aristocracy" "a point of political principle, a fulfillment of hereditary governing responsibilities." He also becomes incongruous as a figure of direct bearing for a Victorian readership, as he is set up by the poet in some sense to be. A monologist conceived in the early 1830s, on the heels of the great debates over the First Reform Bill, was speaking by the early 1880s in the midst of the agitation over the Third Reform Bill, which passed in 1884 ("Tiresias" was essentially finished in 1883). By the end of the century, according to Mandler, "aristocrats advocating political reform could no longer pose as the people's trustees": "The idea of an aristocratic party—a virtuous band—performing services for the people was finally an anachronism when the people were ready, willing, and able to do the job themselves."[86] Stopford Brooke wrote of Tennyson, "He was always an aristocrat, though he would have said, with justice, that it was a government of the best men that he desired, and not a government of rank and birth alone"—although it is the mere, and major, fact of his rank and birth that alone qualify Menœceus for his singular assignment. Brooke continues, "But I do not think that he ever wished that rank should be dissolved, or privileges overthrown; or that he even conceived the idea that the people of themselves were to choose the best men."[87] Menœceus is elected by the prophet, not the people.

Tiresias himself has sought singularity among the Thebans, imagining the memorial to his "yearning" "standing forth," like a monument "to some great citizen," simultaneously recognized and honored by the "all / Who past it." Winning "all praise from all," or unanimous public favor, the statue nevertheless stands apart, a monument to individual distinction ("That was he!"). As in the other classical monologues, the speaker's ambition is the assent to his will by an audience. For Tiresias, all discourse but his own is as a lion's roar, threatening but inchoate, while Menœceus, for all his valor, never once questions Tiresias's literal authority: making no reply, he does and dies. We have already seen that Tiresias's words are inextricable from the city's foundation or government, and we might now see that his dramatic monologue is itself expressive of the polity he privileges. Tiresias not only implicitly endorses an antidemocratic system, but he articulates it in every ostensibly useless word.

We might well ask whether it suits Tiresias, for all his attempts to gain the ear of the populace, not to be believed. His ability only to coerce one, rather than all, serves to illustrate the failure of democratic discourse itself. The speaker's "power of prophesying" constitutes "No power—so chained and coupled with the curse / Of blindness and their unbelief, who heard / And heard not" (57–59). Goslee summarizes the cause of this failure of verbal efficacy more bluntly: it is due not only to "Athene's curse" but to "society's stupidity."[88] The populace itself is the curse; the prophet's characterization of his own twinned curse points not to his failure but to theirs. This is why Tiresias privileges even the tyranny of the one over that of the many, a position articulated by Edmund Burke: "I hate tyranny, at least I think so; but I hate it most of all where most are concerned in it. The tyranny of a multitude is a multiplied tyranny. If . . . I must make my choice (which God avert!) between the despotism of a single person, or of the many, my election is made."[89] Burke's was not an isolated preference; as M. L. Bush observes, "The aristocracy was needed . . . not to safeguard against royal absolutism but the arbitrary rule of the masses which democracy seemed to sanction."[90] Royal absolutism is the fault, indeed, of the rule of the masses, as Tennyson claims in "I loving Freedom for herself," a political poem written in the period 1832–34: "The tyranny of all begins / The tyranny of one" (35–36).

Tiresias bases his theory of government less on finding an adequate voice than on finding an adequate audience. He reminds Menœceus of both his lineage and his individuality, as he urges him on to "one great deed" (157)—undertaken, indeed, in expiation for the death of a dragon called by Tiresias "the multitudinous beast" (15). This description exposes what it is the scion is out to slay, since the beast is thus directly linked to the ferocious, roaring *multitude*. The multitude easily becomes indistinguishable from the mob, monstrous because multiply organed: many-headed, many-footed, many-tongued. Tennyson's 1885 poem "The Fleet," for example, warns elected officials that, should the navy be weakened, "the wild mob's million feet / Will kick you from your place" (18–19). Multitudinousness is a quality linked not only to people in violent revolt, however; it is for Tennyson the salient feature, and problem, of any popular assembly. The Prologue to *The Princess*, one of Tennyson's most revealing representations of contemporary Victorian society, begins, "Sir Walter Vivian all a summer's day / Gave his broad lawns until the set of sun / Up to the people" (Prologue, 1–3). Surveying "the people," this is what one sees: "There moved the multitude, a thousand heads" (Prologue, 57).

Tennyson was officially created a peer on March 11, 1884, in the middle of the turmoil of the Third Reform Bill, and his "first political utterance as a peer" (*Memoir*, 2:305) was the 1884 poem "Freedom." A frequently personified figure in Tennyson's political poems, Freedom is addressed as "Thou loather of the lawless crown / As of the lawless crowd" (31–32). As in the 1883 "Tiresias," however, the crowd poses a greater threat than the crown. "Freedom" ends by warning against Freedom's greatest threat: "Men loud against all forms of power— / Unfurnished brows, tempestuous tongues" (37–38). Possessors of "Brass mouths and iron lungs" (40), they threaten to drown out quieter, more rational voices. The protesting multitude threatens civic well-being in Tennyson's Britain as in Tiresias's Thebes: thus, it is the ungovernable monster of populism that Menœceus is sent to slay.

Tennyson's peerage was proposed by Gladstone, who engaged in a series of epistolary exchanges with Tennyson to enlist the poet's support in the House of Lords for passage of the Third Reform Bill. These letters can sound like a distorted echo of the letters Gladstone and Arthur Henry Hallam had so delighted in some six decades earlier. At the end of the letter in which Hallam calls Gladstone "divine Ulysses," he had imagined his friend's "future government," using his "eloquence" to fight "battles of freedom & justice" (*Letters*, 105–6), as if in anticipation of Gladstone's migration from serving, in Macaulay's famous phrase, as "the rising hope of those stern and unbending Tories" to serving as the nation's leading liberal voice. Tennyson, too, had fulfilled Hallam's prediction, also written in a letter to Gladstone, that he would become the greatest poet not only of his generation but of his age. The poet's political views had remained identifiably Whig, although the party no longer existed; perhaps his unwavering adherence to ideological positions held by the young Arthur Hallam served as another variant of his habitual mourning. The prime minister cajoled the poet laureate, in a series of letters, to support passage of the bill, and Tennyson negotiated with Gladstone in his responses, agreeing to support the extension of the franchise only after extracting a promise on Redistribution. Tennyson and his siblings rang in the First Reform Bill on the church bells at his father's Somersby rectory; he voted in favor of the Third Reform Bill in July 1884 as a member of the House of Lords. He favored the extension of the franchise but remained skeptical regarding a populace he considered erratic and irrational. "Not that he deemed the time altogether ripe for such a measure, on the contrary," Hallam reports. "But the promises of statesmen and agitators had so deeply stirred the popular mind, that delay, he thought, was no longer safe" (*Memoir*, 2:303). Tennyson put it more directly to William Allingham in 1884, declaring, "I voted for the Franchise to avoid worse things."[91] We can hear clearly an echo of Macaulay's more elegant formulation of the same point during debates over the First Reform Bill: Reform that you may preserve.

Instead of debating, in the House of Lords or elsewhere, Tennyson wrote three poems addressed to Gladstone in 1884–85, each of which counsels him to turn a deaf ear to the noisy agitation of the "popular mind." "Compromise," published in *St. James's Gazette* on October 29, 1884, urges Gladstone not to be "precipitate in thine act / Of steering," but rather to resist "Whate'er the crowd…may say" (1–2, 8). Though in the midst of debates concerning Redistribution, Gladstone wrote to thank the poet, with an indefinable degree of irony, for his views: "I think it a great honour to receive from you a suggestion in verse" (*Memoir*, 2:309). Another poem, "Politics" (1884–85), admonishes "you that drive" to "firmly hold the rein, / Nor lend an ear to random cries" (5, 6–7). "'Captain, Guide!'" (1885) again imagines Gladstone charting a course through dangerous waters, urging, "in change of wind and tide, / List no longer to the crew!" (4–5). Each of these poems urges the prime minister essentially to proceed without regard to public opinion, characterized variously as the "random cries" of "the crowd" or "the crew." In his letters Arthur Hallam had compared Gladstone to Homer's Ulysses, and Tennyson too seems to imagine him at the helm, steering the ship of state. But Gladstone by this time had forwarded the argument that the only voice worth hearing is that of the crew, which itself must guide the captain.

Representations of Gladstone's speeches, whether positive or negative, stress the effect he had on his audience, his ability to sway crowds sometimes numbering in the tens of thousands. Many noted the disjunction between the apparent accessibility of these endeavors and his voluminous, highly detailed, generally pedantic writings on Homer. But perhaps his most significant statement regarding the theory behind his oratorical practice appears in his 1858 *Studies on Homer and the Homeric Age*:

> Poets of modern times have composed great works in ages that stopped their ears against them.… The case of the orator is entirely different. His work, from its very inception, is inextricably mixed up with practice. It is cast in the mould offered to him by the mind of his hearers. It is an influence principally received

from his audience (so to speak) in vapour, which he pours back upon them in a flood. The sympathy and concurrence of his time is with his own mind joint parent of his work. He cannot follow nor frame ideals; his choice is, to be what his age will have him, what it requires in order to be moved by him, or else not to be at all. (*SH*, 3:107)

This passage was frequently cited in contemporary Victorian analyses of Gladstone's oratorical abilities and effects, and its elements are important for us to understand in light of my larger arguments about the representation of efficacious speech in Tennyson. In a major modification of Mill's claim· that poetry is overheard and eloquence is heard, Gladstone argues that poets need not be heard at all, while eloquence is not only heard but produced by its contemporary auditors. Indeed, the orator's ontological status depends on his auditors; he is "to be" what his audience requires, or "not to be at all." Oratory is not something presented to auditors, intended to work on them in order to obtain the assent of their will, as Hallam, and Gladstone, had believed as young men. Gladstone now claims a reversal of oratorical cause and effect, whereby a speech is understood to be caused by its auditors rather than its speaker (who labors to articulate the crowd's views), as if an orator were himself the object of the audience's persuasive rhetorical gestures. Oratory is the performance of auditors.

Gladstone's theory developed, presumably, less out of his interpretations of Homeric speakers than out of his own practice, as he increasingly adapted his speeches to his audiences, following their cues.[92] This apparent ceding of a speaker's authority to an audience was widely remarked, and seriously questioned, by Gladstone's observers. One contemporary, the political journalist and *Daily News* editor Frank Harrison Hill, quotes in a reminiscence of Gladstone from this passage from *Studies on Homer*, strongly objecting to it as "self-excusatory." Hill sees this theory as "ignoble" and says of its practice by Gladstone, "If it does not convert him to a demagogue it is because he is demagogued, if one may be allowed to coin a word."[93] While Gladstone accedes to the orator himself being "joint parent" of the work, his theory, if practiced, might ultimately wrest paternity from the orator altogether, resulting in a yielding of his own voice and silencing of the free exchange of opposing ideas. The theory also commits a speaker to the trope of identification rather than similitude, as the orator's views are not considered *like* those of the crowd, but inseparable from them.

In a twentieth-century analysis of Gladstone's rhetorical prowess, D. A. Hamer describes the effects of Gladstone's encouragement of his audience to lead, which placed "more and more emphasis on those parts of his utterance which drew applause and popular acclaim, and less and less on those which did not."[94] In an analysis published in 1860 of the implications of Gladstone's oratory, Walter Bagehot also quotes from his oratorical theory in *Studies on Homer* and observes, "Such an orator may believe his conclusions but he can rarely believe them for the reasons which he assigns for them." More, this method militates against the possibility of rational thought for both the audience and the speaker, Bagehot believes, because the orator will "catch at disputable premises because his audience accepts them" and will "draw inferences from them which suit his momentary purpose."[95]

In "Gladstone on Church and State," Macaulay's 1839 review of Gladstone's first book, *The State in Its Relations with the Church* (1838), the Whig reviewer devotes an extensive analysis to the many points on which he disagrees with Gladstone (at this point in his career, still a staunch conservative). But he commends Gladstone's "laudable desire to penetrate beneath the surface of questions," noting that this quality is surprising in any politician, regardless of party. Macaulay attributes this in part to the fact that political rhetoric, because it is so often spoken, can carry its points by the performance itself, potentially replacing rationality with theatricality: "It is not by accuracy or profundity that men become the masters of great assemblies. . . . This has long appeared to us to be the most serious of the evils which are to be set off against the many blessings of popular government."[96] Macaulay was prescient in making this point in an essay on this particular rising politician: Gladstone was to become the master of vast assemblies, by reason of a personal and rhetorical magnetism, according to his more skeptical contemporary observers, rather than through penetrating rationality. Whether or not this cynical view was merited, there is ample cause to question whether Gladstone's theory was negated by his practice. The historian T. A. Jenkins echoes many Victorians in voicing a reservation over the statesman's efforts and effects: "When we consider the periodic bouts of mass-enthusiasm for Gladstone, which manifested themselves from the 1860s onwards, the hyperbolic praise that was heaped upon him, and the almost mystical, superhuman qualities that were attributed to him, it is difficult to believe that this was the product of a purely rational assessment of the virtues of the policies with which he was associated."[97]

Tennyson read "Tiresias" to Gladstone and Dean Bradley at Westminster on May 1, 1883, and we should understand this dramatic monologue to be as politically urgent as any other of his poems in this period.[98] I would argue, indeed, that this performance constitutes as direct an attempt to persuade the prime minister of the dangers of the demotic as his squibs of the following two years, "Compromise," "Politics," and "'Captain, Guide!'" In an unpublished fragment of "To E. FitzGerald," his dedication of "Tiresias," Tennyson makes his assignment of contemporary relevance explicit. "Ah if I / Should play Tiresias to the times," he fears that he "might but prophecy" various losses and cataclysms, "And fierce Transition's blood-red morn, / And years with lawless voices loud" (*Poems*, 3:108). Transition itself is conceived of as violent disorder, allied to the same popular voices (ignoble ["lawless"] but impossible to ignore ["loud"]) we hear in Tennyson's political poems. This draft offers its own highly conditional prophecy: "one lean hope, that at the last / Perchance—if this small world endures— / Our heirs may find the stormy Past / Has left their Present purer" (*Poems*, 3:109). In revision, Tennyson omitted this hypothetical scene of his own hesitant prediction of the future, thereby evading direct reference to the poet's own relation to civic transformation, as well as to the poet's likeness to his monologue's speaker. As we have seen, a significant generic consistency of the dramatic monologue is the speaker's recurring ambition for rhetorical efficacy, for the accomplishment of some effect in the course of the monologue, through the medium of the monologue itself. This ambition would appear to have taken on the cast of a crude didacticism in "Tiresias," but the genre itself maintains the poet's ideological and rhetorical separation from the dramatic monologist (whom the poet can only *play*), despite any resemblance, and thus interrogates the poet's capacity either to compel or to prevent "Transition." The poet resists playing the prophet, less because of the apparent theatricality than the apparent futility of the role.

By the time Tennyson set about revising "Tiresias," he was himself of advanced years. Begun as a young poet's precocious imagining of an old man's verbal impotence, "Tiresias" was completed by an elderly laureate whose words had long been on every schoolchild's lips. In 1833, Carlyle had described Tennyson, then revising poems featuring classical subjects, as "sitting on a dung-heap among innumerable dead dogs" (*Memoir*, 1:340). As the poet turned to complete "Tiresias," his wife, Emily Tennyson, wrote to a friend, "Ally has been finishing one of his old world poems begun about the *Ulysses* period and discarded as what Carlyle called 'a dead dog' but Ally has come to think that the world will receive lessons thus when it discards them in modern garb" (*Poems*, 1:623). The fifty years between the conception and the completion of this poem made a profound difference for the poet, of course. Not only was he writing from a greatly altered vantage point, but now he was also attempting to alter the vantage point of the genre. "Tiresias" is a product of the poet's revision of the monologue, and with it, the attempted revision of what had become an established literary form.

Tennyson sought similar didactic or intentional roles for other late monologues, such as "Demeter and Persephone" (1889) and "Akbar's Dream" (1892). This pedagogical project fails, though, and for the same reason that he tacitly acknowledged in omitting his introductory conjecture, "if I / Should play Tiresias to the times." He implicitly attempts, in these later monologues, to speak directly through a monologist, in the hope "that the world will receive lessons" from him. The poet thus adopts a stance inseparable from, rather than *like*, that of his speakers, which in itself must trouble our perception of the genre, in which monologists are not identical to the poet. In shackling his own discursive ambitions and regrets to those of the dramatic monologist Tiresias, Tennyson appears to break faith with a genre whose partition between the poet and the poem's speaker, a division both affirmed and breached by similitude rather than identification, is a governing principle. In his suppressed prefatory conjecture, Tennyson raises, and then silences, a central problem posed by the genre of the dramatic monologue, namely, the question of likeness, in political or cultural views, between the poet and the monologic speaker.

In its ideal, according to Gladstone, oratorical speech ought neither merely to "follow" or respond to public sentiment, nor to "frame" or anticipate it, but to be concurrent with it. This ventriloquism of an audience by an orator might be dismissed as mere pandering, but it can also be seen as promoting populism. Gladstone suggests the democratization of the practice of oratory, as auditors themselves determine the articulation of the oration, being not the objects but the proponents of persuasive speech. Whether or not it was borne out by his practice, Gladstone's theory can have fascinating implications for the reading of dramatic monologues, which in many ways are molded by their auditors, even as, in Victorian examples of the genre, there is always an assertion of the *monologic* nature of this discourse. Though a dramatic monologue can appear to have a double speaker (the poet and the monologist), the poet is not a "joint parent" of the work; the notion of joint or multiple authors being anathema to Tennyson, as much as, for example, the notion of a sequence of rhapsodists composing Homer's *Iliad*. In response to Gladstone's claim, Bagehot labels the transformation of a speaker in order to appeal to different audiences "the oratory of adaptation."[99] We might also call it an oratory of identification. According to Gladstone, the orator's voice should loudly echo the voice of its auditors: both the content and the form of a speech ought not merely to articulate but to amplify the vocation of the ma-jority, pouring back in a flood what it receives in vapor. The speaker is uttering not arguments or ideas that are like or resemble those of his auditors, but ideas that are identical to, inseparable from those whom he addresses. In recognizing that he cannot play Tiresias to the times, Tennyson maintains a crucial distinction, ulti-mately, even in this dramatic monologue: he cannot be wholly identified with his speaker, even as his speaker cannot be wholly identified with his audience. Were such absolute concordance possible, there would be no need for the dramatic monologue, as presumably there would be no need for the political oration.

Although Tennyson softened the explicit comparison of himself to his speaker and his times to those of Tiresias, the relevance of this dramatic mono-logue to current issues was established by that most contemporary of publications, *Punch*. The preface to volume 89 (December 26, 1885) features an illustration of an olive glade that encloses three figures: Tennyson in his distinctive cloak and hat, gesticulating in companionable conversation with Tiresias, also seated, and Mr. Punch, standing and facing Tennyson with the muzzled dog Toby at his side (figure 6.1). *Punch* rings out the old year with reference to Tennyson's "Tiresias," as Mr. Punch, clad in a toga and holding a sturdy black umbrella, notes regretfully that Pallas Athene is not at the moment emerging from her bath. Tiresias comforts him: "Better so. / *Your* blindness were the eclipse of Britain's sun." Mr. Punch in turn compliments Tennyson on remaining "Melodious still through Faction's fiercest roar," and Tiresias adds, "The Golden Bough / Bare

FIGURE 6.1 "Preface" [Tennyson, Tiresias, and Punch], *Punch* 89 (December 26, 1885): iii.

never mellower fruit since SAPPHO sang." "Thanks!" Tennyson exclaims, but then disdains "an effeminate song," preferring instead that "my daintiest Art" should fire "the patriot plumed for fight." Mr. Punch reassures Tennyson that all recognize him as "A patriot valiant and wise," whose poems "have dropt on a barren and bellicose day / Of angry and heady word-warfare." He is referring to the recent election, in which Gladstone was defeated by an alliance of conservatives and anti–Home-Rulers. On December 17, Gladstone's son had leaked his father's support for Home Rule in Ireland, and a national furor followed in the days prior to the conclusion of the election on December 19, the first major election in which virtually all male householders were eligible to vote. Mr. Punch imagines an audience will be more receptive to Tennyson's recently published poems, "When Christmas has softened their souls, / And sweetened their tempers, who lately went frantic and fierce at the Polls."

Mr. Punch hopes that Tennyson's poems may come in time to be recognized as being "As sweet as the music, TIRESIAS, to which your loved city was built," and his reference to Tiresias's song-built city prompts the following exchange:

> TIRESIAS   Will they *then* hear him, the mad multitude,
> To whom wise words, if cast against the wind
> Of their wild wishes and vain hopes, are vain,
> Here, as in Thebes?

PUNCH (cheerily)	At last they *must* hear ME!
TIRESIAS (admiringly)	Happy your lot, not blind nor unbelieved!
TENNYSON	Thrice happy, to no faction thrall,
	With Fairness and gay Fun,
	Flouting the tyranny of All,
	As well as that of One!

Unlike Tiresias and Tennyson, neither of whom was ever accused of being a figure of "gay Fun," Mr. Punch is neither blind nor unbelieved and not subject to the tyranny of the one *or* the many. Accepting cheerfully that the "mad multitude" will not hear prophets or poets but will certainly hear him, Punch reassures Tennyson, "Your hour will come," though at the present "The world wants something gay and bright and genial and amusing." With this, he removes the muzzle from the dog and in effect places it on the poet laureate. The closing lines offer Tennyson the volume and the role of reader rather than author, urging, "Take it! There is joy in every line. / Take, read to friend Tiresias, my Volume Eighty-Nine!"[100] Another, smaller cartoon after the end of the poem shows Mr. Punch, now in coat and top hat, helping to steady Tennyson, who stumbles as he tries to carry the massive tome, as if staggering under the weight of public opinion, to the limited extent that *Punch* might be understood to represent it (figure 6.2).[101]

Adopting for himself the role of national poet, Mr. Punch plays Tennyson to the times. In the poem that suggests to him this role, however, not only will Tennyson not play Tiresias to the times, but neither will Tiresias. That is, this dramatic monologue comes in the course of its utterance to reject its own stated discursive goals. In the first of the five 1833 fragments, Tiresias searches for words "potent to coerce, / And to conciliate" (116–17). In the course of his dramatic monologue, he recurs to the spectacle of his physical and rhetorical inutility, lamenting, "These blind hands were useless in their wars" (77) and complaining of "These useless eyes" (105) and "This useless hand!" (159). Of his foresight he also insists, "This power hath worked no good" (76). The internal drama enacted in the monologue would appear, however, to belie Tiresias's claims of futility. Has any reader ever doubted the truth of Tiresias's words, or the effect they will have? The curse of Pallas is far more futile; what reader, seeing Tiresias's name at the title, would doubt his claims? His discursive goals are directly stated and seem directly met, even before they are stated. According to the readings of "Ulysses" and "Tithonus" I have forwarded, each speaker accomplishes what he seeks, chiefly the accession to his will by his auditor, and we know certainly that Menœceus does not even tarry for the conclusion of the monologue, but hurries to his death.

But the death of Menœceus and the consequent salvation of the song-built city of Thebes are not, finally, the goal of Tiresias's speech. Instead, what he seeks to achieve in his dramatic monologue, by way of the dramatic monologue, is

𝔙𝔬𝔩𝔲𝔪𝔢 𝔈𝔦𝔤𝔥𝔱𝔶-𝔑𝔦𝔫𝔢!

FIGURE 6.2 "Volume Eighty-Nine!"
[Tennyson and Punch], *Punch* 89
(December 26, 1885): iv.

the death of the dramatic monologue. His ambition is to attain the death of the
suasive lyric voice. I have been associating the rise of the dramatic monologue, in
Tennyson's practice of the genre, with the rise in liberal democracy in the course
of the poet's career. Gladstone, the man most associated with that rise, wrote of
the classical period, still believed to be so consequential, that the "trait which
is truly the most worthy of note in the polities of Homeric Greece" is "the
substantive weight and influence which belonged to speech as an instrument of
government." He remarks in the Homeric period a "power of speech" that was
"essentially a power to be exercised over numbers," "by man among his fellow-
men" and "also essentially an instrument addressing itself to reason and free will"
(*SH*, 3:102). While one man speaks, he stands "among" rather than above his
fellows or peers, and his speech asks them for the kind of rational response ostensibly sought by Tennyson's "Ulysses," namely, the agreement of "free hearts, free
foreheads." In spite of recognizing oratory's "power," Gladstone sees the oratorical
experience as one of shared potency. For one of the period's preeminent orators,
persuasive efforts not only advanced a democratic agenda, reflecting or increasing
popular support of particular initiatives, but themselves constituted democratic

objects, created communally by a range of equal voices, one of which belongs to the speaker himself. In this way, an orator's speech might be democratic (that is, representing the will of the majority) both in content and in form.

Tennyson's Tiresias hears in this popular voice the discursive tyranny of the many. While Gladstone is boundless in his admiration for the "leading orators" in Homer (Ulysses and Achilles in particular), he admires the auditors as well, arguing that it is not possible "that in any age there should be in a few a capacity for making such speeches, without a capacity in many for receiving, feeling, and comprehending them" (*SH*, 3:107). The speaker of "Tiresias," however, rejects . the capacity of auditors to receive, feel, or comprehend his words, and this includes Menœceus; it is in his utter subjugation to Tiresias's words that the young auditor, assigned to represent all Thebans, does actually represent the populace. Menœceus's response to the monologue can look like an exercise of reason and free will, his answer to the prophet's words of "warning" and "counsel" (terms suggesting the autonomy of an auditor who may choose to reject what he hears). An 1833 fragment of the poem at Trinity shows that, instead, Menœceus is merely following orders: in the early version, Tiresias commands his audience, "Go thou and do my bidding" (*T. Nbk.* 20). According to Tiresias, civic tyranny is a product of the prophet's discursive impotence, and yet what this tyranny realizes is Tiresias's own discursive control. Even as he finally finds a willing audience, this speaker exterminates him, and in this Menœceus stands as representative for the annihilation of any rational audience.

Emily Tennyson's characterization of "Ally's" ambition ally the poet quite specifically with this particular monologist, since it is Tiresias's concern as well that the world discards his lessons and that he must therefore render his teachings more accessible. Tiresias comes to discard the lessons himself, however, having in his monologue interrogated his own vatic role. I would argue that Tennyson did not retreat from engagement with his public; to the contrary, in the decade left to him after completing "Tiresias," Tennyson was more politically active, in his person and his poetry, than he had ever been in his life. He did not play Tiresias—that is, he did not play *Tennyson's* Tiresias—to the age, in that he did not reject engagement with the most pressing issues of his day. But in this dramatic monologue he experiments with the rejection of not only the vocation of the populace, but the vocation of the poet. In assuming the discursive tyranny of one, namely himself, Tiresias rejects suasion in favor of dictation, or dictatorship. In the dramatic monologue, by way of the dramatic monologue, Tiresias accomplishes or performs the failure of the monologue, enacting the failure of the rational, singular voice in an increasingly democratic age. "Poets of modern times have composed great works in ages that stopped their ears against them," Gladstone asserts, yet it is not that the age stops its ear against the dramatic monologist, but that he stops his ears against the age, performing a discursive absolutism whose implications are as political as they are poetical.

The Apotheosis of Tiresias

After Gladstone's death in 1898, Queen Victoria remarked in her diary of a man whose loss it would have been difficult for her to mourn, "He had a wonderful power of speaking and carrying the masses with him."[102] In his theory of oratory published four decades earlier in *Studies on Homer,* Gladstone claims, however, that the masses are largely self-propelled, establishing for an orator what they require of him if they are to be "moved." After commanding the national stage for some years, Gladstone gave this advice (noted in my first chapter) to an admirer: "Remember that if you are to sway an audience you must besides thinking out your matter, watch them all along."[103] Many observers argued, however, that it was virtually impossible to "think out one's matter" under the conditions of an oratorical performance before a great crowd. Moreover, the ambition to "watch" the audience "all along," which might be understood to follow upon Gladstone's argument in *Studies on Homer,* suggests that the speaker might be propelled by public opinion rather than political substance, with a speaker watching an audience watching him watching them. As Walter Bagehot put it in his 1871 essay, "Mr. Gladstone and the People," the prime minister managed to "deal with political topics in the broad, easy, and animated style which touches the people."[104] What remained surprising to critics, as R. H. Hutton wrote in 1894, was that although Gladstone's "own natural style was almost scholastic," he was able to electrify "those modern drill-halls or circuses in which great mass meetings are now addressed."[105]

Bagehot remarks the intellectual limitations of a speech "made to 25,000 people in the open air": "A man who has to exert his voice to the utmost, and to interest a great crowd for a considerable time, cannot by any possibility trace out the fine lines of a national policy, even if he had spare energy enough to concentrate his mind upon them in the face of such physical difficulties."[106] For all of its implicit claims to democratic access, the physical space of vast public arenas may not be conducive to reflection on the part of either speakers or individual auditors. Bagehot had previously noted, in an 1860 essay on Gladstone, "The higher faculties of the mind require a certain calm, and the excitement of oratory is unfavorable to that calm." Exercising analytic faculties becomes unlikely not only for a public that can get "carried away" but also for the orator, since the "force which carries away his hearers must first carry away himself," a transportation that Bagehot likens to a "kind of *seizure.*"[107] The magnitude of the crowd, and the task of appealing to it "naturally inclines" the speaker, Bagehot worries, "to the views which will excite that audience most effectually." Gladstone's orations are "easy," accessible, but they disturb more for being violently transformative. In these most powerful moments of Victorian oratory, both the speaker and the audience are "carried away," "seized." Bagehot, the queen, and the prime minister himself all hear in his performances the act of discursive transportation (carrying, moving) I have been associating in Tennyson with rapture. In his rejection of rhetorical suasion, Tennyson's Tiresias can appear to refuse to enter the state of being carried away, but in this final section we shall attend to this blind seer's final rapturous vision.

Having sought and then rejected popular accessibility, Tiresias now seeks the divine inaccessibility of Elysium. In turning on his own heel to address, as his monologue does from the outset, one rather than all, Tiresias had turned away from the Theban multitude and toward an audience he singled out for address, an auditor from whom he in the end also turns away, the one representing too precisely the many. It is therefore a fitting culmination of the monologue for him to seek the genuinely exclusive company of gods and heroes. Theodore Redpath observes of the poem's didacticism, "It seems to have been intended...to be something of an appeal to the finest of the young not to be afraid to sacrifice themselves for great causes."[108] Contemporary readers recognized this; Alfred Lyall commented on "Tiresias," "The modern poet transfigures the legend into a lofty encomium upon the glory of patriotic martyrdom."[109] *Il faut payer de sa vie.* But Redpath exempts the poem's closing lines from this purpose, explaining that these "were added during...revision, and they seem to express nothing didactic, but rather a yearning for the kind of return which involves a nostalgic *contemplation* of the glory for old times."[110] Because saving the song-built city is accomplished before the end of the monologue (and is indeed virtually prescribed), this final translation of Tiresias to Elysium is what he seeks more broadly to effect. Tiresias has not indicated in his monologue the extent of his foresight into his own future. While he assures himself of what his "eyes will find" there, the subjunctive mode with which he draws toward this vision ("I would that I were") suggests that he cannot yet see, or perhaps that he hopes to dictate an alternative to what he does see. The monologue moves toward replacing his foreknowledge, which he has never desired to be honored, with his "yearning," which he has. But of what does his yearning consist?

Tiresias dismisses Menœceus ("He will achieve his greatness"), as if to acknowledge that he has never been the subject or the object of the monologue, and turns to a vision of his own future, itself a heroic one:

> But for me,
> I would that I were gathered to my rest,
> And mingled with the famous kings of old,
> On whom about their ocean-islets flash
> The faces of the Gods—the wise man's word,
> Here trampled by the populace underfoot,
> There crowned with worship—and these eyes will find

The men I knew, and watch the chariot whirl
About the goal again, and hunters race
The shadowy lion, and warrior-kings,
In height and prowess more than human, strive
Again for glory, while the golden lyre
Is ever sounding in heroic ears
Heroic hymns, and every way the vales
Wind, clouded with the grateful incense-fume
Of those who mix all odour to the Gods
On one far height in one far-shining fire. (161–77)

Although he has sent Menœceus off to great achievement, Tiresias appears to be eschewing any such ambition for himself, to have failed for so long that he no longer seeks existence, let alone honors. He contrasts Menœceus's "one great deed" (157) with his own useless retirement, insisting not only that he desires "rest," but to be "gathered" to it, in opposition to his auditor's strenuous action. Yet Tiresias's withdrawal is not toward "rest" but toward vigorous activity, to whirling chariots and racing hunters and warrior-kings in Olympic competition, conveyed here in a series of enjambed lines that turn with a kind of lyric athleticism on "whirl," "race" and "strive."

Tiresias's final vision is marked by other contradictions. His monologue appears to offer a critique of the authority held by kings and gods ("The Gods . . . / Are slower to forgive than human kings"), and he has been mediating between Cadmus's line of kings and Ares' line of gods. He has compared the motivations of kings not only to the smoldering anger of the gods, but to the headlong irrationality of the populace. In cataloguing the inefficacy of his speech he has lamented, "nor . . . / was mine the voice to curb / The madness of our cities and their kings" (66, 69–70). Nevertheless, he seeks to "mingle with the famous kings of old," in a return to the monologue's first line, in which he longs to return to the "days of old." These ancient kings and days may remind us of the refrain in Tennyson's 1837 "Amphion," "Oh had I lived when song was great / In days of old Amphion." Song, according to the speaker of that poem, had been great because it had been literally propulsive, compelling rocks and persons into movement, and Tiresias too seeks to move his auditors by the compulsive rhythms of his final words.

Tennyson's son tells us that the poet "liked to quote" from this final passage of "Tiresias" "as a sample of his blank verse" (*Memoir*, 2:318). Full of admiration for Tennyson's powers of lyric variety ("He touched no rhythm that he did not adorn, and . . . very few poets have touched so many rhythms"), George Saintsbury reserves special praise for his blank verse: "His extraordinary accomplishment in blank verse is almost unique."[111] Tennyson was an unparalleled judge of the technical quality of his work, but his privileging of the blank verse of this concluding verse paragraph, a distinction invariably remarked in discussions of this poem, should give us pause, partly because not everyone agrees that these are exemplary. Ricks comments, "Some woodenness encumbers the verse... the skill is patent, too much so." "What went wrong?" he asks, and surmises, "Complacency."[112] Even admirers of this verse might well wonder how it was that these particular lines could so distinguish themselves among so many contending examples in Tennyson's oeuvre: what makes them merit being singled out as an "example," even as Tiresias himself had wished to be singled out? To answer this, we must glance toward the great example of English nondramatic blank verse: John Milton's *Paradise Lost*.[113]

Tennyson's admiration for Milton's poetry was vast; speaking of the "grand style," Tennyson told his son that "he considered that of Milton even finer than that of Virgil, 'the lord of language'" (*Memoir*, 2:284). Milton broods over Tennyson in more ways than criticism has yet addressed, but he might be seen especially to hover over "Tiresias," since Milton likened himself to that vatic figure—as well as to the sightless poet Homer—in the invocation to book 3: "blind *Mæonides* / And *Tiresias*" (3.34–35). Marvell's prefatory poem "On Paradise Lost" compares Milton to Tiresias ("Just Heav'n thee like *Tiresias* to requite / Rewards with Prophecy thy loss of sight"), immediately before addressing the problem posed by the epic's use of blank verse, its lack of "tinkling Rime" (43–44, 46).[114] In Milton's explanation for "why the Poem Rimes not," he states that we might find "true musical delight" in "apt Numbers, fit Quantity of Syllables, and the sense variously drawn out from one Verse into another, not in the jingling sound of like endings, a fault avoided by the learned Ancients both in Poetry and all good Oratory."[115] Adumbrating the elements and ambitions of blank verse, Milton shows that he has ample precedent, both in poetry and in oratory, and this can help us track the complex associations Tennyson brings to what is in a sense Tiresias's blank verse oration. M. H. Abrams speaks for many theorists of English prosody in noting that unrhymed iambic pentameter is the "closest to natural rhythms of English speech,"[116] a quality of blank verse that is highly relevant for Tennyson's Tiresias, burdened as he is with finding an efficacious mode of articulation.

In his notorious politicizing of his verse form, Milton calls *Paradise Lost* "the first in *English*, of ancient liberty recover'd to Heroic Poem from the troublesome and modern bondage of Riming," thus associating "ancient liberty" with blank verse.[117] Tennyson's blank verse, however, might appear to resist bondage to a liberal ideology. Reviewing Tennyson's long career and considering his prosody more widely, Harold Nicolson claims that he "passed from an early suspicion of democracy, through a wholesome dislike of democracy, to a loathing of democracy so fierce and so violent that it upset not only his health and temper, but even his prosody."[118] Nicolson maintained that his late, "violent" antidemocratic sentiments "upset" Tennyson's prosody, but Tennyson maintains that his late blank verse is particularly exemplary. Saintsbury concurred; reviewing Tennyson's "later blank verse," he comments, "It is difficult, even with the assistance of the *Life*, to be quite certain of the time when Tennyson attained his absolute zenith in this art," though he considers "Tithonus" a chief example. After quoting the first ten lines of the dramatic monologue in a footnote, he comments, "For once, rhyme has nothing to add to this; the magic of the poet has already given all, or almost all, that it could give." He notes a similar mastery of blank verse in "Tiresias": "Scores of passages in the *Idylls*, in *Tiresias*, and in other poems, would have to be taken into consideration by any one who wants to get a really synoptic view of the matter."[119] In privileging the aesthetic merit of what I believe are openly antidemocratic lines, Tennyson takes what he might have considered a synoptic view. Responding to Milton's association of the form with more radical ends, Tennyson put the resources of the blank verse line to more conservative purposes, if only to suggest that no poetic form bears a necessary political connotation.

Milton points to the liberating potential of blank verse, but in the closing lines of Tennyson's "Tiresias" the dramatic monologist does not seek the kind of unfettering that the verse form, following its greatest literary historical precedent, might be seen to permit. Tiresias's verse paragraph, thick with kings and heroes, culminates in the image of a "golden lyre" that is "ever sounding in heroic ears / Heroic hymns." Tiresias has just dispatched young Menœceus to an act of self-destroying heroism comparable in its way to the sacrifice undertaken by the Son in *Paradise Lost*, but these closing lines confirm our earlier suspicion that it is not his auditor's heroic act that concerns Tiresias but his own heroic discourse. Milton states that his epic employs "*English* Heroic Verse without Rime, as that of *Homer* in *Greek*, and of *Virgil* in *Latin*,"[120] and we recall that iambic pentameter is termed the "heroic line" because it is used so often in epic or heroic poetry in English (its equivalent in classical literature is dactylic hexameter, in French the alexandrine). Tennyson forwards the possibility that Tiresias attains to the heroic by way of his dramatic monologue's metrical affiliations—and yet we can hear in these culminating lines the countermanding suggestion that heroic hymns gain their valorous qualities after all not from their singer but from their auditors.

What might a heroic hymn, as imagined here by Tiresias, sound like? It might sound like Tiresias's dramatic monologue, which is so efficacious that it is capable, in the course of its articulation, of saving the song-built city and thus transforming its auditor Menœceus, and its speaker Tiresias, into heroes. But as performed on a golden lyre in Tiresias's "Pagan Paradise" ("To E. FitzGerald," 64), these worshipful "Heroic hymns" sound in "heroic ears," whose identification with the songs knows no disjunction. How different is such an audience from the Theban multitude whose incomprehension is a daily scourge. Indeed, these heroic hymns sound *only* in heroic ears, signifying a radical deviation in Tiresias's ambitions for his own vatic voice. Emily Tennyson reports that the poet had returned to this "old world" poem because he hoped "that the world will receive lessons thus"; Tennyson had sought, apparently, to teach the many or multitude through efficacious verse. Tiresias's exemplary closing blank verse lines suggest, however, that the audience for heroic hymns must be possessed of heroic ears. The poem therefore develops not only from fragments the poet's son unearthed from his 1833 notebooks, but from Arthur Hallam's 1831 essay on Tennyson, in which he resigns himself and his friend to the fact that poetry can no longer attain to a popular following. Reading poetry, according to Hallam, "requires exertion," which is "not willingly made by the large majority of readers" (*Writings*, 188). Tiresias's heroic lines point to a defeat on his part, an abandonment of a larger potential audience, in favor of an audience fit, because few.

The final verse paragraph offers still other reversals on the part of Tiresias. He has told his auditor that a goddess blinded him when, he says, she "flashed upon me" useless power. He describes how, in punishment for having seen Athena "climbing from the bath," she darkened his sight by way of her "virgin eyes / Remaining fixt on mine" (45–46). But in closing he seeks again to see the faces of divinities "flash" out of bodies of water (now "ocean islets"), as if to recreate in perpetuity not the effects but the cause of his blindness. In her essay "What Tiresias Saw," Nicole Loraux warns, "For a human to behold the faces of the gods, even when they are motivated by friendly intentions, is difficult, even dangerous."[121] Tiresias, at "rest," seeks to recapture the "flash" of his viewing of the "faces of the Gods," to enjoy continually that forbidden spectacle, and this may indicate to us that Tiresias's mistake of happening upon a naked Pallas, like Tithonus's verbal construction "Give me immortality," was intentional.

Critics have remonstrated against the severity of the goddess's punishment; as James Kincaid argues, "She reveals to him the principles on which the universe operates: malignity and pettiness. Because he dared to worship, Tiresias is made the subject of a vicious joke."[122] Athena's swift punishment reflects, however, her wisdom as much as it does her modesty. As she "flashed" her visage upon Tiresias, she apprehended some less worshipful attention, recognizing in his upturned face the unspecified "desire" and "yearning," some ambition for uncommon distinction, to which his monologue freely admits (as do those of Ulysses and Tithonus). The closing verse paragraph emphasizes the restoration of his sight; this can demonstrate an ongoing transgressive voyeurism, but it hints too at a more daring fantasy. In regaining his sight and the company of the "famous kings of old," he points toward a historical regression that contains a personal reversion as well. He does not imagine his entrance into this Elysium as an ancient man with recovered vision; rather, because the sense of sight is associated by him with the state of being a young man, his is a fantasy of being restored not merely to vision but to his own ephebism.

The monologue's closing vision may itself draw the parameters of the "boundless yearning" of Tiresias. Seeking exclusively the company of gods and kings, the only group he would now avoid is the populace, characterized by Lord Henry Wotton in his counsel to Dorian Gray as "the ignorant, the common, and the vulgar." Tiresias tells us that he seeks "the men I knew," and of course Ulysses (who himself seeks always to be known) announces when he finds Tiresias in the underworld of the *Odyssey*, "he knew me well" (11:113, trans. Chapman). In the *Odyssey*, before leaving the underworld where he has learned his future from Tiresias, Ulysses hesitates, in the hope of seeing what Tennyson's Tiresias now also longs to see, namely, "more Heroes of the times before." This desire for the company of what Tiresias calls "warrior-kings" is frustrated, according to Ulysses: "but before th' atchiev'd / Rare sight of these [Heroes] the rank-soul'd multitude / In infinite flocks rose, venting sounds so rude / That pale Feare tooke me" (11:858–61, trans. Chapman). Ulysses' specific fear is that the Gorgon's head will be "thrust up . . . / By grim Persephone" (11:862–63, trans. Chapman). We might also sense, in Tennyson's Tiresias at least, a fear of a multitude "infinite" in dimension, threatening and inhuman in its magnified sound, like that of the roaring crowd of Thebans, or what the excised lines in the dedication to FitzGerald bemoans as the "lawless voices loud" of their own time. Early in the monologue Tiresias describes a Thebes where "To cast wise words among the multitude / Was flinging fruit to lions." He still holds this view at the end of a monologue that in its course has labored first to cement him to his city, then to spirit him away from it.

Tiresias contrasts Thebes, where "the wise man's word" is "trampled by the populace underfoot," with Elysium, where the "wise man's word" is "crowned with worship." Tiresias's "word," presumably his dramatic monologue itself, will enjoy kingly "crowning" and godlike "worship." What Tennyson's Tiresias seeks to accomplish in the monologue, the utterance of the word of a "wise man," by way of the monologic mode itself, is the assumption not only of verbal potency in his honored words, but also of power more broadly defined. He intends by way of the monologue's self-consciously "wise words" to become kingly, godlike, something he may well achieve. In the eleventh book of the *Odyssey*, when Tiresias appears to Ulysses, he is holding not a "golden lyre" but "a golden Scepter"; after Tiresias departs, Ulysses calls him "the kingly soule" (11:113, 190, trans. Chapman). The fire that Tiresias evokes in closing is unlike that of Cassandra, which danced "before her night and day." This seer's senses are filled instead with the flames of the "grateful incense-fume" (175), a sacrifice to the gods whose capricious authority Tennyson has questioned throughout his poems on classical subjects. In offering to the gods "On one far height in one far-shining fire" (177) the kind of offering that Zeus missed when Demeter in her anguish rendered earth a "fruitless fallow" ("he missed / The wonted steam of sacrifice" ["Demeter and Persephone," 116–17]), the dramatic monologue endorses rather than laments the exercise of such arbitrary power. In its repetition of the word "one," the final line also underscores the singularity of voice and vision that the dramatic monologue, as performance and as genre, has emphasized from the start.

In his dedication of this poem to Edward FitzGerald, Tennyson admits that his friend, who predeceased the poem's publication, would not have been pleased with the monologue's conclusion, but would instead prefer "A less diffuse and opulent end, / And would defend his judgment well" ("To E. FitzGerald," 60–61). Not only is Tiresias's discourse opulent, but so are his destination and his means of transportation. In his conditional statement, "I would that I were gathered to my rest," Tiresias asserts unconditionally what it is he most yearns for: to be "gathered" to this paradise, borne away to it. The word "gathered" can sound like he desires a gentle delivery, but it also suggests an ambition to be raptured, to be taken up bodily and transported to a divine community.

That rapture is Tiresias's ambition is borne out by a poem fragment, "Semele" (1833), that serves as a subtext, appearing literally under the manuscript of these final lines. The 1833 draft of "Tiresias" in *Trinity Notebook* 20 contains what would half a century later be published as the final lines of the final version of the poem (lines 161–77). Tennyson's revisions were minor, as in his alterations to the line regarding the "famous kings of old" to whom, in this version, "the faces of the Gods / Flash on a sudden" (*T. Nbk.* 20; 0.15.20 fol. 12r). The revisions are telling, however, as in this instance, in which the swift unexpected quality of this "flash"—so important a word for the speaker—is omitted. Tiresias's willing submission to being gathered into the sudden flashing of the gods represents more clearly, however, that what he desires is to experience the sensation of being divinely overtaken suddenly and without warning. The sharpest association of Tiresias with rapture occurs, however, on the other side of the page on which Tennyson wrote these lines. In his early notebooks, it was fairly common for Tennyson, when he had reached the end of the notebook, to turn it upside down and continue to write in a new sequence on the reversed pages. In the case of this early draft of "Tiresias," this process is unusually revealing. The final lines of what would become the dramatic monologue bear the heading "End of Tiresias" at the top of the page, 12 recto. On page 12 verso there appears, upside down, a draft for the poem "Semele" (0.15.20.fol.12v [reversed]).[123] While this poem may be too fragmentary to be considered a nascent dramatic monologue, it is written in first person, and its female speaker recounts an incidence of rapture, the most vivid and violent Tennyson would ever write.

"Tiresias" became notable, at the instigation of its author, for its exemplary iambic pentameter, but the poem fragment "Semele" is written in free verse, which is, according to his most comprehensive editor, "very unusual for Tennyson" (*Poems*, 1:630). The poem's speaker, Semele, bears similarities to Tiresias, however. Tiresias reminds Menœceus that he is descended from Cadmus; Semele is a daughter of Cadmus and Harmonia. Like Tiresias, she too is the victim of an angry goddess. A lover of Zeus, Semele was, by most mythological accounts, tricked by Hera, who came to her in the form of her nurse and persuaded her, as Lemprière tells the story, to have the god "come to her arms with the same majesty as he approached" his wife. "This rash request was heard with horror" by a god who knew what Tithonus also learned, that humans should not behold a god directly.[124] Zeus's attempt to dissuade her failed, and when he appeared to her in the full force of his fiery godhead, she was burned to death. She was pregnant by the god, and her fetus was rescued from her burning womb and sewn into the thigh of its immortal father, who carried their child, the god Dionysus (or Bacchus), to full term.

"The mortal nature of Semele could not endure so much majesty, and she was instantly consumed by fire," Lemprière reports.[125] The thirty lines we have of Tennyson's "Semele" seem to take place in the instant of the god's approach. She begins:

> I wished to see him: who may feel
> His light and live? He comes.
> The blast of Godhead bursts the doors.
> This mortal house is all too narrow
> To enclose the wonder. (1–5)

In some mythical accounts, Semele is the victim of the cruel, vengeful ruse of a powerful goddess, but in Tennyson's telling, the demands she makes are wholly intentional, like those of her Tennysonian peers Simeon, Ulysses, Tithonus, and Tiresias. Just as the "End of Tiresias" begins with the speaker's stated desire ("I would that I were"), "Semele" begins with a statement of her desire: "I wished to see him." She assumes full responsibility for the consequences of her yearning: the colon following her stated wish indicates her recognition that death will be the result: "who may feel / His light and live?" The first line and a half of the poem span the course of her desire and its known consequences. The caesura of the full stop, after the word "live," marks the end of her life though not of the line. Her death sentence is the sentence "He comes," and yet with his arrival begins the "flash" of her rapture.

The god's sudden, overwhelming arrival constitutes an explosive vaginal intrusion, as his blast bursts apart the doors of her narrow mortal house. This may remind us of another of Zeus's erotic exploits, the rape of Leda by the god appearing in the form of a swan. Yeats's "Leda and the Swan" (1928) begins, "A sudden blow: the great wings beating still / Above the staggering girl," but though the god's arrival is just as sudden for Semele, unlike Leda she is neither "helpless" nor "terrified" ("Leda and the Swan," 1–2, 4, 5). "He came to her bed attended by the clouds, the lightning, and thunderbolts," according to Lemprière, and even as she is, like Yeats's Leda, "caught up" ("Leda and the Swan," 10), Tennyson's Semele observes, "His mighty hands entwine / The triple forks" (6–7). She wished to "feel / His light," and the sensations she describes in the wavy foldings of her enjambed lines have an atmospheric lightness: "Over me, / Fluttering in Elysian airs / His green and azure mantles float in wavy / Foldings" (9–12).

Semele desires to see her lover; now she hears him too, and "when he speaks / The crown of starlight shudders round / Ambrosial temples" (7–9). The god also shudders in "Leda and the Swan," begetting all the woes of the Trojan story: "A shudder in the loins engenders there / The broken wall, the burning roof and tower /And Agamemnon dead" (9–11). Zeus has already engendered Semele's son, Dionysus, whose presence is announced by her turn to address him (as was the case with Ulysses' son, Telemachus, and Tiresias's "son," Menœceus). After describing Zeus's dizzying lovemaking, during which "melodious thunder / Wheels in circles," she says, "But thou, my son, who shalt be born / When I am ashes, to delight the world—" (12–13, 14–15). Dionysus (Bacchus) is a fitting figure not only for this mother, but for this poet to turn to. I have noted the relevance of the Greek god Apollo to Troy's beautiful young men, and Lemprière notes of this originally Theban deity, "His beauty is compared to that of Apollo, and, like him, he is represented with fine hair loosely flowing down his shoulders, and he is said to possess eternal youth." God of wine and the theater, Dionysus is often figured, Lemprière states, as beardless and "effeminate," and sometimes depicted as an old man, thus easily transgressing boundaries of generation as well as of gender. This moment of Semele's announcement of his presence may occur concurrently with his partition from her womb. She speaks with fore-knowledge of his future, "When I am ashes." "As she was a mortal," Lemprière recounts, "and unable to bear the majesty of Jupiter, she was consumed and reduced to ashes."[126] Tennyson's Tithonus looks back upon his ruined self and laments, "And all I was, in ashes," and Semele also locates her transformed identity in her incineration.

At the moment of her speaking, Semele is being consumed by the fire from which her divine offspring is being rescued. She proceeds to describe the Dionysian festivals or Bacchanalia of her son, emphasizing their temporal immediacy with the repetition of the word "now," by which she signifies the temporal sequencing of the festivals ("now" meaning "next"), but also their immediacy:

> Now with measured cymbal-clash
> Moving on to victory;
> Now on music-rolling golden orbs,
> A sliding throne, voluptuously
> Panther-drawn,
> To throbbings of the thundrous gong
> And melody o' the merrily-blowing flute;
> Now with troops of clamorous revelers,

Noisily, merrily,
Rapidly, giddily
Rioting, triumphing,
Bacchanalians
Rushing in cadence,
All in order
Plunging down the viney valleys. (14–30)

Dionysus's role, his mother declares in these closing lines, is "to delight the world"; as *Punch* would remind Tennyson fifty years later, "The world wants something gay and bright and genial and amusing." The Dionysian festivals celebrating this god of impersonation and epiphany were often far from genial, of course, but instead ecstatic, often violent, orgiastic rituals, celebrating the transformations occasioned by wine, theater, or death.

"The infamous debaucheries which arose from the celebration of these festivals are well known," comments Lemprière regarding these Bacchanalia; so well known, apparently, that Connop Thirlwall, in his essay, "On the Attic Dionysia," published in 1833 (the year Tennyson produced this Dionysian fragment) in the Cambridge journal *Philological Museum*, finds no cause to review them. Instead, he presents a detailed response to a recent essay by a German philologist on the relations among differing Dionysian festivals. His interest is academic; because of their direct connection to the Greek dramas performed at them, these festivals "have naturally been objects of peculiar interest to the learned, nor ought it to be believed that the attention bestowed on them has been misplaced." Research into these events deepens our knowledge both of context (increasing our understanding of "the outward conditions and occasions that determined the production of those masterpieces of dramatic art") and of text (enabling "the study of these great works themselves"). But the justification to undertake this study comes to rest less on the appeal of scholarly utility than on the appeal of a Bacchic casting aside of inhibition: "However diminutive may be the object that attracts us in any new direction across the boundless field of antiquity, we may safely abandon ourselves to the impulse which urges us to investigate it." Abandoning himself to these urgent impulses, one of Victorian Britain's most distinguished scholars limns a desire at once exegetical and experiential, as this intellectual pursuit constitutes an abandonment to physical pleasure: "Even if we should not find any use to which it is immediately applicable, we shall assuredly be rewarded for our labour, not merely by the invigorating effect of the exercise, but by the air we shall breathe, the new views that will open on us, and the flowers that we shall gather in our way."[127]

Tiresias bears various connections to Bacchus; he too is a figure capable of gender transformation, from man into woman and back again, and in Euripides' *Bacchae* he labors unsuccessfully to convince Pentheus not to interfere with the celebrations of the god's ecstatic followers. Moving into her own characterization of Bacchic abandon, Semele describes her son "Moving on to victory" on a "Panther-drawn" throne on "music-rolling" golden wheels. The young Tennyson depends on the compound words so characteristic of his early poems, such as "Ilion, Ilion" (1830). He had asked the Trojan city, "To a music merrily flowing, merrily echoing / When wilt thou be melody born?" (8–9), and the Bacchanalians in "Semele" are themselves melody-borne, drawn forward by the "merrily-blowing flute."

This Theban festival evokes the origin of Troy; it also evokes the end of the world. The celebrants "carried thyrsi, drums, pipes, and flutes," as Lemprière notes, "and crowned themselves with garlands of ivy, vine, fir, &c.,"[128] and in Tennyson's version they are attended "Noisily" by the cymbal, gong, and flute. While the sound echoes "merrily, / Rapidly, giddily," however, it also, in its "measured" "cadence," strikes an ominous chord. Amid "the dark and windy waste of Earth" in "Armageddon," an early poem of Tennyson's, there is "a beating in the atmosphere, / An indefinable pulsation," and the "tumultuous throbbings" (4:27, 28–29, 33) of the destruction of the universe sound like the "throbbings" of these "thunderous" instruments and "clamorous," "Rioting," "revelers." Seemingly undisciplined and yet "All in order," the movement of the Bacchanalians seems as free as the movement of this free verse. "Plunging down," they seem also to be rising up, caught up in a cacophonous rapture that seems far removed from the stately heroic hymns Tiresias can hear already, on the reverse page of these closing lines of Semele's incandescent vision.

Although Semele describes the future Dionysia honoring the son torn from her inflamed womb, she is also describing a concurrent event; this clamorous revelry is taking place, she thrice repeats, "Now." Such temporal simultaneity is the result of this present event and that future one constituting one continuous experience of rapture, which is to say, the "blast of Godhead" that Semele calls down upon herself as surely and knowingly as do Simeon, Tithonus, and Tiresias. Like Tennyson's major dramatic monologues begun in the year of this fragment's composition—"St. Simeon Stylites," "Ulysses," "Tithonus," "Tiresias"—Semele narrates an event that takes place in the time of its utterance and performs the rapture her monologue describes. She is burning as she speaks, like Dante's Ulysses, the figure who beckons always to Tennyson's Ulysses, who also speaks from the flames and can, like Oenone, by night or day, "see only burning fire." Semele in the blazing moments of her articulation is also attaining her ambition: to become like a god, or, more specifically, like the goddess Hera, who enjoys unmediated intercourse with the blast of Godhead. During Zeus's thunderous lovemaking, Semele enters his realm of "Ambrosial temples" and "Elysian airs." The speaker feels herself as she speaks already transported to Elysium, and indeed many mythological accounts hold that she was immortalized in the lightning's purifying fire, her apotheosis, according to some accounts, being concurrent with her incineration. (Other accounts claim she becomes an immortal following her rescue from the underworld by her son.) Her deific name, Thyone, is based etymologically on *thyo* (to rush or rage) and is considered to signify fury and ecstasy. Tiresias yearns for his own apotheosis, literally to become a god (Latin, from Greek, *apo*, change + *theos*, god). Exaltation to divine rank or stature, by way of rapture, is also the goal of Simeon and Tithonus, who imagine that deific resemblance constitutes deification. The one far-shining fire he can see as he speaks burns to apotheosize kingly Tiresias, and thus to join him to the performance of transformative discursive rapture that unites these dramatic monologists, and consumes them.

CONCLUSION

Tennyson's Apotheosis

On September 8, 1883, Britain's poet laureate and prime minister embarked together on a sea voyage. Tennyson and his son Hallam joined Gladstone and others aboard the *Pembroke Castle*, a four-thousand-ton, 410-foot ship, for a cruise that took them around the west of Scotland, from Ardnamurchan Point to Tobermory to Gairloch to Kirkwall. From there, they crossed the North Sea to Christiansand in southern Norway, and then sailed on to Copenhagen. They were entertained by the king and queen of Denmark at the Castle of Fredensborg, and in turn hosted a shipboard luncheon for fifty, including not only the Danish royalty but the emperor and empress of Russia and the king and queen of Greece, who happened to be visiting, as well as "Ministers and Diplomatists and Consuls" (*Memoir*, 2:283). An engraving in *The Graphic* depicts this bountiful luncheon, with Gladstone and Tennyson presiding over tables occupied by various monarchs and decorated with bottles of champagne and arrangements of cake, fruit, and potted plants (figure C.1).

Far from delighted by accounts of this hospitable scene, Queen Victoria was furious, or, as she phrased it in a letter to Gladstone on September 20, 1883, "*very much* surprised, to say the least" that Gladstone had ventured into international waters and met with "Foreign Sovereigns" without her prior knowledge or permission.[1] Gladstone had written to the queen on the same day, apparently before receiving her outraged letter, providing her with a lengthy account of diplomatic dealings that seem chiefly to have consisted of extensive rounds of toasts among the sovereigns and ministers, and the illustration in *The Graphic* confirms Gladstone's own participation in these rituals. The afternoon concluded with the "senior Imperial and Royal Personages crowded together into a small cabin on the Deck" (579) to hear Tennyson read a few poems. Surveying the English literary tradition, Douglas Bush is moved to call Tennyson "the greatest English poet

Mrs. Gladstone   Princess of Wales   King of Denmark   Czar of Russia   Sir Donald Currie   Queen of Denmark   Mr. Gladstone   Queen of Greece   Mr. Alfred Tennyson   Crown Prince of Denmark

THE ROYAL BANQUET IN THE SALOON OF THE "PEMBROKE CASTLE" AT COPENHAGEN

of the sea,"[2] but when actually shipboard the laureate read what can seem like curious choices: not "Ulysses," for example, but "The Grandmother" (1859) and what Hallam calls "The Bugle Song," from *The Princess*. Two days later, Gladstone, writing to acknowledge receipt of the queen's reproving letter, admits himself to be "responsible for having acquiesced in the proposal (which originated with Mr. Tennyson)" (580)—thus ostensibly accepting responsibility for what appears to have been a spontaneous excursion while nevertheless placing responsibility firmly upon the queen's beloved laureate.

Victoria had written to Gladstone of her trust that he "will have avoided Politics with the Sovereigns he met at Copenhagen," although she doubts in "the public believing this," and complains, "many remarks & surmises have already been made" (577). In his response of September 22, her minister is elaborately respectful in his dismissal of her concerns, finding "some consolation" that the only complaint appeared in "two secondary Journals" that have never found in any of his acts "anything but guilt and folly" (581). The illustration in *The Graphic* a week later suggests that Gladstone's no doubt prolix toast seems to have been an occasion for polite boredom rather than international intrigue, while, to judge from a full-page cartoon and a fifty-four-line poem published in *Punch* on the same day as Gladstone's letter of theatrical contrition, the journey was cause for general ribaldry more than reproach (figure C.2).

The *Punch* cartoon bears the caption "'A Life on the Ocean Wave.' (Supposed latest Performance of the G. O. M)" and a quotation from the opening scene of Shakespeare's *The Tempest*, when the boatswain, assessing the rising storm, cries out, "Heigh, my hearts. Cheerly, cheerly, my hearts! Yare, yare." On the facing page appears the unsigned poem "On the Skye-Lark," subtitled, "A Song of High Jinks among High Personages in High Latitudes," which narrates *Punch's* version of this escapade.[3] An air to the tune of "Jack Robinson," the poem begins with Gladstone escaping "The perils and pothers of the Session past" aboard the *Pembroke Castle*, casting "to the winds all his longshore troubles" (1, 3). "Chief among his mess-mates" (4) was "Alf Tennyson," whose name, in this form, serves throughout as a refrain. Accepting an invitation to serve "As Minstrel for the voyage," the poet agrees "to twangle and to play" "on a harp he always bore" (8, 10, 6). "On the Skye-Lark" recounts:

> So upon the Pembroke Castle's poop they both sat down,
> A-talking of great statesmen and of bards of high renown;
> And they drank as much—say nectar—as might come to half-a-crown.
>   "This is really very jolly!" says ALF TEN-NY-SON. (19–22)

FIGURE C.1 Opposite, "The Royal Banquet in the Saloon of the 'Pembroke Castle' at Copenhagen," *The Graphic* 15 (September 29, 1883): 316–17.

FIGURE C.2   "'A Life on the Ocean Wave' (Supposed latest Performance of the G. O. M.)," *Punch* 85 (September 22, 1883): 139.

Just as Gladstone is about to embark on "another long yarn," the party is joined by a "Sawbones," the doctor Andrew Clark, who, among other distinctions, would attend Tennyson in his final illness. "The Sawbones he seemed staggered" by the scene, reprimanding the two for the "grog" and "pipes" (afflicted with tuberculosis himself, Clark was a specialist in lung disease), although he soon joins them in these vices, smoking a pipe, pouring himself a drink "Which *wasn't* homeopathic," and listening to the tune Tennyson has begun to play (28, 29, 47).

The *Punch* illustration depicts these three eminences in nautical attire. Dr. Clark, drink in one hand, pipe in the other, sits astride a medicine chest inscribed with his initials. Having assured the doctor, "Just wait," Tennyson "plumped down on a barrel, and the laurels round his head / Took a Bacchanalian rake, and on his harp he twan-gle-ed" (39, 41–42). Crowned with a laurel wreath, smoking his pipe and plucking his instrument, the poet inspires Gladstone to dance "a hornpipe, with a light elastic tread" (43). Arms crossed high on his chest, shifting nimbly from toe to toe, the prancing prime minister, though stern of visage, appears to follow the cheery propulsion of this playing, as Tennyson sings, "To fret and stew about things much is all in vain. / We are off to Skye and Orkney," and "to Norroway o'er the main" (50–51). In his initial account of the voyage, Gladstone reports modestly to the queen that he is "a most indifferent sailor," but that Tennyson "is an excellent sailor and seems to enjoy himself much in the floating castle" (576). *Punch* depicts the Grand Old Man on deck as remarkably light on his toes. *Punch* also depicts these men on a lark, with no more pressing agenda than for the poet laureate to sing nonsense (each stanza ends, "Singing toḍdi-oddi-iddi-iddi-um-tum-tay!") and the prime minister to dance. In fact, on this voyage both Tennyson and Gladstone reflected deeply on the relative public roles of the poet and the orator, a subject each sought to fathom as the ship headed out to sea.

In his account to Victoria of their journey, Gladstone recounts his polite reception by foreign monarchs but omits any mention of his thunderous reception by the British populace. Gladstone's popularity had reached such a pitch that wherever he traveled cheering crowds in the thousands appeared, often overtaking the stations where his train was due to stop.[4] Hallam Tennyson reports in his journal that as the party traveled by train to the *Pembroke Castle*, they passed through "crowds shouting 'Gladstone' at every station." As they boarded the ship and set sail, he exclaims, they "left our native land in a tumult of acclaim! Thousands of people lining the shore, and cheering for 'Gladstone' and 'Tennyson'" (*Memoir*, 2:278). These tumultuous cries might be heard as an echo of one of each man's earliest and most significant cheerleaders, Arthur Henry Hallam. Hallam had committed himself early and avidly to the promotion of Tennyson's poetic career, and he had similarly and still earlier recognized and encouraged in Gladstone his exceptional oratorical talents. His comparison of the conservative young Gladstone's "skill in speech" to that of Homer's Ulysses infuriated his friend, as we have seen, who resisted the comparison because of what he felt were the Whiggish qualities of the character. One wonders if the prime minister recalled this epistolary argument and Hallam's invitation to join him in fighting "battles of freedom & justice," as crowds of the newly or nearly enfranchised gathered to cheer him at every stop.

On its journey along the coast of Scotland, the *Pembroke Castle* anchored at the town of Kirkwall on September 13, 1883. The party disembarked and, after a picnic lunch at Maeshowe, a Neolithic chambered cairn, Gladstone and Tennyson were given the "freedom of the Burgh." Inspired by this ancient site and in response to this civic honor, Gladstone delivered an extended comparison before the crowd regarding the relative duration of their professional accomplishments. Tennyson, so shy in front of a large audience that he had not been able some fifty years earlier to read the poem "Timbuctoo" (which had stymied Gladstone) at the Cambridge prize assembly, refused to speak. In his journal, Hallam Tennyson records that his father told him, "Before a crowd, which consists of many personalities, of which I know nothing, I am infinitely shy. The great orator cares nothing about all this. I think of the good man, and the bad man, and the mad man, that may be among them, and can say nothing. *He* takes them all as one man. *He* sways them as one man" (*Memoir*, 2:280). Tennyson claims that he cannot address a crowd because he cannot see it *as* a crowd; what he sees is a collection of individuals, each with his own history and subjectivity ("good," "bad," "mad"): it is as if he faces an assembly full of potential dramatic monologists. In essence imagining what each auditor might say, the poet "can say nothing." The poet fails as a public speaker because he can address only persons rather than a public, whereas the orator addresses the populace as one person. In his almost lyrical repetition of the phrase "as one man," Tennyson stresses the crowd's wholesale identification into a singular entity that can sound disturbingly indivisible, undivided as well from the "one man" who sways them.

Even as the poet sat silent, Gladstone, rising easily to speak, elevated poetry over political oratory, declaring, "Mr. Tennyson's life and labours correspond in point of time as nearly as possible to my own, but Mr. Tennyson's exertions have been on a higher plane of human action than my own." Distinguishing himself from the apparently secluded poet, Gladstone refers to "we public men," who are, he admits, "subject to the danger of being momentarily intoxicated" by "the kindness, the undue homage of kindness" of the crowd—that is, the mass approbation he so often enjoyed in these years, and certainly on this journey. Gladstone contrasts the momentary intoxication of politics with the grave longevity of poetry, declaring of his silent traveling companion, "His work will be more durable" (*Memoir*, 2:280).

Gladstone imagines the perusal "in distant times" of the Kirkwall annals of this very day, when "some may ask, with regard to the Prime Minister, 'Who was he, and what did he do? We know nothing about him.'" "Were the period of the inquiry to be so long distant as between this day and the time when Maeshowe was built," he posits of a research project some five thousand years in the future, "in regard to the Poet Laureate of to-day there would be no difficulty in stating who he was, and what he had done." Gladstone recalls, "On this and on many other occasions, in a thousand other places, I have declared to the crowd, 'It is our business to speak, but the words which we speak have wings, and fly away and disappear.'" Perhaps it is because his words are so fleeting that he has had to repeat them on so many occasions, in so many other places, to so many people. Gladstone's emphasis on his innumerable speeches to numberless crowds renders this vocational comparison less self-effacing than it may initially seem, but he nevertheless concludes, "The Poet Laureate has written his own song on the hearts of his countrymen, that can never die" (*Memoir*, 2:280–81).

Whether on or off stage or shore, Tennyson and Gladstone spent much of their time together, as *Punch* accurately has it, "A-talking of great statesmen and of bards of high renown." On the first morning of the voyage, they inevitably turned to the abiding topic of their lost friend. Hallam Tennyson reports, "The two at breakfast were deploring Arthur Hallam, and saying what a noble intellect he had, and, as a student, how great a loss he had been to Dante scholarship." As the *Pembroke Castle* headed up the coast of Scotland, from Oban to Loch Hourn, their conversation takes another inevitable turn: "Gladstone and my father conversed on Homer," continuing their unceasing discussion of the comparative merits of various translations. Hallam reports that they "were as jovial together as boys out for a holiday; but they took good care to keep off the quagmire of politics" (*Memoir*, 2:281). And yet it was on this cruise that Gladstone persuaded Tennyson to accept the offer of a more direct political role, through membership in the House of Lords. Gladstone had assured the queen that he did not actively pursue any course of foreign relations while on this journey, but he was far from idle on the domestic front. The shipboard company constituted, according to Martin, a "gathering of Liberals,"[5] and many believe that Gladstone hoped, by thus elevating Tennyson, to gain one more liberal vote in a generally conservative body he considered obstructionist. Some suspect that Tennyson was equally calculating. He had repeatedly during his career declined the offer of a baronetcy; having rejected previous lesser offers, Tennyson ultimately obtained the far more prestigious hereditary peerage.

Hallam gives a riveting account of the shipboard contretemps that led to Tennyson's eventual acquiescence. He is firm in maintaining that the driving force in this endeavor was Gladstone, who at one point found Hallam reading and "beckoned me to walk with him" in order to consult about broaching the topic to Tennyson. Hallam advised Gladstone not to make the offer to his father directly or immediately, because it might "fluster him and mar his enjoyment of the voyage, since he never thought about or cared for titles." The prime minister agreed not to speak to Tennyson on the subject until his son indicated that the time was propitious. Hallam let the matter rest for a day or so and then, under pressure from Gladstone, found his father smoking, informed him of the offer, "and left him to ruminate." His account continues, "When I returned, I found Mr. Gladstone and my father deep in Homer, discussing the beauty of the similes. I said to Mr. Gladstone, 'I have spoken.' 'I may speak then,' he said, and proceeded to urge the peerage" (*Memoir*, 2:298–99).

While Hallam tells the larger, presumably more momentous anecdote regarding the delicately triangulated negotiations over the tremendous reward of a hereditary peerage, one cannot help but wish for a report on their exchange over the beauty of Homeric similes. As I have argued in the previous four chapters, this was a no less consequential conversation, and, indeed, there was no more appropriate subject for them to pursue at this particularly intense moment. We have attended to numerous anecdotes that tell us in the aggregate how enduring were their conversations on Homer, and how revealing. And yet, with rare exceptions (such as the account of Symonds at Woolner's dinner party), anecdotalists neglect to report the details of a conversation "deep in Homer" that for Tennyson and Gladstone was not subordinate to contemporary issues but entirely continuous with them.

Tennyson eventually tells his son, "By Gladstone's advice I have consented to take the peerage, but for my own part I shall regret my simple name all my life." Gladstone cabled the queen to offer the poet a barony, and in a matter of months, Tennyson officially became a new name: Baron Tennyson of Aldworth and Freshwater or, more commonly, Alfred, Lord Tennyson. He claimed to have accepted the peerage for his sons, in what we might see as reparation for the displacement of his father's inheritance. He cannot refrain from telling Gladstone, in a letter determining when he is "to be Peered" and what he is to be called, "The younger branch of my father's family...succeeded to the fortune" (*Memoir*, 2:300). Although he accepts the elevation for the sake of his descendents, he suspects that the political future of the populace is more assured than that of the aristocracy, whether a title was attained through individual labor, as his was, or through inheritance, as he ensured would be the case for his progeny. As he looks toward "the dark days that may be coming on," and perhaps looks back too at his own poetic explorations of the burdens as well as the benefits sons may inherit from their fathers, he cannot help but wonder whether "a peerage might possibly be more of a disadvantage than an advantage to my sons: I cannot tell" (*Memoir*, 2:302). Tennyson's first major dramatic monologues assay the staggering responsibilities placed directly or indirectly on Ulysses' Telemachus, Tithonus's Memnon, Tiresias's Menœceus, and, indeed, the Son of God, whose likeness so preoccupies St. Simeon Stylites. These monologues make clear that each (as would be the case for Tennyson's own eldest son, Hallam) must be about his father's business.

"I anticipate for him...immortality," Gladstone declared of Tennyson at Kirkwall. The speechless poet at his side, however, had he spoken, would have voiced deep skepticism at the notion of his or any poet's immortality. His poem "Parnassus," published in 1889 in *Tiresias and Other Poems*, begins with an epigraph from Horace's well-known proclamation in the third *Ode* regarding the longevity of his verse, loosely translated, "I have constructed a monument that the passage of countless years cannot destroy." Tennyson's poem consists of three

numbered stanzas, in the first stanza of which a risibly ambitious Poet pleads
with the Muses to help him attain to the company of the Bards at Mount Parnassus, that he might join "those crowned forms" "that the mighty Muses have raised
to the heights of the mountain, / And over the flight of the Ages!" (1, 2–3; *fuga
temporum* in Horace). In an earlier version of this poem, the supplicant is repeatedly addressed as "little poet," stressing his minor status. In the final version, the
Poet's potential for canonicity is clouded, but his ambition for it is clear; he desires
to roll his voice "from the summit, / Sounding for ever and ever through Earth
and her listening nations, / And mixt with the great Sphere-music of stars and of
constellations" (6–8).

In the second stanza an answering voice addresses the Poet, mocking any notion of the permanence of poetry itself. Referring to Tennyson at Kirkwall, Gladstone had avowed, "Time is powerless against him," but the speaker here insists
that poetry will be overpowered by time itself, or at least its study: "Astronomy
and Geology, terrible Muses!" (16). Exploring vast tracts of celestial and terrestrial
time and space, these sciences investigate seemingly infinite processes of transformation, far into the distant past and the distant future. These "two known peaks"
cast a "deep double shadow," into which the Poet is urged to "Look" in order to
see "the crowned ones all disappearing!" (11, 13). As the laureates disappear into
the shadows of the science of transformative time, the striving poet is warned not
to "hope for a deathless hearing" (14).

Having provided a thesis regarding poetic immortality in part I and its antithesis in part II, "Parnassus" concludes in part III by offering this synthesis:

> If the lips were touched with fire from off a pure Pierian altar,
> Though their music here be mortal need the singer greatly care?
> Other songs for other worlds! the fire within him would not falter;
> Let the golden *Iliad* vanish, Homer here is Homer there. (17–20)

The poem has moved from the inevitable disappearance of the ludicrously overreaching poet to the more startling disappearance of the poet whose lips, though
touched with fire from the altar at Pieria (home of Orpheus and the Muses), are
also to be silenced in time, and by it. Tennyson had meditated on Homer's longevity more than a half century earlier, contemplating his figure in "The Palace
of Art": "A million wrinkles carved his skin; / A hundred winters snowed upon
his breast, / From cheek and throat and chin," but now the voice of "The Ionian
father of the rest" (138–40, 137) is stilled. I have delineated Tennyson's architec-
tonics of the song-built Troy, long disappeared; here he insists that the music that
constructed the city must also perish from the earth. This conclusion is potentially
consolatory, however. Although on earth even the most inspired poet's music is
"mortal," and we must reconcile seeing even "the golden *Iliad* vanish," the poet
continues to produce different songs in worlds beyond our own, and thus in some
sense continues everlastingly: "Homer here is Homer there."

In an 1889 letter thanking Tennyson for sending him a copy of the *Tiresias* volume, Gladstone comments only on "Parnassus," protesting, "I am not ready to part from the *Iliad* on any terms, not even on the condition of meeting its author." As was the case when Gladstone studied Tennyson's "Timbuctoo" in 1829 (Arthur Hallam having brought it to Oxford for him to read), there is cause to suspect that Gladstone did not entirely follow the argument of the poem. He also responds to another line, in which the preposterously ambitious Poet declares, "Lightning may shrivel the laurel of Caesar, but mine would not wither" (4). "Your 'lightning may shrivel, etc.,'" Gladstone comments, "is the grand expression of what I meanly spoke at Kirkwall as to your vocation and mine" (*Memoir*, 2:367). But of course the point the poem makes in this line is in precise opposition to Gladstone's speech, since it mocks the idea that the poet's laureate is any more flame-retardant than the politician's.

Gladstone is right, however, to associate this poem directly with his oration; Tennyson was silent at Kirkwall, but "Parnassus" (early versions of which were titled "Fame") rings as the response he might have made had he stood that day to answer the prime minister's claim that he had acquired "a deathless fame" (*Memoir*, 2:281). Gladstone refers (with a not entirely credible humility) to the words he "meanly spoke" at Kirkwall, and "Parnassus" would seem to serve as Tennyson's similar assessment of the words uttered so fluently before the crowd. (William Allingham reports an 1884 conversation with Tennyson about "Gladstone's oratory," during which Allingham gives his view that Gladstone's "practiced verbosity" produced "few memorable passages," an opinion with which he does not record disagreement from Tennyson.)[6] Although he dismisses the idea of poetry's immortality, Tennyson maintains the primacy of the poet's memorable words over any other kind of speech. In a sense, though, he had already made his point in the two poems he chose to read to the ministers and monarchs at the *Pembroke Castle* luncheon. The second speaker in "Parnassus" incredulously queries the claim of the first, the mistaken poet, "'Sounding for ever and ever?'" and exclaims dismissively in response, "pass on!" (15). "The Bugle Song" ends with the assurance, however, that "Our echoes roll from soul to soul / And grow for ever and for ever" (15–16). And although the music of the lips touched with Pierian fire may vanish, discursive fire itself will not falter, as the elderly speaker in "The Grandmother" reminds her granddaughter: "the tongue is a fire as you know, my dear, the tongue is a fire" (28).

On the course of their journey in the fall of 1883 the orator and the poet each affirmed his own mode of inspired speech, although they appear to have found accord on the matter of Tennyson's elevation, if not to Parnassus, then at least to the peerage. In a letter to Hallam several months after the events aboard the *Pembroke Castle*, however, the prime minister wrote of his father, "I am very glad to learn that the title is fairly launched and the apotheosis accomplished" (*Memoir*, 2:301). Gladstone's phrasing suggests Tennyson's transportation to a celestial rather than an earthly sphere, as if, rather than being made a lord, he had been made a god.

Other admirers similarly did not heed the warning of "Parnassus" regarding the futility of any ambition for poetic immortality. In a poem on the occasion of Tennyson's funeral, "Apotheosis: Westminster, October 1892 (An allegory)," James Knowles begins, "The peasants of Parnassus come to fling / Their wreaths upon the grave of Orpheus" (1–2).[7] "But there was loftier tribute" (6), he declares. He turns to "the gods, / the deathless gods," who descended to Westminster Abbey in what might be considered an audacious pagan intrusion into the august Anglican ceremony: "They stood around the portals of the tomb / Invisible, yet dimly felt by all" (6–7, 10–11). Knowles catalogues specifically the presence of the deities Diana, Demeter, Persephone, Apollo, and Pallas Athena, who in one way or another help prepare "his pathway to Elysium" (19). Knowles imagines Tennyson caught up and borne away, as the gods' "sovran presence rapt" the dead laureate "in their arms— / Amid his kindred gods and demigods" (26, 27–28). He envisions Tennyson's "translation to the starry realm" (9), which we might understand as an enactment of the ambitious transformations of St. Simeon Stylites, Ulysses, Tithonus, and Tiresias. In the course of their dramatic monologues, these speakers articulate and concurrently perform their own rapture, attaining in the course of their monologues, by way of their monologues, their ambition to be like gods, or, in Simeon's case, like God. Long transported discursively by the poet, the audience at his funeral could not but feel itself witness to Tennyson's own final performance of rapture.

NOTES

Introduction

1. Christopher Ricks, ed., *The Poems of Tennyson*, 2nd ed., 3 vols. (Berkeley: University of California Press, 1987), 2:403. Unless otherwise specified, all subsequent references to the line numbers of Tennyson's poems are from this edition, hereafter cited in the text as *Poems*.

2. Priscilla Johnston, "Tennyson's Demeter and Persephone Theme: Memory and the 'Good Solid' Past," *Texas Studies in Literature and Language* 20 (1978): 81.

3. David Van Biema et al., "The 25 Most Influential Evangelicals in America," *Time*, February 7, 2005, 39. Tim LaHaye and Jerry B. Jenkins's *Left Behind: A Novel of the Earth's Last Days* (1995) has spawned eleven sequels to date.

4. Richard Chenevix Trench, *On the Study of Words*, 22nd ed. (New York: Macmillan, 1892), 8–9.

5. Ibid., 284.

6. K. B. Smellie, "Victorian Democracy: Good Luck or Good Management," in *Ideas and Beliefs of the Victorians: An Historic Revaluation of the Victorian Age* (New York: E. P. Dutton, 1966), 291.

7. W. B. Yeats, *Collected Poems*, ed. Richard J. Finneran (New York: Macmillan, 1989), 214.

8. The classics in the field of Tennysonian classicism are John Churton Collins, *Illustrations of Tennyson* (London: Chatto and Windus, 1891); Wilfred P. Mustard, *Classical Echoes in Tennyson* (London: Macmillan, 1904); Douglas Bush's chapter on the poet in *Mythology and the Romantic Tradition in English Poetry* (New York: Norton, 1963); and Theodore Redpath, "Tennyson and the Literature of Greece and Rome," in *Studies in Tennyson*, ed. Hallam Tennyson (Totowa, NJ: Barnes and Noble, 1981), 105–30. For a comprehensive overview

of classical sources throughout Tennyson's career, see A. A. Markley, *Stateliest Measures: Tennyson and the Literature of Greece and Rome* (Toronto: University of Toronto Press, 2004).

9. Matthew Arnold, *Culture and Anarchy and Other Writings*, ed. Stefan Collini (Cambridge, UK: Cambridge University Press, 1993), 186. "In the middle of the Victorian age Hellenism was subtly pervasive; it was not the name of a fashion or a movement," Richard Jenkyns explains in *The Victorians and Ancient Greece* (Cambridge, MA: Harvard University Press, 1980), 16. The major studies of this phenomenon are those of Jenkyns and Frank Turner, *The Greek Heritage in Victorian Britain* (New Haven, CT: Yale University Press, 1981). For a consideration of the Victorian study of Latin, and its lesser standing, see Frank Turner, "Why the Greeks and not the Romans in Victorian Britain?" in *Rediscovering Hellenism: The Hellenic Inheritance and the English Imagination*, ed. G. W. Clarke with J. C. Eade (Cambridge, UK: Cambridge University Press, 1989), 61–81.

10. D. W. Bebbington offers a probing account of the relation of Gladstone's Homeric writings to his ideological and theological beliefs, in *The Mind of Gladstone: Religion, Homer, and Politics* (New York: Oxford University Press, 2004). Gerhard Joseph compares aspects of Gladstone's and Tennyson's approaches to classical material in *Tennyson and the Text* (Cambridge, UK: Cambridge University Press, 1989), 129–41.

11. Quoted in O. F. Christie, *The Transition to Democracy 1867–1914* (London: Routledge, 1934), 34.

12. Walter Bagehot, "Mr. Gladstone" (1860), in Norman St. John-Stevas, *Bagehot's Historical Essays* (New York: New York University Press, 1966), 253.

Part I

1. See Benjamin Willis Fuson, *Browning and His English Predecessors in the Dramatic Monolog*, State University of Iowa Humanistic Studies, Vol. 8 (Iowa City: State University of Iowa, 1948); Alan Sinfield, *Dramatic Monologue* (London: Methuen, 1977), 46, 49; and Isobel Armstrong, *Victorian Poetry: Poetry, Poetics and Politics* (London: Routledge, 1993), 326.

2. T. H. Vail Motter, ed., *The Writings of Arthur Hallam*, Modern Language Association of America General Series 15 (London: Oxford University Press, 1943), 151; hereafter referred to as *Writings* and cited by page number in the text.

3. John Stuart Mill, "What Is Poetry?" in *John Stuart Mill: Literary Essays*, ed. Edward Alexander (Indianapolis: Bobbs-Merrill, 1967), 56.

4. Ibid., 56–57.

5. For example, Patrick Parrinder, in *Authors and Authority: English and American Criticism 1750–1990* (New York: Columbia University Press, 1991), 132–33, asks, "What are we to make of a utilitarian philosopher whose poetic theory comes so close to that of the aesthetes?" and notes, "Aesthete and utilitarian are united by their opposition to the belief that poetry has a rational content and must therefore be treated on a level with other forms of discourse."

6. Mill, "The Two Kinds of Poetry," in *John Stuart Mill: Literary Essays*, 75.

7. Mill, "What Is Poetry?" 57.

Chapter 1

1. Dorothy Mermin, *The Audience in the Poem: Five Victorian Poets* (New Brunswick, NJ: Rutgers University Press, 1983), 11, 10.

2. J. L. Austin, *How to Do Things with Words*, ed. J. O. Urmson and Marina Sbisà, 2nd ed. (Cambridge, MA: Harvard University Press, 1975), 6. For two probing applica-

tions of Austin's theory to Victorian poetic practice that take different directions from mine, see Eric Griffiths, *The Printed Voice of Victorian Poetry* (New York: Oxford University Press, 1989), 37–59, and E. Warwick Slinn, *Victorian Poetry as Cultural Critique: The Politics of Performative Language* (Charlottesville: University of Virginia Press, 2003), 14–20.

3. A. Dwight Culler, "Monodrama and the Dramatic Monologue," *PMLA* 90 (1975): 368.

4. Samuel Silas Curry, *Browning and the Dramatic Monologue: Nature and Interpretation of an Overlooked Form of Literature* (New York: Haskell House, 1965), 13.

5. Culler, "Monodrama," 85; Alan Sinfield, *Dramatic Monologue* (London: Methuen, 1977), 42.

6. John D. Jump, *Tennyson: The Critical Heritage* (London: Routledge, 1967), 120. Daniel A. Harris, *Tennyson and Personification: The Rhetoric of "Tithonus"* (Ann Arbor, MI: UMI Research Press, 1986), offers a penetrating discussion of *prosopopoeia*, although it does not stress the question of oratorical practice.

7. Culler, "Monodrama," 85.

8. John Morley, *The Life of William Ewart Gladstone*, 2 vols. (London: Macmillan, 1905), 1:192.

9. Quintilian, *The Institutio Oratoria of Quintilian*, trans. H. E. Butler, 4 vols., Loeb Classical Library (London: William Heinemann, 1921), 3.4.49, 50, 49, 55.

10. Matthew Campbell, *Rhythm and Will in Victorian Poetry* (Cambridge, UK: Cambridge University Press, 1999), 125–26.

11. Isobel Armstrong, *Victorian Poetry: Poetry, Poetics and Politics* (London: Routledge, 1993), 138.

12. Herbert F. Tucker, *Tennyson and the Doom of Romanticism* (Cambridge, MA: Harvard University Press, 1988), 23, 16.

13. Robert Langbaum, *The Poetry of Experience: The Dramatic Monologue in Modern Literary Tradition* (New York: Random House, 1957), 89.

14. Campbell, *Rhythm and Will*, 127.

15. Langbaum, *Poetry of Experience*, 182–83.

16. Adena Rosmarin, *The Power of Genre* (Minneapolis: University of Minnesota Press, 1985), 107.

17. Sinfield, *Dramatic Monologue*, 7.

18. Rosmarin, *The Power of Genre*, 122.

19. Sinfield, *Dramatic Monologue*, 9.

20. For an application of this argument to a range of dramatic monologues by a number of other Victorian poets, see my essay, "The Dramatic Monologue," in *The Cambridge Companion to Victorian Poetry*, ed. Joseph Bristow (Cambridge, UK: Cambridge University Press, 2000), 67–88.

21. See, for example, the essays "A Plea for Excuses," "Pretending," "How to Talk— Some Simple Ways," and even "Other Minds," in J. L. Austin, *Philosophical Papers* (Oxford: Clarendon, 1961).

22. According to Bloom, "No really magical poem by Tennyson ever became quite the work he intended it to be, and this gap between his intention and the actual achievement saved him as a poet, though it could not save him altogether." *The Ringers in the Tower: Studies in Romantic Tradition* (Chicago: University of Chicago Press, 1971), 147.

23. J. L. Austin, *Philosophical Papers*, 3rd ed., ed. J. O. Urmson and G. J. Warnock (London: Oxford University Press, 1979), 284. Shoshana Felman remarks that in Austin's view intention itself is for anyone "scarcely conscious." *The Literary Speech Act: Don Juan*

with J. L. Austin, or Seduction in Two Languages, trans. Catherine Porter (Ithaca, NY: Cornell University Press, 1983), 100.

24. W. K. Wimsatt, Jr., and Monroe C. Beardsley, "The Intentional Fallacy," reprinted in W. K. Wimsatt, Jr., *The Verbal Icon: Studies in the Meaning of Poetry* (Lexington: University of Kentucky Press, 1954; rptd. New York: Noonday Press, 1958), 3, 4.

25. Sinfield, *Dramatic Monologue,* 26.

26. Among the most comprehensive examples of this approach are Ralph W. Rader, "The Dramatic Monologue and Related Lyric Forms," *Critical Inquiry* 3 (1976): 131–51, and Culler, "Monodrama."

27. Herbert F. Tucker Jr., "From Monomania to Monologue: 'St. Simeon Stylites' and the Rise of the Victorian Dramatic Monologue," *Victorian Poetry* 22 (1984): 121–22.

28. Alastair Fowler, *Kinds of Literature: An Introduction to the Theory of Genres and Modes* (Cambridge, MA: Harvard University Press, 1982), 38. Daniel Karlin's chapter "Genre and Style" in John Woolford and Daniel Karlin, *Robert Browning* (New York: Longman, 1996), 38n, makes this point and notes that the term was first applied to Browning in 1864. Culler dates the first use to 1857, as a title to a collection of poems by George W. Thornbury (Culler, "Monodrama," 356).

29. Armstrong, *Victorian Poetry,* 13.

30. Langbaum, *Poetry of Experience,* 77, 85.

31. Morley, *Life of Gladstone,* 1:192.

32. Austin, *How to Do Things with Words,* 100.

33. Mary Louise Pratt, *Toward a Speech Act Theory of Literary Discourse* (Bloomington: Indiana University Press, 1977), 86.

34. Judith Butler, *Excitable Speech: A Politics of the Performative* (New York: Routledge, 1997), 11. For further discussions of the construction of identities through a range of citational processes, see Judith Butler, *Gender Trouble: Feminism and the Subversion of Identity* (New York: Routledge, 1990) and *Bodies that Matter: On the Discursive Limits of "Sex"* (New York: Routledge, 1993). See Felman, *The Literary Speech Act,* for a development of the insight that speaking itself is a bodily act, one that signifies in ways both intended and unintended.

35. Quintilian places a moral imperative on the definition of rhetoric, insisting in *Institutio Oratoria* on the restriction of both "the name of orator and the art itself to those who are good," since "no man can speak well who is not good himself" (2.15.1, 34).

36. Ibid., 2.15.6.

37. Langbaum, *Poetry of Experience,* 75.

38. Ibid., 77.

39. Alex Preminger and T. V. F. Brogan, eds., *The New Princeton Encyclopedia of Poetry and Poetics* (Princeton: Princeton University Press, 1993), s.v. "Simile" (by Jaqueline Vaught Brogan); all citations are to this edition.

40. Steven G. Darian, "Similes and the Creative Process," *Language & Style* 6 (1973): 51.

41. Marsh H. McCall Jr., *Ancient Rhetorical Theories of Simile and Comparison* (Cambridge, MA: Harvard University Press, 1969), 178, 229 (trans. McCall).

42. The extensions and discontinuities between the dramatic monologue and Romantic lyric are considered in Langbaum's *Poetry of Experience* and developed in Tucker's *Tennyson and the Doom of Romanticism.* The most compelling studies of Romantic influence on Victorian and other poets remain Harold Bloom, *The Ringers in the Tower,* and *Poetry and Repression: Revisionism from Blake to Stevens* (New Haven, CT: Yale University Press, 1976).

43. William Allingham, *A Diary* (London: Macmillan, 1908), 88–89.

44. Robert Browning, *The Poems*, 3 vols., ed. John Pettigrew and Thomas J. Collins (New Haven, CT: Yale University Press, 1981), 1:347; hereafter cited in the text.

45. Austin, *How to Do Things with Words*, 21–22. See Felman on the playfulness and richness of Austin's language and examples. Despite contesting Austin's claims, Jacques Derrida, in "Signature Event Context," calls his tone "patient, open, aporetic, in constant transformation, often more fruitful in the recognition of its impasses than in its positions." In *Margins of Philosophy*, trans. Alan Bass (Chicago: University of Chicago Press, 1982), 322. Christopher Ricks discusses Austin's uses of literary language in "Austin's Swink," *Essays in Appreciation* (Oxford: Clarendon: 1996), 260–79. Austin was aware of the aesthetic dimensions of his own writing; defining the word "performative," he called it "a new word and an ugly word." "Performative Utterances," in *Philosophical Papers* (Oxford: Clarendon, 1961), 220.

46. Andrew Parker and Eve Kosofsky Sedgwick, "Introduction: Performativity and Performance," in *Performativity and Performance*, ed. Andrew Parker and Eve Kosofsky Sedgwick (New York: Routledge, 1995), 4; Derrida, "Signature Event Context," 325. For further consideration of the problem raised by Austin's apparent exclusions, see also Stanley Cavell, "Counter-Philosophy and the Pawn of Voice," in *A Pitch of Philosophy: Autobiographical Exercises* (Cambridge, MA: Harvard University Press, 1994), 86–105.

47. Tucker, "From Monomania to Monologue," 134 n10.

48. Pratt, *Toward a Speech Act Theory*, 173.

49. Jack Kolb, ed., *The Letters of Arthur Henry Hallam* (Columbus: Ohio University Press, 1981), 433. All subsequent references to Hallam's letters are taken from this edition and are referred to as *Letters* and cited by page number in the text.

50. Sinfield, *Dramatic Monologue*, 42, 25, 30.

51. Jacqueline Vaught Brogan, *Stevens and Simile: A Theory of Language* (Princeton: Princeton University Press, 1986), 125–26.

52. For an important analysis of the gender implications of Langbaum's theory, see Cynthia Scheinberg, "Recasting 'Sympathy and Judgment': Amy Levy, Women Poets, and the Victorian Dramatic Monologue," *Victorian Poetry* 35 (1997): 173–91.

53. Quoted in Brogan, "Simile," in *New Princeton Encyclopedia of Poetry*.

54. Alexander Bain, *English Composition and Rhetoric*, 2nd ed. (London: Longmans, 1869), 3.

55. Steven G. Darian, "Similes and the Creative Process," *Language & Style* 6 (1973): 48.

56. Bain, *English Composition*, 171, 174, 178, 182.

57. Brogan, *Stevens and Simile*, 126.

58. Bain, *English Composition*, 10.

59. Ibid., 212.

60. W. E. Gladstone, *Studies on Homer and the Homeric Age*, 3 vols. (Oxford: Oxford University Press, 1858), 3:114; hereafter cited in the text as *SH*.

61. Langbaum, *Poetry of Experience*, 92.

62. Robert Bernard Martin, *Tennyson: The Unquiet Heart* (Oxford: Clarendon, 1980), 546, 68, 68.

63. Tucker, *Tennyson and the Doom of Romanticism*, 15.

64. Sir Charles Tennyson, "Tennyson's Politics," in *Six Tennyson Essays* (Totowa, NJ: Rowman and Littlefield, 1972), 39.

65. G. M. Young, *Victorian England: Portrait of an Age* (London: Oxford University Press, 1967), 10.

66. Peter Mandler, *Aristocratic Government in the Age of Reform: Whigs and Liberals, 1830–1852* (Oxford: Clarendon, 1990), 273–74.

67. Edgar Finley Shannon Jr. reviews the politically charged reception of Tennyson's early volumes in *Tennyson and the Reviewers: A Study of His Literary Reputation and of the Influence of the Critics upon His Poetry, 1827–1851* (Cambridge, MA: Harvard University Press, 1952), 5–26.

68. [Hallam Tennyson], *Alfred Lord Tennyson: A Memoir by His Son*, 2 vols. (New York, Macmillan, 1905), 1:42. All subsequent references to this work are taken from this edition, and are referred to as *Memoir* and cited by page number in the text.

69. Charles Tennyson, "Tennyson's Politics," 39.

70. Jonathan Parry, *The Rise and Fall of Liberal Government in Victorian Britain* (New Haven, CT: Yale University Press, 1993), 73.

71. Benjamin Disraeli, "The Spirit of Whiggism" (1836), in *Whigs and Whiggism: Political Writings*, ed. William Hutcheon (New York: Macmillan, 1914), 331, 352–53.

72. T. A. Jenkins, *The Liberal Ascendancy, 1830–1886* (London: Macmillan, 1994), 6. In *The Great Reform Act* (London: Hutchinson University Library, 1973), 142, Michael Brock observes that the "ideas of the ministers on Reform cannot be compressed into a single, internally consistent theory."

73. Benjamin Disraeli, "What Is He?" (1833), in *Whigs and Whiggism*, 19.

74. Charles Tennyson, *Alfred Tennyson* (New York: Macmillan, 1949), 59.

75. Charles Tennyson, "Tennyson's Politics," 39. He adds, "The boy shared his uncle's political views" (30).

76. Armstrong, *Victorian Poetry*, 4.

77. W. E. Gladstone, "Macaulay," in *Gleanings of Past Years, 1843–79*, 7 vols. (London: John Murray, 1879), 2:267–68.

78. [Thomas Babington] Macaulay, *Speeches and Poems*, 2 vols. (New York: Hurd and Houghton, 1877), 1:23, 39, 38.

79. G. P. Gooch, *History and Historians in the Nineteenth Century* (New York: Longmans, 1913), 292, 294.

80. Eugenio F. Biagini, *Liberty, Retrenchment, and Reform: Popular Liberalism in the Age of Gladstone, 1860–1880* (Cambridge: Cambridge University Press, 1992), 372.

81. Charles Tennyson, *Tennyson*, 299, 295.

82. William Ewart Gladstone, *Arthur Henry Hallam*, Companion Classics (Boston: Perry Mason, [1898]), 18; rptd. from *The Youth's Companion*, Jan. 6, 1898.

83. William G. Gordon, *The Social Ideals of Alfred Tennyson: As Related to His Time* (Chicago: University of Chicago Press, 1906), 239.

84. Raymond Williams, *Keywords: A Vocabulary of Culture and Society*, rev. ed. (New York: Oxford University Press, 1983), 94; *Culture and Society: 1780–1950* (1958; New York: Columbia University Press, 1983), xiv. In *Keywords*, Williams remarks, "This is the most striking historical fact" (94).

85. Macaulay, "Parliamentary Reform" (March 2, 1831), in *Speeches*, 1:22.

86. Charles Tennyson, *Tennyson*, 477.

87. Quoted in Jump, *Critical Heritage*, 349.

88. H. C. G. Matthew, "Rhetoric and Politics in Great Britain, 1860–1950," in *Politics and Social Change in Modern Britain: Essays Presented to A. F. Thompson*, ed. P. J. Waller (New York: St. Martin's Press, 1987), 39, 35.

89. Richard Holt Hutton, "Mr. Gladstone," *Contemporary Review* 65 (1894): 619.

90. Biagini, *Liberty, Retrenchment*, 379. Macaulay's characterization (cited by Biagini) is from the first sentence of his essay, "Gladstone on Church and State" (1839).

91. Gladstone and others "gravitated towards the Whigs during the course of the 1850s," according to Jenkins; he "finally threw in his lot" with the liberals in June 1859 (Jenkins, *Liberal Ascendancy*, 50, 112).

92. Young, "The Liberal Mind in Victorian England," in *Victorian Essays*, ed. W. D. Handcock (London: Oxford University Press, 1962), 113.

93. Jenkins, *Liberal Ascendancy*, 111, x.

94. Years later, Tennyson accompanied Macaulay, Henry Hallam, and Francois Guizot to the Houses of Parliament and Westminster Hall. He told Carlyle, "Macaulay said to me on going away, "I am delighted to have met you, Mr. Tennyson'; but I never saw him afterwards" (*Memoir*, 2:236).

95. Arthur Sidgwick, "Tennyson," in *Tennyson and His Friends*, ed. Hallam, Lord Tennyson (London: Macmillan, 1911), 325.

96. Martin, *Tennyson*, 67.

97. Quoted in Jenkins, *Liberal Ascendancy*, 8.

98. Stopford A. Brooke, *Tennyson: His Art and Relation to Modern Life* (New York: G. P. Putnam's Sons, 1894), 42.

99. A. Dwight Culler, *The Poetry of Tennyson* (New Haven, CT: Yale University Press, 1977), 96.

100. Armstrong, *Victorian Poetry*, 56. For another approach to Tennyson that pays close attention to his early political poems and political leanings but does not consider the poet's Whig affiliations, see Alan Sinfield, *Alfred Tennyson* (Oxford: Basil Blackwell, 1986), chapter 2.

101. Jenkins, *Liberal Ascendancy*, 33.

102. Brooke, *Tennyson*, 47, 45.

103. Raymond Macdonald Alden, *Alfred Tennyson: How to Know Him* (Indianapolis: Bobbs-Merrill, 1917), 271–72.

104. Brooke, *Tennyson*, 42–43.

105. Sidgwick, "Tennyson," 331.

106. G. K. Chesterton, *The Victorian Age in Literature* (New York: Henry Holt, 1913), 72.

107. W. B. Yeats, *Collected Poems*, ed. Richard J. Finneran, new ed. (New York: Macmillan, 1989); all citations to Yeats's poems are from this edition and cited in the text by line number.

108. Walter Bagehot, "Tennyson's Idylls" (1859), in *The Collected Works of Walter Bagehot*, ed. Norman St John-Stevas, 4 vols. (Cambridge, MA: Harvard University Press, 1965), 2:198.

109. J. F. A. Pyre, *The Formation of Tennyson's Style: A Study, Primarily, of the Versification of the Early Poems*, University of Wisconsin Studies in Language and Literature 12 (Madison: University of Wisconsin, 1921), 114.

Chapter 2

1. William Hone, ed., *The Every-Day Book; Or, Everlasting Calendar of Popular Amusements*, 2 vols. (London: For William Hone, 1825), 1:35.

2. George Saintsbury, *A History of English Prosody*, 3 vols. (New York: Russell & Russell, 1961), 3:198.

3. John D. Jump, *Tennyson: The Critical Heritage* (London: Routledge, 1967), 133.

4. Letter of July 13, 1842, in *Robert Browning and Alfred Domett*, ed. F. G. Kenyon (New York: E. P. Dutton, 1906), 41.

5. Edward Gibbon, *The Decline and Fall of the Roman Empire*, 3 vols. (New York: Modern Library, 1932), 2:16.

6. Jump, *Critical Heritage*, 148.

7. Ibid.

8. Ibid., 120.

9. Peter Allen, *The Cambridge Apostles: The Early Years* (Cambridge: Cambridge University Press, 1978), 162–63.

10. Jump, *Critical Heritage*, 120.

11. Herbert F. Tucker Jr., "From Monomania to Monologue:'St. Simeon Stylites' and the Rise of the Victorian Dramatic Monologue," *Victorian Poetry* 22 (1984): 127.

12. Quintilian, *The Institutio Oratoria of Quintilian*, trans. H. E. Butler, 4 vols., Loeb Classical Library (London: William Heinemann, 1921), 9.3.66.

13. Jonathan Culler, "The Call of the Phoneme: Introduction," in *On Puns: The Foundation of Letters*, ed. Jonathan Culler (New York: Basil Blackwell, 1988), 3.

14. Alex Preminger and T. V. F. Brogan, eds., *The New Princeton Encyclopedia of Poetry and Poetics* (Princeton: Princeton University Press, 1993), 1005.

15. Tucker, "From Monomania to Monologue," 130.

16. Umberto Eco, *The Role of the Reader: Explorations in the Semiotics of Texts* (Bloomington: Indiana University Press, 1979), 72, 74.

17. Ibid., 74.

18. Robert Bernard Martin, *Tennyson: The Unquiet Heart* (Oxford: Clarendon, 1980), 92.

19. Richard Deacon, *The Cambridge Apostles: A History of Cambridge University's Elite Intellectual Secret Society* (London: Robert Royce, 1985), 3, 5. "Apostolicans" had been the name of a thirteenth-century French mystical society.

20. [Henry Hallam, ed.,] *Remains, in Verse and Prose, of Arthur Henry Hallam* ([London]: W. Nicol, 1834), xxii.

21. W. C. Lubenow, *The Cambridge Apostles, 1820–1914: Liberalism, Imagination, and Friendship in British Intellectual and Professional Life* (Cambridge, UK: Cambridge University Press, 1998), 359.

22. Harold Nicolson, *Tennyson: Aspects of his Life, Character, and Poetry* (New York: Doubleday, 1962), 261.

23. Ian Bradley, *The Call to Seriousness: The Evangelical Impact on the Victorians* (London: Cape, 1976), 22.

24. Jerome H. Buckley, *Tennyson: The Growth of a Poet* (Cambridge, MA: Harvard University Press, 1960), 25.

25. Hugh Evan Hopkins, *Charles Simeon of Cambridge* (London: Hodder and Stoughton, 1977), 209.

26. Buckley, *Tennyson*, 25.

27. Hopkins, *Simeon of Cambridge*, 59.

28. T. Wemyss Reid, *The Life, Letters, and Friendships of Richard Monckton Milnes, First Lord Houghton*, 2 vols. (New York: Cassell, 1891), 1:51.

29. Bradley, *Call to Seriousness*, 20, 23.

30. Buckley, *Tennyson*, 25-6.

31. A. Dwight Culler, *The Poetry of Tennyson* (New Haven, CT: Yale University Press, 1977), 24.

32. Hone, *Every-Day Book*, 38.

33. Charles Simeon, *The Offices of the Holy Spirit: Four Sermons preached before The University of Cambridge, in the month of November, 1831*, 1st American ed., from the 2nd London ed. (New York: Swords, Stanford and Co., 1832), 57.

34. Hopkins, *Simeon of Cambridge*, 185.

35. Simeon, *Offices of the Holy Spirit*, 50.

36. Hopkins, *Simeon of Cambridge*, 186.

37. Culler, *Poetry of Tennyson*, 14.

38. Ernest R. Sandeen, *The Roots of Fundamentalism: British and American Millenarianism 1800–1930* (Chicago: University of Chicago Press, 1970), 40.

39. Hopkins, *Simeon of Cambridge*, 185.

40. Richard Chenevix Trench, *Letters and Memorials*, 2 vols., ed. Maria M. Trench (London: Kegan Paul, Trench, 1888), 1:114. All subsequent references to Trench's correspondence are taken from this edition and are cited by page number in the text.

41. Hopkins, *Simeon of Cambridge*, 184.

42. Simeon, *Offices of the Holy Spirit*, 99.

43. Francis Trench, *A Few Notes from Past Life: 1818–1832* (Oxford: John Henry, 1862), 270, 286–87.

44. Sandeen, *Roots of Fundamentalism*, 14.

45. Edward Miller, *The History and Doctrines of Irvingism*, 2 vols. (London: Kegan Paul, 1878), 1:22–23, 24.

46. Thomas Carlyle, "Edward Irving," in *Reminiscences*, ed. James Anthony Froude, 2 vols. (London: Longmans, Green, 1881), 1:280.

47. Ibid., 1:244.

48. Miller, *Irvingism*, 1:71.

49. P. E. Shaw, *The Catholic Apostolic Church, Sometimes Called Irvingite: A Historical Study* (New York: King's Crown Press, 1947), 34; see also Miller, *Irvingism*, 1:71.

50. Carlyle, "Irving," 1:319.

51. Miller, *Irvingism*, 1:149.

52. Hopkins, *Simeon of Cambridge*, 186.

53. Miller, *Irvingism*, 1:7–8, 12.

54. L. E. Elliott-Binns, *Religion in the Victorian Era* (London: Lutterworth Press, 1946), 54.

55. Miller, *Irvingism*, 1:24, 25.

56. Peter Allen, *The Cambridge Apostles: The Early Years* (Cambridge: Cambridge University Press, 1978), 124.

57. Reid, *Milnes*, 1:87.

58. Robert Baxter, *Narrative of Facts Characterizing the Supernatural Manifestations in Members of Mr. Irving's Congregation, and Other Individuals in England and Scotland, and Formerly in the Writer Himself* (London: J. Nisbet, 1833), 134–35. All subsequent references to Baxter's book are taken from this edition and are cited by page number in the text.

59. Miller, *Irvingism*, 1:64, 74.

60. Sandeen, *Roots of Fundamentalism*, 26.

61. Carlyle, "Irving," 1:320.

62. H. C. G. Matthew, *Gladstone 1809–1874*, 2 vols. (Oxford: Clarendon, 1986), 1:25.

63. Sandeen, *Roots of Fundamentalism*, 28.

64. Frances M. Brookfield, *The Cambridge Apostles* (New York: Scribner's, 1906), 256.

65. December 11, 1831; quoted in Allen, *The Cambridge Apostles*, 125–26.

66. Quoted in Allen, *The Cambridge Apostles*, 126.

67. Cecil Y. Lang and Edgar F. Shannon, eds., *The Letters of Alfred Lord Tennyson*, 2 vols. (New York: Oxford University Press, 1981), 1:71.

68. Ibid.

69. Trench maintained this skeptical attitude, writing to Donne a year later that Tennyson was "certainly the best of the young Poets and the perversest, but this must chiefly be laid to the charge of his Cambridge advisers (Hallam, Blakesley, Kemble and Co) who in a short time did much to spoil and pervert him, flattering in every way his Antinomian Spirit, which needed rather a check and no such encouragement" (quoted in Martin, *Tennyson*, 112).

70. Hallam, Lord Tennyson, ed., *Poems*, annotated by Alfred Lord Tennyson, Eversley ed., 2 vols. (London: Macmillan, 1907), 1:363.

71. Culler, *Poetry of Tennyson*, 71.

72. Culler tracks Trench's own aesthetic and political interests prior to his return to Cambridge (and the turn to millenarian theology I detail here) to support the compelling claim in *Poetry of Tennyson* that "Trench had himself in mind more much more than Tennyson" when he warned against living in art (64). Culler argues in his article "'Tennyson, we cannot live in art,'" in *Nineteenth-Century Literary Perspectives: Essays in Honor of Lionel Stevenson*, ed. Clyde de L. Ryals et al. (Durham, NC: Duke University Press, 1974), that the dedicatory poem was addressed to Hallam or Spedding rather than to Trench, but this is not widely accepted; see Jack Kolb, ed., *The Letters of Arthur Henry Hallam* (Columbus: Ohio University Press, 1981), 550 n2, and *Poems*, 1:435–36.

73. Shaw, *The Catholic Apostolic Church*, 36.

74. Carlyle, "Irving," 1:310.

75. Allen, *The Cambridge Apostles*, 170.

76. J. Bromley, *The Man of Ten Talents: A Portait of Richard Chenevix Trench 1807–86, Philologist, Poet, Theologian, Archbishop* (London: SPCK, 1959), 229.

77. For discussions of Trench's major originating role, see Hans Aarsleff, "The Original Plan for the *OED* and Its Background," *Transactions of the Philological Society* 88 (1990): 151–56, and Simon Winchester's lively account in *The Meaning of Everything: The Story of the Oxford English Dictionary* (New York: Oxford University Press, 2003), 38–50. Trench inscribed the cover of his "On Some Deficiencies in our English Dictionaries: Two Papers Read Before the Philological Society, 1857" (London: Parker, 1857) to "A. Tennyson Esq. from the author."

78. Lang and Shannon, *The Letters of Alfred Lord Tennyson*, 1:101.

79. Ibid., 1:95.

80. Lubenow, *The Cambridge Apostles*, 370.

81. Edward Irving, *Babylon and Infidelity Foredoomed of God: A Discourse on the Prophecies of Daniel and the Apocalypse, which relate to these Latter Times, and Until the Second Advent*, 2 vols. (Glasgow: Chalmers and Collins, 1826), 2:149.

82. Shaw, *Catholic Apostolic Church*, 42. The date also commemorates (significantly, given the attitude of Irving and others to the French Revolution) the storming of the Bastille on July 14, 1789, although Bastille Day did not become an official national holiday in France until 1880.

83. Sandeen, *Roots of Fundamentalism*, 31.

84. H. A. Ironside, *A Historical Sketch of the Brethren Movement* (1942; rptd. Neptune, NJ: Loizeaux Brothers, 1985), 185.

85. Peter E. Prosser, *Dispensationalist Eschatology and Its Influence on American and British Religious Movements* (Lewiston, NY: Edwin Mellen, 1999), 183.

86. Larry V. Crutchfield, *The Origins of Dispensationalism: The Darby Factor* (Lanham, MD: University Press of America, 1992), 174.

87. Ibid., 191.

88. Timothy P. Weber, *Living in the Shadow of the Second Coming: American Premillennialism, 1875–1982* (Chicago: University of Chicago Press, 1987), 21.

89. Sandeen, *Roots of Fundamentalism*, 64.

90. Paul Boyer suggests that Darby forwarded the interpretation at a Powerscourt conference in 1831, though the idea had been voiced at prophecy conferences at Henry Drummond's Albury Park estate beginning in 1826 and published in prophetic journals and tracts; see Paul Boyer, "The Growth of Fundamentalist Apocalyptic in the United States," in *The Encyclopedia of Apocalypticism*, 3 vols., ed. Stephen J. Stein, (New York: Continuum, 1999), 3:151, 148. Sandra L. Zimdars-Swartz and Paul F. Zimdars-Swartz note earlier and later nineteenth-century British and Continental versions of apocalypse in "Apocalypticism in Modern Western Europe," in *The Encyclopedia of Apocalypticism*, 3:151, 148. A common source for both Darby and Irving may have been Margaret Macdonald, a mystic in Port Glasgow, Scotland, whom both Irving and Darby visited (Weber, *American Premillennialism*, 22; Crutchfield, *Origins of Dispensationalism*, 190).

91. Sandeen, *Roots of Fundamentalism*, 65. Sandeen claims that Irving and his followers did not advocate the doctrine of the secret rapture (64), though it is worth noting Baxter's account of the utterance of another speaker in tongues at Irving's church in the early 1830s: "She most emphatically pronounced, that Christ would come at an hour when even his own people would not be looking for him—that the time of his coming would not be known to his own people" (Baxter, *Narrative*, 93).

92. Crutchfield, *Origins of Dispensationalism*, 172.

93. Sandeen, *Roots of Fundamentalism*, ix.

94. Craig Unger, "American Rapture," *Vanity Fair*, December 2005, 204.

95 Nicholas D. Kristof, "Hug an Evangelical," *New York Times*, April 4, 2004, A17.

96. Culler, *Poetry of Tennyson*, 18.

97. Eric Griffiths, *The Printed Voice of Victorian Poetry* (New York: Oxford University Press, 1989), 111.

98. Linda K. Hughes, *The Manyfacèd Glass: Tennyson's Dramatic Monologues* (Athens: Ohio University Press, 1987), 109.

99. T. S. Eliot, "*In Memoriam*," in *Selected Prose of T. S. Eliot* (1936; New York: Harcourt Brace Jovanovich, 1975), 246.

100. Hallam, *Remains, in Verse and Prose*, xxviii–xxix.

101. Quoted in Christopher Ricks, *Tennyson*, 2nd ed. (Berkeley: University of California Press, 1972, 1987), 101.

102. William E. Fredeman, "'A Sign Betwixt the Meadow and the Cloud': The Ironic Apotheosis of Tennyson's 'St. Simeon Stylites,'" *University of Toronto Quarterly* 38 (1968): 71.

103. Hughes, *The Manyfacèd Glass*, 109; Fredeman, "'A Sign Betwixt the Meadow and the Cloud,'" 73.

104. James R. Kincaid, *Tennyson's Major Poems: The Comic and Ironic Patterns* (New Haven, CT: Yale University Press, 1975), 48.

105. Martin, *Tennyson*, 54. Martin reports that Tennyson's tutor William Whewell "turned a blind eye to the fact that Alfred read Virgil under his desk when he was supposed to be working at mathematics" (56).

106. William Ewart Gladstone, *Arthur Henry Hallam*, Companion Classics (Boston: Perry Mason, [1898]), 19, 20.

107. Hallam, *Remains, in Verse and Prose*, xiv, xv.

108. James Spedding, "English Hexameters," in *Reviews and Discussions, Literary, Political, and Historical, Not Relating to Bacon* (London: C. K. Paul, 1879), 321.

109. Culler, "The Call of the Phoneme," 4.

110. Ricks, *Tennyson*, 101.

111. Matthew Campbell, *Rhythm and Will in Victorian Poetry* (Cambridge, UK: Cambridge University Press, 1999), 129–30.

112. Fredeman, "'A Sign Betwixt the Meadow and the Cloud,'" 73.

113. Campbell, *Rhythm and Will*, 129.

114. Gibbon, *Decline and Fall*, 2:16.

115. Hone, *Every-Day Book*, 37–38.

116. David Ferry, *The Epistles of Horace* (New York: Farrar, Straus and Giroux, 2001), 169.

117. Paul Fussell, *Poetic Meter and Poetic Form*, rev. ed. (New York: McGraw-Hill, 1979), 20.

118. Yopie Prins, *Victorian Sappho* (Princeton: Princeton University Press, 1999), 147.

119. W. H. Thompson, quoted in Allen, *The Cambridge Apostles: The Early Years*.

120. Langbaum, *Poetry of Experience*, 87.

121. Prins, *Victorian Sappho*, 151.

122. Langbaum, *Poetry of Experience*, 87.

123. Saintsbury, *History of English Prosody*, 3:194.

124. Kincaid, *Tennyson's Major Poems*, 48.

125. Hone, *Every-Day Book*, 38.

126. Tucker, "From Monomania to Monologue," 129.

127. Edmund Gosse, *Father and Son: A Study of Two Temperaments* (New York: Norton, 1963), 229–30.

128. Hone, *Every-Day Book*, 38.

129. Fredeman, "'A Sign Betwixt the Meadow and the Cloud,'" 76.

130. Edward Irving, *The Last Days: A Discourse on the Evil Character of these our Times*, 2nd ed., preface by Horatius Bonar (London: John Nisbet, 1850). Irving also quotes here from 1 Corinthians 15:51–52: "We shall not all sleep, but we shall all be changed. In a moment, in the twinkling of an eye, at the last trump: for the trumpet shall sound, and the dead shall be raised incorruptible, and we shall be changed."

131. Gibbon, *Decline and Fall*, 2:16, 16 n72.

132. Roger S. Platizky, "'The Watcher on the Column': Religious Enthusiasm and Madness in Tennyson's 'St. Simeon Stylites'" *Victorian Poetry* 25 (1987): 184.

133. J. F. A. Pyre, *The Formation of Tennyson's Style: A Study, Primarily, of the Versification of the Early Poems*, University of Wisconsin Studies in Language and Literature 12 (Madison: University of Wisconsin, 1921), 151.

134. *New Princeton Encyclopedia of Poetry and Poetics*, s.v. "Blank Verse" (by T. V. F. Brogan).

135. Hone, *Every-Day Book*, 37–38.

136. Gibbon, *Decline and Fall*, 2:16 n71.

137. Hone, *Every-Day Book*, 38.

138. Saintsbury, *History of English Prosody*, 3:198–99.

139. Carlyle, "Irving," 1:281.

140. [Margaret] Oliphant, *The Life of Edward Irving*, 2 vols. (London: Hurst and Blackett, 1862), 2:278.

141. Sandeen, *Roots of Fundamentalism*, 59.

142. Frank Kermode, *The Sense of an Ending: Studies in the Theory of Fiction with a New Epilogue* (Oxford: Oxford University Press, 2000), 17, 8, 14.

143. Crutchfield, *Origins of Dispensationalism*, 178.

144. Langbaum, *Poetry of Experience*, 157.

145. J. F. C. Harrison, *The Second Coming: Popular Millenarianism, 1780–1850* (New Brunswick, NJ: Rutgers University Press, 1979), 12.

146. Hone, *Every-Day Book*, 38, 39.

147. Hughes, *The Manyfacèd Glass*, 110.

148. Fredeman, "'A Sign Betwixt the Meadow and the Cloud,'" 72.

149. Platizky, "'The Watcher on the Column,'" 182, 183; Fredeman, "'A Sign Betwixt the Meadow and the Cloud,'" 75; Tucker, "From Monomania to Monologue," 133.

150. Hone, *Every-Day Book*, 38.

151. Ricks, *Tennyson*, 104.

152. Fredeman, "'A Sign Betwixt the Meadow and the Cloud,'" 71.

153. Tucker, "From Monomania to Monologue" 131.

154. Ricks, *Tennyson*, 103.

155. Fredeman, "'A Sign Betwixt the Meadow and the Cloud,'" 72.

156. Ibid., 78.

157. Bradley, *Call to Seriousness*, 21.

158. For an analysis of Irving's arguments regarding the person of Christ, see Graham McFarlane, *Christ and the Spirit: The Doctrine of the Incarnation According to Edward Irving* (Cumbria, UK: Paternoster Press, 1996).

159. Bromley, *Man of Ten Talents*, 239.

160. Richard Chenevix Trench, *On the Study of Words*, 22nd ed. (New York: Macmillan, 1892), 318.

161. Hallam, *Remains, in Verse and Prose*, xxxix.

162. Marsh H. McCall Jr., *Ancient Rhetorical Theories of Simile and Comparison* (Cambridge, MA: Harvard University Press), 182.

163. Ibid., 95 (trans. McCall).

164. Platizky, "'The Watcher on the Column,'" 186, quoting from John Coulson, ed., *The Saints: A Concise Bibliographical Dictionary* (New York: Hawthorn Books, 1958), 400.

165. Fredeman, "'A Sign Betwixt the Meadow and the Cloud,'" 78, 79.

166. Gibbon, *Decline and Fall*, 2:16.

167. Fredeman, "'A Sign Betwixt the Meadow and the Cloud,'" 79.

168. Tennyson, *Poems* (Eversley ed.), 1:363–64.

169. M. R. D. Foot, ed., *The Gladstone Diaries*, 14 vols. (Oxford: Clarendon Press, 1968), 2:63.

170. Anne Ritchie, *Records of Tennyson, Ruskin, Browning* (New York: Harper, 1893), 18, 21.

171. Eco, *The Role of the Reader*, 72. Eco compares puns to metaphor rather than simile: "The force of the pun (and of every successful and inventive metaphor), consists in the fact that prior to it no one had grasped the resemblance" (73).

172. Julia Butterfly Hill, *The Legacy of Luna: The Story of a Tree, A Woman, and the Struggle to Save the Redwoods* (New York: HarperSanFrancisco, 2000), 118. All subsequent references are from this edition and are cited by page number in the text.

173. Jump, *Critical Heritage*, 133.

174. Eco, *Role of the Reader*, 74.

175. Julia Butterfly Hill, as told to Anthony Lappé, "'There Is No Average Day When You Live in a Tree,'" *New York Times Magazine*, December 12, 1999, 128.

176. Ibid.

177. Sandeen, *Roots of Fundamentalism*, 41.

178. Carlyle, "Irving," 1:309–10.

179. Harrison, *The Second Coming*, 222–23.

180. Hone, *Every-Day Book*, 37.

181. Gibbon, *Decline and Fall*, 2:15, 16–17.

182. Fredeman, "'A Sign Betwixt the Meadow and the Cloud,'" 71.

183. Quoted in S. Baring-Gould, *The Lives of the Saints* (1872), rev. ed., 16 vols. (Edinburgh: John Grant, 1914), 1:76.

184. Hone, *Every-Day Book*, 35.

185. Gibbon, *Decline and Fall*, 2:17–18.

186. Fredeman, "'A Sign Betwixt the Meadow and the Cloud,'" 74.

187. Matthew Heller, "The Power of One: Butterfly's Hard Landing," *Los Angeles Times*, January 20, 2002, http://pqasb.pqarchiver.com/latimes/doc...968d878e89140a392 7&did=101387859&FMT=FT.

188. Ibid.

189. Fredeman, "'A Sign Betwixt the Meadow and the Cloud,'" 74.

190. Exceptions include Hughes, who comments in *The Manyfacèd Glass*, "He really is pitiful as well as absurd" (111), and Platizky, who argues in "'The Watcher on the Column,'" that Tennyson "humanizes Simeon and invests him with cultural significance" (181).

191. Fredeman, "'A Sign Betwixt the Meadow and the Cloud,'" 73.

192. Baring-Gould, *Lives of the Saints*, 1:77.

193. Alban Butler, *Butler's Lives of the Saints*, complete ed. ed. Herbert Thurston, SJ, and Donald Attwater, 4 vols. (New York: P. J. Kenedy, 1956), 1:36.

194. Associated Press, "To Dismay of Scholars, Syrians Use 'Dead Cities,'" *New York Times*, September 6, 1998, A4.

195. Tucker, "From Monomania to Monologue," 16.

196. Nicolson, *Tennyson*, 264.

197. Langbaum, *Poetry of Experience*, 182.

198. Heller, "The Power of One," online source. Hill also writes poems, a number of which she includes in *The Legacy of Luna*.

Part II

1. G. M. Young, "The Age of Tennyson," in *Victorian Essays*, ed. W. D. Handcock (London: Oxford University Press, 1962), 47. The perceived intimacy between Tennyson's poetry and classical authors was so strong as to inspire a number of translations of Tennyson's verse into Greek or Latin (translators included Gladstone and R. C. Jebb).

2. John Churton Collins, *Illustrations of Tennyson* (London: Chatto and Windus, 1891), iii.

3. Robert F. Horton, *Alfred Tennyson: A Saintly Life* (London: J. M. Dent, 1900), 147.

4. Martin, *Tennyson*, 55.

5. Frank M. Turner discusses Grote's claim that readers cannot look to Greek myth for empirical evidence regarding ancient elements of Greek history, as well as the influence of Grote's arguments regarding *mythopoesis*, in *The Greek Heritage in Victorian Britain* (New Haven, CT: Yale University Press, 1981). 83–103.

6. Tennyson's imaginative returns to Troy have been mentioned by critics, but never explored in a sustained way. Herbert F. Tucker in *Tennyson and the Doom of Romanticism* (Cambridge, MA: Harvard University Press, 1988), 219, observes, for example, "The agonistic theater of Troy lies as surely behind Ulysses as it lies behind Oenone," and Matthew Rowlinson in *Tennyson's Fixations: Psychoanalysis and the Topics of the Early Poetry*

(Charlottesville: University Press of Virginia, 1994), 98, notes that the legend "preoccupied Tennyson throughout his career." The most comprehensive tracing of the dense network of Tennyson's allusions to Troy is provided by Ricks's cross-references and notes to individual poems in his three-volume edition of Tennyson. For more focused discussions of other classical patterns that interested Tennyson, see Gerhard Joseph's reading of the figure of Pallas Athene in *Tennyson and the Text* (Cambridge, UK: Cambridge University Press, 1992), 141–58; Robert Pattison's treatment of Tennyson's uses of classical precedent in the context of the idyllic tradition in *Tennyson and Tradition* (Cambridge, MA: Harvard University Press, 1979); and especially W. D. Paden's indispensable *Tennyson in Egypt: A Study of the Imagery in His Earlier Work*, Humanistic Studies 27 (Lawrence: University of Kansas Publications, 1942).

7. Tennyson recalled that he "received a good but not a regular classical education" (*Memoir*, 1:16). "Biography is lamentably sketchy on the formative years of Tennyson's intellectual life," as Isobel Armstrong remarks in "Tennyson's 'The Lady of Shalott': Victorian Mythography and the Politics of Narcissism," in *The Sun Is God: Painting, Literature and Mythology in the Nineteenth Century*, ed. J. B. Bullen (Oxford: Clarendon Press, 1989), 105n1.

8. Herbert Paul, "Aspects of Tennyson, IV: The Classical Poems," *Nineteenth Century* 33 (1893): 436–37. Gladstone died in 1898.

9. S. G. W. Benjamin, *Troy: Its Legend, History and Literature* (New York: Scribner's Sons, 1880), 103.

10. Joseph, *Tennyson and the Text*, 136.

11. William Ewart Gladstone, *Juventus Mundi: The Gods and Men of the Heroic Age*, 2nd ed. (1869; London: Macmillan, 1870), 310.

12. George Chapman, *Chapman's Homer*, ed. Allardyce Nicoll, Bollingen Series 41, 2 vols. (New York: Pantheon, 1956). Tiresias tells Ulysses his fate in *Odyssey* 11:100–37, one of the sources for "Ulysses" specified by Tennyson in the Eversley edition.

13. Horace, *Works*, trans. into verse by Christopher Smart, 4 vols. (London: Flexney, 1767), 1:201.

14. Gladstone, *Juventus Mundi*, 310.

15. Douglas Bush also considers "Lucretius" stylistically different, stating that it "out Brownings Browning." *Mythology and the Romantic Tradition in English Poetry* (New York: Norton, 1963), 214.

16. Anne Ritchie, *Records of Tennyson, Ruskin, Browning* (New York: Harper, 1893), 52.

17. Virgil, *Opera* (Oxford: Clarendon Press, 1817); No. 2281 in Nancie Campbell, *Tennyson in Lincoln: A Catalogue of the Collections in the Research Centre*, 2 vols. (Lincoln: Tennyson Society, 1971), 1:103. A. A. Markley in *Stateliest Measures: Tennyson and the Literature of Greece and Rome* (Toronto: University of Toronto Press, 2004), 33, notes this quotation and judges this volume one of "the most heavily annotated books in the collection."

18. In Homer, Troy is often called "sacred," "holy," "lofty," "well-built"; Stephen Scully, in *Homer and the Sacred City* (Ithaca, NY: Cornell University Press, 1990), notes, "When the subject concerns the destruction of Troy, references to the city rarely lack an epithet" (69).

Chapter 3

1. Richard Jenkyns in *The Victorians and Ancient Greece* (Cambridge, MA: Harvard University Press, 1980), 194–95, provides further examples of Victorians encountering Homer, by way of Pope, "even in the nursery."

2. Tennyson continues, "& we followed the same command of his, writing in our Horaces, Virgils & Juvenals &c &c the criticisms of their several commentators." Robert Bernard Martin, *Tennyson: The Unquiet Heart* (Oxford: Clarendon, 1980), 29.

3. Yopie Prins, *Victorian Sappho* (Princeton: Princeton University Press, 1999), 8.

4. Heinrich Schliemann, *Ilios: The City and Country of the Trojans* (1881; Salem, NH: Ayer, 1989), 5.

5. Ibid., 3.

6. David A. Traill, *Schliemann of Troy: Treasure and Deceit* (London: John Murray, 1995), 5.

7. Ibid., 198.

8. Jeffrey Moussaieff Masson, trans., *The Complete Letters of Sigmund Freud to Wilhelm Fleiss, 1887–1904* (Cambridge, MA: Harvard University Press, 1985), 353.

9. Peter Gay, *Freud: A Life for Our Time* (New York: Norton, 1988), 172, 170, 171.

10. Ibid., 171–72.

11. Caroline Moorehead, *The Lost Treasures of Troy* (London: Weidenfeld and Nicolson, 1994), 235.

12. A. Dwight Culler, *The Poetry of Tennyson* (New Haven, CT: Yale University Press, 1977), 84.

13. M. L. Clarke, *Classical Education in Britain, 1500–1900* (Cambridge, UK: Cambridge University Press, 1959), 104. See also Martha M. Garland, *Cambridge before Darwin: The Ideal of a Liberal Education, 1800–1860* (Cambridge, UK: Cambridge University Press, 1980), which describes the academic excellence of Trinity, as well as its "longstanding association with the British liberal political world" (18).

14. Judith Anne Merivale, ed., *Autobiography and Letters of Charles Merivale* (Oxford: H. Hart, 1898), 89.

15. Clark, *Classical Education*, 158, 109. According to Clark, Thirlwall had in fact dissuaded Milnes from studying Greek and Latin texts, saying, after their initial meetings, "You will never be a scholar. It is no use our reading classics together" (158).

16. Such interaction between tutors and students was itself novel; Robert Robson, in "Trinity College in the Age of Peel," writes that tutors like Thirlwall and Hare "in particular began to break down the rather rigid barrier which separated the Fellows from the undergraduates." In *Ideas and Institutions of Victorian Britain: Essays in Honour of George Kitson Clark*, ed. Robert Robson (New York: Barnes & Noble, 1967), 324.

17. Cecil Y. Lang and Edgar F. Shannon, eds., *The Letters of Alfred Lord Tennyson*, 2 vols. (New York: Oxford University Press, 1981), 1:111.

18. Quoted in John Connop Thirlwall, *Connop Thirlwall: Historian and Theologian* (London: Society for Promoting Christian Knowledge, 1936), 48.

19. Ibid., 60.

20. For a discussion of the Germano-Coleridgeans that works closely with the historical writings of Hare, Thirlwall, Grote, and others, see Robert Preyer, *Bentham, Coleridge, and the Science of History* (Bochum-Langendreer, W. Germany: Verlag Heinrich Pöppinghaus, 1958). For further discussion of philology in the Germano-Coleridgean sense ("embracing literature, language, ancient law, history and archeology"), see Hans Aarsleff, *The Study of Language in England, 1780–1860* (Princeton: Princeton University Press, 1967), 194. Merivale recalled, "Coleridge and Wordsworth were our principal divinities, and Hare and Thirlwall were regarded as their prophets" (Merivale, *Autobiography*, 98). The philological method was itself a matter of great controversy; leaders both of the Evangelicals and the Oxford Movement strongly resisted and disapproved of the influence of Continental (especially German) philological scholarship.

21. B. G. Niebuhr, *The History of Rome*, trans. Julius Charles Hare and Connop Thirlwall, 2 vols. (Cambridge, UK: Printed by John Smith, 1828), 1:ix.

22. Frances M. Brookfield, *The Cambridge Apostles* (New York: Scribner's, 1906), 8.

23. Hayden White, *Metahistory: The Historical Imagination in Nineteenth-Century Europe* (Baltimore: Johns Hopkins University Press, 1973), 147.

24. Thirlwall, *Thirlwall*, 47–48.

25. T. Wemyss Reid, *The Life, Letters, and Friendships of Richard Monckton Milnes, First Lord Houghton*, 2 vols. (New York: Cassell, 1891), 1:71.

26. For a detailed account, see Aarsleff, *Study of Language*, 211–63.

27. Thomas Carlyle, *The Life of John Sterling* (London: Chapman and Hall, 1871), 29.

28. *Philological Museum*, 2 vols. (Cambridge, UK: J. Smith for Deightons, 1832–33), i, ii, iv.

29. For a study of Whewell's influence, see Richard Yeo, *Defining Science: William Whewell, Natural Knowledge, and Public Debate in Early Victorian Britain* (Cambridge, UK: Cambridge University Press, 1993). See also Garland, *Cambridge before Darwin*.

30. Robson, "Trinity College in the Age of Peel," 321.

31. Isobel Armstrong, "Tennyson's 'The Lady of Shalott': Victorian Mythography and the Politics of Narcissism," in *The Sun Is God: Painting, Literature and Mythology in the Nineteenth Century*, ed. J. B. Bullen (Oxford: Clarendon Press, 1989), 87.

32. Charles Tennyson, *Alfred Tennyson* (New York: Macmillan, 1949), 123.

33. E. P. Thompson, *The Making of the English Working Class* (London: V. Gollancz, 1963), 817. For accounts of these disturbances, see John Stevenson, *Popular Disturbances in England, 1700–1832*, 2nd ed. (New York: Longman, 1979, 1992), 254–304, and Derek Fraser, "The Agitation for Parliamentary Reform," in J. T. Ward, *Popular Movements, c. 1830–1850* (New York: St. Martin's Press, 1970), 31–53.

34. Martin, *Tennyson*, 125.

35. John Stuart Mill, *Autobiography*, in *Autobiography and Other Writings*, ed. Jack Stillinger (Boston, Houghton Mifflin, 1969), 75. In his essay "Civilization: Signs of the Times" (1836), Mill declared Thirlwall "one of the few great scholars who have issued from either University for a century." He was unable to resist the parenthetical jibe at these institutions, "(and he was such before he went thither)." In *John Stuart Mill: Literary Essays*, ed. Edward Alexander (Indianapolis: Bobbs-Merrill, 1967), 123. Like Mill, Thirlwall was prodigious in his learning, reading Latin at age three and Greek, fluently, by the age of four.

36. Thirlwall, *Thirlwall*, 16.

37. William Ewart Gladstone, *Arthur Henry Hallam*, Companion Classics (Boston: Perry Mason, [1898]), 9.

38. Ibid., 16.

39. Quoted in Martin, *Tennyson*, 74.

40. Hallam is attentive to the potential dangers in a mind "whose conformation is oratorical"; he warns that the process of persuasion is inevitably "in danger of being inverted and confused," leading to the deception both of the self and of others. But he insists, "Those who debase...the persuasive art, are commonly called rhetoricians, not orators." T. H. Vail Motter, ed., *The Writings of Arthur Hallam*, Modern Language Association of America General Series 15 (London: Oxford University Press, 1943), 152, 153. In his essay on Cicero, he suggests that oratory in itself is not intrinsically either ameliorative or destructive.

41. James Knowles, "Aspects of Tennyson, II," *Nineteenth Century* 33 (1893): 185.

42. Linda Dowling, *Hellenism and Homosexuality in Victorian Oxford* (Ithaca: Cornell University Press, 1994), xiii, 85. The term "Apostles" came to denote something of a

"homosexual code," especially in the days when Lytton Strachey and J. M. Keynes were members. See the chapter "The Higher Sodomy" in Richard Deacon, *The Cambridge Apostles: A History of Cambridge University's Elite Intellectual Secret Society* (New York: Farrar, Strauss and Giroux, 1985), 55–68.

43. Reid, *Milnes*, 1:59, 72.

44. November 26, 1831, in Francis Trench, *A Few Notes from Past Life: 1818–1832* (Oxford: John Henry, 1862), 286.

45. Culler points out that in the earliest Tennyson publication, *Poems by Two Brothers* (1827), "there are some eight or ten poems which deal with this same theme of the fall of empire or the destruction of cities," but he only briefly mentions Troy, and indeed leaves many of Tennyson's cities off the list. He concludes, "All these cities, historical and visionary, may be reduced to two, Jerusalem and Babylon, the City of God and the City of Wrath" (*Poetry of Tennyson*, 22).

46. Lang and Shannon, *The Letters of Alfred Lord Tennyson*, 1:109.

47. W. E. Gladstone, *Homeric Synchronism: An Enquiry into the Time and Place of Homer* (New York: Harper, 1876), 9. For discussions concerning the broader relevance of Gladstone's Homeric writings, see Jenkyns, *Victorians and Ancient Greece*, 199–210; Frank Turner, *The Greek Heritage in Victorian Britain* (New Haven, CT: Yale University Press, 1981), 159–70, 236–44; and D. W. Bebbington, who argues in *The Mind of Gladstone: Religion, Homer, and Politics* (New York: Oxford University Press, 2004), 142–215, that Gladstone's Homeric arguments changed over time, in ways corresponding to his shifting political views.

48. George Grote, *A History of Greece*, new ed., 12 vols. (London: John Murray, 1883), 1:277.

49. Connop Thirlwall, *A History of Greece*, 2 vols. (New York: Harper, 1845), 1:880; Niebuhr, *History of Rome* (trans. Hare and Thirlwall), 1:151.

50. Quoted in James Kissane, "Victorian Mythology," *Victorian Studies* 6 (1962): 7.

51. Turner, *Greek Heritage*, 139; W. D. Paden, *Tennyson in Egypt: A Study of the Imagery in His Earlier Work*, Humanistic Studies 27 (Lawrence: University of Kansas Publications, 1942), 192n. Jenkyns comments, "The public was deluged with Vindications and Expostulations" by and in response to Bryant (*Victorians and Ancient Greece*, 9).

52. Turner suggests, "Although until the 1860s reviewers complained about the continuing use of Bryant [*A New System* in particular] there is little evidence that his ideas...exercised any appreciable influence" (*Greek Heritage*, 79). This may be because the work requires inordinate patience; even Paden, a virtually indefatigable reader of source materials, admits of reading *A New System*, "I must confess that his thousand-odd infinitely repetitious pages, thickly studded with names in grotesque connections, have several times put me to sleep" (*Tennyson in Egypt*, 193n).

53. Jacob Bryant, *A Dissertation concerning the War of Troy and the Expedition of the Grecians, as Described by Homer: Showing, that no such expedition was ever undertaken, and that no such city of Phrygian existed*, 2nd ed. (London: T. Payne, 1799), vi, 2, 4, 40.

54. Armstrong, "Tennyson's 'The Lady of Shalott,'" 55.

55 Julius C. Hare, "Preface," *Philological Museum*, iii.

56. Connop Thirlwall, *Letters Literary and Theological*, ed. J. J. Stewart Prone and Louis Stokes (London: Bentley, 1881), 96.

57. Thomas Keightley, *The Mythology of Ancient Greece and Italy*, 3rd ed. (New York: Appleton, 1866), viii, v.

58. Keightley, *The Mythology of Ancient Greece and Italy*, 1st ed. (1831), 2 n2.

59. Grote, *History of Greece*, 1:43, 312, 324, 312.

60. John Addington Symonds, *Studies of the Greek Poets*, 3rd ed. (1873; London: A. and C. Black, 1920), 1:33–34.

61. Turner, *Greek Heritage*, 95.

62. Ibid., 161.

63. Jenkyns, *Victorians and Ancient Greece*, 200.

64. William Ewart Gladstone, *Juventus Mundi: The Gods and Men of the Heroic Age*, 2nd ed. (1869; London: Macmillan, 1870), 7. Bebbington discusses the revisions in *Mind of Gladstone*, 178–79. The proofs of *Studies on Homer* were read by Thirlwall, with whom Gladstone corresponded extensively on matters Homeric.

65. W. E. Gladstone, *Landmarks of Homeric Study* (London: Macmillan, 1890), 106–7.

66. Ibid., 113.

67. Gladstone, *Juventus Mundi*, 413.

68. See Turner, *Greek Heritage*, 187–263.

69. Herbert M. Schueller and Robert L. Peters, eds., *The Letters of John Addington Symonds*, 3 vols. (Detroit, MI: Wayne State University Press, 1967–69), 1:594; hereafter cited by page number in the text.

70. The passage he read was "Achilles Over the Trench" (*Iliad*, 18:202 ff), describing the turning point in the Trojan War when Achilles rejoins the battle. For a comparison of Tennyson's translation of *Iliad* 8:542–61 with the original, see Theodore Redpath, "Tennyson and the Literature of Greece and Rome," in *Studies in Tennyson*, ed. Hallam Tennyson (Totowa, NJ: Barnes and Noble, 1981), 107–10. Tennyson adopted most of Gladstone's suggestions. For other fragmentary blank verse translations, see Christopher Ricks, ed., *The Poems of Tennyson*, 2nd ed., 3 vols. (Berkeley: University of California Press, 1987), 3:603–4; for a prose translation of *Iliad* 6:503–14, see [Hallam Tennyson], *Alfred Lord Tennyson: A Memoir by His Son*, 2 vols. (New York, Macmillan, 1905), 2:15–16.

71. Gladstone, *Juventus Mundi*, ix–x; Keightley, *The Mythology of Ancient Greece*, 3rd ed., v.

72. For a survey of Tennyson's classical versification, see A. A. Markley, "Barbarous Hexameters and Dainty Meters: Tennyson's Uses of Classical Versification," *Studies in Philology* 95 (1998): 456–86.

73. Herbert Paul, "Aspects of Tennyson, IV: The Classical Poems," *Nineteenth Century* 33 (1893): 453.

74. Jenkyns, *Victorians and Ancient Greece*, 206.

75. Arthur Coleridge, "Fragmentary Notes of Tennyson's Talk," in *Tennyson and His Friends*, ed. Hallam, Lord Tennyson (London: Macmillan, 1911), 271; H. D. Rawnsley, *Memories of the Tennysons* (Glasgow: James MacLehose, 1900), 142.

76. Paul, "Aspects of Tennyson, IV," 450.

77. W. E. G. to A. T., 19 December, 1873, Tennyson letter 5943, Tennyson Research Centre, Lincolnshire.

78. Martin, *Tennyson*, 458; Gerhard Joseph, *Tennyson and the Text* (Cambridge, UK: Cambridge University Press, 1989), 133.

79. Frank Turner, "Why the Greeks and Not the Romans in Victorian Britain?" in *Rediscovering Hellenism: The Hellenic Inheritance and the English Imagination*, ed. G. W. Clarke with J. C. Eade (Cambridge, UK: Cambridge University Press, 1989), 64.

80. G. W. Benjamin, *Troy: Its Legend, History and Literature* (New York: Scribner's Sons, 1880), 141.

81. Walter Pater, "The Beginnings of Greek Sculpture," in *Greek Studies: A Series of Essays* (London: Macmillan, 1897), 220–21.

82. Jenkyns, *Victorians and Ancient Greece*, 200.

83. W. E. Gladstone, "Preface," in Henry Schliemann, *Mycenae: A Narrative of Researches and Discoveries at Mycenæ and Tiryns* (New York: Scribner's, 1877), v.

84. Traill, *Schliemann of Troy*, 165–66. For further discussion of the complexities of this relationship, see Bebbington, *The Mind of Gladstone*, 202–4.

85. Percy Lubbock, ed., *The Letters of Henry James*, 2 vols. (New York: Charles Scribner's, 1920), 2:53.

86. Ibid.; Martin, *Tennyson*, 518.

87. Virginia Woolf, "The Letters of Henry James," in *The Essays of Virginia Woolf*, ed. Andrew McNeillie (San Diego: Harcourt Brace Jovanovich, 1988), 3:200.

88. Gladstone, *Homeric Synchronism*, 36–37.

89. Heinrich Schliemann, *Troy and Its Remains*, ed. Philip Smith (New York: Scribner, 1875), 345.

90. Wilfrid Ward, "Tennyson and W. G. Ward and other Farringford Friends," in *Tennyson and His Friends*, 230.

91. Traill, *Schliemann of Troy*, 208.

92. Turner, *Greek Heritage*, 180.

93. Heinrich Schliemann, *Troja* (1884; Salem, NH: Ayer, 1989), 236, 237, 240, 241.

94. Quoted in Traill, *Schliemann of Troy*, 236.

95. R. C. Jebb, review of *Ilios: The City and Country of the Trojans: Researches and Discoveries 1871–73, 1878–79* (London, 1880), in *Edinburgh Review* 153 (1881): 539, 544, 547, 525.

96. Turner, *Greek Heritage*, 180.

97. Jebb, review of *Ilios*, 524.

98. Turner, *Greek Heritage*, 180; R. C. Jebb, *Homer: An Introduction to the Iliad and Odyssey* (1887), new ed. (Boston: Ginn, 1893), 147.

99. Sigmund Freud, "A Disturbance of Memory on the Acropolis" (1936), ed. James Strachey in *The Standard Edition of the Complete Psychological Works of Sigmund Freud, Volume XXII (1932–1936): New Introductory Lectures on Psycho-Analysis and Other Works*, 243, 242, 241, 245, 243, 244.

100. Gay, *Freud*, 89.

101. Freud, "Disturbance of Memory," 245.

102. Symonds, *Studies of the Greek Poets*, 1:6.

103. Turner, *Greek Heritage*, 181.

104. Walter Leaf, *Troy: A Study in Homeric Geography* (London: Macmillan, 1912), 168. Leaf also provided the introduction to C. Schuchardt's *Schliemann's Excavations: An Archaeological and Historical Study* (London: Macmillan, 1891), a copy of which Tennyson owned.

105. [Agnata Frances] Butler, quoted in Rev. H. Montagu Butler, "Recollections of Tennyson," in *Tennyson and His Friends*, 216.

106. Jebb, review of *Ilios*, 527, 547.

107. 16 October 1829, in M. R. D. Foot, ed., *The Gladstone Diaries*, 14 vols. (Oxford: Clarendon Press, 1968), 1:263.

108. John Morley, *The Life of William Ewart Gladstone*, 2 vols. (London: Macmillan, 1905), 1:59.

Chapter 4

1. "Every language is really untranslateable," Tennyson mused. [Hallam Tennyson], *Alfred Lord Tennyson: A Memoir by His Son*, 2 vols. (New York, Macmillan, 1905), 1:278.

In tacit agreement with this observation, I employ in what follows a range of translations, attempting to balance a historicized approach to translation (that is, to make use of translations from Victorian and earlier periods) with contemporary versions (which are sometimes, though not always, more accurate). Because Tennyson read the works of Homer, Virgil, Dante, and others continuously over the course of his lifetime, generally in the original language, projecting his translations in a given period is a complicated matter. We do have a few of his translations (of Horace and Claudian from childhood, of Homer from the 1860s), and these figure in my study.

When quoting from Homer, I make frequent use of Alexander Pope's translation of the *Iliad*, intimately known to Tennyson. Pope's *Iliad* is augmented here by later nineteenth- and twentieth-century translations that render the text more literally, as Tennyson also would have known it. Pope translated parts of the *Odyssey* (books 3, 5, 7, 9, 13, 14, 17, 21, 22, 24). I also draw from George Chapman's sixteenth-century translation. I augment Pope and Chapman with prose translations (owned by Tennyson) by Andrew Lang, Walter Leaf, and Ernest Myers, several of whose personal connections to Tennyson I note. I employ their *The Iliad of Homer* (1882), rev. ed. (London: Macmillan, 1930); Leaf translated books 1–9; Lang, books 10–16; Myers, books 17–24. Andrew Lang and H. S. Butcher, *The Odyssey* (1879; London: Macmillan, 1921), and Andrew Lang, *The Homeric Hymns* (London: G. Allen, 1898) were also consulted; Lang's admiration for Tennyson is expressed in his *Alfred Tennyson* (London: Blackwood, 1901). I have also drawn from the *Iliad* translations of Richmond Lattimore (Chicago: University of Chicago Press, 1951) and Robert Fitzgerald (New York: Anchor, 1975), as well as A. T. Murray, *Iliad*, Loeb Classical Library, 2 vols. (London: W. Heinemann, 1924) and Apostolos N. Athanassakis, *The Homeric Hymns* (Baltimore: Johns Hopkins University Press, 1976).

I have employed Dryden's translation of the *Aeneid* (Dryden did not translate the entire work), supplemented with H. Rushton Fairclough, Loeb Classical Library, 2 vols. (London: W. Heinemann, 1916–18) and Robert Fitzgerald (New York: Random House, 1983). I use Tennyson's own translations of Horace, as well as H. Rushton Fairclough, *Horace*, Loeb Classical Library (Cambridge, MA: Harvard University Press, 1936). I have also consulted a translation of Virgil from Tennyson's father's library, *Works; tr. into English prose, with the Latin text...for the use of schools*, 4th ed., rev. (London: Davidson, 1763).

Tennyson owned numerous editions of Dante, but the translation he would have been most familiar with in the 1830s was that of H. F. Cary (1805), the 1814 edition of which was in his father's library (though incomplete); all citations are from this translation (London: Taylor, 1814). One of Tennyson's volumes had belonged to Arthur Hallam. Hallam referred to Cary's use of blank verse in place of terza rima in his 1832 "Review of an Italian Translation of Milton" (*Writings*, 237). All citations refer to line numbers and the translator(s).

2. Richard Shannon, *Gladstone*, 2 vols. (London: Hamilton, 1982), 1:34.

3. Coleridge, "Fragmentary Notes," in *Tennyson and His Friends*, ed. Hallam, Lord Tennyson (London: Macmillan, 1911), 263.

4. H. C. G. Matthew, *Gladstone 1809–1874*, 2 vols. (Oxford: Clarendon, 1986), 1:25, 11.

5. William Ewart Gladstone, *Arthur Henry Hallam*, Companion Classics (Boston: Perry Mason, [1898]), 11–12.

6. Bruce Coleman, *Conservatism and the Conservative Party in Nineteenth-Century Britain* (London: Edward Arnold, 1988), 10.

7. Shannon, *Gladstone*, 1:29.

8. Eugenio F. Biagini, *Liberty, Retrenchment, and Reform: Popular Liberalism in the Age of Gladstone, 1860–1880* (Cambridge: Cambridge University Press, 1992), 387, 390.

9. Gladstone's opinion of Ulysses altered significantly; in 1858 he insisted, "Whatever the Ulysses of Virgil or of Euripides may be, the Ulysses of Homer...has nothing about him of what is selfish, tricky, or faithless" (*SH*, 3:47).

10. R. H. Horne, *A New Spirit of the Age* (1844; London: Henry Frowde, Oxford University Press, 1907), 257.

11. Gladstone, "Tennyson," in *Gleanings of Past Years, 1843–79*, 7 vols. (London: John Murray, 1879), 2:132–33.

12. For an articulation of the claim that this section of the monologue constitutes "public silence," see Claire Berardini, "The Tennysonian Paradox: Privacy and Sociality in 'Ulysses' and 'St. Simeon Stylites,'" *Victorian Poetry* 31 (1993): 377.

13. Christopher Ricks and Aidan Day, eds., *Tennyson: The Harvard Manuscripts*, in *The Tennyson Archive*, 31 vols. (New York: Garland, 1987), 3:10–11; hereafter cited in the text as *H. MS.*

14. Herbert F. Tucker, *Tennyson and the Doom of Romanticism* (Cambridge, MA: Harvard University Press, 1988), 217–18.

15. William Ewart Gladstone, *Juventus Mundi: The Gods and Men of the Heroic Age*, 2nd ed. (1869; London: Macmillan, 1870), 464.

16. Tucker, *Tennyson and the Doom of Romanticism*, 217.

17. Jerome H. Buckley, *Tennyson: The Growth of a Poet* (Cambridge, MA: Harvard University Press, 1960), 86.

18. Christopher Ricks, *Tennyson*, 2nd ed. (Berkeley: University of California Press, 1972, 1987), 117; Dorothy Mermin, *The Audience in the Poem: Five Victorian Poets* (New Brunswick, NJ: Rutgers University Press, 1983), 30.

19. A. Dwight Culler, *The Poetry of Tennyson* (New Haven, CT: Yale University Press, 1977), 95.

20. James Knowles, "Aspects of Tennyson, II," *Nineteenth Century* 33 (1893): 182.

21. Ricks notes the Virgilian qualities of the ending of "On a Mourner," which "is poised, waiting," and compares this to the "fateful pause and poise" in Tennyson's 1863 translation of the passage from book 8 in the *Iliad* in which, by the light of their fires, "a thousand on the plain," the Trojans "waited the golden dawn." Ricks, *Tennyson*, 112. I would add that such pausing appears anathema to Ulysses, who declares, "How dull it is to pause" (22).

22. In *The Manyfacèd Glass: Tennyson's Dramatic Monologues* (Athens: Ohio University Press, 1987), 93, Linda K. Hughes posits, "Perhaps this simile suggested the subject of Ulysses," but says that the differences show that Tennyson "had grown to use the dramatic monologue for (relatively) more objective ends, the lyric for (relatively) more subjective ends."

23. Dante may draw on the brief address of Aeneas to comrades whom he calls *iuvenes* ("My men," trans. Loeb ed.; "Brave souls," trans. Dryden). He tells them, "*si vobis audentem extrema cupido, certa sequi,*" which Dryden renders, "So bold a speech encouraged their desire / Of death and added fuel to their fire" (2:477–78).

24. R. C. Jebb, review of *Ilios: The City and Country of the Trojans: Researches and Discoveries 1871–73, 1878–79* (London, 1880), in *Edinburgh Review* 153 (1881): 539–40.

25. G. W. Benjamin, *Troy: Its Legend, History and Literature* (New York: Scribner's Sons, 1880), 85.

26. Stephen Gwynn, *Tennyson: A Critical Study*, Victorian Era Series (London: Blackie, 1899), 135, 139.

27. Frank Turner, *The Greek Heritage in Victorian Britain* (New Haven, CT: Yale University Press, 1981), 239.

28. Henry Kozicki, *Tennyson and Clio: History in the Major Poems* (Baltimore, MD: The Johns Hopkins University Press, 1979), 43.

29. Raymond Williams, *Keywords: A Vocabulary of Culture and Society*, rev. ed. (New York: Oxford University Press, 1983), 96.

30. Benjamin Disraeli, "The Spirit of Whiggism" (1836), in *Whigs and Whiggism: Political Writings*, ed. William Hutcheon (New York: Macmillan, 1914), 331 and "What Is He?" (1833), in *Whigs and Whiggism*, 19; George Eliot, *Felix Holt, the Radical*, ed. Fred C. Thomson (Oxford: Clarendon, 1980), 247–48.

31. Thomas Carlyle, *Past and Present* (1843; London: Oxford University Press, 1909), 35, 37, 38.

32. Ibid., 38.

33. J. F. A. Pyre, *The Formation of Tennyson's Style: A Study, Primarily, of the Versification of the Early Poems*, University of Wisconsin Studies in Language and Literature 12 (Madison: University of Wisconsin, 1921), 120–21.

34. Douglas Bush, *Mythology and the Romantic Tradition in English Poetry* (New York: Norton, 1963), 210.

35. Elaine Scarry, *On Beauty and Being Just* (Princeton: Princeton University Press, 1999), 105, 104.

36. Elizabeth Sewell, *The Structure of Poetry* (London: Routledge, 1951), 131.

37. The Harvard manuscript also has "the men that in one night" (*H. MS*, 1st reading).

38. J. Lemprière, *A Classical Dictionary*, 8th ed. (London: Printed for T. Cadell and W. Davies, 1812), s.v. "Troja."

39. Tucker, *Tennyson and the Doom of Romanticism*, 235.

40. W. E. Gladstone, "Preface," in Henry Schliemann, *Mycenae: A Narrative of Researches and Discoveries at Mycenæ and Tiryns* (New York: Scribner's, 1877), xvi.

41. In Tennyson's source, Quintus Smyrnaeus's *The Fall of Troy*, Oenone has been incinerated with Paris: "the blast of the devouring fire / Had made twain one, Oenone and Paris, now / One heap of ashes" (10:483–85). Trans. Arthur S. Way, Loeb Classical Library (London: W. Heinemann, 1913), 453.

Part III

1. Robert Bernard Martin, *Tennyson: The Unquiet Heart* (Oxford: Clarendon, 1980), 148.

2. Stephen Scully, in *Homer and the Sacred City* (Ithaca, NY: Cornell University Press, 1990), 50.

3. Douglas Bush, *Mythology and the Romantic Tradition in English Poetry* (New York: Norton, 1963), 200 4n.

4. A. Dwight Culler, *The Poetry of Tennyson* (New Haven, CT: Yale University Press, 1977), 27.

5. J. Lemprière, *A Classical Dictionary*, 8th ed. (London: Printed for T. Cadell and W. Davies, 1812), s.v. "Troja."

6. Scully, *Homer and the Sacred City*, 51; see *Iliad* 21.441–57.

7. W. E. Gladstone, "Preface," in Henry Schliemann, *Mycenae: A Narrative of Researches and Discoveries at Mycenæ and Tiryns* (New York: Scribner's, 1877), viii, ix.

8. William Ewart Gladstone, *Juventus Mundi: The Gods and Men of the Heroic Age*, 2nd ed. (1869; London: Macmillan, 1870), 162.

Chapter 5

1. For two studies of the iconographic and literary history of Ganymede's rapture, see James M. Saslow, *Ganymede in the Renaissance: Homosexuality in Art and Society* (New Haven, CT: Yale University Press, 1986), and Leonard Barkan, *Transuming Passion: Ganymede and the Erotics of Humanism* (Stanford: Stanford University Press, 1991).

2. William Ewart Gladstone, *Juventus Mundi: The Gods and Men of the Heroic Age*, 2nd ed. (1869; London: Macmillan, 1870), 418, 459.

3. Walter Pater, "The Beginnings of Greek Sculpture," *Greek Studies: A Series of Essays* (London: Macmillan, 1897), 228.

4. Charles Tennyson, *Alfred Tennyson* (New York: Macmillan, 1949), 509.

5. Robert Bernard Martin, *Tennyson: The Unquiet Heart* (Oxford: Clarendon, 1980), 242.

6. "Wills & Bequests: Lord Tennyson's Gifts," *Daily Telegraph*, February 19, 1929.

7. Pater was disappointed in this respect when he saw Carlyle himself; he observed, "He is far from being as beautiful as his prose," a comment others in turn made about Pater. Quoted in James Eli Adams, *Dandies and Desert Saints: Styles of Victorian Masculinity* (Ithaca, NY: Cornell University. Press, 1995), 227.

8. Martin, *Tennyson*, 82.

9. Roy Jenkins, *Gladstone: A Biography* (New York: Random House, 1995, 1997), 16; William Ewart Gladstone, *Arthur Henry Hallam*, Companion Classics (Boston: Perry Mason, [1898]), 23.

10. Martin, *Tennyson*, 53.

11. Ibid., 203.

12. Douglas Bush, *Mythology and the Romantic Tradition in English Poetry* (New York: Norton, 1963), 205 n13, 204. Bush also regrets "the artifice and refinement" of "The Lotos-Eaters," calling the poem "incomparably pretty" (208) and remarking that in the "delicacy" of their observations they lack any resemblance to "tough, hairy, brine-stained Greek mariners" (207).

13. Gladstone, *Juventus Mundi*, 511.

14. Bush, *Mythology and the Romantic Tradition*, 208.

15. T. S. Eliot, *The Use of Poetry and the Use of Criticism: Studies in the Relation of Criticism to Poetry in England* (Cambridge, MA: Harvard University Press, 1933), 98.

16. M. R. D. Foot, ed., *The Gladstone Diaries*, 14 vols. (Oxford: Clarendon Press, 1968), 1:263.

17. Herbert F. Tucker, *Tennyson and the Doom of Romanticism* (Cambridge, MA: Harvard University Press, 1988), 239.

18. Henry Kozicki in *Tennyson and Clio: History in the Major Poems* (Baltimore, MD: The Johns Hopkins University Press, 1979) notes that Tithonus "can be taken to represent in his immobility both aristocracy and Troy dead in history" (40), an insight that he does not develop. Daniel A. Harris in *Tennyson and Personification: The Rhetoric of "Tithonus"* (Ann Arbor, MI: UMI Research Press, 1986) dismisses Kozicki's suggestion, arguing, "Political argument seems as extraneous to the poem (and to its literary sources) as Tithonus's familial connections" (126 n70).

19. Samuel Clarke, ed., *H. Ilias Graece et Latine*, 14th ed., 2 vols. (London: Johnson, 1806).

20. Gladstone, *Juventus Mundi*, 325.

21. I am grateful to Justina Gregory for alerting me to the controversies surrounding the translation of the Greek *amumon*; see Anne Amory Parry, *Blameless Aegisthus* (Leiden: Brill, 1973).

22. *Georgics* 1:501–2, trans. Stephen Scully, in *Homer and the Sacred City* (Ithaca, NY: Cornell University Press, 1990), 39.

23. J. Lemprière, *A Classical Dictionary*, 8th ed. (London: Printed for T. Cadell and W. Davies, 1812), s.v. "Ganymedes."

24. Andrew Lang, *The Homeric Hymns* (London: G. Allen, 1898), 177. The translator of the Loeb edition considers Aphrodite disgraceful, observing in a footnote, "Aphrodite extenuates her disgrace by claiming that the race of Anchises is almost divine, as is shown in the persons of Ganymede and Tithonus." Hugh G. Evelyn-White, trans., *Hesiod, the Homeric Hymns, and Homerica*, Loeb Classical Library (Cambridge, MA: Harvard University Press, 1967), 419.

25. K. J. Dover, *Greek Homosexuality* (Cambridge, MA: Harvard University Press, 1989), 7, 197, 75, 93.

26. *Homeric Hymns*, trans. Lang, 179.

27. Gladstone, *Juventus Mundi*, 517.

28. Ibid., 460.

29. As Tucker points out, "Commentators cannot decide whether to name her Aurora in Latin or Eos in Greek" (*Tennyson and the Doom of Romanticism*, 245). This indecision reflects the Victorian debate over Latin and Greek nomenclature generally (as Gladstone and Tennyson discussed at the Woolner dinner party). In Tennyson's note to "Tithonus" in the Eversley edition he favors the Latin, referring to "Aurora" rather than Eos, and to "Venus" rather than Aphrodite.

30. For the full translations, see [Hallam Tennyson], *Alfred Lord Tennyson: A Memoir by His Son*, 2 vols. (New York, Macmillan, 1905), 1:15, and Christopher Ricks, ed., *The Poems of Tennyson*, 2nd ed., 3 vols. (Berkeley: University of California Press, 1987), 3:604.

31. Thomas Keightley, *Mythology of Ancient Greece and Italy*, 1st ed. (New York: Appleton, 1831), 97.

32. Lemprière, *Classical Dictionary*, s.v. "Apollo."

33. J. M. Kemble to A. T., [January 1833], in Cecil Y. Lang and Edgar F. Shannon, eds., *The Letters of Alfred Lord Tennyson*, 2 vols. (New York: Oxford University Press, 1981), 1:85–86.

34. Ovid, *Heroides and Amores*, trans. Grant Showerman (Cambridge, MA: Harvard University Press, 1977); subsequent quotations are cited in the text.

35. Gladstone, *Juventus Mundi*, 511.

36. Quoted in Bush, *Mythology and the Romantic Tradition*, 205.

37. For a discussion of Tennyson's gods, with their Homeric interventionism and Lucretian indifference, see Gerhard Joseph, *Tennyson and the Text* (Cambridge, UK: Cambridge University Press, 1989), 138–39.

38. Gladstone's translation of this passage reads, "That dame of alien tongue, / That Judge befooled by Fate and Lust, / Have shattered Ilion into dust." *The Odes of Horace* (New York: Scribner's, 1894), 77.

39. Gladstone, *Juventus Mundi*, 459.

40. Tucker, *Tennyson and the Doom of Romanticism*, 157.

41. Ibid., 172.

42. Ibid., 256.

43. Lemprière, *Classical Dictionary*, s.v. "Aurora."

44. George Grote, *A History of Greece*, new ed., 12 vols. (London: John Murray, 1883), 1:291.

45. Oskar Seyffert, *A Dictionary of Classical Antiquities: Mythology, Religion, Literature and Art*, rev. and ed. by Henry Nettleship and J. E. Sandys (London: Swan Sonnenschein, 1891), s.v. "Memnon."

46. Lemprière, *Classical Dictionary*, s.v. "Memnon."

47. Seyffert, *Dictionary of Classical Antiquities*, s.v. "Memnon."

48. Lemprière, *Classical Dictionary*, s.v. "Memnon."

49. Ibid.

50. Thomas Hutchinson, ed., *The Complete Poetical Works of Percy Bysshe Shelley* (London: Oxford University Press, 1923), 546.

51. Connop Thirlwall, "Memnon," *Philological Museum* 2 (1833):146.

52. Ibid., 165, 166, 167.

53. Gregory Nagy, "The Name of Apollo: Etymology and Essence," in *Apollo: Origins and Influences*, ed. Jon Solomon (Tucson: University of Arizona Press, 1994), 6.

54. Thirlwall, "Memnon," 167.

55. W. E. Gladstone, *Homeric Synchronism: An Enquiry into the Time and Place of Homer* (New York: Harper, 1876), 9, 166.

56. Ibid., 168, 169–70, 182.

57. Thirlwall, "Memnon," 153, 165.

58. Ibid., 153.

59. John Milton, *Complete Poems and Major Prose*, ed. Merritt Y. Hughes (New York: Macmillan, 1957, 1985).

60. William Wordsworth, *Selected Poems and Prefaces*, ed. Jack Stillinger (Boston: Houghton Mifflin, 1965).

61. Isobel Armstrong, *Victorian Poetry: Poetry, Poetics and Politics* (London: Routledge, 1993), 81. See also Armstrong, "Tennyson's 'The Lady of Shalott': Victorian Mythography and the Politics of Narcissism," in *The Sun Is God: Painting, Literature and Mythology in the Nineteenth Century*, ed. J. B. Bullen (Oxford: Clarendon Press, 1989), for a reading of "The Lady of Shalott" by way of Hallam's contemporaneous writings.

62. Michel Foucault, *Technologies of the Self: A Seminar with Michel Foucault*, ed. Luther H. Martin, Huck Gutman, and Patrick H. Hutton (Amherst: University of Massachusetts Press, 1988), 19.

63. For a rich discussion of this simile that views Aurora's discourse "as in itself summoning objects and their properties into being," see Matthew Rowlinson in *Tennyson's Fixations: Psychoanalysis and the Topics of the Early Poetry* (Charlottesville: University Press of Virginia, 1994), 149–51.

64. Alan Sinfield, *The Wilde Century: Effeminacy, Oscar Wilde and the Queer Movement* (New York: Columbia University Press, 1994), vii, 26, 27.

65. Joseph Bristow, *Effeminate England: Homoerotic Writing after 1885* (New York: Columbia University Press, 1995), 7.

66. Sinfield, *Wilde Century*, 57, 60.

67. Bristow, *Effeminate England*, 7–8.

68. Jeffrey Weeks, *Against Nature: Essays on History, Sexuality and Identity* (London: Rivers Oram, 1991), 71. For a comprehensive examination of the history and discourses of sexual classification, see Joseph Bristow, *Sexuality*, New Critical Idiom (London: Routledge, 1997), 12–61.

69. Michael E. Green, "Tennyson's 'Gray Shadow, Once a Man': Erotic Imagery and Dramatic Structure in 'Tithonus,'" *Victorian Poetry* 18 (1980): 295.

70. Armstrong, *Victorian Poetry*, 82.

71. Jennifer Larson, *Greek Nymphs: Myth, Cult, Lore* (London: Oxford University Press, 2001), 66.

72. Armstrong, *Victorian Poetry*, 81. Herbert F. Tucker, in "When the Soul Had Hips: Six Animadversions on Psyche and Gender in Nineteenth-Century Poetry," in *Sexualities*

in Victorian Britain, ed. Andrew H. Miller and James Eli Adams (Bloomington: Indiana University Press, 1996), 157–86, explores some versions of the physical, gendered, lyricized Victorian soul.

73. See, for example, Eve Kosofsky Sedgwick, *Between Men: English Literature and Male Homosocial Desire* (New York: Columbia University Press, 1985, 118–33; Richard Dellamora, *Masculine Desire: The Sexual Politics of Victorian Aestheticism* (Chapel Hill: University of North Caroline Press, 1990), 16–41; Christopher Craft, *Another Kind of Love: Male Homosexual Desire in English Discourse, 1850–1920* (Berkeley: University of California Press, 1994), 44–70; and James Eli Adams, *Dandies and Desert Saints*, 43–51, 116–21.

74. Havelock Ellis, "Eonism," in *Studies in the Psychology of Sex*, 7 vols. (Philadelphia: F. A. Davis, 1928), 7:8; hereafter cited by page number in the text.

75. Edmund Burke, *A Philosophical Enquiry into the Origin of our Ideas of the Sublime and Beautiful*, ed. J. T. Boulton (New York: Columbia University Press, 1958), 44.

76. I dissent from those who argue that Aurora departs midway through the monologue; Tithonus describes in lines 44–45 her habitual departures, not a present one.

77. For exemplary articulations of this argument see Christopher Ricks *Tennyson*, 2nd ed. (Berkeley: University of California Press, 1972, 1989), 121; Eric Griffiths, *The Printed Voice of Victorian Poetry* (New York: Oxford University Press, 1989), 138–39; and Rowlinson, who argues that these lines "enact Tithonus's death" (*Tennyson's Fixations*, 152).

78. E. S. Dallas, *Poetics: An Essay on Poetry* (London: Smith, Elder, 1852), 9; hereafter cited by page number in the text.

79. M. H. Abrams, *A Glossary of Literary Terms*, 6th ed. (Fort Worth: Harcourt Brace Jovanovich, 1993), 67.

80. John R. Searle, *Expression and Meaning: Studies in the Theory of Speech Acts* (Cambridge, UK: Cambridge University Press, 1979), 94.

81. Abrams, *Glossary*, 66.

82. Sinfield, *Wilde Century*, 85.

83. For an exploration of the implications of gender identification for another Victorian poet, see Joseph Bristow, "Coventry Patmore and the Womanly Mission of the Mid-Victorian Poet," in *Sexualities in Victorian Britain*, 118–39. Bristow explores the troubling ramifications for Patmore of the "gendering of the male poet's vocation" (119) and briefly considers the "male femininity" that Patmore confronted in Tennyson's poetry at midcentury (131).

84. Havelock Ellis, *Man and Woman: A Study of Secondary and Tertiary Sexual Characteristics* (Boston: Houghton Mifflin, 1929).

85. Benjamin Jowett, "Personal Recollections by the Late Master of Balliol," quoted in *Memoir*, 2:465.

86. R. H. Horne, *A New Spirit of the Age* (1844; London: Henry Frowde, Oxford University Press, 1907), 258.

87. J. C. Heywood, *How They Strike Me, These Authors* (Philadelphia: J. B. Lippincott, 1877), 136, 137.

88. George Saintsbury, *A History of Nineteenth Century Literature (1790–1895)* (New York: Macmillan, 1896), 267.

89. Stephen Gwynn, *Tennyson: A Critical Study*, Victorian Era Series (London: Blackie, 1899), 22, 135.

90. Horne, *A New Spirit of the Age*, 257.

91. Lionel Trilling, ed., *The Selected Letters of John Keats* (New York: Farrar, Straus and Young, 1951), 88.

92. A. S. Byatt, "The Lyric Structure of Tennyson's *Maud*," in *The Major Victorian Poets: Reconsiderations*, ed. Isobel Armstrong (Lincoln: University of Nebraska Press, 1969), 77.

93. Walter Bagehot, "Wordsworth, Tennyson, and Browning; or, Pure, Ornate, and Grotesque Art in English Poetry" (1864), in *The Collected Works of Walter Bagehot*, 15 vols., ed. Norman St. John-Stevas (Cambridge, MA: Harvard University Press, 1965), 2:344, 350, 348.

94. Ibid., 2:343, 347.

95. Matthew Arnold, "Last Words," in *On Translating Homer* (London: Routledge, 1905), 274, 275.

96. Bagehot, "Pure, Ornate, and Grotesque Art," 346–47.

97. Burke, *Sublime and Beautiful*, 72–73.

98. Sinfield, *Wilde Century*, 88.

99. Ricks, *Tennyson*, 130, 131.

100. Harold Bloom, *Poetry and Repression: Revisionism from Blake to Stevens* (New Haven, CT: Yale University Press, 1976), 161, 168.

101. Rowlinson, *Tennyson's Fixations*, 162.

102. James A. Harrison, ed., *The Complete Works of Edgar Allen Poe*, 17 vols. (New York: AMS Press, 1965), 14:275. For a discussion of the relation of Poe to Tennyson, see Joseph, *Tennyson and the Text*, 26–46.

103. Eric Griffiths hears in this renewal not transformation but "the very changelessness which pains [the] speaker" (*Printed Voice*, 140).

104. J. F. A. Pyre, *The Formation of Tennyson's Style: A Study, Primarily, of the Versification of the Early Poems*, University of Wisconsin Studies in Language and Literature 12 (Madison: University of Wisconsin, 1921), 121, 123, 124.

105. Thomas Carlyle, *On Heroes, Hero-Worship and the Heroic in History*, ed. Carl Niemeyer (Lincoln: University of Nebraska Press, 1966), 82. Carlyle admits that German critics are not always "very intelligible at first" and hopes that "if well meditated, some meaning will gradually be found in it" (82–83), preferring the "old vulgar distinction of Poetry being *metrical*, having music in it, being a Song" (83).

106. Eliot, *Use of Poetry*, 148.

107. Ricks, *Tennyson*, 131; Bloom, *Poetry and Repression*, 167.

Chapter 6

1. Oscar Wilde, *The Picture of Dorian Gray*, ed. Isobel Murray (New York: Oxford University Press, 1981), 24–25; hereafter cited in the text by page number. There are Tennysonian references throughout the novel, as when Sybil Vane, echoing the Lady of Shalott, tells Dorian she is "grown sick of Shadows" (86).

2. M. L. Bush, *The English Aristocracy: A Comparative Synthesis* (Manchester, UK: Manchester University Press, 1984), 75.

3. Thomas Carlyle, *Past and Present* (1843; London: Oxford University Press, 1909), 186.

4. Edmund Burke, *Reflections on the French Revolution*, ed. A. J. Grieve (London: J. M. Dent, 1955), 49.

5. Ibid., 73, 108. Jack Kolb notes these echoes in *The Letters of Arthur Henry Hallam* (Columbus: Ohio University Press, 1981), 673.

6. Burke, *Reflections on the Revolution*, 49, 31.

7. Quoted in J. T. Ward, *Popular Movements, c. 1830–1850* (New York: St. Martin's Press, 1970), 13.

8. Edmund Burke, *A Philosophical Enquiry into the Origin of our Ideas of the Sublime and Beautiful*, ed. J. T. Boulton (New York: Columbia University Press, 1958), 42–43.

9. Peter Mandler, *Aristocratic Government in the Age of Reform: Whigs and Liberals, 1830–1852* (Oxford: Clarendon, 1990), 1, 85, 5.

10. Ibid., 282, 5, 2–3.

11. According to Robert Bernard Martin, "There was hardly another friend of Tennyson's with whom he was ever so much at ease except Hallam." *Tennyson: The Unquiet Heart* (Oxford: Clarendon, 1980), 241–42.

12. Carlyle, *Past and Present*, 184, 145, 179.

13. Mandler, *Aristocratic Government*, 44, 45.

14. Matthew Arnold, *Culture and Anarchy and Other Writings*, ed. Stefan Collini (Cambridge, UK: Cambridge University Press, 1993), 93, 105, 90, 91.

15. Ibid., 90–91.

16. Ibid., 114.

17. G. K. Chesterton, *The Victorian Age in Literature* (New York: Henry Holt, 1913), 70, 73.

18. G. K. Chesterton and Dr. Richard Garnett, *Tennyson* (London: Hodder and Stoughton, 1903), 4.

19. Clyde de L. Ryals and Kenneth J. Fielding, eds., *The Collected Letters of Thomas and Jane Welsh Carlyle*, 33 vols. (Durham, NC: Duke University Press, 1970–2005), 19:228, 20:185, 22:188.

20. Thomas Carlyle, *Shooting Niagara: And After?* (London: Chapman and Hall, 1867), 28.

21. *Letters of Thomas and Jane Welsh Carlyle*, 22:182.

22. Norman Page, ed., *Tennyson: Interviews and Recollections* (Totowa, NJ: Barnes & Noble Books, 1984), 193.

23. Hippolyte Taine, *History of English Literature*, trans. H. Van Laun (New York: Crowell, 1873), 716, 713, 714.

24. Henry James, "Tennyson's Drama," in *Views and Reviews*, ed. Le Roy Phillips (Boston: Ball, 1908), 176.

25. Taine, *English Literature*, 716.

26. William Allingham, *A Diary* (London: Macmillan, 1908), 119.

27. Benjamin Jowett, "Notes on Characteristics of Tennyson," in *Tennyson and His Friends*, ed. Hallam, Lord Tennyson (London: Macmillan, 1911), 186–87.

28. Martin, *Tennyson*, 44.

29. James, "Tennyson's Drama," 170.

30. Christopher Ricks, *Tennyson*, 2nd ed. (Berkeley: University of California Press, 1972, 1989), 124.

31. Daniel A. Harris, *Tennyson and Personification: The Rhetoric of "Tithonus"* (Ann Arbor, MI: UMI Research Press, 1986), 7, 8.

32. James, "Tennyson's Drama," 174.

33. Herbert F. Tucker, *Tennyson and the Doom of Romanticism* (Cambridge, MA: Harvard University Press, 1988), 242, 246.

34. In his use of alternating words such as grasshopper, cicada, and cicala, Tennyson may have been following classical precedent. Don Cameron Allen claims, "The Greeks do not distinguish clearly between the various singing insects." *Image and Meaning: Metaphoric Traditions in Renaissance Poetry*, 2nd ed. (Baltimore: Johns Hopkins University Press, 1968), 155 n1.

35. Ricks, *Tennyson*, 125, 124.

36. Taine, *English Literature*, 31.

37. Taine acknowledges his debt to German philological study, which his opening paragraph describes as having taught "that we might recover, from the monuments of literature, a knowledge of the manner in which men thought and felt centuries ago" (*English Literature*, 17).

38. Hilary Mackie, *Talking Trojan: Speech and Community in the Iliad* (New York: Rowman and Littlefield, 1996), 66. For another sympathetic reading of the Trojans, see James Redfield, *Nature and Culture in the Iliad: The Tragedy of Hector* (Chicago: University of Chicago Press, 1975).

39. Thomas Keightley, *The Mythology of Ancient Greece and Italy*, 3rd ed. (New York: Appleton, 1866), 92.

40. Wilde, *Dorian Gray*, 22.

41. William Empson, *Some Versions of Pastoral* (Norfolk, CT: New Directions, 1960), 271.

42. Hugh G. Evelyn-White, trans., *Hesiod, the Homeric Hymns, and Homerica*, Loeb Classical Library (Cambridge, MA: Harvard University Press, 1967), 421.

43. A precedent for this may be Chapman's translation of the *Homeric Hymn*, which claims parenthetically regarding Tithonus that "(To satisfie him) she bad aske of Jove / The gift of an Immortall for her Love" ("A Hymne to Venus," 369–70).

44. Matthew Rowlinson suggests that with this image, "the poem poses the problem of reading a woman's meaning." *Tennyson's Fixations: Psychoanalysis and the Topics of the Early Poetry* (Charlottesville: University Press of Virginia, 1994), 149.

45. Linda Dowling, *Hellenism and Homosexuality in Victorian Oxford* (Ithaca: Cornell University Press, 1994), 82 n6; she is referring to Pater's persistent exploration of this theme.

46. Carlyle, *Past and Present*, 292.

47. Bush, *English Aristocracy*, 73.

48. Arnold, *Culture and Anarchy*, 91.

49. Arnold, "Democracy," in *Culture and Anarchy and Other Writings*, 3.

50. Quoted in Donald Southgate, *The Passing of the Whigs, 1832–1886* (New York: St. Martin's Press, 1962), 197.

51. In Gladstone's translation her declaration reads, "Where Priam and where Paris rest, / Beasts must be safe to breed, and kine to trample." *The Odes of Horace* (New York: Scribner's, 1894), 78.

52 Wordsworth calls a beetle "a mailèd angel on a battle-day" (61) in "Stanzas on 'Castle on Indolence,'" while Tennyson declares, "Thou art a mailèd warrior" (13). Edgar Finley Shannon Jr., *Tennyson and the Reviewers: A Study of His Literary Reputation and of the Influence of the Critics upon His Poetry, 1827–1851* (Cambridge, MA: Harvard University Press, 1952), 195.

53. John Keats, *Poems*, ed. Gerald Bullett (London: J. M. Dent, 1951), 37; hereafter cited by line number.

54. Thomas Moore, *Odes of Anacreon* (London: Printed for John Stockdale, 1800), 131–34; hereafter cited by line number.

55. Allen, *Image and Meaning*, 159.

56. Ibid., 156.

57. Carlyle, *Past and Present*, 185.

58. Keats's grasshopper withstands the midday heat: "When all the birds are faint with the hot sun, / And hide in cooling trees, a voice will run / From hedge to hedge about the new-mown mead; / That is the Grasshopper's—" ("On the Grasshopper and the Cricket," 2–5).

59. Gladstone, "Tennyson," in *Gleanings of Past Years, 1843–79*, 7 vols. (London: John Murray, 1879), 2:159.

60. Ibid.

61. *Hesiod, the Homeric Hymns, and Homerica*, trans. Evelyn-White, 421–22.

62. William Ewart Gladstone, *Juventus Mundi: The Gods and Men of the Heroic Age*, 2nd ed. (1869; London: Macmillan, 1870), 511.

63. Herbert Paul, "Aspects of Tennyson, IV: The Classical Poems," *Nineteenth Century* 33 (1893): 443.

64. Douglas Bush, *Mythology and the Romantic Tradition in English Poetry* (New York: Norton, 1963), 211.

65. Theodore Redpath, "Tennyson and the Literature of Greece and Rome," in *Studies in Tennyson*, ed. Hallam Tennyson (Totowa, NJ: Barnes and Noble, 1981), 125.

66. Oskar Seyffert, *A Dictionary of Classical Antiquities: Mythology, Religion, Literature and Art*, rev. and ed. by Henry Nettleship and J. E. Sandys (London: Swan Sonnenschein, 1891), s.v. "Tithonus."

67. *Homeric Hymns*, trans. Lang, 179.

68. Robert Langbaum, *The Poetry of Experience: The Dramatic Monologue in Modern Literary Tradition* (New York: Random House, 1957), 157; W. E. Gladstone, *Studies on Homer and the Homeric Age*, 3 vols. (Oxford: Oxford University Press, 1858), 3:241.

69. Carlyle, *Past and Present*, 176.

70. "The Waste Land," 37–55 in T. S. Eliot, *The Complete Poems and Plays, 1909–1950* (New York: Harcourt, Brace, 1971); hereafter cited by line number.

71. For discussions of Tennyson's sources, see Bush, *Mythology and the Romantic Tradition*, 216–19, and A. A. Markley, *Stateliest Measures: Tennyson and the Literature of Greece and Rome* (Toronto: University of Toronto Press, 2004), 130–39.

72. J. Lemprière, *A Classical Dictionary*, 8th ed. (London: Printed for T. Cadell and W. Davies, 1812), s.v. "Tiresias."

73. A. Dwight Culler, *The Poetry of Tennyson* (New Haven, CT: Yale University Press, 1977), 88.

74. David F. Goslee, "Three Stages of Tennyson's 'Tiresias,'" *Journal of English and Germanic Philology* 75 (1976): 158.

75. Carlyle, *Past and Present*, 210.

76. Goslee, "Three Stages," 159; Tucker, *Tennyson and the Doom of Romanticism*, 204.

77. Goslee, "Three Stages," 158.

78. Christopher Ricks and Aidan Day, eds., *The Tennyson Archive*, 31 vols. (New York: Garland, 1987), 11:166; hereafter cited by line number in the text.

79. Darice Birge, "Sacred Groves and the Nature of Apollo," in *Apollo: Origins and Influences*, 13.

80. Tucker, *Tennyson and the Doom of Romanticism*, 197.

81. See Keightley's review of the story in *Seven against Thebes*: "[Eteocles] consulted Teiresias, who declared that victory would fall to Thebes, if Menoeceus the son of Creon gave himself a voluntary victim; and that heroic youth learning the response, slew himself at the gates of the city" (*The Mythology of Ancient Greece and Italy* [1831], 432.

82. Lemprière, *Classical Dictionary*, s.v. "Amphion."

83. Quintilian, *The Institutio Oratoria of Quintilian*, trans. H. E. Butler, 4 vols., Loeb Classical Library (London: William Heinemann, 1921), 3.2.4.

84. Jerome H. Buckley, *Tennyson: The Growth of a Poet* (Cambridge, MA: Harvard University Press, 1960), 229.

85. Goslee, "Three Stages," 163.

86. Mandler, *Aristocratic Government*, 276, 282, 277, 279.

87. Stopford A. Brooke, *Tennyson: His Art and Relation to Modern Life* (New York: G. P. Putnam's Sons, 1894), 32.

88. Goslee, "Three Stages," 163.

89. Quoted in Frank O'Gorman, *British Conservatism: Conservative Thought from Burke to Thatcher* (New York: Longman, 1986), 104–5.

90. Bush, *English Aristocracy*, 146.

91. Allingham, *Diary*, 325.

92. Gladstone reflected in an 1840 letter to his brother-in-law, "It is my nature to lean not so much on the applause as upon the assent of others to a degree which perhaps I do not show.... I wish you knew the state of total impotence to which I should be reduced if there were no echo to the accents of my own voice." John Morley, *The Life of William Ewart Gladstone*, 2 vols. (London: Macmillan, 1905), 1:191.

93. Frank Harrison Hill, in Lionel A. Tollemache, *Gladstone's Boswell: Late Victorian Conversations and Other Documents*, ed. Asa Briggs (New York: St. Martin's Press, 1984), 219.

94. D. A. Hamer, "Gladstone: The Making of a Political Myth," *Victorian Studies* 22 (1978): 46.

95. Walter Bagehot, "Mr. Gladstone" (1860), in *Bagehot's Historical Essays*, ed. Norman St. John-Stevas (New York: New York University Press, 1966), 247.

96. Thomas Babington Macaulay, "Gladstone on Church and State," in *Critical and Historical Essays*, 2 vols. (London: J. M. Dent, 1907), 2:239, 238.

97. T. A. Jenkins, *The Liberal Ascendancy, 1830–1886* (London: Macmillan, 1994), 117.

98. Richard Shannon, *Gladstone: Heroic Minister, 1865–1898* (London: Allen Lane, Penguin Press, 1999), 316.

99. Bagehot, "Mr. Gladstone," 247.

100. "Preface," *Punch, Or the London Charivari* 89 (December 26, 1885): iii–iv.

101. Although radical in its early leanings, by the 1880s *Punch* offered, according to Richard D. Altick, "a mingling of moderate liberalism in political matters and non-reactionary social conservatism." *Punch: The Lively Youth of a British Institution 1841–1851* (Columbus: Ohio State University Press, 1997), 734. As Ruskin declared sardonically in an 1883 lecture, "You must be clear about Punch's politics. He is a polite Whig" (735).

102. Quoted in O. F. Christie, *The Transition to Democracy 1867–1914* (London: Routledge, 1934), 34.

103. Morley, *Life of Gladstone*, 1:192.

104. Bagehot, "Mr. Gladstone and the People" (1871), in *Bagehot's Historical Essays*, ed. Norman St. John-Stevas (New York: New York University Press, 1966), 270.

105. Richard Holt Hutton, "Mr. Gladstone," *Contemporary Review* 65 (1894): 618.

106. Bagehot, "Mr. Gladstone and the People," 271.

107. Bagehot, "Mr. Gladstone," 253.

108. Theodore Redpath, "Tennyson and the Literature of Greece and Rome," in *Studies in Tennyson*, ed. Hallam Tennyson (Totowa, NJ: Barnes and Noble, 1981), 113.

109. Alfred Lyall, *Tennyson* (London: Macmillan, 1902), 145.

110. Redpath, "Tennyson and the Literature of Greece and Rome," 113.

111. George Saintsbury, *A History of English Prosody*, 3 vols. (New York: Russell & Russell, 1961), 3:297, 298.

112. Ricks, *Tennyson*, 125.

113. For Tennyson's recorded comments on *Paradise Lost*, see Hallam's notes in [Hallam Tennyson], *Alfred Lord Tennyson: A Memoir by His Son*, 2 vols. (New York, Macmillan, 1905), 2:518–23.

114. Andrew Marvell, "On Paradise Lost," in Milton, *Complete Poems* (ed. Hughes), 209.

115. John Milton, "The Verse," in *Complete Poems* (ed. Hughes), 210.

116. M. H. Abrams, *A Glossary of Literary Terms*, 6th ed. (Fort Worth, TX: Harcourt Brace Jovanovich, 1993), s.v. "Blank Verse."

117. Milton, "The Verse," in *Complete Poems* (ed. Hughes), 210.

118. Harold Nicolson, *Tennyson: Aspects of his Life, Character, and Poetry* (New York: Doubleday, 1962), 252.

119. Saintsbury, *History of English Prosody*, 3:213n, 213.

120. Milton, "The Verse," in *Complete Poems* (ed. Hughes), 210.

121. Nicole Loraux, *The Experiences of Tiresias: The Feminine and the Greek Man*, trans. Paula Wissing (Princeton: Princeton University Press, 1995), 213. Laroux also remarks the significance of Tiresias's "flash" of insight just prior to the moment of his blindness: "It will not be Tiresias, the voyeur in spite of himself or the blind seer, who will retain our interest here, but the blinding flash that shrouded the ephebe with night" (211–12).

122. James R. Kincaid, *Tennyson's Major Poems: The Comic and Ironic Patterns* (New Haven, CT: Yale University Press, 1975), 139.

123. Ricks and Day, eds., *The Tennyson Archive*, 12:197, 199.

124. Lemprière, *Classical Dictionary*, s.v. "Semele."

125. Ibid.

126. Lemprière, *Classical Dictionary*, s.v. "Bacchus."

127. Ibid.; C[onnop] T[hirlwall], "On the Attic Dionysia," in *Philological Museum* (1833), 2:273.

128. Lemprière, *Classical Dictionary*, s.v. "Dionysia."

Conclusion

1. Philip Guedalla, *The Queen and Mr. Gladstone* (Garden City, NY: Doubleday, 1934), 577; excerpts from the letters of Victoria and Gladstone hereafter cited by page number.

2. Douglas Bush, *Mythology and the Romantic Tradition in English Poetry* (New York: Norton, 1963), 210.

3. "On the Skye-Lark," in *Punch, or the London Charivari* 85 (22 September 1883): 138; hereafter cited by line number.

4. For an account of these episodes and the unprecedented public magnitude of Gladstone's Midlothian campaigns (1879–92), when his "manifestations of charismatic power reached their zenith" (405), see Eugenio F. Biagini, *Liberty, Retrenchment, and Reform: Popular Liberalism in the Age of Gladstone, 1860–1880* (Cambridge: Cambridge University Press, 1992), 405–16.

5. Robert Bernard Martin, *Tennyson: The Unquiet Heart* (Oxford: Clarendon, 1980), 539.

6. William Allingham, *A Diary* (London: Macmillan, 1908), 336.

7. James Knowles, "Apotheosis: Westminster, October 1892 (An allegory)," *Nineteenth-Century* 32 (1892): 843–44; hereafter cited by line number.

INDEX